Routledge Revivals

A Critical Edition of George Whetstone's 1582 an Heptameron of Civill Discourses

A Critical Edition of George Whetstone's 1582 an Heptameron of Civill Discourses

Edited by
Diana Shklanka

The Renaissance Imagination
Volume 35

First published in 1987 by Garland Publishing, Inc.

This edition first published in 2019 by Routledge
2 Park Square, Milton Park, Abingdon, Oxon, OX14 4RN
and by Routledge
605 Third Avenue, New York, NY 10017

Routledge is an imprint of the Taylor & Francis Group, an informa business

© 1987 by Diana Shklanka

All rights reserved. No part of this book may be reprinted or reproduced or utilised in any form or by any electronic, mechanical, or other means, now known or hereafter invented, including photocopying and recording, or in any information storage or retrieval system, without permission in writing from the publishers.

Publisher's Note
The publisher has gone to great lengths to ensure the quality of this reprint but points out that some imperfections in the original copies may be apparent.

Disclaimer
The publisher has made every effort to trace copyright holders and welcomes correspondence from those they have been unable to contact.
A Library of Congress record exists under ISBN:

ISBN 13: 978-0-367-19758-2 (hbk)
ISBN 13: 978-0-429-24310-3 (ebk)

The Renaissance Imagination
Important Literary and Theatrical Texts
from the Late Middle Ages
through the Seventeenth Century

Stephen Orgel
Editor

Volumes in the Series

1. *Arte of Rhetorique* by Thomas Wilson
   edited by Thomas J. Derrick
2. *An Enterlude Called Lusty Iuuentus* by R. Wever
   An old-spelling critical edition
   edited by Helen Scarborough Thomas
3. *The True Tragicomedy Formerly Acted at Court.* A Play by Francis Osborne Transcribed from the Manuscript in the British Library by John Pitcher and Lois Potter
   edited, with an introduction, by Lois Potter
4. The Comedies of John Crowne
   A critical edition
   edited, with Prolegomena, by B. J. McMullin
5. The *Pearl* Poems: An Omnibus Edition.
   Vol. 1: *Pearl* and *Cleanness*
   edited by William Vantuono
6. The *Pearl* Poems: An Omnibus Edition. Vol. 2: *Patience* and *Sir Gawain and the Green Knight*
   edited by William Vantuono
7. *The Swisser* by Arthur Wilson
   edited by Linda V. Itzoe
8. *Greene's Tu Quoque Or, The Cittie Gallant* by J. Cooke
   A critical edition
   edited by Alan J. Berman
9. A Critical Edition of *I Sir John Oldcastle*
   edited, with an introduction, by Jonathan Rittenhouse
10. The Tudor Interludes: *Nice Wanton* and *Impatient Poverty*
    edited by Leonard Tennenhouse
11. Pageants and Entertainments of Anthony Munday
    A critical edition
    edited by David M. Bergeron
12. *The Fancies, Chast and Noble* by J. Ford
    A critical edition
    edited by Dominick J. Hart
13. Buckingham: Public and Private Man. The Prose, Poems and Commonplace Book of George Villiers, Second Duke of Buckingham (1628–1687)
    edited by Christine Phipps
14. *The Pastyme of People* and *A New Boke of Purgatory* by J. Rastell, with a facsimile of *The Pastyme*
    A critical edition
    edited by Albert J. Geritz

15. *The Passions of the Mind in General*
by Thomas Wright
A critical edition
edited by William Webster Newbold

16. *Thomas Heywood's Pageants*
A critical edition
edited by David M. Bergeron

17. *The Obstinate Lady* by Aston Cokayne
edited by Catherine M. Shaw

18. A Critical Old Spelling of the Works of Edward Sharpham
edited by Christopher G. Petter

19. *Sicily and Naples, Or, the Fatall Union.*
A Tragœdy by S. Harding
edited by Joan Warthling Roberts

20. The *Aeneid* of Thomas Phaer and Thomas Twyne
A critical edition introducing Renaissance metrical typography
edited by Steven Lally

21. A Critical Edition of Abraham Cowley's *Cutter of Coleman Street*
edited by Darlene Johnson Gravett

22. A Critical Edition of Abraham Cowley's *Davideis*
edited by Gayle Shadduck

23. An Old-Spelling Critical Edition of William Davenant's *The Platonic Lovers*
edited by Wendell W. Broom, Jr.

24. A Critical Edition of John Fletcher's *The Humorous Lieutenant*
edited by Philip Oxley

25. A Critical Edition of John Fletcher's Comedy *Monsieur Thomas or Father's Own Son*
edited by Nanette Cleri Clinch

26. The Prose of Fulke Greville, Lord Brooke
edited by Mark Caldwell

27. A Critical Edition of *The Play of the Wether* by John Heywood
edited by Vicki Knudsen Robinson

28. A Critical Edition of *The Isle of Ladies*
edited by Vincent Daly

29. A Contextual Study and Modern-Spelling Edition of *Mucedorus*
edited by Arvin H. Jupin

30. A Critical Edition of Ferdinando Parkhurst's *Ignoramus, The Academical-Lawyer*
edited by E. F. J. Tucker

31. A Critical Edition of Alexander Ross's 1647 *Mystagogus Poeticus, or The Muses Interpreter*
edited by John R. Glenn

32. A Critical Edition of Thomas Salter's *The Mirrhor of Modestie*
edited by Janis Butler Holm

33. An Old-Spelling Critical Edition of James Shirley's *The Example*
edited by William F. Jones

34. Stuart Academic Drama: Three University Plays
edited by David L. Russell

35. A Critical Edition of George Whetstone's 1582 *An Heptameron of Civill Discourses*
edited by Diana Shklanka

36. An Edition of Robert Wilson's *Three Ladies of London* and *Three Lords and Three Ladies of London*
edited by H. S. D. Mithal

37. The School of Cyrus: William Barker's 1567 Translation of Xenophon's *Cyropaedeia (The Education of Cyrus)*
edited by James Tatum

A Critical Edition of George Whetstone's 1582 AN HEPTAMERON OF CIVILL DISCOURSES

edited by
Diana Shklanka

The Renaissance Imagination
Volume 35

GARLAND PUBLISHING, INC.
NEW YORK & LONDON
1987

© 1987 Diana Shklanka
All rights reserved

Library of Congress Cataloging-in-Publication Data

Whetstone, George, 1544?–1587?.
   A critical edition of George Whetstone's 1582 An heptameron of civill discourses.

   (The Renaissance imagination; v. 35)
   Thesis (Ph.D.)—University of British Columbia, 1977.
   Bibliography: p.
   I. Shklanka, Diana, 1941–   . II. Title.
III. Series.
PR2386.H47   1987   823'.3   87-7439
ISBN 0-8240-8415-2

Printed on acid-free, 250-year-life paper
Manufactured in the United States of America

A CRITICAL EDITION

OF

GEORGE WHETSTONE'S <u>AN HEPTAMERON OF CIVILL DISCOURSES</u>
(1582)

by

DIANA SHKLANKA

B.A. Honours, University of Saskatchewan, 1961
M.A., Cornell University, 1963
M.Sc., Simmons College, 1966

A THESIS SUBMITTED IN PARTIAL FULFILLMENT OF
THE REQUIREMENTS FOR THE DEGREE OF
DOCTOR OF PHILOSOPHY

in

THE FACULTY OF GRADUATE STUDIES

Department of English

We accept this thesis as conforming
to the required standard

.... *[signature]* ....

.... *[signature]* ....

.... *[signature]* ....

THE UNIVERSITY OF BRITISH COLUMBIA

March, 1977

TABLE OF CONTENTS

	page
Prefatory Note	v

CRITICAL INTRODUCTION

Whetstone's Life and Works	vii

The <u>Heptameron</u> of <u>Civill</u> <u>Discourses</u>:

1. Italian Influence	xxvi
2. The Ideal of Civility	xxxix
3. Renaissance Courtesy Literature	xlix
4. Dialogue Literature	lix
5. Marriage Literature	lxvi
6. The <u>Heptameron</u> and Prose Fiction	lxxii
7. Whetstone's Sources	lxxxv
8. The Structure of the <u>Heptameron</u>	xcvii
Footnotes	cxii

TEXTUAL INTRODUCTION — cxviii

Footnotes	cxxv
Bibliographical Description of the <u>Heptameron</u>	cxxvii
Substantive Emendations	cxxix
Emendations of Accidentals	cxxxi
Press Variants	cxlvi
Collation with <u>Aurelia</u>	cli
Title pages of the <u>Heptameron</u> and of <u>Aurelia</u>	clx

Contents

AN HEPTAMERON OF CIVILL DISCOURSES 1
    The First Day's Exercise 13
    The Second Day's Exercise 44
    The Third Day's Exercise 75
    The Fourth Day's Exercise 114
    The Fifth Day's Exercise 144
    The Sixth Day's Exercise 168
    The Seventh Day's Exercise 198

EXPLANATORY NOTES 231

Glossary 386

Index of Proper Names 399

Index of Stories 403

Index of First Lines of Poems 404

LIST OF WORKS CONSULTED
    Primary Texts 405
    Secondary Sources 410

PREFATORY NOTE

This edition seeks to make available, for the scholar and the student of Elizabethan literature, an accurate text of <u>An Heptameron of Civill Discourses</u>, a work that has received insufficient critical attention. I am of course indebted to Thomas C. Izard's pioneer study, <u>George Whetstone, Mid-Elizabethan Gentleman of Letters</u> (1942), which attempts to uncover the few facts of Whetstone's life and which suggests some of his literary sources. The work of David N. Beauregard, however, whose critical edition of the <u>Heptameron</u> remains an unpublished dissertation (Ohio State University, 1967), is not duplicated here. Beauregard's edition is incomplete and does not provide an adequate textual and critical apparatus. His introduction outlines a few of the specific literary influences on Whetstone, focusing primarily on Castiglione and Tilney, whereas my critical introduction discusses the social and literary ideals and traditions that give rise to and merge in the prose narrative that is the <u>Heptameron</u>.

In the Introduction and the Explanatory Notes, when quoting from Renaissance texts I have modernized the usage of u-v and i-j and have expanded typographical abbreviations. Dates given are those of first publication, unless otherwise noted. Except where accurate modern editions are available, references are to the primary texts, which I have generally consulted in the University Microfilm series of <u>STC</u> books. My authorities for names, titles, and dates are A. W. Pollard and G. R. Redgrave, <u>A Short-Title Catalogue of Books Printed in England, Scotland and Ireland</u>, and of English Books Printed Abroad, 1475-1640 (London: Bibliog. Society, 1926; 2nd ed., 1976, only Vol. 2 available); Dizionario enciclopedico della letteratura Italiana, 6v. (Unedi: Laterza, 1966-70); and Alexandre Cioranesco, Bibliographie de la littérature française du seizième siècle (Paris: Klincksieck, 1959).

I am indebted to Dr. E. Bongie for her help in translating the Latin passages in the Heptameron.

CRITICAL INTRODUCTION

Whetstone's Life and Works

Few details of Whetstone's life are known, and even fewer are verifiable. Although the name of George Whetstone repeatedly creeps into discussions of Shakespeare's sources, into works on Sir Philip Sidney, and into literary histories -- for Whetstone is still most often recalled only as the author of Promos and Cassandra and of a metrical eulogy of Sidney -- the biographical information provided is sketchy and incomplete, if not inaccurate. Even the dates assigned to Whetstone's birth and death are often unreliable and sometimes misleading. Authorities such as the Dictionary of National Biography and the Encyclopaedia Britannica perpetuate a largely legendary, highly coloured account of the author of the Heptameron. According to Sir Sidney Lee in the DNB, Whetstone squandered his patrimony in wild living at court then "subsequently devoted much energy to denunciations of the depravity of London, and declared that he was fraudulently deprived of his property," met George Gascoigne and Thomas Churchyard while fighting in the Low Countries in 1572, returned to London to take up writing only as a last resort in an unsuccessful attempt to earn his living, sought adventure on a voyage with Sir Humphrey Gilbert, finally returned to the life of a professional writer and soldier, witnessed the Battle of Zutphen, and died at an unknown date and place. Lee's account is not far-fetched, but his stereotyped picture of Whetstone the reformed rake and Elizabethan adventurer cannot be authenticated. Whetstone may very well have been such a swashbuckling figure, or he may have been the sober English nationalist and Protestant suggested by his later works and by Watson's description of him as "Morall Whetstone":[1] we simply do not know. Nor are bibliographers more reliable as a source of information about Whetstone's life and works; for instance, the "G.W." who wrote The Cures of the Diseased, in Remote Regions (London, 1598) is frequently identified in library catalogues, apparently on the authority of a conjecture made by Charles Singer in 1915, with the George Whetstone who died in 1587.[2]

It is to Thomas C. Izard, whose study George Whetstone, Mid-Elizabethan Gentleman of Letters first appeared in 1942, that we owe the first scholarly attempt to sift out historical data from unsubstantiated hearsay.[3] Izard suggests that the commonly accepted version of Whetstone's life most likely originated with John Berkenhout's Biographia Literaria (1777), which in turn is indebted to George Steevens "the Shakespearean commentator, phrasemaker, practical joker, and wag extraordinary":

> Berkenhout reports that Steevens said of Whetstone, "He is certainly the most quaint and contemptible writer, both in prose and verse, I ever met with." This picturesque asperity stuck. From that day to this it has been the routine ending for accounts of Whetstone. Also in this Steevens-Berkenhout sketch the misinformation that Whetstone turned soldier early in life and was as a result reduced to beggary seems to have originated.[4]

What little we are now able to reconstruct of Whetstone's life is based primarily on information from an inquisition post mortem after the death of his father Robert Whetstone, who died 10 August 1557; from the will of Robert Whetstone; and from a few references in the Calendar of State Papers. Further information may be gleaned, less certainly, from supposedly autobiographical passages in George Whetstone's writings.

Whetstone's father, Robert, was a haberdasher who owned property in London and York as well as in the counties of Essex, Leicester, Stafford, Kent, Somerset, and Middlesex. By his first wife he had one son, Robert, and by his second wife, Margaret Barnard, he had four sons, Bernard, George, John, and Francis.[5] The ingenious calculations of early biographers, based on the recorded fact that the eldest son Robert was seventeen in 1557 when Robert senior died, conclude that George was probably born in 1544 -- the date accepted by Sir Sidney Lee in the DNB; however, Izard's equally ingenious but more convincing calculations, based on the fact that Margaret Whetstone was carrying her fifth child in 1557, arrive at a birthdate for George of 1551.[6] After Robert senior's death, Margaret married Robert Browne of Walcot in Northamptonshire,[7] and George may have been a frequent visitor to their country home -- such a visit may be behind Thomas Churchyard's reference, in the prefatory remarks to Whetstone's The Censure of a Loyall Subject, to "my good friend M.G.W. at his departure into the Countrey" (sig. A1v). Whetstone's claim, on the title page of one of his many elegies,[8] that he was present at the death of his friend George Gascoigne at Stamford in Lincolnshire is thus easily credited, for Stamford is only four miles from Walcot. In Northamptonshire also, Whetstone may have experienced at first-hand the hospitality of Holdenby, the showpiece of its age, the palace built by Sir Christopher Hatton, to whom he dedicated the Heptameron.

The education of George Whetstone is not documented, but his writings reveal a traditional Renaissance humanist background and training. The Heptameron exhibits the author's familiarity with classical and contemporary Renaissance texts, rhetorical skills, and literary devices. We do know that Whetstone's brothers Bernard and Francis matriculated from St. John's College at Cambridge in 1563 and 1573 respectively, and that Francis was admitted to Gray's Inn in 1578.[9] The evidence for believing that George was similarly educated may not be conclusive but is certainly persuasive: in the epistle prefacing The Rocke of Regard, his first published work, Whetstone refers to his lodgings in Holborne, a district near the Inns of Court (sig. ¶3^r), and he addresses one of the poems in the same work to "my especiall friends and companions, the Gentlemen of Furnivals In" (sig. O1^v); Whetstone's fellow-writers and associates George Gascoigne, Thomas Watson, and Thomas Churchyard had been law students at the Inns of Court;[10] and William Webbe in his Discourse of English Poetrie (1586) singles out Whetstone as one "of the learned company of Gentlemen Schollers, and students of the Universities, and Innes of Courte" (sig. C4^r).

Further details of Whetstone's life in the early 1570's may be gathered from passages in The Rocke of Regard which are autobiographical in tone. Whetstone himself claims that The Rocke of Regard is based on his own experiences: he addresses his first book "To all the young Gentlemen of England, . . . For whose behalfe and forewarning, I have collected together a number of my unlearned devises (invented for the most, of experience)" (sig. ¶2^r); and he describes the fourth section, which portrays "the miseries of dice, the mischiefes of quarelling, and the fall of prodigalitie" (sig. K1^r), as "the Ortchard of Repentance, the which for the most part, I planted with experience" (sig. ¶2^v). Ignoring the significant phrases "invented for the most" and "for the most part," literary historians have traditionally read two narratives in "The Ortchard of Repentance" as undiluted autobiography. The first narrative, "The honest mans adventures" (sigs. K3^r-L7^r), is a poem telling how the speaker, as a young man, seeks to make his way at court; "When coine, and clothes were spent," he finds it "Hie time to trudge" and takes up soldiering; he grows old, is wounded, and leaves the wars penniless; he ends as a farmer, poor and embittered. Since the speaker is obviously an old man and since Whetstone was about twenty-five when The Rocke of Regard was published, the poem may be dismissed as a record of Whetstone's life. The second narrative, "Inventions of P. Plasmos touching his hap and hard fortune" (sigs. O8^{r}ff.), a collection of poems and prose commentaries, is more convincing as autobiography. Plasmos confesses that an unhappy affair with a light woman made him spend his living -- he complains of being in want -- and involved him in "a certaine quarel" in which he "a litle before" maimed his right hand (sig. P3^v). In an earlier poem in the same book, addressed to "his especiall friend and kinseman, maister Robert Cudden of Grayes In," the speaker, Whetstone, had also mentioned a maimed hand acquired as a result of his rashness and rage (sig. M3^r); thus, the way is clear to identify Plasmos with Whetstone. Nevertheless, how much of the "Inventions" is Whetstone's own story? The prodigal son motif appeared frequently in Renaissance fiction, in both courtly and popular works:[11] it was made fashionable by Lyly as a result of the vogue of Euphues (1578), and it was later exploited by Greene in The Repentance (1592) and in Greenes Mourning Garment (1590). In writing the "Inventions of P. Plasmos," Whetstone undoubtedly drew on his own experience, but he cast that experience into a traditional literary frame (as he was later to do in the *Heptameron*); in fact, he may have helped to popularize the prodigal son theme.

That the story of Plasmos is largely autobiography is further corroborated by Whetstone at the end of *A Touchstone for the Time*:

> No man was ever assaulted with a more daungerous strategeme of cosonage then my selfe, with which my life and living was hardly beset. No man hath more cause to thanke God for a free delivery than my selfe, nor anie man ever sawe more suddaine vengeance afflicted upon his adversaries, than I myselfe of mine: as lively appeareth in the ende of my booke intituled *The rocke of regarde*, imprinted many yeares past. (sig. K4^v)

Whetstone goes on to bemoan the huge deceitfulness of friends as well as of strangers, to complain of his more than three years of "costly sute" and "greevous oppression," and to praise the wisdom and grave judgement of the Lord Chancellor who relieved and released him from "the toile of Law."

After publishing *The Rocke of Regard*, Whetstone appears to have travelled abroad. Plasmos mentions a projected trip to France, and a commendatory poem in "The Ortchard of repentance" is headed "A caveat to G.W. at his going into Fraunce, written by his friend R.C." (sig. O3^r). Such a trip might account for the fact, extensively documented by Izard, that Whetstone's later writings reveal a marked indebtedness to French literary works, especially to Marguerite de Navarre's *Heptaméron* and to the translations of Mexia by Antoine du Verdier and Claude Gruget. In 1578, Whetstone participated in one of Sir Humphrey Gilbert's voyages: the dedicatory letter to *Promos and Cassandra* (1578) announces his intentions to accompany Gilbert (sig. A3^r), and that he did so is shown by references in the *Calendar of State Papers* and in accounts of Gilbert's

1578 expedition.[12] Thomas Churchyard hurriedly commemorated the occasion by a poem entitled "A matter touching the Journey of Sir Humfrey Gilbarte Knight," included in his *Discourse of the Queenes Majesties Entertainement in Suffolk and Norfolk* (1578), in which he singles out a few sailors:

> Miles Morgan gaynes good Fame,
>   and Whetstone steps in place,
> And seekes by travell, and by toyle,
>   to winne him double grace. (sig. H4^v)

The exact purpose of this expedition is not known. It consisted of ten or eleven ships; Whetstone served on the vice-admiral ship, the *Hope*, commanded by Sir Humphrey Gilbert's half-brother, Carew Raleigh. Dissension broke out among the commanders of the ships, and only seven ships, including the *Hope*, finally sailed with Gilbert on November 19, 1578.[13]

There are no records for Whetstone's life between 1578 and his military career after 1585, but he did publish several works, including the *Heptameron* and sections of *The English Myrror*, at this time, and he claims to have made a journey to Italy in 1580. References to this Italian journey occur not only in the *Heptameron*, but also in *The Honorable Reputation of a Souldier* (1585), in *The English Myrror* (1586), and in *The Censure of a Loyall Subject* (1587). In the *Heptameron*, Whetstone's epistle to Sir Christopher Hatton states that he wrote the book in order to acknowledge "many received favours, of a Right noble Italian Gentleman" (p. 3):

> I have likewise committed to memorie, the civill disputations, and speaches of sundry well Courted Gentlemen, and Gentlewomen, his Guestes, during the time of my intertainment, with Segnior Phyloxenus (for so covertly I name him, least

> in giving him, his true honorable Tytles in England, I
> should make a passage for Envie, to injurie him in Italy) . . . .
> (p. 4)

In the epistle "Unto the friendly Reader," Whetstone repeats his assertion that the book is a factual account, based on his visit to Italy:

> I have, with well advised Judgement, bethought mee, of suche
> memorable Questions and Devices, as I heard and sawe presented,
> in this most noble Italian Gentlemans Pallace, the Christmas
> twelvemoneths past . . . . (p. 6)

And he hints at his own unfortunate experiences:

> Some will (perchaunce more of envie to heare a stranger commended,
> then of pittie to bemone my hard fortune, or fowle usage)
> say, I have as just cause to complaine, of injuries received
> at Roane, Rome, and Naples, as to commend the vertues and good
> intertainment, of Segnior Philoxenus . . . . (pp. 7-8)

Whetstone begins the Heptameron by describing, in the first person, his supposed visit to Philoxenus's palace, but he soon adopts the persona of Cavaliero Ismarito, "in whiche name heereafter, I will present those actions that touch my selfe" (p. 23). In his prefatory remarks to The Honorable Reputation of a Souldier, Whetstone says that he was present at a quarrel involving an insolent Spaniard in Thurin in 1580 and was lodged in Milan near the River Po (sigs. A2^r-A3^v). In The English Myrror, in order to establish the credibility of his report of the actions of Catholic Englishmen in Italy, he declares that he speaks as an eye-witness: "In the beginning of November 1580, I returned from Naples to Rome" (sig. K6^v). Finally, in The Censure of a Loyall Subject, one of the three speakers, "Weston," says that he was in Rome in 1580 before he visited Venice (sig. F4^{r-v}). Weston may be identified with Whetstone on the grounds that he appears to represent the author's views and that his name is possibly a variant spelling of "Whetstone." If we believe Whetstone's statements that he was in Italy in 1580, we may then accept Izard's reconstruction, based on these passages and on references in the Heptameron, of Whetstone's itinerary to include Roane (or possibly Rouen), Turin, Bologna, Rome, Naples, Tivoli, Loreto, Ravenna, and Venice.[14] Whetstone's return to England seems to have plunged him into litigation, for at the end of A Touchstone for the Time (1584) he refers to his legal problems (sig. K4^v). Did these stem from settlements of his father's estates?

We know that George Whetstone and his brother Bernard served in Leicester's campaign in the Low Countries sometime after 1585, but there has been some confusion as to whether George witnessed Sidney's death, which he describes in his poem Sir Phillip Sidney, His Honorable Life, His Valiant Death, and True Vertues (1587). Izard, contending that Whetstone's account of Sidney's death is secondhand and largely derived from his brother Bernard, does not place George in the Low Countries until after the Battle of Zutphen.[15] However, recent research by R. C. Strong and J. A. Van Dorsten shows that there were two Whetstones in Leicester's train, the second most probably being George. Billeting lists indicate that, whether or not George Whetstone was present at the Battle of Zutphen, he certainly was in the Low Countries as a member of the same army at the time of Sidney's death.[16]

The Sidney elegy was printed in the fall of 1587, and in a letter prefacing the poem, the publisher Thomas Cadman refers to the death of Whetstone in the Low Countries (sig. A4^r). The episode surrounding Whetstone's death is easily reconstructed from entries in the Calendar of State Papers.[17] In August 1587, at Burghley's prompting, Whetstone was appointed a commissary of musters under Thomas Digges, "although all places were furnished" (p. 244). As mustermaster, Digges frequently complained of the trouble he was experiencing over his military accounts and of the abuses perpetrated by his captains; and in a letter to Burghley, dated September 12, he laments the death of Whetstone, saying that he was honest and just and was slain "no doubt because he could not be corrupted" (p. 311). Whetstone quarrelled with one of the captains, Edmund Udall (whom he had praised in the Sidney elegy, sig. B1^r), and in the ensuing duel, Whetstone was fatally wounded. Digges suggests that the quarrel broke out because Whetstone, in the course of his duty, attempted to check Udall's accounts; and Sir Richard Bingham reports to Walsingham that the two men "falling out into some speeches overnight, met by chance the next day, and so unknown to any went themselves without the town, where it was the said Whetstones' chance to be slain" (p. 321). Udall, formerly in Sidney's service, was at first held responsible, but was eventually cleared by the Council of War on the ground that the fight was "Whetstone's own seeking" (p. 369). Sir Thomas Morgan, then governor of Bergen ap Zoom, tried unsuccessfully to re-open the case. Udall returned from the Low Countries campaign to become Master of the Revels at Lincoln's Inn. Whetstone left a widow, Anne[18] -- but the date of his marriage is unknown and the identity of his wife remains a mystery.

In addition to a commendatory verse prefixed to The Posies of George Gascoigne (1575), another in Timothy Kendall's Flowers of Epigrammes (1577), and two poems in The Paradise of Dainty Devices (1578 and 1580),[19] Whetstone published the following works, all of which are extant:

The Rocke of Regard (1576).

A Remembraunce of George Gaskoigne (1577).

Promos and Cassandra (1578).

A Remembraunce of Sir Nicholas Bacon (1579).

An Heptameron of Civill Discourses (1582).

A Remembraunce of Sir James Dier (1582).

A Remembraunce of Thomas late Earle of Sussex (1583).

A Mirour for Magestrates of Cyties (1584); published with

A Touchstone for the Time (1584).

A Mirror of Treue Honnour and Christian Nobilities (1585).

The Honorable Reputation of a Souldier (1585).

The English Myrror (1586).

The Censure of a Loyall Subject (1587).

Sir Phillip Sidney (1587).

On the verso of the title of The Enemie to Unthryftinesse (a re-issue in 1586 of A Mirour for Magestrates of Cyties and A Touchstone for the Time), Whetstone's major publications are listed; under the subtitle "Books redy to be printed" are included A Panoplie of Devices and The Image of Christian Justice, now lost works, although the latter may refer, as Izard points out, to the third book of The English Myrror.[20]

The Rocke of Regard, called by Whetstone "the first increase of my baren braine" (sig. ¶3^r), is an exercise in metrical and prose fiction. It is divided into four parts, "The Castle of Delight," "The Garden of Unthriftiness," "The Arbour of Vertue," and "The Ortchard of Repentance." The narratives, drawn largely from Italian authors, are designed as exemplary tales, driving home lessons on the benefits of virtue and good conduct and the evils of prodigality and loose living. Too often the lessons have a preaching tone; at other times, however, the morals are merely tagged on to the otherwise unedifying novella material. Included in the series of laments, in the style of The Mirror for Magistrates, are the stories of Bianca Maria, Cressid, Dom Diego, and the Bohemian Lady Barbara. These are intermingled with clusters of admonitory, didactic, Petrarchan, and laudatory verses, such as the "Fiftie apples of admonition, late growing on the tree of good government" (sigs. O1^{v}ff.), "Whetstons Invective against Dice" (sigs. N1^r-O1^v), and a variety of poems on "Loves woes." Of especial interest is the "Discourse of Rinaldo and Giletta" (sigs. B4^{r}ff.), "first written in Italian by an unknowne authour," a prose tale which frequently reveals narrative techniques similar to those of Gascoigne's The Adventures of Master F.J. (1575) and Grange's The Golden Aphroditis (1577), and which looks forward to the narrative skill exhibited in the Heptameron.

Promos and Cassandra apparently was never played upon the stage. The title page and the oft-reprinted preface point out that this play was also written with marked moral intent. Again, Whetstone reveals a susceptibility to Italian influence, for the story of Promos and Cassandra, which he retells in the Heptameron (pp. 125-37), occurs also in Cintio's Ecatommiti (1565). As the primary source of Measure for Measure, Whetstone's one play has acquired a secure slot in Shakespearean studies, but in so doing has sacrificed recognition of its own merits. The play is lively and entertaining; the narrative pace is rapid and skilfully varied with frequent songs; and the scenes of low life are convincing. Charles T. Prouty is not alone in wondering why Promos and Cassandra failed to attract an Elizabethan audience.[21]

The four books entitled A Mirour for Magestrates of Cyties, A Touchstone for the Time, The Honorable Reputation of a Souldier, and The English Myrror, were originally conceived as parts of one great work to be called The English Mirror.[22] These works are patriotic and moralisti concerned with right conduct, with the attainment of virtue and the defeat of vice, especially of the vice of envy. They draw from a variety of classical and contemporary sources, but rely heavily on certain French works, notably Antoine du Verdier's and Claude Gruget's translations of the encyclopedic Silva de varia lección by Pedro Mexia (see Explanatory Note 168.21-22), which Whetstone had already used extensively in the Heptameron.[23] A Mirour for Magestrates of Cyties holds up Alexander Severus as a type of ideal ruler whose reforms are worthy of imitation by contemporary governors. It attacks the taverns, dicing houses, and brothels of Rome and warns the gentlemen of the Inns of Court to beware similar dens of iniquity in London. Designed as a companion piece, A Touchstone for the Time attacks the vices, particularly dicing, drinking, and usury, in the bowels of London; it condemns stage plays and insists on the elimination of abuses in the playhouses -- but points out that "the Playes of dice" are more vicious and dangerous; and it praises the Inns of Court as islands of much honour and reputation. In The Honorable Reputation of a Souldier, a conduct book for the military man, Whetstone asserts that he intends to speak not of military technique, in which he lacks experience, but of the "Morall government necessarie for a perfect Souldier" (sig. A2^r). First published in London in 1585, The Honorable Reputation of a Souldier was re-issued in Leiden in 1586, in a dual-language version, in German and English; Geoffrey Whitney, who was then a member of Leicester's train in the Low Countries, supplied a commendatory verse (sig. A4^{r-v}), and the Dutch poet Jacob Walraven translated the entire book. Thus, Whetstone's book exemplifies the close Anglo-Leiden assocation of the 1580's.[24] The main text ends with the author's address to the soldiers fighting in the Low Countries, urging them to do their best in a just war. The Protestant cause is further supported in The English Myrror, a treatise which attacks Envy, praises the English government as "A Fortris against Envy," condemns both Turks and Papists, and eulogizes Queen Elizabeth, the Protestant champion who has been preserved through God's protection. The language verges on the apocalyptic, as Whetstone proclaims that England is to be the Saviour of the world, the North Wind of the Song of Songs that will blow upon the garden of the world and will cleanse and refresh the earth (sig. H6^v).

The Censure of a Loyall Subject is a dialogue discussing the deaths of fourteen Catholics recently executed in London for treason. Wilcocks, "a substantial clothier," gives an eyewitness account of the deaths of the traitors who, persuaded by Anthony Babington, sought the Queen's life. Walker, "a godlie devine," preaches and asks most of the questions that elicit Wilcocks' observations. Weston, "a discreet Gentleman," attacks the Papacy in strong language, underlines the moral lessons, and in general provides a running commentary; he seems to represent Whetstone himself. The Censure, hopes Whetstone, "will merite the acceptance of my former bookes, which hetherto have escaped the disgrace of publique reproofe. Protesting, in the behalfe of my writing, that my desire hath evermore bene, to instruct all men, and not to injure the worst of the wicked" (sig. A2^v).

The elegies on the deaths of notable persons -- George Gascoigne, Sir Nicholas Bacon, Sir James Dyer, the Earl of Sussex, the Earl of Bedford and his son Lord Russell, and Sir Philip Sidney -- appear to have been dashed off, generally with unseemly haste, as the occasions arose -- possibly in order to flatter the dead men's relatives into becoming Whetstone's patrons. They are unremarkable poems, replete with moral commonplaces, repeated phrases, and extravagant praises.[25]

The Heptameron of Civill Discourses marks a transition in the types of writing undertaken by Whetstone. His earliest books, The Rocke of Regard and Promos and Cassandra, were consciously composed as literary works, the first modelled on the complaint and the novella, the second designed as a tragicomedy. In the Heptameron, several literary traditions merge, resulting in a greater and more successful combination of literary design with didactic intent. Whetstone's moral aim does not often harmonize with his artistic aim in his early works, and the reader of The Rocke of Regard especially is frequently distracted by the overt preaching that seems to be tagged on to otherwise entertaining stories; however, such a clash in tone is avoided in the Heptameron which successfully uses the conventions of dialogue, marriage conduct book, courtesy literature, and prose fiction to fuse morality with art. After the Heptameron, Whetstone's works are primarily didactic; the literary aspect is almost lost -- except in The Censure of a Loyall Subject, in which the propagandistic attack on Papacy is constructed as a dialogue, thus reflecting a revival of Whetstone's interest in the dialogue form.

Since Protestantism is a recurring motif in Whetstone's works -- and the Heptameron is no exception, for it portrays Segnior Philoxenus,

the ideal gentleman, as a Protestant, even though he is Italian -- it
is fitting that his literary career ended with his eulogy of the Protestant
hero Sir Philip Sidney, also a soldier and a writer. Sidney and Whetstone
were not of the same social class, yet they shared similar religious
convictions, political ideals, and literary contacts. Whetstone's friends
Thomas Watson and Thomas Churchyard were associated with the Sidney
family: Watson, through his connections with Walsingham, appears to
have known Sir Philip Sidney; and Philip's father, Sir Henry Sidney,
was one of Churchyard's patrons. Another friend, George Gascoigne,
knew Leicester and probably had contact with Sidney as well. Although
I can find no concrete evidence that Whetstone was part of the Sidney
circle, the paths of the two men -- the courtier and the soldier-writer --
often crossed. It may even be argued that Segnior Philoxenus, a bachelor,
represents Sir Philip Sidney and that Aurelia, Philoxenus's sister,
represents Mary Sidney Herbert, the Countess of Pembroke, who was frequently addressed in poetry as "Aurelia": in the fall of 1580, the time
of the Christmas festivities described in the Heptameron, Sidney was
in disgrace at court and spent his retirement in the country, perhaps
at Wilton; and in December 1581, since he was preparing to marry Frances
Walsingham, he might be expected to be interested in discussions of
marriage. However, such an identification presupposes that Whetstone is
not in fact describing an Italian experience; it ignores the fact that
Sidney was back at court on New Year's Day 1581 when he presented the
Queen with the gift of "a juell of golde" in the form of a whip garnished
with diamonds and pearls as an emblem of his penitence; and it does
not reconcile Sidney's violent stand against the proposed marriage of

Queen Elizabeth and the Duc d'Anjou with Philoxenus's admiration of Anjou.[26]

Although we may not assume a link between Segnior Philoxenus and Sir Philip Sidney, we may still posit a connection between Whetstone and Sidney. Such a connection is made more likely by the recent studies by J. A. Van Dorsten, who has uncovered the active relationship between the Protestant circles of England and the Low Countries in the late 1570's and early 1580's, especially at the University of Leiden.[27] George Gascoigne, Thomas Churchyard, Thomas Wilson, and Sir Philip Sidney all had literary or political contact with the Low Countries, as there was a constant interchange of poets, scholars, printers, and ambassadors. In fact, Leicester's campaign in 1585 was a gathering of literary men in the Low Countries. Sidney associated with the Leiden humanists, and for both the Dutch and English literary men, he was the ideal Christian knight, taking the place of Gaspard de Coligny and William of Orange who had been Protestant martyrs before him. (Both Coligny and Orange are depicted as Protestant heroes in the Heptameron, pp. 116-17). The first literary product of this general Anglo-Leiden integration was Geoffrey Whitney's A Choice of Emblemes, published in May 1586. It was followed by Whetstone's The Honorable Reputation of a Souldier, "a small mirror of Anglo-Leiden contacts," according to Dorsten:

> A few months later [after May 1586] there appeared a booklet, now rare and almost forgotten, that in a small compass contains a summary of much of this story. It brought together soldiering and language courses, Dutch, English, and traditional Latin, practical linguistics and Anglo-Leiden 'schools' of verse. And it linked the principal groups of agents: the Dousas, Lipsius, and Van Hout -- the English printer-schoolmaster Basson -- Gilpin's host Van Brouchoven -- Geoffrey Whitney -- Leicester himself -- the Dutch poet Walraven -- and Sidney's

eulogist George Whetstone, 'a man singularly well skyld in this faculty of Poetrie'. The book was Whetstone's The honourable reputation of a souldier of 1585, translated by Walraven as De eerweerdighe achtbaerheyt van een soldener in 1586, and together printed in parallel columns by Paedts -- at one time printer of Stanyhurst's Aeneis -- for Thomas Basson, the publisher.[28]

Thomas Basson was an English refugee who had set up a printing press and an informal English school in Leiden. The scholars Walraven, Van Hout, Dousa, and Van Brouchoven had come together at Basson's in January, 1586 in a serious attempt to study English. Walraven's contribution to the school was a translation of Whetstone's book, one of three textbooks to be used. Basson's license to publish The Honorable Reputation of a Souldier was granted by Leicester on August 14, and Walraven's dedication to the magistrates of Hoorn is dated August 30. By what coincidence did Whetstone's book attract the interest of this circle of poet-scholars, a circle which included Sir Philip Sidney? Whetstone himself may have brought his work to their attention, for he was a member of Leicester's train, which entered Leiden on January 12, 1586. Thus, his presence in Leiden "would almost coincide with the sudden English interest of a Dutch poet, Jacob Walraven, who 'had never set foot in England.'"[29]

Now generally dismissed as a hack writer, in his own age Whetstone appears to have been respected as an author. William Webbe (who was possibly a friend of Whetstone, Izard cautions)[30] in his Discourse of English Poetrie (1586) mentions in passing "the learned company of Gentlemen Schollers and students of the Universities and Innes of Courte," but pauses to add:

> One Gentleman notwithstanding among them may I not over-slyppe, so farre reacheth his fame, and so worthy is he, if

> he have not already, to weare the Lawrell wreathe, Master George Whetstone, a man singularly well skyld in this facultie of Poetrie. (sig. C3^v)

Gabriel Harvey, referring to "Our late writers" in Pierces Supererogation (1593), allots qualified praise to Whetstone and his contemporaries:

> In Grafton, Holinshed, and Stowe; in Heywood, Tusser, and Gowge; in Gascoigne, Churchyarde, and Floide; in Ritch, Whetstone, and Munday; in Stanyhurst, Fraunce, and Watson; in Kiffin, Warner, and Daniell; in an hundred such vulgar writers, many things are commendable, divers things notable, some things excellent. (sigs. 2A4^v-2B1^r)

And Francis Meres in Palladis Tamia (1598) lists Whetstone between Shakespeare and Gascoigne as one of "the most passionate among us to bewaile and bemoane the perplexities of Love" (sig. 20^{4r}).

The image of Whetstone that finally emerges from a study of his life and works is indeed that of an increasingly "Morall Whetstone." Although he was a literary opportunist who tried his hand at a variety of popular types of writing as he had tried a variety of professions, in his books Whetstone never strays from his narrow and pronounced patriotic, moral, and religious convictions. His self-confessed goal is to create "A perfect Myrror for the followers both of Mars and Mercury" (Sir Phillip Sidney, t.p.) -- to supply a guide to ideal conduct that would appeal to both soldier or governor and scholar. The Heptameron marks but one stage towards that goal, yet it is Whetstone's most successful literary achievement.

THE HEPTAMERON OF CIVILL DISCOURSES

1.

Italian Influence

In the Heptameron Whetstone claims that he is describing the holiday festivities in which he participated in Italy "the Christmas twelve-months past" (p. 6) -- that is, in December 1580. I have already suggested that since Whetstone refers in three of his works -- and possibly in a fourth -- to his journey to Italy in 1580, it is probable that such a journey did in fact take place; but whether he actually participated in a social occasion similar to the one he describes in the Heptameron cannot now be determined. Fact or fiction, the Heptameron as an imaginativ work shows considerable Italian literary influence -- in its conversazione form, its discussions of love and marriage, its descriptions of social customs, its use of novellas, and its relation to courtesy literature. Although such influence may have reached Whetstone indirectly through French imitations and translations or through French-English literary contacts -- for Italian culture flourished at the French court after 1533 when Catherine de' Medici married the future Henry II -- I propose to show that he almost certainly had direct personal experience of Italian literature and social customs.

The Heptameron was written at a time when the English interest in Italy was at its peak.[31] English travellers had been enduring the seven-week horseback journey between London and Rome since the time of Chaucer (who had himself brought back Italian books in his saddle bags), for Italy had long been venerated as the center of learning and culture, especially of letters and architecture. Merchants and traders, diplomats and courtiers, scholars and writers maintained economic, political, and cultural ties with Italy; and in the sixteenth century the literary interest which had almost died with Chaucer rapidly revived. The new learning, which had been cultivated even in the fifteenth century within the literary circle of Humphrey, Duke of Gloucester,[32] strove to keep in touch with the latest trend in Italian letters and hence encouraged contact with Italy. The humanists set a fashion for Italy as the place to study -- for both scholars and diplomats. William Lily and William Grocyn visited Italy, and Thomas Linacre studied there for twelve years. Reginald Pole's household in Padua from 1521 to 1526 attracted Thomas Lupset, a friend of Erasmus, and Thomas Starkey, an historian.[33] Sir Thomas Wyatt, after a three-month diplomatic mission to Italy in 1527, imported the Petrarchan sonnet and its conventions into England. Even during the Reformation in the reign of Henry VIII, when diplomatic relations with Rome were severed and when, for fear of Catholic influence and of the dangers of the Inquisition, all ties with Italy were discouraged, Thomas Cromwell continued to patronize writers who translated Italian books or otherwise showed interest in Italian studies. During this time Cardinal Pole spent his years of exile in Italy; he was welcomed back by Queen Mary in 1554, bringing with him an appreciation of Italian culture. With the death of Henry in 1547, travel to Italy became easier: the upper classes began to send their young men to Italy for education, and the English admiration for things Italian reached a new height. Sir Thomas Hoby, sent to Padua in 1548 when he was eighteen, translated Castiglione's <u>Il cortegiano</u> into English as <u>The Courtier</u> (1561), a book that both reflected and helped to feed the rising enthusiasm for Italy. William Thomas returned from a visit to Italy to write The Historie of Italie (1549) and to become a professional teacher of Italian, publishing the Principal Rules of the Italian Grammer, with a Dictionarie for the better understanding of Boccacce, Petrarche, and Dante (1550). Roger Ascham, whose Scholemaster (1570) gave fame to what he calls an Italian proverb, "An Englishman Italianate is a devil incarnate," was able to condemn Italy from personal experience:

> I was once in Italy myself; but I thank God my abode there was but nine days; and yet I saw in that little time, in one city, more liberty to sin, than ever I heard tell of in our noble city of London in nine year.

Yet even Ascham could not reject all Italian culture:

> To join learning with comely exercises, Conte Baldesar Castiglione, in his book Cortegiane, doth trimly teach; which book advisedly read and diligently followed but one year at home in England, would do a young gentleman more good, I wis, than three years' travel abroad spent in Italy.[34]

Later literary travellers included courtiers such as Sir Philip Sidney (and his friend Lodowick Bryskett) and professional writers such as Thomas Watson, Anthony Munday, and Robert Greene.

In the late sixteenth century Italian became a useful language to know at court. It always remained a gentleman's rather than a businessman's language, for although English traders were of necessity accomplished linguists, conducting transactions in Dutch or German or Spanish, they had no control over the Venetian-dominated Italian trade and thus had little need to learn Italian. At court Italian was fashionable among courtiers and indispensable for politicians. Elizabeth had studied Italian since at least 1543 when she was eleven, spoke that language fluently, and wrote in the Italian script.[35] Burghley and Walsingham wrote Italian letters; Raleigh read Italian; Hatton owned a large number of Italian books; Leicester employed Italian musicians. As Lievsay puts it, "Almost every cultivated Elizabethan had at least a smattering of Italian."[36] The vogue supported professional teachers such as William Thomas, Claude Desainliens (Hollyband), and John Florio. Italian books were printed in England, especially by John Wolfe; translations from the Italian increased; and Italian proverbs proliferated in English writings. Interest in Italian was so great at Oxford, especially at Magdalen College, that by 1576 tutors were offering informal language instruction in Italian as well as in French.[37] Italians in England responded to the demand for Italian fashions by teaching deportment, dancing, music, fencing, and horsemanship. Italian sculptors and architects were eagerly sought out by the aristocracy.[37a]

Thus, even without visiting Italy, Whetstone may have learned Italian and certainly would have absorbed considerable Italian culture. Within Whetstone's own circle, George Gascoigne translated from the Italian two plays, Supposes (1572) and Jocasta (1572), and at least one prose work, The Droomme of Doomes Day (1576); and Thomas Watson earned high repute as an Italian scholar, chiefly for his Hecatompathia (1582), Amyntas (1585), a collection of Italian madrigals (1590), and Amintae Gaudia (1592). Whetstone's own Rocke of Regard (1576) contains several stories of Italian origin, as does the Heptameron, for which there are no known earlier English versions.

The well educated Renaissance gentleman, however, would not have been satisfied with a book knowledge of other languages and cultures -- and Whetstone appears to have been no exception. The Renaissance gentleman travelled for study, for further education; and from other countries he brought home new manners and ideals. Many Englishmen, especially dilettantes like the Earl of Oxford, undoubtedly travelled only for pleasure and affected Italian fashions upon their return: these were the "Italianated" Englishmen, as Ascham contemptuously refers to them. But ideally, travel was supposed to be of benefit to the gentleman, for it provided him with an opportunity to learn new languages and to observe the politics, manners, and customs of other countries. Such is the conviction of Jerome Turler in <u>The Traveiler</u> (1575), the first treatise on travel written in English: after admitting that "this is an auncient question, <u>whether traveyling do a man more good or harme</u>?" (sig. B2^v) and warning young men to "Beware corruption" (sig. C3^v), Turler concludes that travel is "honeste, pleasant, profitable, and commodious" (sig. I2^v), a highly educating experience and a duty to the state. No small part of the wisdom acquired through travel is the added skill in dealing with people, the increased knowledge of "the nature and maners of men, and how to live with everybody" (sig. D3^r). Furthermore, travel was of course sanctioned by antiquity. Was not Ulysses, who knew many men's manners, the first famous traveller? Did not Plato and Pythagoras, Abraham and Moses, Darius and Alexander -- to name but a few -- travel widely? For "there was never man that performed any great thinge, or atchieved any notable exploit, unlesse hee had traveilled" (sig. G4^v).

The courtier's duty, then, was to travel and to bring back reports of his travels; the middle class gentleman could also derive profit and pleasure from travelling or from hearing and reading travellers' reports. This moral attitude towards travel is exhibited by Whetstone in the _Heptameron_ through his _persona_, Ismarito. It underlines his purpose in writing that work: to make available in England the Italian ideals of civility, ideals which he himself learned to appreciate fully in Italy. In _The Rocke of Regard_, "his friend R.C." expresses concern for Whetstone's ability to profit from his travels (this time, to France):

> My joye thy profite great, if thy returne do showe,
> Thy travell tends to countries good, not french man like to goe.
> (sig. O3^r)

R.C. (probably Robert Cudden) looks forward to receiving an account from Whetstone of the state of the foreign countries, of the latest news abroad: "These fruits thy friends expect, at thy returne to reape" (sig. O3^v). Perhaps the _Heptameron_ is Whetstone's attempt to fulfil similar expectations, to assure his acquaintances that he did indeed take his travels seriously, and to present his friends with the fruits of his Italian journey.

Whetstone may also have wished to allay any suspicion that he himself had been corrupted by his visit to Italy -- for the English admiration of Italy was by no means universal. One of the earliest and strongest attacks on Italy was that of Ascham in _The Scholemaster_ (1570): he views Italy as Circe's court, where plain Englishmen are transformed into right Italians, where men are turned into beasts by the enchantments of licentious pleasure and seductive sin. Even Jerome Turler in _The Traveiler_ (1575) admits that sometimes his countrymen "bringe three thinges with them out of _Italye_: a naughty conscience, an empty Purse, and a weake stomacke," and acknowledges that "it is growen into a proverbe amonge the _Italians_, _Thedesco Italionato_, _Diabolo incarnato_:

that is to saye, a Dutchman become in manners lyke an Italian putteth on the nature of the Devill" (sig. Fl^{r-v}). Henry Wotton, in A Courtlie Controversie of Cupids Cautels (1578) condemns Italian fashions and "Italionated" Frenchmen (sig. 2Kl^r), pointing out that in the Golden Age there had been no need to travel (sig. 2I4^r). Burghley, in Certain Precepts for the Well Ordering of a Man's Life (c. 1584) advises his own son, "Suffer not thy sons to pass the Alps, for they shall learn nothing but pride, blasphemy, and atheism." Thomas Nashe, in Pierce Penilesse his Supplication to the Divell (1592), lashes out at "Italie, the Academie of manslaughter, the sporting place of murther, the Apothecary-shop of poyson for all Nations"; and in The Unfortunate Traveller (1594) he both uses and mocks the admonitory tradition.[38] This wave of "Italophobia" did not leave Whetstone untouched; although he never condemns all foreign travel, his later works do reveal an awareness of the dangers of travel to Italy. In Sir Phillip Sidney (1587), he praises Sidney because "He spake the French and Italian language, but their vices defiled him not":

> The Frenche he sawe, and at their follies smil'de,
> He sildome did theire gawdes in garments ware:
> In Italy his youth, was not begilde.
> By vertue he, their vices did forbeare:
> Of this bie-speache he evermore had care,
> An English-man that is Italionate:
> Doth lightly prove a Devell incarnate.   (sig. B2^r)

Whetstone's mockery, in the Heptameron, of the "superstitious cermonies" of the Papist Italians later turns to angry denunciation in The English Myrror and The Censure of a Loyall Subject.

G. B. Parks, in "The First Italianate Englishmen" suggests that the negative view of Italy arose largely as a result of strong political repulsion and gained currency after the excommunication of Queen Elizabeth in 1570 and the conviction of Ridolfi for his part in the Norfolk conspiracy. The two pictures of Italy -- as a model of manners and as a pattern of sin -- then existed side by side into the seventeenth century. The term "Italian" became ambivalent, sometimes meaning "dangerous"; but "Italianate" was always derogatory, implying "immoral," "irreligious," "vicious," "wicked," and (after 1572) "deceitful," then "treacherous."[39]

Nevertheless, in spite of the growing chorus of warnings against the atheism, immorality, violence, treachery, and lasciviousness of the Italians -- and especially of the Neapolitans -- Italy remained the usual ultimate destination of the English traveller. Scenery was not the chief interest of the Renaissance traveller: beautiful as the Italian landscape may have been, it was barely commented upon in travellers' reports. Instead, the reports spoke of the dazzling pageantry, the magnificent architecture, the inspiring music, and the splendidly luxurious manner of living. Painting was barely mentioned. When Ismarito comments on the architecture and luxury of Segnior Philoxenus's palace, he is reflecting the typical traveller's fascination with the great palaces of Italy; for instance, William Thomas had also admired the Palazzo Farnese and the Italian gardens which, he felt, transformed the palaces into paradises.

Above all, Italy was the center of culture, and its gentlemen were considered to be models of behaviour -- as Segnior Philoxenus is "a president of behaviours." In his preface to The Historie of Italie (1549), Thomas refers to "the Italian nation, which seemeth to flourish in civility most of all others at this day."[40] The Elizabethans looked to sixteenth-century Italy, focusing chiefly on Venice and Florence, for standards of "civility," for guides to courtesy, taste, conversation, speech, and manners. These ideals were popularized in England largely through courtesy books, especially Castiglione's Il cortegiano and Guazzo's La civil conversazione, and through collections of novellas, especially adaptations and imitations of Boccaccio and Bandello. They determined the shape and intent of Whetstone's Heptameron.

Has Whetstone pieced together a description of Italian social customs based solely on literary sources, on his reading rather than on his own experience? And does he then claim to have been in Italy to provide an aura of verisimilitude to his fictional account? Other writers of his day also describe Italian customs and also claim to have visited Italy, but none, I believe, does both in the same work. Anthony Munday spent some time at the English College in Rome in 1578 or 1579; in 1581 he acted as a witness for the Crown in the trial of Edmund Campion and other Jesuits; and in 1582 he published The English Romayne Lyfe in an attempt to re-affirm his reliability as an eyewitness, "Because a number have been desirous, to understand the successe of my journey to Roome, and a number beside are doubtfull, whether I have beene there or no." In the dedicatory epistles in the Heptameron, Whetstone presents his credentials as a reliable "truchman" or reporter, but unlike Munday, whose work is a factual account, Whetstone casts his material into an obviously traditional literary form. Framed discourses and tales set in Italy, similar in form to the Heptameron, were penned by Robert Greene: Morando, The Tritameron of Love (1587) takes place in Bologna, and Greenes Farewell to Folly (1591) begins in the Golden Age of Florence.

In these works, however, Greene does not pretend to be recording his own experiences. His assertion that he left Cambridge to travel to Italy and Spain, probably in 1580, "in which places I saw and practizde such villainee as is abhominable to declare," occurs in the supposedly autobiographical Repentance of Robert Greene (1592); thus, Greene sets apart his confessional narratives from his fictional ones. Similarly, in the writings of Thomas Nashe, the Italian setting and the personal reference to an Italian journey appear in different works: in The Unfortunate Traveller (1594) Jack Wilton's adventures culminate in Italy, while in An Almond for a Parrot (1590) the author (often identified as Nashe) states that he has been in Venice.[41]

These works do not present the complex problem of the relationship of fact to fiction as does the Heptameron, for they are either blatantly fictional narratives or supposedly autobiographical reports. Except for Munday's The English Romayne Lyfe, they do not purport to be eye-witness descriptions of Italian customs. Even where Italy is the setting of the narrative, the references to things Italian are perfunctory or -- more usually -- non-existent. In the Heptameron, on the other hand, the numerous comments on Italian art and architecture suggest a tourist's observations and are, in fact, corroborated by travel books such as The Diary of Montaigne's Journey to Italy in 1580 and 1581 and A True Description and Direction of What is Most Worthy to be Seen in all Italy (c. 1600).

The Italian atmosphere of the Heptameron, then, is more than literary. Whetstone's prefatory statements (pp. 3-8) that this book is based on his own experience of Italy are supported by his consistently accurate references to Italian art, architecture, music, literature, social entertainments, words, and proverbs.[42] Segnior Philoxenus's palace is Italian in design: it follows the "H-plan" and makes emphatic use of elaborate decoration, plasterwork, and sculpture (pp. 14-18). The device embossed in the plaster ceilings is Italian in form and employs a motto not yet well-known in England but known on the continent (pp. 15-16). Whetstone accurately refers to local features, often giving correct historical details: these include the pine forest of Ravenna (p. 13), the garden of Tivoli (p. 18), Cardinal Farnese's palace (p. 18), Loreto and the legend surrounding its shrine (pp. 44-45), the Pope's palace at Lateran (p. 115), and Cosimo de Medici's library (p. 169). The reference to Capua Verde as the ancient capital of Naples (p. 92) does not occur in Whetstone's source, Marguerite de Navarre's Heptaméron 32, and may reflect knowledge acquired by a visit to that city (in The Honorable Reputation of a Souldier, sig. G2^r, Whetstone admits to visiting Naples). Among the social entertainments of clearly Italian origin described in the Heptameron are two differently structured masques (pp. 66ff. and 227ff.), a show by mountebanks -- Whetstone takes care to indicate how these differ from the English mountebanks (p. 109) -- and a performance by a travelling troupe of players that recalls the commedia dell'arte (pp. 163ff.). Although the commedia dell'arte had already appeared in England, perhaps as early as 1547, it was not yet widely performed in 1582, at least not outside the court circle. K. M. Lea, in Italian Popular Comedy, claims that Whetstone's descriptions of mountebanks and improvising comedians "show that he was perfectly acquainted with both kinds of professional entertainers."[43] Furthermore, the names of several of Whetstone's characters -- Aurelia, Fabritio and Isabella, Franceschina, and Farina -- may have been suggested by actors and characters in the commedia dell'arte (see notes for pp. 19, 23, and 120); the figure of Doctor Mossenigo combines traits of the Pedant and of Pantalone (the old man in love); and a clever servant, suggesting a zanni, makes a brief appearance (pp. 172-73). Philoxenus's guests are frequently entertained by a soloist singing to the accompaniment of a lute; this was also the practise in England. But what is remarkable in the Heptameron is that the soloist is a "Eunuke" (p. 25, etc.) -- in keeping with Italian but not English practise. The sources of the songs, where they have been discovered, are Petrarch's poems. Not only does Whetstone use words that are of Italian origin and not yet assimilated into English, such as "bollytine" (p. 14) and "zanni" (p. 109), but he also uses one proverb for which the only known source is Italian, "After dynner, talke a while, After supper, walke a mile" (p. 49). None of these examples taken alone would prove that Whetstone visited Italy -- although the references to the commedia dell'arte and to the eunuch singer are persuasive -- but they create a total cumulative impression of thorough acquaintance with Italian customs, language, and geography.

Whetstone's indebtedness to Italian literary sources and traditions cannot be denied, but he supplements his reading with personal experience. There is nothing described in the frame of the Heptameron that may not have been found or may not have occurred in Italy of 1580. If Whetstone is not writing from his own experience, if he is in fact composing a merely literary description of Italian customs, as did other writers of his day, then he was a most thoroughgoing and accurate sociologist to a degree unheard-of in the Renaissance, when such fidelity to social and historical detail in literature is unknown. The Heptameron is not a translation or a slavish literary imitation; nor is it a factual report; it is an imaginative embodiment of Whetstone's own reading and own experience.

2.

The Ideal of Civility

An understanding of the peculiarly Renaissance ideal of civility is essential to a proper appreciation of Whetstone's <u>Heptameron</u>. It is an ideal that grew out of the civilized urban life as opposed to the unsophisticated country life. Whereas the isolated castle was the center of medieval social life, in ancient Greece and Rome and in Renaissance Italy the city was the center of society. In Italy, the focal point narrowed to the court, especially in Urbino, Ferrara, Mantua, Milan, and Naples, and to its offshoots, the city palace or <u>palazzo</u> and the gentleman's country villa. The city-states with their many small courts fostered an ideal that valued social contact and urban life. The term "civil" which originated with the city came by extension to refer to a type of living that need not be particularized by place or setting. It could still be used to define good government, in the political sense, but more often "civil" identified an ordered, harmonious, virtuous social life, the life of social harmony that made the city possible. This is the sense in which Guazzo employs the word in his <u>Civile Conversation</u> (1581):

> You see then, that we give a large sense and signification to this woorde (civile) for that we would have understoode, that to live civilly, is not sayde in respect of the citie, but of the quallities of the minde: so I understand civile conversation not having relation to the citie, but considera-tion to the manners and conditions which make it civile. And as lawes and civile ordinances are distributed not onely to cities, but to villages, castles, and people subject unto

> them, so I will that civile conversation appertaine not
> onely to men inhabiting cities, but to all sortes of persons
> of what place, or of what calling soever they are.
> Too bee shorte, my meaning is, that civile conversation
> is an honest commendable and vertuous kinde of living in
> the world.44

Two other dialogues show that this interpretation of "civil" was consistent throughout the sixteenth century. In <u>A Discourse of Civill Life</u> (1606), Lodowick Bryskett, while discussing the two kinds of felicity, civil and contemplative, describes the former thus:

> you shall understand that the civill felicitie is nothing
> else then a perfect operation of the mind, proceeding of
> excellent vertue in a perfect life; and is atchieved by the
> temper of reason, ruling the disordinate affects stirred
> up in us by the unreasonable parts of the mind, (as when
> the time shall serve will be declared) and guiding us by
> the meane of vertue to happy life.45

And Thomas Starkey in his <u>Dialogue Between Cardinal Pole and Thomas Lupset</u> (c. 1538) gives the following speech to Lupset:

> Nay, Maystur Pole, you take the mater amys. Thys ys not
> the cyvyle lyfe that I mean, -- to lyve togydur in cytes and
> townys so fer out of ordur, as hyt were a multytude conspyryng
> togeddur in vyce, one takyng plesure of a nother wythout
> regard of honesty. But thys I cal the cyvyle lyfe, contrary,
> lyvyng togyddur in gud and polytyke ordur, one ever redy to
> dow gud to a nother, and, as hyt were, conspyryng togydur
> in al vertue and honesty. Thys ys the veray true and cyvyle
> lyfe.46

"Civility" is not to be defined simply as city life or social intercourse; rather, it is the more general and abstract ideal which makes possible the social life. The formulation of such an ideal of social harmony was important to an age in which Order -- universal order -- was the first law of nature and hence of God.

That the word "society" came into common use in the sixteenth century indicates the extreme self-consciousness of Renaissance social life. In an age of upheaval and change in all dimensions of life, men looked for new ideals to provide a sense of stability. Social and family relations assumed great importance at a time when the feudal order was dissolving, governments were rapidly falling and rising, the authority of the Church was diminishing, religions were taking new forms, economic conditions were constantly altering, and when there was unprecedented social mobility. Increasingly concerned with ways of achieving happiness in this life, the sixteenth-century Englishman became very conscious of the clash between the individual's instincts and passions and society's codes of behaviour. Civilized life was possible only if the disruptive instinctual forces were disciplined; thus, rules of conduct were established and all details of life were organized.[47] The classical ideal of <u>urbanitas</u> or <u>civilitas</u> was absorbed into the broader concept of civility, giving rise to a code of gentlemanly behaviour that was within reach of every educated citizen. The result was the rapid growth of a literature of manners, generally referred to as courtesy literature. Civility is the ideal of which courtesy is the virtue as it is manifested in the interrelationships of persons; such social behaviour is referred to as "manners" or "conversation."

Because the ideal harmonious life is possible only in society, the civil life is of necessity an active life. The emphasis on life in this world owed a great deal to the impact of Renaissance humanism which encouraged the belief that happiness could be achieved on earth. Happiness is available only to the truly virtuous man, and since virtue must be practised to be known, the virtuous man must live in society. A moral end, it is assumed, implies a public end. The civil man, then, rejects the medieval ideal of the contemplative life:

> But being as we are among men, and set to live and converse
> with them civilly, the civill man must not give himself to
> contemplation, to stay upon it as wisedome would perswade
> him, untill he have first employed his wit and prudence to
> the good and profit as well of others as of himselfe.[48]

The anonymously written dialogue between an English courtier and a country gentleman, <u>Cyvile and Uncyvile Life</u> (1579), points out that the life of man is like iron: it must be used if it is to be bright and shining, otherwise it rusts away. The dialogue concludes that the gentleman should dwell in the town. Starkey's <u>Dialogue Between Cardinal Pole and Thomas Lupset</u> (c. 1538) similarly draws a parallel between the conflict of active versus contemplative life and the conflict of city versus country life. It is not enough for men to pursue knowledge and virtue in isolation, as did the old philosophers, maintains Starkey; they must communicate their knowledge to others. Such communication of virtue and knowledge is the end of civil life, to which man is born as a politic creature, argues Starkey's spokesman, Thomas Lupset. When Cardinal Pole counters that city life is evil and corrupt and that man is better off in a natural world as in the Golden Age, Lupset points out that the civil life is not necessarily the life of the city. In any case, continues Lupset, it is not society that causes disorders, but the lack of wise governors; and without cities men would still be living rudely and wildly as do the beasts. Thus, Starkey's dialogue suggests the opposition inherent in the ideals of civility and of pastoralism.

The extent to which the ideal of the active civil life, as opposed to the medieval ideal of the contemplative life, pervades Renaissance imaginative literature is reflected in Spenser's <u>Faerie Queene</u>. Thomas P. Roche links Spenser to Lodowick Bryskett, pointing out that <u>The Faerie</u>

Queene "is a fulfillment of the ideal of civil life that is to occur historically during the reign of the Tudors . . . . The action of the poem is the evolution of the civil ideal and is conceived as a reciprocal interchange between England and Faeryland." The civil man finds his fullest expression in a society centered on the city, and such an ideal city, representing the civil life, is the city of Cleopolis in Book II of The Faerie Queene.[49]

The active expression of civility is manifested through manners, social behaviour, speech, and virtue -- all closely related terms in Renaissance thought. In The Faerie Queene, Spenser links courtesy, an aspect of civility, with virtue and manners and suggests the importance of knowing how to behave towards others:

> Of Court it seemes, men Courtesie doe call,
> For that it there most useth to abound;
> And well beseemeth that in Princes hall
> That vertue should be plentifully found,
> Which of all goodly manners is the ground,
> And roote of civill conversation.
> (The Faerie Queene VI.i.1.)
>
> They teach us, how to each degree and kynde
> We should our selves demeane, to low, to hie;
> To friends, to foes, which skill men call Civility.
> (The Faerie Queene VI.x.23)

"Conversation" is defined by Guazzo as relationships between people, and in his book he attempts to discuss the importance and the basis of social intercourse. Guazzo is not alone in refuting the value of the solitary life: love of solitude, he claims, arises out of dangerous melancholy, and true pleasure is possible only when it is shared with others or given to others, for man is a social animal. Similar views are presented by Bryskett:

> For as concerning civill felicitie, man cannot, nor ought not to be alone: in which respect conversation and friendship are necessary for the accomplishment of the same.
>   Aristotle sayd, that he that lived alone could be none other than either a God or a brute beast.
>
> Besides that, solitarinesse bereaveth a man of the sweetest part of his life that is conversation among friends, increasing the contentation of a happie man, as he is to be a civill man.[50]

Whetstone expresses the same feeling indirectly in the Sixth Day of the Heptameron: when Ismarito retires alone to a quiet place to read Mexia, Segnior Philoxenus, the perfect host, seeks him out "to geve his solytarinesse, a disgrace, by conversing with him, in some Gentlemanly Discourse" (pp. 168-9).

    The ideal of civility presupposes that social interaction is the chief means by which we learn to know ourselves; through knowing ourselves and knowing how to interact with others, we may achieve happiness. Hence, to the Renaissance man, no aspect of social life is trivial. Etiquette, gestures, games, jokes, anecdotes, and ceremonies all have their place in social life, for they are vehicles of subtle communication. Guazzo points out that although some ceremonies may seem superfluous, their proper use in society is important; they create expectations and are therefore to be observed. In Whetstone's time, even clothes might be expected to make statements; accordingly, the masquers' apparel in the Second Day of the Heptameron communicates their states of mind. This universal Renaissance concern with ceremony reflects the play element inherent in the notion of civility:[51] as men become more obsessed with the importance of creating order and beauty, they create rules for all aspects of life and enjoy consciously playing their roles in society. The Renaissance to a large degree lived out the concept of the world as a stage. The significance of games and ceremonies as a basis for social intercourse is overshadowed only by the importance of fine and witty speech, the mark of a gentleman. All educated citizens cultivated the graces of conversation, and their enthusiasm fostered the publication of many specialized manuals of conversation, dictionaries of similes, proverbs and anecdotes, and manuals of letter-writing.

Related to the ideal of civility is the idea of the gentleman; and in the <u>Heptameron</u> Whetstone's discussion of civil discourses is linked to a description of the courteous Segnior Philoxenus, an Italian gentleman who is worthy to be a model of behaviour. As civility took root in the city life in general, the concept of gentlemanly behaviour, usually characterized as courtesy, developed out of the ideals of conduct at the court. Courtesy was thought of as an exhibition of good will between the classes and an expression of the beauty of the highly civilized life.

> To sum up, courtesy as a gentlemanly virtue was fundamentally a preserver of society, helping to keep the lines between classes that the aristocratic ideal created by prescribing the kind of treatment due to each, and helping also to maintain obedience by gaining the good will of the lower classes to the upper; it was also a beautifier of society adding grace to the actions of men; and last of all even according to Elyot it adorned the individual, allowing his real worth and accomplishments to shine forth and draw the eyes of all men to him.[52]

The Italian Renaissance courtier was the counterpart of the Greek philosopher-king and the Roman orator, each the mirror for a particular society; the Renaissance gentleman, however, was a broader and more democratic ideal than that of the courtier. Whereas the courtier performed primarily within the limited world of the court, the gentleman was found throughout the middle classes as well as the aristocracy, for the new commercial wealth enabled merchants to live as noblemen. Catering to this shift in values, writers devoted entire works to the discussion of the meaning of nobility, voicing the Renaissance consensus that high birth and virtue are not necessarily synonymous. In the new idea of the gentleman were merged classical, Christian, and chivalric values. Neither a philosophical and civil leader as was the classical statesman, nor a military and religious hero as was the medieval knight, the Renaissance gentleman nevertheless shared many values with his predecessors.

In addition to the privileges he enjoyed by virtue of his position between the king and the common people, the gentleman bore many obligations. He was expected to administer justice, to provide leadership in war, and to advise the king. Conduct books stress the importance of this sense of social responsibility because they all aim ultimately at furthering the social life and especially the public life. The gentleman's first loyalty is to his country, and the courtier's first loyalty is to his prince; Whetstone depicts Segnior Philoxenus as a nobleman who owes allegiance primarily to the Protestant cause. Although the Renaissance ideal of courtesy has much in common with the medieval concept of <u>cortesia</u> and with chivalry -- manuals of knighthood emphasize the knight's personal development and his need to seek the glory bestowed by noble deeds -- the courtier must put selflessness and devotion to the service of his country first and his own personal glory second. For the gentleman, the striving after personal glory fades even more in the face of social goals. In general, English works tend to accentuate the moral qualities of the gentleman, while Italian works ascribe more importance to his personal perfection and social grace. The Italian emphasis on the aesthetic aspect of courtesy, including the art of loving, is virtually non-existent in England where writers preoccupied with morality lose sight of the merits of grazie and sprezzatura, of grace, nonchalance, and ease.

Because education is the means of perfecting a gentleman, every treatise on civility or courtesy or conduct pays attention to the training of the gentleman. Furthermore, education was valued by the middle class as a means of rising from low to high estate and by the Protestants as an aid to approaching the kingdom of God. Hence it comes as no surprise to find Whetstone describing Philoxenus's studies as "the true patterne for a Gentleman to imitate" (p. 170). The subjects of study are Theology, Physick, Law, Heraldry, Morality, Cosmography, History, and Armory. That this is a typical Renaissance gentleman's education is supported by Ruth Kelso's Doctrine of the English Gentleman in the Sixteenth Century:[53] to Philoxenus's list Kelso would add logic and rhetoric, poetry, mathematics, natural philosophy, modern languages, especially French and Italian (which Philoxenus speaks in addition to English), drawing (which he practises), and travel, especially to the French court (where Philoxenus spent some years as a young man).

In a society where man strives for perfectibility as a social being, the role of women becomes more significant. In sixteenth-century Italy, women of the upper classes were neither expected to be menial servants nor exalted to the position of presiding deities. They were educated and cultivated, moving in courts and palaces as the courtiers' social equals and companions. The art of conversation acquired an added importance as a way of promoting social intercourse between the sexes. Castiglione's Il cortegiano is generally gracious towards women and Guazzo's La civil conversazione tends to be charitable, but English works do not always share their attitude. English Renaissance literature frequently adopts a more pragmatic view of woman as a helpmate and companion in the home. In Whetstone's _Heptameron_, the Italian courtly ideal of woman appears in the frame characters, especially in Aurelia, and the practical approach to the role of women in marriage dominates the discussions.

3.

Renaissance Courtesy Literature

Because the virtues requisite for social living could be learned, the Renaissance generated a mass of literature that discussed in detail the ideals of civility and of conduct. Such works reflect in their forms the belief that civil ideals are best manifested in society through action and talk. Hence, books on civility are not mere philosophical treatises or collections of precepts; they are almost always dialogues that exhibit civil virtues in action. Books of parental advice, social conduct, policy in government, etiquette, and domestic affairs, all reflect the assumptions that conversation and courtesy are arts that may be learned and practised, that the end of courtesy is practical conduct, and that civility is acquired not inherited. The term "courtesy book" traditionally refers to any work that is intended to be a guide to conduct, ranging from books of table manners to volumes outlining the broad conception of the gentleman. The courtesy books that are works of art generally depict an ideal rather than an actual picture of gentlemanly behaviour. According to Thomas Greene, they are types of the "institute," a genre which inspired numerous ideal portraits of a society, an institution, or an occupation; which expressed the constant Renaissance search for perfection; and which reflected the Renaissance faith in man's ability "to mold and transform the self," a faith that was summed up in the saying of Erasmus, _Homines non nascuntur, sed finguntur_ ("Men are fashioned, not born").[54]

Very few works adopt a philosophical approach to civility, and those that do cannot properly be called courtesy books. The Italians published some discussions of civility, but the emphasis in literature quickly shifted to courtesy and manners. Palmieri's <u>Della vita civile</u> (c. 1528) describes society as a whole and draws a picture of the ideal citizen as one who is well educated, skilled in public affairs, and respected for his own virtues rather than for his title. At the same time as ideals of the courtier and of the prince were being formulated, Palmieri helped to define the ideal citizen. Cintio's <u>Ecatommiti</u> (1565), from which Whetstone adapted several novellas, includes a second part entitled <u>Tre dialoghi della vita civile</u>, freely translated by Lodowick Bryskett as <u>A Discourse of Civill Life</u> (published 1606 but written around 1582). Bryskett's version gave voice to the growing English preoccupation with the meaning and value of the civil life, a preoccupation that more often resulted in practical essays on conduct than in abstract discussions of ideals of civility.

Among classical works on conduct that served as models in the Renaissance were Cicero's <u>De Officiis</u> and <u>De Oratore</u>, Aristotle's <u>Ethica</u>, Seneca's <u>De Beneficiis</u> and <u>Epistulae Morales</u>, and Plutarch's <u>Moralia</u>; but there is no classical precedent for a work that deals exclusively with the fine points of conduct. In contrast, the Middle Ages produced a host of books on manners in the narrower sense of the word, intended for scholars, knights, princes, husbands and wives, or children; such medieval conduct books were often in verse and sometimes in dialogue form. The limited medieval approach to conduct persisted into the English Renaissance in works such as <u>The Babees' Book</u> (c. 1475), <u>The Institucion of a Gentleman</u> (1555), and Thomas Twyne's <u>The Schoolemaster, or Teacher of Table Philosophie</u>

(1576). Later conduct books typically combined the broader classical approach to virtuous behaviour with the medieval concern for pragmatic detail. English literature tended to examine specific topics related to both conduct and the civil life: the question of nobility, the relative merits of court life and country life, the duties of the administrator and of the soldier, the duties of husband and of wife, the obligations of children, the conflict between the sexes, the advisability of marriage and the management of domestic affairs, the composition of letters, and the practise of social recreations. The encyclopedic description of the total gentleman received its fullest expression in English literature only in the seventeenth century, in Henry Peacham's Compleat Gentleman (1622) and in Richard Brathwaite's The English Gentleman (1630) and The English Gentlewoman (1631). However, the most important Renaissance courtesy books in England and throughout Europe were Italian: Della Casa's Il Galateo (1558), Guazzo's La civil conversazione (1574), and Castiglione's Il cortegiano (1528).

Galateo was translated into English by Robert Peterson in 1576. Subtitled "A Treatise of the Manners and Behaviours, it behoveth a Man to use and eschewe, in his Familiar Conversation," it is a book of specific, utilitarian advice. It emphasizes the importance of manners, which are founded in a desire to please others, and is aimed at the ordinary educated man. The popularity of Della Casa's essay is evidenced by the currency in Italian of the phrase "To teach the Galateo" which became synonymous with "To teach good manners."[55]

The first three books of Guazzo's dialogue were translated by George Pettie in 1581 as The Civile Conversation; the fourth book was added by Bartholomew Young in 1586. Whetstone, however, may have known the two French translations of Gabriel Chappuys and François Belleforest, both published in 1579. Guazzo's aim is to outline the theory, then to illustrate the practise of polite society; he discusses the philosophy of right conduct, analyzing the principles of conduct which underlie social intercourse, attempting to define the quality of behaviour that brings about harmony in society. His moral intent is obvious: he is interested primarily in making his reader a better person. He does so by casting his discussion into the form of a dialogue between William Guazzo (his brother) and the physician who has been called upon to cure William's melancholy. "Civil conversation," the avoidance of solitude, is the proper cure. In Book Three Guazzo deals with relations between husband and wife, describing domestic life, providing instructions on marriage, and emphasizing that marital happiness depends on mutual trust. Book Four describes a banquet, thus showing how the theory discussed in the previous three books might manifest itself in an actual social occasion. Such a description of an informal gathering of friends engaged in talk is termed the <u>conversazione</u> form. Guazzo's book, both in the original Italian and in English translation, was sufficiently popular in England to give wide currency to the phrase "civil conversation."

The <u>Courtier</u>, translated by Sir Thomas Hoby in 1561, presents an ideal that is aesthetic as well as moral. Castiglione's book is concerned with "the self as a work of art" as well as with manners defined as "that range of conduct which must be both ethical and beautiful at the same time, the kind of behaviour which eases and graces the conduct of life."[56] The courtier attains perfection by balancing within him the contrary impulses and feelings that are part of the human condition, and by developing and disciplining all his potentialities. Even erotic impulses, always destructive, are transformed into courtly love and into Platonic ideals of love and beauty. Always a performer and above all an artist, the courtier consciously shapes his self and his life into things of beauty. Because aesthetic and moral considerations overshadow political realities in his book, Castiglione has been accused of evading reality; but surely this is in some sense his aim, for he is sharing with the reader his vision of what life might be, not his perception of what life is. And this vision is a flowering of the ideals of the civil life, which is a life of harmony and beauty, of both seriousness and playfulness.

> If ever an élite, fully conscious of its own merits, sought to segregate itself from the vulgar herd and live life as a game of artistic perfection, that élite was the circle of choice Renaissance spirits. We must emphasize yet again that play does not exclude seriousness. The spirit of the Renaissance was very far from being frivolous. The game of living in imitation of Antiquity was pursued in holy earnest . . . . And yet the whole mental attitude of the Renaissance was one of play. This striving, at once sophisticated and spontaneous, for beauty and nobility of form is an instance of culture at play.[57]

Both The Civile Conversation and The Courtier are compilations and discussions of commonplace themes: of nobility, education, friendship, love, the war of the sexes, the value of arms versus letters, humor, dress, and language. Guazzo, however, addresses a middle class audience and his aim is therefore more overtly moral and less aesthetic; although he recognizes the court as the arbiter of conduct, his book is anti-courtly in tone. Whereas Castiglione, addressing the aristocracy, emphasizes the importance of appearance, Guazzo stresses the need for honesty to oneself and to others. Guazzo incorporates a discussion of marriage as a type of civil conversation, but Castiglione, although he gives women a prominent place in his book, does not discuss marriage. The tone of The Courtier, with its preoccupation with self-advancement, is essentially pagan; The Civile Conversation constantly recognizes the importance of religion, that is, of Christianity. In both works dialogue is important, in the first as an instrument to be used in forming a sense of self, and in the second as a way to social harmony; but Castiglione's style is the more flexible and varied, for flexibility and variety of response are important attributes of his courtier.

> In a world which has vanished or is about to vanish, Castiglione is intent upon a theoretic and impossible ideal for a narrow coterie of the elite; Guazzo is engrossed in a practical, workaday mode of conduct for all levels of society in a world in process of becoming.[58]

The ideas of The Civile Conversation are more important than the occasion framing them; in The Courtier, the social occasion predominates. It is not surprising, then, that Whetstone is indebted to Guazzo for many of the ideas in the Heptameron and to Castiglione for its style and structure. Nor was he alone in profiting by both works. Late sixteenth-century England had not yet exchanged the ideal of the cortegiano for that of the gentiluomo, as had Italy, for both Castiglione's book and Guazzo's became available in England at the same time. With characteristic eclecticism, the Elizabethans absorbed these contradictory models of conduct into their own social outlook; for instance, as Daniel Javitch points out, in The Faerie Queene Spenser also conflates Guazzo's civility and Castiglione's courtliness.[59]

In England, The Courtier was read chiefly as a treatise on education, on the code of polite society. However, the spirit of Castiglione's work may have had a direct bearing on the development of poetic style (Puttenham's Arte of English Poetrie (1589) links artistic norms with courtly conduct),[60] and it does penetrate -- though not very deeply -- Elizabethan prose fiction. The aesthetic consideration, the sense of play, may be felt in works such as John Grange's The Golden Aphroditis (1577), John Lyly's Euphues (1578), and Whetstone's Heptameron (1582). Vividly aware of life as role-playing, of the world as a stage, and strongly bent on making social intercourse beautiful as well as good, these writers reveal in their works a predilection for social games of all kinds -- for proverbs, riddles, discourses, masques, and story-telling -- largely drawn from Italy but found also in antiquity.

The influence of courtesy books on Elizabethan prose fiction was magnified through the popularity of Euphues and its sequel, Euphues and His England. Aimed at the gentleman rather than the courtier, both works describe a variety of social customs: in Euphues, questions on love are debated after supper, and in Euphues and His England, arbitrated discourses, questions on love, and masques are part of the after-supper entertainment. According to Bond, at a time when prose fiction was based on stories from history, mythology, or chivalry, Euphues stands out as the first English work modelled on the social intercourse of the modern world; it is really a courtesy book in novel form.[61] Although undeniably influenced by Italian literature, Euphues attacks Italy and condemns the Italianization of English manners. Whetstone, who does not borrow directly from Euphues yet shares many of Lyly's aims and topics, perhaps deliberately intended the Heptameron to be a rejoinder to attacks such as Lyly's. In contrast to Lyly's picture of Italy as a place of disruptive passions, of violence

and treachery, of atheism and Papistry, the Heptameron presents us with
an Italian country palace that is a model of civility, of order and harmony
and good will -- though it must be admitted that Whetstone's praise of
Italy is somewhat qualified by his making the palace the home of a Protestant
gentleman.

Courtesy literature and the prose fiction influenced by it may be
viewed as outgrowths of an ideal that is both akin to and opposite to
the pastoral ideal. Pastoral literature glorifies nature for its goodness
and condemns society for its corruption; it celebrates a free, innocent
love; it values simplicity; and it generally adopts for its setting a
forest, field or garden that is symbolic of the natural world. On the
other hand, courtesy literature despises the state of nature as being
evil and brutish and glorifies the life of the city and of the court,
or of the villa that is in reality an extension of the court; it puts
forth a Platonic concept of love and views marriage as a social contract;
it recognizes the value of ceremony and role-playing; and it usually chooses
as its setting a glittering palace or a cultivated garden that is symbolic
of civilizing order. Yet both types of literature are arcadian in tone;
that is, they express a nostalgic desire for what was or what might have
been. Both long for a return to the Golden Age, whether it be in Arcadia
or Urbino -- or at Segnior Philoxenus's palace. In the pastoral romance,
the knight finds peace and contemplation in a retreat to nature; in the
courtesy book, the traveller or visitor finds security and social harmony
in the court or castle. The courtly refuge, however, seems to be extremely
short lived, almost ephemeral in comparison to the pastoral retreats.
The courtier, who is also an artist in the way he shapes his life, seeks

to re-create a perfect unfallen world, not by rediscovering the primal
order in nature, not by going back to a prelapsarian state -- for that
is impossible -- but by imposing on nature a new order that redeems it,
by creating a civilization that supplants nature. This new civilization
is better than the primitive world, even as, in the <u>Heptameron</u>, the sophisticated life of Juno is more attractive than the simple life of Diana (pp.
33-34).

Hence, in Renaissance art that seeks to communicate civil ideals,
a common motif is the contrast between the violence of the wilderness
and the serenity of the civilized city or castle. This is a motif that
hearkens back to the literature of chivalry. For example, Ismarito's
wanderings in the desert forest of Ravenna, where he has "strayed out of
knowledge" (pp. 13-14), are reminiscent of the aimless quests of the
knights-errant. Just as, in <u>Sir Gawain and the Green Knight</u>, the heartsore
and weary Gawain on Christmas Eve suddenly comes across the magnificent
castle, and is overcome by a rush of joy at his anticipation of warmth
and companionship, the lost Ismarito is delighted to spot the bright
glimmerings of the stately palace that promises him a "spedie Harbour"
for Christmas. With the knights of medieval romance Ismarito shares a
sense of isolation from society, a sense of "world-alienation":[62] he
cannot even bring himself to trust the porter's courteous invitation,
thinking that his polite words are but "an <u>Italion</u> curtesie" and not
sincerely intended (p. 14). A similar sense of the meaninglessness and
uselessness of the world recurs in many of the framed discourses of the
Renaissance and is even more pronounced in framed collections of novellas.
The Urbino of Castiglione's book is a safe, bright haven amidst the violence

and turmoil of sixteenth-century Italian politics. In the Windsor Castle of Ascham's *The Scholemaster*, the company of scholar-courtiers has found respite from the plague that is ravaging London. In this way, the authors of courtesy books try to make their readers aware that terrible as the outside world may be, all may yet be put right -- at least, by men and women striving together to create a highly civilized and perfect society. Because social harmony is all-important in the world of courtesy literature, disruptive social forces cannot be tolerated. Envy, slander, ambition, and ingratitude are threats to civility. This in part explains Whetstone's obsession with the dangers of envy and helps us to understand why the *Heptameron* concludes with a masque that dramatizes the threat of Envy to a Golden World.

4.

Dialogue Literature

Segnior Philoxenus's reading "For Government, and Civil behaviours" (p. 171) includes Plutarch's <u>Moralles</u>, Castiglione's <u>Courtier</u>, and Guevara's <u>Dial</u> <u>of</u> <u>Princes</u>. The first two books are largely dialogues; the third, a collection of essays chiefly in the form of letters, is closely related to the literary dialogue.

The Renaissance passion for dialogues is more than a reflection of writers' desire to coat the pill, to make their books more attractive and their moral lessons more palatable to prospective readers. As conversation is both the manifestation of civility in society and the bond that makes the civil life possible, so the dialogue is the practical expression in literature of the ideal of civility:

> it is emphasized that man can best realize his potential in civil conversation, in human communication that is relatively unhampered by artificial barriers to genuine understanding. This kind of social intercourse will cultivate individuality and nurture proper societal goals, and the basis for all this is an extension of the rhetorical tradition to its logical conclusion in interpersonal communication. As Garin summarizes, "The whole concept of humanity exhausts itself in this concept of conversation, in this dialogue, in this speech which gathers in itself the concrete meaning of the life of the mind."[63]

Furthermore, in an age that delighted in discussing questions that are ultimately insoluble because this world is not the ideal world, the dialogue enabled an author to present a variety of viewpoints, to examine a proposition from every possible angle, to balance and juxtapose different modes of experience, and to commit himself to a judgement as definitely as he dared, or to remain as detached and ambiguous as he liked. The element of play that is characteristic of the civil life is apparent in most dialogue literature. Bembo's discourse on Platonic love in Book Four of *Il cortegiano* is not unique in supplying scholars with a fruitful field for controversy: the degree of seriousness of the discussion and the exact position of its author have similarly been questioned in criticism even of Plato's dialogues. Like Plato, the Renaissance writer sought to portray the multiplicity and ambiguity of experience, not the absolute truth of existence, for he believed that the latter is found only in Heaven. The popularity of free-ranging discussions and debates in academic circles also prompted scholars to employ the dialogue form in their writings; indeed, it was not unusual for academic exercises to arise out of the telling of a story, a practise that is put to effective use by Marguerite de Navarre in her *Heptaméron* and by Whetstone in his *Heptameron of Civill Discourses*. The fact that Guazzo took the lead in re-establishing the academy of the "Illustraty in Italy, where debates were virtually synonymous with academies, undoubtedly influenced the structure of his *Civil conversazione*. The wide range of the dialogue is also attributable to the humanist emphasis on rhetoric as a mode of persuasion, for the dialogue was considered to be a most effective means of moving men to use their knowledge and talents in the service of society. In short, the dialogue was a common form for ethical treatises, philosophical essays, conversation books, and language manuals, and the most frequent form for courtesy books.

For civil conversation, Guazzo specifies that there be no more than ten persons, and the dialogue as a vehicle of enquiry generally features from two to eight speakers. The talk is lively, and although the final effect is one of ambiguity, the interchange clarifies and focuses the ideas. Often the opinions of one speaker are drawn out extensively, for he alone is worth heeding: in the <u>Heptameron</u> Segnior Philoxenus provides a definitive point of view. The setting of a dialogue is always tranquil, establishing an atmosphere that is the social counterpart to contemplation, in which thoughts are easily communicated. The informal tone facilitates the author's rapport with his readers and extends his appeal to a wider audience beyond the closed circles of the court and the study. The conventions of dialogue literature, then, are admirably suited to realize the aims of courtesy books and of works such as Whetstone's <u>Heptameron</u>.

Classical precedents for the use of the dialogue in serious writing are abundant. Plato's dialectics characteristically record an earlier conversation and describe the external scene in some detail. This is especially true of the <u>Symposium</u>, <u>Phaedo</u> and the <u>Republic</u>, of which the first two were current in the Renaissance. Lucian provided a model for ironic and satirical dialogues, and Cicero, as in <u>De Oratore</u>, for expository dialogues. A later example was Boethius's <u>De Consolatione Philosophiae</u>, an exchange between the author and Lady Philosophy, a book much admired by Ismarito (p. 76). In their drive to imitate the best of antiquity, the humanists cast many of their writings as dialogues. A well-known collection of dialogues was Erasmus's <u>Colloquia</u> (1516), including the "Convivium Religiosum" or "Religious Banquet." Two of the most popular humanist examples of philosophical dialogues were the <u>Paradiso degli Alberti</u> by Giovanni Da Prato (c. 1389) and Pietro Bembo's <u>Gli Asolani</u> (1504).

The European literary conventions with which Whetstone's Heptameron has most in common are the Italian discorso, questione d'amore, and conversazione. The discorso, discourse or discussion, could frame any subject matter from the lightest racy anecdote to the most elevated philosophical speculation. The questione d'amore, in which some lovers gather to discuss a general proposition about love, probably originated in the Court of Love that became a medieval device for rendering judgements in poetry. The conversazione is a dialogue most often following a banquet, and is usually a work on conduct. Other traditional models, perhaps related to the dialogue, are the débat of the Middle Ages, a semi-dramatic form epitomized by the Roman de la Rose; the dubbi, or doubts about love; and the French trattato d'amore, a treatise on love.[64] This type of discussion of love was given impetus by Boccaccio, whose Filocolo (c. 1336) contains an episode in which thirteen questions are debated in a garden by a company who choose Fiammetta to preside over them as their queen. The relevant section of Filocolo was translated into English by H.G. (Henry Grantham or Humphrey Gifford) as A Pleasaunt Disport of Divers Noble Personages Entitled Philocopo (1567) and reissued as Thirtene Most Plesant and Delectable Questions (1571). Boccaccio's influence may be traced in courtesy literature and in collections of novellas, but his questions serve no serious purpose, being intended as pure entertainment. Castiglione, however, transforms dialogue into a mode of self-realization and illustrates its flexibility and possibility for achieving wit; hence, Il cortegiano represents the peak flowering of the dialogue form.

In addition to Castiglione's Il cortegiano and Guazzo's La civil

Dialogue Literature lxiii

conversazione, Whetstone's immediate literary sources for the dialogue appear to be Edmund Tilney's The Flower of Friendshippe (1568) and Plutarch's Moralia. Tilney, admittedly influenced by the Filocolo, suggests that the *conversazione* reported in his book was a type of social diversion in actual practice at Elizabeth's court:

> But M. Pedro, nothing at all lyking of such devises, wherein the Ladies should be left out, sayde that he wel remembered how Boccace, & Countie Baltizar with others recounted many proper devises for exercises, both pleasant, & profitable, which quoth he, were used in the courts of Italie, and some much like to them, are practised at this day in the Englishe court, wherein is not only delectation, but pleasure joyned with profite, and exercise of the witte.[65]

Set in an English country garden in springtime, the Flower of Friendshippe is essentially a domestic conduct book which discusses the duties of a married man and a married woman. The group who are thrown together include the usual emancipated woman, Lady Isabella, and the misogynist, Master Gualter; they proceed to choose a sovereign and a topic of conversation for two days. R. G. Johnson claims that this is the first original work in English literature in which a queen is chosen to preside over the discussions.[66]

Another book containing dialogues assimilated by Whetstone is Plutarch's Moralia, especially the "Quaestionum Convivialium" or "Table-Talk" (612-748), which purports to reproduce the after-dinner conversation of Plutarch and his friends on various occasions. According to the speakers, a dinner "always requires friendly sociability for seasoning" (697); a group of men who stuff themselves without speaking are "downright swinish"; and a drinking-party without orderly and profitable conversation is ridiculous, "wholly inconsistent with culture and refinement" (716). In fact, the dialogue consists entirely of a series of questions, propositions to be debated: they are put forth as examples of appropriate dinner-time diversions, and range from "Why we trust our dreams least in the autumn" (734) to "Whether it is more plausible that the total number of the stars is even than that it is odd" (741). The Moralia also contains the "Amatorius" or "Dialogue on Love" (748-71), which refers to the poet Philoxenus; the "Conjugalia Praecepta" or "Advice to Bride and Groom" (298-343); the "Septem Sapientium Convivium" or "Dinner of the Seven Wise Men" (146-64), in which riddles are featured and a leader is chosen; and a tale illustrating the "Mulierum Virtutes" or "Bravery of Women," the story of Pieria (253-54), which is the basis of Philoxenus's narrative in the Heptameron (pp. 215-26).[67] Plutarch emphasizes the importance of order in life, the importance of drink and food and especially of conversation in forming friendships; he describes entertainments, relates tales, and discusses questions that are both moral and light. These are the qualities that must have attracted Whetstone to the Moralia as a source for his Heptameron.

Although Bryskett's Discourse of Civill Life also invites comparison with the Heptameron, I am unable to trace a direct relationship between the two. Bryskett's dialogue, published in 1606, was probably written in 1582 or shortly thereafter. Edmund Spenser and seven other friends -- all male -- visit Bryskett in a cottage near Dublin, and their discussions extend over three days. No questions of courtly love are raised, and no series of novellas are narrated, for the discourses are markedly serious and moral. However, like Whetstone, Bryskett claims to be recording his own experience; and although some of the frame of the Discourse of Civill Life is undoubtedly original, much is borrowed from Guazzo, and most is translated from Cintio.

In keeping with the tradition of civility and of courtesy literature, Whetstone chooses a social setting to frame his own discussion of marriage. Christmas is an appropriate time for social entertainments. The travellers assembled in Philoxenus's palace at Ravenna are varied in character and nationality. They include Italians, a Frenchman, a German, a Scotsman, a Neapolitan, and an Englishman. The traditional plain-speaking cynic surfaces in Doctor Mossenigo, and the sharp-tongued Katherina Trista enlivens the discussions. Bergetto and Soranso are played off against Ismarito, and the modest Lucia Bella and Franceschina Sancta serve as foils to the lively Isabella and Maria Belochy. For some unexplained reason, Segnior Philoxenus, though he appears at dinner and at other occasions throughout the holiday, is not present during the discourses until the last day, when he sums up and describes the ideal to be sought in marriage. The book has been moving in the direction outlined by Philoxenus's speech, but Whetstone allows some ambiguity to remain as to how the ideal might be reached in this life -- and Philoxenus, himself unmarried, protests that he lacks experience of the subject on which he is asked to hold forth. On the whole, although Whetstone's dialogue is carefully shaped to the author's purpose of defining civil ideals and shows flashes of deft characterization and wit, it is derivative and unremarkable.

5.

Marriage Literature

Throughout the Middle Ages there was a mass of literature dealing with marriage, and the popularity of such books came to a peak in England in the sixteenth century. Interest in the problems of marriage was undoubtedly fed by public curiosity about the marital difficulties of Henry VIII -- including widespread gossip about the King's Great Matter -- and by the speculations and negotiations surrounding Elizabeth's possible alliances. Yet the Elizabethan preoccupation with marriage goes deeper than political interest, for the institution of marriage lay at the foundation of Renaissance society and made possible the civil life. In the Middle Ages, books of manners were distinct from books on marriage; in the Renaissance, when marriage was viewed as one aspect of civility, the two kinds of literature were often combined. Hence, most Renaissance works that deal with courtesy and civility discuss marriage in more or less detail; and the responsibilities of the married life are frequently included in descriptions of the complete gentleman.

In the increasingly commercial society of the Renaissance, the stability of the home assumed a new significance as the means of ensuring the continuity and safety of property, of goods, of "livings." The aim of early domestic treatises since the fourteenth century was simply to clarify and codify the complexities of domestic relations in order to facilitate the efficient running of the home, without friction or waste. The wife's primary duty was considered to be the wise use of the income which the husband earned. Renaissance works, however, while not losing sight of this practical approach to household economy, tend to focus more closely on relations between the sexes. Even in academic debates, a favourite subject was the question of advisability of marriage. Influenced by the Italian conception of marriage as an equal partnership and a source of companionship, by the sixteenth-century trend towards greater liberty for women, by the increasing importance of women in polite society, and by the reign of Elizabeth which did a great deal to reinforce the position of women in society, Elizabethan literature reflects the trend towards greater freedom of choice in marriage. Middle class writers still argued about women's position in society; humanists continued to express traditionally misogynist opinions; and many satires and moral attacks were continually published. Women were condemned for their pride, vanity, jealousy, temper, talkativeness, extravagance, and love of pleasure. Nevertheless, the sixteenth century also nurtured an increasingly widely-read number of defences of women.

The typical domestic conduct book is described by C. L. Powell in his English Domestic Relations, 1487-1653:

> In its most complete form, a book of this type contained four principal subjects: (1) discussion of the marriage state from religious and secular standpoints, (2) the legal elements involved in contracting matrimony, (3) mutual relations of husband and wife, (4) the government of the family, including housekeeping, the upbringing of children, the management of servants, and general household economics. The ultimate sources of all these books were the New Testament (especially the teachings of St. Paul), the classics, and the church fathers.[68]

According to Powell, the first book on the family printed in England is William Caxton's Book of Good Maners (1487), translated from the French of Jacques Legrand. The first book to focus specifically on marriage and the first such work of English origin is William Harrington's Commendacions of Matrymony (1528), which, however, is intended as a manual for clergymen and retains a medieval tone. The most popular English domestic conduct works were translated or adapted from foreign books. David Clapham's The Commendation of Matrimony (1540) from the Latin of Cornelius Agrippa, Miles Coverdale's The Christen State of Matrimonye (1541) from the German of Heinrich Bullinger, and Thomas Becon's The Golden Boke of Christen Matrimonye (1542) from several European sources, largely determined the pattern of the marriage literature to follow. More influential in courtly circles were the works of Erasmus and Juan Luis Vives. Richard Taverner's A Ryght Frutefull Epystle in Laude and Prayse of Matrymony (1530?), Thomas Wilson's "An Epistle to perswade a young gentleman to Mariage" in his Arte of Rhetorique (1553), and N.L.'s A Modest Means to Marriage Pleasantly Set Foorth (1568) are derived from Erasmus. Richard Hyrde's The Instruction of a Christen Woman (1529?) and Thomas Paynell's The Office and Duetie of an Husband (1555?) are translations from Vives. These books monotonously echo the same arguments and probe the same questions. Is marriage a necessary evil? or an honorable and natural estate? Is the single life or the married life more valuable? Who should marry? How should a husband choose a wife? What are the duties of the wife? the duties of the husband? of the children? of servants? And so on.

  The discussions are based ultimately on the authority of the Scriptures: it is better to marry than to burn (I.Cor.vii); the wife is the weaker vessel (I Peter iii.7); the wife must submit to the husband (I Cor.vii, Eph.v.22ff.); a virtuous woman is a rare and glorious thing (Proverbs 31).

The Christian attitude towards woman, which assumes that she is weak, deficient in moral strength and hence extremely prone to sinning, is somewhat modified in Renaissance literature as a result of classical and Italian influence. Together with a more charitable, though hardly less practical, view of women, the Renaissance imported from the ancients the dialogue form. Gentian Hervet's _Treatise of House Holde_ (1532), a translation from Xenophon, is a dialogue modelled on works of Plato, Cicero, and Seneca. From Italy arrived more courtly attitudes towards women and the ideals of cultivated social life. Italian influence is apparent in John Heywood's _A Dialogue . . . Concernynge Two Meanes of Maryages_ (1561) and Edmund Tilney's _The Flower of Friendshippe_ (1568). The growing number of books in defence of women, most drawing on classical examples, is exemplified by Sir Thomas Elyot's _The Defence of Good Women_ (1545) and Barnaby Rich's _The Excellency of Good Women_ (1613); Whetstone's list of famous women is part of this tradition (pp. 138-42).

The Renaissance consensus was that marriage is a duty, a joining of families and fortunes as well as a binding of two individuals, a social contract. Women have no place in society unless married. The duties of the husband and wife are to love one another, to beget children, and to live virtuously. The husband is to exercise his authority paternally, acting as guide and friend and protector, governing his wife with kindness and understanding. The wife is to obey her husband, to be clean and modest, to manage the household effectively, and to live chastely. However important a good marital settlement may be, marriage ought not to be forced -- and in fact, few marriages were forced -- but it should be planned by the parents. An attraction based on fancy is less likely to lead to happiness than a love rooted in duty. Hence, although mutual consent of the man and woman to be married is advocated by most Renaissance marriage books, the degree of parental authority remains a very live issue. Writers voice concern about young people entering wedlock rashly and foolishly, ignoring parental advice. Suitability for marriage is to be sought in equality of rank, age, and wealth; Guazzo, for instance, points out that unhappy marriages are due to inequality of age or condition or to their being forced upon the children.[69] Whetstone's Heptameron faithfully reflects this typical Renaissance attitude to marriage. Out of the many topics that might be included in a domestic conduct book, Whetstone chooses to focus on the one question of the suitability for marriage, echoing Guazzo's views, and thus gives his discussion unity.

Elizabethan marriage books are practical and down-to-earth. Even Tilney, who reveals an idealistic view of the married life and who mirrors some Italian courtly attitudes, is domestic rather than courtly in the over-all tone of The Flower of Friendshippe; his subjects are the mundane ones of how a wife ought to be chosen and how the wife and husband ought to behave. To a great extent, literary works on marriage served as an antidote to Petrarchan love stories and poems. The Petrarchan conventions which portray love as a disruptive passion and a violent force and which elevate women to a level at which domestic affairs and household management are unheard-of, have no place in domestic conduct literature. The courtly view of women as heavenly creatures of love and beauty jars harshly with the less exciting domestic view of women as wives who fulfil natural, commonplace, and valuable roles in society. Whetstone makes effective use of such a contrast in the Heptameron: the Petrarchan love poems set off the practical tone of the framework discussions, and the novellas reveal how courtly ideals do not work in real life. To Whetstone, the significant question to be faced as a result of love is not how to live -- or die -- with an all-consuming passion, but how to cope with love and how to shape love into a constructive social force capable of sustaining the civil life.

6.

The "Heptameron" and Prose Fiction

Whetstone's <u>Heptameron</u> has generally found a place in histories of Renaissance prose fiction as a collection of novellas. To categorize as a collection a work which contains only six brief tales is misleading. Nevertheless, Whetstone's tales -- and especially the ways in which they contribute towards the cumulative effect of the discussions in the <u>Heptameron</u> -- do owe a great deal to the novella tradition in Europe.

"Novella" is an imprecise literary term. Generally, it refers to a short prose tale, non-aristocratic in tone, in which the primary interest is the sequence of events (character portrayal is weak and psychological motivation is rare) and in which the setting is one of realistic ordinary life. Robert J. Clements, in his "Anatomy of the Novella," an attempt to define the genre, identifies four structural characteristics of the Italian novella: "the cornice, the time unity, the evolving length, and the thematic classification centering on the everyday dramas of men and women during the Middle Ages and Renaissance,"[70] The usual themes are sexual love, the vanity of women, the immorality of priests and friars, and the cleverness of clerks, often related with coarse humour and rhetorical ornamentation. Such tales in English are most frequently Italian in origin.

Both literary and oral traditions probably influenced the development of the novella. Collections such as the <u>Milesiae Fabulae</u> are known to have existed in classical times, and anecdotes were frequently woven into longer classical narratives for purposes of both illustration and entertainment. In the Middle Ages, the popularity of jests and of racy fabliaux and the proliferation of preachers' manuals which contain exempla (stories designed to serve as illustrations in sermons), attest to a lively taste for story-telling of all kinds. These anecdotes, jests, fabliaux, and exempla all provide pictures of contemporary life designed to engage the attention of a lower class audience. But, as Schlauch points out, in the novellas the settings become more urban and mercantile, until by the sixteenth century the economic and social details are adding considerable realism to the tales, and the stories are told at a more leisurely pace, with fashionable decorations.[71] Apparently intended originally for entertainment at social occasions, especially at court and in polite society, novellas were quickly adapted for didactic ends and were aimed at a new audience -- that is, at the new group of readers, the middle classes. Thus, the novella style is more down-to-earth and coarse than the highly mannered style of courtly fiction, yet also more sophisticated and self-conscious than the racy colloquial style of popular oral narrative.

Novellas are always found in collections or embedded in longer narratives. The earliest European vernacular collection of novellas is the anonymous thirteenth-century Il novellino or Le cento novelle antiche, probably written as a manual for story-tellers in polite society. But it was of course Boccaccio's Decameron (c. 1350) which accomplished for the novella what Petrarch's Rime or Canzoniere (c. 1374) did for the sonnet, inspiring such a host of imitations that no well-bred Renaissance Italian gentleman dare admit that he lacked the skill either to relate a novella or to sing a sonnet, as the occasion demanded. Boccaccio's collection was followed in Italy by Franco Sacchetti's Trecentonovelle (c. 1378), Ser Giovanni Fiorentino's Pecorone (c. 1378), Masuccio Salertano's Novellino (1475-76), Agnolo Firenzuola's Ragionamenti (1525), Matteo Bandello's Novelle (1554), Gianfrancesco Straparola's Piacevoli notti (1550-53), and Giovan Battista Giraldi's (Cintio's) Ecatommiti (1565).

In France, similar short tales were called nouvelles, contes, or devis; almost all French collections were translations or imitations of the Italian. The most widely read French novellas in the sixteenth century were Les Cent Nouvelles Nouvelles attributed to Antoine de la Sale (adapted by William Copland as The Deceyte of Women, 1560?), Marguerite de Navarre's Heptaméron (1559), Bonaventure Des Périers' Nouvelles Récréations et joyeux devis (1558) (adapted into English as The Mirour of Mirth and Pleasant Conceits), Jacques Yver's Le Printemps d'Iver (1572) (translated by Henry Wotton as A Courtlie Controversie of Cupids Cautels, 1578), and Noel du Fail's Baliverneries, ou contes nouveaux d'Eutrapel (1548). Of these collections, the Heptaméron is the most original -- only six of Marguerite's tales are known to have literary sources -- and the most significant for English literary history. Later French translators adopted Marguerite's didactic method, but with less subtlety and far less wit. Marguerite's first editor, Pierre de Boaistuau, collaborated with François de Belleforest to translate Bandello into French; their Histoires tragiques (1559) bristles with the moral earnestness that later permeates the English collections. Boaistuau and Belleforest added anecdotes, discourses, moral discussions, poems, and rhetorical ornaments; they emphasized the sensational and the sentimental elements of Bandello's stories; and they created a vogue for this type of writing. After 1560, Bandello replaced Boccaccio as the source most commonly used by writers of novellas.

The first English collection of novellas was William Painter's *The Palace of Pleasure* (1566-67). Painter drew on classical as well as European literature, and he shared with Whetstone sources such as Plutarch, Quintus Curtius, Aulus Gellius, Boccaccio, Bandello, Marguerite de Navarre, and Pedro Mexia. Geoffrey Fenton's *Certaine Tragicall Discourses* (1567), derived from the French Bandello, includes digressions, moralizing comments, and discussions of marriage; by calling his stories "Discourses," Fenton directs attention to his use of rhetorical skills. *A Petite Pallace of Pettie His Pleasure* (1576) by George Pettie continues to rely heavily on Bandello, but also retells love stories from classical myth and history, giving them the style of novellas and strongly emphasizing the importance of the sanctity of marriage. Other English Renaissance works which contain novellas, and which may have been read by Whetstone, are *The Forrest of Fancy* (1579) by H.C. (possibly Henry Chettle), *The Schoolemaster, or Teacher of Table Philosophie* (1576) by Thomas Twyne, *Straunge, Lamentable, and Tragicall Hystories* (1577) by Robert Smythe, and *Tragical Tales* (1587, but probably written before 1577) by George Turberville. The only framed collection of novellas in English before Whetstone's *Heptameron* is Henry Wotton's *A Courtlie Controversie of Cupids Cautels* (1578), a loose translation of Jacques Yver's *Le Printemps d'Iver*. In Wotton's version, five gentlemen and gentlewomen relate five "Tragicall Histories," thus exhibiting a skill which Wotton claims is necessary for the courteous gentleperson and even more so for the courtier. Since the *Courtlie Controversie* is closer in tone and intent to the *Heptameron* than are the other English collections, it is not surprising that Whetstone draws on Wotton for some ideas and phrases, especially in the masque of the Seventh Day.

Unlike their English counterparts, most Italian and French collections of novellas use a framework device, a "cornice," to unify the tales, to maintain the illusion that the novellas are oral in nature, to create authenticity, and to give perspective to the work as a whole. As in the popular courtesy books, the work is often set in a country villa or a garden, stories are linked together, and social games are described. Whereas courtesy books picture a world of reason and order, the novellas depict a world of violence and passion ruled by chance. Courtesy books stress man's god-like potentialities; novellas dwell on his animal nature. Both types of literature face the same problem -- how to impose order and beauty on life without rejecting or denying its vitality and multiplicity -- and both generally contrast the two kinds of reality. The anarchic, comic, and often obscene world of the novellas is set apart from the ordered world in which they are narrated; the reality of the tales clashes with the ideal of the frame. From the secure setting, suggests Rodax, the interlocutors and hence the reader may view the world realistically.[72] However, collections of novellas go a step further than most courtesy books, for the ideal society in which the story-telling occurs is itself a refuge from the ugliness of the world beyond. Boccaccio's garden in the Tuscan countryside is for ten days a place of light and gaiety and security; outside is the nightmare of the Black Death. In the Novelle (c. 1374) of Giovanni Sercambi of Lucca, the travellers are fleeing the plague in Lucca in 1374. Cintio's Ecatommiti (1565), a collection of tales of conjugal fidelity and infidelity, is set on a ten-day sea voyage as ten men and women escape to Marseilles from the Sack of Rome in 1527. Girolamo Parabosco's Diporti (1550) are related by a shooting party kept indoors by bad weather. In her Heptaméron, Marguerite de Navarre claims to be reporting the discussions and tales heard at an Abbey in the Pyrenees where a group of travellers are marooned by floods for ten days. The five gentlemen and ladies of Yver's Le Printemps d'Iver (1572) are gathered at the feast of Pentecost to escape their memories of the recent civil wars in Poitou. A villa near Florence in springtime is the setting for the six-day gathering of young people that provides the frame for Firenzuola's Ragionamenti (1525). A convent parlor is the site of Fiorentino's Pecorone (c. 1378), and carnival time in Venice is the scene of Straparola's Piacevoli notti (1550-53). Even Bandello achieves the same effect by framing his Novelle (1554) with dedicatory letters, many of which are fictional in character, for the letters provide details of historical events and social happenings of the time and by so doing create a courtly, realistic setting for the sensational tales.

Among the numerous framework devices there is only one winter setting. Anton Francesco Grazzini (known as "Il Lasca") describes in his Le cene a dinner that takes place in 1540 at the house of a wealthy Florentine widow and her brother on the last day of January; five men and five women are present; a snowstorm rages outside; and names are drawn by lot. The parallel to Whetstone's Heptameron must be coincidental, however, for Le cene was not published until the eighteenth century.

The frame of Boccaccio's Decameron includes descriptions of nature that add to the decorative quality of the work; it depicts a refined, aristocratic group of young people who establish a tone of elegance; and above all, it makes clear the theoretical reasons and ideals which inspire the novellas.[73] Progressing from the harsh reprehension of vice in Day One to the eulogy of virtue in Day Ten, the novellas themselves form a "moral itinerary of ideas." This progression is emphasized by the frame, in which the discussions and interactions of the interlocutors highlight the important movements without overtly declaring the themes. The pretense to historicity in the characters and the setting of the frame helps to create an illusion of actuality, while the stylization of the characters and their dialogue lends their behaviour -- and their stories -- an exemplar and ideal value. "That is, the action in the 'frame' does not represent a human world psychologically alive and real, but only a felicitous visualization of those ideal, longed-for, conditions of life, weightless and remote from any daily concern."[74] For later novella writers, the frames became mere decorations, literary devices; they do not succeed in holding the reader's attention in the same way as did Boccaccio's frame. Yet Whetstone does shape the frame and novellas of the Heptameron in a way that sometimes stirs up an echo of the Decameron.

The sixteenth-century writer who most adroitly manipulates the framework device, and from whom Whetstone undoubtedly learned a great deal, is Marguerite de Navarre (also known as Margaret of Angoulême), elder sister of Francis I, wife of Henri d'Albret King of Navarre, and the most famous patroness of letters of her day. She set out to collect true histories that reflected contemporary French life and to organize them, after the example of the Decameron, into ten days of ten stories each. The seventy-two tales that were completed at her death were published by Boaistuau in 1558 as Histoires des amans fortunez, a badly edited book.

In 1559 Claude Gruget published a superior new edition and gave it the title of L'Heptaméron.

Although the frame device was commonplace in sixteenth-century French collections of novellas, Marguerite's handling of it is unique. The characters in the frame of the Heptaméron are exceptionally well-realized, perhaps because they represent Marguerite's close friends disguised by pseudonyms. The continual sparring of the sexes, as the men seek to conquer and the women seek to preserve their honor, the touches of banter, and the author's success in dramatization help to enliven the dialogue. More significant, however, is the way in which Marguerite uses the characters' conversation to draw the reader into the discussion and to give moral direction to the work as a whole. The tales also advance and dramatize the discussion, and they encourage the reader to participate in the talk of the framework characters. The novellas are not mere entertainments or illustrations; they are part of the fabric of the whole work. The characters are well motivated and generally sympathetic. Their actions are the raw material of human experience on which the framework characters comment, and the relation between the narrated tale and real life is thus emphasized. The technique of making the discussion after each tale an epilogue to the story is Marguerite's contribution to the history of the novella after Boccaccio.

The tone of the Heptaméron is skilfully varied, yet Marguerite's work is fundamentally serious. Her subjects are love and religion. Very much aware of the clash between the demands of the flesh and of the spirit, she finds a solution in Christian marriage. For Marguerite, love is a means of reaching the ideal in this world; human love is a ladder to the divine. Marriage, both a social and divine institution, is the necessary compromise. It enables men and women to fulfil their love in this world, but it also concerns the family and the community and connects property and status. Social rank, wealth, and parental consent are all to be considered in the search for the ideal marriage, but love too is essential. Romantic love is insufficient as a basis for the social institution of marriage; companionship is more important. Marguerite cautions, however, that the ideal marital state is not often reached in our fallen world, that the condition of married life is often hellish. She would have agreed wholeheartedly with Whetstone's dictum "That Marriage, was a Parradice on earth, if her Lawes be observed: and a Hell in the House, where her Statutes are broken" (p. 36).

Whetstone, then, echoes many of Marguerite's ideas; but the philosophical and spiritual dimension of the Heptaméron, its religious theme and Platonic idealism, are not approached by the more practical English book. Marguerite's Protestant tendencies would also have attracted Whetstone, for although she always remained a Catholic, she was influenced by Protestant humanism and exhibited sympathy for Reformers. She attacks the Order of St. Francis, as does Whetstone (see the adventure of Friar Inganno, pp. 120ff.), and her hatred of monks is conspicuous. Above all, Marguerite de Navarre's Heptaméron provided Whetstone with a model for effectively combining frame and novellas so that the resulting clash culminates in the emergence of truth, for examining love as it functions in society, and for fusing courtesy book and novella and philosophical treatise.

In The Rocke of Regard Whetstone had collected prose and verse tales, many derived from Italian sources (the stories of Dom Diego, Lady Barbara, and Bianca Maria are adapted from Bandello), and one -- "The Discourse of Rinaldo and Giletta" -- that reveals considerable originality in spite of its claim to be translated from an unnamed work by an unknown Italian author; but the Heptameron of Civill Discourses shows a more sophisticated use of the prose tale, probably reflecting Whetstone's indebtedness to Marguerite de Navarre. Of the six tales in his Heptameron, only one has no known source, the story of Sicheus and Clearches in Day Two (pp. 57ff.). The adventure of Friar Inganno (pp. 120ff.) is taken from Boccaccio; the stories of Borrihauder and Ophella (pp. 40ff.) and of Malipiero and Felice (pp. 92ff.) are borrowed from Marguerite de Navarre; the story of Promos and Cassandra (pp. 125ff.) is found in Cintio; and the tale of Phrigius and Pieria (pp. 182ff.) occurs in Plutarch. Another anecdote, the metamorphosis of Rinautus (pp. 182-83) is not a novella, for it is presented not as fact (as history) but as fable, that is, as a poetic embodiment of moral truth; and its main function in the book is primarily to display Ismarito's wit. The six tales that may be called novellas are more than exempla. Into the framework discussion of ideal marriage and of life as we might make it, these tales bring the world of action, a reminder of life as it is. The novella characters illustrate through their actions some qualities that are being examined by Segnior Philoxenus's guests; thus their adventures are the experiences by which the precepts are tested. In turn, the result gives rise to further discussion.

Whetstone's novellas, then, are not the tools of a preacher, but an integral part of his mode of apprehending experience imaginatively. Nothing like his technique appears in English literature before the Heptameron, though it is approached by Greene later in the century. Tilney and Wotton unify their works by means of an enveloping narrative, but in The Flower of Friendshippe the stories are simply illustrative, and in A Courtlie Controversie of Cupids Cautels they are primarily diverting. Among Robert Greene's framework tales -- others being Morando (1584), Alcida (1588), and Perimedes (1588) -- it is Greenes Farewell to Folly (1591) that is closest in narrative design to the Heptameron. In the Golden Age of Florence, Jeronimo Farneze, his wife, three daughters (including the sharp-tongued Lady Katherine), and four gentlemen escape from the "mutinous factions" of the Guelphes and Ghibellines to a farm near Vienna. The discourses and discussions by which they pass the time provide occasions for narrating tales. However, Greene's tales here suggest more the medieval exempla than the Italian novelle, for they are more illustrative than entertaining. Greenes Farewell to Folly contains other parallels to the Heptameron: the first after-dinner discussion is sparked by the device of a death's head on Cosimo's ring, as the pictures of Ixion and of a "Rhinocerot" give rise to discussions in the Heptameron; Cosimo draws Benedetto out of his dumps, as Philoxenus brings Ismarito out of his melancholy musing; and the question of why love is painted blind occurs in both works. Nevertheless, in over-all structure, in the ways in which the novellas interrelate with the frame, the Heptameron has more in common with the Decameron and the Heptameron than it has with any English work.

In other respects, Whetstone's treatment of his novellas is competent and traditional. The tales are appropriate to the characters of their narrators, and the listeners react appropriately. Rhetorical exercises are worked into the fabric of the story, but not to an extent associated with the euphuism of the late sixteenth century. In the Heptameron, such exercises are not mere rhetorical decoration: laments and debates heighten dramatic moments, long monologues focus attention on the disruptive force of passions, and the frequent exchanges of letters further the plots. The common motif of the go-between appears in the figure of Macrello in the story of Malipiero and Felice, and the motif of the elder man giving wise advice appears both in the same story and in the story of Sicheus and Clearches. Whetstone maintains the sense of detachment required in a successful novella, but his attitude -- or at least Ismarito's attitude -- is basically good-humoured and compassionate to a degree not often known in continental tales. Friar Inganno's punishment, although justly cruel, is quickly curtailed; and the macabre revenge of Malipiero is toned down by his reconciliation to Felice. Another noteworthy feature of Whetstone's novellas is his occasional regard for economic motives.[75] Elisa and Felice both go astray because they are seduced by wealth, thus illustrating how want destroys marriage. The emphasis on the need for thrift is bourgeois in tone, and Whetstone's middle class leaning is also revealed in the portrayal of his characters. Tryfo is a rich merchant and Clearches a wealthy neighbour; Malipiero is a gentleman, but not a nobleman; Promos is a governor, but not a king. Pieria and Phrygius are royal, but their story unfolds an ideal case and is related by the courtly Segnior Philoxenus. Finally, Whetstone's novellas reflect his Protestant morality: he tones down any suggestion of lasciviousness in his originals (Farina retains her virtue), and he always seizes opportunities to satirize Papacy.[76]

Each tale in the Heptameron contributes to the total effect. The first tells a story of a disorderly and comic marriage; the last describes an ideal marriage in which love triumphs over enmity and in which public and private goals are combined. The progress from first to last is gradual matching the pace of the framework discussions, until at the end of the book the concepts of marriage treated in both frame and tales coincide. The ideal of civility merges with the reality of the novella world.

7.

Whetstone's Sources

The Elizabethan middle class audience demanded information and entertainment, profit and pleasure, from their reading, and professional writers such as Whetstone strove to satisfy their tastes, finding in the classics precedents for literary didacticism. Writers of Elizabethan prose fiction frequently compare their work to that of the bee which sucks the sweet and profitable honey out of both weeds and flowers. Their usual method of teaching is to stock their books with precepts, instructions, and examples. Pettie, in his translation of Guazzo's Civile Conversation, declares that he is making his discussion of serious matters more palatable by sweetening it with commonplace illustrations, jests, popular proverbs, and classical authorities.[77] He praises plain speaking, because goodness and weight of matter are more important than ornaments and flowers, but he admits the need for some art to alleviate boredom. Similarly, Whetstone declares in The Rocke of Regard, "And sure I hold it necessarie, that matter of devise (to worke attention) be sometimes mingled with delight" (sig. ¶2^r), and he calls the Heptameron "A Worke, intercoursed with Civyll Pleasure, to reave tediousnesse from the Reader: and garnished with Morall Noates to make it profitable, to the Regarder" (t.p.). Whetstone's method of achieving these goals is identical to that outlined by Pierre de la Primaudaye in The French Academie: (1) to praise virtue and dispraise vice, (2) to define the subject of discourse, (3) to give precepts, and (4) to provide examples that move with delight -- all in order to compare motives and reasons until truth is sought out and the best conclusion chosen.[78] Whetstone arranges the discourses and novellas to form a progression from the dispraise of vice to the praise of virtue; in the First Day's Exercise he sets out the order of the entertainments, defining the topic of each day's discourse; in the frame he outlines the precepts by which marriage may lead to happiness; and in the tales and anecdotes he tests those precepts.

The need for amplification and ornamentation is stressed in rhetorical treatises such as Thomas Wilson's Arte of Rhetorique (1553) and Henry Peacham's The Garden of Eloquence (1577). The approved means of achieving "copy" and revealing "invention" include causes, effects and consequences, examples, similes, antitheses, notable sayings and proverbs, moral sentences, dreams, fictitious narratives, theological allegories;[79] these may all be illustrated from the text of the Heptameron. In this way, a writer may display wit. Whetstone uses "wit" both in the sense of mental ability and in the sense of quickness of intellect and flow of ideas; at one point in the Heptameron (p. 111) he seems to echo Lyly in warning against the superficiality of wit, but on the whole, it is a quality he seeks and praises. The Renaissance model for such highly rhetorical writing is the classical oration. The Inns of Court and the universities trained students in the arts of persuasion, stressing that the way to argue effectively was by citing authorities and giving illustrations. The orations at the Inns of Court (where Whetstone probably studied) used jests and comic tales for illustration and to attract attention Letter-writing was also taught as an art in composing written orations. Thus, Whetstone's Heptameron may be "built along the lines of a deliberate oration," as is argued by Beauregard in his unpublished dissertation.[80]

Books of useful information, such as William Baldwin's <u>A Treatise of Morall Phylosophie</u> (1547) and H. C.'s <u>The Forrest of Fancy</u> (1579), were extremely popular, and similar compilations became the handbooks of Renaissance writers.[81] Whetstone would have had these books at hand since his schooldays:

> The school libraries of the Renaissance were made up largely of collections of proverbs, maxims, apophthegms, fables, examples, similes, descriptions, and selected quotations from such authors as Cicero, Plutarch, Aristotle, and Seneca.[82]

The <u>Heptameron</u> provides evidence that Whetstone preferred compendia of moral philosophy and historical anecdotes to general dictionaries. In the sixteenth century, history was second in importance to the Bible as a source of examples of good conduct, and Whetstone's fascination with historical narrative is demonstrated in his later works, <u>A Mirour for Magestrates of Cyties</u> and <u>The English Myrror</u>, which combine pseudo-biographical stories with moralizations.

The encyclopedias of miscellaneous information, largely historical, which Whetstone apparently used in writing the <u>Heptameron</u> include versions of Mexia's <u>Silva de varia lección</u> and Guevara's <u>Rélox de principes</u>. Mexia may today be forgotten, but the attraction which his book held for Whetstone is not difficult to understand:

> Pedro Mexía, like Antonio de Guevara, is now among the least read of sixteenth-century Spanish writers, and yet in his own age was one of the most famous. His <u>Silva de varia lección</u> (1540), put into English as <u>The Forest or Collection of Historyes</u>, went through more than thirty editions during the sixteenth century in Spain and enjoyed exceptional success in France, where it possibly encouraged Boaistuau to compose his <u>Histoires prodigieuses</u>. It was also translated into Italian as well as English. It stands as one of the most important of Spanish witnesses to the taste of the time for compilations and miscellanies of random information -- the taste that prompted

Erasmus to put together his <u>Apophthegms</u> and <u>Adages</u>, carried
the <u>Nine Books of Memorable Deeds and Sayings</u> of Valerius
Maximus through over a hundred editions, and lay behind Montaigne's
<u>Essais</u>. Mexía explains his title by saying that he has brought
together his material 'without arrangement or order' so that
it is like many different kinds of trees in a wood. It is,
indeed, there to be wandered through this way and that. He
may tell us how the empire of the Turk arose, or about Tamberlain
the Great, the wisdom of animals or the ages of the world --
and all in a straight-forward prose which, though lacking
outstanding excellence, invites one to read on. Mexía shares
the sixteenth-century love of extraordinary and amazing events
and its delight in curious information, drawn often from ancient
writers, the 'authorities', and pointing to a practical moral
lesson.[83]

The Explanatory Notes of this edition attempt to indicate the extent of Whetstone's debt to Mexia through the French translations of Claude Gruget and Antoine du Verdier, first published in 1554 and 1577 respectively (see especially Note 203.8). Further evidence that Whetstone borrowed from Mexia in his later works is provided by Thomas C. Izard throughout his <u>George Whetstone</u>, <u>Mid-Elizabethan Gentleman of Letters</u>. Although Gruget's translation of the <u>Silva</u> formed the basis of T. Fortescue's <u>The Foreste</u> (1571), there is no indication in any of Whetstone's works that he knew the English version.

Guevara's book, <u>Libro de Emperador Marco Aurelio con rélox de principes</u> (1529), also consists of collections of essays. It reached forty editions in France before 1600, and in England it was translated by Sir Thomas North as <u>The Diall of Princes</u> (1557). Imitating Plutarch, Guevara claims to be putting together the life and letters of Marcus Aurelius, translated from a Greek work found in Florence; but he elsewhere admits that he could not read Greek. Written in the high style, the <u>Relox de principes</u> may have contributed towards the development and spread of euphuism. The Elizabethans read Guevara for his essays, anecdotes, quotations, accounts of customs and superstitions, rhetorical embellishments, advice, and moralizations. Parallels between the *Heptameron* and *The Diall of Princes* are suggested throughout the Explanatory Notes.

Whetstone's interest in history is apparent also in the number of classical references, most of which are illustrative, in his works. In the *Heptameron*, there are unusually few mythological references -- and those few are primarily from Ovid -- but many historical or pseudo-historical ones, drawn chiefly from Plutarch and from the miscellanies written by Valerius Maximus, Quintus Curtius, and their intermediaries. In many cases, it is impossible to determine whether Whetstone used a primary classical source, a classical miscellany, a Renaissance translation, or a Renaissance encyclopedia; but for some of the anecdotes originating in Valerius Maximus I have not been able to trace a Renaissance source. Similarly, there is no indication that Whetstone used Golding's Ovid; in fact, his Ovidian references are closer to the Latin original than to the English translation. Furthermore, Ismarito recommends that the *Metamorphoses* be read in Latin (p. 161). The evidence, then, suggests that Whetstone did not always rely on the most available Renaissance compilation, but used the primary classical sources as well.

Nevertheless, the likelihood that Whetstone referred to some Renaissance dictionaries and manuals of classical myth and history cannot be dismissed. Starnes and Talbert have shown that lexicons including proper names were popular in Renaissance England and were easily available in school libraries. Writers frequently were familiar with classical texts, yet used the lexicons as aids to memory to recall the original or to provide a reference. The most common dictionaries were Ambrosius

Calepine's Dictionarium (1502), Robert Stephanus' Thesaurus Linguae Latinae (1531), Charles Stephanus' Dictionarium (1553), and, pre-eminent in sixteenth-century England, Thomas Cooper's Thesaurus Linguae Romanae & Britannicae (1565).[84] In his introduction, Cooper indicates that his work may be fruitfully used as a commonplace book. While Starnes and Talbert suggest that Pettie drew on Cooper for some of his stories because some details and phraseology correspond, and state that Grange and Gascoigne were probably indebted to the Thesaurus,[85] I find it impossible to distinguish definitely between the similarities of Whetstone to Cooper and those of Whetstone to classical writers. In The English Myrror Whetstone refers to both "Callipin" and "Cooper Dict." (sig. N7^r), but since he supplies no comparable signpost in the Heptameron, the extent of his use of Cooper in the earlier work cannot be conclusively stated.

Encyclopedic works on classical mythology included Natalis Comes' Mythologiae sive Explicationis Fabularum (1551), Vincenzio Cartari's Le imagini dei Dei degli antichi (1556), and Lilius Gregorius Gyraldus' De Deis Gentium (1548). These reveal an attitude towards the function of mythology in literature that is shared by Whetstone: myths transform morality into forms that are pleasant and easy to recall and provide dignity and authority to the author's statements. It was a convention of the high style, a convention common in framed novellas, to mark the passage of time by mythological references -- and Whetstone does so in the Heptameron at the opening of Days 1, 2, 4, and 7. Above all, mythology is another instrument of persuasion, for it may suggest an allegory or spark an argument:

> For undoubtedlye there is no one tale amonge al the Poetes,
> but under the same is comprehended some thinge that perteyneth
> eyther to the amendments of maners, to the knowledge of trueth,
> to the settynge forthe of Natures woorcke, or elles to the
> understandinge of some notable thynge done. (Wilson, <u>The
> Arte</u> <u>of</u> <u>Rhetorique</u>, 1553, sig. 2C4r).

The more common moralistic interpretations of myth appear in the discussions of Juno and Diana (pp. 33-34) and of Ixion (p. 144); an unconventional treatment of myth occurs in the story of Rinautus (p. 182). Both the fable of Ixion and that of Rinautus are inspired by pictures in Segnior Philoxenus's palace and lead to further discussions.

Another traditional way in which Whetstone amplifies and ornaments his theme is the use of proverbs.[86] Important in the rhetorical training of the Renaissance, the proverb was a favourite tool of preachers, politicians, pamphleteers, and dramatists, for it helped to put them as speakers or writers on friendly and familiar footing with their audiences. Initially intended as a means of extending the rhetorical resources of the native tongue -- to increase the "copy" possible in English, in the sixteenth century proverbs were often adopted from foreign languages. A knowledge of foreign proverbs was recommended for travellers as an aid in establishing rapport with strangers, in learning to converse idiomatically in another language, and in understanding foreign customs. Morals and manners were taught through proverbial expressions, especially to children; thus, the proverb came to be closely associated with conduct literature. Because in Latin the proverb had been an important rhetorical figure, both native and classical proverbs were memorized in schools; and in academic circles, a proverb might be the basis for elaboration of a theme, as it sometimes is in Erasmus.

> The Renaissance English schoolboy learned the proverb as
> a rhetorical figure of speech with which he might embellish

his theme, or help an argument by the authority of the wise saw; or, indeed, he might even work out an entire essay based upon a single proverb as topic. The principle behind this educational use of the proverb came ultimately from classical rules of rhetoric. Aristotle viewed the proverb as a figure of speech resembling the simile, the metaphor, and the hyperbole, for each figure conceals a "hidden meaning," which delights in "deceiving the hearer" and in the fact that "there is an acquisition of knowledge" in solving the enigma embodied in the proverb. Furthermore, the proverb was considered an "authority" by virtue of its being universally known and "beyond the reach of corruption," and therefore could reasonably be used as an "ancient witness" in judicial oratory.[87]

Whetstone learned his lessons well, for he does not use proverbs simply for decoration in his works; it is the wisdom expressed in the proverb that is important to him.

The term "proverb" generally refers to a wide range of wise sayings: classical adages and sentences (usually called <u>sententiae</u>), homely proverbs and proverbial phrases, and proverbial similes. Classical sayings had long been fashionable in literature and by the sixteenth century many had become proverbial. Although native proverbs were at first considered to be appropriate only in writing designed for a popular audience, or were assigned by courtly authors only to simple and uneducated characters, by Whetstone's time they were generally respectable in all literature. The late sixteenth century was the heyday of the proverb in England: Gascoigne stressed its use in literature, Pettie's novellas abound in proverbs, and Lyly's <u>Euphues</u> undoubtedly encouraged a heightened taste for a proverbial style of writing.

The first English collection of popular proverbs is John Heywood's <u>Dialogue</u> (1546), a book on marriage, recommended as a sourcebook by Wilson's <u>Arte of Rhetorique</u>, 1553 (sig. R2^r). Classical proverbs had always been recognized and were given still more exposure through Erasmus in his <u>Adagia</u> (1500), <u>Similia</u> (1513), and <u>Apophthegmata</u> (1531). Richard Taverner's <u>Proverbes or Adagies Gathered out of the Chiliades of Erasmus</u> (1539) was the most important collection of proverbs in English up to that date and was plundered by both Heywood and Meres. But by the 1570's, foreign proverbs, especially Italian ones, were in vogue. Italian proverbs are collected in James Sanford's <u>The Garden of Pleasure</u> (1573), a translation from Guicciardini; Charles Merbury's <u>A Briefe Discourse of Royall Monarchie</u> (1581), which takes many proverbs from Guazzo; and John (or Giovanni) Florio's <u>Second Frutes</u> (1591). Many commonplace books were also storehouses of pithy sayings and similes: these include Caxton's <u>The Dictes or Sayengis of the Philosophres</u> (1477), drawn from Diogenes Laertius; Sir Thomas Elyot's <u>The Bankette of Sapience</u> (1539); and John Florio's <u>Florio His Firste Fruites</u> (1578). Whetstone may have drawn, and undoubtedly did draw, on any number of these collections. Many of the proverbs in the <u>Heptameron</u> occur also in Guazzo's <u>Civile Conversation</u> and in Lyly's <u>Euphues</u> and <u>Euphues and His England</u>, but no direction of influence may be determined. The currency of Guazzo's work in England, both in the original Italian and in Pettie's translation, helped to enrich Tudor and Stuart proverb lore, and Whetstone may have learned from it his technique of using proverbs.

Whetstone's comments in the <u>Heptameron</u> indicate that he considers the proverb to be the embodiment of the wisdom of accepted truth: "for well he knewe, that Byrdes of a feather, would flie together" (p. 133); "but she (that knew a leg of a Larke, was better than the whole Carkasse of a Kyte) woulde none God thank him" (p. 180). Thus, he frequently illustrates a point by piling up proverbs as examples, heeding Thomas

Wilson's observation, in The Arte of Rhetorique, that "sentences gathered and heaped together commende muche the matter" (sig. R1^r). Clusters of proverbs serve as warnings ("Al is not gold . . . that glistereth," p. 34; "Crocadyles teares, intrappeth Fooles," p. 90); as wise precepts ("counterfeits will to kinde," p. 53; "fairest colours soonest staine," p. 111); as guides to conduct ("He that crackes the Nut, thinkes the Kernell sweetest," p. 152); and as comforting thoughts ("thinges when they are at the worst, begin again to amend," p. 196). On the other hand, a character in the book will sometimes argue against the force of a proverb, using it to ignite an argument (pp. 52, 83). Proverbs may simply focus and enforce an idea; or they may begin a discourse (pp. 84, 110, 159), provide a proof to cap an argument (pp. 112, 210), supply a neat summary of a discussion (pp. 80, 95, 166), or help to develop the theme of a poem (p. 148).

The most obvious proverbs are those that are used for expansion and embellishment of a theme or simply for ornament; but because their wisdom is so much a part of Whetstone's thought, proverbs are sometimes so embedded in the text of the Heptameron that they are difficult to recognize. When Whetstone writes, "if their wyves love gadding, lyke faire Felice, and be inconstant, do want, or finde in their Husbands, miscontentment: Twentie to one, they wil pawn their honours, to please their fancies" (p. 98), he is expanding the proverb, "Women and hens are lost by gadding." "If a House, were as soone bilded, as the Plot is drawn . . . Shepherds wold disdaine to live in Cotages" (p. 154) may be read as a version of "If wishes were horses, then beggars would ride." The metaphor "Whose eye was able to fire a mountaine of Ice"

(p. 23) echoes the proverb "To strike fire from ice." The exact interpretation of some proverbs depends on their context; for instance, Whetstone writes both "her knowen enemy is not so daungerous, as the fayned friend" (p. 218), and "better to have you a fayned friende, (being so daungerous) then an open enemie" (p. 43). On occasion, Whetstone will go so far as to change the usual meaning of a proverb to suit his theme or to create comic distortion. "An ungodly childe maketh an unthriftie Father" (p. 86) is a reversal of the usual "A sparing father and a prodigal son." The Doctor is described as shrinking "no more at these threates, then an Oke at the Helve af an Axe" (p. 82); that is, he is in less danger than the tree that "falls not at the first stroke." The meaning of one proverb is disputed by Bergetto and Soranso (p. 56), and two interpretations of another are suggested by Maria Belochy and Soranso (p. 190).

It is largely through proverbs that Whetstone establishes the frequently down-to-earth tone of the discourses and narratives, for proverbs characteristically refer to the concrete details of ordinary life and to everyday domestic affairs. For example, "<u>Felices</u> Father hath much adoe, to keepe rayne out of his housetop: then if with difficulties he lieth drye in his Bed, it is impossible he should have anye great cheare at his Boorde" (p. 95); "In deede, want wyll so quicken them, as the Husband wyll leape at a Cruste, and the Wife trot for her Dinner" (p. 90); "she will goe like a Pecock, and you like a meacock" (p. 95); and "for Spannyels and Curres, hardly live together without snarling" (p. 210). Such homely proverbs frequently introduce a note of humour or satire: the company, ready to sing the praises of Hymen, are suddenly "mute as a fishe" (p. 36), and the courtly gentlemen and ladies are "coupled together lyke fowles on Saint Valentines day morninge" (p. 24). Finally, proverbs frequently suggest character traits: the blunt and biting Doctor Mossenigo cites one colorful popular proverb after another, but the grave Soranso prefers weighty classical sententiae.

Although all Whetstone's works reflect his interest in proverbs, the Heptameron has an unusually rich store of pithy sayings. Could this feature be accounted for by the Heptameron's relation to courtesy literature and to the tradition of polite conversation, both of which favor the witty rhetorical application of proverbs? Whetstone's style has much in common with Lyly's -- including the use of proverbs -- but the Heptameron is by no means euphuistic. Euphues may have been the most popular book of its day (1578), and it released a tide of imitative writing, yet it failed to absorb Whetstone completely. The soliloquies, orations, laments, complaints, epistles, and conventional conversations that appear in Euphues and in the Heptameron occur in most sixteenth-century collections of novellas. Unlike Lyly, Whetstone does not create similes from natural history. His dialogue is colloquial and unrefined as often as it is courtly. Because his interest lies more in the movement of the action than in the analysis of sensibilities, he is concerned with capturing the nuances of speech. Whetstone's clauses are shorter, his sentences less involuted. He uses more native proverbs. The rhetorical devices that he does manipulate in the Heptameron were common currency in England in the 1580's and were the usual trappings of a literary work that aimed at moral edification. Whetstone's literary significance rests not in his style, but in his narrative skill and structural technique.

8.

The Structure of the "Heptameron"

In the dedicatory epistle to Sir Christopher Hatton (pp. 3-5), an epistle remarkable for its lack of extravagant praise, Whetstone outlines the three-fold purpose of his book: to praise Segnior Philoxenus as a model civil gentleman, to describe, as a "president of behaviours," "the civill disputations, and speaches of sundry well Courted Gentlemen, and Gentlewomen," and to provide "a true Anatomie" of the inconveniences and the benefits of marriage. The book is presented as an attempt to recall the entertainments which he had "heard and sawe presented in this most noble Italian Gentlemans Pallace, the Christmas twelvemoneths past" (p. 6). I have already argued that, although the extent to which the Heptameron is linked to an historical event is open to question, Whetstone indeed reveals a sound knowledge of Italian culture. But what is the relationship of fact to fancy in the Heptameron? Is Whetstone simply claiming to be reporting his own experience in order to give his narrative credibility? I think not. Nor do I believe that he is a faithful recorder of an actual event. For the Heptameron is perhaps unique in Elizabethan fiction in the degree to which it creates an air of "realism" while obviously assimilating several literary traditions.

Fictional narrative in the Renaissance was often condemned as time-wasting, frivolous, and dishonest. Hence, many writers attempted to make their works respectable by tagging on moral lessons and by frequently drawing the reader's attention to the ways in which the stories might be read for moral profit. Whetstone had done so in The Rocke of Regard. The technique of the Heptameron, however, is more sophisticated: not only does the narrative fully integrate the "profitable" discourses, the wise and witty comments, and the rhetorical sayings, but it is presented in such a way as to increase the book's aura of verisimilitude without sacrificing its artistic integrity.

To avoid the charge of lying, the Renaissance storyteller could insist that his work was a true history; however, rarely did he expect to deceive a reader into accepting fictional narrative as an actual record of historical events.

> Renaissance makers of fiction . . . seek to delight or instruct their readers, not to delude them . . . . If he [an author] presents himself as one who reports things that have happened, his attitude is like that of a masker at a fancy dress ball who hopes that the audience will admire the art of his dress and his acting but certainly not mistake him for the character he is playing. As Frederico remarks in the second book of Il Cortegiano, a young man who masquerades as an old one should so clothe himself as to betray the nimbleness of his person.[88]

Similarly, Whetstone takes care to specify his own role in relation to the Christmas pleasures at Philoxenus's palace. He calls himself a "trouchman", that is, an interpreter of events; but a truchman is a figure usually associated with a dramatic entertainment. Furthermore, he represents himself in the book in the guise of Cavaliero Ismarito. This role-playing and creation of a mask look forward to the storytelling technique of the seventeenth century, when tales were frequently declared "to be no fiction at all but a narration of true events under a veil of feigned names and altered circumstances."[89] Such stories appeared in the sixteenth century only as supposedly autobiographical narratives, generally of the prodigal-son type, like Greenes Mourning Garment (1590) and Greenes Groats-worth of Wit (1592). They resemble novellas in their concern with ordinary people in contemporary settings. "But while the typical novella may make a token assertion of its truth, it asks for tolerance rather than belief."[90] Whetstone portrays real people and describes events which apparently correspond to real happenings, but he rearranges and modifies the characters and actions to suit his artistic purpose, in the manner of a novelist.

This is truth as Whetstone sees it. On the one hand, a writer must ideally speak from experience: in The English Myrror he quotes what he calls an old saying, "Orpheus can describe hell better than Aristotle," for "truly in knowledge is assurance, and in report may be error" (sig. M1^r). On the other hand, Whetstone, in typically Renaissance fashion, looks to classical and other authorities for his models. Hence the ambiguity created by the fusion of experience and art. For instance, Whetstone locates Segnior Philoxenus's palace ".10. miles from Ravenna towards the River of Poo" (pp. 13-14); yet eight years earlier, before his visit to Italy, he wrote in The Rocke of Regard, "In Italie (neare to the river of Poo) there dwelled a noble man" (sig. B4^r). Segnior Philoxenus unaccountably retires after supper, not participating in the civil entertainments until the last day; and in one of Whetstone's sources, The Courtier, "the Duke uses continually, by reason of his infirmitie, soone after Supper to goe to his rest, everie man ordinarily, at that houre drew where the Dutchesse was."[91] Whetstone says that he was an eyewitness of the Italian entertainments which he describes in the Heptameron; yet in the masque in the Seventh Day's Exercise, he describes a shield which had been pictured in an English book, Gerard Legh's Accedens of Armory (1562). Such fusion is of course not unusual in literature; it is remarkable in the Heptameron, however, in that it occurs as early as 1582.

It is the carefully constructed design of the Heptameron that identifies it finally as an imaginative creation. The Heptameron opens with a description of "the dead of Winter." Ismarito, travelling on horseback on Christmas Eve, a stranger lost in "a Countrey farre from home," in which the threat of the plague is never far away, longs for a "spedie Harbour." While most men are comfortably feasting in their homes and all living beings are safe in their nests, coverts, hives, holes, and other havens, he wanders alone in "a desert Forrest." Thus, Whetstone establishes a fairy-tale atmosphere which contrasts domestic security and wild desolation. In the midst of this dark and lonely forest of Ravenna, Ismarito is suddenly amazed by the brightness of a stately palace that symbolizes the beauty and order of the civil life -- for there he meets with gracious hospitality, courtesy, and companionship. Segnior Philoxenus offers hospitality to all passers-by in the great hall; a select few, "the better sort," engage in more sophisticated, refined pastimes in the great chamber. The representative group of Europeans form a social gathering that is a court in miniature, a society in which the art of living is all-important. Once he has set the tone for the rest of the work and has acquainted the reader with the beauty and grace of the palace, Whetstone moves ahead to describe the entertainments and discussions.

An order for the after-dinner pastimes is established by Philoxenus's guests, and this order shapes the book. By means of a marked lot in a cake, a leader is chosen -- she is Aurelia, the queen of the Christmas pleasures -- for it is necessary in a society to have "one to commaund, and all to obay" (p. 19). Laws governing courtly and sociable behaviour are decreed (pp. 21-23). Aurelia defines the topics to be debated and appoints Fabritio and Isabella as judges (p. 23). The order of each day is outlined (p. 24). The day begins at nine; the company assemble in the great chamber, then celebrate morning service in the private chapel; after dinner they retire to the drawing chamber for two hours of civil discourse and disputation -- but Segnior Philoxenus does not participate; after supper they dance, mask, or enjoy other entertainments. Only in the Seventh Day is the pattern disrupted, as Philoxenus joins the company after dinner and acts as an authoritative commentator.

The purpose of the discourses is to bring out truth. "For, as Yron and Flynt, beat together, have the vertue to smite fire: so, mens wittes, encountryng in doutful questions, openeth a passage for imprisoned Trueth" (p. 27). The civil discourses begin with a theoretical consideration of love as an ideal and with a debate on the relative advantages and disadvantages of the married and the single life, judgement being passed in favor of the married life. By the end of the First Day's Exercise, the first skirmish in the battle of the sexes has been fought, and the topic has been progressively narrowed to the practical level of a debate on the inconveniences of marriage, directed towards finding the path to paradise in marriage. The stage is set for the remainder of the discourses, which will attempt to determine how the goal might be achieved in practice. Why does marriage frequently lead to hell? How may joy in marriage be ensured? Is the guidance of parents necessary in choosing a wife or husband? Should free choice be allowed? Is unequal love to be condemned? These are the major questions to be considered.

As the opening scene established a dichotomy between nature and civility, the First Day's Exercise suggests a conflict between love as ideal and love as earthly passion. Isabella questions the validity of Petrarchan love: "If _Love_ be so sweete a passion (quoth she) I muse from what cause proceedeth the complaintes of Lovers, who with showering teares, bedeweth the earth: with misty sights, dimmeth the aire, and with shril outcries pearceth the heavens" (p. 26). Soranso attributes the pains to "our fleshly imperfections, which corruptes the nature of good things, and not of any defect in love"; love on earth must ordinarily result in marriage or wantonness. This contrast is maintained throughout the _Heptameron_. The novellas depict the destructive effects of love, as men and women seek vainly to attain the ideal state. The frequent verses express the pains of love, the inner turmoils of love as passion, through the conventional Petrarchan conceits which compare love to a disease, a battle, an icy fire. In contrast, the frame pictures a fairly ordered, ideal social occasion, reinforced by the references to music as an aid to harmony and the references to classical history and mythology as examples that might be followed or avoided, as the case may be.

The story of Borrihauder and Ophella, told in Day 1 by Doctor Mossenigo to illustrate a marriage ruled by violent passions untempered by love, recalls the _fabliaux_ in its rapid, economical narration and its cynical tone. In Day 2, the story of Sicheus and Elisa, narrated by Faliero to illustrate the results of a marriage forced on the children in an attempt to bring the families together, is more novella-like in its attention to rhetorical details. The marriage ends in murder, revenge, miscarriage, and horrible death, sensationally bringing home the truths of the monstrousness of hatred and the justice of divine retribution. In Day 3, the story of Malipiero and Felice, narrated by Doctor Mossenigo to support his argument against rash marriages, is the liveliest in the book. Poverty destroys this marriage. Felice's adultery is motivated: she is vanquished by the persuasions of gold and of a go-between. The novella is less melodramatic than the tale of Sicheus and Elisa; this time love persists and triumphs, and Felice is redeemed. The story of Friar Inganno, related by Bergetto in Day 4 to entertain the company who are melancholy because Aurelia is ill, shows how lust threatens the religious and moral order. The story leads to a discussion of the sex war, which in turn leads directly to the next story, that of Promos and Cassandra, narrated by Isabella to reveal the treachery of men. In Day 6, Ismarito's implicitly bawdy fable of Rinautus wittily expands the theme of marriage between the very old and the very young. Day 7 ends with an encomium on marriage by Segnior Philoxenus, who climaxes his speech with the tale of Phrygius and Pieria, a tale in the courtly love tradition in which the lovers succumb at first sight in a temple, indulge in love laments, exchange letters, and trust their fortunes to a go-between. Because their private desires correspond with public goals, however, their union is blessed and comes close to the ideal. Thus the last novella ends the discourses on a note of hope and harmony.

Whetstone's verses are similarly integrated into the design of the Heptameron. Unlike the novellas, the verses have little artistic merit, but they are nevertheless appropriate to the discourses and lead up to the theme of each day. The Petrarchan "To realish Love, I taste a sowrie sweete" (p. 50) echoes the first novella's picture of the woes of love. Ismarito's farewell to worldly vanity in Day 3 (p. 76) proves to be short-lived, as his mood of contemplative melancholy is dispersed by "conversation." The theme of the significance of beauty is picked up by the verse in Day 4, "To thee I sende, thou fayrest of the fayre" (p. 81). The company's need for mirth in Day 4 is emphasized in "Care, Care, goe pack" (p. 119). The discussion of lofty love in Day 5 is anticipated by "Who prickels feares, to pluck the lovely Rose" (p. 148). In Day 6, "Regarde my love, but not my frostie haires" (p. 175), "the fruites of Doctor Mossenigoes Muse," both discloses the Doctor's comic predicament -- the arch-detractor of women has fallen in love with the "waspissest Damosel" -- and inspires the ensuing discussion. As might be expected, the final verse, in Day 7, sings the praise of Hymen's rites, of marriage: "O none, nor state, lyke to the married lyfe" (p. 201).

Although Whetstone's dialogue is frequently animated and interesting, the characters tend to be sketchily realized, perhaps because they suggest social types. Fabritio, the elderly courtier, is a diplomat, who manages to avert open conflict between Mossenigo and Bergetto (pp. 91, 142). Soranso is fond of weighty pronouncements; Dondolo is haughty; Bergetto is boastful and hot-tempered -- he clashes with Mossenigo, Ismarito, Franceschina, and Isabella -- and he is a sore loser; Faliero is the one who baits Friar Bugiardo. Isabella is sometimes lively; Lucia Bella is sweet and modest; and Franceschina Sancta is a bit saucy; but the only woman to have any identity is Katherina Trista, "a sowre and testy Dame" (p. 23), whose witty comments make her a fitting opponent for the Doctor. Aurelia is always the beautiful hostess, a faint reflection of Lady Emilia Pia in The Courtier, who controls the entertainments and frequently forestalls outbreaks of excessive feeling.

Against this general background of shadowy gentlemen and ladies, three characters stand out: Segnior Philoxenus, Doctor Mossenigo, and Ismarito. The portrait of Philoxenus, the ideal gentleman who is superior in rank and more accomplished in manners than are the rest of the company, is scarcely individualized, for Ismarito is very much aware of the distance between himself and his host. Like the absent King in the story of Promos and Cassandra, Philoxenus fulfils the role of a deus ex machina: he sets the stage, retires from the major entertainments, then returns to tie up the loose ends. At the end of the book, he presents the case for an ideal marriage, just as Bembo in The Courtier eloquently expounds the subject of ideal love.

The opposite of the courtly Segnior Philoxenus, who represents order, tradition, and conformity, is Doctor Mossenigo, the outsider, cynic, critic, and rebel. As a self-confessed plain-speaking lawyer and misogynist, he calls to mind the character of Gaspar in The Courtier. Doctor Mossenigo quickly becomes the focus of interest in the frame of the Heptameron, for the liveliest parts of the book are his. To him are attributed most of the colloquialisms, the homely proverbs, and the colorful speeches. He wittily twists the meaning of words and sentences. He relates the fabliaux-like tale of Borrihauder and Ophella, and his cynical comments bring to life the story of Malipiero and Felice. Marino, Felice's lover, is said to be burning with love until "he was in daunger to have consumed to Cinders" (p. 99); he is compared to a "sullen swounding Childe" (p. 100); he sends Felice an image of himself wrought in gold, depicting his "bared Carkasse of Death" (p. 101), which ironically foreshadows his fate; and he signs his letter to Felice, "Unto my latter Gaspe" (p. 101). The grotesque dinner which Marguerite de Navarre and Painter mention without comment is neatly summarized by Doctor Mossenigo as being "longer, then pleasant, either to husbande, wife, or friende" (p. 106). The most convincing account of the hell of married life is attributed to Doctor Mossenigo, as he describes the inconveniences of unequal love: "a slut like the furie of lothsomenes, shall bring in dinner, because the Jelious wife, dare not trust her husbande with any maide that is hansome: the husbande offended, throweth the Platters at her head, and axeth if she meane to poyson him: the wife taketh pepper in the nose, and sayth, if hee had not married her, he woulde have beene glade of the worst morsell there" (pp. 186-90). The cynical Doctor clashes with Friar Bugiardo, with Soranso, with Bergetto, and with the thief. As a result of their verbal skirmish, Bergetto and Doctor Mossenigo treat each other coldly, and the hidden anger nearly bursts forth as Bergetto goes so far as to eye his sword (p. 91): even in Segnior Philoxenus's palace, the ideal civil life is easily disturbed. Finally, the old Doctor becomes a figure of ridicule as he is enamoured with the young but shrewish Katherina (p. 175).

Ismarito, not as colorful a figure as Doctor Mossenigo, is nevertheless most convincing as the author's fictional self. He emerges as a solitary, diffident, yet engaging figure, predisposed to melancholy. He does not believe the porter's extended invitation, thinking it to

be a mere formality (p. 14). At the beginning of the civil entertainments, when the others are "coupled together lyke fowles on Saint Valentines
day morninge" (p. 24), Ismarito is yet unmatched. During the discussions
in Day 1, he is silent and has to be drawn out by Aurelia (p. 26). At
the beginning of Day 3, he is again alone, musing on the vanity of the
world and the uncertainty of fortune (p. 75). Because he misses the
gaiety and brightness of the previous night's society, he is now lonely
and melancholy, feeling as though he were in a "desert wilderness."
His song expresses his determination to seek out philosophy, contemplation,
and heavenly knowledge; but the remedy for his depression turns out
instead to be the companionship of the returning guests. In Day 4,
Ismarito is still unhappy, this time because Aurelia is indisposed
(p. 114). Philoxenus brings him out of his dumps by accompanying him
to the gallery. When Philoxenus finds Ismarito once more alone, in
Day 6, "in a quiet place," reading Mexia on the history of Tamberlaine
(pp. 168-69), his cure this time is to show Ismarito the library.
Ismarito is baited by Soranso and Bergetto in Day 5, and by Bergetto
in Day 6 (p. 173). Nevertheless, he is able to hold his own and to
express well-defined, even unpopular views, for which he is sometimes
attacked in the debates: he pleads the cause of the equality of men
and women (pp. 140-41); he wittily explicates the picture of the "Rhinocerot"
(p. 182); he arouses Bergetto's jealousy (p. 174); and he overcomes
his modesty sufficiently to expound theology (p. 145). Since Ismarito
is the most fully realized character in the Heptameron, he may very well
reflect Whetstone's own personality.

    The tone of the Heptameron ranges from the serious and courtly to the humorous and colloquial, but it is rarely admonitory or declamatory and never bitter or sarcastic. Whetstone's moral and Protestant bias is apparent in his didactic debates, in the reference to Christmas as a season devoted to the service of God, when no light mirth should be allowed, and in his view of marriage as a sensible solution to the problems created by undisciplined passion. The ideal is shown to be not always practicable in a world where even economic factors may determine the course of love. Italy emerges as another qualified ideal, a valuable model of manners in spite of its Papistry. Accordingly, the attacks on Roman Catholicism -- the mockery of Friar Bugiardo's sermon, the treatment of Friar Inganno, the scorn of relics and tapers, and the references to the priests' lack of celibacy, to their babbling sermons, and to the superstitious ceremonies -- are critical and comic rather than vicious. Philoxenus embodies this tolerant attitude: he is an Italian Protestant who allows Catholic services in his home (p. 20), and who accepts the role of Roman Catholicism in Italy because it at least provides some hope for a large number of people (p. 45). Whetstone's ability to be critical yet detached in the *Heptameron* undoubtedly results from his skill in maintaining his role as an observer.

In the Seventh Day's Exercise, Whetstone takes care to bring together the various threads of the *Heptameron*, to create a sense of completion. The day is a special one: the New Year is described as a time of new beginnings; the festivities are celebrated not in the main palace, but in the banqueting house; and Segnior Philoxenus is present at the discussions. Whereas the previous days had explored the various ways to hell in marriage, New Year's Day focuses on the path to paradise. Philoxenus emphasizes this note of hope, the promise of a new social order: "Perchaunce you have ended all the inconveniences in the old yeare, and I may begin the New Yeare, in helping to bloome the blessings of Marriage" (p. 197). So eloquent is Philoxenus's description of an ideal marriage that Lucia Bella abandons her resolution to be a nun. Even the final masque is a celebration of a triumph and a reflection of the longing for renewal. The masque picks up the motif of the contrast between desert wilderness and civil order -- the motif with which the Heptameron had opened. It looks back to the Golden Age, but reminds us that we no longer live in that age -- that perhaps the ideal is not now attainable -- chiefly because of the prevalence of Envy. Aurelia and Philoxenus, the hosts of the civil entertainments, have key roles in the masque, and by means of a mirror, they defeat Envy. The action of the masque -- and of the book as a whole -- is reflected in the gift which Uranie presents to Ismarito, a shield which is a representation of the cardinal virtues, often referred to as the civil virtues, by means of which man may defeat the unruly forces that threaten the stability of civilized life. The ending of the book, however, brings us down to earth again with the domestic image of the cock, whose "midnight song" is a reminder of time and of human fallibility: during the Christmas season the cock is said to be especially active, crying "Christus natus est," both celebrating the divine birth and recalling Peter's inability to keep faith. Just as the road to paradise in marriage is constantly, but not eternally, blocked by man's imperfections, so the way to the civil life is not an easy one in this world of passion, discord, and time.

    The Heptameron, then, is more than a domestic conduct book or a collection of translated novellas. It is not as prescriptive as, for example, Tilney's _Flower of Friendshippe_, which sets down rules for the behaviour of husbands and wives; nor is it as deficient in narrative skill and in characterization as are many moral discourses. The discussions and entertainments which frame the tales become at least as interesting as the tales themselves, more so than in other framed collections, such as Wotton's _Courtlie Controversie of Cupids Cautels_ and Greene's _Morando, The Tritameron of Love_. In the _Heptameron_, the enveloping narrative and structure are significant: these, together with the courtly atmosphere, the Italian setting, and the occasional colloquial tone, account for much of the book's artistic merit.

The _Heptameron_ may be read as a literary manifestation of the Renaissance ideal of civility. It may also be studied as a document in the history of Italian-English social and literary relationships. As a work by a professional writer in the pre-Golden Age of Elizabethan England, it may be of interest to literary historians. Since Whetstone's works were probably read by the greatest dramatists of late sixteenth-century England, Shakespeare and Marlowe, by the outstanding poet of the age, Spenser, and by one of the most popular writers, Greene, the _Heptameron_ may be studied with a view to increasing our understanding of those writers. Nevertheless, the value of the _Heptameron_ today is not solely historical and sociological; it is aesthetic as well. The careful patterning of the entire work is evident in the alternation of idealism in the framework discussions and realism in the tales, in the progression towards a hopeful but qualified resolution, in the varied pacing of courtly rhetoric and colloquial idiom, in the flashes of wit and deft characterization -- all held together within the seven days' Christmas exercises and convincingly narrated by a charming Ismarito. These make the Heptameron, not a great book, but an entertaining one, well able "to reave tediousnesse from the Reader." A work which displays sufficient "novelistic talent" to elicit C. S. Lewis's comment, "the ride through the forest on Christmas Eve and the first sight of the palace might well be the beginning of an excellent story,"[92] deserves to be made available outside the vaults of a rare book library.

Footnotes

¹ Thomas Watson, commendatory poem, Heptameron, p. 9 below.

² Charles Singer, "Introduction" to The Cures of the Diseased in Forraine Attempts of the English Nation (1598; facsimile rpt. Oxford: Clarendon Press, 1915), n.pag. See also the comments by Thomas C. Izard, George Whetstone, Mid-Elizabethan Gentleman of Letters (1942; rpt. New York: AMS Press, 1966), pp. 2-4.

³ Izard, especially the chapter "The Hap and Hard Fortune of George Whetstone, Gent.," pp. 1-34.

⁴ Izard, p. 32.

⁵ Inquisition post mortem of Robert Whetstone, 15 July 1558; and the will of Robert Whetstone, 18 Oct. 1560. Izard quotes abstracts of both documents, admitting that he has not consulted the originals in the P.R.O. (pp. 5-7). See his footnote 4, p. 6 for other possibly relevant inquisitiones post mortem.

⁶ Izard, 6-8.

⁷ Izard, p. 8; citing the Visitations of Essex, Part II (Harleian Society Publications, London, 1879), p. 520.

⁸ "A Remembraunce of the wel imployed life, and godly end, of George Gaskoigne Esquire, who deceassed at Stalmford in Lincolne Shire the 7. of October. 1577. The reporte of Geor. Whetstons Gent. an eye witnes of his Godly and charitable end in this world. Formae nulla Fides." in Certayne Notes of Instruction in English Verse, The Steele Glas, [and] The Complaynt of Philomene, by George Gascoigne, ed. Edward Arber (Westminster: Constable, 1901), p. 15.

⁹ Izard, p. 10; citing Alumni Cantabrigienses (Cambridge, 1927), IV, 392, 382.

¹⁰ For information on Whetstone's contemporaries I have relied heavily on Edwin Haviland Miller, The Professional Writer in Elizabethan England (Cambridge, Mass.: Harvard Univ. Press, 1959); Charles T. Prouty, George Gascoigne; Elizabethan Courtier, Soldier, and Poet (New York: Columbia Univ. Press, 1942); and Mark Eccles, Christopher Marlowe in London (Cambridge, Mass.: Harvard Univ. Press, 1934).

[11] Miller, p. 17.

[12] "List of Ships Officers, Ordinance, etc. of Gylberte's Expedition of 1578," State Papers, Domestic, Elizabeth, Vol. CXXVII, No. 49, reprinted in Sir Humfrey Gylberte and his Enterprise of Colonization in America, ed. Carlos Slafter (Boston: Prince Society, 1903), pp. 253-58. George Whetstone, gent., is one of the eight "soldiers and mariners" mentioned (p. 254). Cited by Izard, pp. 17-22.

[13] Ibid.

[14] Izard, p. 22.

[15] Izard, pp. 251-52.

[16] R. C. Strong and J. A. Van Dorsten, Leicester's Triumph (Leiden: Univ. Press, 1964), pp. 131, 133; and J. A. Van Dorsten, Poets, Patrons, and Professors (Leiden: Univ. Press, 1962), pp. 139-40.

[17] Calendar of State Papers, Foreign Series, Elizabeth (London: P.R.O., 1929), XXI, iii (Apr.-Dec. 1587), pp. 244, 311-12, 321, 369; XXI, iv (Jan.-June 1588), pp. 497-98. Cited by Izard, pp. 28-31.

[18] Izard, p. 25. A letter of administration dated Jan. 3, 1587/8 was issued to Whetstone's widow.

[19] George Gascoigne, The Posies (1575) in Complete Works, I, ed. John W. Cunliffe (Cambridge: Univ. Press, 1907), pp. 23-24; Timothy Kendall, Flowers of Epigrammes (London, 1577) sig. a6^v; and Hyder Edward Rollins, ed., The Paradise of Dainty Devices (1576-1606) (Cambridge, Mass.: Harvard Univ. Press, 1927), pp. 108-11; 119-20.

[20] For a bibliographical account of Whetstone's works, see Izard, pp. 280-87.

[21] Charles T. Prouty, "George Whetstone and the Sources of Measure for Measure," Shakespeare Quarterly, 15 (1964), 131-45.

[22] The plan of the projected work is mentioned in The English Myrror (London, 1586), sig. P8^r; and The Honorable Reputation of a Souldier (London, 1585), sig. C1^r.

[23] Izard, pp. 131-218.

[24] Dorsten, especially pp. 138-46.

[25] Miller, pp. 228-30.

[26] John Nichols, The Progresses and Public Processions of Queen Elizabeth (1823; rpt. New York: Burt Franklin, n.d.), II, 301. My discussion of Sidney is indebted to Roger Howell, Sir Philip Sidney, The Shepherd Knight (Boston: Little, 1968), especially ch. 2, "Leicester, Walsingham and the French Marriage," pp. 48-74.

27 Dorsten, passim.

28 Dorsten, pp. 138-39.

29 Dorsten, p. 140. See also A. J. Barnouw, "How English was Taught in Jan van Hout's Leyden," English Studies, 17 (1935), 1-7.

30 Izard, p. 32.

31 This discussion of the relations between England and Italy in the Renaissance is indebted primarily to the following books: Lewis Einstein, The Italian Renaissance in England (1902; rpt. New York: Burt Franklin, n.d.); John L. Lievsay, The Elizabethan Image of Italy (Ithaca, N.Y.: Cornell Univ. Press, 1964); George B. Parks, The English Traveler to Italy, Vol. I (Stanford, Calif.: Stanford Univ. Press, 1954); and Parks, "Introduction" to The History of Italy (1549) by William Thomas (Ithaca, N.Y.: Cornell Univ. Press, 1963).

32 Roberto Weiss, Humanism in England During the Fifteenth Century (Oxford: Blackwell, 1941), especially ch. 3, pp. 39-70.

33 Parks, The English Traveler to Italy, pp. 475-79.

34 Roger Ascham, The Scholemaster, ed. R. J. Schoeck (Don Mills, Ont.: Dent, 1966), pp. 65, 70, 55.

35 Parks, "Introduction," p. xiv. Elizabeth's eloquent command of Italian is praised by Whetstone in The English Myrror, sig. I4^v.

36 Lievsay, p. 9.

37 R. C. Simonini, Jr., Italian Scholarship in Renaissance England (Chapel Hill: Univ. of North Carolina, 1952), p. 32.

37a Parks, The English Traveler to Italy, p. 616.

38 Ascham, pp. 61-65; Louis B. Wright, ed., Advice to a Son (Ithaca, N.Y.: Cornell Univ. Press, 1962), p. 11; Thomas Nashe, Works, ed. R. B. McKerrow (Oxford: B. Blackwell, 1958), I, 186; II, 297-301. See also George R. Hibbard, Thomas Nashe; A Critical Introduction (London: Routledge, 1962).

39 George B. Parks, "The First Italianate Englishmen," Studies in the Renaissance, 8 (1961), 197-216.

40 William Thomas, The History of Italy (1549), ed. G. B. Parks, (Ithaca, N.Y.: Cornell Univ. Press, 1963), p. 3.

41 Anthony Munday, The English Romayne Lyfe, ed. G. B. Harrison (London: Lane, 1925), p. 1; Robert Greene, Repentance of Robert Greene (London, 1592), sig. C1^v; Thomas Nashe, Works, ed. R. B. McKerrow (Oxford: B. Blackwell, 1958), III, 342.

[42] For further information on the Italian features discussed below, see the explanatory notes for the pages cited.

[43] Kathleen M. Lea, *Italian Popular Comedy* (Oxford: Clarendon Press, 1934), especially pp. 345-47; and *New Encyclopaedia Britannica*, 15th ed. (Chicago, 1974), *Macropaedia*, IV, 979-87.

[44] Stefano Guazzo, *Civile Conversation*, tr. G. Pettie and ed. E. Sullivan (London: Constable, 1925), I, 56.

[45] Lodowick Bryskett, *A Discourse of Civill Life* (1606), ed. T. E. Wright (Northridge, Calif.: San Fernando State College, 1970), p. 32.

[46] Thomas Starkey, *England in the Reign of King Henry the Eighth. A Dialogue Between Cardinal Pole and Thomas Lupset*, ed. J. M. Cowper (London: EETS, 1871), pp. 9-10.

[47] Zevedei Barbu, *Problems of Historical Psychology* (London: Routledge, 1960), pp. 197-98.

[48] Bryskett, p. 190.

[49] Thomas P. Roche, *The Kindly Flame* (Princeton: Princeton Univ. Press, 1964), pp. 38-43, 46.

[50] Bryskett, pp. 166, 170-71.

[51] On the play element in culture, see Johan Huizinga, *Homo Ludens* (1949; rpt. London: Temple Smith, 1970), *passim*.

[52] Ruth Kelso, *The Doctrine of the English Gentleman in the Sixteenth Century* (Urbana: Univ. of Illinois, 1929), p. 88.

[53] Kelso, chapter 7.

[54] Thomas Greene, "The Flexibility of the Self in Renaissance Literature" in *The Disciplines of Criticism*, ed. P. Demetz, T. Greene, and L. Nelson, Jr. (New Haven: Yale Univ. Press, 1968), pp. 250, 243, 249.

[55] Mary A. Scott, *Elizabethan Translations from the Italian* (1916; rpt. New York: Burt Franklin, 1969), p. 463.

[56] Joseph A. Mazzeo, *Renaissance and Revolution* (New York: Random, 1967), p. 133.

[57] Huizinga, pp. 205-6.

[58] John L. Lievsay, *Stefano Guazzo and the English Renaissance, 1575-1675* (Chapel Hill: Univ. of North Carolina Press, 1961), p. 44.

[59] Daniel Javitch, "Rival Arts of Conduct in Elizabethan England: Guazzo's *Civile Conversation* and Castiglione's *Courtier*," *Yearbook of Italian Studies* (1971), 179, 197-98.

[60] Javitch, "Poetry and Court Conduct: Puttenham's *Arte of English Poesie* in the Light of Castiglione's *Cortegiano*," *MLN*, 87 (May 1972), 865-82.

[61] R. W. Bond, "Euphues and Euphuism: Introductory Essay" in *The Complete Works of John Lyly* (Oxford: Clarendon Press, 1902), I, 160.

[62] Donald R. Howard, "Renaissance World-Alienation" in *The Darker Vision of the Renaissance*, ed. R. S. Kinsman (Berkeley: Univ. of California Press, 1974), pp. 47-76.

[63] Gerald P. Mohrman, "*The Civile Conversation*: Communication in the Renaissance," *Speech Monographs*, 39 (March 1972), 203. Quoting Eugenio Garin, *Italian Humanism*, trans. Peter Muntz (New York: Harper, 1965), p. 159.

[64] John C. Nelson, *Renaissance Theory of Love* (New York: Columbia Univ. Press, 1958), ch. 2, pp. 67-162.

[65] Edmund Tilney, *The Flower of Friendshippe*, ed. R. G. Johnson, Diss. Univ. of Pittsburgh 1961, p. 73.

[66] Ralph G. Johnson "A Critical 3rd Edition of Edmund Tilney's *The Flower of Friendshippe*," Diss. Univ. of Pittsburgh 1961, p. 56.

[67] Plutarch, *Moralia* (London: Heinemann, 1957-69), 15v.

[68] Chilton L. Powell, *English Domestic Relations, 1487-1653* (New York: Columbia Univ. Press, 1917), pp. 101-2.

[69] Guazzo, II, 4-5.

[70] Robert J. Clements, "Anatomy of the Novella," *Comparative Literature Studies*, 9 (March 1972), 14.

[71] Margaret Schlauch, *Antecedents of the English Novel, 1400-1600* (London: Oxford Univ. Press, 1963), p. 138.

[72] Yvonne Rodax, *The Real and the Ideal in the Novella of Italy, France and England* (Chapel Hill: Univ. of North Carolina Press, 1968), passim.

[73] Vittore Branca, *Boccaccio: The Man and His Works*, trans. Richard Monges (New York: New York Univ. Press, 1976), pp. 201-9, 310-23.

[74] Ibid., p. 209.

[75] Schlauch, pp. 156-57.

76 Giuseppe Galigani, ed. *Il Boccaccio nella Cultura Inglese e Anglo-Americana* (Firenze: Olschki, 1974), pp. 27-57, 185-91.

77 Guazzo, I, 136-37.

78 Pierre de la Primaudaye, *The French Academie*, tr. T. Bowes (London, 1586), sig. A5^r.

79 William G. Crane, *Wit and Rhetoric in the Renaissance* (1937; rpt. Gloucester, Mass.: Peter Smith, 1964), p. 71.

80 David N. Beauregard, Introduction to "A Critical Edition of George Whetstone's *An Heptameron of Civill Discourses*," Diss. Ohio State Univ. 1967, pp. 20-21.

81 Crane, pp. 33-48.

82 Crane, p. 33.

83 A. J. Krailsheimer, *The Continental Renaissance, 1500-1600* (Harmondsworth, Middlesex: Penguin, 1971), pp. 475-76.

84 DeWitt T. Starnes and Ernest W. Talbert, *Classical Myth and Legend in Renaissance Dictionaries* (Chapel Hill: Univ. of North Carolina Press, 1955), pp. 11-28.

85 Ibid., pp. 29-43.

86 For discussions of Renaissance proverbs, see especially Rudolph E. Habenicht, "Introduction" to *A Dialogue of Proverbs* by John Heywood (Berkeley: Univ. of California Press, 1963), pp. 1-94; Charles G. Smith, *Shakespeare's Proverb Lore* (Cambridge, Mass.: Harvard Univ. Press, 1963), and *Spenser's Proverb Lore* (Cambridge, Mass.: Harvard Univ. Press, 1970); and Morris P. Tilley, *Elizabethan Proverb Lore in Lyly's Euphues and in Pettie's Petite Pallace* (New York: Macmillan, 1926).

87 Habenicht, p. 9.

88 William Nelson, *Fact or Fiction: The Dilemma of the Renaissance Storyteller* (Cambridge, Mass.: Harvard Univ. Press, 1973), p. 67.

89 Ibid., p. 93.

90 Ibid., p. 108.

91 Baldassare Castiglione, *The Book of the Courtier*, trans. Sir Thomas Hoby, 1561 (London: Dent, 1928), p. 20.

92 C. S. Lewis, *English Literature in the Sixteenth Century, Excluding Drama* (Oxford: Clarendon Press, 1954), p. 419.

TEXTUAL INTRODUCTION

An entry in the Stationers' Register for 11 January 1582 licenses Richard Jones to print "master" Whetstone's "An heptameron of Civill discourses unto the christmas Exercises of sundry well courted gentlemen and gentlewomen."[1] The title page of the Heptameron bears the statement that it was "Printed by Richard Jones, . . . 3. Feb. 1582." In 1593 Whetstone's book was reprinted by "Richard Johnes" as Aurelia, The Paragon of Pleasure and Princely Delights. Whether Jones did in fact print these two editions is uncertain: it is more likely that he was the publisher who contracted the work to other printers. Katharine F. Pantzer in a letter dated 11 February 1969 writes that "Professor Jackson had the note that this edition [i.e. Aurelia] was printed by (Thomas Orwin for) R. Johnes, 1593." However, since McKerrow indicates that in 1591-92 Orwin's press had been seized by the Stationers' Company and that Orwin died before June 25, 1593,[2] I am unable to support Jackson's statement. Until more background research on sixteenth-century printers' ornaments and types has been completed, the printers of Whetstone's work cannot be identified.

Since Aurelia was published after Whetstone's death and appears to have been edited so as to omit passages that were no longer topically relevant in the London of 1593, it undoubtedly was not set up directly from the author's manuscript. Accordingly, the only authoritative text, the Heptameron of Civill Discourses of 1582, is the copy text for the present edition.

Textual Introduction   cxix

The Heptameron has not been reprinted since the sixteenth century. A bibliographical entry in E. A. Baker's History of the English Novel,³ referring to an edition of the Heptameron apparently published by the Percy Society in 1844, has defeated my attempts at verification, and I can only conclude that the listed work is a ghost. A Ph.D. dissertation by David Beauregard, "A Critical Edition of George Whetstone's An Heptameron of Civill Discourses (1582)" is incomplete, textually inaccurate, and critically inadequate.⁴ The story of Promos and Cassandra in the Fourth Day's Exercise has been frequently included in collections of Shakespeare's sources, and a few brief passages and poems from the Heptameron have been published by the Chetham Society.⁵ The following text, then, is the only complete critical edition of George Whetstone's An Heptameron of Civill Discourses.

I have been able to locate ten extant copies of the Heptameron⁶ -- two at the British Museum, one at the Bodleian, three at the Folger Shakespeare Library, one at the Henry E. Huntington Library, one at the University of Illinois, one at the J. Pierpont Morgan Library, and one at the Rosenbach Foundation; and three extant copies of Aurelia -- one each at the British Museum, the Bodleian, and the Henry E. Huntington Library. I have examined xerox or microfilm reproductions of all these copies: they appear to be in good condition, clean, and readable. The Bodleian copy of the Heptameron, however, lacks the title page leaf. Hazlitt's Hand-Book⁷ describes two issues of the Heptameron, the first with a title apparently identical to the title of this edition, and a second "with a very different title." I have not been able to confirm the existence of two title pages: I suggest that Hazlitt has incorrectly transcribed different sections of the same title page twice. As the control text for this edition, I have used the Folger Shakespeare Library copy 3, which I have collated with the nine other extant copies in order to determine press variants resulting from proof corrections. The final critical text of the <u>Heptameron</u> has then been collated with the Bodleian copy of <u>Aurelia</u> to enable me to construct a historical collation of variants.

Since the printed text of the <u>Heptameron</u> was probably set up from the author's manuscript, I have aimed at preserving its spelling and punctuation in order to retain as much of the author's style as possible. The present edition follows the editorial principles enunciated by McKerrow Greg, and Bowers,[8] who claim that the editor should attempt to reconstruct the text in a form in which it may have been available in the author's fair copy, to put forth the work as the author intended it. The opposing point of view has been argued by John Russell Brown,[9] who favors modernization of spelling of Elizabethan texts on the grounds that an old-spelling edition does not in fact retain the author's intentions, but merely reflects compositorial practice; is not sufficient for a textual student, who must still consult the original books; and does no more than add an unnecessary and antique flavour to the work. However, it may be countered that even if the spelling and punctuation are not always the author's, they do at least reflect the usage of the author's age. Furthermore, as W. W. Greg and Arthur Brown[10] point out, we are at present linguistically unequipped to normalize or modernize Elizabethan spelling: it is difficult to moderniz spelling because of the ambiguity of the original spellings and because of the lack of modern equivalents for some Elizabethan words. An old-spelling critical edition may not be the ideal form in which all readers

would prefer to first encounter the Heptameron, but it remains the most
appropriate text to serve the purposes of the literary scholar, the student
of the Elizabethan age, and the linguist.

    The editorial policy adopted for the present edition, then, is very
conservative: my aim has been to follow the practice of the late sixteenth
century in spelling, punctuation, and paragraphing. The original punctuation
is retained except where it is confusing or obviously incorrect by sixteenth-
century standards. The use of parentheses to set apart the name of the
speaker from the rest of a spoken sentence is standardized for ease of
reading, the changes being recorded in the list of emendations of accidentals.
Obvious compositorial errors such as reversal or omission of letters have
been corrected silently except where they create questionable readings.
Eccentricities of spellings have been retained, in the supposition that
these might reflect the author's rather than the compositor's practice.
Any spelling for which the OED provides authority has been retained; the
notes explain any uncertainties or ambiguities. Names of places and
persons follow the copy-text practice. Variations in spellings of characters'
names have been retained as long as the change in spelling does not result
in a change in pronunciation. Hence, "Cicheus" is accepted for "Sicheus,"
but "Falerio" is not allowed as a substitute for "Faliero." The contemporary
practice of italicizing or setting apart in Roman type proper names and
significant abstract nouns has been followed.

    I have not found it necessary to make many substantive emendations --
the text is carefully and clearly printed -- although I have emended some
of the accidentals in such a way that the changes clarify or alter the
meaning of the text and hence have the status of substantive emendations.

In cases of important or debatable emendations, notes provide the reasons for the decisions to emend. The readings of the corrected formes have been incorporated into the text, but only after each reading has been considered on its own merits; in cases where there is no reason to prefer one reading to another, the reading of the corrected forme has been adopted. Except for a few classes of silent emendations, which are outlined below, the emendations of accidentals and of substantives are listed separately in the textual apparatus. I have not attempted to identify compositors, although patterns of spelling variations, especially variations in the spelling of the characters' names, suggest that such an identification might be possible.

Since the present text is not intended to be a replacement for or a facsimile of the original text, for ease of reading and for typing convenience the typography has been modernized. Bowers in his edition of Beaumont and Fletcher[11] argues that there is no linguistic justification for perpetuating confusing typographical conventions. Accordingly, alterations that involve only the typography and not the spelling or meaning of the text have been made silently -- although differences in typographical styles have been noted in order to help the reader to envisage the texture of the original text.

The following alterations have been made silently:

-- Normalization of the usage of u-v and i-j.

-- Modernization of ſ to s and w to w.

-- Expansion of contractions such as the ampersand, the tilde, ẏ (the or that), ẘ (with), φ (quoth), &c (etc.), and ; in Latin (-que).

-- Reproduction as separate letters of ligatures such as ct, fi, ſt, ſl.

-- Separation of linked letters such as œ, æ, ∞, ee -- except on page 2, where the linked letters in the Latin text are retained.

-- Non-reproduction of ornamental initials, display capitals, swash capitals, type ornaments, and printers' "fillers" such as ◇ and ¶.

-- Correction of wrong-fount and damaged type and turned letters, unless the result of the error is a new word or a questionable reading. In cases where the type is not clear, textual notes indicate the editor's uncertainty.

-- Use of hyphenation only when it occurs in the copy text other than at the end of a line.

-- Regularization of spacing of lines and words and of spacing of lines of poetry. Errors in spacing noted when they result in questionable readings.

-- No indication of size of type.

-- Substitution of curved parentheses for square brackets for the sake of consistency.

-- Correction of the punctuation at the ends of side notes. This generally involves the addition of periods or the change of commas to periods.

Unless otherwise noted, the text of the Heptameron is printed in black letter, with running titles, chapter headings, and the first line of each chapter set in Roman. Side notes are set in small Roman. Poems, letters, and speeches are generally set in Roman type, and are so indicated in the textual notes. Underscoring within the text indicates use of Roman type within black letter in the copy text or italic within Roman type.

Footnotes

[1] Edward Arber, ed., _A Transcript of the Registers of the Company of Stationers of London, 1554-1640 A.D._ (London: privately printed, 1875), II, 185b.

[2] Ronald B. McKerrow, ed., _A Dictionary of Printers and Booksellers in England, Scotland and Ireland, and of Foreign Printers of English Books 1557-1640_ (1910; rpt. London: Bibliog. Society, 1968), p. 208.

[3] Ernest A. Baker, _The History of the English Novel_ (New York: Barnes & Noble, 1936), II, 277.

[4] David Napoleon Beauregard, "A Critical Edition of George Whetstone's An _Heptameron of Civill Discourses_ (1582)," Diss. Ohio State Univ. 1967.
    Beauregard's edition is incomplete, merely summarizing the second and sixth days. The textual editing is inconsistent and careless: for instance, certain words listed as substantive emendations are only obvious spelling errors, and some spellings have been unnecessarily "corrected" even when the _OED_ provides authority for Elizabethan usage of the rejected spellings. Since only American copies have been collated, the list of press variants is incomplete. The introduction is sketchy and does little more than echo Izard's work on Whetstone and discuss the _Heptameron_ in relation to Castiglione and Tilney. The glossary and notes are inadequate. No attempt is made to identify classical and Biblical allusions such as "Parrhasius" and "Labans sheepe," and there are no references for unnatural natural history such as "cockatrice." Only one or two of the very obvious proverbs are identified: the editor draws attention to the proverb "all is not gold that glistereth," but ignores proverbs such as "mute as a fishe" and "for a man can have of a cat but her skin." The glossary purports to include words that cannot be found in Webster's _New World Dictionary_ with the appropriate definitions, yet it omits words such as "baineth," "Pyne Apple trees," and "president" (of behaviours). Words that do occur in Webster and that nevertheless require a gloss include "skreene," "scrip," and "champion" (for _champaigne_).

[5] Thomas Corser, _Collectanea Anglo-Poetica_, Part XI, in _Remains, Historical and Literary_, Vol. CXI (London: Chetham Soc., 1883), pp. 382-92

[6] A. W. Pollard and G. R. Redgrave, _A Short-Title Catalogue of Books Printed in England, Scotland, and Ireland and of English Books Printed Abroad, 1475-1640_, 2nd ed., rev. Vol. 2. (London: Bibliog. Society, 1976) lists ten copies of the _Heptameron_, _STC_ 25337 -- and three copies of _Aurelia_, _STC_ 25338. The R. L. Harmsworth copy of the _Heptameron_ is

now at the Folger and the J. L. Clawson copy is at the Rosenbach Foundation. Cambridge Univ. has a fragment of sigs. L3 and L4.

[7] W. Carew Hazlitt, *Hand-Book to the Popular, Poetical, and Dramatic Literature of Great Britain, From the Invention of Printing to the Restoration* (London: John Russell Smith, 1867), p. 651.

[8] Ronald B. McKerrow, *Prolegomena for the Oxford Shakespeare; a Study in Editorial Method* (Oxford: Clarendon Press, 1939); W. W. Greg, "The Rationale of Copy-Text," *Studies in Bibliography*, 3 (1950-51), pp. 19-36; W. W. Greg, *The Editorial Problem in Shakespeare; A Survey of the Foundations of the Text*, 3d ed. (Oxford: Clarendon Press, 1954); and Fredson Bowers, "The Text of This Edition" in *The Dramatic Works in the Beaumont and Fletcher Canon* (Cambridge: Univ. Press, 1966), I, ix-xxv.

[9] John Russell Brown, "The Rationale of Old-Spelling Editions of the Plays of Shakespeare and his Contemporaries," *Studies in Bibliography* 13 (1960), 49-67.

[10] W. W. Greg, *The Editorial Problem in Shakespeare*; and Arthur Brown, "The Rationale of Old-Spelling Editions of the Plays of Shakespeare and his Contemporaries: A Rejoinder," *Studies in Bibliography* 13 (1960), 69-76.

[11] Fredson Bowers, *op. cit.*

Bibliographical Description of The "Heptameron"

[within a frame of type-orn] An Heptameron / of Civill Discourses. /
Containing: The Christmasse Ex- / ercise of sundrie well Courted Gen- /
tlemen and Gentlewomen. / In whose behaviours, the better / sort, may
see, a representation of their own Vertues: / And the Inferiour, may learne
such Rules of Civil Go- / vernment, as wil rase out the Blemish of their
basenesse: / Wherin, is Renowned, the Vertues, of a most Honou- / rable
and brave mynded Gentleman. / And herein, also, [as it were in a Mirrour]
the Unmaried / may see the Defectes whiche Eclipse the Glorie of MARIAGE: /
And the wel Maried, as in a Table of Housholde Lawes, may cull / out
needefull Preceptes to establysh their good Fortune. / A Worke, intercoursed
with Civyll Pleasure, to reave / tediousnesse from the Reader: and garnished
with Morall Noates / to make it profitable, to the Regarder. / The Reporte,
of George Whetstone. Gent. / Formæ, nulla fides. / AT LONDON. / Printed
by Richard Jones, / at the Signe of the Rose and the Crowne, / neare
Holburne Bridge. 3. Feb. 1582. /

Collation: $4°: A^4¶^2B-Z^4$, 94 leaves unnumbered.

Signatures: $3 (-A3, E2, GUYZ3; +E4) signed; B1 misprinted as A1;
Gothic caps (except A2, P2, X1, Z1 in italic).

Contents: $A1^r$: title. $A1^v$: Commendatory poem in Latin, "Ad Mecœnatem,"
signed Joan: Botrevicus. $A2^r$: Epistle dedicatory "To the right Honourable, Sir Christopher Hatton." $A3^v$: "Unto the friendly Reader." ¶1^r:
Commendatory poem by T.W. ¶1^v: "Verses translated out of Latine . . .
by URANIE." ¶2^v: "A briefe Summarie of the principall Argumentes."
$B1^r$: "The first Dayes exercise." $D3^r$: "The first Nights Pastime."
$E1^r$: "The seconde Dayes Exercie [sic]." $H2^r$: "The thyrd Daies Exercise."
$M2^r$: The fourth Daies exercise." $P2^v$: "The fift Daies Exercise." $R4^r$:
"The syxt Dayes Exercise." $U4^r$: "The .vii. Dayes Exercise."

RT] THE FIRSTE / DAYES EXERCISE. $B1^v$-$D1^v$ [THE .I. DAYES EXERCISE. $B2^v$,
$B3^r$, $B4^v$ (with .I,); FIRSTE. $C3^v$; EXERCIE. $C2^r$]
THE SECOND / DAYES EXERCISE. $E1^v$-$H1^v$ [EXERCIE. $E2^r$; EXERCISE FG3^r4^r]
THE THYRDE / DAYES EXERCISE. $H2^v$-$M1^r$ [THIRD I1-4^v; THIRDE K1^v; THYRD
K2^v-L2^v; EXERCISE I1^r2^r. K3^r4^r]
THE FOVRTH / DAYES EXERCISE. $M1^v$-$P2^r$ [EXERCISE N3^r4^r]
THE FIFTH / DAYES EXERCISE. $P3^r$-$R3^v$ [FIFT P4^v; FYFTH Q1^v, Q3^v, R1-3^v;
FOVRTH Q2^v, Q4^v; EXERCISE Q3^r4^r]
THE SYXTH / DAYES EXERCISE. $R4^v$-$U3^v$ [SYXTE R4^v, U1-3^v; EXERCISE S3^r4^r]
THE SEVENTH / DAYES EXERCISE. $U4^v$-$Z4^v$]

CW] B4^v with D3^v her [the] E2^v inter-[taynment] O4^v verified [veryfied] R1^v (quoth [We] T1^r Fore [The] X3^v unhap- [happye] [no cw on G1^v, H3^v, H4^r, R4^r]

<u>Notes</u>: Row of type orn. at head of A1^v, A2^r, A3^v, ¶1^r, ¶1^v, ¶2^v, D3^r; at foot of A4^v, ¶2^r, ¶2^v, D2^v, H1^v, M1^v, P2^r, R3^v, U3^v. Orn. initials, 6-line, on A2^r, A3^v, B1^r, E1^r, H2^r, M2^r, P2^v, R4^r, U4^r.

TEXTUAL APPARATUS

Substantive Emendations

26.14 uses] use

   No authority in <u>OED</u> for "use" as plural noun.

61.4 breedeth hate in] breedeth in

69.17 Blue,] Blue

   Although "Carnation" may refer to a type of cloth, it is obvious from the context that a sequence of colours is intended.

75.9 yet] ỹ

82.26s.n. counterbuff] counterbuse

   <u>ODEP</u> emends to "counter use"; however, "counterbuff," "a blow given in return" is more appropriate in the context.

85.10 teather] teacher

93.16 as much for] as

94.22 as] a

113.2 <u>Cicuta</u>] <u>Cienta</u>

113.2s.n. Cicuta] Cienta

119.30 crownd] grownd

   "grownd" may mean "advanced in age," but "crownd" makes better sense.

119.32 hop] hope

   "Hope" is an acceptable Elizabethan spelling for "hop"; however, I have emended the word to avoid ambiguity. The emended spelling occurs at 120.6 and 120.12, and in <u>Aurelia</u>.

143.4 contention] contention,

145.30 <u>Will</u>] <u>Wit</u>

In Whetstone's source, Du Verdier's Mexia, the original word is <u>la volenté</u> (Izard, p. 263).

148.29 through] though

164.23 <u>Ismarito</u>] <u>Soranso</u>

Ismarito might be expected to answer, since the question was addressed to him. It is less likely that Ismarito is too diffident to respond.

198.27] own] one

<u>OED</u> cites "one" as an obsolete but erroneous spelling of "own." In any case, "one" is confusing here.

226.6 the] that the

Emendations of Accidentals

pp. 1-5] text in Roman, underscored words in italic.

    1.19 The Reporte,] black letter.

    1.19 Gent.] black letter.

    3.3-4 chamberlaine . . . Majesties] black letter.

    3.18 REVENGE] revenge

    7.27 Aucthor,] Aucthor.

    9.5 ours,] ours

    9.7 art.] art

    9.9 frost.] frost

    9.13 abuse.] abuse

    9.17 consent:] consent

pp. 10-11] text in Roman.

    10.12 smoke,] comma not clear.

    10.15 the Townes] the' Townes

    10.26 renowne,] renowne

p. 12] text in Roman.

    12.3 these . . . Pleasures.] black letter.

    13.8 Aestas] aestas

    13.22 Tyme.] Tyme:

    15.19 Why] Why?

    15.24 service.] service

    16.1 French] french

    17.3 s.n. but] But

Emendations of Accidentals   cxxxii

17.17 service,] service.

18.15 certenly] certertenly

19.17 s.n. used] uesd

19.28 admiration] admiraion

21.2 Queene] queene

21.6 Wandring] wandring

21.10-11 (quoth Aurelia?)] quoth Aurelia?

21.15 (quoth I,)] quoth I,

21.28 Misterisse] Misterisse.

22.10 bounde] bonnde

23.26 priveledge] priveldge

23.32 Sancta] sancta

25.8-25 No joy . . . in love.] text of poem in Roman.

25.11 fyre.] fyre

25.16 imbrace,] imbrace.

25.18 fight,] fight

26.6 heavens.] heavens

26.7 (quoth Soranso,]] quoth Soranso,

26.15 (quoth Soranso,)] quoth Soranso,

26.18 frends.] frends

27.1 (quoth Franceschina,)] (quoth Franceschina,

27.7 instruction.] instruction

28.9 Mariage.] Mariage?

29.9 (quoth Soranso,)] quoth Soranso,

29.25 (quoth Ismarito,)] quoth Ismarito,

29.32 needed.] needed

30.7 ever-springing] hyphen occurs at end of line.

30.20 then] then then

31.32 other] over

32.16 (quoth Ismarito,)] quoth Ismarito,

33.10-11 (quoth Queene Aurelia,)] quoth Queene Aurelia,

33.13 (quoth Ismarito.)] quoth Ismarito.

33.16 Vechio] vechio

33.23 Boare] Board

34.23 he] he

35.13 question] qustion

36.8 Statutes] Satutes

36.10 Fabritios] Fabririos

36.19-20 (quoth Doctor Mossenigo,)] quoth Doctor Mossenigo,

36.29 (quoth Katharina Trista,)] quoth Katharina Trista,

37.22 testimonie] testionie

37.26-27 by your] by : your [colon not clearly printed]

39.10 selves.] selves:

39.21 Doctor Mossenigos] Doctor mossenigos

40.33 Ophella] Orphella

42.2 Crabtree.] Crabtree:

42.3 (quoth Katherina Trista,)] quoth Katherina Trista,

42.23 Faliero] Falerio

43.3 evermore] ever-/evermore

44.2 EXERCISE] EXERCIE

44.11 brighte] brighte,

Emendations of Accidentals   cxxxiv

45.14-15 (quoth he,)] quoth he,

45.34 himself] hmself

45.35 (quoth Philoxenus)] quoth Philoxenus

46.28-47.7 Noble Allexaunder . . . of the poore.] text in Roman.

47.7 poore.] poore:

47.11-17 Do (gratious . . . water of lyfe.] text in Roman.

47.14 inspiration,] inspiration. [punctuation not clear]

47.18 Philoxenus] PHILOXENUS

47.19 Ismarito] ISMARITO

47.22 Bugiardos] Buiardos

47.34 Faliero] Falerio

48.6 Faliero] Falerio

48.7 (quoth he:)] quoth he:

48.18 Doctour] doctour

48.22 Bugiardoes] Buiardoes

48.30 intertaynment] taynment [inter- occurs as catchword]

49.13 Mistres,)] Mistres,

49.24 with] wtth

50.1 Sonnet] Sennet

50.2 Italion] Italon

50.3-20 To realish . . . paaste my way.] text of poem in Roman.

52.10 Plato] Plato

52.14 (quoth he,)] quoth he,

53.1 he.] he

53.29 Experience.] Experience:

54.26 foresight] foresight, [comma not clear]

55.4-7 The Prince . . . yeeldes to none.] text in Roman.

55.5 mone.] mone

57.18 Faliero]   [in italic]

57.23 affection.] affection

58.14 (quod he,)] quod he,

62.1-28 Chions Letter . . . Chion.] letter in Roman

63.19 Chion] CHION

63.24 death:)] death:

63.26 lyves.] lyves:

64.17 Elisa] ELISA

64.33 offence:] offence. [punctuation not clear]

65.4 Elysaes] Eysaes

65.17 (quoth Soranso)] quoth Soranso)

66.7 (quoth Doctour Mossenigo)] quoth (Doctour Mossenigo)

66.17 (quoth hee,)] quoth hee,

66.17 you] your

66.18 love,] love.

67.4 times,] times;

67.33-68.8 In these . . . fayre wife.] text of poem in Roman

68.1-2 gayne,) / As] gayne, / As)

68.14 s.n. Sclaunder] sclaunder

68.23 company, Supper] company Supper,

69.2 Posie,] Posie.

69.23 hid)] hid

69.24-70.10 Two Soveraigne . . . the world.] text of poem in Roman.

70.20-71.7 Hence burnyng . . . Mistresse good.] text of poem in Roman.

Emendations of Accidentals   cxxxvi

71.9 Orange,] Orange

71.18-72.13 Even as . . . your owne.] <u>text of poem in Roman</u>.

72.11 face,] face?

72.13 Dame,] Dame. [<u>punctuation uncertain</u>]

72.25-73.12 From shore . . . in hope.] <u>text of poem in Roman</u>.

73.20-29 If one firme . . . of Grace.] <u>text of poem in Roman</u>.

73.20 one] on

73.22 lawde,] lawde.

73.24 woe,] woe.

73.27 smart,] smart.

75.1 <u>Exercise</u>.] <u>Exercise</u>

76.5 Sunne.] Sunne:

76.21 <u>Consolation of</u>] consolation of

76.24-77.16 Farewell, bright . . . crowne.] <u>text of poem in Roman</u>.

77.8 blame.] blame

77.18 Musick, the] Musick. The

78.3 Musick:] Musick.

79.24 aunsweare,] aunsweare.

81.14 places, the] places. The

81.17-27 To thee I . . . of zeale.] <u>text of poem in Roman</u>.

81.29 Doctor] <u>Doctor</u>

86.7 death,] death.

88.7 <u>Forma numen habet</u>] <u>in italic</u>.

88.14 <u>Thisbie</u>,] <u>Thisbie</u>.

91.26-27 (quoth . . . controversies:)] quoth . . . controversies:

92.12 (quoth Queene <u>Aurelia</u>,)] quoth Queene <u>Aurelia</u>,

92.20 reasons.] reasons

92.24 Disputation,)] Disputation,

93.9 of] of of

94.5 s.n. reporter] eeporter

95.8 contentment] content ment

96.2 not,) yet] not, yet)

96.10 Philippo Provolo] PHILIPPO PROVOLO

96.23 Malipiero] Maliperio

98.34 with all] withall;

99.17 furious] surious

100.16 Chamber] Camber

101.13-32 Fayre Mistresse . . . MARINO GEORGIO.] letter in Roman.

102.13-27 I am not . . . FELICE.] letter in Roman.

102.21 sighes:] sighes.:

104.16 world.] world,

106.22 dishonour,] dishonour?

106.25 (quoth Cornaro,)] quoth Cornaro,

107.28 (quoth Fabritio,)] quoth Fabritio,

108.1 slaunder] slannder

108.3 (quoth Isabella,)] quoth Isabella,

108.8 (quoth Soranso,)] quoth Soranso,

108.15 (quoth Queene Aurelia:)] quoth Queene Aurelia:

108.18-19 correction. [Begins new paragraph.] After] correction. After

108.20-21 Historie: Maddam] Historie. [Begins new paragraph.] Maddam

108.21 (quoth Don Dolo,)] quoth Don Dolo,

108.22 s.n. instructeth] instuceth

108.24 (quoth Queene Aurelia,)] quoth Queene Aurelia,

Emendations of Accidentals   cxxxviii

109.8 Aurelia] AURELIA

109.11 Snakes,] Snakes

110.2 true (quoth] (true quoth

110.21 retayne] retayno

110.29 that] that)

117.17-18 coun-/terfeits] coun-feits [catchword: terfeits]

117.20 (quoth Ismarito,)] quoth Ismarito,

117.25 (quoth he,)] quoth he,

118.3 countenaunce] conntenaunce

119.27-120.12 Care, Care . . . for joye.] text of poem in Roman.

120.22-23 (quoth Queene Aurelia,)] quoth Queene Aurelia,

120.27 Inganno] in italic.

120.28 Bergetto] in italic.

120.30 Sainct] S.

120.31 intombed, there] intombed. There

121.2 Sainct] S.

121.16 Saint] saint

121.32 fayre,] fayre

124.17 Maister] maister

124.27 Vechio,)] Vechio,

126.6 voutchsafe] voutchsafe,

126.22 s.n. more] mors

129.32 Andrugio,)] Andrugio,

130.26 Andrugios] Andrugio

132.10 (quoth shee,)] quoth shee,

133.21 s.n. pollicye.] pollye

134.27 s.n. bere] beres

134.28 s.n. of] ot

134.28 s.n. Officers] Officsrr

135.27 Pegasus] PEGASUS

135.30 Promos] PROMOS

136.9 Promos:] Promos,:

136.29 (possibly)] (possibly

136.33 revived] revined

136.34 Hermyt,)] Hermyt,

137.20 every partie] everypartie

137.21 desire] dessre

137.26 had] had, had

138.4 Aurelia,)] Aurelia,

138.21-22 away,) Alvisa Vechio] away.) [Begins new paragraph] Alvisa vechio

140.11 Nero] NERO

140.17 Madame, with] Madame (with

140.17 (quoth] quoth

140.28 skanse] skause

140.29 saye,] saye.

140.32 (quoth Ismarito,)] quoth Ismarito,

141.3 reasons,)] reasons,

142.11 (quoth Ismarito,)] quoth Ismarito,

142.16 Saint] S.

142.19 Saint] S.

142.24 (quoth he,)] quoth he,

144.18 (quoth he,)] quoth he,

Emendations of Accidentals cxl

144.22 (quoth Ismarito,)] quoth Ismarito,

144.34 (quoth Soranso,)] quoth Soranso,

145.5-6 (quoth Ismarito,)] quoth Ismarito,

145.13 (quoth Soranso,)] quoth Soranso,

145.25 absurdity] obsurdity

146.22 body:] body.

146.27 Christall] Chrstall

146.34 (quoth Soranso,)] quoth Soranso,

147.8 (quoth Ismarito,)] quoth Ismarito,

147.34 (quoth Soranso.)] quoth Soranso.

148.1-2 (quoth Ismarito:)] quoth Ismarito:

148.7 (quoth Soranso,)] quoth Soranso,

148.27-149.12 Who prickels . . . my breast.] poem in Roman.

149.13-14 (quoth Queene Aurelia,)] quoth Queene Aurelia,

149.17 (quoth Dondolo,)] quoth Dondolo,

149.24 (quoth the plaine Doctor,)] quoth the plaine Doctor,

149.25 sighe] (sighe

149.26 but] but)

149.30 Ladies] Laides

150.6 omitted.] If there sight be. so quick, quoth Franceschina Santa, then /

152.1 (quoth Soranso:)] quoth Soranso:

152.6 basenes:] basenes?

152.9 greevous] greevons

154.4 Cotages] Co, tages

155.4 Saints.] Saints,

156.31 s.n. reproofe] repoofe

Emendations of Accidentals   cxli

158.1 shee,] shee.

158.14 reputation] reputatiton

159.33 Husband,] Husband.

161.17 <u>Italian</u>,] <u>Italian</u>.

162.28 (quoth <u>Dondolo</u>.)] quoth <u>Dondolo</u>.

162.29 (quoth <u>Alvisa Vechio</u>?)] quoth <u>Alvisa Vechio</u>?

162.30 of] of of

162.32 (quoth <u>Dondolo</u>:)] quoth <u>Dondolo</u>:

163.2 (quoth <u>Soranso</u>,)] quoth <u>Soranso</u>,

163.6 (quoth <u>Fabritio</u>, and <u>Isabella</u>:)] quoth <u>Fabritio</u>, and <u>Isabella</u>:

163.11 Queene] <u>Queene</u>

163.15 controversies] controver-/versies

163.32 pleasaunt] pleasannt

164.3 (quoth he:)] quoth he:

164.6-7 (quoth <u>Soranso</u>:)] quoth <u>Soranso</u>:

164.12 Queene] <u>Queene</u>

164.33 the Doctor] <u>the Doctor</u>

166.2 overmuche] over-/muche

166.16 (quoth <u>Segnior Philoxenus</u>:)] quoth <u>Segnior Philoxenus</u>:

166.19 (quoth <u>Katherina Trista</u>,)] quoth <u>Katherina Trista</u>,

166.21 (quoth <u>Segnior Philoxenus</u>,)] quoth <u>Segnior Philoxenus</u>,

166.25 (quoth <u>Fabritio</u>,)] quoth <u>Fabritio</u>,

166.27 <u>Philoxenus</u>] <u>Philox</u>.

166.34 in] is

168.1 <u>Exercise</u>:] <u>Exercise</u>,

168.28 lived] li-/lived

168.34 companie,)] companie,

169.5 Segnior] Seg.

169.29 Bookes, (and] (Bookes, and

170.3 Sciences,] Sciences.

170.18 Friers,] Friers.

171.9 (to] to

171.27 Hystoriographer] Hystorigrapher

172.29 pilfering] piylfering

173.24 Doctor,)] Doctor,

173.28 (envying] envying

174.22 remembraunce] remembrannce

175.4-19 Regarde my . . . your friende.] text of poem in Roman.

176.11 Platoes] PLATOES

176.34 have] havo

178.15 Infancie: In whose] Infancie. [begins new paragraph] In whose

178.16 there] there,

178.21 You] (You

179.5 Smoake] Somake

180.22 Orchard] Orchad

181.25 words:] words.

181.30 disgrace] disgace

182.7 straunge] strannge

182.33 horne] borne

183.7 faire] faire.

183.30 (that] that (

183.32 because] hecause

185.7 s.n. enemie] enemies

185.26 (quoth she,)] quoth she,

186.9 contentment] coutentment

187.12 Doctor.)] Doctor.

187.13 Maister] M.

188.27 perforce] perfore

188.29 hideth.] hideth

189.11 like unto *Iris*,)] like) unto *Iris*,

189.20 (sayth he,)] sayth he,

190.14 Maister] maister

190.25 you] yon

190.27 to an] an to

190.29 affection] affction

190.32 Belochye.)] Belochye.

191.1 (quoth the Doctor,)] quoth the Doctor,

192.4 men,] *comma not certain*.

192.7 (quoth the Doctor,)] quoth the Doctor

193.3-6 I that . . . sugred joyes.] *text of poem in Roman*.

194.28 (quoth] quoth

194.29 *Aurelia*,)] *Aurelia*,

195.2 *Phyloxenus*] *italic*

195.7 past,] past.

195.15 s.n. striving] strivng

195.31 pryson) so] pryson so)

196.1-2 (quoth *Signior Philoxenus*,)] quoth *Signior Philoxenus*,

196.14 s.n. the] the the

196.21 (quoth Dondolo,)] quoth Dondolo,

196.29-30 (quoth Segnior Philoxenus,)] quoth Segnior Philoxenus,

198.5 Phrigius] Pyrigeus [in italic]

198.5 Pieria] italic.

198.6 Segnior Phyloxenus] italic.

198.32 Chamber,] Chamber.

199.7 lively] livelely

200.21 (withall)] (withall

200.24 Aurelia,] Aurelia.

200.27 sownded.] sownded:

201.12-29 Even as . . . married lyfe.] text of poem in Roman.

201.13 beare:] beare

201.19 breede.] breede

201.23 Gold.] Gold

201.26 greeve,] greeve

204.11 (quoth Cornelia,)] quoth Cornelia,

206.18 abylytie) to] abylytie (to

206.30 wordes:] wordes.

207.11 loved] lo

207.15 s.n. King] king

207.21 Augurers] Angurers

207.29 unhappye] happye

209.25 perfected] pefected

209.29 Reported, by] black letter.

Emendations of Accidentals   cxlv

209.34 choyce.] choyce:

210.2 (advisedly)] (advisedly

211.29 s.n. Philosophie] Philosophit

212.19 breake it,] breake, it

214.24-25 reasons to,] reasons, to

215.5 Phrigius] italic.

215.6 Pieria] italic.

215.7 Segnior Phyloxenus] italic.

219.29 (quoth he,)] quoth he,

220.15 mee.] mee:

220.27-221.33 Faire PIERIA . . . PHRIGIUS.] text of letter in Roman.

221.23 crueltie,] crueltie.

222.5 Pythes] Pythes,

222.19 who,] who [punctuation not clear]

222.26-223.13 SIR PHRIGIUS . . . PIERIA of MYOS.] text of letter in Roman.

223.8 Hostilyty] Hostliyty

225.31 IONIA.] IONIA

226.8 cupple)] cupple

228.34 show,] show

229.31 Triumph] Trumph

230.1 A lookyng Glasse] A lookyng Glasse

230.2 a payre of] a payre of

230.3 a Pyller of] a Pyller of

230.4 a standing Cup] a standing Cup

230.4 ARGENT] Argent

230.5-21 The Muses . . . and steepe.] text in small Roman.

cxlvi

Press Variants

Copies collated:

    B   Bodleian Library, Oxford.

    BM^1 British Museum, London, C59ff.21.

    BM^2 British Museum, London, 10445.

    F^1 Folger Shakespeare Library, Washington, D.C., copy 1.

    F^2 Folger Shakespeare Library, Washington, D.C., copy 2.

    F^3 Folger Shakespeare Library, Washington, D.C., copy 3.

    H   Henry E. Huntington Library, San Marino, Calif.

    I   University of Illinois, Urbana, Ill.

    P   J. Pierpont Morgan Library, New York, N.Y.

    R   Rosenbach Foundation, Philadelphia, Pa.

Sheet B (Inner forme)

Corrected: B, BM^1, BM^2, F^1, F^2, F^3, I, P, R.

Uncorrected: H

Sig. $B1^v$: 14.27 won] one

Sig. $B2^r$: 15.24 any] my

Sig. $B4^r$: 21.16 expect] except

    (Note: in 21.16, F^3 possibly reads "best," instead of "best."; but I believe the comma to be a smudged period.)

Sheet D (Outer forme)

Corrected: BM^1, BM^2, R.

Uncorrected: B, F^1, F^2, F^3, H, I, P.

Sig. $D1^r$: 34.4 Dianaes] Dianes

Sheet F (Inner forme)

Corrected: F^2, F^3, I, P, R.
Uncorrected: B, BM^1, BM^2, F^1, H.
Sig. $F1^v$: 55.3 defyneth] devyneth
Sig. $F3^v$: 60.28 coursest] crossest

Sheet G (Outer forme)

Corrected: F^3.
Uncorrected: B, BM^1, BM^2, F^1, F^2, H, I, P, R.
Sig. $G1^r$: 63.30 sore] fore

Sheet N (Outer forme)

Corrected: B, BM^1, BM^2, F^1, F^2, H, I, P, R.
Uncorrected: F^3.
Sig. $N1^r$: 121.8 manye] mauye

Sheet N (Inner forme)

First Stage Corrected: F^2, R.
Uncorrected: B, BM^1, BM^2, F^1, I.
Sig. $N4^r$: 129.12 s.n. For-/tune] for-/tune
Second Stage Corrected: F^3, H, R.
Sig. $N2^r$: 124.24 s.n. subtilly] subilly

Sheet P (Outer forme)

Corrected: B, BM^1, BM^2, F^1, F^2, H, I, P, R.
Uncorrected: F^3.

Sig. P1^r: 141.13 judgement, and he] judgement, he
Sig. P2^v: 144.17 heardled] headled
Sig. P3^r: 145.29-30 to wit, Intendment] to witte, Intenment
           145.33 Intendment] Intenment
           145.33 both] bothe
           146.12 Alexander] Alexanders
Sig. P4^v: 149.11 all passions] at passion
           149.21 geve] gave
           149.25 their] this
Sig. P4^v: 149.26 chastẽ] chasten
           149.29 would] should

Sheet Q (Inner forme)

Corrected: B, F^1, F^2, F^3, H, I, P, R.
Uncorrected: BM^1, BM^2.

Sig. Q1^v: 152.20 ẙ evyl, maketh] the evyll, make
Sig. Q3^v: 157.19 Death] Deth
           157.19 ẙ] that
           157.21 hee] shee
           157.25-26 in an errour] in errour
           157.28 mẽt] ment
           157.28 if] of
           157.29 Brethrẽ er] Brethren

Sheet S (Outer forme)

Corrected: B, BM^1, BM^2, F^1, F^2, H, I, P, R.
Uncorrected: F^3.

Sig. S3^r: 176.5   prophesieth] propheiseth

Sheet S (Inner forme)

Corrected: B, BM^1, BM^2, F^1, F^2, H, I, P, R.
Uncorrected: F^3.

Sig. S4^r: 178.24   concludeth] concludes

Sheet T (Inner forme)

Corrected: BM^1, BM^2, H, P.
Uncorrected: B, F^1, F^2, F^3, I, R.

Sig. T2^r: 183.16   Metamorphosis] Metamorphossi

Sheet U (Outer forme)

Corrected: BM^2, F^3, H, I, P.
Uncorrected: B, BM^1, F^1, F^2, R.

Sig. U3^r: 196.12   your] you

Sheet U (Inner forme)

Corrected: B, BM^1, BM^2, F^1, F^3, H, I, P, R.
Uncorrected: F^2.

Sig. U1ᵛ: 192.21 her entrayles] her owne entrayles

193.8 lawe] awe

Sig. U2ʳ: 194.6 ẙ whole world: which is, wher the Tennaũt] the whole world: that where the Tennaunt

Sig. U4ʳ: 198.13 Tithon] Titan

198.17 shrill] still

Sheet Z (Outer forme)

Corrected: B, BM¹, BM², F¹, F², I, P, R.

Uncorrected: F³, H.

Sig. Z4ᵛ: 230.16 were] wore

Collation with "Aurelia" (Bodleian copy)

/[Within a factotum at head:] AURELIA. / [below factotum] The Paragon of plea- / sure and Princely delights: / Contayning / The seven dayes Solace (in Christmas / Holy-dayes) of Madona Aurelia, Queene of / the Christmas Pastimes, & sundry other well- / courted Gentlemen, and Gentlewomen, in a / noble Gentlemans Pallace. / A worke most sweetely intercoursed (in civill and / friendly disputations) with many amorous and / pleasant Discourses, to delight the Reader: and / plentifully garnished with Morall Notes, to make / it profitable to the Regarder. / By G. W. Gent. / [printer's device & motto, McKerrow 283] / At London printed, by Richard Johnes. / 1593. /

pp. 2-5 omitted in Aurelia

   6.1 Unto] To

   6.1 Reader] Readers, both Gentlemen and Gentlewomen

   6.3 Friendly Reader] Gentlemen & Gentlewomen

   6.3 thee] you

   6.22 twelvemoneths] omitted.

   6.24 thou] you

   6.25 art] be

   6.25 thee] you

   6.27 thee] you

   6.27 thee] you

   6.27 wherin] herein

   6.27 thee] you

   6.30 thee] you

   6.32 thou] you

   6.33 receivest] receive

Collation with Aurelia   clii

6.33 sweete] omitted.

6.34 thy] your

7.2   thou mayste] you may

7.6   thou haste] you have

7.7   thee] you

7.8   thou shalt] you shal

7.9   a] you

7.18 Reader] Gentlemen and Gentlewomen

7.18 thou haste] you have

7.25 withall] with al

7.26 thee] you

7.28 thee thou shalt be] you, you shalbe

7.29 thou makest thy] you make your

7.29 thy] your

7.30 thou mayest] you may

8.22 gentle Reader] Gentlemen and Gentlewomen

8.23 thee mine] you friendly

8.24 Thine] Your

8.25 George Whetstone.] G.W.

9.5   ours,] ours:

9.6   So Morall Whetstone, to his Countrey] This Morall Author so, to us he,

9.9   frost.] frost,

9.13 th'abuse.] th'abuse,

11.15 twincking] twinckling

Collation with Aurelia cliii

13.1   The first Dayes exercise.] Madona Aurelia, her first dayes pleasures.

13.5   in] on

14.18 I] omitted.

14.22 replyed] replying

17.2   Souldiers] shoulders

24.22 Caviliero] Signior

26.14 uses] use

26.14 love. The] love. [Begins new paragraph] The

26.24 wantonnesse. There] wantonesse [Begins new paragraph] There

26.28 it deserveth] deserves

26.30 defences. Madame] defences [Begins new paragraph] Madame

26.34 chast. Well] chast. [Begins new paragraph] Well

30.7   ever-springing] everspringing

31.29 Pans] Paris

33.14 Yea] I

36.10 bittersweete] bitter-sweete

37.22 s.n. ignoraunce] ignorant

40.33 Ophella] Orphella

41.5   toule] knole

41.9   that] so

42.23 Faliero] Falerio

42.31 Gentlewomen] Gentlewomens

43.15 they] wherewith they

44.1-2 The seconde Dayes / EXERCISE.] MADONA AURELIA, Her second daies pleasures.

44.14 Jubiter] Jupiter

45.7   as if] if

46.11   s.n. Dennis Bull] Phalaris Bull

51.1   cause?] causes

61.4   breedeth hate in] breedeth in

61.5   overpayseth] overpoyseth

61.9   s.n. quited] quieted

61.20   foorthwith] forth with

62.12   wordes.] words,

63.14   yet] omitted

63.17   CICHEUS] SICHEUS [Aurelia continues to use this spelling.]

63.30   sore] fore

64.33   offence:] offence.

65.1   unknow] unknown

65.17   Metamorphos] Metamorphosis

66.11   woulde] it would

68.1-2 gayne,) / As] gaine, / As)

69.17   Blue,] Blew,

75.1   The thyrd Daies Exercise.] MADONA AURELIA, Her third daies pleasures.

75.9   yet] omitted

82.26   s.n. counterbuff] counterbuse

83.19   credit] credit?

83.29   growe] groweth

83.34   agreeeth] agreeth

84.6   Mariage:] Mariage?

85.10   teather] teacher

86.7   death,] death:

86.15 seeeth] seeth

86.32 the dishonesty] this dishonesty

87.15 seeeth] seeth

90.2   the] their

92.17 imployment. / But] imployment. [Begins new paragraph] But

93.16 as much for] as

96.4   containe] attaine

98.34 with all] withall

99.14 leaft] left

100.13 Jubiter] Jupiter

101.29 I remayne.] I remaine,

103.6 not indured] indured not

104.16 world.] world?

107.30 Amonition] admonition

108.19 [Begins new paragraph] After] no paragraph.

108.21 no paragraph] [Begins new paragraph] Madame

108.21 Don Dolo] Dondolo

109.21 generall] omitted.

113.2 Cicuta] Cienta

113.2 s.n. Cicuta] Cienta

113.3 of] omitted.

Collation with Aurelia   clvi

114.1 The fourth Daies exercise] MADONA AURELIA, Her fourth daies pleasur

114.14 hart.] hart,

114.25 misling] mistie

115.1 service] service,

116.12 writ.] writ:

116.13 Europe] Europae

116.13 Africe] Africae

116.31 their] there

116.31-117.13 And by her . . . meintiendray] omitted.

118.23 avenged] avenge

119.24 Eunick] Eunuch

119.26 away.] away,

119.30 crownd] grownd

120.15 currant:] currant.

120.29 little] omitted.

121.27-28 countrey-wemen] countrie women

121.30 after,] , after

124.15 seeeth] seeth

125.14 free] omitted.

126.6 voutchsafe] vouchsafed

131.11 expect?] expect,

131.12 villany.] villàny?

133.17 and] omitted.

133.22 the] this

135.19 injustly] unjustly

135.23 afflictions] affections

136.27 give hym leave to] omitted.

Collation with Aurelia   clvii

136.29 (possibly)] (possibly

136.29 satisfied] satisfied)

137.26 had] have had

137.34 likelie] like

138.19 Gentlemens.] Gentlemens,

138.22 Alvisa] [Begins new paragraph] Alvisa

138.26 man] men

138.32 Husband,] Husband?

138.33 himselfe.] himselfe?

139.17 aunswered.] answered,

139.20 men. / It] men. [Begins new paragraph] It

140.28 skanse] skawse

141.14 man] men

141.19 qualyted] qualified

143.4   contention] contention,

144.1   The fift Daies Exercise:] MADONA AURELIA, Her fift daies pleasures.

145.8-9 where some / ever] wheresoever

145.30 Will] Wit

147.7   man.] man?

148.29 through] though

149.3   flye.] flie:

149.25 sighe] (sigh

149.26 but] but)

149.25 one] owne

Collation with Aurelia clviii

151.9 againe.] againe?

152.6 basenes:] basenesse?

156.25 blessing] blessings

159.10 neither] omitted.

159.11 they contrary] they are contrary

161.12 via] Via

164.23 Ismarito] Soranso

166.7 Death?] death:

166.19 s.n. 13. Pride.] omitted.

167.22 FINIS.] omitted.

168.1 The syxt Dayes Exercise:] MADONA AURELIA, Her sixt daies pleasures.

169.9-14 s.n. a gentleman . . . the evyll.] omitted.

169.29 (and] and

169.32 resolutions)] resolutions,

170.10 imitate.] imitate,

170.2 s.n. sene] severe

170.10 his worthines] whom

170.13 course] cause

171.9 (to] to

171.9 Commentaries)] commentaries,

172.32 present. / Some] present. [Begins new paragraph] Some

174.9 hymselfe. / But] himselfe. [Begins new paragraph] But

174.10 unkindnesse] kindnesse

175.25 waspissest] waspishest

177.12 whyther] whether

177.31 stronge,] strong?

Collation with Aurelia   clix

178.15 Infancie: In] Infancie: [Begins new paragraph] In

189.26 Thus] [Begins new paragraph] Thus

190.27 to] omitted.

197.11 FINIS.] omitted.

198.1 The .vii. Dayes Exercise:] MADONA AURELIA, Her seventh daies pleasures.

198.27 own] owne

199.24 Earles,] Earles to

200.23 Discourse. When] discourse. [Begins new paragraph] When

202.11 s.n. qualitie] a qualitie

206.14 the] that

207.21 Augurers] Augurs

207.30 him.] him?

210.2 (advisedly)] (advisedly

210.2 consider,] consider)

212.32 s.n. sollomnes] sullennes

214.24 reasons] reasons)

214.25 to,)] to

222.21 peace. After] peace, after

226.6 the] that the

230   no colophon] colophon

Text of colophon:

/ At London / Printed by Richard Johnes, at the / signe of the Rose and Crowne, neere / Holburne Bridge. / 1593. / [printer's device McKerrow 283] /

Title pages

of

An Heptameron of Civill Discourses (1582)
STC 25337, Folger Shakespeare Library, copy 3.

Aurelia, The Paragon of Pleasure and Princely Delights (1593)
STC 25338, Henry H. Huntington Library

An Heptameron
of Ciuill Discourses.

Containing: The Chriſtmaſſe Exerciſe of ſundrie well Courted Gentlemen and Gentlewomen.

In whoſe behauiours, the better sort, may see, a repreſētation of their own Vertues. And the Inferiour, may learne such Rules of Ciuil Gouernmēt, as wil raſe out the Blemiſh of their baseneſſe:

Wherin, is Renowned, the Vertues, of a most Honourable and braue mynded Gentleman.

And herein, also, [as it were in a Mirrour] the Vnmaried may see the Defectes whiche Eclipſe the Glorie of MARIAGE: And the wel Maried, as in a Table of Houſholde Lawes may cull out needefull Preceptes to eſtabliſh their good Fortune.

A Worke, intercourſed with Ciuyll Pleaſure, to reaue tediouſneſſe from the Reader: and garniſhed with Morall Noates to make it profitable, to the Regarder.

The Reporte, of George Whetſtone. Gent.

Formæ, nulla fides.

AT LONDON.
Printed by Richard Iones,
at the Signe of the Roſe and the Crowne,
neare Holburne Bridge. 3. Feb. 1582.

AVRELIA.

The Paragon of pleasure and Princely delights:

Contayning

The seuen dayes Solace (in Christmas Holy-dayes) of Madona Aurelia, *Queene* of the Christmas Pastimes, & sundry other well-courted Gentlemen, and Gentlewomen, in a noble Gentlemans Pallace.

A worke most sweetely intercoursed (in ciuill and friendly disputations) with many amorous and pleasant Discourses, to delight the Reader: and plentifully garnished with Morall Notes, to make it profitable to the Regarder.

By G. W. Gent.

At London printed, by Richard Iohnes.
1593.

A CRITICAL EDITION

OF

GEORGE WHETSTONE'S AN HEPTAMERON OF CIVILL DISCOURSES

TEXT

An Heptameron

of Civill Discourses.

Containing: The Christmasse Exercise of sundrie well Courted Gentlemen and Gentlewomen.

In whose behaviours, the better
sort, may see, a representation of their own Vertues:
And the Inferiour, may learne such Rules of Civil Government, as wil rase out the Blemish of their basenesse:

Wherin, is Renowned, the Vertues, of a most Honourable and brave mynded Gentleman.

And herein, also, (as it were in a Mirrour) the Unmaried
may see the Defectes whiche Eclipse the Glorie of MARIAGE:
And the wel Maried, as in a Table of Housholde Lawes, may cull
out needefull Preceptes to establysh their good Fortune.

A Worke, intercoursed with Civyll Pleasure, to reave
tediousnesse from the Reader: and garnished with Morall Noates
to make it profitable, to the Regarder.

The Reporte, of George Whetstone. Gent.
Formae, nulla fides.

AT LONDON.
Printed by Richard Jones,
at the Signe of the Rose and the Crowne,
neare Holburne Bridge. 3. Feb. 1582.

Ad Mecœnatem, in laudem Aucthoris:
CARMEN HEROICUM

Mecoenas proceres inter celeberrime nostros,
Et Clario dilecte deo, castisque Camaenis;
5 Accipe Pierios tibi quos sacravit honores,
Troianovantaei vocalis Musa Georgii.
    Non Apinas Tricasve canit, sed conscia laudis
Musa vacat studiis gravioribus: arctaque junctae
Conditione pari commendat foedera vitae;
10 Conjugiique refert incommoda disparis Aucthor.
    Nec solum haec; sed vera ducis praeconia magni
Pandit, et Aonio tollit super aethera plectro.
    Divisitque operis seriem per tempora, miro
Ordine, juditioque pari: septemque dierum
15 (Judice me) certant cum Castilione labores.
    Et quae tam parvo descripsit Nymphia libro,
(Crede mihi) tanto non sunt indigna Patrono.

                JOANNES BOTREVICUS. /

To the right Honourable, Sir Christopher Hatton,   A2^r
Knight, Captaine of the Queenes Majesties
Garde: Viz-chamberlaine to her Highnesse,
and of her Majesties moste Honourable
Privie Connsell: GEORGE WHETSTONE,
wissheth long continuance of Honor,
Health and Happynesse.

    Right Honourable, in the Interpretation of
the wise: PARRHASIUS, in painting of INGRATITUDE
and ENVIE, like Feends: rather performed a worke
of Judgement, then Arte: for so soyled with infamie
are these passions as hell ought to be their
harbour, and not the heart of man. All other
defeactes of the minde have their cause of nature,
or colour from reason. PRIDE proceedeth from mans
overweening, of his owne excellencie: the Sourse
of AMBITION, is the glory and reverence given unto
Aucthoritie. ANGER, and REVENGE, groweth from the
injurie of others. But these two yokefellowes
INGRATITUDE and ENVIE, doe degenerate from kinde,
and maske without visard of excuse. The other
pursue their enemies and seeke to breake but the
barres of their advauncement: but the one of
these woundeth his friend, whom he ought to honour,
and the other reprocheth / vertue, whom the wicked   A2^v
reverence: And least, Time, the true exposer of
Secrets, reproche me, as a Fosterer of both these
dampnable vices. Of Ingratitude, in not
acknowledging, many received favours, of a Right
noble Italian Gentleman. Of Envie, in smouldring
his most cleare vertues: who with a zealous
affection, oftentimes in my hearing, made his
tongue, an honorable Trumpet to sounde the bright
renowne of her Majesties excellencie (as he sayd,
and I beleeve uppon earth) the fountaine of grace

and goodnes: who used her sacred name, with such
a reverent regard, as in his behaviour, I noted
the full consideration of a dutifull subject,
denized by the eternall fame, of her Highnes
5 devine Grace.

So that desirous to erect some Memorial
Monument of his worthines, I have taken upon me
to be the Secretarie of a few, of many his precious
vertues: Which I humbly present unto your honor,
10 with a hand redy to doe you effectuall service:
and a tongue confessing, that you shall herein
beholde, the least part of those glorious giftes,
which eternize your name, and binde the generall
multitude, to honour your Counterfet, for whose
15 benefite, I have likewise committed to memorie,
the civill disputations, and speaches of sundry
well Courted Gentlemen, and Gentlewomen, his
Guestes, during the time of my intertainment,
with Segnior Phyloxenus (for so covertly I name
20 him, least in giving him, his true honorable Tytles
in England, I should make a passage for Envie, to
injurie him in Italy) whose exercises, if my penne
hath not maimed them in the reporting, may be a
president of behaviours to the indifferent well
25 qualited Gentleman and / Gentlewoman: Besides,   A3^r
a true Anatomie of the inconveniences, which
eclypse, and of the vertues which expresse the
glory of Marriage: an estate both honorable and
divine: honorable, in that, she is imbraced of
30 all men: divine, because in the last yeare of
their life she (in dispite of death) maketh men
to live a new terme, in their children and
posteritie: not unlike to a leafe fallen Rose,
which in his stalke hath many tender buddes:

Which bare report of mine: I reverently protect
under the Garde, of your honors regarded vertues:
A bare report, I Christen it: for, whatsoever is
praise worthy in this Booke, belongeth to Segnior
5 Phyloxenus and his Courtly favourers: and what is
worthlesse, is the blame of my imperfect judgement:
So that, besides the protection, I am humbly to
crave, that your Honor will receive whatsome-ever
is due to them, with a favorable countenance, and
10 to pardon the unsufficiencie of their Trowchman:
with an imagination, that his Present, is the
testimonie of a duetiful affection: Who zealously
prayeth, that your vertues maye have as full power
over Envie, as they have Aucthoritie to command
15 the willing mindes of the best inclined dispositions:
Of which number, it may please you of favour,
though not of merit, to account me.

¶ Your Honors most bounden,
GEORGE WHETSTONS. /

Unto the friendly Reader, Wealthe and welfare.

Friendly Reader, I present thee heere (as I thinke) a profitable, unpolyshed labour: For,
5 he that is the Troucheman of a Straungers Tongue, may well declare his meaning, but yet shall marre the Grace of his Tale: And, therefore, Themistocles, the noble Captayne and Philosopher of Athens, compareth suche forced Speaches, to Tapistrie
10 Hangings rowled up: which, beyng open, appeare beautifull: and fowlded, reserve their Vertue, but lose their showe: But I expect (somwhat) a better event, then may an Interpreter, that is bownd to a present Reporte: for my Respit, hath ben
15 sufficient to consider of Segnior Phyloxenus, and his honorable companies vertues: and (least by rash acquitall of their favours, I should do injurie, to their reputation) I have, with well advised Judgement, bethought mee, of suche
20 memorable Questions and Devices, as I heard and sawe presented, in this most noble Italian Gentlemans Pallace, the Christmas twelvemoneths past: and aunswerable to my weake capassitie, have exposed the same, in such sort, as if thou
25 art not too curious, may delight, and content thee: and if not too carelesse, may directe, and benefit thee: And to satisfie thee, wherin: I give thee friendly knowledge, that Segnior Philoxenus reverent regard of the Queenes Majesties high
30 Vertues, is a President for thee: with a dutiful, and unfained heart, to love, feare, and obay her Highnesse, from whome, next under / God, thou receivest such sweete blessinges: as through the whole world, her excellencie is renowned, and thy

prosperitie envied. By this noble Gentlemans
civill intertainment of strangers, thou mayste
perceyve with what Garland, Courtisie, is
principally crowned: By the civill behaviours,
5 of <u>Soranso</u>, <u>Dondolo</u>, <u>Bergetto</u>, and other
Gentlemen herein named, thou haste a President
of government, which will commend thee: and by
well regarding their speeches, thou shalt finde
a discreete methode of talke, meete for a
10 Gentleman. The lyke benefit, shall Gentlewomen
receive, in Imitating, of <u>Madona</u> <u>Aurelia</u> (Queene
of the Christmas pleasures) <u>Maria</u> <u>Belochi</u>, <u>Lucia</u>
<u>Bella</u>, <u>Franceschina</u> <u>Santa</u>, and the rest of the
wel qualited Gentlewomen. Besides, a number of
15 other Morall documentes, needefull reprehensions,
and witty sayinges, to perfect the commendation,
both of a Gentleman, and Gentlewoman. (Courteous
Reader) thou haste heare, the honorable institution
of Marriage, so perfectly Anatomed, as a verye
20 weake Judgement, may see the causes, which make
Houshould quarrelles, to resemble Hell. Againe,
the man, which is willing to live happily, may
here learne such directions, and lawes, as will
chaunge his private house, into a Paradice on
25 earth. If civill and Morall pleasures, withall
these benefites, may make thee intertaine thys
booke and report well of the Aucthor, I assure
thee thou shalt be pleased, and I satisfied. But
if thou makest thy tongue, enemie to thy owne
30 reputation, thou mayest detract, but not reproche
the worke: Injure, but not hurt the writer, for
both will live, and laugh such Callumniators to
scorne, when either are readie to doe the discrete
Reader service. Some will (perchaunce more of

Epistle to the Reader   8

envie to heare a stranger commended, then of pittie
to bemone my hard fortune, or fowle usage) say, I
have as just cause to complaine, of injuries
received at <u>Roane</u>, <u>Rome</u>, and <u>Naples</u>, as to commend
the vertues and good intertainment, of <u>Segnior</u>
<u>Philoxenus</u>: But to give such Suggestioners a /
double good example, both of patience and   A4^v
thankefulnesse: I heare protest, that as these
injuries begunne, with my hard fortune, so they
ended, no wayes in my discredite: And as I
forgeve the causes of my mishaps, so scorne I,
to recount them, to receive amendes, in a little
pittie. But, for that they, and all such as
vew my Report, may learne of me to bee gratefull
for received benefites: I make it knowen: That
this travell, is <u>Segnior</u> <u>Philoxenus</u> due: And I
still his debter, and so shall remayne during my
life: reserving a good affection, to bestow on
such as receive his Vertues: and my paynes to
profite and commend them selves. And in my
opinion, it is just they doe so: Wherfore, to
give a disgrace to ceremonies, gentle Reader I
ende: as I hope to finde thee mine.

                         <u>Thine assured friend</u>,
                         <u>George Whetston</u>. /

T. W. Esquier, In the commendation of the Aucthor, and his needefull BOOKE.

Even as the fruictfull Bee, doth from a thousand Flowers,
5 Sweet Honie draine, and layes it up, to make the profit ours,
So, Morall Whetstone, to his Countrey doth impart,
A Worke of worth, culd from the wise, with Judgement, wit and art.
No Stage Toy, he sets foorth, or thundring of an Hoast,
But his rare Muse, a passage makes, twixt burnyng fier and frost.
10 Suche Vertues as beseeme, the worthy Gentles breast,
In proper colours he doth blaze, by followyng of the best:
The Vertue is but rare, and Vice not yet in use,
That modestly he not commends, or mildely shewes th'abuse.
Such matter in good wordes, these few leaves doo reveale,
15 Unforst, or strainde, as that it seemes, a naturall common weale.
Of forced Marriage, he dooth shew the foule event,
When Parents joyne, the Childrens hands, before their harts consent:
And how these fortunes eke, in wedlock seeldom prove,
Unequall choice, in birth, in yeeres: and Childrens hasty love.
20 Yet he with learned prooffes, this sacred state dooth raise,
(As it deserves) above the Skies, in wordes of modest praise.
More, every Page, heere dooth present, the Readers eyes,
With such regardes, as help the weake, and doo confirme the wise.
Which needelesse were, to blase, in prayses to allure:
25 The holy Bush, may wel be sparde, where as the Wine is pure. /

¶1ᵛ

       Verses translated out of Latine, and delivered
       by URANIE, with a Silver Pen, to ISMARITO, in
       a Device, contayned in the seventh daies
       Exercise: placed in this Forefront, for the
5   excellencie of PANDORA.

   The mighty JOVE beholding from above,
The mistes of sinne, which from the earth arose,
In angry moode, sent IRIS downe to moove,
Throughout the worlde, the exercise of foes,
10   With vengeance armde: who poured downe her Ire,
     And with debates, set Monarchies a fyre.

   Whole Countries burnde, did dim the Sun with smoke,
The Cannon noyse, the Ayre with Thunder rent:
The wounded men, with shrikes the Heavens shoke:
15 The Temples spoyld: the Townes to ruine went:
   Unwillyng yet, to worke the worlds decay,
   JOVE, CYLLEN sent, in part his wrath to staye.

   Who hastes his charge, with winges as swift as winde,
But comming to, the Region next the grounde,
20 He could no way, for clowdie darknes finde:
And fearing, in the Ocean to be drownde:
   He hovered till, in fine, he did espie,
   A PHAROS light, which was a PHENIX eye.

   Led by this Starre, amaine he commeth downe,
25 And footing sets, uppon a fruitfull Ile:
Where liv'd a Queene, crownd with the worlds renowne,
Upon whose rule, Grace, Peace, and Wealth did smyle.
   Her Senate, grave, her Citties, Mansions weare,
   For such as fled, for persecutions feare. /

¶2ʳ

30   To whom he gave the tokens that were sent,
Faire PALLAS forme, and VENUS lovely face:
Sweete PITHOS tongue, and DIANS chaste consent:

And of these giftes, PANDORA nam'd her Grace:
    And joynes with all, JOVES blessings to the same,
    To make her live, in everlasting fame.

These monsters fell, which publike order breake,
5   Dissention, Wrath, and Tiranny, he bounde:
This office done (he thought as JOVE would leake)
To Heaven he hyes, and blessed leaves the grounde:
    Where this good Queene, and Subjects quiet lyve,
    When civill warres, her neighbor kingdomes greeve.

10   Even this is she, whose sacred fame is knowne,
Through out the worlde, in Envie, Feare, and Love,
Envi'd, because, she raignes in peace alone:
Feared, in that, she shielded is by JOVE:
    Lov'd, for desarte, whose vertues shine as bright,
15   As twincking Stars, do in the frostie night.

This Silver Pen, meete for a Virgins praise,
URANIE heere, doth ISMARITO give:
With charmed charge, this Queenes renowne to raise:
As she in spight of Death, and Time may live:
20   Which right is hers, the labour is but thine,
    Then (Judging) write, as she may seeme devyne.

              Vaticinium URANIES./

A breefe Summarie of the principall
Argumentes handled, in
these seven Dayes Pleasures.

1. Of the difference betweene the Married state and the single lyfe.
2. Of the inconveniences of forced Marriages.
3. Of the inconveniences of rash Marriages.
4. Of divers speciall poyntes concerning Marriage, in generall.
5. Of the inconveniences of over loftye, and too base Love, in the choyce, of either Husband or Wyfe.
6. Of the inconveniences of Marriages: where there are inequalytie of yeares.
7. Of the excellencie of Marriage: with manye sounde Lawes and lawdable directions, to continue Love betweene the Married.

All which Principles, are largely intercoursed, with other Morall Conclusions of necessarie regarde.

FINIS. /

The first Dayes exercise. B1ʳ

Chiefly contayning: A civill Contention, whyther, the maryed or single lyfe, is the more worthy: And after many good Reasons, alleadged on either
5 parte, Sentence is given in the behalfe of Mariage.

    At what tyme, the Earth dismantled of her brave Attyre, lamented the absence of Dame Aestas company, and that faire Phaebus in his Retrogradation,
10 entring the Tropique of Capricorne, and mounting in the Zodiacke, licensed naked Hyemps, to powre down her wrath, upon the face of the whole worlde: through dread of whose boysterous stormes, every lyving creature, by the direction of Nature
15 retired himselfe unto his safest succour, as the Birde to his Nest, the Beast to his Covert, the Bee to his hyve, the Serpent to his hole: onely Man excepted, who (being beautified with a devine spirite, and armed with reason, farre
20 above the reache of Nature) scorneth to be chayned unto any place, through the violence or injurie of Tyme.

    In this dead season, suche were my Affayres, that Necessytie sent me into a Countrey farre
25 from home, where as I was no lesse unacquainted with the people, then ignorant of the wayes: And having travayled the great part of a Christmas Eve in a desart Forrest, strayed out of knowledge, I tooke me to a deepe beaten way, which promised
30 a likelyhood to finde out some spedie Harbour: And after I had jornyed the space of an hower, in a sweete Groave of Pyne Apple trees, mine eye fastened upon a stately Pallace, the brightnes wherof, glimmered through the Braunches of the

Marginalia:
- A description of the dead of Winter.
- Man by reson inlargeth the boundes of Nature, within whose lymites every other creture lyveth.
- This was the Forrest of Ravenna in Italye, (for the most part) of pine Apple trees.
- This Pallace was .10. miles from Ravenna

The Firste Dayes Exercise 14

younger woodde, not unlyke the Beames of the Sonne   towardes the
throughe the Crannelles of a walle, assuryng then   River of Poo.
my selfe, too receyve best Instruc-/tions, of the
better sort of people: such was my haste, as I   B1^v
5 soone arrived at this sumptuous place: but
according to the condition of time, in Christmas,   The custome
sooner to fynde a friende feasting in the Hall,   of Christmas.
then walkinge in the Feelde: other then a few
of ignoraunt peysauntes, I could perceive no
10 person. The delight I tooke to beholde the
scituation, and curious workmanship of this
Pallace, made mee so long forget the cause of
my arrivall there, as in the ende one of the
well qualyted Servaunts (havinge knowledge of my
15 being without) in a servisable order, came and
presented mee with his Lordes curteous welcome,
and reverently requested mee to alight, and enter
the Pallace: I which imagined this entertainment
to be but an <u>Italion</u> curtesie, after thankes geven,
20 by a modest excuse, refused so great a favour,
and onely craved, to be directed the rediest
way to <u>Ravenna</u>: the Servaunt cunninglye replyed,
that I could not bee received into the Cittie
without his Lordes <u>Bollytyne</u>, and at this time   BOLLYTINE,
25 hee sealed no mans safecundit, without knowledge,   a warrant of
that his affayres requyred great haste: in so   health
much, as won with his importunities, and overcome   without which,
with wearynesse of Travell, I commytted my Horse,   no man may
to the orderinge of my man, and accompanied this   travell in
30 officious Servant, towardes the Pallace, and by   Italy.
the way, over a lardge entraunce into a faire
court, I might read these two breefes in <u>Italion</u>.

<u>Pisano é Forresterio.</u>
<u>Entrate, e ben venuto.</u>   A liberall
    welcome.

The Firste Dayes Exercise 15

    Which generall invyting, imboldned mee so
far, as I hardely marched towardes the great Hall,
the Skreene wherof, was curiously fronted with
clowdy Marble, supported on every side the passadges,
5 with stately Pillers of Geate: and over the three   Welcom and
Portalles, stood the Images of two men: the one   Bountie, the
of Allablaster Marble, bare headed, representing   Porters.
the vertue of welcome: the other of blewe/ Marble,   B2^r
attyred lyke a Cooke, and by him were artifycially
10 painted, Pheasants, Partriges, Capons, and other
costly Cates, as the Figure of <u>Bountie</u>: At the
entry of this stately Hall, I was received by the
Lord of the Pallace, accompanied with divers
Gentlemen of good quallytie, with so civill and
15 friendly intertaynment, as his behaviour blazoned
the true knowledge of Curtesie: before we past
any further, I began to recount the Adventure
which brought me thither, and craved his honourable
favour for my dispatch: Why then (quoth <u>Segnior</u>
20 <u>Phyloxenus</u>) for so (for some cause) I name the
Lord of the Pallace, I thanke your hard Fortune
for arrivyng you here, to do me this honour: No
hard, but happy Fortune (quoth I) if I may live
to honour you with any effectual service.
25   Well (quoth he) after your weerie travaile,
it is more needeful to provide for your repose,
then for a further Jorney, and so lead me the
way into a faire great Chamber, richly hung with
Tapistrie: the Roof wherof, was Allablaster
30 plaister, embost with many curious devises in
gold, and in sundrie places in proper colours
was ingraved his devise, which was <u>A Holly Tree,
full of red Beries: and in the same, a fluttering
MAVIS fast limed to the bowes</u>, with this posie

in French, _Qui_ _me_ _nourit_, _me_ _destruit_: And, in
verie deed, the beries of the tree feedeth this
Bird, and the barke maketh Lime to fetter her.
But I afterwardes learned, Segnior _Philoxenus_
5 used this _Ensigne_ as a covert description of — A covert description of desyre.
desire: whose sweete torments nourisheth the
minde, but consumeth the bodie to the grave. In
this bewtifull place, I imbraced the salutations
of such a brave troupe of Gentlemen, and
10 Gentlewomen, as the honour of the householde
might well give envie unto some Princes Court.
And least, at my first comming, I might be
abashed through small acquaintance, Segnior
Philoxenus, emboldened mee with a familiar — A civill foresight meete for a Gentleman.
15 communication, and in the ende uppon a
convenient occasion, demaunded of me the name
of my Countrie?/ I aunswered him, I was a
Gentleman of _England_, voluntarily exiled with
a burnyng desyre, to see the Monuments of
20 other Countries, the order of their government, — A necessary regard for Travelers.
and manners of the people. And are you of that
blessed Ile (quoth he?) where the people live in
peace and prosperytie, under the rule of a
Mayden Queene, crowned with such devine vertues,
25 as the whole world may hardly containe her fame. — The vertues of the Queenes Majestie, maketh the Iland of Englande famous through out the whole Worlde.
Sir (quoth I) your good testimony of her
worthynesse, being a Straunger, taketh all
occasion from mee (her dutiful subject) to
inlardge her renowne. O (quoth he) if _Envie_
30 durst detract her openly, as she secretlye
conspireth her overthrowe, in these partes you
should be driven to stop your eares, or endure
a torment (to a faithfull subject) more violent
then Death. But the vertue of her Shielde,

B2^v

The Firste Dayes Exercise 17

    I meane her grave Senate, hath returned the   Vertue
Dartes of <u>Envy</u> so thick upon her Souldiers, as   stoppeth the
she hath no power to eclips her bright renowne,   mouth of
whose vertue shineth in <u>Envies</u> dispight as a Diamond   Envye, but
5 in an obscure place, or as the Sunne through smal   fyreth her
passadges, into the bowels of the earth: so that   hart with
happy and thrice happye are you, the Subjectes of   mallyce.
the good Queene of <u>England</u>, whose gratious
governement, filleth your Coffers with wealth,
10 sealeth your dores with peace, and planteth
quietnesse in your Conscience: so that (blessed
above other Nations) you live abroad, without
suspition of daunger at home: and at home
fearelesse of enemies abrode. Wherefore, in
15 honour of your Soveraigne, whose fame armeth al
true knights, with an earnest desire to doo her
service, I am glad of the meane, to bestow on you,
or any of hir nation, the affection of a friend.
Sir (quoth I) the vertue of these honorable
20 thoughts blaseth the true magnanimity of a noble
mind, which measureth not your favour by the
desart of others, but with the ryaltie of your   The true
heart, and so binde thousands in recognisance of   Blazon of
service: among which debters I desire to bee   a noble
25 inrolled, although I can discharge but litle   mynd.
After we had bestowed a smal time in these like
speches, he commanded some of his servantes to
direct me unto a lodging (if I pleased) to bee/
dispoiled of my riding attyre: who straight   B3^r
30 waies brought mee into a Bed Chamber, so well
accommodated with every necessarie pleasure,
as might have served for the repose of <u>Cupid</u>
and his lover <u>Ciches</u>: having a fayre prospect
into a goodly Garden, beautified, with such

rare devises, as deserved to be compared with
the earthly Paradice of <u>Tivoly</u>. And to be
breefe, this Pallace, with all her conveiances,
as well necessarie, as of pleasure, fully
5 mached the statelynesse of Cardinall <u>Furnesaes</u>
Pallace, buylded and beautified, with the
ruinous Monumentes of <u>Rome</u>, in her pride: so
that the curiousnesse thereof, was of power
to have inchaunted my eyes with an immodest
10 gase, had I not remembred, that it belongeth
unto a Gentleman to see, and not to stare upon
the straungest Novell that is: for bace is
his mynde, whose spirit hourely beholdeth not
greater matters then eyther beautie, buylding
15 or braverie. And certenly, at this instant, I
delighted more to contemplate of <u>Segnior</u>
<u>Phyloxenus</u> vertues: then to regarde his
sumptuous buyldings, who (as I learned of one
of the Servantes) all the yeere opened his
20 dores to everie civill Gentleman, and at
Christmas, invited all commers, as a customarie
dutie: so large was the prescription of his
curtesie. But, which shined above the rest,
he was in his youth, brought up in the French
25 Courte, where, by the grace of God, and labour
of some good freend (as his behavyours could
not but winne many) he learned to serve God,
with purenesse of heart, and not with painted
ceremonies, as his superstitious Countrie
30 men do: which was one chief cause, why he
spake so reverently of the Queenes majestie,
whose vertues make her enemies dumbe, for
malice will not let them say well, and shame
forbids them to speake amis, of her sacred

Tivoly .12. miles from Rome, where the Cardinall of Esta hath a most rare Garden.

Cardenal Furnesaes pallace in Rome.

A necessarie observation for a Gentleman.

A worthye Custome.

He was a Protestant.

lyfe: by the time I had talked awhile, with
one of the servantes, and put my selfe in a
more civill order, then was necessarie for
travel, Supper was in a redinesse: whiche
5 although it exceeded the common order of fasts,
yet it passed not far the bounds of auncient
custome: for my place at the Table, I had the/
pryveledge of a Stranger, set above my degree,
and with the same intertainment, were <u>Frenchmen</u>,
10 <u>Almain</u>, <u>Duchmen</u> and other Gentlemen, Straungers,   Other
intreated. The Grand Maister of the feast, in   straungers
wordes gave us one welcome for all, but not so   arrived by
few as a thousand in affable countenaunces.   the lyke
Supper being ended, according to the custome   adventure.
15 of the place, a Cake was cut in peeces, to the
number of the Gentlemen and Gentlewomen present,   A custome
and if the marked peece were allotted unto a   generally used
man, he should be King, if to a woman, she   in Fraunce,
should be Queene of the Christmas pleasures: and in some
                                                                       places of Italy.
20 for it was agreede, there should be but one
to commaund, and all to obay. <u>Madona Aurelia</u>,
Sister to the Lorde of the Pallace, was crowned
with the Lot, whose worthynesse was such, as
herein it seemed Fortune obayed desert: for
25 there was no Gentlewoman in the trowpe, that
<u>Aurelia</u> excelled not in beautie, and singularity
of wit, nor no Gentleman, that her vertues
inchaunted not, with more admiration, then
the <u>Sirens</u> sweete songes, the wether weried
30 Sayler, so that of the one shee was crowned with
<u>Envy</u>, and of the other with <u>Honor</u>. But in as
much, as this was but the fyrst night of her
raigne, she referred the Proclamation of her
lawes untill the next daye, and so dismist the

attendaunce of her subjectes for that night,
which (in sooth) lasted me but a sleepe, so
soundly after travell, I imbraced mine ease.

    The next Day no sooner appeared, but the
5 Trumpets sounded the honour of Christmas:
uppon which Sommons, the Companie rose, and
(attired in their most sumptuous weedes) in
the greate Chamber attended their Queene
<u>Aurelia</u>, who about Service time, (with the
10 Majestie of a Goddesse) presented her selfe:
on whome, all the Trowpe waighted unto the
Chappell, wheare the Service was not so
ceremonious, as in other Churches of Italy,
and yet more then agreed with <u>Segnior Phyloxenus</u>
15 conscience, onely to geve no offence, to the
superstitious zeale of others. The Service
ended, against the returne of the company, the
Tables were covered in a most/ stately Order,   B4^r
and with the sownd of Trumpettes, were furnished
20 with so many severall daintie Disshes, as the
Rialtie of the Feaste, might have pleased
<u>Heliogabalus</u>.
                                                                Heliogabalus
    After Queene <u>Aurelia</u> was set, the rest   a most
tooke their accustomed places: but (God knowes)   voluptuous
25 the eyes of the greater parte, were more   Emperor
hungrye, then their stomackes: for their   of Rome.
appetites were dulled, with the overplentie
of meates, and their desires quickened, with
the regarde of the faire Gentlewomen.
30   The Dinner and every solempne service
ended, <u>Segnior Phyloxenus</u> committed the company,
to the good intertainment of his Sister <u>Aurelia</u>,
and (with a speciall sute) recomended me unto
her favour: After vewe was taken of the

Attendantes, certaine Gentlemen and Gentlewomen (by the appoinctment of Queene Aurelia) were addopted with the names of their Fortunes, as occasion will manifest hereafter: and for that I was a Traveler, she calde mee Cavaliero Ismarito, in Englishe, The Wandring Knight: whereuppon, Madam (quoth I) you have christened mee with the true name of my fortune: for I was but late out of my way, and now am straied out of my self: where are you then (quoth Aurelia?) at your only direction (quoth I:) well (quoth she) since so cunningly you prefer your selfe, I admitte you my servant, and as you deserve so will I reward: and Madam (quoth I,) if I bee not loyall, let mee not lyve: well (quoth she) I expect the best. The rest of the affaires set in good order, the Harold proclaimed the lawes, whereunto the Gentlemen and Gentlewomen were bounde, with the penallties for the breach of them.

The Lawes of Queene Aurelia.

First, everie Gentleman, and Gentlewoman, were conjured faithfully to execute all the charges, and offices assigned by their Queene Aurelia, and that they should be attendant of her pleasure./

Item every Gentleman was bound, to serve some one Misterisse befor the next day at noone, uppon paine, to bee turned into the great Hall, among the Countrie Trulles the whole Christmas. And every Gentlewoman that had not a Servant, was judged unworthye, to bee courted for one weeke: for his merrit was holden very small,

that coulde bee intertained of none, and her
conditions very crooked that was beloved of none.

    Item every Gentleman, was bound to geve
his owne Mistresse the honour of his servise,
and the chiefe place in his commendations,
uppon paine, to lose her service, and to bee
entertained of no other. For he that was
disloyall to one, coulde not be holden faithfull
unto an other.

    Item every Gentlewoman, was bounde to
imploye her owne Servaunt uppon paine to be
reputed symple. For she that affyed not in
her owne Servant, had no reason to trust an
others.

    Item every Gentleman was bound, to defende
the honor of his Misterisse, both with worde
and sworde, uppon paine to be reputed a Coward,
and not to were her glove. For he was holden
very unsufficient, that prysed not his Misterisse
honor above his owne lyfe.

    Item evrey Gentlewoman was bound, to
incouradge her Servant with Good countenances,
and uppon the execution of any worthy service
to rewarde him, with the kissing of her hand,
upon paine to be deemed, unworthy to be served.
For she of all the world is acounted to rigorous
a Dame, that with scorne, receyveth dutifull
service.

    Item every Gentleman was bounde to Court
his misterisse with Civill speaches, upon
paine to be forbidden, to talke of love for
three daies. For he was accompted bace mannered,
or verie grose witted, that coulde not pleasantlye
intertaine time with a civill discourse.

Item every Gentleman was bound, either by
some exercise of value, or by some shew of
excellency of wit, to approve him selfe worthy
of his Mistrisse: upon paine, to be spoyled
of his Armes, and the whole Christmas to attende/
with the Pages: for he was holden unworthy
the societie of men, or the affection of women,
that was neither valiant nor wise.

These Lawes proclaimed, Queene Aurelia
appoynted an elderly Courtier named Fabritio,
and a well spoken Gentlewoman, called Donna
Isabella, to be Judges of the controversyes,
in disputation: and to attend her in her
affaires of pleasure, she chused Segnior Soranso,
a Gentleman Italion, of Wit quick and sharp,
and for his devices, sweete and pleasant: Don
Dondolo, a Napolitan, haughtie and proude in
his conceits. Monsier Bargetto a Frenchman,
amourous and light headed. Doctor Mossenigo,
a Germaine, so called, for the plaine discoverie
of his mind. Segnior Faliero a Scot, subtill
and cunnyng in his devyces: and my selfe
Cavaliero Ismarito, an English man, in whiche
name heereafter, I will present those actions
that touch my selfe.

Courtisie unto straungers, is a marke of Gentilytie.

This wise, choice she made to priveledge the
Strangers with the hyest favour.

Of Gentlewomen, she chused Maria Belochy,
a Damsell whose eye was able to fire a mountaine
of Ice. Lucia Bella, for fairenesse and sweete
behaviour an Angel. Hellena Dulce, a loving
and affable Gentlewoman. Franceschina Sancta,
so called for hir modest and lowlye countenance:
Katherina Trista, a sowre and testy Dame: Alvisa

<u>Vechio</u>, who although shee were in the wayne of
her yeeres, yet was she in the pride of yong
desires.

    This done, Queene <u>Aurelia</u>, by consent,
5 devided the exercises of every day, into
these times: the forenoone to bee bestowed   A division of
in the service of God: after dinner, two houres   their pleasurs.
to be intertained in civell discourse, and
disputation: the rest till Supper at pleasure:
10 and after supper to spende a time in daunsing,
maskinge, or in other like pastimes, as occasion
presented.

    The greater part of Christmas day, was
spent in establishing these orders, the rest
15 was overcome with solempne Musick, for, among
the better sorte, that day is honoured, with
no light mirth./

    The next daye by nine a Clocke, according   C1^v
to one of the charges in the Proclamation, you
20 might see the yong Gentlemen and Gentlewomen,
coupled together lyke fowles on Saint <u>Valentines</u>
day morninge. But <u>Caviliero Ismarito</u>, having the
eyes of his hart setteled upon his Mistresse
beautie, with carelesse regarde, behelde the
25 rest of the company: and leanyng by a dore,
thorow which she should passe, he awayghted
Queene <u>Aurelias</u> comming. Who at her accustomed
howre, presented her self with an advauntage
of braverie, whom the whole trowpe reverently
30 saluted, and honorably accompanyed unto the
Chappell.

    After Service, Dinner, and all were
solempnlye ended: Queene <u>Aurelia</u> with a chosen
company, retyred her selfe, into a pleasant

The Firste Dayes Exercise 25

drawing Chamber, to execute the reported Musick
ordenaunce. But to quicken the Spirites of the refresheth
company, before they entred into discourse, the wits.
she commaunded a faire <u>Eunucke</u> Boy, to singe
5 some one songe, as hee thought good, who
obaying her commaundement, with a heavenly
note, unto the Lute sunge this lovyng Laye.

    No joy comes neare the heavenly joy of love,
When we imbrace, the wish of our desyre.
10 All pleasures els, that kinde or Arte may move,
To love, are lyke, the heate of paynted fyre.
        Love is the roote, whereon swete thoughts do grow,
        Love is the sowrce, from whence content doth flow.

    When I behould my Mistresse in the face,
15 Love from her eyes, a thousand Graces throwes.
But when in armes, I doe her selfe imbrace,
One smyling looke exileth all my woes.
        Then straight our lippes prepare them selves to fight,
        And on eche kys, Love seales a new delight.

20   What would you more? I wish me in my grave,
Were but my soule with halfe these pleasures crownde:/
And heare on earth to be my Misterisse slave, C2^{r}
I hold me free, and others to be bounde.
        Wherfore, I sing which I in sollace prove,
25   There is no heaven, to lyfe bestowed in love.

    The sweet deliverie of this sonet, so
inchanted the harts of the hearers, as for a
space, their sences gave place to the contemplation
of their soules. In the end, <u>Madona Isabella</u>
30 by this motion, made the whole company a passadge

The Firste Dayes Exercise 26

for speech.

   If <u>Love</u> be so sweete a passion (quoth she)
I muse from what cause proceedeth the complaintes
of Lovers, who with showering teares, bedeweth
5 the earth: with misty sights, dimmeth the aire,
and with shril outcries pearceth the heavens.

   The cause (quoth <u>Soranso</u>,) proceeds of our
fleshly imperfections, which corruptes the
nature of good things, and not of any defect in
10 love: for love is a simple devine vertue, and
hath his being in the soule, whose motions are   Love simplye
heavenly.   is good.

   I have read (quoth <u>Isabella</u>) that there be
sundry kindes of love. The uses of love, are
15 divers (quoth <u>Soranso</u>,) as in zeale towardes God,
in duty towardes our Countrie, in obedience
towards our parents, and in affection towards our   The
frendes. All which motions proceedeth forth of   distinctions
one love, although som are more vehement then   of love.
20 the other, even as many Rivers doo run out of
one Spring, whereof som have a more swift course
then the other. But of that passion which we
ordinarily call love, the wish either tends to
Marriage or wantonnesse. There is matter of
25 disputation in Marriage (quoth <u>Franceschina</u>,)
because the estate is honorable, and yet subject
to crosse fortunes: But touching your conclusion
of wantonnes, it deserveth to die in silence, for   Knowne evils
known evils are to bee chastened, without allowing   are not to bee
30 their defences. Madame (quoth <u>Faliero</u>) unlesse   defended.
you revoke this sentence, we wil have you indited
at <u>Rome</u>, as an heretick, for by the Popes <u>Cannons</u>,
<u>Priests</u> <u>may</u> <u>not</u> <u>marry</u>: and they have a custom
among them selves, not to live chast. Well

(quoth Franceschina,) if the Pope for this
opinion, burne mee as an heretick, good men will
cannonise mee for a vertuous Virgin./

    Thease Digressions (quoth Queene Aurelia,)
are the meanes (rather) to worke a confusion of
our memories, then to conclude any beneficial
matter for our instruction. And therefore, I hold
it to greater purpose (substantially) to handle
one Argument, then (sleightly) to overrunne many
causes, where the doubts we leave unresolved, wyl
be more daungerous unto the hearer, then the
Counselles we use, profitable unto the follower.

    Madame, (quoth Fabritio) I hold it good, we
obay your direction. And for that Mariage, is
the most honourable event of Love: and that a
Single lyfe, is the greatest testimonie of
Chastytie: A civill Contention, to proove which
is the most worthy of the two, would conclude
much contentment: For, as Yron and Flynt, beat
together, have the vertue to smite fire: so, mens
wittes, encountryng in doutful questions, openeth
a passage for imprisoned Trueth.

    Queene Aurelia, and the rest of the company,
lyked verie well of the Subjeat: and studing, who
weare the fittest to deale in this Controversie,
Aurelia (with a glaunsinge eye) beheld, that her
servant Ismarito, witsafed no greater Token,
that he tooke delight in thease actions, then
(sometime) the secrete bestowyng of a modest
smile: wherupon she forethought, that as Floods,
when they are most hyest, maketh least noise:
even so (perchaunce) his styll tongue, was
governed by a flowyng witt, and desirous to
sounde his sufficiencie, she quickned him with

Marginalia:
- A necessarye note.
- A contention whether Mariage or the single lyfe, is the worthyer.
- Argument decideth doubtes.
- Wise scilence worketh mor regarde then foolish talke.

this crosse surmise.

    Servant (quoth she) your sober lookes, promiseth a hope that you will undertake <u>Dianaes</u> quarrell: but (which wil serve in this question)
5 I feare me, you commaund <u>Love</u>, so much, as you contempne <u>Mariage</u>: And the greater is my suspicion, in that you are a Travayler: the nature of which sort of people, is to swell, with a monsterous disdayne of <u>Mariage</u>. The reason is (say they)
10 their Affections are poysoned, with the knowledge of womens so haynous evyls, as thei dare not venter of that vocation: But my opinion is, they have learned so many subtilties to deceive a shiftlesse woman, as dandled with the imbracements
15 of sundry/ <u>Loves</u>, they forsweare <u>Mariage</u>, who bindes them to one only wyfe: And if you be infected with the humour of thease sorte of Travailers, you may wel undertake this charge: for <u>Venus</u>, though she love not <u>Diana</u>, yet is she
20 the sworn enemie of <u>Juno</u>. And if you be sound from this infirmitie, the little haste you make to marry, witnesseth, you honor <u>Hymen</u>, with no great devotion, and therfore, I commaund you too use all your possyble proofes, in the Defence of
25 a <u>Single lyfe</u>: and for your Assistaunce, I do appoinct you, <u>Lucia Bella</u>, whom, this Charge can not mislyke, because (as I understand) she meanes to be a professed Nun: You are to encounter the opinions of many, and therfore,
30 arme your selves, with as good reasons, as you may.

    Madame (quoth <u>Ismarito</u>) I am so deeply bound unto your commaundement, as I am driven to leave youre suggestions not answeared, and my

A fault in many travellers.

Al unmarried, pass under the name of chast.

owne innocency, unexcused, and only attend the
incounter of him, that wil maintaine Marriage,
to be more worthy then a syngle life: which
vocation of Marriage, though I reverently
5 honour, yet I so zealously affect the other, as
I hope (where the Judges are indifferent) to
make the glory thereof to shine as the faire
white, above every other colour.

  Syr, (quoth Soranso,) though white be a   Defences of
10 fayre colour, yet are the choyse of all other   Marriage.
colours, more rich and glorious: so, though
Virginitie (which is the fayrest flower of a
single lyfe) be precious, in the sight of God,
and in the opinion of men, yet is Marriage more
15 precious, in that, it is a sacred institution
of God, and more honoured of men: the Marryed
are reverently intertained, when the unmaryed
are but familiarly saluted. The Maried in
assemblies, are honoured with the hyghest
20 places, the unmarryed humble them selves unto
the lowest. To be short, Virginitie is the
handmayde of Marriage. Then, by how much the
Master is greater then the servaunt, by so much
Marriage is more worthy then is single lyfe.

25   I confesse (quoth Ismarito,) Marriage is   Defences of
an honourable estate, instituted of God, and   a single lyfe.
embraced of men, but wher-/on had she her
beginning? upon this cause, to keepe men from   C3^v
a greater inconvenience: as the Lawe was
30 founded uppon this reason, to punishe the
trespasses of men. But if no offence had ben
given, the Law had not needed. So if man had
lyved within boundes of reason (whiche before
any commaundement geven; was unto him a Law)

Marriage might have ben spared: and therefore
in the hyest degree, is but a vertue uppon
necessitie: where <u>Chastitie</u>, is a devine
vertue, governed by the motions of the soule,
5 which is immortall, and perticypating of the
same vertue, is alwaies fresh and greene. The
ever-springing <u>Baye</u>, is the <u>Metamorphos</u> of chast
<u>Daphne</u>, whom <u>Appollo</u>, although he weare a
soveraign GOD, could not allure to <u>Mariadge</u>:
10 which prooveth <u>Chastitie</u>, a true spark of
<u>Divinitie</u>, whose twinkling reflexions, so
daseleth the eyes of imagined Gods (whose powers
must needes be more great then the greatest of
men) as they cannot see an ende of their incontinent
15 desires: where as the beautie of <u>Marriadge</u>, is
many times blasted by fortune, or the frailtie of
the Married.
 Therfore (think I) by how much devyne thinges
are of greater emprise then earthlye, by so much
20 the <u>Single lyfe,</u> is more worthy then the maryed.
 And in advauntage, (quoth <u>Lucia Bella</u>) where
<u>Soranso</u> sayth, that there is great honour done
unto the married, and to the <u>Single</u> is given
light regard, I pray you whether are <u>Baccus</u>
25 minions or the <u>Muses</u>, most reverensed? Among
men, whose places are hyer then the Cleargies?
and amonge women, whose greater then the religious
Dames?
 They have not this preheminence (quoth   Defences of
30 <u>Faliero</u>) because they professe a <u>Single life</u>,   Mariadge.
but because their function is more sacred then
other mens, who if their prayers to GOD bee no   The cause
more zealous, then their vowes to chastytie are   why the
stedfast, you flye to the authoritie of a company Cleargie are
                                                  reverensed.

as spotted as <u>Labans</u> Sheepe./

    But where Sir <u>Ismarito</u> saith, that <u>Mariage</u>
is but a vertue upon necessytie, to restrayne
man from a greater evyll: I approove it an estate,
5 set downe by Nature, and that man hath but
amplified it, with certain Ceremonies, to make
perfect the determination of nature: For we
dayly see, in unreasonable Creatures, <u>Mariage</u> is
(in a sorte) worshypped: Fowles of the Ayre
10 (I meane) the he and the she, cupple together,
flie together, feede together, and neast together.
The Turtle is never merie after the death of her
Mate: and in many brute Beastes, the lyke
Constancie is fownd: But (generally) there is
15 never jarre nor mislykyng betwene the Male and
Female, of unpollitique creatures: and among
the most barbarous people that ever lyved, by
the Impression of Nature, <u>Mariage</u> hath (evermore)   Unpollitick
ben reverenced and honoured: Muche more, civill   creatures
                                                                                         reverence
20 people, ought to affecte this holy estate: And   mariadge.
where <u>Ismarito</u>, attributes suche Glorie unto a
<u>Single lyfe</u>, because that <u>Daphne</u> was metamorphosed
into a <u>Bay</u> Tree, whose Branches are alwayes
greene: In my opinion, his reason is fayre lyke
25 the <u>Bay</u> Tree: for the <u>Bay</u> Tree is barren of
pleasant fruict, and his plesing words of weighty
matter.

    Furthermore, what remembrance is theare of
faire <u>Sirinx</u> coynesse, refusing to be God <u>Pans</u>
30 wife? other then that she was metamorphosed
into a fewe unprofitable Reedes: Or of <u>Anaxaretes</u>
chaste crueltie towardes <u>Iphis,</u> other then that
she remaineth an Image of Stone in <u>Samarin</u>.

    Many other suche lyke naked **Monumentes**

remayne, of nice contempners of <u>Marriage</u>.

But in the behalf of <u>Mariage</u>, thousands
have ben changed into <u>Olyve</u>, <u>Pomegranate</u>,
<u>Mulberie</u>, and other fruictfull trees, sweete
5 flowers, Starres, and precious Stones, by whom,
the worlde is beautified, directed and noorished.

In many well governed common wealths,
Sterylitie hath ben reputed so vile, as the Aged
was of no man honoured, that had not children of
10 his own, to do him reverence./

Then, by how much those thinges, which   C4^v
noorish with increase, are more necessarie then
those things, which but simply please the eye:
by so muche, the marryed, is more worthy then
15 the single lyfe.

Sir, (quoth <u>Ismarito</u>,) it seemeth that you   Defences of
have read a Leafe more then Sainct <u>Katherynes</u>   a single lyfe.
Nun: for she (simply) tried all thinges, and
you (subtilly) use, but what serveth your owne
20 tourne: You reproach a <u>Single lyfe</u>, with
<u>Barrennesse</u>, and commend the fertilytie of
<u>Mariage</u>: But had you showen the weedes with
the Corne, bare pasture wold have retourned as
great a benefit, as your harvest. The Monsters,
25 Serpents, and loathsome Creatures, mentioned
by <u>Ovide</u>, in his <u>Metamorphosis</u>, were they not
I praye you the fruicts of <u>Marriage</u>? as wel as
the blessings, whiche you so affectedlye reported?
<u>Oedippus</u> was glad to scratch out his eyes,
30 because he could not indure to behold the vices
of his Children. The good Emperour <u>Marcus</u>
<u>Aurelius</u> in his aged daies, never rose that he
sighthed not: never dyned that he fretted not:
nor never went to bedd, that he weeped not: to

heare, see, and consider, the mounstrous evylls
of his Children. Admit the Married, have vertuous
Children, they may dye when they are yonge, then
the goodness of their lyves, increaseth sorrowes,
by their deathes: and where the comfort is so
doubtfull, it is not amisse to refuse the hazard
of the greefe: neither dyeth there any of Dianas   Vertuous
band, but that their vertues reviveth them as the   fame, is
ashes of the Phenix, tourneth into an other Phenix.   an other
                                                                                         lyfe.
     It is for some Phenix sake, (quoth Queene
Aurelia,) that you thus stoutly defend a Single
lyfe.
     I doo but your commaundement, (quoth Ismarito.)
     Yea (quoth shee) it is at my commaundement,
but yet for some others merit.
     Alvisa Vechio, fearing that Marriage wold   The impatiencie
receive som disgrace, if that Queene Aurelia   of women, will
favoured the Defence of a Single lyfe, could   not be hidde.
not longer suppresse her affections, but with
a womans Impatiencie, blamed the rigour of
Diana, who condempned Acteon to be devoured   D1^r
of his own Howndes: who caused sweete Addonis
to be slayne by a wylde Boare: with many
other cruell partes, unseemyng the naturall
pittie of a woman: but (which might have saved
a great deale of Argument, or at the least,
which wyll now soone ende the Controversie:)
compare (quoth she) Juno and Diana together, and
by their callings, you may easely judge who is
the worthyer. Diana (poore soule) is but a
Goddesse here on earth, and Juno is Queene of
Heaven: Dianaes force, is in her Bow and
Arrowes, Juno bestoweth Thunderbolts, upon her
enemies: Diana, is attyred with greene leaves,

and Juno with glorious Starres: Diana, feedeth
on rawe Fruictes, and drinketh cold water:
Junoes Feastes, are of Manna, and her Bowles are
fild with Nectar: Dianaes Musick, is no better
5 then the voyces of a fewe Nymphes: Juno is
recreated with the Harmonie of Angelles: Dianaes
pastime, is (a foote) to chace the fearefull Roe,
where Juno (in Phaetons wynged Chariot) pursueth
a thousand several pleasures: then, by how
10 much the pompe of Juno, exceedeth the naked
Triumphes of Diana: by so much, Mariage must
needes be more worthye then the Single lyfe.

    Lucia Bella, that shuld have answered
Alvisa Vechio, (not unlyke the Marygoulde, that
15 cloaseth her Beautie, when Phebus is attyred
with his brightest Rayes) so admyred the glory   Vaine glorious
of Juno, that, as an inchaunted creature, her   shewes
tongue forgot her naturall office: the reason   bewicheth
was, her hart was sodenly surprised with an   women.
20 ambitious desire of honor.

    Which change, Ismarito perceyved, with the
first: and least, her scilence shuld conclude a
yealding: Al is not gold (quoth he) that   Contentment
glistereth, nor every thyng counterfet that is   neither
    followeth the
25 not curiously garnished: a smyling countenance   greatest, nor
is no full testimonie of a merie hart, nor costly   scorneth the
Garments, of a rich Purse: And (perchance) the   meanest.
griefe of Junoes secret discontentmentes, is
greatter then the delight of her gloryous pompe:
30 where Diana, who (as a Diamond in the darcke,
shineth of her selfe) needeth not the Ornaments
of Juno./

    And as shee is (symplye) of a pure substaunce,
so her thoughtes, must needes be sweete, and quiet.

Sir (quoth Maria Belochy) our soundest
judgements, are of those things that we our selves
see: therfore, if the apparaunce of Mariage, be
worthier then the apparaunce of the single lyfe:
if sentence be truely pronounced, it must be in
the behalfe of Juno.

Queene Aurelia perceyving the increase of
Ismaritos adversaries, (for who can stop a
streame? measure the fire? weygh the winde? or
hynder Fancyes passage?) and withall considering
how that the controvercy was sufficiently debated,
commaunded the contenders, to keepe scilence:
and referred the question, to be Judged by Fabritio,
and Isabella.

Who having advisedly considered, the reasons
on both sydes, agreed that a single chast lyfe
pleased God, because, Chastitie is pure: and
also delighteth man, because, shee quieteth the
mynde: but a chast marryed lyfe, bothe pleaseth,
and honoureth God: because Marriage, howrely,
presenteth the world, with the Image of himselfe:
pleaseth, and profiteth man, because, she giveth
him a companyon, by affection, chaunged into his
owne disposition: of whom he hath children, who
in dispight of death, preserveth him alyve. And
therefore, the sentence of them both, was
pronounsed by Fabritio, in the behalfe of
Marriage: who with all, enlarged her prayses,
with the reporte of many sweet Blessinges, whiche
shee liberallye bestoweth, uppon her Subjectes.

But least the company, should have ben fyred
with too hasty a desyre of Marriage, he cooled
theyr affections, with such caveats, as they that
had their voyces ready tuned, to synge the

Sentence gyven, in the behalfe of Mariage.

prayses of God Himen, were of the suddayne, as
mute as a fishe: by reason whereof, Fabritio,
had free passage: for his counsellinge reporte:
who, after many wordes, to either purpose
5 delivered, concluded with the opinion of Plato,   Platoes
That Marriage, was a Parradice on earth, if her   opinion of
Lawes be observed: and a Hell in the House,   Mariage.
where her Statutes are broken./

    The Gentlewomen wist not what to say, to   D2^r
10 Fabritios bittersweete commendation of Marriage,
untyll Bargetto quickned their tongues, by this   Pleasant
pleasaunt suggestion.   talk is good
    If (quoth he) Platoes opinion be lawe, by   physicke for
the same reason, women are either Angells, or   sorrowe.
15 Devills.

    And why not men, as well as women (quoth
Isabella) whose disposition beareth the greatest
swaye in this vocation.

    I will showe you a reason, (quoth Doctor
20 Mossenigo,) men with a meane, canne temper their
passions: when a woman hath no measure in her   The extreme
love, nor mercye in her hate: no rule in her   passions of a
pittie, nor pietie in her revenge: no Judgement   woman.
to speake, nor patience to dissemble: and therfore
25 she is lykened unto the Sea, whych (one whyle)
is so mylde, as a small Gundelo indureth her   A GUNDELO,
might, and anon, with outrage, she overwhelmeth   is a little
the taullest shippe.   Boat like a
    Ah Master Doctor, (quoth Katharina Trista,)   wherie.
30 I feare me you are so learned, as like the Hyen,   HIEN,
you change your self sometimes into the shape   somtimes a
of a woman: but yet, of this malitious purpose,   man, and
to learn their dispositions: only to reproch   somtimes a
their kinde: but had any of us the cunning, to   woman.

become a man but a while, I imagine, we should
ever after, love the better to be a woman.

You have rather cause (quoth <u>Dondolo</u>) to
let Mayster Doctor kisse your hand, (for
5 commending your kynde) then to blame him, by a
surmise, of injurye, offered unto women, for if
there be a few good, they cover the faults of a
number that are evill: as a litle golde,
guildeth a great quantitie of iron: and for any
10 thing he sayde, you have as generall an interest
in vertue, as in vice.

Yea, but (quoth Queene <u>Aurelia</u>) he is to be
blamed for his intent, which was evyll, and   The intent of
deserveth not to be praysed for the good which   evyll, is to
                                                                                          be punished.
15 came of it, which was our meryt.

Madame (quoth the Doctor) so much greater
is the good, you receive by my Trespasse, as
therby you are honoured with the vertue, to
forgive./

20 Yea, but (quoth she) remission is to be used   D2^v
in ignorant offences, and not in wilfull.   Pardon is to
                                                                                     be used in
My Habit (quoth he) is a testimonie that   ignoraunce
I spake not of mallice.   and not in
                                                                                     wilfull faultes.
So much (quoth she) the greater is your
25 fault, in that it proceeded upon pleasure: and
where you thinke to priviledge your selfe by
your Habyt: for Example sake, you shall at   The punishment
(open) Supper, bothe renounce your Heresie and   of great
make satisfaction, or abide the Judgement of   offenders dooth
                                                                                      most good in
30 these Gentlewomen.   example.

If there be no remedie (quoth he) I must
obay.

The Doctor thus taken tardie, gave occasion
of laughter unto the whole company.

Which, blowne over, (quoth _Soranso_) we have travailed this day to an unfortunate ende: for that now, towardes night, we are entred into an open Champion, wheare we finde many broade wayes
5 to Hell, and but one crosse Path to Heaven.

Well (quoth Queene _Aurelia_) we wyll take other tymes, to beate out the true passage: And (least we be lated) wee wyll no further too daye.

Wherupon, after a Courtly reverence don:
10 Queene _Aurelia_, with her Attendantes, shewed her selfe in the great Chamber, where she might repose her minde with the choice of sundrie pleasures: For his, or her disposition was very strange, that in that company, could not finde
15 both a Companion and sport, that pleased his humour.

FINIS./

The first Nights Pastime.

Among wise men, these Orders, have evermore
ben observed, or allowed: In the Church, to be
devoute: in place of Justice, to be grave: at
5 home to be affable, and at meales to be mery:
for in the Churche we talke with God, who seeth   Devotion.
our hartes and hateth Hypocrysie: in Justice,
we sitt to chasten light demeanours, then, great   Gravitie.
were the shame, that our countenaunces shuld
10 condempne our selves.
    At home we rule and commaunde, then were   Affabilitie.
it Tyranny, to use severytie, there, where, is
no resistaunce.
    At meales to bee merrie, disgesteth meate,
15 and refresheth the witte: then is he an enemy
unto himselfe, that contemneth the rule of   Myrthe.
health, and the helper of knowledge. Howsoever
the three first preceptes were observed, Segnior
Philoxenus and his honourable guestes duly
20 executed the last, who in the midst of supper
hearinge of Doctor Mossenigos pennaunce, hasted
the execution.
    The Doctor seeing there was no remedie,
openly confessed that hee had praysed women
25 against his wyll, for which he was condemned to
singe Ab re nuntio, and to make satisfaction by
some other meanes: And as hee thought the
contrarie was the amends of everie trespas, and
therfore, where as he had praysed them against
30 his will, hee was ready to dispraise them with
his will.   Subtiltie beateth true meaning with his owne sword.
    Queene Aurelia, woulde have taken exceptions
to these wordes, but that the company cryed, The

Doctor speaks Law, which shee coulde not with
Justice violate, wherupon Mossenigo, reported as
followeth./

DOCTOR MOSSENIGO HIS
5　Satisfaction, for praysing women against his will.

　　In the famous Citie of Viena, in Austria,
somtimes dwelled a simple Sadler, named Borrihauder,
who was married to an olde crabbed shrew, called
Ophella: the agreement of this couple was so
10 notable, as the Emperour Charles the fift,
commaunded his Paynter Parmenio, to draw their
counterfeats, as a Monument of fury: Parmenio,
commyng to doe the Emperours commaundement, found
Borrihauder weeping with the agony of his wives
15 stripes, and Ophellas cheeks as red as fire with
the heate of her tonge: which straunge sight,
chaunged his determination, into a pleasaunt
conceit, and in place of their Counterfets, in a
fayre table, he drew an Element troubled with
20 lightnyng, and underwrit Ophella, and in another
Table fastened to the same, he likewise drew an
Element darkned with rayne, and under wright,
Borihauder. Parmenio presented this travel unto
the Emperour. The Emperour seeing the two names,
25 and not the shape of those, hee commaunded to be
drawne, demaunded the Paynters meanyng heerein,
who pleasantly aunswered, that he could not take
the view of Ophellas face, for feare of being
fyered with the lightning of her tonge, and that
30 Borihauder was drowned with teares, which as
showers of Raine folowed the thunder claps, of
his wives Fistes: But in good time (had she
died) this Demidevill Ophella fel so extremely

sick, as in every mans judgement, it was needefull
to give Phisick to her soule, but bootelesse to
bestow any of her body: _Borihauder_ seeing her,
as he thought at a good passe, was so accustomed
5 to sorrow, as hee determined to toule her passing
bel, with this counterfet mone. Ah deare God
(quoth he) how unhappy am I to lose my loving
wife, my good wyfe, my sweet wife? O how happy
were I, that as we have lyved together, that we
10 might nowe dye together. This pittyous sound of
her husband, so melted/ the dying harte of
Ophella, that lyke a Candle consumed, that leaveth
a little smoke in the weeke, she lay both speechles,
and senceles, save that the panges of death,
15 sometymes threwe a weake breath out of her mouthe:
but lyke unto wilde fire, that burneth in water,
the Corsive, that would have killed the devill,
in her case, recovered her to health, which was
her husband, out of feare of her life, in dispight
20 of the injurie of time past, fell to kisse and
coll his Maide, which watched his gasping wife,
before hee tooke order with the Clarke, to ring
her knell: which _Ophella_, as dim as her sight
was, perceived, and Furie, which was the last
25 motion, that accompanied her in life, like a whirl
wind, that with a suddaine violence, draweth things
into the ayre, so fired her hart with malice, to
see her husband in this jolity with her maide,
as madnes, gave her the strength to crye. Ah,
30 ah, Traytour, I am not yet dead, ah villain,
villaine, I am not yet dead: and through this
passion, choller so dryed her _Catar_, as shortly
after, she perfectly receyved her health: and
so canvassed her husband _Borrihauder_, as by the

D4^r

motions of sorrow, and payne, he hung himselfe
in a Crabtree.

O (quoth Katherina Trista,) it was great
dammage that Thymon of Athens was not in the
town, to show al malitious men that tree. The
devill might have put in their myndes, to have
hanged themselves.

This suddayne answeare of Katherina Trista,
tickled all the companye with a laughter, a good
parte whereof, were reddy to scandall women, with
a frowarde nature, beyng by this example, more
fostered with dyspight, then good usage: who,
nowe for feare of theyr owne reproche, amplyfied
not Master Doctors tale, with any other spightfull
authorityes.

For the Hystorie of Thymon of Athens dogged
nature, was so well knowne to everie Gentleman,
as the remembraunce of his name, assured them,
that there never lyved woman of so frowarde a
condityon: neyther is it possible, that ever
any man agayne, shoulde be so great an enemye
to Humanitie./

And there upon (quoth Faliero) Thymon of
Athens was without heyre or successor, and
therefore is no able example, to blame us.

Neither had Ophela (for any thinge we
heare) either heyre or successor, (quoth Alvisa
Vechio:) then, by your owne reason, is of no
authoritie to slaunder our sexe.

This one quip for an other (although more
myldelye handled of the Gentlewomen side,
according to their naturall modestie) quieted
either parte. In so moch as Doctor Mossenigo
humbly desired to be received, into the grace

A cunnynge aunswere, taketh away the grace of a shrewd tale.

THYMON of Athens was the sworn enemie of humanitie.

of women againe.

    Nay, (quoth Queene Aurelia) you deserve to bee evermore banyshed the presences of women.

    Alas good Madam, (quoth he) I did but your commandement, and therupon I appeale to the report of the company.

    Yea, but (quoth she) my meanyng was otherwise.

    O Madame (quoth he) Subjects, are bounde to execute their Soveraignes woordes, and are not priveledged, to interpret their charge, to their owne fancy.

A dutiful subject is bound to obay his Princes wordes, and not linger upon the effect.

    I see well, (quoth Queene Aurelia) that there is no dealyng with a Lawyer, for they can defend their owne trespasses, with the same sworde, they punish other mens offences, and therefore better to have you a fayned friende, (being so daungerous) then an open enemie: wherefore, we pardon you.

A fayned friend is better then a dangerous open enimy.

    By this time, Supper, and everie service of the Table ended. Whereuppon, Queene Aurelia, and the whole company rose, and saluting one an other, with a civill reverence. The Musick sommoned the yonge Gentelmen, and Gentlewomen, to daunsinge: for (this night) they expected no other pastime, unlesse it were dicing, carding, or such like unthrifty sports. And therefore as the night grew on, or they waxed wearie, untill the next mornyng they commytted one an other, a dio.

FINIS./

The seconde Dayes EXERCISE.

Contayning (with many other necessarie Questions,) a large Discoverie, of the inconveniences of forced Marriadges.

    Aurora had no sooner forsaken her Husband Tithons bed, but that Phebus ashamed of his over drowsy sleeping, in the darke Caves of Tartessus: hastely harnesed up his Horses, and in his fierie Chariot, clymed the Mountaine Oeta, the painefull travell whereof made brighte Pyrois and sparklinge Phlegon, breathe flambes lyke the burninge Furnace, wherein Vulcan forgeth the Thunderboltes of Jubiter: In so much as Phaebus golden rayes (which beautifieth the Heavens, and comforteth the earth) pearced through everie small passadge, into Segnior Philoxenus Pallace: and glimmering in the yong Gentlemens faces, wakened them, with an imagination, of their Mistresses beauties (who scorning their Beds, as Graves which buried the one half of their pleasures, and the Cannapies, as Clowdes, that shadowed the brightnesse of their Loade Starres) now started up, to honour and salute the Images, of their hartes delighte: and to waken the Ladies and Gentlewomen (who of the suddaine, could not be attyred) the tingling of a small Bell, gave them warning of a Sermon. In so much, as by nine of the Clocke, Queene Aurelia, and her stately Attendants entered the Chappel, in such Equipage, as I think, the Preacher, Fryer Bugiardo, immagined our Lady was come from Loretto, to honor Segnior Phyloxenus Aultar: and therefore to welcome her the more, he so extolled our

A Discription of the Sunne risinge.

Pyrois and Phlegon fained to be two of the Sunnes Coche horses.

The Bed resembleth the Grave.

Laureta, commonly called Loreto, the great pilgrimage of Italy where

is a small Chappell, sometymes made, by the cunning of certaine
Fryers, and the consent of some of the Cittizens of RACANATI: only,
to bring Trafficke to their Cittie, destroyed by the Goathes, and
Vandals: and in the night, stole it out of the Towne: and spread
a rumoure, that our Ladye by Aungells, had brought it out of JURY:
Ladies vertues, and the good and pitifull woorkes
of our Cannonyzed Ma-/trons, and Virgins: as if
the Crown of Heaven, had stode upon our Ladyes
head, and that the earth (cheefely Italy) was
blessed for pittyfull womens sakes: of whych,
they could have no greater testimonie, then that
our Ladye by myracle, had possessed them, with
her earthlye Mansion: which she dayly visiteth,
with a thousand blessinges. And therfore, (quoth
he,) repayre her Churches, cherish her Preestes,
praye before her Aulters, and your sinnes,
whatsoever, shallbe forgeven: O she is pittifull,
as a woman: and can rule her son, as a Mother:
and with such lyke owld tales, and Tapers, he
lighted the people, as they thought, to Heven:
but in verye trueth, into blinde Ignoraunce Cave,
from whence, the devill carryed them to Hell.

    Ismarito smiled, to heare the subtiltie of
the Fryer, and sorrowed to see the simplicitie
of the people, in causes that appertayne unto
the soule, who in the affaires of the flesh, are
as wylye as Serpents: whose countenaunce, when
Philoxenus beheld, he pleasauntly demaunded, how
Ismarito lyked Fryer Bugiardo his sermon.

    Ismarito merely aunsweared, it was pittie
that Judas had not harde the lyke, after he had
betrayed his Maister Christ: it might have ben,
uppon these large promyses of forgivenes, he
wold not so desperatly have hanged himself.

    Then (quoth Philoxenus) these pleasing

Marginalia:
- the mansion House, wherin she ther lived: whych Fable, an number hold for a trueth.
- Ignoraunce Cave, the hye waye to Hell.
- Italians, a most subtyle kinde of people.

sermons be not unnecessary in this countrie,
where sinne is so grose: for were not the people   Sinne cannot
in hope, that our Lady, of pitty, wold pardon   indure to here
them, a number would followe Judas in dispaire: of Gods Justice.
5 with feare, that Gods Justice would condemne them.

It seemeth reason (quoth Ismarito) that the
people beleeve what is sayd in the Pulpit: for
they understand not what is read in the Church.

In this especiall case (quoth Philoxenus)   A tiranny ten
10 all our crosses, are curses./   tymes more
                                                   cruell then
So that our first restraint from reading   Dennis Bull. E2^r
the Scriptures, could not but come from as
accursed a spirit as his, that first invented
the Turkes Alcaron, for by the paine of the one,   Alcaron, a
15 Mahomets Idolatry, is unreprehended, and through   Lawe that for
our ignoraunce in the other, the Popes blaspheamye, byddes the
is in us unespyed, and thereby, both God is   Turks to
dyshonoured, and manye a Soull distroyed: so   dispute, of
that happye, and thryse happye, are you of   Mahomet.
20 Englande, that have the sacred Byble, and the   A divine
hard passages of Scrypture, expounded in vulgar   blessinge.
Language: that your common sorte, howesoever
youre Prealates lyve, understande wheather they
erre or no in theyr Doctryne.
25   And synce the Subjectes of the Emperour,
Alexander Severus, honoured theyr Soveraygnes
vertues, wyth these acclamations.

Noble Allexaunder, wee praye the Goddes,   A token of
that they have no lesse care of youre Majestye,   lovinge
30 then you have of us: most happye bee wee, that   Subjectes.
wee have you among us. Noble Alexander: The
Goddes preserve you, the Goddes defende you:
proceede foorth in your purpose: we ought to

love you, as our Father, too honour you as our
Lorde, and to admyre you as a God, heare among
us. And therunto added: Noble Emperour, take
what you wyll of our Treasure and substance to
5 accomplish your Purpose, (only) for buylding of
three Hospitalles, to succour the sicke bodies
of the poore.

By how much more zeale ought you, the good
Queene of Englandes Subjectes, adde to this
10 Prerogative?

Do (gratious Queene Elizabeth) what shall
seeme to you good: for your most blessed nature
cannot erre, or do any thing amis that you
purpose, who by divine inspiration, hath unlocked
15 the fountaine of grace: so that the thirstye
soules both of her rich and poore subjectes, may
freelye drinke the water of lyfe.

Segnior Philoxenus, so affected this speech,
as Ismarito coulde not, but imagyne, hys heart/
20 adjudged him, a straunger to Grace, and unworthy
lyfe, that was her vassaile and sayd not thereunto,
Amen. The end of Fryar Bugiardos clawing Sermon,
broke off thys private talke, and the Gentlewomen,
proude of the commendation, of their pytifull
25 sexe, now wisshed, that Doctor Mossenigo had ben
unpardoned his yesternightes trespasse towards
women: that the holy Frier, might have cited him
before our Ladie of Loretto: who, the greatter
parte of Dinner time, left his victuelles to
30 inlarge his Feminine prayses.

In the ende, tasting the goodnesse of the
meate, he fownd prating verie unsaverie: and
therfore, to recover his losses, his lippes layde
on loade: which Faliero, and some other of the

E2^v
Reconciliation
may take away
revenge, but
not grudge
from enimies
harts.

pleasaunt company perceiving, assayed to reward
the Fryar for his good Sermon, with <u>Tantalus</u>
dinner, and to that end, busied him with many
questions, which he ever aunsweared in a
⁵ <u>monisillable</u>, so that his tongue hyndred not his   Questions
feeding: As, (quoth <u>Faliero</u>) a question or two,   aunswered by
Master Fryer I pray? saye, (quoth he:) who   Monisillable.
strikes wyth the sharpest rod? God: of all other,
who is most evill? Devill: in distresse, who
¹⁰ deserveth most rueth? Trueth: who is charged
with most cryme? Tyme: what houlds the worlde
in most imprice? Vice: who is the greatest
lyer? Fryer: Desier: without flame, what maketh
the greatest fire? Ire: what sin is most accurst?
¹⁵ Lust: what bread is best to eat? Wheat: what
drink is worst for the eyne? Wine: When they
could devise no talke, to put lyfe in the Fryars
tongue, Doctour <u>Mossenigo</u> demaunded, why he was
so breefe, in his aunsweares? O (quoth he) <u>Pauca</u>
²⁰ <u>sapienti</u>: Then (quoth the Doctor) it is good
taking awaye, this plenty of meat, for cloying
Fryar <u>Bugiardoes</u> wit. The hole company, hearing
the Fryar beaten with hys owne sentence, tourned
into a contrary sence, burst out into suche an
²⁵ immoderate laughter, as choller that rose to the
very throat of the Friar would not suffer him to
swallowe, one bitt more of meat: in somuch, as
the boord was taken awaye, and the Friar driven
to saye <u>Benedicite</u>, with an emptye stomacke: an/
³⁰ intertaynment, as fit for a flatterer, as a   E3^r
reward for a faythful servaunt.
     The office of courteous reverence, fully   A good
discharged: the company retyred towards the fyre,   reward for
to pause a little after their dinner, observing   Flaterie.

therein an olde health rule.

After <u>dynner</u>, <u>talke</u> <u>a</u> <u>while</u>,
After <u>supper</u>, <u>walke</u> <u>a</u> <u>mile</u>.

Where the pittifull Gentlewomen, moaned the
5 dysgrace of their prayse Master, the Fryar, but
murmured more that he was crossed (without a
blessing) by theyr enemye, the Doctor. And to
put them out of this matter, <u>Bargetto</u> sayde
merrily, that the Fryar had taught hym such a
10 cunning way to woo, as to melt a woman into pitty,
he woulde wish, but the oportunitie of three howres:
two to love, and one to prayse the thing they lyke.
Yea (quoth <u>Franceschina</u> <u>Santa</u>, his Mistres,)
since women are so mercyfull, it is necessary to
15 brydle the subtilty of men: and to give example,
I enjoyne you, these three dayes to speake no
more of love: And questionlesse, thys payne set
uppon <u>Bargettos</u> head, was no greater then his
oversight deserved: for in doing of these three
20 thinges, is great daunger, and smal discression:
to play with fire: to strive with water: and to   A profitable
give a woman knowledge of our power: therfore,   Note.
he that will discover his owne secreat advauntage,
is worthy to have his heyre cutt with <u>Sampson</u>.
25   Queene <u>Aurelia</u>, by this time was reddy to
walke into the drawing chamber, to continue her
established exercise: and for the execution
thereof, shee called certayne of her chosen
Attendants, (whose appearance being made,) to
30 observe her former course: for auncient customs
profitable, are better then new lawes incertaine,
shee commaunded the <u>Eunuk</u>, to set their witts in
an order, by the vertue of some sweete harmony,
who, taking his Lute, after a dutifull obaysaunce,

played, and sunge, this followinge Sonnet, in
Italion./

To realish Love, I taste a sowrie sweete,
I finde Repose, in Fancies fetters bounde:
5 Amyd the Skies, my wysh I often meete:
And yet I lye, fast staked to the grownde:
    My eye sees Joy, my hart is grypde with payne,
    I know my hurt, and yet my good refrayne.

But how thease hang, the faithfull Lover knowes,
10 And yet can geeve, no reason for the cause:
The power of Love, mans reache so farre out goes,
As bownd (perforce) he yealdes to Cupids Lawes,
    And yet we finde, this Libertie in Love,
    As bard from Joye, Hope doth our griefes remoove.

15 Then Love sitte crownd, as Soveraigne of my thought,
And Fancie see, thou other motions chace,
To do whose wyll, Desire in me hath wrought,
A strength to ronne, in Gyves, sweete Pelops race,
    And those to charme, that studie me to staye,
20   It may suffise: the wisest paaste my way.

    The double effectes of this Sonet, made them
freshly to remember the doubtes, they left
yesterday unresolved. And to avoyde degression,
whiche rayseth many difficulties, and resolveth
25 few: Queene <u>Aurelia</u>, caused a Repeticion of
<u>Platoes</u> opinion of Mariage: which was: <u>She was
a Paradice on earth, where her Statutes were kept:
and a Hell in the House, where her lawes were
broken</u>.
30   Whereupon (quoth <u>Dondolo</u> with the libertie

of Queene <u>Aurelias</u> favour) I demaunde the cause?
why that the Male, and Female, of bruite and wilde
creatures love, cherish and take comfort, in one
anothers companie, onelie by the Impression of
nature: and man and woman, that/ are bewtified
both with the vertues of nature and reason, manie
times matched together, make a hell, of this
holie institution.

    By Queene <u>Aurelias</u> commaundement, to aunswere.
    Sir (quoth <u>Faliero</u>) The advantage of reason,
with which you have previledged man and woman, is
the onelie cause thereof: no man will denie, but
that there is a difference of conditions, in
creatures of everie kynde: some horse, an
unskilfull horseman, can hardly disorder; and
some in dispite of his rider will have a jadish
tricke. Some Hauke though shee bee evill served,
will not stragle foorth: and some, do the
Faulkener what he can, wil continuallie flie at
checkes: some hound by no meanes wil be rated
from riote, and some will never forsake, his
undertaken game: even so some man will filch if
his handes be fast bounde, and some having the
advantage of a bootie, will rather stearve, then
steale: some woman, with an houres libertie will
offende, and tenne yeares loving sute can not
overcome some other. But the vice, and vertue
in every creature, by the opinions of manie sage
Phylosophers, proceedeth from the purenesse, or
the imperfection of nature: which is not to be
founde, but by reason: and the use of reason
onelie belongeth to man: Now, if by oversight
in choice, the maried, are devided in desire,

Marginalia:
- Reason giveth man soverainty over al creatures.
- There is diversitie of condition in every kinde.
- Reason findeth out the imperfection of nature.
- Cause of misliking in mariage.

differ in life, and delight in neithers love: **Causes of**
Reason that findeth out this contrarietie, **comfort in**
soweth contention betweene the unfortunate **mariage.**
couple in Matrimonie thus matched. Againe, when
5 betweene the married there is equalitie, of
byrth, yeares, and manners, no difference in
love, nor suspition of others behaviour: Reason
that delighteth in unitie, maketh the Joyes of
Mariage innumerable.
10   Therefore (thinke I) the opinion of <u>Plato</u>
maye bee imbraced as a sounde judgemente.
    The whole assemblye, allowed <u>Falieroes</u>
reason: And <u>Dondolo</u> hymselfe was reasonably
well satisfied. But (quoth he,) since Mariage
15 bringeth with her unspeakable/ Joy, or uncurable   E4^v
sorrow: How may a man assure himselfe of the
one or avoide the other? when a womans
unsearcheable hart, is the only harbour both of
her good and evil conditions: and (once) in
20 appearance, the honourable, and the dishonest,
the vertuous, and the vicious: and in breefe,
every sorte of Women, are naturally beautifyed
with modestie. If the good repulse dishonest
request with chaste disdaine, the badde with
25 counterfet sobryetie, will blush at incontinent
sutes: If the good useth silence as a vertue,
the bad with well ordered speach, will be as
highly esteemed: If the good with the beautie
and benefites of Nature, delighte: the bad with
30 the florish of Arte, will no lesse be fantasied.
So that, at the first face, the cunningest Clarke
may bee deceived, in judginge who best deserveth.
    The greatest Clarke (quoth <u>Faliero</u>) proves
not alwaies the wisest man, and none more apt to

be beguiled then he. He valueth all, that
glistereth, Golde: he esteemeth fayre wordes,
as friendly deeds: and thinketh that lovely
countenaunces, doo spring from a lovyng condition.
5 When experience knowing the contrarie, will trie
them all by the test.

    The corruptest Canker, bloometh lyke the
sweetest Eglantine: the bitter Bullice,
resembleth the pleasaunt Damson, and the sowre
10 Crab, the savorie Pippin. Even so good and bad,
faire and fowle, chaste and unconstaunt, Women
are made of one moulde, framde of one forme, and
naturaly graced, with a shamfast blushing, but
as in smell the Cankar, in tast the Bullice, and
15 the Crab in relysh, bewray their imperfections,
even so with cunning usage, the subtillest woman,
will shew her unnaturall conditions: counterfeits
will to kinde: Copper holds print, but not touch
with Gold: Fire hid in Ashes, will breake foorth
20 in heat: water courses stopt, find out new
passages: even so the impatient woman, throwly
moved, discloseth her passions: the prowde with
sufferaunce, exceedeth in pompe, and the wanton
sore charged, will fall to folly./

25   Well (quoth <u>Dondolo</u>,) notwithstanding your
directions be good, yet the pathe to heaven, is
so difficult to fynde, as the ignoraunt passenger
without direction, is like to follow the beaten
waye to Hell, and the surest guide is Experience.
30   So that the direction of the Parents, is to
be imbraced of the Chyldren in this behalfe.

    Parents with regarde, foresee the evils that
negligent Children, feele ere they withstand:
Parents provide living, to mainetaine their

Marginalia:
- (line 5) Experience is the best Judge.
- (line 11) The forme deceiveth, but the qualytie sheweth the creature.
- (line 25) F1^r
- (line 30) The foresight of Parentes.

Childrens loove.

    Children often times by matching with beggers, diminish theyr parents inheritaunce.

    Parents labour for necessaries to support an householde.

    Children onely seeke for silken ragges, to upholde their pride.

    Parents have care to matche their Children with those of vertuous condition: and Children lightly regarde no more then their loovers amiable countenaunce.

    I confesse with you (quoth <u>Faliero</u>) the oversights of yonge men in their choyce, but I crye out uppon forcement in Marriage, as the extreamest bondage that is: for that the raunsome of libertie is the death of the one or the other of the married. The father thinkes he hath a happy purchase, if he get a riche young Warde to match with his daughter: But God he knowes, and the unfortunate couple often feele, that he byeth sorrow to his Childe, slaunder to himselfe, and perchaunce, the ruine of an auncient Gentlemans house, by the riot of the sonne in Lawe, not looving his wife. *[A reprehension of forced Mariage.]*

    But admit there be no disagreement betweene the parties, which is rather fortune then foresight in parentes, who regarde that the landes and goods be great, but smally waye, whether the beauty and behaviours please or no: yet loove enforste, taketh knowledge neither of freendes, favour, forme, goods nor good bringing up. *[Love will not be constrained.]*

    Delicate meate, hardely forceth an appetite unto the/ sycke. Pleasure yeeldes no sollace to the sorrowfull, no more can forcement enforce

the free to fancie. The <u>Lyon</u> with gentlenes may
be tamed, but with curstnes never conquered:
much more lordly is <u>Love</u>, for as <u>Petrarke</u> defyneth.

The Prince, the Peere, the Subject and the slave,
5   Love gives with care, to him they make their mone.
And if by chaunce, he graunt the grace they crave,
    It comes of ruthe, by force he yeeldes to none.

    I could report many examples of large authoritie,
to proove this inconvenience, but to a needelesse   The evil of
10 ende: for tediousnes duls the remembraunce of the   tediousnes.
hearer, and tyres the tongue of the Reporter. In
dayly action, you may vew the libertie of <u>Love</u>,
his contempt to be constrained, and the great
compassion he useth when he is with curtesie
15 acquired, which account, inforced Mariage is
sildome considered. There is procurement of
freendes before plightment of faith: safety for
livinges before assuraunce of love, and clapping
of handes before knitting of hartes: an occasion
20 that the sorrowfull partyes morne when they are
Married, and rejoyse when by death they are severed.

    <u>Dondolo</u> replyed, that when there is no
remedy <u>Reason</u> will drive them to <u>Love</u>.

    But <u>Faliero</u> maintayned, that <u>Reason</u> and <u>Love</u>,
25 are at deadely foode: <u>Reason</u> byds thee loove,   Reason and
but where thou art lyked, and <u>Love</u> byds thee   Love, as
fancie where thou art hated: <u>Reason</u> directes for   enemies.
thy benefit, and <u>Love</u> allures to thy detryment:
and to conclude, the office of <u>Reason</u> is to
30 appease olde greefes, and the nature of <u>Love</u> is
to raise new debates.

    Tush, tush, (quoth <u>Bargetto</u>,) among the
married, quarrels in the day, are qualified with

kisses in the night: whereupon groweth this
Adage./

<u>The jangling wordes, that Lovers use in rage</u>:
<u>Gives Love a grace, when anger dooth asswage</u>.

A wytnesse that <u>Unkindnesse</u> inlargeth <u>Love</u>,
as the wracke of Winter dooth the beautie of
Summer: then, although the Parents matche at
first, be without the fancie of the Children, a
reconciliation (in fine) will double their
comforte.

Sir (quoth <u>Soranso</u>, favouring <u>Falieros</u>   An other
opinion) you wrest: the Adage is to a contrary   reprehension
meaning: for it is to be used but where there   of forcement
hath beene sometyme perfect love, and where a   in mariage.
grounded love is, although the Married menace
with their tunges, they malice not with their
hartes: on the contrarie parte: looke what
rule the <u>Lover</u> useth in love, the <u>Enemie</u> observeth
in revenge.

Therefore if the Maried abhorre before
<u>Marriage</u>, they may well desemble with their
tounges, but wyll never bee delighted in their
harts: and where there is such a devision in
the desires of the Married, fayre, fained
semblaunce, wil soone turne to flat fowle falling
out: their thrift goeth forwarde as the carriage
drawen by two Oxen, taile to taile: the Husband
wyll have no delight to get, nor the Wife desyre
to save: Servauntes with negligence will waste,
and hyrelinges, with proloyning, will winne:
and (which is worst) the continuaunce of mallice,
will custom them with mortall hatred: hatred
betweene the Married, breedeth contencion betwixt

the parents, contencion betwixt the parents, raiseth
quarrels among the kindred, and quarrels among the
kindred, occupieth all the neighbours with slaunder:
so that for the most part, these forced Mariages,
5 engendereth sorrowes for the Married, disquietnesse
to both their freends and kindred: but which
still renueth greefe, the scandall of enemyes,
endeth in neyther of theyr wretchednesse.

    This beeing said, lyttle avayled the further
10 prooffes, of the contrary part, so full was the
crie: <u>Fye of forcement in Mariage</u>, so that to
paint out, the inconveniences therof in his proper
coulours, Queene <u>Aurelia</u> commaunded <u>Faliero</u>/ to
confirme his sufficient reasons, with the discourse
15 of some rare Historie. Whose commaundement he
willingly satisfied, and reported as followeth.

<u>   The Historie in the reproche of forced
        Mariage, reported by Faliero.</u>

    In the famous Cittie of <u>Cirene</u>, in <u>Affrick</u>,
20 dwelled sometimes a riche Marchaunt named <u>Tryfo</u>.
This <u>Tryfo</u> had a wealthy neighbour called <u>Clearches</u>,
who of long time entertained one an other with a
neighborly affection. <u>Tryfo</u> to inherite all his
livings, had but one onely sonne, named <u>Sicheus</u>:
25 and <u>Clearches</u> one onely Daughter called <u>Elisa</u>.
The Parents to establish (as they imagined) an
everlasting amitie, betweene theyr houses,
concluded a <u>Mariage</u> for theyr unfortunate Children:
making no doubt, but that they would as well
30 inherite theyr affections, as theyr livings: of
which there was hope enough, if the order had
beene as good to establish theyr <u>Love</u>, as the
haste great, to sollemnize the <u>Mariage</u>: for that
in theyr persons, appeered no signe of disagreement,

nor in theyr abilyties cause of exception: but
loove (that behouldeth no more quicknesse in a
Dyamond, then in a dim Saphyre) though he take
impression by sight, rooteth in contemplation: Loove
5 which devine exercise of the soule, smally   rooteth by
delighteth green Youthe, who intertaine their   Contemplation.
thoughts with a thousand vaine fancies: but to
my purpose; The Mariage day drew neare: and as
at the very push of Battell, the wise Captaine
10 animateth his Souldiers, with some plausible
Oration, even so the night before the Mariage,
Trifo schooled his sonne Sicheus, with this
following advertisement.

    My good sonne (quod he,) so great are the   Advise to a
15 follyes of men, and so cunning the deceits of   booteles
women, as the most (especially the yonger sorte)   purpose.
wyll credite theyr lookes, without looking
into their lives: beleeve their woordes, and
lightly regard their workes: delyght to recount
20 theyr entertainements, and disdaine to reckon
theyr shrewde payments./ For as the sycke   F3^r
pacient, comforted with the Phisitions words,
leaves to examine the quallities of his receites:
Even so, the wretched Lover, cured with the   Loove yeelds
25 yeelding of his beautifull Mistrisse, with   neither to
negligence, bothe over lookes his owne benefit,   wyt, strength
and her behaviour. Salomon was deceyved,   nor learning.
Sampson subdued, Aristotle derided, and Hercules
murthered, by the illusions of errant honest
30 women.

    Kinge Demetrius, notwithstanding he was   An exstreame
bothe wise and valiant, was so bewitched with   affection.
the wyles of the notorious strumpet Lamia, as in
open Schooles, he raysed disputations, whether

the love he bare <u>Lamia,</u> or the Jewels he bestowed
upon her, were the greater: or whether her
merrit exceeded them bothe or noe. Yea when she
died he caused her to be Intombed under his Bed
5 Chamber windowe, to the ende, that with dayly
teares he might worship her engraved bones, who
(living) was of him intirely belooved.
    If the wisest, and the worthyest, be thus
overtaken in their affections, what easie baites
10 may beguile thee, who in yeares art young, of
substaunce delicate and lustie, and therefore apt
to loove: reddy in conceyt, and of consideration
unperfect: whot in desire, and in discretion
colde: My sonne, by experience I know, and to
15 prevent thy overlikely mischaunce in choyce: I
have chosen thee a wife, fayre to please thee,
ritche to continue loove, her Parents my assured
freendes, and she thy affected loover: love her
well, beare with her in small faultes, as a
20 woman and the weaker, and bridle thy owne evill
affections as a man, her head and governour: and
in thus dooing, God will multiply his blessings
upon you, and make your aged Parents to dye in
peace, to see you live in prosperitie. Young
25 <u>Sicheus</u> regarded his Fathers tale, as Schollers
doo their <u>Tutors,</u> who giving them leave to playe,
admonisheth them with all, to keepe good rule,
which they promise, and performe the contrary.
With the like affection, <u>Sicheus</u> embraced <u>Mariage.</u>
30 He was not so soone wearie of dallying with his
Wife, as he was ready to entertayne a Harlot:/
so that in shorte space, he became a common <u>Lover,</u>
and a carelesse Husband: and withall, grew as
arrogant in defending his libertie, as dissolute

in his actions and behaviour: If his freends did gently advise him, he was of age to counsell himselfe: if his Parents did sharply reprehend him, he would impudently aunswer, he was past
5 correction: if his Wife found her selfe agreeved with his hard usage, she might well complaine, but he would take no time to amend: so that his dayly actions of evill, tooke away all after hope of weldooing: in so much as he became
10 odious unto his freends, that beheld his lewde inclination: and a plague unto his Wife, who was dayly oppressed, with his monstrous vices. So that, the overcharge of sorrow made her many times passage, for these and such like passions.
15 O unhappie and over hastie Mariage, which in the pride of my youthe, with discontentments, makest me resemble a fayre Fig Tree, blasted with the after colde, of an untimely Spring: but why blame I Mariage, which is honourable? alas,
20 because the abuse of good things, worke evill effectes: Roses unadvisedly gathered, pryck our hands: Bees ungently used stinge our faces, yet the one pleasaunt, and the other profitable: so that if their come any evil of that which is good,
25 our folly or fortune is cause thereof: Aye me, when I was married, I was to young to be a wife, and therefore have no reason to exclayme on folly. But Fortune, fowle falle thee, which coursest me with cursses, in possessing me with those things,
30 which others holde for blessings: Wealth, that bestoweth pleasures on many, is the orriginall of my woe. Mariage, which giveth lybertye to many, inlargeth my Fetters, and demaundeth death for my raunsome: Beautie that advaunseth many, is to

The title of Mariage, maketh youthe arrogant.

Abuse of good things, worke evill effectes.

That which is blessing to one, may be a curse to an other.

me a disgrace: for that, injoying her forme, I
am of Sicheus not fantasied, of whom every foule
and common Trull is belooved: But therein,
Fortune, thou doost me no wronge, for my hate
5 towards him, overpayseth his light regarde of me.
O but my hart is conti-/nually afflicted with
his evill, and his finger never akes with my
mallice. Yea: but Forberaunce edgeth the sword
of Revenge, when Choller, though it often strikes,
10 it woundes not muche. Raine falleth every where,
yet beateth but the leaves, the thunder Bowlt
lighteth in one place, but yet teareth up the
rootes: so though I dissemble tyll oportunitie,
Sicheus shall feele my hate to death: and though
15 I endure a space, I will redeeme my dying life:
and persevering in this resolution, Elisaes
thoughts, that were lately drowned in sorrow, now
flamed with desyre of Revenge: and the Devill
who is the Executioner of Vengeance, presented
20 her foorthwith this ungratious meane.

    A Yonge Gentleman, named Chion, among a
troupe of other Ladyes and Gentlewomen, beheld
fayre Elisae, with such a burning affection, as
he foorthwith dispossessed his owne hart, to make
25 his bosome the seate of her imagined Image: so
that his soule, that continually eyed her beautie,
and his heart, at the direction of his Mistresse,
gave such a heate to his desire, that had he
beene sure to have received Ixions torments, for
30 his ambitious attempting of Junoes love, he could
neither have left to love, nor have forborne to
seeke for grace: so that follow what would, he
foorthwith presented his affections, in this
ensuing Letter.

Marginalia:
- Carlesnesse of the husband breedeth hate in the wife.
- F4^r
- Choller, is soone quited, but Forberaunce increaseth mallice.
- The Divell is the Executioner of vengeaunce.
- An extreame passion of Love.

Chions Letter to Elisae.

Fayre Mistresse, had I vertue to perswade
you to ruthe, as you have power to make me love:
the discoverie of my blasing affections,/ would
melt you, (were you a Mountaine of Ice) to pitty.
But for that Love is more vehement in the heart,
then in the tongue, I appeale to your owne motions
for grace, if you have ever loved: if not, I
hope for such justice at Venus handes, as you
shall love: and yet thus much I saye, although
I affye nothing in my perswations, because they
be but wordes. I presume of my indevours, for
that I have vowed my life, to death, to do you
service: of which you can have no better assuraunce,
then imployement, nor I a hyer favor, then to be
imployed.

Good Madame, martir me not, with ordinary
doubts, in that my affections are not ordinary.
For as your beautye excelleth all other Dames,
as the fayre Rose eache Garden Flower, even so
the full power of love, hath made me in the estate
of flaming flaxe, that is, presently to receive
grace, or in a moment to perish. Thus longing
for your sweete aunswer, I somewhat succour my
torments, with the imagination, that I kisse
your gratious hand.

No more his owne
Chion.

This Letter sealed, and subscribed, was
delyvered to so cunning a Messenger as needed no
instructions in Chions behalfe. The Letter
presented, and advisedly reade by Elysa, surprised
her with an unmeasurable joye: not so much for

that she had purchased her self a faithfull Loover,
as procured her Husband a mortall enemy: of which
Chions Letter gave her not so great assuraunce,
as the disposition of his countenaunces, in a
former regarde: and theruppon pursuing Sicheus
with more hate, then minding Chion with affection,
she mused uppon an number of mischeefes, invented
by desyre to be revenged, and suppressed by feare
to be defamed./

A naturall feare in a woman, suppresseth many of their evill affections.

In fine, remembring, that she had read: <u>Love
quickeneth a mans wit, although it burieth Reason</u>:
To trie, if he could define, what Service she
desired: she retourned Chion a Briefe, wherin he
had a light to mischiefe, and yet might be read,
without bleamysh of her honour: the Effect wherof,
was this.

G1^r

<u>Whyle CICHEUS doth lyve:
ELISA can not love.</u>

Chion, receyved this Scrowle: But yet before
he presumed to reade the Contents, he kissed and
rekissed the same: houldyng an opinion, that
commyng from his Mistresses handes, it deserved
suche honour (althoughe it contayned Sentence of
his death:) not unlyke the foolishe Mahometians:
who upon their Emperours Commaundementes, are
ready Executioners of their owne lyves.

An example, for Christian Subjectes.

But to my purpose: when Chion had throughly
perused this strange Aunswere: weare it Cicheus
his heavy Destinie, or a just Scourge, for his
sore trespasses: (accursed that he was) he
became too just an Executioner of Elisaes wicked
wil: but yet with this interpretation, that the
love she bare her Husband, directed her in this

Craft hath many times his will, with an opinion of honestie.

answer.

    In so much, as, overcom with a furious hate towards <u>Cicheus</u>, as the Barre of his welfare, lyke a Lyon that bites the Iron grate, which houlds him from his pray: sodenly with this salutation, he sheathed his Sword in <u>Cicheus</u> intrayles.

<u>CICHEUS</u> <u>shall</u> <u>not</u> <u>lyve</u>,
<u>To</u> <u>hinder</u> <u>CHIONS</u> <u>love</u>.

The fact, was so fowle, and withall so publique, as the Officers of Justice, immediatly seased upon <u>Chion</u>: and for that his bloodie sword, was a witnes of the trespas, there was no <u>Plea</u> to save him: for wilfull faultes may be pitied, but deserveth no pardon: and to say trueth, neither did he desire to lyve, because <u>Elisa</u>, the vertue of his lyfe, by the charge of Lawe, was bownd to sue him to death: who/ followed the processe, with an apparance of sorrow, suche as if her Conscience had bene without scruple of guiltinesse, or her harte a thowsande degrees from joye: when God knowes, she was puffed with the one, and the other, so that the wonder, at her dissimulation, equalled the reproche of her notorious hatred.

    To be shorte, this was the Judges sentence: <u>Chyon</u> should be beheaded, as amends for <u>Cicheus</u> death, and the Widdow should be endowed with his goods, for the dammage done unto her: but God which knoweth our seacret faultes (when Judges though they rule as Gods, know, but what they heare and see as men) not willynge to hide such an haynous offence: First, amased all the hearers,

Wilful faults deserve no pardon.

A favour evil bestowed.

This Judge is not parciall, for favor, gain or feare.

with an unknow voice, Elisaes harte, is as Gyltie,
as Chions hand: and therewithal, thundred this
following vengeance, uppon the cleared malefactor.
The Infant in Elysaes wombe, as it were engendred
5 of the Parents malyce, at the verie instaunt,
not obeying the course of Nature, so tyrannised
her Intrailes, as with very agony she dyed, and
with all remayneth an opinyon, that the Husband,
Wife, and Sonne, by the appointment of the Gods,
10 were Metamorphosed into Vipers, whiche venimous
Beastes are thrall to these curses. The female   The curses
after shee hath engendred, murdreth the Male,   geven unto a
because she wil not be ruled as an inferiour: Viper.
and the yong eate themselves, forth of their Dams
15 Intrailes: because they wil not be bound to the
obedience of Nature.

    Well (quoth Soranso) though your Metamorphos
bee unlykly, yet is it not unnecessarilye applyed.
For, for the most part, those which are forced to
20 Mariage, agree little better then Vipers. But
it seemeth to mee (Segnior Faliero) you have too
favourably reported this Historie in Elysaes
behalfe, considering the mortal venyme she
tempered in her harte.

25   O (quoth Faliero) longe fowle wayes, both
tyreth the Horse, and wearieth his Ryder, where   Brevitie is
both the one, and the other, overcommeth the   best in
length of fayre passages, with pleasure: Even   passionate
so, in a ruthfull Historie, over plentie of/   matters, and
30 wordes, both greeveth the reporter, and giveth   effectation,
meane for a thousande sighes to breake from the   in pleasaunt.
hearer, where affected circumstances give a   G2^r
grace to a pleasant tale. Sorow to heare their
kinde thus stayned with crueltye, locked up the   Sorrowes
    causeth
    scilence.

tonges of the poore Gentlewomen a pretie while.
In the end (quoth Alvisa Vechio, a dame more olde,
and bold then the rest,) meseemeth that Faliero
hath but little favored Elysa, for he hath showen
her evill, and the scourge of her evill: and in
charitie, he was bounde to shewe the cause of her
evill: I would (quoth Doctour Mossenigo) that
Frier Bugiardo, had hearde this disputation, it
might have ben the breaking downe of the Altar,
whereupon he but lately committed blasphemie,
woulde have more reformed him, then his pleasing
Sermon, could have confirmed us. These advantages
the Doctor tooke to crosse the Gentlewomen, his
late open enemies, and but nowe his fained
friendes: not unlike a sneaking dog, that never
barkes but bites withall. And to spite them the
more, (quoth hee,) Monsier Bergetto, since you
are bound from speaking of love, you have both
cause and oportunitie to talke of womens hate.
  Pardon me (quoth Bergetto) for this penance
was but a due payne for my presumption, which I
hope to overcome with patient suffering: and
sure in this milde aunswere: Bergetto shewed a
moral vertue, and Doctor Mossenigo, by his
malicious question, a canckred nature: for
simplie to offend proceedeth of frailtie, but to
perceaver in evill is a noate of wilfull frowardnesse.
  Well, notwithstanding Bergettos temperaunce,
a Caveler caught hold uppon this question, as a
Mastive uppon an old drye Mariebone, and to prove
a womans hatred more greater then her love: hee
avouched manye cruell authorities. But Faliero,
who had donne them some injurie in reporting the
late history made them part of amends, and put

We are bound to showe as well the cause as to punnish the evill.

Good morralitie, is better then evil doctrine.

There is no trustinge of a reconcyled enemye.

The example of a naughtye nature.

A necessarie note.

A Caveller, hath colours for everie question.

their adversarie to silence in proving the contrary:
his reason was, that their hate, in the extremest
degree, stretched, but to the death of another,
and their love many times; hath done wilful murder
upon them selves./

    Then it followeth, by how much we pryse our
selves above an other, by so muche, theyr love is
greater then theyr hatred.

    Yea (quoth the Doctor) but their love and
hatred, are both violents: and every violent is
an evill.

    Yea Master Doctor (quoth <u>Maria Belochy</u>) their
evills are the greater for men, for by their
flattering enchauntments, wemen love immoderately,
and stung with mens unsufferable injuries, they
hate mortally.

    The Doctor replied, there was more power in
her lookes, then authoritie in her wordes: but
least he should be subdued by the one, he would
not contend with the other.

    Why (quoth Queene <u>Aurelia</u>) beauty workes no
more impression, in a Doctors eye, then doth
poyson, in <u>Minervas</u> sheelde, for he by <u>Philosophy</u>
can subdue affection.

    Madame (quoth he) you may well compare beauty
and poyson together, for their operations, are a
lyke: save that beauty is the more extreame, in
that she infectes with her lookes, and poyson not,
unlesse wee taste it: or when it is most strong,
not unlesse we touch it: yea, <u>Euripides</u>, compareth
her inchauntement, with the inticementes of a
kingdome, whereas he saith.

In these two thinges, a Kingdome to obtaine,
Or else to worke the fayre to their will,

(margin: $G2^v$)

Wemens love, is more great then theyr hate.
Wemen do amis, but men are the cause.

Beauty overcommeth the wisest.

EURIPIDES comparison, betweene Beauty and Love.

(So sweetely tastes the grace of either gayne,)
As men ne dread, their friendes with foes to kyll:
The reason is, controulment shrinkes the place,
Whereas a Kyng, as soveraigne Judge doth sit,
5 In love, because that reason lackes his grace,
For to restrayne, the selfe conceyghtes of wit,
So that God knowes, in daunger standes his lyfe:
That is a King, or hath a fayre wife.

    To deale in Princes affayres, the companye
10 was too greene: but in Beauties behalfe, there
was neither Gentleman, nor Gentlewoman, that was
not desirous to bee revenged of the Doctours
detractyon: for hee that hath a/ slaunderous
tonge injurieth manie, and is himselfe hated of
15 all men: but for that it was nowe to late, too
decide any other great question, Queene <u>Aurelia</u>
adjorned the ending of anie controversie, untill
the next day.

        <u>The Device of the second Nights Mask</u>.

20   By a secreate foreknowledge of a Maske, with
which <u>Soranso</u>, <u>Bargetto</u>, <u>Ismarito</u>, and others,
purposed to honour <u>Segnior Phyloxenus</u>, and his
company, Supper was hastned, and soone ended:
and after the one had saluted the other, with an
25 accustomed reverence: while the rest of the
Gentlemen interteined Time, with dauncing, or
devising with their Mistresses, the Maskers
withdrew themselves, and about nine of the clocke,
in this disguise, presented themselves agayne.

30   A Consort of sweete Musycke, sounded the
knowledge of their comming: the Musitians, in
<u>Gyppons</u> and <u>Venetians</u>, of <u>Russet</u> and <u>Blacke Taffata</u>,

Sclaunder is generally hated.

G3^r

bended with <u>Murrey</u>, and thereon imbroadered this   A Gentleman
Posie, <u>Spero</u>, <u>Timeo</u>, <u>Taceo</u>: expressing thereby,   is not to
the sundrye passions of Love: and before them   shoe his
two Torchbearers, apparelled, in <u>Yallowe</u> <u>Taffata</u>   passions, by
5 <u>Sarcenet</u>: the Generall apparell of the Maskers,   his attyre.
was short Millaine Cloaks, Dublet and hose, of
<u>Grene</u> <u>Satten</u>: bordered with <u>Silver</u>: <u>Greene</u>
<u>Silcke</u> <u>stockes</u>: <u>White</u> <u>Scarpines</u>: <u>Rapiers</u> and
<u>Daggers</u> <u>sylvered</u>: <u>Blacke</u> <u>Velvet</u> <u>Cappes</u>, and
10 <u>white</u> <u>Feathers</u>. They agreed to be thus attyred,   Men in many
to showe themselves free, in the eye of the world,   cases are to
and covertly bound unto their Mistresses.   be privileadged,
                                                                   for an others
    <u>Ismarito</u> for courtisy sake, because he was   merrite.
a stranger, and withal, in that his Mistres was
15 the most honourable, had the leading of this Maske,
who lighted with a torch, by his Page, apparelled
in <u>Blue</u>, <u>Carnation</u>, and <u>whyte</u> <u>Taffata</u>: the colours
of his Mistres: intred with a <u>Ventoy</u> in his hand,   Ventoie, a
made like an <u>Ashe</u> <u>tree</u>: wrethed about with <u>Ivye</u>:   Fan.
20 expressing this posye: <u>Te</u> <u>stante</u> <u>virebo</u>: with/
which, upon fit oportunitie, he presented Queene
<u>Aurelia</u>, his Mistresse: within which, weare
(covertly hid) these verses in English <u>Italion</u>.

Two Soveraigne Dames, Beautie and Honestie,
25   Long mortal foes, accorded are of late.
And now the one, dwels in my Mistresse eye,
    And in her hart the other keepes her state.

Where both to show the vertue of this peace,
    To garnysh her, make riot of their Grace:
30 In her fayre eye, Dame Beautie doth increace,
    A thousande Gleames, that doo become her face.

And with her harte, thus doth the other deale,
    She lowly seemes, and mountes throw chast disdaine,
So that her thrales doo serve with honest zeale,
    Or fearing blame, doe yeelde unto their paine.

5 The heavenly soules, envies the earthes renowne:
    Such gyftes devine, in humayne shape to see,
And Jove still moves, a Goddesse her to crowne:
    Which is decred, when Nature shall agree.
        Thus happy I (in Fortunes frownes long whyrld)
10   A Goddesse serve, and soveraigne of the world.

    BARGETTO, lighted by a Page, apparayled in
his Mistresse colours, Greene, Carnation and
Whyte, followed Ismarito, having the mouth of his
Mask closed with a small Golden Lock, as a
15 witnesse of the true execution of his Mistresse
Commaundement: and upon hys fist hee caried a
Parrate to pratle to his Mistresse, uppon pausing
betweene every solemne Almayne, and covertlye
under the Parrats winge, was hidden this passion.

20   Hence burnyng sighes, which sparckle from desyre,
To pitty melt my Mistresse frosen Hart:
Her frosen hart, that Fancy cannot fyre,
Nor true intent, perswade to rue my smart.
    Haste, haste, I pray, the Icye passage breake,
25   And pleade for him, that is forbid to speake./

    What though at first, you faile to calme her rage,   G4^r
Yet as the Sunne, from earth doth draw the Rayne,
Your vertues so, the stormes of scorne may swage,
Or feede Desyre, with showers of disdayne.
30   For even as drink, dooth make the Dropsey drye,

So colde disdaine, compels Desyre to frye.

    Her wyll be done, but I have sworne to love,
And with this vow, will nourish my delight:
Her scorne, my woe, nay, time may not remove,
5 A faithful zeale out of my troubled spright.
        Yea more then all, Ile Sacrifice my blood,
        And fyre my bones, to doe my Mistresse Good.

    <u>SORANSO</u>, lighted by a Page, in <u>Orange</u>, <u>Tawny</u>,
<u>Watchod</u> and <u>Greene</u>, was the next that presented
10 him selfe: who uppon his left side, had a <u>Harte</u>,
of <u>Crymson Granado Silke</u>, so artificyally made
and fastened to his dublet, as if his body had
opened, and his hart appeered, which fell downe
at his Mistresse feete, upon such a Fortune, as
15 she was bounde to take it up, which opened, she
might beholde the Picture of her selfe, reading
this submission.

    Even as the Hart, a deadly wounde, that hath
Retires him selfe, with sighes to solace greefe:
20 And with warme teares, his gored sides doth bath,
But finding mone, to render small releefe:
        Impatient Beast, he gives a heavy Bray,
        And hasts the Death, that many woulde delay.

    So I whose Love, beyond my hap doth mount,
25 Whose thoughts as Thornes, yet prick me with Desire:
Whose sute and zeale, return's with no accompt:
Whose hope is drye, set in a harte of Fyre:
        Holde this for ease, foorthwith to spoyle the eye,
        That lookte and lov'de, then in dispaire to dye./

A happy Doome, if it for Law might stande,
But men condemd, them selves may not dispatch.
Their lyves and deathes, are in their Soveraignes hand
So myne in hers, whose Lookes did me attache:
5   And therfore I, to pardon or to kyll,
    Must yeald my selfe, the Prysoner of her wyll.
L'ENVOY.
Then Ladie faire, receive what longes to thee,
A fettred thralle, attyred with disgrace,
10 And at thy feete, his wounded hart here see,
And in the same, the Image of thy face,
    Whiche bleding fresh, with throbs throwes foorth his mone,
    Rueth, rueth, deare Dame, for that I am your owne.

DONDOLO, lighted by his Page, apparayled in
15 Tawnie, Blew and Black Taffata, was the fourth:
who uppon his Breast, bare a Myrrour, set the
outeside inwarde, and yet fastened so slope as
it might receive light, with an Imagination, that
he showed his Hart, the Beautie of his Mistresse,
20 and in the thought, he wrot upon the out side:
Basta che spero: within whiche glasse, this
sonet was coningly convaied: which upon a fit
oportunitie he presented unto his Mistresse,
Lucia Bella.

25   From shore to sea, from dales to mountaines hie,
From meddowes faire, amid the craggie rocke,
Love doth me leade, I know not whether I,
But evermore a passage doeth unlocke.
Nowe doe I fight, now weepe, now death I feare,
30 In all these stormes, yet love the healme doth steare.

In desert woods I wander to and fro,
Where I wilde beastes, and firie Serpentes meete.
Yet safe I passe, Love doth direct me so.
In tempestes rough, my barke doth alwayes fleete,
5 Yea, when Sunne, Moone, and starres forsake the skie,
Love gives me light, from my faire Mistresse eye./

    I mount to heaven, I know not with what winges H1^r
I sinke to hell, yet drowne not in distresse:
Twixt Ice and flame, Love mee in safetie bringes,
10 But to what end? in sooth I cannot gesse:
    Yet hap what shall, Love giveth me this scope,
    In daungers mouth, to live alwaies in hope.

<u>FALIERO</u> lighted by a Page, attired in <u>Peach
colour, yellow, and popenjay greene Taffeta,</u>
15 was the fifte and last that entred: who (as yf
she were climynge up his Arme) caryed a whyght
<u>Turtle</u>, so artifycially made, as it deceyved, no
lesse, then <u>Parrhasius</u> paynted Table Clothe: In
whose Beake, were fynely rowled these Verses.

20 If one firme Faith, one Hart uncharg'd with frawd,
One langour sweete, one wish desire dooth move:
If honest Zeale, a gentle breast doth lawde,
If wanderyng long, in the Lab'rinth of Love,
If wan pale cheekes, are witnesses of woe,
25 If reaking sightes, throwne from a burnyng harte:
If all these, and thousand sorrowes moe:
May charme Mistrust, and make you rue my smart,
    Faire Mistresse, looke but in my Meagre face,
    And you shall reade, that I have neede of Grace.

30   In this order, and with these devises, the

Maskers entred, and after they had saluted Queene
Aurelia, and the honourable of the company, they
placed themselves, some of the one side, of the
greate Chamber, and some of the other, observynge
5 therein a more discreate order then the ordynary
Maskers: who at their first entraunce, either
daunce with them selves, or rudelye sease uppon
the Gentlewomen: but these Maskers, intertained
a smal Tyme, with their Musick, while they had
10 leasure to looke about, and espie who were the
worthyest amonge the Ladies./

In the ende, Ismarito kyssing his hand, with
a Countenaunce abased, humbly desired Queene
Aurelia, to do him the grace, to daunce with him.
15 Next, Bergetto made choice of Franceschina Santa:
after him, Soranso, chewsed, Maria Belochi:
Dondolo, raysed Lucia Bella: and last of all,
Faliero, tooke his Mistresse Catharina Trista:
and thus, they observed in their choyce, the same
20 course they kepte in their entrance.

After this Companie had performed all the
civill Services of Maskers, leavyng behinde them,
their Mistresses honoured, and the whole companie
much contented: they departed in the good order
25 they entred: savyng that their Mistresses were
possessed with their severall Devices.

Which done, the Gentlemen and Gentlewomen
began to shrinck out of the great Chamber, as the
Starres seeme to shoote the Skie, towardes the
30 Breake of Daye.

FINIS./

The thyrd Daies Exercise.

Contayning: sundrie Morall Preceptes: With a large Discoverie, of the inconveniences of Rash Mariages.

    The Aucthorytie, is dayly Experience, that prooveth, how that the bitterest worldly Sorow, soone endes, eyther by Benefit of Fortune, or violence of death: neither is the firmest worldly pleasure, yet of more continuance, then an Imagynation, whiche is straight crost with a contrary Suggestion. *(The uncertaintie of worldly thinges.)*

    What difference was there betwene the Fortunes of Cesar and Pompey, when their endes were both violent? save that I hould Cesars to be the harder: for that, he was murthered in the Armes of Prosperytie, and Pompey, at the feete of Disgrace: but being both dead, unto their Monumentes, Writers adde this Opinion. *(Both POMPEY and CESAR, died violently.)*

    Cesar, in his lyfe, was more fortunate then Pompey: and Pompey, more honest then Cesar.

    A proofe, that some Disgrace, is the ground of Good Reporte: and some good Fortune, the Trumpe of Infamie: therfore, let no man yeld to Adversitie, nor affie too much in Pompe and painted Prosperytie: for the one, is but vexation, the other vanitie, and both in short time vanish.

    A sodayne alteration (as me thought) made me to contemplate of these causes: for that (commynge out of my lodgyng, somwhat tymely) I entred the great Chamber, with as strange a regarde, as he that commeth out of a House full of Torch and Taperlights, into a darke and obscure Corner: knowing that at midnight (aboute whiche

tyme, I forsooke my company) I lefte the place,
attyred lyke a seconde Paradice: the earthly
Goddesses, in brightnesse, resembled Heavenly
Creatures, whose Beauties daseled mennes eyes
5 more then the Beames of the Sunne./

    The sweet Musick recorded the Harmonie of
Angels, the straunge and curious devices in
Maskers, seemed as fygures of devine Misteries.

    And to be short, the place was a verie
10 <u>Sympathie</u>, of an imagined Paradice. And in the
space of one slumbering sleepe, to bee left lyke
a desert wildernesse, without any creature, save
sundrie savadge Beastes, portrayed in the
Tapestrie hanginges, imprest suche a heavy passion
15 in my minde, as for the time, I fared as one,
whose sences had forgot how to doo their bounden
offices: In the ende, to recomfort my throbbing
hart, I tooke my Citterne, and to a solempne Note,
sung this following Sonet, which I a litle before,
20 composed upon a quiet thought, I possessed after
my reading of <u>Boetius</u> of the <u>Consolation of
Philosophy</u>, translated into <u>Italion</u>, by <u>Cosimo
Bartoli</u>.

Farewell, bright Golde, thou glory of the worlde,
25   Faire is thy show, but foule thou mak'st the soule:
Farewell, prowde Mynde, in thousand Fancies twirld:
    Thy pompe, is lyke the Stone, that still doth rowle. SISIPHUS.

Farewell, sweete Love, thou wish of worldly joy,
    Thy wanton Cuppes, are spiste with mortal sin:
30 Farewell, dyre Hate, thou doost thy selfe annoy,
    Therefore my hart, no place to harbour in.

Envy, farewel, to all the world a foe,
    Lyke DENNIS BULL, a torture to thy selfe:
Disdayne, farewell, though hye thy thoughts doe flow,
    Death comes, and throwes, thy Sterne upon a shelfe.

5   Flatterie, farewell, thy Fortune dooth not last.
    Thy smoothest tales, concludeth with thy shame:
Suspect, farewell, thy thoughts, thy intrayles wast,
    And fear'st to wounde, the wight thou faine woul'dst blame./

Sclaunder, farewell, which pryest with LYNX his eyes,
10   And canst not see, thy spots, when all are done:
Care, Care, farewell, which lyke the Cockatrice:
    Doest make the Grave, that al men faine would shun.

And farewell world, since naught in thee I finde
    But vanytie, my soule in Hell to drowne:
15 And welcombe Phylosophy, who the mynde
    Doest with content, and heavenly knowledge crowne.

    During the time, that my thoughtes swounded
with the charme of my passionate Musick, the
Sun decked in his most gorgious Raies, gave a <u>bon</u>
20 <u>Giorno</u>, to the whole troupe: and so many as were,
within the sownde of my Instrument, were drawne,
with no lesse vertue, then the Steele unto the
Addamant. In so much, of the suddaine, to beholde
the statelynesse of the presence, I was dryven
25 foorth of my muse, with a starklyng admyration,
not unlyke unto him, that sleeping over a dying
brand, is hastelye wakened with the lyghtenynge
of a thousande sparcles.
    The offices of Curtesie discharged on every
30 part, <u>Segnior Soranso</u> sayed: the Poets fayned not

without reason, that <u>Amphions</u> <u>Harp</u> <u>gave</u> <u>sence</u> <u>unto</u>
<u>stone</u> <u>Walles</u>. For so devine (quoth hee) are the   A commendation
operations, and vertues of Musick: As he that   of Musick.
shall be bounde, to declare her particuler Graces,
5 shall be no lesse troubled then the Paynter <u>Zeuxes</u>
was in the counterfettinge of <u>Cupid</u>: Who after
much travell, was driven to draw him blynde, for
otherwise, he had under taken <u>Sisiphus</u> taske,
because the twinckling reflections of <u>Cupids</u> eies,   A fayning
10 threw a thousande Beauties upon his face, and   how CUPID
shadowed the worke of the Paynter.   came to be
          Thus through Ignoraunce, <u>Cupid</u> hath ever   called
since bin reputed blinde, and for his owne   blinde.
perfection, is honoured with the title of the <u>God</u>
15 <u>of</u> <u>Love</u>. The name of <u>Love</u> gave/ a large occasion   H3^v
of discourse: but for that an other tyme was
appoynted for those disputations, and the morninge
was wholly dedicated, unto the service of God:
the question drowned in <u>Soransos</u> suggestion, and
20 the whole company scylent, in such affayres,
attended Queene <u>Aurelias</u> comming: who, in chaunge
of gorgious, and rich apparell, kept her
accustomed howre, to go unto the Chappel. By that
time service was ended, and every mans devotion
25 donne, dinner was ready to be set uppon the Tables,
with such choyce of delicate Viandes, as unto the
bountie of the Feast, there might nothing be added.
          After that Queene <u>Aurelia</u> and the rest, had
taken their ordinarye places, every one helped the
30 disgestion of their meate, either in inventing
some civill merriment, or in hearinge it reported
by an other.
          <u>Bergetto</u> all this while, was neither heard
to speake, nor seene to smyle.

The Thyrde Dayes Exercise 79

Which, perceived by <u>Franceschina</u> <u>Sancta</u> his
Mistres, she (moved with the spirit of compassion)
studied, howe with Justice, shee might revoke her
sentence, and unstring her servauntes tongue: and
5 to that ende, shee demaunded, how three good turnes,
might be unrewarded, three offences pardoned, three   A question
injuryes leaft unrevenged, and in everye of these,   to trye a
Justice preserved? This question passed through   quicke witt.
the table: and retourned without his true
10 resolution.

    In the end (quoth <u>Segnior</u> <u>Philoxenus</u>) <u>Monsier</u>
<u>Bergetto</u>, what is your opinion?

    Sir (quoth <u>Bergetto</u>) my Mistresse hath locked
the tongue, that should pronounce it.

15   Why (quoth <u>Franceschina</u>) these be no questions
of love, and therefore you have libertie to speake.

    No Lady (quoth <u>Bergetto</u>) but his vertue may
appeare in the aunsweare.

    Well (quoth his Mystresse) if you canne cleare
20 your trespasse, by one of these questions, I must
do no injurie to Justice, and therefore, saye your
pleasure.

    Uppon this warrant (quoth <u>Bergetto</u>) to your
first/ three, I aunsweare, A Captayne maye betray   H4^r
25 his charge, which is a benefit to the enemy: but   Three good
the betrayer, is not to be received as a friende: turns, may
for he that will sell his countryman, may not be   be received,
held assured, to a straunger. Secondly, a Theefe   unrewarded.
that peacheth his fellowes, doeth good to the
30 Common wealth: and yet, deserveth no reward: for
he that may previleadg his own theft, in bewraying
other mens, will evermore steale upon presumption.
Thirdly, to win a mans money, is a good turne, and
yet the loser is not to be recompenced: for his

intent, was to winne the winners.

    To your second three questions, a man maye offende through ignoraunce, which is excused without a pardon: for ignoraunce, is without intent of evill: therfore to be suffered, though not to be cherished: A man may offend, through necessitie, which commendeth Justice, with the vertue to forgive: for necessity, is bound unto no law, and therefore, deserveth not to be punnished with the rigour of law: To the third, a man may offend through rashnes, and make amends with repentance: which Justice may pardon, without prejudice to equity: and herein (faire Mistres) I have showen my trespas, and the reparation of my trespasse. *(Three offences, may with Justice be pardoned.)*

    To your third three questions, a man may hurt his friend against his will, which is an injurie: yet, ought not to be revenged: for revenge, can but afflict the trespasser, and the misfortune, greeveth him: Before the husband, a man may kisse the wife, by mistaking: which is an injury, not to be revenged: for the wife may wipe away the wrong with her hand, and the husband by revenge, may make worke for the Chirurgion: And to the last, a man must be content to take good wordes of a beggerly debtor: which is an injury not to be revenged: for a man can have of a Cat but her skin, and of a begger, but his scrip: unles he wil sel the Appothecary the greace of the one, and the dice maker, the bones of the other. *(Three injuries, may pas unrevenged.)*

    The whole company gave a verdict, that <u>Bergetto</u>, had expounded his Mistres doubts without blemish to Justice: and therfore were ernest suters for his remission. Whom she

pardoned, with this proviso, that he should
behave himselfe honourably towardes women
heareafter./ For his lybertie, Bargetto
reverently kissed his Mistresses hande, and thus
5 all unkindnesse pacified.

    Queene Aurelia movyng alitle, raisde the
companye, from the Table, who a pretty tyme after
dinner, had respyt, to prepare their wits, for
the accustomed exercise.

10   The Clocke had no sooner sounded the
disputation howre: But Queene Aurelia, and her
Ladies were redy in the drawinge Chamber, and
upon warnyng, the chosen Gentilmen gave their
attendaunce: who havyng taken their places, the
15 Eunuck (knowing his charge) unto the Lute sung
this Sonet,

To thee I sende, thou fayrest of the fayre,
The Vowes and Rites, of an unfayned hart:
Who with my plaintes, doe pearce the subtil Ayre,
20 That Beautie thou, maist heare and see my smart.
Who sues, but that thy Deputie on earthe,
May take in gree, my off'ringes of good wyll,
And in accompt returne my Love in worth.
With charge thy priestes, my bones to Ashes burne:
25 And with the same, thy Aulters all to meale,
That I may make (to serve, eche Lovers turne)
The peace off'ring, with Sacrifice of zeale.

    This Sonet in Beauties behalfe, put the
whole companie in remembraunce of Doctor Mossenigoes
30 last nights lavish speach of Beauty, and the
scandalous comparyng of her to Poyson, or, which
is worse, a more subtil infection: And therefore,

The Thyrde Dayes Exercise   82

to bee resolved of his wronge, or her gyltines,
Queene Aurelia, appointed Monsier Bargetto to be
her Champion, and to assist him, (for it was agreed
that free choice of Mariage, shoulde (this daye)
5 bee disputed: whose affection for the most
proceedeth from the vertue of Beautie,) she
lycensed every one that favoured her cause: which
done, she willed the Doctor and his favourers to
spit their venym./

10   Maddame (quoth the Doctor,) it neither   J1^r
beseemeth the stayednes of my yeares, nor agreeth   Olde men are
with the gravetie of my profession, in such an   bound by
assembly, to speake the thing I dare not avouch,   their gravitie,
and therefore since it cometh to this issue, that   to say no more
15 I must, hazard upon a charge, or shrinke away with   then they will
shame: though my ennemyes be many, my cause is   stand to.
juste: uppon which warrant I am feareles of my
foes, and resolute in myne opinion.

Bergetto likewise glad of this favour,
20 protested before Queene Aurelia and the whole
company, that in the faithfull execution of his
charge, the prodygall spoyle of hys lyfe, should
give contempt to death.

The Doctor, that had given as many deepe   The dashe of
25 woundes with his Pen, as ever he had doone with   a Pen, is more
his Launce, shronke no more at these threates,   greevous then
then an Oke at the Helve of an Axe, but coldely   the counterbuff
wylled him, to use his pleasure, he was ready to   of a Launce.
defend (or to die, in) his oppinion.

30   Whereupon Bergetto, to strengthen himself
the better, made this remembraunce, of the
yesterdayes reporte.

It is (quoth he) already approved, if the   Free choise
married in forced Mariages, could as well finish

with the Church, as they can account with their   in Mariage
consciences: their joy to be Married was not so   defended.
colde, as their desire to be devorsed would be
whot: therfore by this awkeward successe in
5 forcement: a free choise in Mariage, can not
choose, but continue (as I thinke) as much love
betweene the Married, as the other sowed debate.

     Rashnes and constraint (quoth the Doctor)   Reproofe, &c.
are bothe violents and every violent is a vice,
10 then how can a vicious attempt have a vertuous
successe: Men doo evill (quoth <u>Bergetto</u>) that   Defence, &c.
good may come of it, and it is allowed.

     And men doo good (quoth the Doctor) that   Reproofe, &c.
evill may come of it, and it is forbidden: for
15 it is the intent bothe in good and evill, that
commendeth or condemneth: and what good intent
hath the foolishe young man, that by his rashnes
in Marriage, robbeth his parentes of their
comfort, and him selfe of his credit./

20   He satisfieth his fancie (quoth <u>Bergetto</u>) a   J1^v
speciall regarde in Marriage: and where there is
a sweete accorde betweene the married, the
parents cannot but rejoice, and the neighbours
are bound to speake well: and beautie in his
25 wives face, will feede his heart with a thousand
delights: so that he shall sustaine want with
little greefe, and labour to get wealth with a
great desire: for where unitie is, small things
groweth to great.

30   Such may be the unitie (quoth the Doctor) as   Reproofe, &c.
small greefes may growe to great sorrowes: when
the winde is in the neck of a stooping Tree, it
falleth downe right: and when the unthriftines of
the Husband, agreeeth with the evill huswiferie of

the Wife, Sorrow striveth to be in the married
mans bosome, before the maried be in his wives
bead: and what other expectation may there be,
either of the one or the other, when he satisfyeth
5 his fancie, before he considereth of the dutyes
of Mariage: and she in taking an husband, that
is ignoraunt in the affaires of husbandry, and
in offices of Mariage: It is the office of the   Duties
married, to be advised ere he love, and loving to   before
10 be reposed in his choise: It is the office of the   Mariage.
married to provide for an Household, before he
take possession of his hearts delight: and it is
the office of the marryed, to examine the
conditions of his Mistresse, before he enter into
15 any covenaunt of Mariage. And how can he be
advised, that marrieth without the privitie of
his Parents? and how can he supporte an household,
that marryeth with his Parents displeasure, upon
whose devotion he liveth? and how can he judge of
20 his Mistresse conditions, that wanteth discretion
to consider of his owne estate? And where you
alledge, the beautie of his wives face, wyll feede
the husband with delight: his delight will starve
his body, without other supplyes: so that when
25 charge shall increase, and his wealth diminish,
let the foolish younge marryed man, impose him
self upon this fortune, that he cannot so oft
kisse the sweete lippes of his beautifull wife, as
he shalbe driven to fetche bitter sighes, from his
30 sorrowfull hart./

    Sir (quoth <u>Soranso</u>, taking <u>Bergettos</u> parte:)   J2^r
of two evils the least is to be chosen: and it is   Defence, &c.
lesse evill for a man, to lyve a while hardly, and
satisfye his owne fancie, then to live ever

discontented and please his freendes. The good
behaviour of the maryed, may winne the Parents to
consent, and amend their exhibition: or death
may come, and put them in possession of theyr
5   Parentes lyving.
    If either of these chaunce, as one is
shortely like to happen, the penaunce that they
indured, wyll season theyr prosperitie, and
counsell the Married to keepe within their
10 teather, to leape within their latchet, and lyve
within theyr compasse: The loving advise of the
husband, wyll reforme the disposition of evill in
the wife. For (as Plato sayeth,) there is no   No man nor
woman so perfect good, but in some one point may   woman, but
                                                      in some point
15 be reprehended: nor no man so faultlesse, but   deserve to be
that somewhat in him may be amended: so that if   blamed, and
                                                      in some other
the Husband gently reprehend the fault of his   to be praised.
Wife, and the Wife patiently suffer the offence
of her Husband, the abylytie of theire estate
20 wyll sustaine a househould, and their loove and
agreement wilbe an especiall comfort unto them
selves, and a commendable example unto all the
neighbours.
    The best of bothe your evils (quoth Doctor
25 Mossenigo) is starke naught: but our question was   Reproofe, &c.
not, to chuse the least of evyls, but that which
is simply good: notwithstanding, to aunswer to
the sequell of this rashenesse in Mariage, you
saye, theyr good behaviours may recover theyr
30 Parents good wyll, but I Prophesie, that theyr
evill demeanures, are more likely to extinguish
the affection of a Father: for necessitie wyll
accustome the Husband with dishonest shyftes, and
keepes his fayre Wife from beeing ydle: for want

muste be supplyed, what shame so ever ensue.
Then is it lykely, that the Parentes which did
shutte their Pursses in the beginning, to punishe
the contempt of their Chyldren,/wyll now fast
5 locke them, to be revenged of theyr infamie.
And where you gave them a hope, by their parentes
death, I say no man dyneth worse, then hoping
Tantalus, nor none are more wetshod, then they
which expect deade mens shooes, and when they
10 fall, the soules (perhaps) wilbe worne: I meane
the Father in his life tyme, may take order to
dye even with the worlde, or at leaste, leave his
living maimed, and the most of his substaunce
wasted: for in a tempest at Sea, what Pylote hath
15 any care of goodes, that seeeth the ship, at the
poynte to syncke: even so what parents can have
any joye of worldly wealth (more then to defende
necessytye) when he seeth, the heyre bothe of his
labour, and lyving, out of hope of weldooing: so
20 that through this rashnesse many sonnes, during
their fathers lyves, with hard shiftes, shift of
necessity, and after their deathes live disinherited:
and not altogether so much for their owne contempt,
as for their wives incontinencye: and truely in
25 the fyrst, although the parentes may be thought
cruell, yet are they not to be reputed unnaturall,
for that every offence hath his proper scourge:
restitution is the true payne for robbery: an
eye is revenge for an eye, a hand for a hande,
30 death challengeth death, and disobedience in the
sonne, deserveth disinheritaunce, by the father.
Touching the dishonesty of the daughter in lawe
(as it is great hazarde but that necessitie, thus
bestowed, will bend her a little:) the severitie

Their pennaunce is great that live in incertaine hope.

An ungodly childe maketh an unthriftie Father.

The several paines of offences.

Incontinency

is sufferable, if her husbandes father shut her forth of his doores, for that the honour of a mans house is so delicate, as it can awaie with no staine: and (reservyng your favours vertuous dames) where a strumpet entereth, she stuffeth the house with slaunder, as carraine infecteth the ayre with stincke, yea the occasion is just: if the father spare to gette, and the mother cease to save, nay if they spend that which they have, for it weare great pitty, that there should be any thing leafte either of their livyng or labour, to support a harlots pride. O how innumerable are the inconveniences, of this timeritye in Marriage? The wise by conjecture and daylye/ experience seeeth, and the foolish (with sorrowe in theyr own entrailes) feeleth: and therfore as a hainous offence: the aunciect Philosophers (which without partiallitie, checked <u>Vice</u> and cherrished <u>Vertue</u>) punished this contempt of Children. <u>Plutarke</u> saythe, the sonne that marryeth without his Parents consent, among the <u>Greekes</u> was publikely whipped: among the <u>Lacedemonians</u> dishearited, and among the <u>Theabanes</u> bothe disinhearited, and of his Parents openly accursed.

    The yonger company, began to feare a restraint of <u>Freeloves</u> libertie, and their Goddesse <u>Beauties</u> disgrace: The Doctor gave Capitaine <u>Bergetto</u> such crosse blowes, who though he fainted in his opinion, yet (like a Cocke, that hath one of his eyes stricken out, and his head bared to the braines, yet striketh untill he dyeth) he assayled the Doctor with this one more reason.

    Maister Doctor (quoth he) they go farre that never returne, and the battaile is very cruell

Margin notes:
- slaundereth an honest mans house.
- J3ʳ
- Paynes for timerity in Marriage.
- Defence, &c.

where none escapes: what although a number
speede yll in making of their owne choyce, many
have prospered well. In matches of the best
foresight, good Fortune hath not alwayes beene
5 found, and yet foresight is not to be blamed, nor
the other adventure to be dispitefully condemned.
<u>Ovid</u> sayeth, that <u>Forma numen habet</u>, then by
vertue of her Divinitie, it is like she will
sustaine them in adversity, that in prosperity
10 became her vowed Servaunts: neither dooth this
stayne of the wives behaviour often follow, for
where <u>Beautie</u>, <u>Love</u>, and <u>Free choise</u>, maketh the
Mariage, they may be crossed by <u>Fortune</u>, and yet
continue faithfull. <u>Piramus</u> and <u>Thisbie</u>, <u>Romeus</u>
15 and <u>Juliet</u>, <u>Arnalt</u> and <u>Amicla</u>, and divers others
at the point to possesse their loves, were
dispossesst of their lives, but yet unstained
with dishonesty. This want with which you
threaten them, what is it in respect of the
20 pleasures these Lovers possesse? <u>Wealth</u> which is   A discription
the contrarie, what is it, beeing ill used? a   of wealth
beautie in the Chest, a bondage to the minde, and   abused.
a blot in the soule: but a couple united by this
affection, for a little Fleabiting of worldly/
25 pennury, suck <u>Nectar</u> betweene their lippes, Cram   J3^v
<u>Manna</u> into theyr Bowels, and possesse Heaven in   The joye of
their hearts. How farre Maister Doctor argueth   true love.
from the opinion of auncient Philosophers, and
famous Schoolemen, these authorities witnesseth:
30 <u>Ovid</u>, <u>Nigidius</u>, <u>Samocratius</u>, <u>Petrarke</u>, and others
in their life time, addored <u>Beautie</u>, with their
bookes honoured her, and by their deathes eternized
her glorye. But for that her vertues be Divine,
and Maister Doctor is soyled with slaunder,

blasphemy and mallice, he is unworthy to be
perfected, with one thought of her excellencie,
which ignorance maketh him so obstinate. The
yonger company began to take heart, in hearing of
5   this Tale, so that the Gentlewomen strengthened
Bergetto with good countenaunces, for (for modesties
sake) they were silent, and the Gentlemen succoured
him with theyr best reasons. But all this hope
prooved but a lyghtning joye: for Doctor Mossenigo,
10 dubble inraged, partly for the check he receyved,
partly for the countenaunce the company gave his
adversarie: but cheefely for to behold a new
Dye, set upon a stayned matter, so sharpely
refuted Bergetto, as he had no delyght to reply,
15 nor his supporter desire to succor him. (Quod
he) Ovid dreamed of a divinity in Beautie, but
never tasted other then a sweete venim, to
proceede from her: He loved Julia, Augustus
Daughter, and enjoyed her: but with what fortune?
20 marry, he was stript of his living, and spoyled
of his libertie, for her sake. Nigidius, an   Sundry famous
auncient Romaine, and in great favour with the   Philosophers
people, for this folly, tasted of Ovids fortune,   and Poets
which was, to dye in exile. Samocratius was in   punished for
                                                      their loves.
25 youthe, so prodigall of his Love, as in age
hated of his freendes, he dyed in Prison, with
famine. And as for frantick Petrarke, I feare
me Madonna Laura smyled more often in reading of
his follyes, then he himselfe did, with the
30 sweete recompences of his fancies. All these
were men learned, wise, and in their other
actions (for their gravitie) were admyred, and
onely for their lightnesse in love, live to this
day defamed: For your/ other authorities, your   J4^r

owne remembraunce of theyr deathes, shew a
vengeaunce sufficient, for the contempt of the
Children. But where you say **Beautie**, **Love**, and
Free choyse, lade the Maried with such pleasures,
5 that they endure povertie, as a Fleabiting. In
deede, want wyll so quicken them, as the Husband
wyll leape at a Cruste, and the Wife trot for her
Dinner. But suppose the best, thus married (whose
loves are indifferent) with patience doo indure
10 the afflictions of **Fortune**: theyr agreement is   Cause of
no generall warrant. The greater number of these   rashe
Mariages, are not solempnyzed, through equaltye   Mariages.
of love, but through inequaltye of lyvyng. The
coveitous Marchaunt, with no more delight heereth
15 the passing bell of his ritch neyghbour, which
promyseth hym the first loppe of his sonnes
livyng, then the poore gentleman eyeth the able
heyre, with desyre to match him (perhappes) with
his fayre proude Daughter. Then as pleasaunt
20 baytes baineth Fyshe, as counterfet Calles
beguileth Foules, and as Crocadyles teares,
intrappeth Fooles: to lyke destruction, lures
are throwne to lime this gallant: freendly usage
shall intyce hym, good wordes shall welcome hym,
25 curtesy shall cheere hym, **Beauty** shall bewitch hym,
and fayre promises, shall altogeather beguile hym.
Newe Vessels are apt for any licquor, and young
heades (empty of experyence) are seduced, with
easey subtiltyes, to be shorte, he shalbe
30 betrothed by cunning: hys promyse once past (for   An
that in delaye, is daunger) the Mariage must be   unfortunate
in poste haste, and the mislikyng at leasure: Mariage.
but in most of these matches, the sorrowe
begynneth, before the solemnitye of the Marriage

endeth. The father hearyng of the indiscression
of his sonne, galleth his harte with greefe: the
mother, spoyleth her eyes wyth teares, and the
freend occupyeth his tounge, in bemoning of hys
5 kynsemans follye. There is yet a further sorrowe,
bytter to the father and unbenefyciall to the
sonne. The father that thought to bestowe hys
daughter wyth the Marryage money of hys sonne, is
forced/ to diminishe his inheritaunce, for her   J4^v
10 advauncement. And by this meanes, the joye which
begunne in the beautie of his Wife, is like to
end in the beggery of himselfe: and since these
unsaverie effectes, growe from the vertue of
<u>Beauties</u> Divinitie, let <u>Mounsier</u> <u>Bergetto</u> burne
15 in his Heresie.

But Doctor <u>Mossenigo</u> will holde himselfe
happie, never to be warmed by her fyre.

<u>Bergetto</u> had not a worde more to saye, but   A Gentleman
angerly looked upon his Sworde, with a   in his
20 countenaunce that promised vengeance upon the   revenge ought
Doctors blasphemous tongue, had he not beene   not to offend
stayed with a reverent consideration of the   a civill
company.   company.

In the end, because Maister Doctor should
25 not be too proude of his conquest, nor <u>Bergetto</u>
overmuch appalled with his defeate, (quoth
<u>Signior</u> <u>Fabritio</u>, Judge of the controversies:)
in a single controversie the argument of the one,
is to be allowed as truthe, and the caviling of
30 the other, to be rejected as error: but for that
this hath beene a double contention, as in
defence and reproofe, bothe of <u>Beautie</u> and <u>Free</u>
<u>choise</u> of Mariage, <u>Madona</u> <u>Isabella</u>, and I,
pronounce sentence with <u>Bergetto</u>, in the behalfe

of <u>Beautie</u>, for <u>Beautie</u> is a blessing, and if she
worke evill effectes in some, their naughtie
disposition, and not <u>Beautie</u> is to be blamed: and
with Doctor <u>Mossenigo</u> we likewise give judgement
5 in reproofe of rashenesse in Mariage.

    This judgement pleased Queene <u>Aurelia</u> and
the whole company, who were glad that they were
thus forewarned of the inconveniences of <u>Free
choise</u> in <u>Love</u>, which they a little favoured, but
10 yet were more glad of the Triumphe of <u>Beautie</u>,
whom they all affectedly honoured: and therefore
(quoth Queene <u>Aurelia</u>,) good Wine neede no Ivie   Vertue
Bushe, fyne Marchaundise are solde without a Signe,   commendeth
and <u>Beautie</u> is sufficiently commended by her owne   her selfe.
15 excellencie, and therefore we wyll spare
<u>Bergettos</u> ready service, untill oportunitie,
present further imployment./ But for that your   K1^r
Tryumphe shall have his full right, we licence
you to tel some one Historie to confirme your
20 reasons.

    The Doctor glad of this lybertie, who
(althoughe he had receyved no Disgrace, yet he
repined that he had not the whole honour of the
Disputation,) determyned in his Historie, a litle
25 more to nettle the favourers of <u>Beautie</u>: with
which intent, upon Queene <u>Aurelias</u> commaundemente,
he reported as followeth.

    <u>The Historie in reproofe of rash Mariages,
        reported by Doctor Mossenigo.</u>
30   Besides <u>Capo Verdo</u>, in times past, the
capitall Citie, within the kingdome of <u>Naples</u>,
sometime dwelled a forward young Gentleman called
<u>Marco Malipiero</u>: the sonne and heire of <u>Cavaliero
Antonio Malipiero</u>, in his youthe renowned, for

manie valiant services. This young Gentleman in
the pride of his youth, became inamoured of a
most fayre Gentlewoman named Felice, the Daughter
of Philippo Provolo, an auncient Gentleman, by

Beautie, halfe a Dowrie in a woman.

5   harde adventure decayed. But yet in dispight of
fortunes injurie, who disabled him with many
losses, and thereby, of small wealth to advance
his Daughter: Felice her selfe was inriched with
suche perfections of nature, that the friends
10 lamented, but could not blame the affection of
young Malipiero: which in verie deede, grewe so
great, as it contemned the duetie of a childe, and
scorned the advise of a Father: Felice alone
governed him, and none but Felice he obeyed.

15   Provolo intertayned Malipiero, with the
curtisie of a friende, as much for the good partes he
possessed: as for the possibilitie of living he

The poore seeketh to matche with wealthy.

stoode in, who (striking the yron while it was
whote) secreatelie fianced Malipiero to his fayre
20 Daughter. The old Knight stormed at these newes,
and notwithstanding this knowne contract, if by
any perswasions he could have revoked his sonnes
consent, he would have caused the Pope to have
dispensed with his consci-/ence: and to that
25 effect, hee caused sundry of his friendes to
deale with him in these affayres. And among many
an auncient Gentleman, his Governour, and
somtimes his Schoolemaister (whose gravetie,
Malipiero reverensed) in a mylde order commoned
30 with him, and amonge other questions demaunded,
with what reason he could justifye his light
affections, and condemne the sounde advyce of
friendes.

    Malipiero, resolute in his love, boldly

aunswered, that <u>Felices</u> devine beauty, was a
sufficient warrant for ether.

    This wise Governour would not harden his
hart with obstinacy, in a sharp reprehension of
his publike arrogant aunswere, but with an
affable countenaunce, conjured hym to lysten unto
his grave sayinges.

    O (quoth he) is she beautifull? then you
have worke inough to watch her, and mischance
sufficient to suspect her.

    Is she beautifull? then her rashnesse in
consent, showeth that she is indiscreet: so that
the diversitie of quallities will soone finde out
a division in your desires.

    Is she beautifull? then it is lyke (by her
quick agreement) that she is poore, then is her
Love fastened on your riches: so that when you
lacke money to maintaine her pompe, she leaves,
to make much of your person.

    Is she beautifull? then she is withall
(lightly) proude, and the pride of a woman (saith
<u>Periander</u>) is lyke unto a Dropsey: for as drinke
encreaseth the drouth of the one, so (sayeth he)
Cost enlargeth the expence of the other: then
if your Purse be not open to feede her folly,
she will pawne her honour to please her fancy.

    Is she beautifull? then her indiscreation,
in this hastinesse, showes her but a slender
huswife, so that the charge of your house, shall
eate and consume your gaines abroade. Is she
beautiful? then your dispence, must be in her
disposition, or els her lookes will litle repose
you: if she order your goodes, her expences will
be great, and her gettinges small, your house

Marginalia:
- A rash aunswer.
- The wordes sheweth the wit of the reporter, but his gesture causeth attention in the hearer.
- The nature of Pride.

shall be stored with costlye stuff, and your
servants starved with lack of meate: she will/
goe like a Pecock, and you like a meacock: what K2^r
followeth? in her bravery, she must be seene: if
5 she take the lyberty to walk, shee giveth other
occasion to speake, and your selfe to sigh. A
faire picture set in the Market place, moveth
many to gase: if the counterfet giveth contentment,
the creature must needes delight: and if any view
10 your wife with unlawfull affection, his practises
wil be many to win his desyre. Take heede, you
undertake an intisinge course, which without good
order, will make you breathlesse before the midst
of your race: you enter into great charge, see
15 meanes to support it. Your Father lives, and must
maintaine his accustomed reputation: if he spare
to sustaine you, it is much: to defraye the charge,
of your Wife and housholde, he cannot: therefore
so love, that this dispence may be shared betweene
20 you, and your wives Parents: and as far foorth as
I can see, <u>Felices</u> Father hath much adoe, to keepe
rayne out of his house top: then if with
difficultie he lieth drye in his Bed, it is
impossible he should have anye great cheare at
25 his Boorde: what reckonyng can you make, to be
supported by him that hath it not? and howe can
you dare presume, to bee supplyed by your owne
Father? when the timeritie of your marriadge
displeaseth him to death. Looke into these
30 mischeeves, before you feele the miseries they
presage: looke before you leape, leaste you be
wet, before you be a ware: your friendes hath
a comfort, but you the benefite of weldooing.

The Schoolemaister gave <u>Malipiero</u> this

advice, with such a temperate gesture: that
(although good counsell prevailed not,) yet he
reverently told him, that his experience knew   Love
more, then his greene imagination could containe: enjoyneth us
                                                    to do what
5   and therefore, he woulde meditate of his loving we kno is
admonition, and proceede no further without his   amis.
privitie. But ah, these weare but sweete wordes
to betraye himselfe, and to blinde his friende.
For uppon the first oportunytie Malipiero speeds
10 unto Philippo Provolo, and recountes the
importunyties of hys Freendes,/ with a desire to   K2^V
have the Mariage previlie solemnised, since that
he could not obtaine the open consent of his
parentes.

15   Provolo, fearing the daunger of delay, was
as ready to satisfy, as Malipiero was earnest to
request: insomuch as early in a morning, Marco
Malipiero, was set in possession of his hearts   An early
delight: and before night, was dispossessed of   mariage,
                                                    worketh a
20 his whole bodies welfare: For his sorrowful   late
Father, and heavy friends, hearing of this suddaine repentaunce.
Mariage, after they had a while bemoned, the
rashnes of Malipiero, with the Affection of
Parentes, menaced to punish his oversight (in
25 not regarding him) as Strangers.

        Provolo, on the other side, to geve knowledge
to his Sonne in Lawes frendes, that althoughe   The rewarde
Fortune had crossed him, she had not wholly   of pryde, is
consumed him: set out his abylytie to the most   povertie.
30 Advauntage: much like unto a Market Marchant,
that on a Newyears Day mornyng, exposeth his
painted tokens, to the ritchest show: His Sonne
(in lawe) was accomodated with the Attyre and
furnyture of a Gentleman, and his Wife was set

foorth, with the showe, of rich Malipieroes
Heires Espouse, and not as poore Provoloes
Daughter: Insomuch, as the common sorte, blinded   The common
with showes, judged after their eyes affection,   sorte Judge
                                                       as they
5 and reputed old Malipiero a cruel covetous Churle, affect.
for dealing with Provolo so frowardly, that had
intreated his Son so honorably. But these
murmurings, litle moved the good auncient Knight:
for well he wist, this braverie was but a blase,
10 as soone ended as the flame of a drie Faggot.
And which should avenge him, this pride promised
a change, attyred with as much pennurie as the
other with pompe.

 The following effect, confirmed olde
15 Malipieros opinion: for Provolo spent so largely
at the beginning, in hope with this florishe, to
make accorde betweene the Sonne and the Father:
As nowe his Table was furnished with emptie
Platters, and his Audit Bagges with a set of   The miserye
20 Counters. So that want, that will make a tooth-/   of want.
lesse woman to bite at Brasen Walles, entred into
Provolos House, and swore both him and his whole   K3^r
householde unto the statutes of necessitie: whose
lawes were so straite, that although they all had
25 great occasion of sorowe, they had no leasure
for shifting to supplie their wantes: In so much
as in shorte time, there was no neighbour, that
Provolo was not in his debt or daunger, and no
good natured youth there aboutes, that Marco
30 Malipiero had not boorded or coosoned.

 And what shoulde faire Felice doe in this
extremitie? live upon her husbandes travel, and
be idle her selfe? that were no good Huswiferie:
and yet poore Malipiero loved her so dearely,

that hee woulde have ventured uppon a thousande
infamies, to maintayne her in the state of an
honest Gentlewoman: but although his shiftes
helped, they defrayed not her desire to be brave.
5 A Diamond hath not his grace but in golde, nor a
fayre Woman, her full commendation but in the
ornamentes of braverie. So that attyred to her   Braverye
best advantage, faire Felice would manie times   belongeth
                                                             to Beautie.
walke, unto the Piatso Richio, a place where the
                                                             PIATSO, a
10 bravest Gentlemen assembled, and where the fynest   marketplace
devices were sould: she taking this liberty to   or a place
walke, bound the gallant yong Gentlemen, in   of assembly.
curtesie to Court her: curtuous service, is to
be accepted with thankes: acceptance of service,
15 inlargeth acquaintance: acquaintance ingendreth
familiarytie: and famyliaritie, setteth al Folies
abroach: So that, let other Married men take   A necessarye
warnyng, by Malipieroes hard fortune: for, if   note.
their wyves love gadding, lyke faire Felice, and
20 be inconstant, do want, or finde in their Husbands,
miscontentment: Twentie to one, they wil pawn
their honours, to please their fancies.

    Well, Felice lost nothyng by these Jorneyes:
for some one Gallant, would present her with a
25 Ventoie, to coole her selfe: some other, with a
Mirrour, to behould her selfe: and some, with   Courtesy don
Lawnes, Ruffes, Coyfes, and suche necessaries, to   with an evill
                                                             intent.
set out her selfe: and yet upon no dishonorable
condition, but (by your leave) wyth hope of an
30 after favour./

    This trafique, faire Felice used, untill   K3^V
(amonge a number, that temperately affected her,)
Marino Giorgio, the rich Orphant of Capo Verdo
immoderately loved her, and with all the honors

of courtisie served her: But notwithstanding,
his lusty personage, might please: his lovely
countenaunce, might intyce: and his rare wit,
passing through a swete tongue, might bewitch a
5 woman in love: for that Malipiero, was inritched   Disdaine
with these perfections: Felice, regarded Marino   haunteth
Georgio, but with an ordinary grace: and had it   desire.
not ben for that Archinchaunter, Golde (perhappes)
would never have bene inconstant.

10   This light account of Felice, inlarged the   The fyre
affection of Marino: for as drincke increaseth   of Love.
the dropsies drowth, so disdaine, heapeth coales
uppon desire: whereof Marino, (Teste se ipso)
hath leaft an infallible aucthoritie: whose
15 torments were so greevous, as the fire: which of
al flames, burneth most, and appeareth least,
burst out of his mouth, the smoake of such furious
sighes, that where he was but late, of a pure
Sanguine Complection, hee seemed nowe, nothyng,
20 but Choller adust: So that, his friendes mourned,
and many moned his strange alteration: who
counsayled him to take the Physitions advice: But
neither Galen, Hipocrates, nor their Enemie,
Paracelsus, could skyl of his cure: so that he
25 was in daunger to have consumed to Cinders, had
not Macrello, the Physition of Love, undertaken   Phisicke
his helth, who comforted him with many sweete   cureth not
wordes of hope: but, Marino, continually afflicted   love.
himselfe in recounting an impossibilytie of favour.
30   Why (quoth Macrello,) is not your parsonage
seemely? Yes: but it doth not please. Is not
your face lovely? Yes: but it doth not allure.
Is not your wyt quicke and good? Yes: but it
can not perswade. Is not Felice, a woman? Yes:

and more, an Angell.

Well, then (quoth Macrello,) be of good
comfort, Angelles be not cruell, nor steelie
harted.
5   O (quoth Marino,) but Felice, is constant,
and true to her husband, who to continue her
affection, is graced with these and many more
perfections./

Yea (quoth Macrello) but hee wanteth one of
10 your cheefest beauties.

What one is that (quoth Marino?) Even that,   The force
that opened the double locked dores of Acrisius   of Goulde.
brasen Tower, and put Jubiter in possession of
his daughter Danais love. And thinke you this
15 Goulden Beautie, will not make a passage into
poore Malipieros Bed Chamber? I warrant you yeas:
you have Goulde more at commaundement then I, but
I know the vertue better then you.

This short tale quickned dying Marrino, as
20 the flashe of Rose water dooth a sullen swounding
Childe.

Wherupon (quoth he) Macrello, if your
Medicine be of no lesse vertue to restore my lyfe,
then your wordes to geve me hope: the fortune,
25 shall be your profit, as wel as my pleasure.

Well (quoth Macrello) sustaine your selfe   Hope
with hope, and for that your invention is   comforteth
delicate, devise you some curious rich Juell, and   but Love
let mee alone (quoth hee) bothe to charme and to   cureth the
   Lover.
30 present it: and so with a remembraunce in the
hande, he left Marino, to contemplate of his love,
and to consider how to recover his lyfe: who in
the ende, concluded to sende faire Felice, the
Image of himselfe in Goulde, inameled blacke, his

face meager and pale, and by a device, the blacke
mantell throwne aside, for to appeare, the bared
Carkasse of Death, with the intrayles consumed,   Marinos
and in the seate of his lyfe, to place Felice,   Present to
5   attyred with Diamonds, Rubyes, Emrodes, and other his Mistrisse.
precious Stones, looking uppon his smoking harte,
wheruppon, was written these two breefes.

   Love onely gives mee health,
   Not Medicine nor wealth.

10 This Image made unto his fancye, he wrote
this following Letter./

  Marino Georgios letter, to Felice the fayre.   K4^v

  Fayre Mistresse, if I enjoyed any health, I
would wishe you parte: but what I do possesse, I
15 acknowledge to be yours, and my selfe to be, but
your steward. And for this service, because it
is duty, I crave nothing, but leave my merrit
wholly to your consideration. Yet, least my
scylence, shuld rob the glory of your pitty, and
20 my death, reave you of a faythfull Servaunt: more
of zeale, to do you long service: then of any
desyre I have to live. I heare present you my
consumed selfe, only kept alive, by the lyfe of
fayre Felice, who sitteth crowned, in the Pallace
25 of my heart: whych bleeding at her feete,
showeth the meanes of my cure: which if you
witsafe, I live: if not, you see my death. And
thus, doubtfull betweene both, untill I kisse
your sweete aunsweare, I remayne.

30   Unto my latter Gaspe,
       Your faythfull

       MARINO GEORGIO.

This letter Sealed, and Subscribed, <u>To the
hands of the most faire Felice</u>: Macrello was sent
for: to whom Marino delivered, both the Juell,
and the letter, with out instructions to do his
5 message: for Protheus could not chainge himselfe
into moe shapes then Macrello: as well, to
avoide suspition, as to compasse his purpose:
who behaved himselfe so cunningly, in Marinoes
errande, as (to be shorte, vertuous Dames) after
10 many perswasions, Felice returned him with this
Answere.

FELICES Answere, to Marino Georgio.

I am not cruell, althoughe with difficultie,
I consent too love: and for that your passions
15 are so extreame, I kepe your Picture in my Bosome:
But, with what thought, I blush to write, though
Pitie be my warrant: so that I leave the event
of our Love, to your Consideration: and my/
yealding, to Macrelloes Reporte: who, in
20 bewraying your passions, lette fall more teares,
then I could drie up with a thousand sighes: So
that overcom with rueth, to see your Affection
so great, and your passion so daungerous, I can
not but commyt my love, my honour, my selfe and
25 all, to the Affection and wise government of
Marino Georgio.

FELICE.

This Letter, was subscribed: <u>Lyfe, to
MARINO GEORGIO</u>: and delivered to the faithfull
30 Macrello: with charge, that he should make
knowen, his great Importunities, before Felice
woulde graunt so hye a favour: which Proviso,

might have ben spared: for <u>Macrello</u>, (partly
for his glorie, but chiefely, for his owne
benefite) upon delyverie of this Letter, willed
<u>Marino</u>, to receive it, as a Conquest as hardly
5 gotten, as <u>Hercules</u> labours: and if (quoth he)
I had not indured your torments (by Imagination)
it had not ben impossible to have mooved <u>Felice</u>
to rueth: <u>Marino</u>, heard these circumstances,
with no better remembrance, then if he had ben in
10 an Extasie: The Subscription: <u>Lyfe to Marino</u>:
overcame him with suche a sodayne passion of Joye,   Suddaine joy
who read, and a hundred times over read this Life   or sorrow
letter: and for that it came from <u>Felices</u> sweete   dulleth our
hand, he a thousand times kissed the Paper.   senses.

15   Which done, by the direction of <u>Macrello</u>,
this Conquerour <u>Gowlde</u>, made suche a passage,
into a reputed honest Cytizens House, as, without
suspition, <u>Marino Georgio</u>, and fayre <u>Felice</u>, theare
(many tymes) mette, but to what purpose, I leave
20 to your constructions: and yet, thus much I say: Gold maketh
this Fortune followed: <u>Marino</u>, in shorte space,   passage into
recovered his former Complection: and it was not   difficulte
long, before <u>Felice</u> was richer, then either Father   places.
or Husband.

25   But, O that Furie <u>Jelousie</u>, envying this
Accord, sent slie <u>Suspition</u>, to infect <u>Malipieroes</u>
heart: who pryinge with <u>Lynx</u> his eyes, presented   The venomous
him a thousande causes of mistrust, which love   nature of
straite suppress with as manie/ contrarie   Jelosye.
30 imaginations of his Wives good behaviour: inso
much, that with the sharp incounter of Love, and
mystrust, poore man, he was continually afflicted.

    In conclusion, seeing his Wife to exceede in   A shrewde
braverie, and knowing himselfe, to declyne with   suspition.

povertie, he resolved uppon this certentie: this
cost coulde not come from the emptie Coffers of
her undone Parentes: and then proceedinge from
others, it was impossible to bee the favours of   Suspect is
5 honest curtesie: so that armed with furie, he   more cunnyng,
deferred revenge, but to intrap the friende of his   then Argus
wives follyes, and the enymie both of her honour,   was warie.
and his delyght.

   In fine, as heedefull, as these Lovers were
10 in their dealinges, Jelosye directed suspecte, to
Marino Georgio: and moreover, made him an eye
witnesse of the injuries done unto Malipiero:
which when he assuredly knew, hee studied a while   Neapolitans,
of a torture, equall to this treacherie: for who   are most
15 hath not hard the Neapolitan to bee the severest   seveare in
revenger of dishonor in the world. To be breefe,   revenge.
his bait was this: he fayned a journey far from
home, and furnished him selfe, with such an
apparance of trueth, as tooke a way all colour of
20 suspition: whiche done, with a dissembling kysse,   A Judas kisse.
hee committed his wife to God, and the charge of
his house, to her good government: and so set
forwarde towards Rome.

   Malipiero was no sooner a mile on his way,
25 then Macrello certified Marino of this wished
oportunitie: and Love made both him and Felice
so boulde, as in his owne house they determyned
the followinge night, to exercise uppon Malipiero
their wonted injurie: but about mydnyght when
30 mistrust was at repose, Malipiero entred the
house with such a sodaine violence, as these two   A fit time,
unfortunate freendes, were surprysed amids their   to deceave
imbracements, before they had warnyng to shift: mistrust.
I sowrrow to tel the rest, but trueth will have

The Thyrde Dayes Exercise 105

passage.

  <u>Malipiero</u>, in his revenge like a Lyon
hungring after/ his pray: with his Rapier and
these bitter wordes nayled <u>Marino</u> unto the Bed.

L2^r

   <u>Thou Couche (quoth he) soyled with dishonour,
washe out thy staynes, with the Adulterers
blood.</u>

Death is too easie a scurge, for a disloyal wyfe.

But holding death too easy a scurge for his wives
trespas, hee condemned her to this torture, more
extreme then death: Hee made an <u>Anotomy</u> of her
welbeloved <u>Marino</u>, and set him in a fayre Chamber,
within whiche, hee inclosed his wyfe, without
dooing her any bodely injurie, save the cutting
of her haire: and to say trueth, this beautifull
ornament of haire, beseemeth not an Adultresse
head. And to punish her the more, <u>Malipiero</u>
caused her everie dinner and supper to take her
accustomed place, that at meales shee might be
tormented with the sighte of her lyvinge enemie,
and all the daye with the bones, of her martired
friende: neither could she quenche her thirst,
but out of a Mazar, made of <u>Marrinoes</u> skull. But
(to tell her vertue, with her vice) hir patience
was suche, as shee was never harde to complaine
of this crueltie: and yet her penitent sorrowe
so great, as the plentie of her teares, somtimes
moved her injured Husbande to pittie.

Haire, the ornamentes of Chastytie.

The bounden office of a Writer.

  But least he should be overcome with
compassion, manie times from dinner, hee commaunded
her to her pryson: who after an humble reverence,
went behind the Tapestrie Hanginges, and so unto
her solitarie Chamber, barred from other companye,
then the gastly bones of unfortunate <u>Marino</u>:
whiche pennaunce shee patientlye indured, untyll

Justice, must not yealde to the teares of Trespassers.

GOD, who saw that her repentaunce was unfayned,
sent Segnior Cornaro to bee a peace maker betweene   God regardeth
her Husbandes injurie, and her offence: who (when   repentaunce.
Supper was sette uppon the Boorde) seeing from
5 behinde the Tapistrie Hanginges, a fayre Gentlewoman
to appeere, somewhat pale with sorrowe, her head
bare, both of attyre and Hayre, apparrelled all in
black, and in her hand, her drynking Bowle of
Marinoes scul, and saying never a word, with a
10 sober reverence sitting down in the/ cheefest   L2^v
place: was stroken with such a maze, as on the
suddayne he wist not what to say.

Dinner being ended, which was longer, then
pleasant, either to husbande, wife, or friende:
15 Felice, as she entered so departed. Who,
notwithstanding, leaft part of her sorowe behinde
in Cornaros heart, whose cheareles countenance,
when Malipiero perceyved (quoth he) let not the
martyrdome of this Woman afflicte you: for her
20 fault deserveth this vengeaunce, and so recounted
the reported adventure. And in advantage, shewed
him her prison and the Annotomie of her dishonour,   A honorable
and withall licensed him to talke with Felice, to   favour.
heare what plee shee had for her discharge.
25 Uppon which warrant, (quoth Cornaro,) Madame, if
your patience be equall with your torment, I holde
you the most happie Woman of the worlde. Felice
with a countenance abased, and Cheakes dewed with
teares tolde him in humble wordes, that her
30 trespasse was tenne times greater, then the torment
which the Lorde of the House, whome shee was not   The true
worthie to call husbande, had appoynted her. And   ensigne of
therewithall, the sorow of her hart, tooke away   sorrowe.
the use of her tongue. Whereuppon Malipiero,

ledde the Gentleman awaye, who rendred him affected
thankes, in that, besides his good intertaynment,
he witsafed him the honour to knowe so great a
secreasie: withall, moved with compassion, hee
5 effectually intreated Malipiero, to accept Felices   True
sorrow the true witnes of grace and amendement, as   repentaunce,
satisfaction of her offence, which proceeded of   is to be
frayltie, and withall importuned him, with such   recevved in
earnest reasons as Malipiero was content to sende   satisfaction
                                                      of offences.
10 both for her and his owne friendes. To bee partly
ruled, and partly advised by them in her behalfe.

    The parentes and friendes of everie side
seeing the humilitie, sorowe, and patience, of
poore Felice, were all earnest sutors for her   Perfect love,
                                                      cannot be so
                                                      injured, but
15 remission.   it will alwais
                                                      retaine some
    The roote of auncient love not altogether   affection.
dead in Malipiero, was comforted with their
intercessions, and quicke-/ned with the hope of   L3^r
amendement: in so much, as uppon sollemne
20 promise to be hencefoorth of good behaviour, he
receyved her to grace: and to repayre her crased   A reparation
honour, with the favour of both their parentes,   of dishonour.
hee newe married fayre Felice, in which holy
estate, they lived, loved, and agreed manie
25 happie yeares afterwarde together: And with the
Bones of Marino Georgio buried the remembrance of
former injuries.

    Maister Doctor, (quoth Fabritio,) you have
reported a verie necessarie Historie: for it
30 contayneth many heedeful notes, both of Amonition,
and advise. Besides the due punishment of
rashnesse in Marriage. For therein wee may see
howe hungersterved want, compelleth the best
natured man to deceive his friende, and yelde unto

his owne slaunder. Againe, how that monster,
Golde, conquereth the honour of the fayrest. Yea,
(quoth Isabella,) and corrupteth the conscience
of the wisest: so that this is no example of any
5 honour to you men, because Golde intised Felice,
to be disloyall to her Husbande, for it draweth
manie of you, both from the feare and love of God.

   Well, (quoth Soranso,) let it passe, Felice
in her repentaunce, hath made a large amendes of
10 her trespasse, and I feare me, if every lyke
offence were so sharpely punnished, we should
have Mazers of mens Sculles, more ordinarye then
Silver Boules, and powled Women more common then
baulde men.

15   Not so, (quoth Queene Aurelia:) for a fewe
of these examples woulde bridle the incontinent
affections both of man and woman, if not for the
love of vertue, for the feare of correction.

   After these and a fewe other Morrall notes
20 were culled out of Doctor Mossenigos Historie:
Maddam, (quoth Don Dolo,) if we continue this
course, it will be a good while, before, we doe
finde out the Parradice, Plato speaketh of.

   Be it so, (quoth Queene Aurelia,) but if we
25 still continue the way to his House Hel, our
errour will instructe others: and since we have
yet long respyte, it shall not / be amisse everie
day to take a sundrie hie way, untill wee finde
out the true passage: And for that our Question
30 is concluded, and our Howre Glasse ronne: we
will (for this Daye,) make here an ende.

   The Question that arose, by behouldyng, the
   MOWNTIBANKES, in the thirde Nightes Pastime.
   At the accustomed Houre, Supper was served

Feare of correction, brideleth the affexcions of the evill.

What hurteth one, instructeth the other.

L3ᵛ

The Thyrde Dayes Exercise 109

in with manie daintye Dishes: whiche were saused,
with sundrie shorte civill, and pleasaunt eventes
of the Gentlemen, and Gentlewomens wittes: For he,
or shee, was helde of weake capacitie, that either
5 of forestuddie, or upon offered occasion, coulde
say nothing of good regarde.

  In the ende, when Supper was done, and Queene
<u>Aurelia</u>, and the most Honourable of the companie   Brevitie, is
had taken their places uppon a Scaffolde made for   best, for
10 the nonce, there mounted, a <u>Mountebanke</u>, his necke   Table talke.
bechayned with live Adders, Snakes, Eav'ts, and   Mountibanks
twentie sundrie kinde of venemous vermines, whose   of Italie,
mortall stinges were taken away by Arte, and with   are in a
him a <u>Zanni</u>, and other Actors of pleasure: who   maner, as
15 presented themselves onelie with a single desire,   Englysh
to recreate <u>Segnior Philoxenus</u>, and his worthie   Pedlers.
companie: and not with the intent of common
<u>Mountebanckers</u>, to deceyve the people with some
unprofitable Marchandize.

20   In the middest of this pastime, an aunciente
Gentleman (of the generall Societie) seeinge these
Viperous Beastes, by cunninge usage, to be made so
Domesticke and affable, whether it were uppon an
impression of his owne greife or of the experience
25 he had of an others mans Plague, I know not: but
sure I am, he burst into these passions./

  O GOD, (quoth hee) of what mettell is a   L4^r
Womans tongue, which correction cannot chastise,   The strange
nor lenitie quiet, when these dumbe Serpentes, by   nature of a
30 the one or the other are tamed?   Womans tongue.

  Marie (quoth a pleasant Companion) it is made
of the same mettle, that <u>Virgils</u> Brasen Flayle
was off, which strooke both his friendes and foes.

  But (quoth the Gentleman) <u>Virgyll</u> knew, and

taught others howe to pacifie this engine.

It is true (quoth the other:) but in teaching the secrete unto his Servant, coste him his owne life. So a woman knowes howe to holde her Tongue, by haveinge of her will, but if a man thinke to stay it, he must beate her to death.

A young Youth named <u>Phrisio</u>, thinking to winne the Spurres, by building a Fortresse for women, who have no weapons but their tongues, to defend, and offend, tooke uppon him, to proove a chiding wife, though shee bee a little unpleasaunt, both profitable and necessarie: his reasons were these.

<small>Defences, for a chidynge wyfe.</small>

Unsaverie receytes tourne to holsome effectes: The strongest Poyson is pleasaunt in taste, and the remedie for the poysoned, offendeth the mouthe with tartnesse: Nettles that stinges the Hande, maketh Pottage to comforte the heart: the bloude of the Scorpion cureth the biting of the Viper. If poysoned, unpleasant, and bitter thinges retayne a vertue for the benefite of man: in my imagination (quoth hee) an unquiete wife is not unprofitable though shee bee a little unpleasaunt: Her anger keepeth Servauntes in awe, and her quicknesse overseeth their negligence: If her tongue runne at ryot, where shee huntes, there is store of abuse, which must be chased either with blowes or wordes: If the furye of her speache offende her Husbande, it is lyke, that her outrage, groweth from his faulte: And where an injurie is offered, it is sufferable, yf the wronge bee blamed:/ but which maketh a full amendes, for her furious moode: as the clowdy and raynie daie, lightly cleareth towardes night: even so, though

she bitterly scowld at boorde, shee will be sure,
to kisse sweetely a bedde.

  The auncient Gentlemen, commending the quick   In blaming,
wit of this yong Gentleman, used thys circumstaunce   mildnes is
5 before he refelled his error.   to be used.

  Ah (quoth he) if witt were as advised in
Judgement, as he is ready in conseight: his
imaginations, would turne to wonderfull effectes:
but as fairest colours soonest staine, as sweetest
10 flowers are blasted with a breath: as beautyful
creatures, are blemished with a little care, as
the brightest Sunne threateneth suddaine raine:
yea, as everye mortall thing hath his imperfection:
even so, witt beinge mortall, and assigned by   Wit simply is
15 Nature, to make man glorious, above other creatures,   imperfect.
by rashnes, corrupts the ripenes of his conseightes:
and to good purpose, his pryde is thus abated: for
otherwise, man which enjoyeth witt, to worshippe
his Creator, and to lyve content, with the liberties
20 of the sea, and to keepe him with in the limits of
the earth, woulde search the secreats of heaven:
and I thinke, dispossesse <u>Pluto</u> of hell.

  Yong Gentleman (quoth he) I use not this
ceremony to represse your libertie of speache:
25 for the error of youre rashnes, I will refell
with reason and experience: but least heareafter
you should be as arrogant in opinion, as you are
ripe in conseight: I have thought good, friendlye,
and breefelye to signifie your imperfection: and
30 nowe to aunswere your late suggestion.

  I affirme that Nature hath created nothing
to a needlesse purpose: but notwithstanding, our
abuse, or mischance, changeth hurtefull thinges,
into occasions of our healpe: Surfit, and

Sicknes only, commendeth Medicine: and as you
affirme, the bloud of a Scorpion, cureth the
biting of the Viper.
    But take away the cause, which proceedeth
5 from our greefe, and you shall finde medicine, an
enemye to health:/ and the stinge of a Scorpion,
no better then death: and trust me, he is to be
reckened a foole, and his misfortune to passe
unreleeved, that wilfully indammageth his health
10 in hope of remedy. In like sorte let him live
unpittyed, to oversee the slacknesse of his
servaunts, who wyll marry a wife, whose tongue
shall over-rule himselfe. But more perticularly
to discribe the properties of an unquiet wife,
15 and more largely to discourse the displeasures of
her unfortunate husband: I will approove her
lowrings, as unprofitable, as his life is
unpleasaunt: you say her quicknesse overseeth
the negligence of servaunts: but I affirme, that
20 her curstnesse maketh them as swift to runne away,
as they were slowe to serve her: and common use
avowes, that often shyfte is neyther beneficyall
for Mayster nor Servaunt: for proofe, as the
rowling Stone gathereth no Mosse, and want of use
25 canckereth Iron, in likewise thrifte flyeth the
fleeting Servaunt, and idlenesse consumeth his
abylytie of service. Now touching the evill
reckening of those which are served: their
wanderyng servantes not onely charge their common
30 accountes, with double wages, but with secret
pylferyng, they sette theyr Maisters in more
deepe arrerages. The Gretians that in tymes
paste neither used medicyne for sycknesse, nor
patience in adversitye, but uppon every great

M1^r

Shift, is
unprofitable,
for Maister
and Servaunt.

vexation, poisoned them selves with venemous
Cicuta. In their Histories remember more, that   Cicuta, a
have voluntarily died, through the violence of   venomous
                                                  Herbe, one
theyr Wyfes tounges, then of any other calamitye. sort wherof
                                                  is supposed
5 Diogenes beeyng demaunded the diversitye in evill, to be Hemlocke.
betweene a Scoulde and a Harlot? aunswered: They
differ as the Viper dooth from the Crockadil:
for the Scoulde, sayeth he, with outrage destroyeth
her Husband, and the other with dissemblyng love,
10 consumeth hym to death. And so concluded them
bothe ennemyes to lyfe, and quiet lyving of man.   A needefull
Phrisio, beeing bothe modestly warned, and   regarde for
                                                   yonge
throughly aunsweared, with a bashefull grace   Gentlemen.
replyed: that the gravetye of hys person, and
15 the sounde reason in his wordes, had taken from   M1^v
hym, all occasion of fur-/ther Question, unlesse
that Women were his Judges. This wittie shift   An ill cause
mooved such as were within the hearing to smyle,   asketh a
                                                   partiall
for where the cause is ill, it is necessarie to   Judge.
20 seeke a Judge that is partiall, and which
commended Phrisios government, uppon a small
check he left to contend, with this auncient
Gentleman: for yonge men, although theyr wittes
be good, are not Priviledged to Dispute with the
25 graver sort, without lycence, intreatie, or great
reverence.

By this time the Mountibanck, with discribing
the quallities of his Vermin, and the Zanni in
showing the knavish conditions of his Maister,
30 had wasted a good part of the night, and wearyed
the moste part of the company, so that desyre of
repose, sommoned them unto their lodgeings.

FINIS./

<u>The fourth Daies exercise:</u>

<u>Containing: varietie of necessarie Discourse, and
yet withall, the greater part appertaining to the
generall argument of Marriage.</u>

     So deepe are the impressions of Sorrow, as   The great
the fayning of Poets, may be held for Morrall   impression.
truthes, where as they affirme, that the bytter
mone of <u>Orpheus</u> tongue, together, with the
passionate sound of his Instrument, mooved suche
ruthe in infernall creatures, as while he was a
suter to <u>Pluto</u>, for the restitution of his Wife
<u>Euridice,</u> his plaints so Charmed the torments of
Hell, as for the time, the <u>Gripe</u> forbare to teare
upon <u>Titius</u> growing hart. <u>Tantalus</u> indevoured
not to drinke: <u>Danaes</u> Daughters, lefte filling
of theyr brincklesse Tub: toyling <u>Sisiphus,</u>
sate and eased himselfe upon his rowling Stone:
yea and <u>Pluto</u> overcharged with pittie, made
restitution of <u>Euridice.</u> This sorrow to heare,
that Queene <u>Aurelia</u> by some distemperature, was
sick, and kept her Chamber, wrought such greefes
in the heartes of the whole company, that they
hounge theyr heads in disgrace, like Garden
Flowers: which (seeming as teares) are cloyed
with the dewe of a fowle misling daye. Among the   True sorrowe
rest <u>Ismarito,</u> although he used not so many words   is knowne
of lament, as some other did, yet, with the teares   rather by
of his heart, he solemnized the true Rites of a   sighes then
Mourner: and to saye truthe, where the tongue   words.
hath free passage to talke, the heart is occupied
with no great greefe./

     <u>Segnior Phyloxenus,</u> seeing <u>Ismarito</u> in this
passion, and that occasion entertayned him with
no other businesse: while the rest of the company

were hearing of a lyttle superstitious service
lead him into a very beautifull Gallerie, where
the Mappes of the worlde were so artificially
set foorth in Painting, as I doubt the Popes
5 Microcosmos at Latteran, which hath beene this
sixteene yeares a making, wylbe ended with no
more perfection. In this Gallerie were the
Pictures of all Christian Princes: and in an
other place by themselves, the Pictures of
10 certaine Heathen Rulers: and in an other rancke,
the Pictures of so many learned men and grave
Magistrates, as he could through freendship or
rewarde obtaine.

After much discourse of the especiall
15 Monuments, wherewith this pleasaunt Gallerie was
attyred, Segnior Phyloxenus brought Ismarito a
fayre booke, wherin were divers rare devises, and
(directing him to Pensils, Colers, and other
necessaries of Harrowldry) requested that he
20 would helpe to beautify the sayd Booke, with some
ingenious remembraunce.

Sir (quoth Ismarito) I have already recorded
your good favours in the Table of my heart: and
I beseeche you that this fayre Booke may not be
25 blemished by me, or remaine a wytnesse to you of
my indiscression.

This nicenesse (quoth Philoxenus) professeth
more then ordinarie knowledge, and therefore I
conjure you, by the affection you beare me, to
30 satisfye my request.

Ismarito upon this importunitie, because he
would not leave a suspition, that his curiositie
grew rather of simplicitie then discression: and
missing among the Moderne Monuments, their

The Pope hath begun, and not yet finished a moste rare Gallerie.

Beautifull attires for a Gallerie.

An espetiall Booke of devises.

Ismaritos devise, Pharos, a Lanterne or

Pictures, the vertues of whose Fame, are blazed
in the Capitols of the whole world: he tooke a
Pensill, and with the same drew an Ileland and
over the middest thereof, made a <u>Pharos</u>, which
5 shyned lyke the Sunne, and therein a <u>Phenix</u>,
bathing of her selfe, whose gleaming reflexions,
shined over all <u>Loegria</u>, <u>Cambria</u>, and the greatest
part of <u>Albania</u>, and extended unto a great/ parte
of the <u>Continent</u>, espetially unto that parte that
10 lay betweene the <u>Occean</u>, the <u>Mediterrane</u>, and the
great Sea called <u>Euxinus</u> <u>Pontus</u>, and underneath
writ.

light, devised by King Ptolome, surnamed Philadelphus, for the benefit of Navigation in those parts, which cost 800. Talents.

M3^r

<u>Pharos Europę, non Africę.</u>

<u>Phyloxenus</u> advisedly regarded this devise,
15 before he would either require <u>Ismaritos</u> intent,
or give his owne judgement. In the end, devining
what should be the secret meaning of this Simbole
or Ensigne: quoth he, <u>Segnior</u> <u>Ismarito</u>, this
Cognizance of your quicke wit, pleaseth me much,
20 and withall remembreth me of a neglected curtesie,
which (I thinke) will showe you the Image of your
<u>Phenix</u>, and blason the secresie of your whole
devise: and thereuppon he lead <u>Ismarito</u> into a
moste curious privie Gallerie, where (drawing a
25 faire Curtaine, and reverently kissing his hand)
he shewed <u>Ismarito</u> the Picture of a Royall
Princesse, moste ritchly and lively set foorth,
with which a Marchaunt of <u>Venice</u>, who traffiqued
toward the Westerne Islands, presented him: which
30 <u>Ismarito</u> beheld, with a regarde so duetifull, as
their needed no glose, to expound the zealous
affection of his heart. And by her was stalled
a goodly Gentleman, Crowned with a Scepter, whom

An honourable favor.

Ismarito knew not, other wise then by imagination, in beholding his Armes, who bare Gu, an Eagle displaied Crowned Ar.

And (quoth Phyloxenus,) when I followed the Frenche Court, I admyred a young Prince of rare towardlinesse, whose counterfeit at my departure I brought with me, and there withall shewed Ismarito a Picture, which he verye well knew, and in it were written in Charracters, these three woordes: Hercules Franciscus valesius. And by this Prince stoode an other counterfeit, whose Armes Ismarito forgot, but well he remembred his Posie was, Je le meintiendray. The counterfeits of other Potentates there were, which Philoxenus placed in the ranck of these Princes, for some regarded vertues, knowne unto himselfe. And by his owne testimonie, he prised these coun-/terfeits, aboove all the Monuments (aunciant or Moderne) which beautified his Pallace.

Upon which warrant, Sir, (quoth Ismarito,) the Honourable regarde that you have of these Princes shaddowes, beeing a strainger, prescribeth rules of dutie, unto theyr Subjectes, humbly to reverence their sacred Persons.

A regard in straungers, to teache Subjectes their dutie.

In deede (quoth he,) it is but just, their tongues crie, God save their Highnesse, and theyr hearts aunswer, So be it.

After Segnior Philoxenus and Ismarito had had some conference, as well touching the meaning of this Pharos, as of some other devises figured in Philoxenus Booke: the Trumpets sound, gave knowledge of Dinner: so that this private conference was adjorned, till Segnior Philoxenus pleasure should renue it. When Ismarito entered

into the great Chamber, and among so many fayre
Flowers, missing the glorious Rose, his
countenaunce well showed, that his mornings
sorrowe had beene but a sleepe, which new
5 awakened, streaked with the increase of passion,
yea such was the pensivenesse of the whole
company, as the fyrst service, represented rather
a Funerall Dinner, then a Christmas feaste. But
in the mydest of a storme, as Phebus sometymes
10 behouldeth the Earth, with a cheerefull
countenaunce, so in the deapth of this heavines,
there was newes brought of Queene Aurelias
amendment, who commaunded the chosen company,
after Dinner, to attend her comming, in the
15 chamber of pleasure. This knowledg so quickned
the dulled spyrytes of the Gentlemen, and
Gentlewomen, as they agreed, for one day (if
Queene Aurelia pleased) to alter the sollemne
course in theyr ordenarie exercyse: for where
20 the malladie is not mortall, mirth cureth as
much as medicine, and houlding this determynacion,
they, the rest of Dinner, in actions of pleasure,
fullie avenged themselves of the injurie of
former sorrowe. After Dinner was ended, and the
25 company had a while pawsed, to set themselves
in good order: upon a new sommons, the appointed
number, martched into this Chamber of Pleasures,
which was hanged with a ritche Ta-/pistrie of
voluntarie devise, every Tree, Flower, Byrde,
30 Beaste, or what somever was therein resembled,
in his proper coloures of Silke, was portrayed.
The Sheepe with theyr Fleeces fryzeled, the
Beastes curiously raysed with rawe Silke, like
unto theyr naturall heayre, the Trees beautified

The Rose is the most glorious of Flowers.

An unexpected good newes, is double welcome.

Myrthe cureth as much as Medicine, where the malladie is not mortall.

M4^r

A sumptuous Tapistrie.

with proper leaves and fruite, the Rose with his
Buds, Sprigs, and other attyre: and to be breefe,
every other Flower was counterfaited with such
Arte, as they seemed to be naturall. Yea a man
might have beene indifferently wise enough, in
other ordinarie matter, and yet have adventured
to have gathered a Flower, or have plucked an
Apple, in these hangings, and who so was best
acquainted, could not wearie his eyes in the
beholding of them: so that the very attyre of
this Chamber walles, had an intertaining vertue,
were there no other creature in the place.

Men may be deceived without the slaunder of simplycitie.

Curious sights, please more then uncivill people.

    Queene <u>Aurelia</u> attended with the Ladyes and
Gentlewomen, presented her selfe, before the
younge Gentlemen had halfe gazed theyr will.
The company saluted theyr Soveraigne with a
reverent curtesie, whose cheekes, somewhat more
bleake then ordinary, with this distemperature,
resembled in colloure the perfect white
Gilliflowre, a little streaked with Carnation.

A lyttle sicknesse maketh an alteration in beautie.

    After some private talke betweene her, and
one or two of her favoured Servaunts, she tooke
her place where she pleased, and the rest as
they were accustomed, which doone, the <u>Eunick</u>
with a well tuned voyce, unto the Lute, Songe
this following, <u>Care away</u>.

Care, Care, goe pack, thou art no mate for me,
    thy thornie thoughts, the heart to death doth wound:
Thou makest the fayre, seeme like a blasted Tree,
    by thee greene yeares with hoarie heares are crownd.
      Which makes me singe, to solace mine annoy:
        Care, Care, adewe, my hart doth hop for joye./

Care, Care, adewe, thou rivall of delight,
    returne into, the Cave of deepe Dispayre:
Thou art no Gueste, to harbour neere my spright,
    whose poisoned syghtes, infect the very Ayre.
      Wherefore I singe, to sollace myne annoye:
    Care, Care, adewe, my hart doth hop for joye.

Care, Care, adewe, and welcome pleasure now,
    thou wishe of joye, and ease of sorowe bothe:
To weare thy weede, I make a sollemne vowe,
    let Tyme, or Chaunce, be pleased, or be wrothe.
    And therefore singe, to sollace myne annoy:
    Care, Care, a dewe, my heart doth hop for joye.

    The note of this Songe, was farre better then the Ditty, but for that it aunswered the determination of the company, it passed for currant: whereupon, Maddame (quoth _Fabritio_) if it be your pleasure, we wyll this day varrie from our wonted course, and according to our Theame, begin with some myrthe, to sharpen our wittes: for graver discourses, we have time inough besides, to beate out the passage to _Platoes_ Paradise.

One square breaketh no custome.

    Use your discressions (quoth Queene _Aurelia_,) and by her commaundement _Bergetto_ was appointed to begin the exercise, who obaying, reported this following adventure, of Fryer _Inganno_.

The adventure of Fryer _Inganno_, reported by _Mounsier Bergetto_.

    In a little Village among the _Appenine_ Mountaynes not far from the place, where Sainct _Fraunces_ lyeth intombed, there sometymes dwelled a fayre younge countery woman named _Farina_: and

for that her house was in the hye waie, to
Sainct Fraunces holy relykes, she was many tymes
visyted with Friers of his order, who were
intertayned,/ rather for their habyt, then their
honestie: for the poore ignorant people,
reverenced Sainct Fraunces, as a seconde Christe,
for whose sake, they hould his Disciples, not
inferiour to Saincts: amonge manye that visited
Farinas house, Fryer Inganno, a smugge Chapleine,
ever sealed his blessings, uppon his dames lippes,
and yet, without suspicion of the husband, or
dishonest intent of the wife: for such greeting
was ever taken for a holly favour.

    Uppon a time, after Fryer Inganno, had wel
beaked himselfe, with a warme fire, and a good
breakefast, the spirit that Saint Fraunces, was
driven to conjure downe, by tumbling naked in the
frost and snowe, tempted his Disciple with suche
sweete motions, as he was mynded willfully to
abjure heaven, rather then to deale so roughly
with the devill. And taking advantage, of the
good opinion, the ignoraunt, heald of his holynes:
and was so bould, with Saincte Fraunces (his
Maister) as to make a wanton match in his name:
so that after he had a while considered, of his
perswasion, uppon a quiet oportunitie: Blessed
art thou (quoth he) among the Appenine countrey-
wemen, for Sainct Fraunces, from Heaven, hath
behelde thy charitable usage of his Disciples,
and the last Night after, I had prayed with great
devotion, before his Image, I behelde him in the
Majestie of an Angell, fayre, yonge, lustie, and
in every proportion like my selfe, and nothyng
at all, like his meagre Cripple Image: So that

Marginalia:
N1^r

It is saide, S. Frances subdued incontinent desires, by tumbling naked in frost and Snowe.

A premiditated sinne.

The tricke of a knavish Servaunt.

A gentle perswasion.

I was in doubt, of beynge transfourmed out of my
selfe, tyll with a meeke voice, he sayd: Be not
dismayde, I am thy Maister, Inganno, and am come,
to bestow my blessinges upon the good Appenine
5 dames, that for my sake cherish you, my Disciples:
But with an especiall Affection, I wil visite the
good Dame Farina: And for that, her Feminine
weakenes, can not indure my Heavenly presence,
I wyll many times borrowe thy earthly shape: and
10 in my name, go salute Farina, and showe her, that
this night, in that her Husbande is from home, I
meane to visite her: wyll her to leave open the
Doores, because/ I purpose to come as Fryer
Inganno, and not as Saint Fraunces.

15   This is his message, therfore, as I began,
I end: blessed art thou among the Appenine
countrie Dames: The poore woman, as apparant as
this trecherie was, had not the power to mistrust,
but gave the Fryer a good almes for his newes,
20 and saide she would attende Saint Fraunces blessed
will.

    Away goeth the Fryer, with a light hart and
a heavy Cowle: but God, to punish his lewde
intent, and to preserve her from sinnyng through
25 ignoraunce, so tyckled her hart with joy, of this
blessinge at hande, as to welcome Saint Fraunces
shee must needes have the Belles roonge: The
Prieste of the Parrishe hearing the cause, smelt
out the Fryers counning, and was glad to take one
30 of those Beggers in a Pitfall, that with glorious
lyes, had robbed him of his Parishioners devotions,
and withall, perswaded her with suche reasons, as
shee was fully resolved of the Fryers deceite:
And to bee advenged, by the Parsons direction,

Ignoraunce heareth every tale as trueth.

Flatterie eateth the bread of the Just.

A note of litle secreacy in a woman.

Envy setteth hatred betweene fellowes of every vocation.

shee caused Leayda to lye in her Bed, a Mayde so
ougly, sluttish and deformed, as thorough the
Parish, shee was called, the Furie of Lothsomnesse.
Aboute ten of the Clocke, findynge the Doores
5 open, Frier Inganno mountes into Farinas Chamber,
and without light or leave, leaps into her bed:
but hee had not blessed Leaydaes lyppes, before
the Priest, Farina, and others, entred with Taper   An unwelcome
and Torchlighte, singing Salve Saincte Francisce: salutation.
10 And kneeling about his Bed sides, sung, Sancte
Francisce, ora pro nobis.

    The poore Fryer, lyke a Fox in a grin, being
both intrapt, and imbraste by a Hag of Hel, cryed
from his hart: Pleasure in
15   A dolore inferni, libera me Domine.   others
    After the Prieste and the rest of the companye,   increaseth
were wearye of laughinge: and the Fryer almost   sorrow in the
dead with weeping: It is an office of Charitie   afflicted.
(quoth the Priest) to put Saint Frances againe
20 in his Tumbe: for it is so long/ since hee was   N2^r
in the Worlde, that he hath forgot the way backe,
into Heaven.   Envy, and
    The Fryer learing lyke the Theefe, that   rude people,
honge on the left side of Christe, tooke all with   are not
                                                                             passifyed
25 patience: for well hee wyst, Prayer booted not.   with praiers
    Well, for that night, they bounde and stript   of the
him, lyke a dead Coarse: and in stead of sweete   afflicted.
Flowers, laid him in a bundell of Nettles.   Rude people
    The next mornyng, the rude Countrie people   extreame
30 (who in revenge are without civyllytie or order)   revengers.
cruelly scourged the poore Fryer. And (setting
hym the forenoone naked in the Sunne) annoynted
his bodie with Honey: so that the Hornets,
Waspes and Flyes, tormented him with the paynes

of Hell.

In the afternoone, with a hundred Torches, Tapers, and other waxen lyghtes: this rustick multitude, caryed seconde Saint <u>Fraunces</u> unto
5 his Tumbe: and had not other Fryers used mylde and plawsible requests, in his behalf, they would surely have buried him alive: for threatning, increaseth a tumult: when faire wordes, may peradventure staye it.

The best way to win the communaltie.

10   The poore Fryer discharged from the handes of these ungentle people, learned afterwardes to be more warie: but for all this punishment, was nothinge the honester. For amonge men of his Habit, remayneth an opynion, that the faultes,
15 whiche the Worlde seeeth not, GOD punnisheth not.

After the Company had wel laughed at Fryer <u>Ingannoes,</u> pennaunce, Queene <u>Aurelia</u> axed Maister Doctor, the Archedetracter of Women, how many suche stories he had read of the religious Dames?

20   None (quoth hee) that hath beene so sorely punished, but of an number that have as hyghly trespassed.

What (quoth <u>Helena Dulce</u>) by suche subtyll practises?

Men offende subtilly, and women simply.

25   No (quoth the Doctor) but through simple affection./

Well (quoth <u>Alvisa Vechio,</u>) their evyls are written in their foreheades, that slaunderous mens tongues may reade and inlarge them. And your
30 great evils are buried in the bottome of your hartes that unlesse the Devill meane to shame you, the worlde knoweth not how to blame you.

Wemens evyls are wryt in their forheds.
Mens faultes, lye hydde in their hartes.

This was the Gentlewomens day, wherefore the civill Gentlemen, would not offer to crosse them

much: so that following their advantage, Madam
(quoth Isabella,) with your favour and patience,
I will reporte an Historie, that shall open suche
a haynous trecherie done by a man, as shall take
away all possibilytie from a woman to commit so
impious an Act.

> A civill curtesie in a Gentelman.

Queene Aurelia, willed her to proceede, and
the whole company seemed to be attentive: whereupon
Isabella reported as followeth.

The rare Historie of Promos and Cassandra, reported by Madam ISABELLA.

At what time Corvinus the scourge of the
Turkes, rayned as Kinge of Bohemia: for to well
governe the free Cities of his Realme, hee sent
divers worthy Majestrates. Among the rest, he
gave the Lorde Promos the Lieutennauntship of
Julio: who in the beginning of his government,
purged the Cittie of many ancient vices, and
severely punished new offenders.

> This Historie for rarenes therof, is lively set out in a Commedie, by the Reporter of the whole worke, but yet never presented upon stage.

In this Cittie, there was an olde custome
(by the suffering of some Majestrates, growne out
of use) that what man so ever committed Adulterie,
should lose his head: And the woman offender
should ever after be infamously noted, by the
wearing of some disguised apparrell: For the man
was helde to bee the greatest offender, and
therefore had the severest punishment.

> A hard Lawe for incontinent persons.

Lorde Promos, with a rough execution, revived
this Statute, and in the hyest degree of injurie,
brake it hym-/selfe, as shall appeare by the
sequell of Andrugioes adventures.

This Andrugio by the yeelding favour of
fayre Polina, trespassed against this ordinaunce,
who through envie, was accused, and by Lorde

Promos condemned, to suffer execution.

    The wofull Cassandra, Andrugioes Sister, prostrates her selfe at Lorde Promos Feete, and with more teares then wordes, thus pleaded for her Brothers lyfe.

    Most noble Lorde, and worthy Judge, voutchsafe mee the favour to speake, whose case is so desperate, as unlesse you beholde mee with the eyes of mercie, the frayle trespasse, of condemned Andrugio my Brother, will bee the death of sorrowfull Cassandra, his innocent Sister. I wil not presume, to excuse his offence, or reproche the Lawe of rigor: for in the generall construction, hee hath done most evill, and the Law hath judged but what is right: But (reverent Judge, pardon that necessitie maketh mee here tel, that your wisdome already knoweth.) The most Soveraigne Justice, is crowned with Laurell, although shee bee gyrt with a Sword: And this priveledge shee giveth unto her Administrators: that they shall mitigate the severetie of the Law, according to the quallyty of the offence. Then, that Justice bee not robbed of her gratious pitty, listen Good Lorde Promos, to the nature of my Brothers offence, and his able meanes to repayre the injurie. Hee hath defyled, no Nuptiall Bed, the stayne wherof dishonoureth the guyltlesse Husband: Hee hath committed no violent Rape. In which Act the injuried Mayde can have no amends. But with yeelding consent of his Mistresse, Andrugio hath onlye sinned through Love, and never ment but with Marriage to make amendes.

    I humbly beseeche you to accept his satisfaction, and by this Example, you shall be as

Lawe adjudgeth, by the generall offence.

Justice, is more renowned by lenytie, then severitie.

A good cause to moove pytie.

much beloved for your clemencye, as feared for
your severitie. Andrugio shalbe well warned, and
hee with his Sister wofull Cassandra, shall ever
remayne, your Lordships true Servantes./

  Promos eares were not so attentive, to heare
Cassandras ruethful tale, as his eyes were settled
to regarde her excellent Beautie. And Love, that
was the appoincted Headsman of Andrugio, became
now the Soveraigne of his Judges thought. But
because he would seeme to bridle his passions, he
aunswered: fayre Damsell, have patience, you
importune me with an impossybylytie: he is
condempned by Lawe, then without injurie to Lawe,
he can not be saved.

  Princes and their Deputies Prerogatives (quoth
she) are above the Lawe. Besides, Lawe, truelie
construed, is but the amends of Injurie: and
where, the faulte may bee valued, and amendes had,
the Breache of Lawe is sufficiently repayred.

  Quoth Lorde Promos, your passions mooveth
more then your proofes: and for your sake, I wyll
reprive Andrugio, and studie how to do you ease,
without apparant breache of Lawe.

  Cassandra, recomforted, with humble thankes
receyved his favoure, and in great haste goeth too
participate this hope, with her dying Brother:
But oh, that Aucthorytie, should have power, to
make the vertuous to doo amisse, as well, as
throughe Correction, to enforce the vicious to
fall unto goodnesse.

  Promos, is a witnes of this Priviledge: who
not able to subdue his incontinent love, and
(withal) resolved, that Cassandra would never be
overcome, with fayre wordes, large promises, or

marginalia:
- Love, favoureth no degre.
- Princes Prerogative, are above Lawe.
- The true intent of the Lawe.
- A good turne upon an evyl cause.
- Aucthorytie, in evyll Majestrates, is a Scourge unto the good.

riche rewardes: demaunded the spoyle of her
Virginitie, for raunsome of her Brothers lybertie.

 Cassandra, ymagyned at the first, that Lorde
Promos, used this speache, but to trie her
5 behaviour: Aunswered hym so wisely, as if he had
not ben the Ryvall of Vertue, he could not but
have suppressed his lewde Affection, and have
subscribed to her just petition: But to leave
circumstaunces, Promos was fiered with a vicious
10 desyre, which must be quenched with Cassandraes
yeldyng love, or Andrugio must dye.

 Cassandra, mooved with a chaste disdayne,
departed,/ with the resolution, rather to dye her
selfe, then to stayne her honour: And with this
15 heavie newes, greeted her condemned Brother:
poore man, alas, what should he do? Life was
sweete: but to be redeemed with his Sisters
Infamie, could not, but be alwayes unsaverie.

 To perswade her to consente, was unnaturall:
20 too yealde to Death, was more greevous.

 To choose the leaste of these evylles, was
difficult: to studie long was daungerous.

 Fayne would he lyve, but Shame cloased his
mouth, when he attempted to perswade his Sister.
25 But Necessytie, that maistereth both Shame
and feare, brake a passadge for his imprysoned
intent.

 Sweete Cassandra, (quoth he) that men love,
is usuall, but to subdue Affection, is impossyble:
30 and so thornie are the motions of incontinent
Desire, as to finde ease, the tongue is only
occupied to perswade. The Purse, is ever open
to entice, and wheare neither words nor Giftes
can corrupt (with the mightie) force shall

Side notes:
A monstrous request.
Unlesse they be reprobate, good Examples, may refourme the wicked.
A hard choice of two evyls.
The force of Necessytie.
The force of Love.

constrayne, or dispight, avenge. That <u>Promos</u> do
love, is but just, thy Beautie commaundes hym.
That <u>Promos</u> be refused, is more just, because
Consent is thy Shame.

5   Thou maiste refuse and lyve: but he beynge
rejected, I die: For wantyng his wyll in thee,
he wyll wreake his teene on mee.

    This is my hard estate: <u>My lyfe, lieth in
thy Infamie, and thy honour in my death</u>. Which
10 of these evylles be leaste, I leave for thee to
judge.

    The wofull <u>Cassandra</u>, answered: that Death,   *A hard
was the leaste: whose Darte, we can not shunne: Fortune.*
when Honour, in Deathes dispight, outlyveth tyme.

15   It is true (quoth <u>Andrugio</u>,) but thy   *Death is to
Trespasse, wyll be in the leaste degree of blame: be preferred,
For, in forced Faultes, Justice sayth, there is   before
no intent of evyll.   dishonorable
   lyfe.*

    Oh <u>Andrugio</u>, (quoth she) Intent, is now
20 adayes, lytle considred: thou art not condemned
by the intent, but by/ the strickt worde of the
Law: so shall my crime bee reproched, and the   *The venemous
forced cause passe unexcused: and such is the   nature of
venome of Envye, one evill deede shall disgrace   Envy.*
25 ten good turnes: and in this yeelding, so shall
I be valued: Envye, Disdaine, Spight, Mallice,   *The vertuous
Sclaunder, and many moe furies will endevour to   are assured
shame mee, and the meanest vertue, wyll blush to   of many
help to support my honour: so that I see no   enemies, and
   incertaine of
30 lybertie for thee but Death, nor no ease for mee   any friendes.*
but to hasten my ende.

    O yes (quoth <u>Andrugio</u>,) for if this offence
be known, thy fame will bee enlarged, because it
will lykewise bee knowne, that thou receavedst

The Fourth Dayes Exercise   130

    dishonor to give thy Brother lyfe: If it be
secreat, thy Conscience wyl be without scruple
of guiltinesse. Thus, knowne, or unknowne, thou
shalt be deflowred, but not dishonested, and for
5 amends wee both shall lyve.

    This further hope remaineth, that as the
Gilliflower, both pleaseth the eye and feedeth
the sence: even so the vertue of thy chast
behaviour may so grace thy bewty, as Promos
10 filthie lust, may bee turned into faithfull love:
and so move him, to salve thy honour in making
thee hys wife. Or for conscience, forbeare to
doe so heynous an injurie.

    Soveraigne Maddame, and you faire Gentlewomen,
15 (quoth Isabella) I intreate you in Cassandras
behalfe, these reasons well wayed, to judge her
yeelding a constrainte, and no consent: who
werie of her owne life, and tender over her
brothers, with the teares of her lovely eyes,
20 bathed his Cheekes, with this comfortable sentence.

    Lyve Andrugio, and make much of this kisse,
which breatheth my honour into thy bowels: and
draweth the infamie of thy first trespasse into
my bosome.

25   The sharpe incounters betweene life and death,
so occupied Andrugios sences, that his tongue had
not the vertue, to bid her fare well. To greeve
you with the hearing of Cassandras secreate
plaints, were an injurie: vertuous/ Ladies, for
30 they concluded with their good fortune, and
everlasting fame: But for that her offence grew
neyther of frayltie, free wyl, or any motion of
a Woman, but by the meere inforcement of a man,
because she would not staine the modest weedes of

Margin notes:
- A cause that may excuse the breach of honour.
- A faint hope.
- A lovyng kys.
- 01^r
- A good consideration in Cassandra.

her kynde, shee attired her selfe in the habit of
a Page, and with the bashfull grace of a pure
Virgin, shee presented wicked Promos, Andrugioes
precious ransome.

5   This Devill, in humaine shape, more vicious
then Hyliogabalus of Rome: and withall, as   A damnable
cruell as Denis of Sicyll: receaved this Juell   offence.
with a thousande protestations of favour. But
what should I say? In the beginnyng of his love,
10 Promos was metamorphosed into Priapus: and of a
Feende what may we expect? but vengeaunce heaped
upon villany. And therefore, let it not seeme
straunge, that after this Helhound, had
dishonoured Cassandra, hee sent his warrant, to
15 the Gayler pryvely, to execute Andrugio, and
with his head crowned with these two Breefes, in
Promos name, to present Cassandra:
                                                    A villanous
    Fayre Cassandra, as Promos promist thee: Ingratitude.
    From Pryson loe, he sendes thy Brother free.
20 This was his Charge, whose cursed wyll had
ben executed, had not God by an especiall
providence, at the howre of his Death, possessed
Andrugio with the vertues of the two brave   An especiall
Romanes, Marcus Crassus, and Marius, the one of   providence
                                                    of God.
25 whiche, by the force of his tongue, and the
other by the motions of his eyes, caused the Axe
to fall out of the Headsmans hand, and mollyfyed
his cruell mynde.

    With lyke compassion, the Gayler (in hearinge
30 Andrugios hard adventure) left his resolution:
And uppon a solempne othe, to live unknowne, yea
to his deare Sister, he gave him life, and in
the dead of the night, betooke him to God, and   A signe of
                                                    an honest
to good fortune: which done this good Gayler   nature.

tooke the head of a yonge man newe executed, who
somewhat resembled Andrugio: and according to
lewde Promos commaundement made a present
thereof to Cassan-/dra. How unwelcome this
5   Present was, the testimonie of her former sorowes
somewhat discover: but to give her present
passion a true grace, were the taske of Prometheus,
or such a one as hath had experience of the
anguishes of hell.
10   O (quoth shee,) sweete Andrugio, whether
shall I firste lament thy death? exclaime of
Promos injurie? or bemone my owne estate,
deprived of honour? and which is worse, cannot
die, but by the violence of my owne hands. Alas,
15 the least of these greefes, are to heavie a
burden for a man, then all joyned in one poore
womans hearte, can not be eased but by death:
and to be avenged of injurious Fortune, I wil
forthwith cut my Fillet of life. But so shall
20 Promos lewdnesse escape unpunished: what
remedie? I am not of power to revenge: to
complayne, I expresse my owne infamie, but
withal, proclaime his vilanie: and to heare his
lewdnes reproved, woulde take away the bitternesse
25 of my death. I will goe unto the King, who is
just and mercifull, hee shall heare the ruthfull
events of Promos Tyrannie: and to give him
example of vengeaunce, I will seale my complaintes
with my dearest bloode.
30   Continuing this determination, Cassandra
buried her imagined brothers heade, and with
speed jornyed unto King Corvinus Court: Before
whose presence when shee arrived, her mourninge
Attyre, but especially her modest countenaunce

01^v

An unwelcome
present.

moved him to beholde her with an especiall
regarde.

    Cassandra (uppon the graunt of audience)
with her eyes overcharged with teares, reported,   A mischiefe
well
5 the alreadie discoursed Accidentes, with suche   prevented.
an apparaunce of greefe, as the King and his
Attendants were astonied to heare her: and sure
had shee not been happily prevented, shee had
concluded her determination, with chast Lucretias
10 destiny. The King comforted her with many   A noble
gratious words and promised to take such order,   favour.
that (although he could not be revived) her
brothers death should fully be revenged,/ and   02^r
her crased honour, repayred, withoute blemysh of
15 her former reputation.

    Cassandra, upon these comfortable wordes, a
lytell succoured her afflicted hart, and with
patience, attended the Justice of the King: who
with a chosen companie, made a Progresse to Julio,
20 and entred the Town, with a semblaunce of great   A necessarie
favour towardes Promos: by that colour, to learne   pollicye.
what other corrupte Majestrates, ruled in the
Cittie: for well he knewe, that Byrdes of a
feather, would flie together, and wicked men
25 would joyne in Affection to boulster each others
evil.

    After this gratious King, had by heedfull
intelligence understoode the factions of the
people, unlooked for of the Magistrates, he
30 caused a proclamation to be published: in which
was a clause, that if anie person coulde charge
anie Magistrate or Officer, with anie notable or
haynous offence, Treason, Murder, Rape, Sedition,   A Ryal grace.
or with any such notorious Crime: where they

were the Judges of the multitude, hee woulde
himselfe bee the Judge of them, and doe justice
unto the meanest.

    Uppon this Proclamation it was a hell to
5 heare, the exclamations of the poore, and the
festered consciences of the rich, appeared as
lothsome, as the River of Stix.

    Among manie that complayned, and received
judgement of comfort, Cassandras Processe was
10 presented, who lead betweene sorrow and shame,
accused Promos to his face.

    The evidence was so playne, as the horrour
of a guiltie conscience reaved Promos of all
motions of excuse: so that holding up his hande,
15 among the worst degree of theeves, the litle hope
that was leaft, moved him to confesse the crime,
and with repentance to sue for mercy.

    O (quoth the King) such espetial mercy were
tyrannie to a common wealth. No Promos no, Hoc
20 facias alteri, quod tibi vis fieri: You shall be
measured with the grace you bestowed on Andrugio./

    O God (quoth hee) if men durst bark as
Dogges, manie a Judge in the world would be
bewrayed for a theefe: It behoveth a Prince to
25 know to whom hee committeth Authoritie, least the
Sword of Justice, appointed to chasten the lewde,
wound the good: and where good subjects are
wronged, evill Officers receave the benefit, and
their Soveraignes beareth the blame.

30   Well, wicked Promos, to scourge thy impious
offences, I heere give sentence, that thou
foorthwith marry Cassandra, to repayre her
honour by thee violated, and that the next day
thou lose thy head, to make satisfaction for her

Marginalia:
- The clamors of the poore, and the consciences of the rich, like Hell.
- Sorrowe and Shame, the Attendantes of Cassandra.
- An unusual place for a Judge.
- 02ᵛ
- A necessarie regarde in a Prince.
- Princes bere the blame of evyll Officers extortion.
- A just Judgement.

Brothers death.

    This just Judgement of the good Kinge, in
the first point, was foorthwith executed: But
sacred is the Authoritie, that the vertues of
5 the good, are a Sheelde unto the lewde: So   *The good*
sweete <u>Cassandra</u>, who (simply) by vertue   *protect*
overcame the spight of Fortune: In this   *the lewde.*
marriadge was charged with a new assault of
sorrow: and preferring the dutie of a wife,
10 before the naturall zeale of a Sister, where she   *The duetie*
before prosecuted, the revenge of her Brothers   *of a wyfe,*
death, shee now was an humble suter to the Kinge   *truely*
for her Husbands lyfe.   *showen.*

    The gracious Kinge, sought to appease her
15 with good words, but hee could not do her this
private favour, without injurie unto the publyke   *The comon*
weale: for though (quoth he) your sute be just,   *weale, is to*
and the bounden dutie of a wife, yet I in   *be regarded*
fulfillyng the same should do injustly, and   *before private*
20 (generally) injure my Subjects: and therfore,   *favour.*
good Gentlewoman, have patience, and no doubt
vertue in the ende will give you power over all
your afflictions.

    There was no remedie, <u>Cassandra</u> must departe,
25 out of hope, to obtayne her sute. But as the
experience, is in dayly use, the dooinges of   *Sive bonum,*
Princes post through the world on <u>Pegasus</u> backe: *sive malum,*
And as theyr actions are good or badde, so is their   *Fama est.*
fame. With the lyke speede, the Kynges Justice,
30 and <u>Promos</u> execution was spred abroad: and by the
tonge of a Clowne, was blowen into/ <u>Andrugioes</u>
eares, who tyll then lyved lyke an Outlawe in the
Desart wooddes.

    But upon these Newes, covertly, in the Habyt

of an Hermyt, by the Divine motion of the sowle,   Good motions,
who directes us in thinges that be good, and the   proceede
Flesshe in Actions of evyll, <u>Andrugio</u>, goes to   from the soule,
see the Death of his Capitall enemie: But on the   and evyll from
                                                                          the flesh.
5   other parte, regardyng the sorrow of his Sister,
he wisshed him lyfe, as a friende.

      To conclude, as well to geve terrour to the
lewde, as comfort to his good Subjectes, the Kyng
(personallie) came to see the execution of <u>Promos</u> :
10 who, garded with Officers, and strengthened with
the comfortable perswasions of his Ghostly
Fathers: Among whom, <u>Andrugio</u> was, meekely
offered his lyfe, as a satisfaction for his
offences, which were many more, then the Lawe   A gratefull
15 tooke knowledge of: And yet, to say the trueth,   parte.
suche was his Repentance, as the multitude did
both forgeve and pittie him: yea, the King
wondred that his lyfe was governed with no more
vertue, consideryng the grace he showed at his
20 death.

      <u>Andrugio</u>, behouldyng this ruethfull
Spectackle, was so overcome with love towardes
his Sister, as to give her comfort, he franckly
consented anew to emperill his own life: And
25 followinge this Resolution, in his Hermyts weede,
upon his knees, he humblye desired the Kinge too
give hym leave to speake. The Kyng (gratiously)
graunted hym Audience. Wherupon (quoth he) regarded
Soveraigne, if Lawe may (possibly) be satisfied:
30 <u>Promos</u> true Repentance meritteth pardon.

      Good Father (quoth the King) he can not live,   Murther
and the Lawe satisfied, unlesse (by Miracle)   asketh death,
<u>Andrugio</u> be revived.   and no other
                                                                             Satisfaction.

      Then (quoth the Hermyt,) if <u>Andrugio</u> lyve,

the Law is satisfied, and Promos discharged.

 I (quoth the King,) if your Praier can
revive the one, my mercie shall acquit the other.

 I humbly thanke your Majestie (quoth
Andrugio) and discoveryng himselfe, shewed the
Providence of God and the meane of his escape:
and tendrynge his Sisters/ comfort, above his
owne safetie, hee prostrated him selfe at his
Majesties Feete: humblye to obay the sentence
of his pleasure. The Kinge uppon the reporte of
this straunge Adventure: after good deliberation,
pardoned Promos, to keepe his worde, and withall,
houldyng an opinyon, that it was more benefitiall
for the Citezens, to be ruled by their olde evell
governour, new refourmed, then to adventure uppon
an newe, whose behaviours were unknowne: And to
perfect Cassandras joye, he pardoned her Brother
Andrugio, with condition, that he should marrie
Polina. Thus, from betweene the teethe of
daunger, every partie was preserved, and in the
ende establyshed in their hartes desire.

 Madam (quoth Soranso) your good conclusion,
hath likewise preserved us from a great daunger:
for had you ended with the sorrow you began, wee
had beene all like to have bene drowned in teares.

 Indeede (quoth Katharina Trista) you men had
cause sufficient of sorrowe, by hearing your
kynde reproched with such monstrous evils: and we
women free passage to lament, in behoulding none
but crosse fortunes to succeede the good
indevours of a vertuous Ladie.

 It is true (quoth Fabritio) but to participate
of their joye, wee men have learned out of Promos
example of evil, for feare of his likelie

o3^v

Princes are bounde to their word.

Of two, the least evill is least daungerous.

Ruthfull tales, raiseth remorce in the hearers.

By example of evill, the evill are feared.

By example of the good, the good are strengthned.

punishment of evil, to doo well: and you Women,
by example of Polinas vice, and Cassandras vertue,
are both warned and incouraged to weldooing.

    Indeede (quoth Queene Aurelia,) there are
many Morall precepts in either Historie, to be
considered: whiche I hope the company have so
regarded, as there needeth no repetition. And
further, because I will not be to bould of the
victorie, over my late distemperature: we will
heare ende: And therwith she rose, and retired
into her Chamber: with charge that the company
should attende her, in the same place, until
Supper, who obaying, intertained time, every one
with their speciall fancy./

Good order is to bee kept among such as have bene late sick.

    The Question that arose at Supper upon
        the fourth Dayes exercise.

04r

    Many prettie nyps, passed (betweene the
retyred Companye) this Night at Supper, as well
on the Gentlewomens parte, as of the Gentlemens.
In so much as presumyng upon this Daies honour
(when the Table was readie to be taken away,)
Alvisa Vechio, tooke upon her, to mayntaine a
woman, to be a creature every way, as execellent
and perfecte as Man. For naturall shape (quoth
she) they are more beautifull, of a better
temperature, and complection then man. In
valiaunt exploytes, what difference was there
betweene Semiramis and her Husbande Ninus?
betweene the Amazon women and Alexender. For
constantnesse of mind, did not Loadice imbrace
deathe, with lesse feare, then Mithridates her
Husband, Asdruballes Wife, then Asdrubal himselfe.
And what man hath kept a constant resolution of
death, so long as Lucretia. In Morall vertues,

Comparison breedeth contention.

Excellent vertues in women.

you men that reade Histories and Cronicles of
all ages, shall finde Women, renowned for
learnyng, Government, and pollycie. In
Mecanycall Artes, there are Women, lykewise
5 experienced. In the vertue of Devining, what
man hath come neare the <u>Sibels</u>? To bee shorte,
what Man hath bene so perfect in any vertue:
but Histories make mention of a woman as perfect?

Yea (quoth <u>Dondolo</u>) but there be so few of   Cavelers
10 these women, as an easy wit may remember them.   never answere
    directly.

But it will cumber your Tong to report them
(quoth <u>Katharina Trista</u>.)

The other Gentlemen although they were
willinge to give place unto the Gentlewomen in   A disgrace in
    honour, a
15 small matters, yet this comparison of equal   Gentleman may
soveraignty, netteled them a lytil. In as much,   not beare
as <u>Soranso</u> aunswered. Madam <u>Alvisa</u>, you have   with.
made a bould comparison, and but a bare proofe:
Where you vaunte, to be more excellent in shape,
20 and more delicate in substaunce then men./ It is   O4^v
an over ruled question, that Women receive
perfection by men, and men imperfection by Women:
then by how much the vertue is of more emprise,   Aristotles
that is simplye of it selfe, then that which is   probleames.
25 compounde of an other: by so farre wee exceede
you in this perfection.

Your honour of valyantnes, died with your
examples, and although there hath bene Women
learned, and experienced in Mecanicall craftes,   Extraordinarie
    thinges, are
30 yet to heare a Woman plead at the Barre, preache   not to be
in a Pulpit, or to see her build a House, is a   compared with
wonder and no example in use. How shorte your   ordinarie.
devinyng <u>Sybels</u>, come of the credit, of the
Prophets in the olde Testament, is no question

disputable: For your constancie at deathe, you
knowe not how precious lyfe is, which maketh you   Life is
rash and not constant: and in trueth, what you   pretious.
have frowardely determined, you will not bee
5 forbidden. As shee that had her Tongue cut, for
callyng of her Husband Theefe, woulde yet
notwithstandinge, make the signe of the Gallowse.

    Well sir (quoth Queene Aurelia) Epicarias   Epicaria, in
obstynacy, who endured to bee rent in peeces,   the trembling
                                                                    passage of
10 before shee woulde confesse the conspyracie   death, was
agaynst Nero, would have ben holden for a Vertue   constant.
of staiednesse in a man.

    And what say you of Leena, that byt off her
tonge, and spit it in the Tirant Hippias face,   PLIN. lib. 34.
15 because she would not bewraye a conspiracy   Cap. 2.
against him.

    Madame, with your favour, (quoth the Doctor)
had she not had this foresight, it had ben lyke
the Athenians shuld have bene driven to have
20 made a brasen Bell, as a Monument of her talke:
rather then a tongueles Lionnesse, as they did   An envious
in honour of her silence, for had she not   Suggestion.
mistrusted her imperfection, she would never
have committed that tirannie upon her selfe.

25   Had her tongue beene venomed with your
mallice, it is like (quoth Queene Aurelia) that
the Athenians had/ veryfied your slaunderous   P1^r
opinion: herewith she looked a skanse, upon her
favoured servaunts, as who would saye, I check the
30 omission of your dutie, in not defending of my
right. Upon which warning, and espetially, for
the excellencie of this sexe, (quoth Ismarito,) a   A man may
man may doo justice unto an other, without   praise a
injurie to himselfe: and sure without the   Woman without

The Fourth Dayes Exercise 141

reproche of men, a man may commend the excellencie
of Women: in whose behalfe (although I wyll not
condemne Sir Soransos reasons,) yet in my opinion,
he erred in the first Article, where he toucheth
5 the perfection of Men, and the imperfection of
Women: for neither of themselves are perfect,
nor may have essentiall substaunce without the
other: But to dispute of this secret in nature
at large, were unpleasing to their chaste eares,
10 and too breefely to misticall, for theyr
understandings. But who so is so curious in
searche, let him reade the Philosophers Probleames,
with an unpartiall judgement, and he shall finde
them in substaunce every way as perfect as man.
15 And in the opinion of the eye, of all the sences,
who is the moste perfect Judge, they farre excell
man in purenes of complection: Where exception
is taken to the few in number, of singulerly well
qualyted Women, I affirme that it is not the
20 quantity, but the quallity that commends: a
little Salte, relisheth more then a great deale
of Sugar. Judeth with her owne hands, atchieved
a more honourable conquest, then all the Cilisions
besides.
25   Alexandra, the wife of Alexander, King of the
Jewes, (when the uncivill multitude, were ready
for his tiranie) to make the intrailes of Dogges,
a Sepulture for his dead body: yea and to be
further avenged, to murther his two Sonnes: by
30 her sweete behaviour, so mollified theyr cruell
hearts, as losing theyr resolutions, they gave
her husband an honourable buriall, and prostrated
themselves, at her Childrens feete: which
pacification, the strength nor wisdom of her

Marginalia:
- reproching a man.
- Chaste talk, ought espetially to be used in the presence of Women. Aris. Prob.
- The quallity and not the quantity commends.

counsel could not obtaine. By what instrument
did God first showe the vigor of his vengeaunce?   Eave.
by a Woman. And by what instrument did he showe
the / vertue of his mercie? by a Woman.   Our Lady.   P1^v

5 Soveraigne Vertue is Feminine, and (I blush to
tell it,) Irkesome Vice is Masculine. The Ladies
laughed out right, to heer Ismaritos difference.
But Soranso, halfe angrie, aunswered, that if
Ismaritos countrimen, were of his minde, they
10 might be ashamed that they were so effeminate.

    Pardon me, (quoth Ismarito,) it is theyr   Where an
commendation to yeelde unto Women, and to conquer   injurie in
Men.   words, may
    Tush, tush (quoth Bergetto) to nip himself   be revenged
in words, a
15 by the nose, Ismarito is to be pardoned: for his   Gentleman is
Captaine Saint George, is shackled in a Womans   not bound to
Garter.   his sword.

    It is true (quoth Ismarito) but thus fettered,
he hath many times chased Saint Michael to his
20 Mounte.

    Fabritio, fearing that these crosses would
turne to the Devils blessing, studyed how to
accorde this contention, and with that intent,   Discreete
(quoth he,) Ismarito, you have well deserved to   standers by
pacifieth
25 kisse these Ladyes handes, for your honourable   contentions.
commendation of theyr sexe: But where you say
Vertue is the Feminine, and Vice the Masculine,
bothe Men and Women, are understood in either.   Vertue and
The old Divines, tooke Vertue to be God, and Vice   vice, bothe
Feminine, and
30 the Divill, and either to be bothe Feminine and   Masculine.
Masculine. Orpheus sayde, that Jupiter and Pluto,
were bothe Male and Female. It is also read in
Scripture: That God fashioned bothe Man and
Woman to his owne likenesse. Moreover this worde

Homo, signifieth bothe kindes: so that since Man and Woman, are not simply of themselves, but compounded one of an other, I blame this unnaturall contention for excellencie, for neither can obtaine Soveraigne victorie, without dooing injurie unto themselves: The head among some is taken for the Man, and the heart for the woman, (for bothe are of an indifferent gender) and all the other members indifferently at their commaundement.   *Note.*

   Queene Aurelia, with a smiling countenaunce, aunswered, that she was content, that a Man should governe as the head, and women direct as the heart, and because we will not doo injurie, unto our naturall vertue of Modesty, / we will give place to you, in contention for Soverainetyes, and binde you to serve us for our vertues, and therewithall in rising, she broke of this controversie.   P2^r

Modesty an naturall vertue in a Woman.

   After Supper, there was a little time bestowed in the hearing of sweete Musique, but for that Queene Aurelias late distemprature, grew of over watching: the company this night, went unto their lodging in a good howre.

FINIS./

The fift Daies Exercise:

Containing a breefe discourse, touching the excellencie of Man: and a large discoverie of the inconveniences of over lofty, and too base Love: with other Morall notes, needefull to be regarded.

    The last nights good howre of repose, was the cause of the companies this daies early rising: who by nine of the Clock, entered the great Chamber, armed for any lawdable exercise. And after an accustomed duty of salutation discharged, every man be thought himselfe of some pleasing matter, to entertaine the present time. Soranso and Ismarito were severed from the rest of the company, upon private discourse: which beeing ended, Soranso, casting his eye aside, beheld in the hangings, the picture of Ixion, heardled to his tormenting Wheele. See yonder, (quoth he,) the worthy scourge of Ambition, and withall reported the Fable, of his presumptuous making of love to Juno. *[The Fable of Ixion.]*

    Naye (quoth Ismarito,) Ixion is rather the example of Vaine Glorie punished: for Jupiter, so well allowed of Ixions hie minde (in that he represented his Image) as he raysed him from Earthe to Heaven, and because he should not perish in his affection, he satisfied his desire with the embracement of a counterfeit Juno, and so sent him backe unto the Earth: where vaine glorious Ixion Proclaymed, that he was the Minion of Juno, and had Acteoned Jupiter: for which arrogancie, Jupiter threw him to Hell, with this pictured vengeaunce. *[To be proude in vertues, is commendable.]* *[The scorge of vaine glory.]*

    Questionlesse, (quoth Soranso,) this

The Fifth Dayes Exercise 145

imagination of the Heathen Poet, could not but
be the travell of a Divine spirit, it exposeth
such needefull matter, for Christians to
contemplate of./

5   You neede not doubt of your opinion, (quoth
Ismarito,) for after God had created Adam after
his owne Image, he scattered the seede of Adam
uppon the face of the whole world, and where some
ever the essentiall forme of Adam was, there was
10 also the Image of God, which in the moste
barberous and Heathen creature, laboureth to
bring out, hye and excellent things.

 I beseeche you, (quoth Soranso,) to inlarge
this discourse. I am not so simple to beleeve,
15 that we are like the Image of God, in our
outwarde shape: yet my knowledge is not perfect,
in what vertues we resemble the Image of God.

 Referring you, for your better knowledge, to
graver judgements (quoth Ismarito) I wyll onely
20 to satisfye your request, say what I have reade,
and what in my oppynyon, standeth with reason.

 In our exterior body, to say we resemble God,
were a grose ignoraunce: but in that our soule
is closed within our body, and giveth life, and
25 moving, to the whole body: it is no absurdity to
conclude the lesse within the greater, to showe
how the soule resembleth God: who consisteth in
a Trinity. Notwithstanding she is but one, yet
she comprehendeth in her three dignities, to wit,
30 Intendment, Will, and Memorie. And as the sonne,
is ingendered of the Father, and the holy Ghost
proceedeth from bothe: even so Will is engendred
of Intendment, and Memorie proceedeth from both:
and as the three persons of the Trinitie, are but

P3^r

The soule
traveleth to
bring forth
Divine
monuments
in the heathen.

A discreete
exordium,
for yong
men that
argue.

The excellencie
of man through
the vertue of
the soule.

Three
dignities, of
the soule.

one God, so the three powers of the soule, are
but one soule: and in that man is created in
this sorte, according to the image of God, because
he should resemble his creator in excellencie, he
5 is formed straight and not curbed: to behould
the earth, not thereby to shewe a dyfference
betweene him and other brute Beastes, but only
because he should raise his spirite, and heave
hys eyes to heaven, his originall, to contemplate
10 of divine and dureable thynges, and not of earthly
and such as peryshe. And sure the monuments,
that to this day renowne heathen <u>Alexander</u>, <u>Julius
Cesar</u>, <u>Scipio</u>, <u>Haniball</u>, and manye other stoute
warriors, <u>Plato</u>, <u>Pithagoras</u>, <u>Socrates</u>, <u>Solon</u>, and
15 ma-/ny thousand grave <u>Philosophers</u> weare the
exercyses of the soule, who in her function is
alwaies occupied, to make men shine like Angels.
And doubtles, the exploits of man, would be
wonderful, and glorious, were not the passages
20 of the three powers of the soule, <u>Intendment</u>,
<u>Will</u>, and <u>Memory</u> stopped, with these three evils
or defects of the body: <u>Ignorance, of that which
is good</u>, <u>Covetousnes, of that which is evill</u>, and
the <u>Infirmitie, and langor of the body</u>. These be
25 the evilles, that eclipseth the excellencie of
many who otherwise would appeare more glorious
then the Sonne, Moone, Starres, and Christall
Firmament, into whose motions, revolutions, and
influences, his knowledge foreseeth: or the earth
30 with all her faire furniture which he governeth,
and therfore he is called <u>Microcosmos</u>, for that
in excellencie, he egalleth the beautie of the
whole worlde.

    Sir (quoth <u>Soranso</u>,) you have inchaunted my

Side notes:
- Man is formed straight, because he should behold heaven, and contemplate one great matters.
- Three evils or defects of the body.

P3^v

Eares with such a pleasing regarde, as if you
were as tedious in discourse, as I would be
attentive in hearing, we should bothe lose our
dinners, without any great repining: but in
advauntage I beseech you, what may be the remedy
of these three evils, which thus obscure the
excellencie of man.

    Three soveraigne remedyes (quoth Ismarito,)
to witte Wisdome, Vertue, and Necessitie, which
to chase the other three evils, are thus ordered:
Wisdome against Ignoraunce: Vertue against Vice,
and Necessitie against Infirmitie. Wisdome is to
be understoode according to the condition of the
things, wherein we be ignorant. Vertue is an
habit of the soule, which without great
difficultie cannot be shaken out of his place and
subject: By Necessitie, absolutely is intended,
a supply against those wants, with which
Infirmitie hath charged us, as if we be lame, to
have Horse to ride: if we be sycke to have
medicine: if our bodyes be weake, to have
nourishing meates, etc. And by these three
remedyes, all Artes and Disciplines have beene
invented, to acquire Wisdome: Theorique, which
is contemplative, and consists in these three
parts, Theologie, Phisick, and Mathematique, was
found, for Vertue. Practise, which is active,
and devi-/ded, into Solitarie Private and
Publike, was put in use. And for Necessitie,
all Mecanicall craftes were invented. These
three vertues if we imbrace them, will chase the
other three evilles bothe out of our body, soule,
and remembrance. You have given me a short
sweete reason (quoth Soranso.) And a longe

Three remedies against the three evils of the body.

The originall of all Artes and Sciences.

Theorique.

Practise.

P4^r

Mecanicall craftes.

remembrance of my weake understanding (quoth
Ismarito:) but for that I have made this Sermon,
uppon your importunity, your curtesy I hope will
pardon me, as well as your wisdome will correct
5 my errours.

    I had thought Ceremonies had beene in
disgrace, among you Englishmen, (quoth Soranso,)
but I finde you superstitious in curtesie, and
therefore will take no example by you: but let
10 it suffise, I am your freend, and wyll deserve
this favour, in any resonable service.

Curtesie is commendable, but superfluous savours of flatterrie.

    By this time, Dinner was ready to be set
upon the boarde, and Queene Aurelia came againe
unto the open viewe, whose presence was as
15 welcome unto the generall company, as the cleare
Sunne (after roughe stormes) to the wether-weried
Sayler. After she had acquited the courteous
salutations of the whole troupe, she fyrste toke
her place, and then the rest as they pleased, or
20 were accustomed. At this Dinner there passed
much pleasaunt Table talke, impertinent for this
report: which beeing doone, at the accustomed
howre, Queene Aurelia sent for the chosen company,
who placed in the drawing Chamber: the Eunuck
25 knowing his charge, tuned his Lute, and songe
this following Sonet.

Who prickels feares, to pluck the lovely Rose,
    By my consent, shall to a Nettle smell:
Or through fainte heart, who dooth a Ladie lose,
30   A droyle I wishe, or to leade Apes in Hell.
    On Thornes, no Grapes, but sowre Slowes do growe:
    So from base love, a base delight dooth flowe. /

Then minde crowne thou, my thoughts above the skie,
    For easie gaynde, the Conquest is not sweete:
My fancie swift, with Icarus wings dooth flye.
    Yet fastined so, as fyre and Froste may meete.
5   For pleas'd am I, if hope returne but this:
    Grace is obtaynde, thy Mistrisse hand to kisse.

A Grace indeede, far passing all the joye,
    Of egall love, that offereth wish in wyll:
For though her scorne, and light regard annoy,
10   Dispaire of grace, my fancie can not kill.
    For why this joye, all passions sets in rest:
    I dayly see, my Mistresse in my breast.

    Who so invented this sonet (quoth Queene Aurelia,) deserveth to be well favoured of his
15 Mistresse, in that he kept her so carefully in his bosome.

    Nay (quoth Dondolo,) if his eyes were so subtyll, as absent, he could see her behavior, his affection were more daungerous then his
20 service necessarie.

    We geve you to know (quoth Isabella) that we waye not though our husbandes, a hundred myles of, knowe our behaviours at home.

    I thinke so (quoth the plaine Doctor,) for
25 so farre off they may sighe at their one mischaunce, but not chasten your amisse. Perchaunce they should not be charged with such injurie, as this company should be (quoth Maria Belochy) if wee would offer to aunswer your envious sugiestions.

30   Ladies I speake not with intent (quoth Soranso) to make a question of your behaviors, but admit you of all creatures the most perfect:

yet for that you have motions, as well bad, as
good, you maye many tymes make showe of evill,
and yet not doo amysse, which if your husbandes
be so quicke sighted, as to perceive, they will
5 judge by their owne eyes, and not by your hartes,
and so from shaddowes may growe evill effectes. /

If their sight be so quick (quoth Franceschina
Sancta) then, though by a negligent trespasse,
their wives sometime give them cause to sigh, with
10 a number of loving usadges, they will give them
daylye occasion of rejoysinge.

I graunt as muche (quoth Soranso) but this   The evyll of
will follow, the Husband will turne his owne   Jelousie.
mistruste, to hys Wives sorrow, and receave her
15 good usage to his owne pryvate comfort.

Indeede (quoth Alvisa Vechio) the love of a
jelous husband, is sawced with such frowarde
motions, as I had rather be matched with him,
that regardeth mee not at al, then with him that
20 loveth mee too muche: for of the one, though I
am not beloved, yet I shall not be much crossed:
of the other, I being too much beloved, I shall
never be in quiet.

I am not of your mynde (quoth Helena Dulce)   Harde is the
25 I had rather have my Husbande jelous, then   difference,
carelesse: for being carelesse, no good usage   betweene a
will reconcile him: and being Jelous, the Wife   carelesse
may studie out how to please him.   and a jelous
    Husbande.

Yea, but (quoth Katharina Trista) Men are so
30 easye conceited, that if they perceive a woman
studdieth how to please them, they straight
waies, imagine, she will lykewise studdie how to
deceive them: and therefore, God sheelde mee
from a Jelous Housbande. I have heard, the

whightstreaked Carnation Giliflower, was the
Metamorphos of a Faire Gentlewoman, beheaded by
her husband, upon this Jelous thought, that his
wife beinge so faire, could not but be beloved of
5 the Gods, although hee had no cause to suspect   Ovid. Meta.
men. And where have yee a larger Example of Love,   lib. 10.
then the Adventure of Orpheus, who by extreame
sorrow and sute, recovered his Wife out of Hell,   Eurydice.
and by over Jelous Love sent her thither againe.

10   Doctor Mossenigo was smyling out a scoffe,   Prevent a
upon this tale, which Queene Aurelia intercepted,   Scoffer, and
by ending of the Gentlewomens contention. By   he becommeth
your talke of Hell (quoth she) I see we are out   a Sotte.
of the way to Platoes Parradice: and / therfore,
15 good, we tourne backe agayne.   Q1^v

     In deede Madame (quoth Fabritio,) if we
travell styll, to choose the leaste of Evylles,
it wyll be longe before we come to the Fountayne
of Goodnesse.

20   Me thinkes (quoth Isabella,) the Sonet,
which mooved the late Question, directes a fayre
way to happinesse in Mariage: for it commendeth
loftie Love: And if, accordyng to the oulde
Proverbe: The best, is best cheape: this   A Commendation
25 Adventure, geveth Hope, and promiseth good   of lofty Love.
Fortune.

     It is true (quoth Soranso,) and I dare
undertake to approove it, the happiest estate in
Mariage.

30   Dondolo, because he would not be disgraced,
by mariyng a Burgoys fayre Daughter of Ravenna,
offered to proove the contrarie.

     Queene Aurelia, licensed them to shew their
reasons.

Wherupon, (quoth <u>Soranso</u>:) to geve great
Ladies and Gentlewomen of calling, their true
right and honor, who lightly, marry not their
Inferiours in reputation, but for some especiall
5 Vertue, that doth commende their choice, and
cleareth the Bleamish of their Husbandes basenes:
I must confesse, that he which rayseth his
thought so hye, undertaketh (no doubt) a tedious
sute: his delayes wyll be greevous, and his
10 Solliciters wyll be well rewarded, in what sort
so ever he be regarded. But what of this? <u>Quo
quid difficilius, eo pulchrius</u>: Perryll maketh
honor perfect: the styngyng of the Bee, mendes
the sweetenes of Honie: Roses best refresheth
15 our Sences, when we prick our handes to reache
them: He that crackes the Nut, thinkes the
Kernell sweetest. The reason is, not for that
the goodnesse of a thing, is the better, for the
evil therunto belonging: but, for that the
20 remembrance of the evyl, maketh us holde the good
in more reputation: especially, in love. The
Affection, whiche is forced with teares, wonne
with sighes, gaind with expence, and compassed
with sorow, is held most pleasant, most perfect
25 and of longest continuance. Againe, easie gotten
good wyll, becommeth in a while lothsome: the
cause is, as I conceive, for that the pleasure
was ne-/ver seasoned with paine. Once, a man,
in loving his better, to encrease his passion,
30 shal lack no occasion, both to seeke, sue, sigh
and serve: and yet, to feede his hope, he shal
want, neyther faire lookes, good wordes, nor
possybilytie of favour. For, for to obtain a
great Ladie, acquireth many circumstaunces, not

*The evyll of
a thyng,
commendeth
the goodnesse.*

Q2^r

for that shee is precise to love, but for that
shee is wise, (or woulde bee so thought) in her
proceedinges. But whether she love or no: <u>Ovid</u>
saith, there is no woman, but wil indure the
5 demaund: she is contented with service to be
courted: and in recompence, rewardeth with good
countenance. But, which most sustaineth hope,
the example is in continual use: that love
spareth no degree, transgresseth every law, and   Love spareth
10 bringeth the mightiest in bondage to the meanest. no degree.
King <u>Cofetua</u>, the <u>Affrican</u>, became enamoured of
a Begger: faire <u>Venus</u>, espoused yll favoured
<u>Vulcan</u>: <u>Pigmalion</u> doted upon an Image: <u>Narcissus</u>
was drowned in imbrasing his owne shadow: and
15 mightie <u>Jove</u>, many times, cast aside his divinitie,
to dallie with simple country trulles: then, why
shuld the affected (how bace so ever his estate
be) dispaire to attempt a great Ladie, when his
warrant is signed with so large Aucthoryties?
20 But whether he speede or faile: be accepted or
rejected: well entertained, or yll intreated:
the ymagination, that time wil invest his desire   Hope to
with delight, is to the Affected, a Paradice,   compasse
farre exellyng the possession of equall love: great matters
   comforteth
25 But if in the end, her affection, or his good   more then the
fortune, concludeth his wish in desire: her   possession of
love, whiche can not choose but be great: in   tryfles.
that she marieth beneth her callyng: And her
Abylytie, which allured at the first, with his
30 inhabylytie: to realysh both, can not but make
the Husbande fortunate, and the Wife well pleased:
for that in recompence of this advancement, she
may presume, somwhat, to rule her Heade: but,
which most contents, she shal have the satisfaction

of her fancie a bed.   Reproofe of
    If a House, were as soone bilded, as the Plot   loftie Love.
is drawn (quoth Dondolo) Shepherds wold disdaine
to live in Cotages; even so, if every man could
5 as soone compasse a Lady for / himselfe, as he   Q2^v
can report the fortune of other: there must be
an Act to make Ladies, or Lords must be glad of
mean Women. But admit, by the example of other
mens Advauncements, that the meanest may be raised,
10 by the yeelding fancye of the mightie: I
prophesie that such an upstarte, had more neede
of ten Eyes, to warde the mallice of his Wives
kindred, then one tongue to move her to kindnesse.
A woman cannot myslike affectionated profers,
15 because they proceede of love: But her kindred
disdaineth his attempte, for that the conclusion,
tendeth both to their and her dishonour: A woman
seeing her servaunts passions, cannot but sustaine   One kinsman
him with pittie, her Kindred seeinge him in good   hath an
                                                                                                 Interest in an
20 way to bee beloved, will lye in waite for his   others honor.
lyfe: For though she may dispose of her affection,
her kindred hath an interrest in her honour, which
if she consent to staine, or deminishe, shee dooth
injurie to her whole house.
25   The Cardinal of Aragon, advenged the base   An inhumain
choice of his Sister, the Duchesse of Malfy, with   parte.
the death of her selfe, her Children, and her
Husband: and alleadged in defence, that he had
done no injurie to Nature, but purged his House
30 of dishonour: for Nature (quoth he) is perfect,
and who blemisheth her is a monster in Nature,
whose head, without wrong to Nature may be cut
off.
    Yea (quoth Soranso) but, this Cardinall, for   Defence. &c.

all his habit, and glose of Justice, is for this
Act, so often regestred for a Tirant, as I feare
mee he will never come among the number of
Saints. But the example of these Mariages are
usuall, and such ensuing vengeaunce is but rare,
and besides her espetiall contentment, a woman
looseth none of her general titles of dignitie
by matching with her inferior.

    In deede (quoth Dondolo) in common curtesie
she enjoyeth them, but in the strickt construction
of the Law, she is degraded. And by this meane
is bounde to intertaine the meaner, with
familyaritie, least, they (being prowde, or
reputing her scornfully) doo crosse her over the
thumbes with the follyes of her fancy. But admit
the meane servant, / marrie his Mistresse, and
escapeth the mallice of her friendes: which
successe, one amonge tenne suche Suters hardly
attaineth. Let him yeelde to pay this rent for
his good fortune: To suffer his Wife, to rule,
to direct, and to commaunde his owne determynations.

    And where shee ordereth: The uncontrouled
Wife, desireth to be served with pompe, and to be
set foorth with pride: whiche the ruling Husband
would represse, as wel for saving his wives
honour, as for sparing his owne pursse.

    The uncontrouled wife desireth to walke at
lybertie, and to be visited of many: of which
the ruling Husbande, woulde barre her: as well
to preserve his mynde from mistruste, as to keepe
his Chimney from being fyred.

    The uncontrouled wife disdayneth the
Countrie and desireth the Citie: which the
rulyng Husband would mislyke, for that in the

Marginalia:
Reproofe. &c.

A woman that abaseth her selfe in Mariage, in Law loseth her reputation, but not in curtesie.

Q3^r

The naturall desires of a woman.

Countrie, the exercise of huswiverie inlargeth
his Wives estimation, and in the Cittie, Idlenesse
hazardeth her reputation.

    The uncontrouled Wife, desireth without
checke to pratle, and without discreation to
governe: which the rulyng Husbande in no wise
would allowe, for that manye wordes is a bleamish
to his wives modestie, and the rule of his Wife,
is warrant sufficient, for the wise to over rule
him for a Woodcocke.

    Many other vanities, follow the desires of
Women: which a man thus advaunst, must forbeare
to chasten, least hee expose himselfe to a
thousande daungers: for the wife taking pepper
in the nose, will suffer him, (yea perchaunce,
agree to make him) a pray, to the displeasure of
his enemies: I meane her able Friendes and
kindred: which bondage is not within the
Paradice, Plato speaketh off: For according to
the opinion of sundrie Philosophers, as Nature
will not be controuled, for that she createth:
as Fortune is won with no praiers, because shee
is blinde, and shooteth at adventure: no more
dooth Marriage alow of inequallitie, because her
will is to devide her be-/nyfites, and blessing
among the married with indifferencie.

    To this ende Marriage is lykened to Sienes
grafted in a stocke of contrarie qualitie: for
as by groweth and good order, they both become of
one nature, even so, man and woman united in this
honourable estate, with good usage, become of one
disposition. Againe, as Sienes thus grafted
without speciall Husbandrie, while they bee
tender, come to no proofe: even so man and woman,

Judgement in reproofe of lofty love.

thus joyned in Matrimonie: unlesse in the prime
of their Mariage, with equall care, they love and
cherrish one an other, in the waine of their
yeares, the sweete Fruites of wedlocke, will be
blasted with repentaunce.

Segnior Fabritio, to conclude Don Dolos
opinion, with his owne Judgement, saide in trueth,
that Marriage coulde not away with such servitude:
as the Husband, who is wise and the cheefe,
shoulde obay the wife, who in common construction,
is simple, weake and the inferiour. And where a
Rich woman (as Don Dolo hath said) Marieth her poore
Servant, because she is the cause of his
advancement, she will looke to governe: which if
she doo, her indiscression, will move others to
speake, and her Husband to sorrow: and if he
challenge the previledge of a husband to direct,
hee shall bee bounde to a lyfe more bitter then
Death. Not, but that in respect of his former
estate, he may endure these crossinges of his
wife, but because, as hee is growne in estimation:
so is hee growne in hautinesse of mynd, and can
now wurse brooke an unkinde word, then in times
past, an injurious deede. And therefore in
Don Dolos behalfe, I doo judge Soranso to be in an
errour.

I wil not dispute, against the Authoritie of
your judgment (quoth Soranso) but at adventure if
yonger Brethren er in Mariage, God send them to
stumble upon no worser fortune.

> Men must have regarde how they blame, least they byte themselves.

Queene Aurelia, who regarded, that Dondolo
was somewhat to lavish, in painting out, of the
natural desires of a woman, knew as well, how to
set foorth his follyes and oversight: and therefore

to take a modest revenge (quoth/ shee,) If
happinesse in <u>Mariage</u> consisteth so much in the
Lordly rule of the Husbande, then where a man
maryeth his inferriour in reputation, there is
5   a lykelyhood of good agreement: Wherfore
<u>Segnior Dondolo</u>, because I think you married
your wife, with the same Judgement, with which
you manyfested the inconveniences of loftye Love:
I beseeche you, show us the blessinges of this
10   inferiour choyce.

    <u>Soranso</u>, and the rest began to smyle, to
heare this commaundement: for well they knew
<u>Dondolo</u>, was intrapt with a slaunder of his owne
reputation: but <u>Dondolo</u>, although, he were a
15   litle gauled, set a reasonable florish, upon his
bace fancie: and therefore (quoth he) as it is
alreadie adjudged, if a man marrie above his
callyng, he must beare with his Wife in folly,
as much as shee was blynded in fancying of him:
20   which bondage, <u>Mariage</u> can hardly endure: Then   Defence of
if hee match with his inferiour, if contraries   bace love.
have contrarie qualyties, <u>per consequence</u>: she
will be as lowly, as the other is loftie: as
pacient, as the other is prowde: and as dutiful,
25   as the other is disdainfull: if the other
prodigally spend, because her portion is large,
she wil with huswiverie spare, because her
substaunce was small: If the other presume,
because of her Gentrie, shee will seeke reputation,
30   with her good conditions: And if the other
bolster her faults, with the countenaunce of her   A riche
able Friendes, she dooing amisse, will crie her   Dowrie with
Husbande mercie, because she lackes succourers,   a woman.
to sustaine her evill: a course, as <u>Plato</u> sayeth,

that maketh the dowrie of the poore virgin of
greater vallue then the possessions of a riche
Ladie.

  You are nothing deceived in the course   Reproofe. &c.
5 (quoth Faliero) but much mistaken in the creature.
As touching your Contraries, I mislike your
Consequent: For Fyre and Water have contrarye
woorkynge, and unorderlye used, both hurtfull,
Prodigallytie, and Coveitusnesse, are contraries,
10 and neither necessarie: even so, the courtly
dame, and / the Countrey Droyle, as they contrary,   Q4^v
in callyng, so are they contrary in conditions:
and so they may be matched, neither profitable.

  A Diamond is blemisht, by the settyng in
15 Brasse, and a Flynt, not the beautyfuller, for
beynge garnishte with Gold: even so, the honour
of a woman, is Eclipst, in matchyng with her
Servaunt, her slave, or her Inferiour: for that
Straungers wyll valewe her by her Fortune,
20 although her haughtie nature, wyll not lose the
name of her reputation: Neither is the estimation
of a Kitchynstuffe inlarged, by marriyng with a
Courtier: for that the Best wyll disdayne her
Basenes, not so much for her byrth, as her
25 bryngynge up: Yet, presumyng on her Husbandes
callyng: in Pryde, she wyll pearch with the
hyest: whiche Soveraigntie, in the one, and   Kytte wyll
saucines in the other, separats pleasantnesse   to kynde.
from their Husbandes, and quietnesse, both from
30 themselves and their Houshouldes: where, as if
the Gentlewoman, marrie with a Gentleman, and a
Kitchin stuffe with a Cooke: the one with
duetifull regarde of her Husband, may hold her
reputation, and the other shal not be driven, to

dissemble with their kinde.

 Well, let this suffice, to refell their Suggestions, that thinke pleasantly to spende their dayes, by marrying eyther their better or inferiour.

 Now, touchynge the generall disposition, of suche wemen, as from the Cart, are raysed unto this account: they will use the better sorte with straingenesse, because they lacke the order of honest curtesie to entertain them, and with the basest wyl be famyliar, because the rudenes of the one answereth the ignorance of the other: So that, it is more requisite for him that is thus married, to watch his wyves goyng into the Stable, for feare of his Horsekeeper, then in her Parlour, to eye her behaviour, in entertayning the Gallant.

 Examine Kyng <u>Astolphus</u>, what constancie he found in his three halpenie Juell, whome he had tourned out of Sheepes Russet, into Cloth of Silver: In such honours, / had no otherwise altered her manners, but that she thought the Lyppes of a Captaine was a sweete as a Kings, and therfore in all her braverie, she fell to her kinde.

 If this suffice not, heare the usage of <u>Bianca</u> <u>Maria</u>, Daughter and onely Heire of <u>Giaccomo</u> <u>Scapardon</u>, a notable Userer of <u>Baetta</u>. <u>Biancas</u> beautie, made her sufficiently knowne, but her Fathers Bagges, made her wonderfully desiered: so that both joyned together, advaunst her, from a Shop Maide, firste, to be the wife of <u>Vicount</u> <u>Hermes</u>: after whose death, clyming up to further honor, and declyning in honestie, she

R1^r

The fall of Maria Bianca is written by the Aucthor in his Booke, intituld, The Rocke of Regarde.

espoused the Counte of Zelande. Long after the
seconde Mariage, shee dallyed not with her
disposition, which was rather in an open Shop, to
bee courted with men, then in a secreat Chamber
to be accompanied with wayting women: so that
following her unmodest fancy, with a few Prentices,
she fled from her Husband to Padua, where she set
up for her selfe: and thus she unworthely raised
to bee a Countesse, wickedly, and wilfully fel to
be a Courtisan.

    Andrea Zeno, a Gentleman of Vennice, was as
slutishly served with via a Cookes Daughter, who
upon her Mariadge day, made an easye way for her
Husband, with no better man, then a Carpenter.

    If you coveit more Authorities, to approve
so common a mischiefe, read Ovid Metamorphosis in
Latine, Segnior Lodovicus Regester, in Italian,   Aucthoryties
Amadis de Gaule, in French, and the Pallace of   for amorous
pleasure, in English, where you shall finde store Histories.
of Histories to the like purpose.

    Sir (quoth Dondolo) without offence, either
to your person or your proofes (for that the one
I love, and the other I allowe) to confirme my
oppinion I can likewise, summon women as base as   Defence.
these in birthe, and as hie as these in fortune,
which with their good behaviours, gave a grace to
their reputacion. Chaste Epethia, the welbeloved
wife of Hanno Prince of Carthage, was a Sailers
daughter. The vertuous Virginia, espoused to
Sextillius a worthie Senator of Rome, was a
Laundresse. Both these / were beautified with   R1^v
such singuler vertues, as while they lyved, their
honest lyves instructed the greatest Lady, in
poincts of honor: and being ded, the remembrance

of their worthinesse is a special commendation to
the whole sexe of wemen.

    Sir (quoth <u>Faliero</u>) as the Proverb goeth: Reproofe, &c.
<u>One or two Swallowes, prooves not Summer</u>: two
5 or three, may thrive by Dice, yet is dicyng yl
Husbandrie: because for the inrichyng of a few,
it beggereth many: so, though two or three
worthy Parsonages were wel wived out of worthles
parentages: a thousand, following the same course,
10 have had a contrary fortune: and wher the
knowledge of evil, is more then the possibility
of good: vertue, warrants not the venter: In
warre, the miraculous escape of two or three rash
persons, is no safecundit, for every man to ron
15 upon the pikes: yet I graunt that in war,
desperate men are nedeful, for the safetie of the
discreate, and so are homely women, necessarie
for their service: but if you will use either to
your benefit, incourage the one with gret pay, and
20 the other with good wages: for if you commit a
charge to a harebraine Souldior his timeritie in
one houre, wil hinder more, then his yeres hazard
did further. And as I have said, if you make of
your Kitchen maid, a companion, her pride in one
25 dayes libertie wil anoy more, then her seaven
yeres love wil comfort.

    Seeing the company begin to smyle, I am
satisfied (quoth <u>Dondolo</u>.)

    But how? (quoth <u>Alvisa Vechio</u>?) doe you
30 repent you of your bargaine, or disalow of
<u>Falieros</u> proofes?

    Neither (quoth <u>Dondolo</u>:) For in general
choice, this course is out of the way, to <u>Platos
Paradice</u>: but for that my especial Fortune is

good, I am pleased.

    Yea, (quoth Soranso,) or if the contrary had happened, this might have comforted you, that your wife should not have been the only blamed woman in the Parish, nor you the sole unfortunate man.

    Wel, (quoth Fabritio, and Isabella:) There needes no further judgement in this Question, then Dondolos confession and his yealding, to Falieros proofes. /

    We have in this exercise taken three sundrie wayes, (quoth Queene Aurelia) and yet never a one the right way to our Paradice: and nowe it is too late to traivel any further. Therefore we will refreash our spirites with a little Musicke, and so adjourne our further controversies untill too Morowe: but as the Eunuke was a tuning his voyce, to have fulfilled his Ladies commaundement, Knowledge was given of certaine honourable Personages arival: by occasion wherof, the company left their determination to furnish the great Chamber.

A confession is a prety Judgement.

R2^r

The wittie device of Segnior Philoxenus, to give certayne Comedians a Theame, to present some pastime in action, the fift night, after Supper.

    By that time, Supper was done, certayne Comedians of Ravenna, presented their service to Segnior Philoxenus, and his honourable companie, who are not tide to a written device, as our English Players are, but having certayne groundes or principles of their owne, will, Extempore, make a pleasaunt showe of other mens fantasies: So that to try the quicknes of the Gentlemen, and Gentlewomens wittes, to give the Comedians a

Theame, Segnior Philoxenus, demaunded the meaning
of certaine Questions.

    Segnior Soranso, (quoth he:) What passion is
that, that tormenteth a man most, and hath least
power to overcome?

    To thinke of a Womans Inconstancie, (quoth   1. Inconstancie.
Soranso:) which greeveth every man, and cannot
be subdued by women themselves.

    Madame Aurelia, (quoth Philoxenus:) What
thing is that, which most delighteth, and most
deceiveth a Woman?

    A mans dissimulation, (quoth Queene Aurelia:)   2. Dissimulation.
Which hath such a sweete passage, through his
Tongue, as it delighteth like the Sirens Songes,
and yet turneth to as deceitefull a conclusion,
as the Crocadiles Teares. /

    This yet, was but quid pro quo: so that   R2^v
neither one parte, nor the other was displeased.

    The modest laughter being ceased, Segnior
Philoxenus demaunded of Ismarito, what was the
cause of most Devotion? and yet the greatest
replenisher of Hell.

    Ignoraunce (quoth Ismarito)whiche causeth   3. Ignorance.
men to worship Stones, and dishonour God.

    Madame Maria, what is that (quoth Segnior
Philoxenus) that of men is least esteemed, and
of God most regarded?

    Chastitie (quoth Maria Belochy) whiche is   4. Chastytie.
precious before God, and a laughing stock among
men.

    Doctor Mossenigo (quoth Segnior Philoxenus)
amonge men who is the most cruell?

    A Dycer (quoth the Doctor) for he teareth   5. A Dicer.
God in peeces. This answer, was both true, and

moved newe laughter: Although it were propounded
to discover the nature of the Envious, who   6. Envie.
murthereth the lyving, and the fame of the dead.

    Madam Lucia (quoth Segnior Philoxenus)
5 wherein doth a man please a woman best, and
displease himselfe most?

    The modest Gentlewoman began to blush, and
with great difficultie resolved this Question.
In the end, by the tongue of Alvisa Vechio
10 (quoth she) In giving of her, her Wyll.   7. Will.

    It is true (quoth the Doctor) for her delight
is to governe, wherin her discretion, giveth
others cause to laugh, and her Husband to hang
the Lyp.

15   Segnior Dondolo (quoth Segnior Philoxenus)
what is the greatest freende to men at libertie,
and the most enimie to such as are condemned?

    Hope (quoth Don dolo,) whiche incourageth men   8. Hope.
at lybertie, to attempt great matters, and maketh
20 such as are condemned, unprepared for death.

    Madam Helena (quoth Segnior Philoxenus) what
is that which woundeth the hart, and yet is
worshipped of the eye?

    Beautie (quoth Helena Dulce) for it pleaseth   9. Beautie.
25 a mans eye, and pearceth his hart. /

    Segnior Bergetto, (quoth Segnior Philoxenus)   R3^r
What is that which oweth most and payeth least,
and of all evils is the worst.

    Ingratitude: (quoth Bargetto:) For that   10. Ingratitude.
30 Monster receiveth good turnes, and payeth
vengeance.

    Madame Franceschina, (quoth Segnior
Phyloxenus:) What is that, whiche in lovynge too
muche, baneth with Hate?

The Fifth Dayes Exercise   166

    Jelousie: (quoth Franceschina Sancta:)   11. Jelosie.
whiche, by overmuche lovyng, raiseth Suspition:
Suspition mooveth Contention, and Contention
tourneth to mortall hatred.

5   Segnior Faliero: I demaunde (quoth
Phyloxenus:) who he is, that profiteth his
frendes, but by Death? is a Stewarde, for other
men: and maketh his Account (only) with God?

    A Coveitous man (quoth Faliero:) who, whyle   12. Covetousnesse.
10 he lyveth, is enemie unto hymself, and therfore,
unlykely, to be friende to others: also is but a
Stewarde of the goods hee gathereth, for he
spareth for others, and spendeth little or nothing
uppon himselfe: and at the judgement day, before
15 God, must make account of all his deceit.

    Madam Katherina, (quoth Segnior Philoxenus:)
what is that, which is couldest clad in Friese,
and warmest attyred in pretious Stones?

    Pride, (quoth Katherina Trista,) which hath   13. Pride.
20 no grace, but in braverie.

    Lovely Guestes, (quoth Segnior Philoxenus,)
you have so lively devined my meaning in your
sharpe answeres: as I expecte wonders, of your
dayly disputation.

25   Sir, (quoth Fabritio,) we hitherto, have but
exposed, and refelled errours.

    If you have done so muche (quoth Philoxenus)
you have made a fayre passage for the glorie of
Trueth, which by the refelling of Error, you   Vertue is
30 shall finde: for everie vertue is commended by   commended by vice.
his contrarie. A Diamond seemeth the fairer, for
his foyle. Blacke best setteth foorth White:
Good is most praysed in the reprehension of Evill:
and Trueth in / the hyest degree is renowned by   R3^v

the refelling of errour: and therfore follow your
purpose, the conclusion, cannot, but bee profitable.

Heere **Segnior Philoxenus** stopped his
digression, and commaunded the **Comedians**, to
5 bethinke themselves of some action, that should
lyvelie expresse the nature of **Inconstancie**,
Dissimulation, **Ignoraunce**, and the rest of the
passions, before named: Which charge being given,
while the Actors, were attiring themselves, for
10 the stage, Queene **Aurelia**, and her Attendaunts,
tooke their places, with such advauntage, as every
Gentleman, had lyberty, to devise with his
Mistresse.

After the **Comedians** had put themselves in
15 order, they patched a Comedie together, and under
the resited names, showed some matter of Morallytie,
but a greate deale of mirth: who with their
pastime, kept the companie up so long, as drowsie
sleepe, which delighteth in nothing but scilence,
20 arrested the greater part of them, and caried them
close prisoners, unto their Chambers.

FINIS. /

The syxt Dayes Exercise:

Contayninge: Many needefull regardes, for a Gentleman: with a Discoverie of the inconveniences of Marriages, where there are great inequalitie of yeares.

  The chearefull Sunne, which comforteth everie earthlye Creature, as the Lanterne of broade day, so lightened every Chamber of Segnior Phyloxenus Pallace: as the Gentlemen and Gentlewomen, to bee avenged of the injurie of Night, (who being the Mother of confusion, had seperated them, from their companions of pleasure) hastely rose and attired themselves: and (like unto Partryges, that how so ever they are seavered, know (and retire unto) their meetyng places) presented them selves, in the great Chamber. The office of civill courtesie discharged, such as were coupled, intertained Time, with the device of their especial fancyes: others, contemplated of their private affaires: and Ismarito amonge the rest, in a quiet place, was reading in Peter Mesiere his Cronicle of Memorable things: The rare Historie of Tamberlaine the Great, surnamed Flagellum Dei, where he much admired, the vertues of the man, who of a laboring Pesaunt, or (in the best degree) of a poore Souldier, by his vertues and Invincible valure, became a great Monarch: Yea, and while Tamberlayne lived, was as much feared as Alexander. But Ismarito, more lamented, that so mightie a Monarchie, erected by the Father, should end, by the envy, and civill dissention of the Children.

  Segnior Philoxenus (after he had given a Bon giorno, to the companie,) seing Ismarito, not

Tamberlaine the Great, in the beginning a Pesaunt.

chained to a companyon, determined to geve his
solytarinesse, a disgrace, by conversing with him,
in some Gentlemanly Discourse: but finding him
accompanied with so sweet a companion, as
5 Mesires Cronicles, Segnior Ismarito, (quoth hee)
you have deceived my imagination, which perswaded
mee that you were solitarye, and therefore,
bounde mee (in courtesye) to visite you. / But,
seeing the great personages, with whom you
10 devise, I envie your happy contemplation.

    But your Envie (quoth Ismarito) is lyke that
of Mutius Seavola, desirous to excell the better
sort in vertue, as you exceede the rascall
multitude in curtesie.

15   This encounter, and a litle other pryvate
talke ended: Segnior Philoxenus, lead Ismarito,
into a fayre Lybrarie, beautified with such a
number of goodly Bookes, of all Sciences, Lawes,
Customes, Governmentes, and memorial Monuments,
20 as wel auncient as Modern, as it came very neare
in excellencie, to the famous Lybrarie of Cosmos
de Medicis in Florence: who imitated in his
Monument, Ptolomey, surnamed Philodelphus: who
had the seventie Interpreters of the Jewes, to
25 translate the Sacred Bible, into the Egiptian
Language: and with great dyllygence, soughte to
have the severall Coppyes of all Bookes.

    After Ismarito had well regarded, the orderly
sortinge of these Bookes, (and how, by a shorte
30 Kallender, a Man without greate paine, mighte
turne unto anye harde Question, in any Science,
and have large resolutions) and had taken a note
of the title of certayne Bookes that hee had not
seene, and yet necessarie to be read.

Side notes:

He is not alone that hath good Bookes.

R4^v

A Gentleman tooke advantage of a worde to praise the good, as to check the evyll.

A most famous librarie in the Dukes Pallace at Florence left by Cosmos de Medicis.

Segnior Philoxenus ledde him into his owne
private studie which was furnished with
Summaries, or Abridgementes of all Sciences,
which he studied, with such a judgement, as there
5 was no Arte, wherein he had not a speciall
knowledge, whiche in argument, he exposed, with
so good a wit and memorie as, manie times, he
grounded Masters in that science. And for that
in al his actions he was the true patterne for a
10 Gentleman to imitate. In honour of his worthines
and for the benefite of such Gentlemen, as will
folow his example, in Vertue, I am bounde to set
briefely downe, the chiefest course of his Studie.

First and principally, for the comfort both
15 of his bodie and soule. In Theologie, he reade
those bookes, that / cleared the mistes of
Ignoraunce, and unmasked the deceiptes of the
superstitious Monkes, Friers, etc. And contemplated
in the sweete comfort of those Aucthors, that
20 expounded the hard passages of the Scripture.

And for that Health, is the most precious
Juell of the worlde, knowyng the Constitution of
his owne bodie, he studied so muche in Phisicke,
as without the direction of Doctors, hee knewe,
25 what meate and Medicine, agreede with his nature.

To minister Justice, unto the Ignorant
multitude, and to keepe hymselfe out of the
Forfaites of Lawe, he studied the civill Law, and
specially, the Statutes of his Countrey: And
30 (questionlesse) the Gentleman, that is ignoraunt
in the Lawes of his Countrey, is an enemye to
hymselfe, and a Cipher in the comon weale.

In Militarie Knowledge, he was experienced, as
wel, by service in the Field, as in readyng

Margin notes:
- It belongeth to a Gentleman to be sene in many things.
- Divinitie.
- S1^r
- Phisyck.
- Lawe.
- Art Militarie.

Vegetius and other Aucthors in his Studie. And
some travell in this Arte, is needefull, as well
as comendable for a Gentleman: for it is not
ynough for hym, to be Togatus, as a Romayne
5 Oratour, nor Paliatus, as a Gretian Phylosopher:
in that he must as well in the field, looke his
enemie in the face, as imbrace his frend in the
house: and therfore, though he bare a Pen in his
eare, (to write his owne Commentaries) hee is
10 bounde to weare a Sword by his side, to doo his
Countrie service.

    For Government, and Civil behaviours, he
read Plutarches Moralles: Guevaraes Dial of   Moralitie.
Princes: The Courtier of Count Baldazar,
15 Castillio: and others. And (in trueth,) it is
not so necessarie, to be well borne, as to be
well quallyted and of good behaviour: wherfore,
the studie of Morallytie, is verie needefull for
a Gentleman.

20   He (likewise) studied Cosmographie, and had
therin commendable knowledge: which studie, can
not, but much please and commende a brave minded
Gentleman: For by the vertue therof, he shalbe,   Cosmographie.
in his Studie, able to sur-/vaye the whole worlde: S1^v
25 and with an agreable Discourse, shall bound out a
Stranger his owne Countrey.

    He was a good Hystoriographer, and had read
manie rare Chronicles. How pleasing this studie   Hystoriografie.
is to a Gentleman, is lively expressed in his
30 owne nature, greedy of newes. And where may hee
have better intilligence, then Cronicles? in which,
quietly in his owne Study, he may receive
knowledge, of Actes done throughout the whole
worlde.

He was a good <u>Harrolde</u>, and had read much in
<u>Armorie</u>: An Arte most needefull, for a Gentleman,   Armorie.
in that it is the Cognisaunce of himselfe. And
in my opinion, he that is not able to blason his
5 owne Armes, is not worthie to beare them.
    These Gentlemanly studies he used, intermedled
with others of more pleasure, whiche I had not
leasure to regarde, nor memorie to beare away:
but in all his actions, and behaviours, he exposed
10 a Gentleman so perfect, as in regarding of hym,   Segnior
but one halfe yeare, a man might have noted downe   Philoxenus
a Courtier, not inferriour to that of Count   a perfect
<u>Baldezar</u>.   Courtier.
    By that time <u>Segnior Philoxenus</u> had
15 sufficiently fed <u>Ismaritos</u> eyes, with this
honourable favour: the sounde of the Trumpet,
gave knowledge of dinner, so that <u>Ismarito</u>, was
driven to leave, that earthly Paradice, to
attende honourable <u>Philoxenus</u>, into the great
20 Chamber: against whose comming, the Table stoode
furnished with manye daintie Dishes. And Queene
<u>Aurelia</u>, and the rest of the Companie, were readie
to salute him: whiche curtesye perfourmed, she
tooke her appointed place and the rest, as they
25 pleased.
    Towardes the latter ende of this dinner, a
meane fellow, garded between, two Furies of the
Kitchen, was brought <u>coram nobis</u>: for some pettie
pilfering in the Scullerie.
30   <u>Segnior Philoxenus</u>, referred his paine to the
Judgement, of the Gentlemen, and Gentlewomen there
present. / Some of the Gentlemen, appointed him
some pleasaunt paine, in the office, where hee
dyd the trespasse: some other of the Gentlewomen

overcome, with a natural pitty, accepted his
teares in satisfaction, and so discharged him:　　　Wemen are
But the Doctor more rougher then the rest, tooke　　to pitifull
him up so short, as the poore fellow was driven　　to be judges.
5 to say, Sir, where you may help, hurt not: The
Doctor, to satisfie his request, and to keepe
his first determination, aunswered, to help hange
a Theefe, is no hurte, to the common weale, your
petition shalbe signed. The rascall Theefe,
10 hearing this severe Judgement (as the Italians
are naturally quicke witted) replyed: If cheefe
Majestrates shoulde set their handes to this
Justice, There would bee more Lawyers hanged, for　　A scoffer is
stealing of Houses, then Roges for robbinge of　　　many times
15 Headges. The aunswere of the Doctor, and the　　　smiten with
replye of the poore Fellow, made the company so　　his owne
merrie, that for the pastime, the trespasser had　　weapon.
made them, they remitted the punishment of his
offence.
20　　The laughter quieted: in the commendation
of his Countriemans capassitie (quoth Soranso)
Master Doctor, this poore Snake, spake true
Italian.
　　Yea (quoth the Doctor,) but he lackes the
25 vertues of the auncient Romaines: covertly
expressing thereby, that their wits were good,　　　Italions are
but their conditions were evill.　　　　　　　　　　wise, but
　　Bargetto (envying the favours, Ismarito　　　　evill
receaved, and for some pryvate grudge, about　　　condicioned.
30 crossing in Argument) sought by some pleasant
scoffe, to raise an unkinde quarel: And with that
intent (quoth he) Segnior Ismarito, I drink unto
you, with a better affection, than I bare you in
my sleepe, for I dreamed, with my Rapire drawne,　　Envy evermore
　　　　　　　　　　　　　　　　　　　　　　　　　　quarreleth,

I chased you, to your Chamber.

    Ismarito, quickly aunswered, I pleadge you (Segnior Bergetto) but with lesse feare then you supposed to bee in mee, when you were asleepe:
5 for men after they are awake, expounde dreames by contraries.

    Bergetto, deceaved of his expectation, was dryven by patience, to salve the wounde, he had given hymselfe. / But Segnior Philoxenus: to take
10 away the cause of after unkindnesse, reaved the companie, of leasure, to judge of Bergettos quarrilynge dreame, or of Ismaritoes crosse exposition, by keeping of them exercised with a newe device.

15   In deede (quoth hee) Dreames are incertaine, and therfore, not to be regarded, but there is a true kinde of divination, in Palmestrie, and so in looking in Maria Belochi's hand, hee used certaine names of Arte, and gave a voluntarie
20 pleasing Judgement: which fired all the Ladies and Gentlewomen, with an earnest desire, to know their fortune: and by this meanes, the remembraunce, of former questions was taken away. Wherein Segnior Philoxenus wisdome, may be a president,
25 for other Gentlemen, that heare quarrels a breedinge, to smoulder them in the shell: for men that bee angrie, are bounde to their passion, when such as are not moved, have libertie, to pacifye, with discreation.

30   Thus, with their spirites well pleased, Queene Aurelia, and the reste of the companie, rose from the table, and after ordenarie curtesie ended, they paused a time by the Fire, to put their witts in order, for the following disputation:

with those that are favoured.

Quarrelers seeke their owne mischiefe.

S2^v

A wise foresight in a Gentleman.

Palmestrie a pretye idle quallitie, for a Gentleman.

A necessarie note for a Gentleman.

who at the ordinarie howre, entred the drawing
Chamber, where the Eunuke readie to discharge his
dutie, unto the Lute sung this following Sonet.

Regarde my love, but not my frostie haires,
5   Although faire Dame, the least may move content:
For Love, Faith, Zeale, standes firme in aged yeares,
    When light greene youth, is fickle in intent.

The aged knowes, the leaves and fruite of youth,
    The leaves they leave, and with the fruite doe love:
10 The sayinges of olde Age, are judged trueth.
    Let love and trueth, mislyking then remove. /

What though my chin, be clothed all in white,
    Whight in your cheekes, the chiefest coulour is:
Which fayre dye, doth make you seeme so bright,
15   As men holde you, the source of beauties blisse.

Sweete Mistresse then, of all the fayre, the Flower,
    Let not condemne, what doth your selfe comend:
Ruthe seemes your face, let rigor not devour,
    His love, and lyfe, that lives and dies your friende.

20   This Sonet, mooved the company to smile, not
because the invention was unwittie, but in that,
it was the fruites of Doctor Mossenigoes Muse,
who to revenge uppon himselfe all the injurie,
which he had done to the sexe of Women, became
25 inamoured of Katharina Trista, the waspissest
Damosel, among the whole troupe of Gentlewomen:
But knowing the Doctors Phylosophie, could not
so subdue his affection: but that time would
make them all sporte and him smarte, they

dissembled their knowledge of his folly, as
deepely as hee covered the passions of hys fancy:
notwithstanding to raise some speach, and to set
the Doctor a work with hope.
5   (Quoth Alvisa Vechio) this Sonet prophesieth
a hapie lyfe to a young woman, and much comfort
to an olde man if their fortunes be so good, as to
be maried together. And if I had as good a
passage, for my opinyon, as I have Reason to
10 mayntayne the same: I woulde thinke to proove
this couple, worthye of a place in Platoes
Paradice.
       Among so manie good Orators (quoth Queene
Aurelia) you cannot want an Advocate.
15   Whereupon Katharina Trista, with a false eye,
conjured the Doctor, in this question, to
maintaine his Love: who thus injoyned, tooke
upon him to maintaine Alvisa Vechioes opinion.
       Queene Aurelia licensed him, and no adversary
20 appea-/red to discourage him: whereupon (quoth
he) where an old man marieth a yonge woman, the
contentment seemes too be muche, and the comfort
more: my reason is, the oulde man hath not onlye
chosen a Wyfe, to recreate him as a companyon,
25 but a Cooke to prepare chosen meates for his
impayred appetite, and a Staffe to sustaine his
Age. The yonge wife also may hold her selfe
happie in this fortune: for she hath chosen one,
whom she may not onely rule, but commaund: and
30 for a litle paynes, who will leave her possest
of a great deale of lyvyng. And this is most
certain, that cruel and wilde Creatures do most
hurt, where their wyll is moste resisted: and
have great compassion, where they finde no

S3^v

Defences
where an old
man marrieth
a yonge
woman.

proffer of repulse: The Lyon in his greatest
hunger, hurts not the wounded sheepe: the
Crocadile with teares wassheth the blood from
a murthred man, and the raging Sea refressheth
the yealding Reede: much more, a woman (that by
nature is beautified with pittie) if she rule
without checke, wyll glorie in the good usage of
her Husbande: and this is in dayly use, that
the olde man, in assemblies, findes his yonge
wife, modest in her speache, basshefull in her
lookes, and nice, in occasion of suspition: and
whyther this behaviour proceedes of desire to be
praysed, or of feare to be blamed, I conclude
the cause with her commendation: for that to do
well in hope of praise, commes of the
incouragement of vertue: and to do well for
feare of reprehension, is the signe of a good
inclination.

    By Sainct <u>Anne</u> Sir (quoth <u>Soranso</u>,) you
well deserve a Fee, (especiallie, of the yonge
wyfe) in that you so connyngly have coloured her   Reproofe, &c.
oversight, and so Clarckely have commended her
good usage of her olde Husband: but your
Suggestion tends to as small effect, as the
Fortune is evyl, of a couple thus unequallie
matched: for that common reason wil refute your
weake opinion, and dayly experience recordes the
miseries of the other.

    What likelyhood of continuance, hath the
House, whose grounde worke is rotten, although
the prospect be beautifull and stronge, God
wotte the feeblenesse of the Foun-/dation, wyll
overthrow the firmenesse of the upperframe.

    Compare this unequall estate in Marriage,

with this oversight in building, and you shall
finde the discorde as great betwene the one, as
the ruyne and decay, speedie in the other. The
good and able Government of the Husbande, is the
5 foundation and grounde worke of Mariage: and
the Beautie of the Wife, the blessynge in havynge
of Children: and the benefite of possessyng
lyvinges, are the outwarde buyldinges of Mariage:
And as they are pleasant in the eye of the worlde,
10 even so, they greatly please the mindes of the
maryed, and geve a singuler Grace to this
honourable vocation. But, if the Government of
the Husbande, be inabled, with Age: (as in
trueth) Olde Age is no other then a seconde
15 Infancie: In whose desire, direction, discrescion
and delight, there are imperfections. The Beautie
of the wyfe, wyll be blasted with sorrowe: for
the insufficiencie of her Husbande: evyll
Education wyll accurse their blessyng in havyng
20 of Chyldren, and negligence wyll waste their
benefites of livyng. You hould a yonge wife, a
Companion to recreate an olde man, but he shal
finde her a Corsive that wyl consume him to
death. A yong man concludeth, the sweetest
25 sollace in love with sighes: it is then, lyke,
an olde man endes it with teares: And God, he
knowes, he often weepeth, more of desire, to
please his wyfe, then of any Devotion he hath to
wantonnesse: yet is al his paynes to a fruitlesse
30 purpose, for that the Game finissheth in his
griefe, and neither began nor endes in his wyves
contentment.

    You are too quicke, in Advauntage, <u>Segnior
Soranso</u>, (quoth the Doctor) Oulde Wine, thoughe

it be dead in the mouthe, yet is it warme in the
Stomacke, when the Newe, fumes in the Heade, but
comforteth not the heart. Dry woodde, maketh a
bright Fyre, where greene Bowes consume halfe
awaye in Fume and **Smoake**.

The Sonne riseth watrishlye, and is longe
before it / geveth heate, where, in the After
noone, it scorcheth the face: So, a Yonge man
devideth his Love, into a hundreth Affections,
and every fancie pleased, there wyll but a little
fall to his wyves share: where an Olde mans
Love is settled, and his fancie is fixed upon
one: And as the resighted Examples, in Age, are
in best hart: so to prove an olde mans
sufficiencie, there is a common Proverbe: <u>Gray
Haires are nourished, with greene thoughts</u>.

Now, to content his yong wyfe, she shal
have no cause to suspect his Affection abroad,
and shall not lacke to bee belooved at home.

Moreover, whiche delighteth a yong woman,
(who naturallye, is Ambitious) shee shall take
her place, accordyng to the gravitie of her
Husband, and not as her yong yeares requyreth.

And to conclude, to give her an honourable
name, the most precious Juell, with which, a
woman may be beautified, she shall receyve grave
Directions from her Husbande: and through the
sweete delight, she taketh in hearyng her good
Government commended, she wyll put them in
Execution.

Doctor <u>Mossenigo,</u> replied not with this
vehemencie, for any delight he had to commende
this unequall estate in Mariage, but to flatter
<u>Katharina Trista,</u> with an Ambitious Hope, of

great Reputation, in matchyng with his aged self:
but she (that knew a leg of a Larke, was better
then the whole Carkasse of a Kyte) woulde none
God thank him.

5   And to make him horne wood (if hee persevered
in his opinion,) in <u>Soransoes</u> behalfe (quoth
<u>Bergetto</u> his auncient crosser:) Maister Doctor,
theare is more pryde in your wordes, then
Substance in your proofes: your hartie olde Wine,
10 must be drawen out, when it is broached: your
drie woodde is but a blaze, and your hot Sunne,
doth but sweate, for sorow, that he is goyng to
cowche in the dark Caves of <u>Tartessus</u>. But as
touching Old men, they may well be sufficient in   Reproofe. &c.
15 greene thoughts, as you terme them, / but I am   T1^r
assured, that in deedes, they are weake, and
wythered: And therefore, a man cannot speake
too muche evill, of this excesse in dotage:
withered Flowers, are more fit for a Dunghill,
20 then meete to deck a house: olde rotten Trees,
are needefull for the fyre, but unnecessarie to
stande in an Orchard; even so, olde decaied
creatures, are comely in the Church, but
unseemely by a yong womans side.

25 The olde man, which marrieth a yonge Wyfe,   The
is sure of this sowre sauce, to rellish his   mischaunces of
sweete Imaginations: his beloved wife (how so   an oulde man
ever she dissembleth) disdayneth hym: his   yongly maryed.
neighbors al to be flouteth him, and soothing
30 Parisites, beguileth him: common opinion will
counterfeit him lyke <u>Acteon</u>, not so much for the
ficklenesse, they see in his wife, as for the
infirmities, they know in himselfe. And breefely,
to conclude his joye: hee may (perchaunce) lyve

two yeares, with his faire wife: but the
mischaunce of his Children, will remember his
infamie, for ever: Greene Ivy, which catcheth
an olde Tree, maketh quicke worke for the fire:
and the imbracements of a faire Woman, hastneth
an olde man to his Grave. And although it be a
haynous wronge, causelesse to condemne the Wyfe:
yet this will be the opinyon, shee killed her
Husband with thought, to heare and see, how she
trespassed, both against, his and her owne
honour.

    Foule fall, suche a Marriadge (quoth Maria
Belochy) where the vertuous Wife, shal be
slaundered, through the imperfections of her
Husbande.

    It is some wrong (quoth Fabritio) but she
might have foreseene the mischiefe, while she
was free.

    Well (quoth Queene Aurelia) upon this
knowledge of mischaunce, our companie, are
sufficiently warned. Proceede in Judgement, as
you allow eithers opinion.

    Whereupon, Fabritio with Isabella, with one
accord, gave sentence, against Doctor Mossenigo,
in these words: An olde man amourous, of a yong
Woman, is an enemie, both to his health and
reputation, for the causes aforesaid. /

    The rest of the companie, smyled to heere
this judgement: but the Doctor, brake foorth
many a secret sigh, not for the disgrace he tooke
in his pleading (for he defended an yll matter,
with colour sufficient) but in that he knew this
verdict would alwaies be a barre in his sute.

    While the Doctor and Soranso argued: Queene

Marginalia:
- A yong wyfe is death to an old man.
- An honest woman is lightly slaundered, by the imperfections of her Husband.
- Repentance to late.
- The wise are warned by the mischaunces of other.

Aurelia, espyed in the Cloath of Arras: a Beast
fourmed like an Unicorne, save that he bare his   A Rhinocerot.
Horne in his nose: whiche beast, sleeping, laide
his murthering Horne in a yong Maidens lap: and
5 after the question was decided, shee demaunded,
what that Beast was? and what the misterie
signyfyed: but the meaning was as straunge, as
the sight, to most of the companie.

    In the ende (quoth Ismarito) Madam, I have   The Metamorphose
10 read of a gallant yong Gentleman of Naples named   of Rinautus, a
Rinautus, that was Metamorphosed into such a   Gentleman of
Beast, by this adventure: passing through the   Naples.
Iland Circeiun (that Homer speaketh off) which
is now annexed unto the Continent: he was espied
15 of Circes, who inhabited that Ilande. This
wrincled, yll favoured Witch, at the first sight,
was surprised in Love, with the goodly shape and
beautie of this seemely Gentleman: but for al her
charmes, and Inchauntments, her Arte failed,
20 either to force him to Love, or to free her selfe
from loving: for, notwithstandinge, shee was a
Goddesse, he disdained her over worne, foule and
wythered visage: and shee presumyng of her
Sorcerie, powred fresh Coales, uppon her kyndled
25 desyre, in hope that necessitie would force him
to consent, to the requeste, freewill contemned:
but Cupid (to whom such power onely belongeth) to
scourge her presumption, in suche sorte hardened
Rinautus harte, that all Circes Sute and Sorceries
30 tended unto a fruitlesse successe. In so much,
as in her rage she turned him into a Rhinocerot,
a Beast of unconquerable force, who in his nose,
beareth a horne, much like to the Unicorne: But
notwithstanding hee was thus transfourmed (as

King <u>Nabucadonizer</u>, in the fourme of an Oxe,
retained the spirit of a man) so hee in his
altered shape, nou-/rished his auncient disdaine
of yll favoured <u>Circes</u>: and to bee fully avenged,
with all hys force, pursueth olde Creatures: and
such as hee overtaketh, hee goreth to death: yet
is he by this polycie subdued: Place a faire
Maide, in his walke, and foorth with hee will
with a lovinge countenaunce, repaire unto her,
and in her bosome, gently bestow his murthering
Horne: and sodainlye, (as one ravished with
contentment) hee fauleth a sleepe, by which
meanes he is slaine before he recovereth the use
of his force.

    The Companie laughed well, to heare this
straunge <u>Metamorphosis</u>.

    In the end (quoth Queene <u>Aurelia</u>) I would
Maister Doctor had hard this Hystorie, when hee
so invayed against Beautie, perhaps, he would
have bene affraide of her vengeaunce, seeing her
power able to conquere savage and wilde Beastes.

    But the Doctor, glad of this advantage, not
unlyke the cunning Lawier, that buyeth Robin
hoodes penniworthes, and yet with some nice
forfaitures, threatneth the seller, with
continuall bondage: and many times, bringeth
backe his money, and keepeth his bargen: not
caring for his Concience, so that hee have a
colour for his offence: or as the wysest sorte
of <u>Atheistes</u>, (that live as though, they hoped
neyther after heaven, nor feared Hel) yet confesse
God with their mouth, because the contrarie
woulde make them hated of men: so he by this
tale, found out both a warrant, to maintayne his

Evyll men care not for the conscience, so they have a colour for their offences.

former Blasphemie, and to excuse his present
Follie in Love: And to Aucthorize either:
Madame (quoth he,) the inchaunted Beaste,
approoveth myne opinion of Beauties power, and
5   his Death is a greater witnesse of her crueltie,   The force of
then is Doctor Mossenigo, who confesseth that   Beautie.
men, in vayne prescribe Remedies for the Affected,
or Receites, to preserve men from the Infections
of Beautie.
10 You are welcome under our Lee (quoth Alvisa
Vechio.)
  But, to take awaye all hope of good   No Affliction,
intertaynment: (quoth Katharina Trista) no, no,   but hath his
Maister Doctor, you deceyve your selfe: Beautie,   remedie.
15 neyther retaineth the power, / nor poyson, which   T2^v
you speake of, and with you, Ovid and all the
amorous Poets are mistaken: who say, Affection,
riseth from Beautie, and not of the free wyll of
man: But say you all what you please: good
20 foresight wyll contrary your opinions. There is
no sore, but hath his salve: no griefe, but hath
his remedie: nor no daunger, but may be forstoode,
eyther by prayer or good indevoure.
  In deede (quoth Faliero) Socrates altred his   Examples to
25 inclination, by the Studie of Phylosophie: The   be regarded.
Nynivites preserved their Cittie by prayer: and
Virbius dubled his life, by mastering of his
disposission.
  Floradin, bewitched with the love of faire   Idlenes
30 Persida, his deare friend Pericles Wife, wrote in   noorisheth
a table Booke: fye Floradin, fye, shee is thy   and exercise
friend Pericles Wife: and so often as idlenes   remedieth
presented him with thys passyon, he read his   love.
written remembraunce: and by some honest exercise,

remooved his imagination.

    This is not your day Maister Doctor (quoth Soranso) I beleeve, there is some unkindnes betweene Saturne and Venus, by the envious aspeckt of some other Plannet this howre.

    It maye be (quoth the Doctor) by the flatterie of Mercurie, who is evermore enemie to the plainnes of trueth.

Flatterie, the enemy of trueth.

    Well (quoth Queene Aurelia) let us leave this bye matter, and consider better of Ismaritos Metamorphosis: me thinks it prophesieth muche mischaunce to an Oulde Wydowe, whiche marieth a Yonge man, and no greate pleasure to the yonge maried Bacheler.

    O good Madam, say not so (quoth Soranso) for in this fortune, lyeth a yonger Brothers welfare: and the cause that maketh happinesse accompanie olde wemen to their Grave.

Mariage commended betwene an olde woman and a yong man.

    It may well be to their Grave (quoth the Doctor) but it bryngeth sorow into their House, and maketh their life more unpleasant then death: and if Soranso followe this Course, perhappes his day wyll be no better then Doctor Mossenigos. /

Reproofe. &c.

    Queene Aurelia smilinge, saide, shee feared this contention woulde bring the companie to hell gates. Yet (quoth she,) In that I imagine the way will be pleasaunt, I licence you to persever in your purpose.

T3^r

    Uppon which warrant (quoth Soranso) to maintaine that to be true, which I have alreadie alleadged in the commendation of this estate in marriage. This further reason (in my conceite) you will neither disalowe, nor the married couple shall have cause to mislike: which is where a

Defence. &c.

fresh young Gentleman, either of small living, or
farre spent with lustinesse, lights of a rich
olde widow, for that both their desires in this
fortune shall bee satisfied. He shall have   *A good*
5   plentie of Coyne, the onelie Grace hee lacked,   *exchange of*
and she the possession of a goodlie Parsonage,   *Marchandice.*
the cheefest Jewel she loveth: which exchaunge
of Marchandise can not chuse, but continue their
liking and raise much contentment.

10   Cleane contrarie (quoth the Doctor) for the
follies of a yong man is sufficiently punished,
by marrying an olde woman: and the sins of an olde
widdow, ar fully plagued, in matching with **a yong**
man: for that (contrarie to your suggestion)
15 neither can injoye, the cause of their Mariage,
without annoyance to their mindes: for his lyking,
is fastned on her riches, which she will not, but
by necessitie leave: and her love is setled on   *The evylles*
his person, which for her pleasure, he disdaineth   *in an olde*
20 to punish. The unfortunate yong man, knowes not   *wydowe.*
what greefe hee joynes to his gaine, in matchinge
with an olde widdow, till that experience breakes
them forth in sighes: If his wife be ritche, shee
will looke to governe, if shee bee poore, he is
25 plagued, both with beggery, and bondage: If she
be proude, she will hide her abylytie, to maintaine
her pompe: If she be testie, he is forst to
pacience: If she bee Jelous, hee canne hardlye
indure her rages. And to conclude, if the olde
30 doting widdow be free from one of these faults,
she is tied to forty evils of lesse sufferaunce:
for if her Husbande commaunde her will, shee
straight waies sayeth, her other Husband was **more**
kinde: If hee chance / to dine from home, she

wyls him to sup with his harlots: if he spend
beyond her allowance, thus she reviles hym:
 <u>A Begger I fownd thee, and so thou wylt leave mee.</u>
 To chastice her talke, setteth an edge of her
5 tongue: to suffer her in her rage, maketh her
raylynges irrevocable.
 By your wordes, Maister Doctor (quoth <u>Lucia
Bella</u>,) the wife is the greatest cause of this
contention, and yet in common opinion, the Husband
10 is most blamed.
 Madame, you are too hastie in an advauntage,
I ment no such parciallytie (quoth the Doctor.)
 Yea Madame, (quoth <u>Bargetto</u>) Maister Doctor
is now so conquered, as his tong is the Trumpet of
15 your pleasure.
 It is so (quoth the Doctor) to sound out those
thinges which are true: and in trueth, the yonge
Husbande often tymes, maketh the evilles, good in PLATOES Hell
deedes, which the olde wyfe useth but in wordes: in Mariage.
20 for no lenger then she feedeth him with Coyne,
shall she enjoy his companie: If she rob not her
Children to inrich him, she shall lack no froward
lookes, nor fowle usage: If she put him in
possession of her lyving, he straight wayes
25 dispossesseth her of his love: for having, what
he sought, he wyl els where be enamoured. And,
uprightly to speake, she lacketh neither occasion
too lament, nor cause to be inraged: for who is
so patient, as can dissemble her unsufferable
30 passions? both, to be spoyled of her lyving, and
to be exyled from that she loveth: And, in verie
trueth, so egall are their evilles, as it were a
harde matter to judge, who deserveth leaste blame,
or most excuse: She reprocheth him, of Beggerie,

Hooredome, Unthriftinesse, yll usage: and of the
ruine, both of her selfe and her Children. He
blameth her of Olde Age, Jelousie, curstnesse,
scowldyng: and for hidyng of her goods, which he
5 hath bought, with doyng Injurie unto his person.
If she be determined to be merie, he (scornfully)
telleth her, that it is as sightly, for a toothelesse
Mare to eate Marchpane, as for suche a wrinckled
Mumpes to fawle a bylling. If he come in wel
10 disposed, and affably intreateth her, she calleth
him dissembling Hipocrite, and saith, he salu-/teth
her with his tong, but his hart imagineth of his
minions abroade: she runneth to the neighbors to
complaine: In the meane while he sendeth her
15 corne to the Market, and her cattel to the Faire.
If the frends, of good wil, or neighbours, of
charytie, labour to accord their contention (as
she imagineth to shame him) she thundreth out a
thousand Injuries that he doth her: for her owne
20 praise, she saith, that of pure love she maried
him with nothing: and to reproch him, she
sweares, he hath spent her substance, and hateth
her person: To show her owne good Huswiferie,
she tels that she worketh al day at her Distaffe:
25 and to blase his unthriftinesse, she showeth how
he plaieth away her gaines at Dice: She crieth
out, that (perforce) he taketh what he openly
findeth, and privylie stealeth, what she secretly
hideth.
30   These, and many moe complaints, she preferreth
against her Husband, with the vehemencie of a
womans passion.

   Her Husband, that knoweth how to be revenged
in deedes, (for his own credit) is more milde in

T4^r

words: he layeth al these blames upon her own
crooked disposition: who though she be so olde,
as a man can hardly love her, yet with a cankred
jelous froward nature, she wold force a man to
hate her: But what remedie, since his fortune
was so hard? he wold starve her with patience:
and only adde this Suffrage to his Letanie: <u>A
prava muliere</u>, good Lord, deliver mee.

    These drie scoffes, sets her hart in a light
fire, and (save that she hath not so many colours
like unto <u>Iris</u>,) thundreth out the venome of her
cankred Spirit in revylings, and raylyngs against
her Husbande: And (to say trueth) her case is to
be pittied, as much as her tong is to be blamed:
for Injurie is not so grevous unto a man, as to
see his Adversarie soothe his trespasse with an
honest shoe.

    But to my purpose, her Husband crosseth her
with a quiet Aunswere: you may see friendes,   *A great cause of Impatience.*
(sayth he,) wyld fire wyl burne in water, Drinke
wil make the Dropsie dry, and mildnes in mee,
mooveth madnesse in my wife: by her example here,
you see my lyfe at home, as **tedious as Hel**: then
(perhaps) som flowting Marchant, sayth: lyke
ynuffe, and the shee Devill weareth the hornes. /
Thus with their own mischeefes, they greve their
friends, delight their foes, and wearie their
Neighbors, in according their debates: and if
they be in the morning quieted, and go home in
peace, at Noone like enemies they ar redy to
throwe the house out at the window: a slut like
the furie of lothsomenes, shall bring in dinner,
because the Jelious wife, dare not trust her
husbande with any maide that is hansome: the

husbande offended, throweth the Platters at her
head, and axeth if she meane to poyson him: the
Wife taketh pepper in the nose, and sayth, if hee
had not married her, he woulde have beene glade
of the worst morsell there.

    The Husband replieth that if he had not
beene so mad, the divell would not have married
her.

    Then beginneth the old Musik, tuned perchance
with a rap or two of the lippes, and when they
have brawled their fill, shee runneth and bemoneth
her selfe at her neighbors, and he goeth and
maketh himselfe merie with his Mistrisses.

    In sooth, Maister Doctor, it seemeth to mee
(quoth Sir Soranso) that you have verie substancially
proved my opinion: for Marriage equallye devideth
her blessings, and mischaunces, betweene the   Defence. &c.
married: and as farre as I can see, neither of
these knoweth, who hath the better or worser
bargen: there is raylinges and unquietnesse of
both sides: but what of that, pleasure is best
seasoned with paine: and though they sometimes
jarre at home, they agree wel when they are
seperated among their neighbours. And although
you have streatched their debates, upon the rack
of vengeaunce: yet at adventure, I wish my selfe
no worse bestowed, then marrie to an old welthy
Widdow. I doo not thinke, but by good usage, to
continue her first affection geeven, even unto
hir verie Grave.

    You will kill her with kindnesse, (quoth
Maria Belochye.)

    Yea, Madam, (quoth Soranso) if her nature be
so froward, as to die with good usage. /

In deede Ladyes (quoth the Doctor,) there are
some men, that entertaine their olde wives, with
such a fayre showe of flattering loove, as they
bewitche them even to theyr latter gaspe. But
5 at what rate dooth she purchase this kindenesse?
O even with the undooing of her selfe and Children:
yea, and which is worse, it is the pollicie of
Father in lawes, to dandle the infancie of theyr
wives Children, in the lap of Ignorance, to this
10 ende, that beeing of lawfull age, they may with
lesse fetches beguyle them of theyr living: so
that the unfortunate childe, knowes not whether
he may more bemone his losse of living, or lacke
of good bringing up: and in my judgement, of
15 bothe the evils: want of education is the
greatest: for learning and vertue purchaseth
living, and lyving corrupteth, but coyneth not
good conditions: and as Seneca sayeth, libertie
without learning is a bondage to the minde: and
20 further, the Childe were better to be dead borne,
then barren of good Letters, for that Ignoraunce
is a grave which buryeth life.
  Maister Doctor (quoth Queene Aurelia) me
thinketh your wordes doo too much wrong to the
25 wife, though they cannot sufficiently blame the
husband. I graunt that father in lawes, esteeme
their owne profiets, before theyr wives Chyldrens
preferments: but yet (I suppose) Nature dooth
direct the naturall Mother, to eye theyr good
30 bringing up, who with muche sorrowe brought them
foorthe: For (as the Proverbe goeth) things that
are dearely bought, are of us intirely beloved,
and nothing is more dearely purchased, then what
is attayned with the hazarde of life, which venter

A most wicked pollysie.

Senecas opinion that Children were better to be dead borne then ignoraunt of good letters.

Thinges that are beast esteemed.

the Mother maketh, before she is assured of her
Childe: then this cruelty towardes her Children,
to satisfye the wyll of her second husbande, wyll
make indifferent men, holde her an unnaturall
5 Mother, whether her husband esteeme her a duetifull
wife or no.

  Oh good Madame (quoth the Doctor,) how can   Reproofe. &c.
the / Hen succour her Chickens, when she her selfe   U1^v
is at the mercy of the Kite? how can the Conny
10 preserve her Rabets, when the Ferret is in
possession of her Burrowe? and how may the
unfortunate Mother, Foster her shiftlesse Children,
either as she should or would, when her fancie or
folly hath enthralled her to a second Husband,
15 whose power is to direct, and displeased, to check?
This severitie of Father in lawes, hath bred much
division in Marriage: but still the quarrels are
concluded, with the detryment of the Children: A hard
for the unhappie wife, is bound to one of these   extremitie.
20 two evils, either to agree to the tyrannizing of
her entrayles, or to yeelde to her owne continuall
sorrow and unquietnesse: And where the case is so
desperate, it may be lamented, but not wondred at,
that necessitie breake the boundes of nature.

25   To staye this mischeefe (quoth <u>Helena Dulce</u>)
Honourable is the custome of <u>Spaine</u>, where the   An honorable
vertuous Dame holdeth the second Mariage, a   custome of
retrograding of her reputation, and a wrong to   Spaine.
her deceased husband: for by this stayednesse,
30 she is in possession of her libertie, and hath
the disposing of her living.

  I holde this precise custome (quoth <u>Dondolo</u>)
more profitable then necessarie: for the penaunce
were to harde, yea, unpossible to be indured, that

the lusty young Widdowe should be constrayned to
a Virgins chastytie, for as <u>Ovid</u> devineth.

>I that some times of Nuptiall rites,
>   Have taste the pleasant toyes:
>5   Now cannot chuse, but call to minde,
>   Dame <u>Venus</u> sugred joyes.

But if the aged widdow, could live within
this lawe, it would bring honour to her yeares,
and happinesse to / the ende of her life. What   U2ʳ
10 better husbands may she have, then her owne   Meete
Children, whom shee may bothe commaund and   husbandes
controule, whose dutyes are to labour in her   for aged
causes, and to unburden her heart of cares? and   widdowes.
when she departeth this life, where may she better
15 dispose her living, then upon her own Children,
whom to releeve, she is conjured by nature, and
to bring up in good nurture, bound in conscience:
But from the beginning so rife hath beene the
dotage of Widdowes, that when their feeble legges,
20 faintely supporteth their consumed bodyes, when
at hie noone, their mistie eyes hardly discerneth
the hye way, and when (forste) thorough lack of
teethe, they swallowe theyr meate, theyr lippes
notwithstanding, take delight in kisses, and their
25 mindes thirst after wantonnesse.

Mens follyes are as great as Womens
simplicities, in this oversight in dotage (quoth
Queene <u>Aurelia</u>) but I thinke it necessarie, that
heere we staye our jorney, least we enter into
30 Hell, before we be aware: and therefore <u>Segnior</u>
<u>Fabritio</u>, I pray you let us have your sentence, to
over rule this question.

Madam (quoth <u>Fabritio</u>) the evill of this

inequallitie in Mariage, is bothe so auncient and
so common in use, as there needeth no other
judgement, then experience of our neighbours
mischaunces, but to succour the injured children,
I would that one of <u>Laertius</u> lawes, were common to
the whole world: which is, wher the Tennaunt sued
his Lorde, the Servaunt his Maister, or the Childe
his Parents, that Judges themselves, should
foorthwith looke into the Processe, and determine
the same, for it is vehemently to be supposed,
that these sutes are foreced upon vehement injuries,
otherwise the Servaunt would feare to sue his
Maister, who hath power moderately to chasten him:
the Tennant would quake to unquiet his Lord, who
hath many meanes to crosse him, and without whose
grace he may never live in peace. Shame and dutie
(in any sufferable matter) would make the childe
forbeare to molest his Parents, for (but where his
cause is known) / <u>Reporte</u> like a two edged Knife,
would (besides his injurie) wound him with blame,
and omission of dutie. Therfore, where the least
of two daungerous evils, foreceth the above sayd
to sue, it is much to be lamented, that delaye,
countenaunce of freends, corruption with bribes,
and other supporters, which the riche hath, should
torment the poore complaynant, more then his
originall injurie.
    Your reason is but just, (quoth Queene
<u>Aurelia</u>,) and the rest of the company: who
wearie with the multitude of the resited
mischaunces, heere broke of the Disputation,
and went and reposed themselves in the great
Chamber.

Marginalia:
- Experience is a judgement it selfe.
- A worthie lawe, made by Laertius.

The speeche which passed the sixt night at Supper, betweene Segnior Phyloxenus, and his Honourable Guestes.

According to the order of Merchaunts, who at the latter ende of the yeare, survey theyr accounts, to see what fortune and mischaunce they have receyved thorough the whole yeare past, Segnior Philoxenus (towards the latter end of Supper) smilelingly, demaunded an account of the benefit of the chosen companies sixe dayes Disputation.

Sir (quoth Soranso, with a modest merry countenaunce) we are like to present you a Banckrupts reckoning, who the longer he occupieth, the worse he thriveth: so we these sixe dayes, have travailed to finde out a way, to the Parradise in Mariage, and every day we have been further and further off, of our determination, one day we thought that the wealthy matches of Parentes, would have speeded our jorney, but there, lack of love in the Children, cast us behinde hand: an other day, we imagined that free choise in the Children, would have directed us to happinesse in Marriage: but want of maintenaunce and frowardnes in the parentes, marred this match. In lofty love we found dainger: in base love lothesomnesse and inconstancy: and where there is inequality of yeares, fume and smoke of Hell: so that now wee shall be dryven to renounce our profession: and runne awaye with the Banckrowt, least (if he staye, as he is chopped up in pryson) so we, if wee proceede any further be drowned in the ryver Stix.

If you travaile with as much pleasure, as

It is no striving against the streame.

U3^r

you report your adventures with ease, (quoth
Signior Philoxenus,) I wonder but a little though
errour carryed you to Hell gates: but to
incourage you to persever in your fyrst purpose,
5 let this comfort you: that thinges when they are
at the worst, begin again to amend. The Feaver
giveth place to health, when he hath brought the
pacyent to deathes doore. The Bee, when he hath
lefte his stinge in your hand without dainger may
10 playe with your eye lidde: so, when all the
inconveniences of Marriage, are in your eares,
you may very well receive her into your heart:
and to conclude your benifytte with your owne
example, there is no such husband as the unthrifte,
15 when he fasteneth uppon the worlde: for in
spending of other mennes goodes he learned howe
to spare his owne, when he gettes them: so in
the pleasaunt beating out of these inconveniences,
you knowe what maketh Marriage bitter, and the
20 greefe knowen, the remedye is easie.

  With your favour, Sir, (quoth Dondolo,) to
be sicke is common to all men, but to restore to
health, under God, is the offyce of the Phisition:
so we all knowe by our owne travaile, the
25 infirmities of Marriage, but to fynde out the
blessinges, muste proceede from your sound
directions which favour to obtaine we are all
earnest suters.

  Your request is so juste (quoth Segnior
30 Philoxenus,) that if I were able (as I am not) to
better your judgementes, I would not be daintye
in this pleasure: but for that the more the
opinions are, in the end, the more pro-/found the
sentence is: I wyll too morrowe (in part, to

The thriving unthrift proves the best husband.

U3ᵛ

satisfie your demaund) joyne with you in your
ordinarie sweete exercise. Perchaunce you have
ended all the inconveniences in the olde yeare,
and I may begin the New yeare, in helping to
5 bloome the blessings of Marriage.

    Queene <u>Aurelia</u> and the rest of the company,
affectionately thanked <u>Signior Philoxenus</u> for this
hye favour: and so rose from the Table, who after
a little pawsing, daunsing and devising: at theyr
10 pleasures, went unto theyr lodginges.

<u>FINIS</u>. /

The. vii. Dayes Exercise:

Containing: a Discourse of the excellencie of Marriage: with many sound Lawes and directions, to continue love betweene the married: with the rare Historie of Phrigius and Pieria, reported by Segnior Phyloxenus: And other good notes of regarde.

    Like as when the royall Armie, lies incamped before a Towne of warre, the sound of Trumpets, noyse of Drums, and neying of Horses, dooth awake the Souldiors and Cittizens, before Aurora be willing to leave the sweete embracements of her husband Tithon: so, even with the departure of the day Star, in honour of the New yeare, the Trumpets, Drummes and Flutes, sounded through every small passage, into the lodgings of Segnior Philoxenus Pallace, such shrill salutations, as the company envying the confusion of night: broade waking, attended the Mornings light, to apparell themselves: who in theyr moste brave and sumptuous araye, by nine of the clock, made the great Chamber resemble a fayre Garden in Maye. In the imbroderies of whose Garments, Flowers and fancies, were so naturally and artificially wrought: some of Pearle, some of golde, some of Bugle, every one according to their own humour: More over, every Gentlemans head was armed with his Mistrisses favor, and every Gentlewomans hart, was warmed with her servaunts affection.

    In the most soveraigne place of the great Chamber, Janus, God of Time (as the Poets faine) was hung up, in the likenes of a Serpent, winding his body into a circkle and holding his taile in his mouth, expressing under / this figure his revolution, who through his continuall motions environing and compasing the world, retourneth into himselfe, and endeth and beginneth in himselfe: and in joyfull token of the newe yeare, he was garnished with many sweete flowers, garlandes, and devices: some artificiall lively counterfeited. Segnior Philoxenus although he hated superstitious Ceremonies, and shund them, yet he honored auncient lawdable customes, and kept them: who according to the custome of the countrey, presented every one of his guests, with a riche new years gifte, which explayned some morrall vertue. Among the reste he gave his sister Queene Aurelia, a fayre plaine tablet, which opened, represented the picture of a faire Lady garnished with many precious stones: covertly, expressing thereby, that gorgeous apparell was but base and counterfeit, in respect of the brave vertues of the mynde. This order the Italians use, the best giveth newe yeares giftes to his inferior freendes, and in England cleane contrarie. The Tennaunt giveth his Lord: the meane Gentlemen, to Knightes: Knightes to Barrons: Barrons to Earles: Earles, Marquises: and Dukes, to their soveraigne Prince: but it seemeth the Englishmen, observe this custome more neere the originall then the Italians: for the founders therof were the auncient Romaines, who bounde theyr Knights, the first day of Januarie, in the Capitole, to present theyr Newyeares giftes, to Caesar Augustus, were he absent, or present: but so many Countryes, so many customes. And (to my purpose) Segnior Philoxenus, thus bountifully solemnized the use of his owne Countrey. This

The yeare endeth and beginneth in it selfe.

Ancient customs are to be kepte.

The vertues of the minde are more glorious then any outward garment.

Custome in Italye in giving of new yeares giftes, contrarie to the custome of England.

The originall of new yeares giftes.

The Seventh Dayes Exercise   200

memorable curtesie perfourmed, <u>Segnior Phyloxenus</u>,
with some of the graver company, went before unto
the Chappell, and Queene <u>Aurelia</u> and her
attendantes, followed with such a glyttering show,
5 as the Preests needed no other Tapers to see to
say service by, then the glimmering reflexions
of the Gentlewomens eyes, and the pretious Stones
they wore in theyr Jewels: and in my oppinion,
God was better plea-/sed, and more honoured, with   X1^r
10 the Braverie of the companie, then with the
babling and Ceremonies of the Priest: who in the
honour of the <u>New yeare</u>, sets forth his relikes
to the best showe: By that time Service was
ended, and the companie retourned: the Tables
15 were furnished with many daintie Disshes: to
wreake her hunger of some few wherof, Queene
<u>Aurelia</u>, tooke her Royall place, and the rest of
the companie, as they pleased. This Dinner was
spent in Discourse of certain Ceremonies and olde
20 Rites used in times past, in the celebrating of
God <u>Janus</u> Feast, too tedious, and (withall)
impertinent for this Discourse. When Dinner, and
a little other pausyng talke was ended, the
companie arose: and Queene <u>Aurelia</u>, with the
25 reverent Salutations of the whole troupe, retyred
into her owne Chamber, tyll the howre of
Disputation sownded.

About which time, she, with <u>Segnior Phyloxenus</u>,
and the rest of her Attendauntes, entred into a
30 moste delycate Banquetinge House, where, uppon   Segnior
the Walles, in so good order, and representation   Philoxenus
of Nature: were painted, all maner of Fruictes,   banqueting
Flowers, Vines, Arbors, and causes of Pleasure,   hous.
either in Orchard or Garden: as a man (without

blushing) might have adventured, to gather upon
the bare Walles, a Pomegranate, a Cluster of
Grapes, a Gyllyflower, or suche lyke: had not the
dead of Winter, reaved the likelyhoode, that they
5   should be perfect.
    After Queene <u>Aurelia,</u> and the rest of the
companie, had taken their places, in this earthly
Paradice: <u>Segnior</u> <u>Phyloxenus</u> (secretly) wylled
the <u>Eunuke,</u> to chaunt out the prayses of <u>Hymen</u>:
10 who obaying this Charge, tuned his Lute, and to
a sweete Noate, sung this following Sonet.

Even as the Vine, that clasps the tender Elme,
   Amonge greene leaves, his purpled Grapes doth beare:
When (wanting props) himself doth overwhelme,
15   And for the fire his Braunches doth prepare. /

So two in one, with Hymens ryghtes fast bound,   XI^v
   Of their sweete love, live always in the seede:
When Death, or time, the single doth confounde,
   Which ruine of fame, the barren thought doth breede.

20 Sweete Hymen then, thy Godhead I adore,
   And bow my selfe, by thee to be controlde:
In foulded Armes, my Spouse my eyes before:
   Yeelds more content, then Dymonds, Pearle, and Gold.

In quiet home, uncheckt, to rule, and lyve,
25 What lyfe more sweete? what hartes ease like to this?
Or through mischaunce, my mind when care doth greeve,
What Medicine, is better then a kysse?
   At unawares, geven by a lovyng wife,
   O none, nor state, lyke to the married lyfe.

The Seventh Dayes Exercise 202

    This Sonet ended, and well considered: Sir
(quoth Queene <u>Aurelia</u> to <u>Segnior Philoxenus</u>) to be
revenged of the injurie, of our former disputations,
who have painted Marriage with a thousand
5 inconveniences, I beseeche you, and binde you, by
your promise, to blazon the blessinges and
excellencie of this sacred Institution: that she
who is devine, may have her due prayses, and we
that are ignoraunt, may knowe how to receave her
10 benefites, and with the same to honour her.
    Madame, (quoth <u>Segnior Philoxenus</u>) you
charge me, beyonde my promise, and binde mee to
an impossibilitie: I promist but to joyne with
this quick witted Company in opinion, which I am
15 readie to accomplish.
    To blaze the excellencie of Marriage, is a
worke of no great difficultie, because her vertues
illustreth the same through the whole worlde,
but to direct the maried, is a labor of Art, wit,
20 and experience: in the fyrst, wherof, I am
ignoraunt, in the second unperfect, and to the
thirde a Strainger: so that, as I am sorry to
injurie your expectation, so am I loth to expose
my insufficient judgement. /
25   Sir (quoth Queene <u>Aurelia</u>) if wee were not
assured of a lyberal contentment, in contemplating
of your waightie Censure, we would receive your
modest refusall, for just excuse. But for that
we have all an intrest in your vertues, and you
30 should be enemie, to your owne honorable
commendation, in keeping of them close prisoners
in your brest (although you be Lord of the Pallace)
yet I, as soveraigne of the Civill Pleasures,
commaund you to give Cerimonies a disgrace, and

Marginalia:
- Among the just, promise is kept.
- To praise, or blame, is qualitie of wit, but to direct is a worke of judgement.
- We have interest in an other mans vertues.
- Princes commandements must be obayed.

X2^r

sincerely to obay my will.

 Madam (quoth <u>Segnior Philoxenus</u>) so strickt is your charge, as I must adventure, of this waighty labour, hoping, that as by aucthoritie you commaund my opinion, so by the motion, of some one of your vertues, you wil pardon my errours.

 Upon which incouragement, to obay your wyll, I say, and approove, by sacred Authoritie, that this holy Institution of Marriage, was erected by God, in the earthly Paradice, before the transgression of <u>Adam</u>, when he joyned him to <u>Eve</u>, with these wordes of blessing, <u>Increace, multiply, and replenish the earth</u>. Againe, after <u>Adams</u> fall, and the deluge: to strengthen his fyrst institution, God commaunded, the good Patriarcke <u>Noe, to encrease and multiply the earth a new</u>. Moreover, God would have no more women, then men, in his Ark, to show there shoulde be a <u>Sympathie</u> in number, as well as agreement in love betwene man, and wife: for if the one might lawfullye have many Wives, and the other, many Husbandes: how should this expresse Commaundement of God be unviolated? <u>You shall be two bodies in one flesh, and no more</u>.

 Compare the Joye, honour and reverence, geven unto Mariage, by the delight, that proceedeth from any other cause, and you shal see her gleame, lyke a blasyng <u>Comet</u>, and the other, but twinckle as an ordinarie Starre.

 Gorgeous and rich Apparayle, delighteth the Gasers eye: and (perhaps) offendeth the wearers hart: where Maryage, in homely Attyre, is every where honored, and reaveth unquiet wandring

Of the exelencie of mariage.

Mariage instituted before the fall of Adam, by God in the earthly Paradice.

A confirmation of the fyrst institution by God.

Man and wife are two bodies and but one flesh.

The joye of marriage shineth above al other delightes.

thoughts, from the Maried: to / abounde in riches, is a glorious fortune, but they charge men with a dubble care, extreame in the getting, and fearefull in the keeping: the married, hath as
5 great, or greater ritches, in their children.

    When the stately Dames of Rome, bragged of theyr Juelles, Cornelia boasted that hers, excelled them all. A Ladye of the company, seeing her, set forth with none, that was
10 precious, demaunded where her Juelles were? Yonder (quoth Cornelia,) and poynted to her children.

    When certaine most rare, and precious Juelles, of King Darius, and his wives, were
15 presented to Olympia, Mother of Alexander the great, she bestowed them upon her Ladyes, as to lowe prised for her wearing, who was continually, adorned with a Juell, in value, as riche as Asia, Affrica, and Europa. And sure Queene Olympia,
20 and Ladye Cornelia, gloried not in their Juelles, without reason: for golde, and precious stones, set but a glose, uppon beautie, when vertuous children, geveth a newe lyfe unto their parentes.

    The administration of Justice, and aucthoritie,
25 in a common weale, are the proper offices of the married: for that the care of wife, and children, presupposeth them to be setled: when the unmarried, though their wittes be good, rayseth a suspition in the wise, that their thoughtes, are
30 vagrant. The unmaried, hath no agreable Companion, to participate of his pleasure, or to lessen his sorrowe. The Maried, hath a Companion of his owne flesh, of his owne wyll, and of his owne Spyryt, so wrought to his owne Affection: that

Margin notes:
- Children are the most rich Juelles in the worlde.
- This Juell, was her sonne Alexander.
- The blessing of Children, is a duble life.
- Offices of Justice apartaine to the maried.
- The sweete Sympathie betweene the married.
- Love to our Parents, reverent.

betweene them, there is seene two bodies, and but
one thought, perceived: The Maried joy alike, — Love to our
sorrow alike: are of one substance, one concord, Bretheren,
one wealth, one povertie, Companions at one naturall.
5   Boorde and in one Bed. The love we beare unto
our Parents, is (or ought to be) reverent and
duetifull, because, they gave us lyfe: Unto our Love to our
Breetherne, naturall, because of the privitie in Friendes,
blood: To our frendes, affectionate, by certaine affectionated.
10 Motions and consents of the minde: Notwithstanding,
that these Loves be / thus greate, yet are there $x3^r$
divers causes too lessen them.

   But betweene the married, no mischaunce, or Love betwen
infirme Fortune, is cause sufficient of hatred: the married
15 for none, governed by reason, is so inhumaine, as irrevocable
to mallice his owne fleshe: Compare their severall
affections, by sorrow, and you shal see the
weakenes of the one, in regarde of the strength
of the other. The greatest mone we make, for the
20 death of our Father, Brother, or friend, appeareth A good mean
in sighes, or (most vehement) in teares: whereas to trye the
if wee our selves, are but a little wounded, we love of the
crye outright: so that by howe much we exceede, married.
in sorrowing our owne mischaunces, above another
25 mans: by the same reason, so much we love our
selves, more then another. The Rynge that is The rynge, a
geven by the Husbande, and put on the Wives triall of the
finger, ought to be of Gould, to witnes, that as love betwene
gould is the most precious of Mettalles, so the the married.
30 love of the married, exceedeth all other loves.

   To which effecte, <u>Propertius</u> sayth, <u>Omnis
amor magnus, sed aperto in conjuge major</u>:
moreover, the close Joyning of the ringe, is a   An other
figure of true unitie of the married: betweene   fygure of
                                                 the rynge.

The Seventh Dayes Exercise 206

whom, there should be no division in desire, nor
difference in behaviour. To honour this holy
institution of God, God would have his onely
begotten sonne, to be borne of a Wife, perfectly
5 married, save that shee was not Carnally soyled.

      <u>Licurgus</u>, the good King of the <u>Lacedemonians</u>,
so reverenced this sacred estate, as he made a
Lawe, that what <u>Lacedemonian</u> soever were unmaried,
after the age, of thyrtie and eyght yeares, should
10 be chased and hissed out of all publique playes,
and assemblies, as one, unworthy to be seene:
and that, in the cold winter, he shuld (naked)
indure the reproches of the people: and withall,
was bounde to confesse, how he justly suffred the
15 punishment, as a Mispriser of Religion, a contemner
of Lawes, and an enemie to nature. The <u>Romaines</u>
were not so severe: but yet the Aged, unmaried,
were condempned (accordyng to their abylytie) to
pay unto the Treasurer, for publique use, a good
20 Summe of Money. /

      <u>Plato</u>, in his Lawes, enacted: that the
Unmaried, shuld execute, no honourable Office,
Estate, nor dignytie, in the Common wealth.

      The good Emperour, <u>Alexander Severus</u>, although
25 he maryed, rather, to geve ende to his Mother,
<u>Mammeas</u>, Importunyties: then (as he thought) to
begin a more happie lyfe: yet fayre <u>Memmia</u>, his
wyfe, so naturally accorded with his disposition,
as when she died, he would often renewe his
30 Sorowe, and remember her Vertues, in these wordes:
<u>So great a Treasure, as I have lost, a man seldome</u>
<u>findeth: Death were gentle, if he tooke nothyng</u>
<u>but that whiche offendeth: but, oh, he hath</u>
<u>reaved the better parte of my selfe.</u>

Christ was
borne of a
married
woman.

Licurgus law
for the
unmaried.

The Lawe of
the Romains,
for the
unmaried.

X3ᵛ

Platos lawes
for the
unmaried.

Alexander
Severus love
to Memmia
his wife.

How wonderfullie, was the Love of <u>Paulina</u>, sage <u>Senecaes</u> Wife, who opened her Vaines, not onely, with an intent to accompanie him to death, but also, with a desire to feele her Husbandes maner of deathe.   *Paulinas rare love, to her Husbande Seneca.*

<u>Quintus Curtius</u>, resiteth, that Kyng <u>Darius</u>, with an unapauled Spirit, tooke his Overthrowes, by <u>Alexander</u> the Great, the ruine of his kingdome, and the daunger of his royall parson: But having knowledge of his wives death, he wept bitterly, shewing by this sorrow, that he loved his Queene, farre above his Crowne.   *The precious love of King Darius to his wife.*

King <u>Admetus</u>, being sore sicke, received this answer from the Oracle: that if he lived, his best friend must dye: which when the good Queene heard, shee presently slewe her selfe, and in the trembling passage of Death, constantly saide: <u>To give King Admetus lyfe, his Queene and dearest friende dooth die.</u>   *The devine love of King Admetus Wife.*

<u>Tiberius Graccus</u>, finding two Serpents, in his chamber, went to the <u>Augurers</u>, to know what they devyned? who answered, that he was bound to kill the one of these two Serpents, if hee slew the Male, he should die himselfe: if hee killed the Female, he should lose his wife: who (murtherer of himselfe) slew the Male, and saved his wife: and so by his rare love, raised a question, whether his Wyfe were more fortunate in havinge suche a Husbande, or / unhappye in loosing of him.   *The exceeding love, of Tiberius Graccus, towards his wife.*

One of the seven wonders of the worlde, is an eternall testimonie of the love whiche Queene <u>Artemesia</u> bare to her Husbande <u>Mausolus</u>, who for to engrave his dead coarse, erected a Sepulchre, so royall and sumptuous, as tooke away   *The wonderfull love, of Queene Artimesia, towards her husbande Mausolus.*

the glorie of all princely Tumbes, before her time,
and lefte no possibilitie, for any (in time to
come) to excel the same: but holding this too
bace a Mansion, for his Kingly hart, she dried
5 the same to powder, and spising her wine there
with, she buryed it in her owne bowels: and to
crowne his fame, with an everlasting memorie, for
that the ruine of his Sepulcher was subject to
the injurie of time, with great rewardes she
10 incouraged Theopompus, Teodectes, Naucrites, and
Isocrates foure of the most famous Crators of
Greece, to renowne his vertues.

    Amonge whom, Theopompus (as we read) received
the triumph of victorie, in that learned skirmish.
15   I coulde reporte manye other Authoryties, of
unseperable Love betweene the Married: the least
of a hundred whereof, would equall, the friendshippes
of TITUS and GISIPPUS: Or of DAMON and PITHIAS,
the two woonders of mens affections. But for
20 that I know, the able wittes heere present, can
cloth my naked prooffes, of the excellencie of
Marriage, and of the devyne Love, betweene the
Marryed, with manye other sounde reasons, I wil
give place Madam, that you, and the rest of your
25 Ingenious Companie, may doe better service to the
one, and Justice to the other, desiring that, that
which is saide, may discharge my promisse, though
not saitisfy your expectation.

    Sir (quoth Queene Aurelia) if you give us
30 good lawes to preserve Love amonge the married,
as you have with precious authorities set forth
the excellencie of Mariage, and the devine
operations of her blessings, with a ful performance /
of your promisse, you shal binde us al to be your

One of the seven wonders of the worlde.

Aul. Gel. in lib. de noeti. atti.

Debters.

    Madame (quoth Phyloxenus) you set me to a verie hard taske: the Rose, is Hostesse, as well for the Butterflie as the Bee: the Sunne shineth, both upon the good and bad: yea, Christe him selfe, was (aswell) Maister to a Theefe, as to a true Disciple: Even so, divine Mariage, can not have, but some Devillysh Subjectes, whome Examples wil not feare: much lesse, may Lawes, keepe in unitie.

    I graunt (quoth Queene Aurelia:) the evyll are fearelesse of the Lawe, untyll they be scourged with the vengeaunce therof: but the good embrace Lawes, as their Directors in Vertue, and Defenders from daunger: for whose Benefite, I intreate you now, with as large a power, as I lately commaunded you: that (in this behalfe) you wyl commyt, some counsaylyng Lawes, to our attentive Memories.

The Lawe is a scourge to the evill, and comforte to the good.

    Madame (quoth Segnior Phyloxenus,) to showe that your Vertues, have as great power to commaund me, as your Aucthorytie to enjoyne mee: I wyll set downe my owne Imagynations, to preserve (and multiplye) Love, peace, wealthe, and Joye, among the Maried: leavyng the same to be perfected, by the hearers better Judgementes.

Householde Lawes, to keepe the Maryed, in Love, Peace, and Amytie: Reported, by Segnior Phyloxenus.

    The Satisfaction of Fancie, is the Sowrce of Joye in Maryage: But, there be many meanes too damne up the Course of Delight, betweene the Maried, if the Match be not made, aswell, by foresight, as free choyce.

Marriage consistes as well in

The Office of Foresight, is to prevent, folowyng Mischaunces: and (advisedly) to consider, if present Abylytie, wyll support an Househoulde, and (according to their callyng) leave a Portion, to their Posterytie. / In this point, the experyence of the Parents, is to be preferred before the rashe imaginations of the sonne: for the aged Married, by proofe know, that in time many accidents of mischaunce, will hinder the indevours of the best husbands. *foresight, as free choyce.*

Y1^r

The office of foresight, is likewise to consider, of the equallitie in yeares, least the one growing, and the other declining in perfection, after a while, repent, when remedie comes too late: the Rose full blowne, seemeth fayre for a time, but withereth much sooner then the tender Bud. *Equallity in yeares.*

It is the office of foresight, to consider of the equallitie of bringing up, least a diversity in manners, betweene the married, make a devision of desires: for Spannyels and Curres, hardly live together without snarling. *Equallity in manners.*

And it is the office of foresight, to see that there be a consent in Religion, betweene the marryed, for if theyr love be not grafted in theyr soules, it is like theyr Marriage will be infyrmed, with the defects of the body. *Consent in religion.*

The office of <u>Free choise</u>, is the roote or foundation of Marriage, which consisteth onely in the satisfaction of fancie: for where the fancie is not pleased, all the perfections of the world, cannot force loove, and where the fancie delighteth, many defects are perfected, or tollerated among the Marryed. *Free choise in satisfaction of Fancie.*

When Marriage is solemnized, there are many
things to be observed one the parte bothe of the
husband and the Wife.

The Husband is to consider, his house is a
petty Common wealth, whereof himselfe is cheefe,
and his Servaunts Subjects: therefore, for the
welfare bothe of himselfe and householde, it is
needefull, that he set downe such orders, as God
may be gloryfied, himselfe profitably served,
the good servaunt well rewarded, the evill
chastened, and the neighbour pleased: And as it
is the Husbands office, to set downe these orders,
so it is the Wives dutie to see them executed. /

The charge of the Husband, is to get abroade
for the provision of his householde: and the
Wife is bounde to spare at home, towards the
maintenance of her children.

The office of the Husband, is to see his
ground Tilled, his Cattell cherished, his fences
sound, his labourers worke, and their wages
paide.

The dutie of the wife is to see her Garden
weeded, her Vines cut, and in her Orcharde her
fruite Trees pruned: within doores her house
well ordered, her Maidens busied, her Children
instructed, the freend intertained, and the
Tables well furnished. And in this Oeconmie,
many women have so excelled, as Socrates
affirmeth: that he learned of Women more Morrall
Philosophie, then naturall reason of Anaxagoras
and Archelaus: wherein Socrates testifyeth no
more then theyr woorthy sexe deserveth: for
many Women governe theyr Families with such
Prudence, Temperance, Pietie, and other

Marginal notes:
- A mans house is a pettie common weale.
- The office of the Wife.
- Y1ᵛ
- The husbandes care appertaineth to thinges abroade.
- The wives charge is huswivery within doore.
- Morall Philosophie to be learned by women.

commendable vertues, as may well instruct the
wisest.

    The Husband ought to beware, that in the
presence of his wife, he useth no filthie
5 lascivious talke: for besides the witnesse of
his owne indiscression, he maketh her a passage
for many an unhappy thought.   *Lacivious talke to be shunned of the husband.*

    The Wife ought to be nice, in occasion of
suspition, for her husband that see'th open cause
10 of mistrust, cannot but feare, that in secret, he
receiveth injurie: and Jelowsie though she
proceedes from exceeding love, yet is she the
greatest enemie of the Married.   *The wife ought to be nice in cause of suspition.*

    The Husband is bound to keepe his wife in
15 civill and comely apparell, as well to make her
seeme beautifull unto himselfe, as to prevent the
reproche of the neighbour: for this hath beene an
aunctient custome among the Romaines, and it is to
be feared, that if the Husband breake it, to
20 spare his Purse, the Wife will repayre it, though
she gage her person.   *Comelye apparell the husband should give his wife.*

    The Wife that will please her Husband, and
make a great showe of a little, though her Gownes
be plaine, in her lynnen she must be curious and
25 fine: for otherwise, / were she attyred all in
Silke: if her sleeves, Partlet and other Linnen
be coorse, torne, or sluttishly washed, she shall
neither be praysed of straungers, nor delight her
Husband.   *Cleane lynnen commendable in a wife.*

Y2^r

30   The Husband, after householde jarres, if the
Wife seeme to be sorie, he ought not to be sullen:
for if shee perceive him of a frowarde nature, it
is like in other suche squares, she wilbe negligent
to please him.   *The husband must beware of sollomnes.*

The Wife, if she offend her husband, by some
ignoraunt trespasse, she must please him with a
loving countenaunce: least if he finde her of a
crooked condition, he will take delight to crosse
5 her with continuall foule usage.

    The wife must be amyable towardes her husband.

    The olde Husband, is to accompany his young
Wife with grave Matrons, and to set her foorth
with costly civill attyre, that seeing the
reverence and honour that is given her for her
10 Husbandes gravitie, she will studdie how to please
him, though she displease her owne disposition.

    A lawe for a younge womans olde husband.

    The younge Wife that hath an olde Husband, is
bound to make much of him at home: for the
reputation she receaveth in his life, and for the
15 wealth she is like to have by his deathe: and
abroade must be sober in her behaviours, discreete
in her talke, and no harkener to young mens tales,
least her owne lightnesse, make her openly
infamed, where her Husbands imperfections, could
20 cause her but to be secreatly suspected.

    A regarde for an olde mans young wyfe.

    The young Husband is too beare with his olde
Wife, in her will, as well for the reverence due
to her yeares, as for the advauncement, the love
bringeth to himselfe: least the neighbours terme
25 his Wife an unfortunate old Woman, and himselfe,
a naughtie, frowarde, vile natured young man.

    A regarde for an olde womans younge husband.

    The olde Wife, to give excuse to her dotage,
must in open assemblies, commend her young
Husband of modest and staied governement: and
30 secreatly, to be lovingly used, must kisse him:
with <u>Midas</u> lippes for, if she fyll not / his
Purse by fayre meanes, with foule intreatie he
will be his owne Carver: if she complayne, she
joyneth but scorne to her owne mischaunce.

    A regard for a young mans olde wife.

Y2^v

Generally, the Husband ought not to forbid his Wife, in assemblyes modestlie, to intertaine time, in devising with the better sorte: for in such jelous restraint, he shall leave a suspition, that he injoyneth her this open pennaunce, for some secret trespasse, and so bothe slaunder himselfe, and injurie his wife.

Modest familiaritie not to be forbidden the Wife.

The Wife should have an especiall care, to shun the company of light Women: for the multitude, though they can charge her with no misdemeanour, yet they well condemne her honor, by the known evils of her companions.

Light company to be shunned of the Wife.

Many other needefull directions, may be given to preserve unitie in Mariage (quoth Segnior Phyloxenus) too cumbersome for me to reporte, and too tedious for this honorable company to heere, whose patience I have already injured too much: but finding my error, I end my tale, and remaine ready to make satisfaction in some other service.

Sir (quoth Fabritio) the end of your Tale, puts us in remembraunce of our duetie and your right, which is for this honourable favour, to remaine your indebted Servaunts, to embrace your counsels, and to commend (and submit our reasons to) your learned Censure.

It is your favour and not my merit (quoth Segnior Phyloxenus.)

Sir, (quoth Queene Aurelia) I will beare the blame of this dayes importuning of you, and you alone shall have the honour, in graunting of my requests, who to the former joyneth this one more favour, which is, that you conclude this your worthy exercise, with some rare Historie at large.

Madam (quoth Segnior Philoxenus) this is the

least of your commaundements, considering that
Histories make mention of thousands, who in their
unseperable looves, have sounded the excellencie
of Mariage, wherefore I obey your pleasure. /

The woorthy Historie of Phrigius and Pieria. Reported by Segnior Phyloxenus.

In the Register of Fame, wherein the
Monuments of the vertuous are Cronicled, as
presedents for theyr posteritie, I reade, that in
the famous Cittie of Miletum in Ionia, as
soveraigne Prince and governour, there raigned a
worthy Duke, called Nebeus, who to comfort and
supporte his aged yeares, had to his sonne and
onely heayre, Phrigius, a young Gentleman of such
rare towardlines, as it may be a question, whether
he weare more beholding to Nature for the
perfections of his body, to Vertue for the
qualities of his minde, or to Fortune in suffering
him to be so nobly borne.

In Myos, a neighbour Cittie to Miletum, there
was also a Prince of much renowne, named Pythes,
whose Daughter and heyre, was fayre Pieria, by
whose vertues all Ionia was renowned. The auncient
envie betweene the Cittizens of Miletum and Myos,
was tourned into amitie: and the open warre
betweene Duke Nebeus and the noble Pithes, was
peaceably and honourably ended: All such happie
events, succeeded this following adventure. Upon
the Feastivall day of Diana, the Cittizens of
Myos, with out the injurie of Souldiers, might
lawfully repayre to Miletum, to sacrifice to Diana,
upon which safe conduct, with many other Ladyes
and Gentlewomen of Myos, fayre Pieria waighted on

her Mother to Dianas Temple, whose rare beauty was
such, as dazeled the eies of the behoulders, like
the reflections of a Myrror, placed against the
Sunne.

  Among many that looved, and few or none that
saw possibility of grace, such was the renowne of
her chaste disdaine, young Phrigius beheld Pieria
with such a setled eye, / as Dianas Temple sheelded
him not against the Arrowes of Loove: but as a
wounded Stag, at the first seemeth little dismayde:
so Phrigius with an unappalled cheere, returned to
the Dukes Pallace, and as pledge of truce, he sent
his heart to Myos. The Ceremonies and Sacrifices
of Diana ended, the Warres renued, the wonted
Massacres, Murthers, Rapines, and outragious
cruelties practised by the Souldiours of either
part: in so much as Lawe gave place to Armes,
equitie to violence, and all publique order was
perverted, and upon the point to be destroyed.
The Captaines of Myos encouraged theyr Souldiours
of the one part: but the Souldiours of Miletum,
were driven to comfort theyr Captaine with a
threatening of disgrace. But ah poore Phrigius,
what aunswer shouldst thou make? To see thy
Souldiours slaine, and thy Citties spoyled,
without proffers of rescue were dishonourable:
to bend thy forces against thy owne heart, were
unnaturall: to make the best choyse of these two
evilles, required leasure: and judgement. And
therefore advisedly to consider of his estate,
at this time Phrigius satisfied his Souldiours
with hope of some speedy venturous exployte, and
daungered not his enemies, with the proffer of
any violence: so that either power kept their

trenches peaceably, but yet with this indifferent
perryll, that they attended oportunitie, to make
the one Conquerors, and the other Captives: for
the long Civill contention, had now made the
5 estate of either as desperate, as the fortunes
of two that have their substaunce upon the chaunce
of Dice, the one to have all, the other to be
undoone.
  When Phrigius had with slender hope thus
10 quieted the acclamations of the people, he retyred
himselfe into a solitary Chamber, to be the sole
companion of his **outragious passions, with whom**
he thus devised.
  Ah trayterous eyes, betrayers of my whole
15 body, the scourge of Miletum, and enymies of my
honour: the vengeaunce of Oedippus is too gentle
for your injuries: what doost thou say? oh
blasphemous tongue, rivall of / humanitie,
callumner of Beautie, and hinderer of thy
20 countryes peace: thou reprocher of vertue, and
Phrigius welfare: know to thy shame, the
perfection of my eyes have constantly behelde
Pieria, whose devine beauties, emblemed in
humaine shape, dazeleth the youngest sight in
25 Ionia: Then to revile them thus, thou tyrannisiest
nature: to demaunde why I love and serve Beautie,
thy question is blinde, and deserveth a double
aunswer: But aye me, though my eyes, and Love,
have doone but what is just, Fortune hath dealt
30 too rigourously with me, to render my heart
Captive to his Daughter, who is the rivall of my
father: what hope may I give to my afflictions?
when possibility of comfort is taken away: the
Parents are ready to sheath their Swords in one

$Y4^r$

an others entrayles: is it then like, the
Children shall embrace a mutuall affection? O no:
for though mylde Venus consent that they love,
wrathfull Mars wyll sever theyr affection. O
5 cruell Warre, thou art not unproperly called the   The vengeaunce
scourge of God, for in thee is contayned a   of Warre.
greater vengeaunce then might be imagined by man:
thou armest the Sonne against the Father, the
Uncle against the Nephew, the Subject against his
10 Soveraigne: Thy Drinke is blood, thy foode the
flesh of men: thy Fiers are flaming Citties:
thy pleasures, spoyling of Widdowes, ravishment of
Virgins, subvertion of Lawes and publique benefit:
thy Judges, Tyrannie, and Injustice: and where
15 thou remaynest, her knowen enemy is not so
daungerous, as the fayned freend.
    But why exclaime I of Warre, who double
Crowned Alexander with the ritches of Asia and
Affrica? who honoured Caesar, with imperiall
20 triumphes? and rewarded Hanniball, for the
travailes of his life, with renowne after death?
by whom Millions of men, are regystred in the
life Booke of Fame: and thorough whom, Phrigius
giveth expectation of benefit unto his Countrey,
25 comfort to his aged Father, and honour to his
posteritie.
    I receyved my wounde in the tyme of peace,
nay in the Temple of Diana: shall I then exclayme
of / Peace, and upbrayde Chastitie: fowle fall
30 the heart that should moove, and shame worme the
tongue that pronounceth such blasphemie: O
blessed Peace, thou fast chainest Treason, Tirannie,
Murther, Theft, and Wrathe, with all disturbers
of common tranquillitie, and in the hyest dignities,

placest <u>Justice</u>, <u>Pietie</u>, <u>Temperaunce</u>, <u>Concorde</u>
and <u>Love</u>, with many other Morrall vertues, by   The blessings
whom the lewde are chastened, the good are   of peace.
cherished, and Common weales prosper and florish.
5   O <u>Chastitie</u>, thy divine vertues deserve a better
Trumpet, then my injurious tongue: thy excellencie
is written in the browe of <u>Pieria</u>. And is <u>Pieria</u>
the Deputie of <u>Diana</u>? O yes: and <u>Phrigius</u> the
servaunt of <u>Venus</u>? too true: it is then impossible
10 they should agree in affection? yea sure. O
unfortunate <u>Phrigius</u>, through <u>Peace</u> which
receivedst thy wound, before <u>Dianas</u> Aulter, and
by cruell Warre art seperated from the Surgion
that should cure thee. These sundrye conflictes
15 <u>Phrigius</u> had with his bitter passions, which
pursued theyr advantage, with such thorny feares,
as if he had not beene suddenly succoured, by the
advise and comfort of Lorde <u>Miletus</u>, a favoured
Counseller to Duke <u>Nebeus</u>, and an assured freend
20 to his sonne <u>Phrigius</u>, he had beene like to have
yeelded to <u>Dispaire</u>. <u>Miletus</u> was glad to see him
thus affected, and sorry to behold him so
daungerouslie afflicted: for in this loove he
foresawe an end, of the auncient envie and enmitie,
25 betweene the Cittizens of <u>Miletum</u>, and <u>Myos</u>: whose
civill Fraies, had buried more young men in the
Fieldes, then aged in the Churches and Churchyardes.
Therefore to confirme his affection, and to comfort
him with hope: Lord <u>Phrigius</u> (quoth he,) to blame
30 your affection were cruelty and no sound counsell:
for you love <u>Pieria</u>, the Parragon of the worlde,
to discomfort you with an impossibilitie of her
favour, were cleane against the possibilitie of
your fortune: for besides that, your person

alluringly pleaseth, your authorities commaund:
yea Pithes cannot but rejoyce, Pieria consent, and
all Myos desire is to solemnize this Mariage. /
   My selfe, and the graver sort of the counsell,
will motion the matter to the Duke your father,
who I trust wil holde the affection of his sonne,
rather to proceede from the justice of Diana, then
the injurie of Cupid. Who regarding the zelous
offeringes of Pieria, agreed that you shoulde be
wounded, that Pieria might have the honour to cure
you, in whose vertues, all Ionia hopeth to be
blessed. Therefore, to make your affection
knowen, in some pleasing Letter, to Pieria commend
your service, and to deale with both your fathers,
refer the care to mee. How sweete the smallest
hope of grace is to a condemned man? or the leaste
woorde of comfort, from the Phisition, to the
infirmed patient: the soden chaunge of Phrigius
mone, truely manifesteth: who nowe began to
looke cheerefully, and with hope appeased his
passions: so that imbrasing Miletus, he committed
his life to the fortune of his discresion: and
while his passion was quicke, hee presented both
love and service to Pieria, in this following
letter.

Phrigius Letter to Pieria.

   Faire PIERIA, sith it is a common thing to
love: and a miracle to subdue affection, let it
not seeme strange, that I am slave to your bewtie,
nor wounder though I sue for grace. The wounded
Lion, prostrateth himselfe at the feete of a man:
the sicke, complayneth, to the Phisition: and
(charged with more tormentes) the lover, is inforced

to seeke comfort of his Mistresse. To prove that
I love, needeth no other testimony, then the witnes
of your rare perfections, and to give me life is
the only work of your pittie. Wherfore (Madame)
5 since the Vertue of your eye, hath drawen away
my heart, as the Adamant doeth the steele, I
beseech you that my hartlesse bodie may so live
by your ruth, as I may have strength (as well as
wil) to do you service: and let it suffice for
10 more honor of your tryumph, that by the power of
beutie, your vertues have achived, a more glorious
conquest, then might the whole strength of MYOS,
and whiche is more, of a puissant / enemie, you
have made so perfect a friende, as Phrygius, shal
15 hold him self in no fortune, so happie, as to
encounter with the oportunytie, to do Pieria, and
her favourers service, or their enemies damage:
If which amendes, may repayre all Injuries past,
I shall hould, the Safecundict blessed, that
20 licensed you to enter Myletum: If greater ransom
be demaunded, it must be my life: which (if it
be your wyl) shall foorth with be sacrificed,
notwithstandinge, in such crueltie, Dianas
Temple shalbe prophaned, before whose Aulter, I
25 received my wound from the eyes of fayre Pieria:
but houldynge it unpossible, that a stonie harte,
may bee enemie to so manye Graces as live in your
face: I Balme my woundes, with hope that I kisse
your gracious hand: and that your Aunswere wyll
30 returne an acceptaunce of service.

      He, whose hart waighteth
       on your beautie.
        PHRIGIUS.

This Letter sealed and subscribed: <u>To fayre
Pieria, Tryumph after victorie</u>: was delivered
unto a trustie Messenger: who (having Safecunduict,
to passe through both the Armies) in good houre,
arrived at Prince <u>Pythes</u> Pallace: and in the
presence of her Mother and other friends
reverently kissyng the same, delivered <u>Pieria</u>,
with <u>Phrygius</u> lovyng commendations, his letter.
Who so in the Spryngtime, in one Moment had seene
rayne and Sunshine, might againe beholde the lyke
chaunge in <u>Pierias</u> troubled countenaunce: who
found no lesse Joye in reading the Letter, then
cause of wonder, in beholding the superscription,
who (by the consent of <u>Diana</u>, to bring peace into
<u>Myletum</u>) was by love, with the selfe same Arrowe,
and at one instant wounded in as deepe Affection,
as <u>Phrygius</u>: notwithstandynge, bounde to no
desire so muche, as to the Direction of her
Parentes, she shewed them this Letter: who,
weerie of the warres: and embracynge this meane
of peace. After they had advisedly considered
the Contentes: to comforte <u>Phrygius</u>, without
injurie to <u>Pieriaes</u> chaste behaviour: in her
name, they returned this Aunswere. /

<u>PIERIAS</u> Answer to <u>PHRIGIUS</u> Letter.

SIR PHRIGIUS, I received your Letter, and as
I confesse, that your prayses, so far passe my
meryt, as I wunder at the errour of your
Judgement: so, I doubt whither so honourable a
personage, as your Lordship, can yeelde your
service, to so meane a Lady: or if love were of
that power, whether you woulde obay, to bee
Servante to her, whose Fathers ryvall, your

parentes, and you are: but on the other part: I
entertayne a faint hope, that you are not so much
enemie to your honor, as to leave in your
Adversaries possession, a Monument of Dissimulation:
5 Upon which warant, and your free offer of service:
I bind you, by a curtuous request, to indevour to
conclude a speedie peace: that I may without
danger of Hostilyty repaire to Dianas Temple: In
compassyng of which gratious League, you shal
10 receive great glory: the countrey much quiet, and
I, whom you wysh such welfare, shalbe bownd to do
you any honourable favour.
      PIERIA of MYOS.

  This aunswer sealed, and subscribed, To my
15 Lorde Phrygius: delyvered by the handes, and
blessed with the loving countenaunce of Pieria,
was returned to Phrigius, by his owne messenger:
who, after hee had read and reread this Letter
(not for that, the Contents, gave him any
20 assuraunce of Love: but for because, they
commaunded an imployment of Service) hee comforted
his Spirit, with hope, that his indevour in this
charge, shoulde, both reave all doubte, of
dissimulation, by hym, and smoothe Pierias Browe,
25 of Chaste disdayne: and to further a happy ende
of the Countries calamitie. In the beginnyng of
Phrigius contentment, Lorde Miletus had so dealt
in these affaires, as in shorte time Duke Nebeus,
and Prince Pythes came to parle of peace: and
30 while the Counsels of either parte, considered
uppon the Articles of agreement: Safecundit of
Trafick, was geven to the Inhabitants of either
Citie.

  How sweete the friendly incounters, of these

aunciente enemies were: is the office of him, that
hath beene scour-/ged with warres: who, though
they were but in the estate of reprived men, yet
the hope of assured peace lightned their hartes
of former sorrowe, and replenished the place with
gladnesse.

    The vertue of Peace.

    Faire Pieria, nowe safely repaired to the
Aulters of Diana: and Phrygius, more of desire,
to salute his Mistris, then of zeale to sacrifice,
to Chastetie: fayned many Devotions, to visit
her Temple: where these Lovers, for the reverence
they bare to the place, forbare to encounter in
any speeche of Love: Yet if Diana, wolde have
publyshed their thoughts, shee shoulde have
confessed, that the most devotionate of them both,
in their hartes, honoured Juno, in the eye of her
owne Image and Aulters. But Diana, though shee
be the Soveraigne of single Nimphes: yet is she
friende to Juno, and the Chast Married: and only
enemie, to Venus and the wanton sort: so that shee
tooke in worth, this light trespasse: yea, held
her self honoured, that her sacred Temple, should
bee the originall cause of Myletum and Myos, peace
and amytie: and the ende of their aunceint envy,
and enmitie. Wherfore, to conclude, the begun
agreement, she sent Concorde and Charitie, to
chayne up Grudge, and Dissention.

    Duke Nebeus and Prince Pythes, freed from
the vexation of these furies, with affable and
friendly intertainment, reasoned of their affayres:
and while the Parents parled of their common profit:
the Children, uppon lawfull oportunities, devysed
of their pryvate Loves: but yet with suche a
dutifull regarde, of their friendes consent, that

although their hartes were lynked together, by
free choyce, the clapping of hands was referred to
the forsight of Parentes: who burying former
injuries, in the Cave of Oblivion, made an Edict
5 of Amyty, sealed, and strengthned, with the
Marriage of Phrygius and Pieria, Heires of eithers
renowne and dignytie. Beholde heere the worke of
Love, grafted in the honorable hartes of the
vertuous. The wrath and stormes of war, is
10 turned to calm and temporate peace: the blossoms
of enmytie are altered into fruts of amyty: and
the roote of mallice, grown to the tree of pitie. /
The Nobles in honour of this Mariage, lavisht out
their treasure, in all their triumphes and showes
15 to be in good equipage. The meaner Gentlemen, by
exceeding cost, learned by experience, how
afterwarde to spare. The Citizens with giftes of
great Emprice, presented their dutiful affections.
The learned eternised this marriage peace, in
20 Tables of Memorie. The Cleargy song Himnes of
joy, The common people ronge the Belles, and
everie sorte showed some token of delight. So that
Phrigius and Pieria, after the deathes of their
aged fathers, were crowned with the dignities of
25 Myletum and Myos, and all their happie life, were
honoured with these acclamations of their
subjectes. Live, blessed Princes: the appeasers
of Jupiters wrathe, by whome War, the Monster of
humanitie, is fast chayned: And peace the
30 soveraigne of morall vertues, Triumpheth in the
Capitals of IONIA. Live blessed princes, and
long enjoye the heartes of your subjectes. In
your vertues who have multiplied wealth: and to
doe you service are readie to spende their lives.

The power of vertuous Love.

Z3^r

This zeale and reverence of their subjectes, Phrigius and Pieria, manie yeares possessed, betweene whome there was such equallitie in disposition, as fortune knew not, by anie accident
5 of joye, or mischance, howe to sever their desires. And when the time came, the heavens (envying the glorie of the earth, in possessing this divine cupple) charged nature, to render their right. Who obaying the will of Jove, sent
10 sickenes to summon both Phrigius, and Pieria, and licensed death to doe his worst. And (as there yet remaineth an opinion in Miletum) as their loves began in one houre, so their lives ended in one momente: whose spirites Metamorphosed, into
15 white Turtles, tooke their flight, towardes that heavenly Paradise. Where I wish all faithfull lovers, and this lovely companie, abiding places.

    Segnior Philoxenus, by the vertue of this dayes exercise, the onely travell of his learned
20 wit, so raysed the heartes of the companie, with the desire of Mariage, that Lucia Bella, who, in the beginning of Christmasse, was / determyned to have beene a vestall Nunne, now confessed that they were enemies to Nature, and not worthy the
25 society of men, which scandylised, or scorned this sacred Institution. The rest of this honorable company, by plawsible speeches, confirmed Lucia Bellas opinion, or by silence shewed a willyng consent. And to conclude the exercise,
30 (quoth Queene Aurelia,) Segnior Philoxenus, your sweet vertues, have described so devyne a Paradice, as our soules cannot, but long, after this holy Institution, and our hartes honour your perfections, by whose bountie this company is not onely highly

intertained, but by your most precious treasures
richly inriched. Madam (quoth hee) the vertue you
speake of, belongeth to Mariage: the benifit to
this gracious assembly: and the bare words, to
5 Phyloxenus. Such bare wordes (quoth Fabritio)
deserve to be registred amonge the lyfe deeds of
Memorie. Upon this Judgment, Queene Aurelia, arose,
and the company performyng the office of reverent
curtesy, returned into the great Chamber to salute
10 some other of the New yeeres Pleasures.

<u>The Device of a Stately Show, and Mask,
the seventh Nyghte, by Segnior PHILOXENUS,
to honoure Queene AURELIA, and the other
Ladies and Gentlewomen.</u>

15   Upon Newe yeeres daye at Night, about nine of
the Clocke, in an inclosed place in the great Hall:
after Queene Aurelia, and her chosen attendants,
had daunced certein solemne Almaynes, appeared a
hye Mountain, the Forestery wherof, was of faire
20 Bay Trees, Pomgranate, Lymons, Orenges, Date Trees,
and other fruites of most pleasure: among the
Mossy Rocks appeared Snailes, Lysards, Moles, Frogs,
Greshoppers, and such lyke unvenymus vermin, and
by the fountaines, which run aslant the side of
25 the Mountain, Lions, Unicorns, Elephants, Camelions,
Camels and other beasts of honor: as if they were
appointed by Nature, to garde those sacred streames,
from being troubled with the raskall multitude of
Cattel, which domesticall desart, was perfected
30 with such art, as nature confessed her ex-/cellent
cunning, to be vanquished by mans industrie. This
Mountaine which resembled, some wildernes in
Arabia, dewed with the pleasant springs of Africa,
by a still motion, removed towards the upper end
35 of the hall, into the ful presence of Queene

24^r

Aurelia, and the most statly company. In the
mydst of this Mountaine was an Arbor of sweete
Eglentine, intercoursed with Roses, and fully
shadowed with the spreadinge Branches, of the
5   purpled Vine: in which, upon a statly throne
sate Diana attired all in whyte, and at her feete
weare the nyne Muses, clothed in severall colours,
according to their several qualyties, sounding
heavenly harmony, both with voice and instrument:
10 out of this arbor sprang a Bay Tree, in which was
the Hyen, which at pleasure being both Male and
Female, expressed the ful power of vertue: who
though shee hath the forme and habit of a woman,
yet is her essentiall substance compounded of
15 both kindes: At the foote of this Hil, was the
Monster Envy armed with fire and sword, to hinder
their passage, which adventred to clime the Mount:
a forest Nimph clad all in flowers, in a short
speech, declared, that Diana, and the Muses, who
20 in the golden age, had their Pallaces, in the
Forrests, Mountaines, and rivers of pleasure,
through out the whole world: now by the injury of
time, were driven to their sanctuary of Parnassus:
at the foote wherof the Monster Envy kept, to
25 hinder the passages of such as attempted with their
renown, to set those Ladies at lyberty: who hering
by fame, the glory of this honorable company, were
arived by hope, that the vertu of some of the
troupe, should redeeme them from captivytie, and
30 therfore, she summoned the Knightes present, to
make tryall of their vallors, and the Ladies of
their vertues: whiche saide, she retired back into
the Mountaine: The Gentlemen and Ladies, having
a cunning foreknowlege of the intent of this show,

The Seventh Dayes Exercise

armed themselves, with sundry attempts to
overcome this Monster. Soranso, Dondolo, Ismarito,
and Faliero, drew their rapiers, and assailed
Envy, but dry blowes availed not: so that they
5 were conquered, and committed to the gayle of
Tediusnesse. Maria Belochy, Franceschina Sancta,
Lucia Bella, Helena Dulce, and other Ladies, and
Damosels, indevored to charme hym, with the sweete
sounde, and Heavenlye / impressions of Musick.
10 But Envy more warie then Argus, and lesse pitifull
then the Tormenters of Hell: the first whereof,
was overcome with Inachus Oten Pipe: the other
moved to ruthe with Orpheus passionate Musick (to
show himselfe composed of all the vennom of Hell)
15 coulde not bee conquered, by the sharp swords of
the Knightes, nor would not be intreated with the
sugred Harmonie of the faier Ladies: But amidst
this Monsters Triumphes, there was a voyce heard
in the Mowntayne: Non vi, sed virtute: Wherupon,
20 Queene Aurelia, with a Myrrour, devised by Segnior
Philoxenus, peaceably, made towards Envie: whiche
Monster, presumyng of his force, lifted his Club
against this vertuous Dame: who, by the reflections
of the Concave Superficies, of this Myrrour,
25 daunted with the feare of his own weapon, imagining
that he stroke him selfe, recoyled backe with such
haste, as he fell downe: Wherupon, Segnior
Phyloxenus, seasyng on his Club, and laying him
on, therwith, said: As Phallaris, dyd to Perillus:
30 die with the weapon, thou preparst for other.

    In Triumph of this glorious Victorie, Diana
sent down the Nymphe Chlora, to salute Queene
Aurelia, with this Present: which was a Shield,
wherin was quartred, four severall Honours.

Envy is murdered with his owne wepon.

The first. VERT: A lookyng Glasse of Christall.
The second. AZURE: a payre of Ballance, Argent.
The thyrd. OR: a Pyller of Porphier.
The fourth. ARGENT: a standing Cup of Ruby Rock.

5   The Muses them selves, came also downe, and
crowned her with a Garland of Roses, parted, perpale,
ARGENT, and GULES: and electing her for their
Soveraign, to comfort the five Knights that were
discomforted by ENVY, two and two leading a Knight,
10 between them, daunced a statly Almain, of XV. which
ended: thei bestowed a favor, and certain Latin
verses, upon every one of the Knights: and returned
unto their Mount. The Silver Pen, and Verses
delivered by URANIE to ISMARITO, stand in the
15 forefrunt of this Booke: the rest, for that they
were proper unto them selves, and impertinent for
this matter, I omit: By this time, the Cock was
ready to sing his midnight song: and the company
(fully satisfied with pleasure) departed unto their
20 lodgings, to spende the rest of the night in
Contemplation and sleepe.

FINIS. /

EXPLANATORY NOTES

Works Frequently Cited

Full bibliographic citations are given below, or in the Explanatory Notes, only for works that are not listed in the bibliography. Classical references in the Notes are to texts in the Loeb Classical Library; Biblical references are to the Geneva Bible (1560; facsimile rpt. Madison: Univ. of Wisconsin Press, 1969).

Whetstone's Works:

Bacon	A Remembraunce of Sir Nicholas Bacon (1579)
CLS	The Censure of a Loyall Subject (1587)
Dier	A Remembraunce of Sir James Dier (1582)
EM	The English Myrror (1586)
HRS	The Honorable Reputation of a Souldier (1585)
MMC	A Mirour for Magestrates of Cyties (1584)
PC	Promos and Cassandra (1578)
RR	The Rocke of Regard (1576)
TT	A Touchstone for the Time (1584)

The Bestiary	T. H. White, trans., The Bestiary; A Book of Beasts, 12th Cent. (New York: Putnams, 1954).
Cartari	Vincenzo Cartari, The Fountaine of Ancient Fiction, trans. Richard Linche (London, 1599).
Castiglione	Baldassare Castiglione, The Book of the Courtier, trans. Sir Thomas Hoby, 1561 (London: Dent, 1928).
Cooper	Thomas Cooper, "Dictionarium Historicum et Poeticum" in Thesaurus Linguae Romanae et Britannicae (1565; facsimile rpt. Menston, Eng.: Scolar Press, 1969).
Du Verdier's Mexia	Pedro Mexia, Les Diverses Leçons d'Antoine du Verdier . . . suivans celles de Pierre Messie (Lyon, 1592), as quoted in Izard (see below).

Gascoigne, The Adventures of Master F.J.
       In A Hundreth Sundrie Flowres, ed. C. T. Prouty (Columbia: Univ. of Missouri, 1942).

Gruget's Mexia Pedro Mexia, Les Diverse Leçons de Pierre Messie, trans. Claude Gruget (Lyon, 1592).

Harl.M. A True Description and Direction of What is Most Worthy to be Seen in All Italy, c. 1600, Harleian Miscellany (1810; rpt. New York: AMS, 1965), V, 1-41.

Izard Thomas C. Izard, George Whetstone, Mid-Elizabethan Gentleman of Letters (1942; rpt. New York: AMS, 1966).

Lyly John Lyly, Euphues: The Anatomy of Wit; Euphues and His England, ed. M. W. Croll and H. Clemons (1916; rpt. New York: Russell, 1964).

Montaigne Michel de Montaigne, The Diary of Montaigne's Journey to Italy in 1580 and 1581, trans. E. J. Trechmann (New York: Harcourt, 1927).

ODEP The Oxford Dictionary of English Proverbs, 3rd ed., rev. F. P. Wilson (Oxford: Clarendon Press, 1970).

OED The Oxford English Dictionary, ed. Sir J. A. H. Murray et al., 12v. and Suppl. (Oxford: Clarendon Press, 1933, 1972).

Ovid Met. Metamorphoses, trans. F. J. Miller, 2v. (Cambridge, Mass.: Harvard Univ. Press, 1921).

Painter William Painter, The Palace of Pleasure, 1566-67, ed. Joseph Jacobs, 3v. (1890; New York: Dover, 1966).

Pliny Natural History, trans. H. Rackham, 10v. (London: Heinemann, 1938-62).

Tilley Morris Palmer Tilley, A Dictionary of the Proverbs in England in the Sixteenth and Seventeenth Centuries (Ann Arbor: Univ. of Michigan Press, 1950).

Topsell Edward Topsell, The Historie of Foure-footed Beastes (London, 1607), STC 24123.

Topsell, Serpents.
       The Historie of Serpents (London, 1608), STC 24124.

Title Page

1.1 <u>An Heptameron</u>] A work divided into seven days. From Greek ἑπτά (<u>hepta</u>) = seven, and ἡμέρα (<u>haemera</u>) = day. Whetstone is undoubtedly echoing the title of Marguerite de Navarre's framed collection of tales published in 1559, <u>L'Heptaméron</u>, which in turn is modelled on Boccaccio's <u>Decameron</u>. In both the <u>Heptaméron</u> and the <u>Decameron</u>, a group of people entertain themselves, in times of flood and of plague respectively, by narrating a series of novellas or tales on successive days. The <u>OED</u> suggests that Boccaccio may have entitled his work on the analogy of the <u>Hexameron</u>, an account by Ambrose of the six days of creation -- a work which inspired many imitations in the Renaissance. The fact that the word "hexameron" became current in English after 1573 testifies to the popularity of this type of writing in Whetstone's time. For a discussion of other framed novellas, see Introduction, p. lxxvi.

1.2 <u>Civill Discourses</u>] Entertaining discussions appropriate to a refined society; also, discussions on social questions. As T. F. Crane has pointed out in his <u>Italian Social Customs of the Sixteenth Century</u>, such discussions were a popular social game imported from Italy into England in the late sixteenth century. The word "civill" includes the connotations of "educated," "well-bred," "polite," and "polished," and is derived from the Renaissance ideal of civility, of the civil life (see Introduction, p. xxxix). It might also suggest a type of exposition, civil narration, which deals with "facts in controversy." (Richarde Rainolde, <u>A Booke Called the Foundacion of Rhetorike</u>, 1563, as quoted by W. G. Crane in <u>Wit and</u>

Rhetoric in the Renaissance, (p. 66). Crane also mentions (p. 124) that "discourse" was "a word much in vogue at that time" -- that is, in 1577.)

Both "Civill" and "Discourses" are words that appear frequently in the titles of Renaissance books. Examples that Whetstone may have known are Fenton's Certaine Tragicall Discourses (1567), Lodowick Bryskett's A Discourse of Civill Life (written about 1582 but published 1606), Pettie's translation of Guazzo's Civile Conversation (1581), and the anonymous Cyvile and Uncyvile Life (1579).

Thus, Whetstone's title sets up definite expectations: a Renaissance reader would expect his book to be a pleasant series of debates on some topic or topics (in this case, marriage) appropriate to, and of interest to, a polite social gathering, set within a framework of seven days, and including some novellas.

1.4 well Courted] Well behaved in a courtly manner. The phrase originally meant "of the court," but Whetstone uses it to refer to gentlemen rather than to courtiers.

1.6-8 the better sort . . . the Inferiour] Superior or inferior in rank or station, in social standing. These phrases are not to be interpreted in an absolute moral sense; however, since social rank and proper conduct were often linked in the Renaissance, Whetstone is probably suggesting some moral judgment.

1.8-9 Civil Government] Well-bred, polite behaviour.

1.16 Civyll Pleasure] Pleasure appropriate to well-bred, cultured persons.

1.17 Morall Noates] Observations of a moral, as opposed to a ribald, nature that are worthy of notice. Whetstone makes the common Renaissance claim that his work combines pleasure and profit -- a claim derived ultimately from Horace, Ars Poetica, 343: Omne tulit punctum, qui miscuit utile dulce (so quoted on the title page of Pettie's Petite Pallace of Pettie His Pleasure, 1576, and in Timothy Kendall's Flowers of Epigrammes, 1577, sig. a4^v).

1.20 Formae, nulla fides.] Latin, "Beauty is not to be trusted." Whetstone also used this motto at the end of his poem in The Paradise of Dainty Devices (1578) and on the title pages of The Rocke of Regard (1576), A Remembraunce of George Gaskoigne (1577), Promos and Cassandra (1578), A Remembraunce of Sir Nicholas Bacon (1579), A Remembraunce of Thomas late Earle of Sussex (1583), and A Remembraunce of Sir James Dier (1583). He then used a succession of different mottoes: Virtute Non Vi ("By virtue, not by might") in A Mirour for Magestrates of Cyties (1584) (see note 229.19); Malgre de fortune ("Inspite of Fortune") in A Mirror of Treue Honnour and Christian Nobilitie (1585) and in The Honorable Reputation of a Souldier (1585); Malgre in The English Myrror (1586); and Mors honesta, vita ignominiosa preferenda ("An honourable death is preferable to a disgraceful life") in Sir Phillip Sidney (1587) (see RR, sig. N1^r, and Tilley H576).

In his edition of The Paradise of Dainty Devices, p. 263, H. E. Rollins notes that Whetstone's first motto is an adaptation from Juvenal II. 8, frontis nulla fides ("Men's faces are not to be trusted," in the Loeb translation). An autobiographical passage at the end of A Touchstone for the Time (1584) may explain the significance of this motto for Whetstone: after complaining of the deceitfulness of friends as well as of enemies, he adds, "but I finde the old Larkes song true: <u>There is no trust in faire words, nor assurance in natures obligations</u>" (sig. K4^v).

1.22 <u>Richard Jones</u>] Or Richarde Jhones. Printer and bookseller in London, 1564-1602. From 1581 to 1602, his shop was located "At the Rose and Crown, over against the Falcon, near unto Holborn Bridge without Newgate." (R. B. McKerrow, ed., <u>A Dictionary of Printers and Booksellers in England, Scotland and Ireland, and of Foreign Printers of English Books 1557-1640</u>, 1910; rpt. London: Bibliog. Society, 1968, p. 159.) We do not have sufficient information to state whether the imprint here identifies Jones as the printer or as the publisher of the <u>Heptameron</u>. Whetstone may have met him through Gascoigne, whose <u>Spoyle of Antwerpe</u> had been printed or published by Jones in 1576 or 1577. Although it was not Jones who gave Whetstone his start as a published author, he has the distinction of being the only printer or bookseller whose imprint appears on more than one of Whetstone's title pages: <u>Promos and Cassandra</u> (1578), <u>A Mirour for Magestrates of Cyties</u> (1584), <u>A Mirror of Treue Honnour and Christian Nobilitie</u> (1585), <u>The Honorable Reputation of a Souldier</u> (1585), and <u>The Censure of a Loyall Subject</u> (1587) bear the name of Richard Jones.

Robert Waley and Edward Aggas preceded Jones as Whetstone's publishers or printers. <u>The Rocke of Regard</u> was apparently Waley's as well as Whetstone's first published book. Other printers or booksellers associated with Whetstone are, in succession, Miles Jennings, John Wolfe (with Richard Jones), John Charlewood, John Windet for Gregory Seton, and Thomas Cadman.

Jones appears to have been interested in works dealing with manners and civility, especially those influenced by Italian social ideals. Among the books published by him before 1582 were the following: Thomas

Twyne's <u>The Schoolemaster, or Teacher of Table Philosophie</u> (1576), a work
showing "howe a yonge gentleman may behave him self in all companies etc."
(<u>SR</u> 17 July 1576); <u>A New Yeeres Gift:</u> <u>The Courte of Civill Courtesie</u>
(1577), "Out of Italian" by Simon Robson; and <u>Cyvile and Uncyvile Life</u>
(1579).

1.24 <u>neare Holburne Bridge</u>] Whetstone's Epistle in <u>The Rocke of
Regard</u> is signed "From my lodging in Holburne the 15. of October 1576"
(sig. ¶3). However, there is no evidence to indicate whether he was still
residing in the vicinity of Jones's shop in 1582.

1.24 <u>3. Feb. 1582</u>] This date might be questioned since sixteenth-
century England officially followed the Julian calendar, in which the year
began on March 25. (Most continental countries, including Italy, adopted
the Gregorian or New Style calendar on October 15, 1582, but England
held back until 1752.) Nevertheless, the New Year was popularly celebrated
on January 1 -- as it is in the festivities described in the <u>Heptameron</u>.
As a result, official documents dated between January 1 and March 24,
1582 would in fact belong to the year 1583, but non-official writings
might be correctly dated by our present reckoning. To confuse the issue
further, printers were inconsistent in their practises: even though
Whetstone's <u>A Remembraunce of Sir Nicholas Bacon</u> bears the date 20 February
1578 yet was apparently printed in 1579, we may not assume that the
<u>Heptameron</u> similarly bears an Old Style date. On the contrary, since Arber,
in the <u>Stationers' Register</u>, enters the <u>Heptameron</u> on 11 January 1582,
and since it is extremely unlikely that a delay of more than one year
occurred before the book was published, we may accept the title-page date,
1582, as the year of publication of the <u>Heptameron</u>.

Explanatory Notes 238

Commendatory Verse

2.1-17 Translation] To Maecenas, in praise of the author: a Heroic Poem.

Maecenas, most celebrated among our leading men, beloved by the Clarian god and the chaste Muses, accept the Pierian honors that the singing Muse of the Troianovantean George has dedicated to you.

The Muse does not sing of useless or worthless things, but mindful of praise, she devotes herself to more serious concerns: confined by this same aim, she recommends the compact of marriage between equals. The author reports the disadvantages of unequal marriage.

Not only this: he reveals the true celebration of a great leader, and he raises him above the heavens with Aonian lyre.

He has divided the sequence of the work day-by-day, in marvellous order, with equal judgement: the labours of the seven days contend (in my considered opinion) with Castiglione.

And the things that the Muse has described in such a small book are not, believe me, unworthy of such a great patron.

2.1 Mecoenatem] Maecenas (d. 8 B.C.), a great patron of Latin literature. In English, simply, a patron.

2.2 CARMEN HEROICUM] A poem in dactylic hexameter.

2.4 Clario] Clarian, from Clarus, a surname of Apollo derived from the name of a town in Asia Minor where one of his major oracular shrines was located. Apollo was the god of song and poetry, as well as of prophecy and medicine, and was associated with the Muses.

2.4 Camaenis] The Camenae, Italian prophetic nymphs of springs, were identified by the Romans with the Muses.

2.5 Pierios] Pieria, a district at the foot of Mount Olympus, was believed to be the birthplace of the Muses. Hence, Pierian = poetic.

2.6 Troianovantaei] New Trojan; hence, British. The legendary capital of Brutus on the Thames was called Troia Nova ("New Troy").

2.6 Georgii] George; that is, Whetstone.

2.12 Aonio] Aonia, part of Boeotia, the region containing Mount Helicon and the spring of Aganippe, haunts of the Muses.

2.15 Castilione] Baldassare Castiglione (1478-1529), author of Il cortegiano, translated by Sir Thomas Hoby in 1561 as The Courtier.

2.18 JOANNES BOTREVICUS] Botrevicus also contributed a Latin verse to Whetstone's A Mirour for Magestrates of Cyties (1584). Franklin B. Williams in his Index of Dedications and Commendatory Verses in English Books Before 1641 (London: Bibliog. Society, 1962) identifies him with the Joannes Butterwike who contributed a commendatory verse to William Blandy's translation of Osorio's The Five Bookes of Civill and Christian Nobilitie (1576). Both these works, like the Heptameron, are concerned with civil behaviour, and both are associated with the Inns of Court: Blandy is described on the title page as "fellow of the middle Temple," and the Mirour for Magestrates of Cyties is addressed "To yong Gentlemen of Innes of Court." Izard believes that Botrevicus may have been an acquaintance of Thomas Watson, another student at the Inns of Court, who wrote the English commendatory verse to the Heptameron (p. 9 below). It is likely that Botrevicus, Blandy, Watson, and Whetstone were contemporaries at the Inns of Court.

If Botrevicus were an Englishman, his name would appear in English historical records as John Butterwick or Boterwike. The name "Butterwick" does appear frequently in Lincolnshire and Yorkshire, and in the <u>Sussex Record Society</u>, Vol. XLI: <u>Sussex Wills</u>, Vol. I (Lewes, 1935-41), but a search of the published records of students at Oxford, Cambridge, and the Inns of Court and of a variety of biographical dictionaries have failed to uncover the author of this verse. However, since Botrevicus retains the Latinized "Joannes" even while anglicizing his surname to "Butterwike," it is possible that he was a foreigner in England. The practice of adopting Latinized pen names was more common on the continent than in England, and it was a practice that foreign visitors often brought with them. (F. B. Williams, "Renaissance Names in Masquerade," <u>PMLA</u>, 69, 1954, 314-23.) "Botrevicus" does not yield to direct translation into English, but it may be a transliterated form of a Germanic name such as "Botterweck," "Buytewech," "Beuterrich," or "Bouterwek" or of the Italian "Boterus."

Izard also suggests (p. 228) that Botrevicus might be the J.B. (John Bodenham) who wrote "In Commendation of Gascoigne's Posies" (1575). Bodenham (fl. 1600) is associated with the publication of <u>Englands Helicon</u> (1600) and is the author of <u>Belvedere, or the Garden of the Muses</u> (1600), but the <u>DNB</u> states that of his life "no particulars have been discovered."

The Epistle Dedicatory

3.1 <u>Sir Christopher Hatton</u>] c. 1540-1591. A favourite of Queen Elizabeth, Sir Christopher Hatton was educated at Oxford and at the Inner Temple before he came to court "by the galliard" (Sir Robert Naunton as quoted in Brooks, <u>Sir Christopher Hatton</u>, p. 31). At the Inner Temple, Hatton participated in the writing and acting of dramatic entertainments: he was one of a group of Inner Temple authors who wrote <u>Tancred</u> and <u>Gismund</u>, a tale from Boccaccio in dramatic verse, which was acted before the Queen in 1566 or 1567 and printed in 1591. Since he was Master of the Game at the Christmas celebrations in 1561, Hatton probably came to the attention of the Queen during the court performance of <u>Gorboduc</u> on January 6, 1562. The tradition that he owed the Queen's favor to his dancing ability was already widespread in 1582, for Anthony Munday in <u>The English Romayne Lyfe</u> quotes a priest in Rome as saying "Sir <u>Christopher Hatton</u>, he pleased the Queene so wel, dauncing before her in a Maske, that since that time he hath risen to be one of the Counsell . . ." (sig. C4^r). In 1564 he became Gentleman Pensioner (a member of the palace guards), in 1569 Gentleman of the Privy Chamber, in 1571 a Member of Parliament, in 1572 Captain of the Queen's Bodyguard, and in 1577, the year of his knighthood, Vice-Chamberlain and a member of the Privy Council. As Vice-Chamberlain, Hatton was responsible for organizing the progresses and all major ceremonies at court, for planning the Revels, and for maintaining order in the Banqueting Hall. In 1582 he was made Lord Chancellor, a position he held until his death in 1591.

Hatton's rise at court is attributable not only to his personal charm and fine appearance, but also to his skills as an excellent speaker and outstanding parliamentarian. In religion, the Protestant Hatton who had been brought up a Catholic pursued a policy of toleration; in foreign affairs, he adopted a firm anti-Spanish position; and in domestic politics, he exercised his tact and good temper. At first, with Leicester and

Walsingham, he supported the proposed marriage of the Queen and the Duc d'Anjou, but by 1582 he was trying to dissuade the Queen from what was obviously an unpopular match. (For a discussion of the French marriage question and the Heptameron see Note 117.5.)

Already in 1578 Burghley was describing Hatton as "a lover of learned men"; certainly many writers were dedicating their works to him in the hope of recognition and financial reward. F. B. Williams, Index of Dedications, lists 23 works dedicated to Hatton before the Heptameron was published. One writer who did benefit from Hatton's patronage was Whetstone's friend, Thomas Churchyard, whose The First Parte of Churchyardes Chippes (1575) is "the first occasion in which Hatton figures as a patron of literature" (Brooks, p. 120); another was Barnabe Rich, whose praise of Holdenby in the epistle "To the noble Souldiours" in Riche his Farewell to Military Profession, 1581 (sigs. B3^v-B4^r) calls to mind Whetstone's description of Philoxenus's palace (pp. 15 ff. below).

Holdenby was built by Hatton in Northamptonshire, his family seat; it was the most splendid mansion of its day, with the exception of Hampton Court, and even before its completion in 1583 it had developed a reputation for hospitality, luxury, and magnificence that rapidly became legendary.

Thus, it is appropriate that Whetstone should have dedicated to Sir Christopher Hatton a work which is set in a palatial country home, which describes a variety of social entertainments including masques and banquets, which relates novellas reminiscent of Boccaccio, which praises the hospitality of an unmarried gentleman who is a converted Protestant, and which discusses the subject of marriage at a time when the court is preoccupied with the French marriage question. Furthermore, the Italian character of the

Heptameron might be expected to appeal to Hatton, who was interested in Italian works, as is evidenced by the number of Italian volumes -- over 75 -- listed in the library of Sir Edward Coke that bear Hatton's coat of arms or his inscription, including a 1582 edition of Boccaccio's Decameron. (See W. O. Hassall, "The Books of Sir Christopher Hatton at Holkham," The Library, 5th Ser., 5 (June 1950), 1-13. Hatton apparently retained very few of the English works dedicated to him, and there is no record of the Heptameron in his library.)

A full, well-documented account of Hatton's life is Eric St. John Brooks, Sir Christopher Hatton, Queen Elizabeth's Favourite (London: Cape, 1946); other useful studies are Sir Harris Nicholas, Memoirs of the Life and Times of Sir Christopher Hatton (London: Richard Bentley, 1897); and Paul Johnson, Elizabeth I, a Study in Power and Intellect (London: Weidenfeld, 1974).

3.9 PARRHASIUS] Celebrated Greek painter, perhaps 4th century B.C., praised by Pliny (XXXV.36) for his accurate drawing and power of expression. I have not been able to locate any reference to pictures of Ingratitude and Envy painted by Parrhasius: Whetstone is undoubtedly inventing this "authority." Cf. the beginning of the Epistle Dedicatory in Lyly: "Parrhasius drawing the counterfeit of Helen, Right Honourable, made the attire of her head loose . . ."; and Croll's note: "Pliny does not mention, in his account of Parrhasius, a picture of Helen by him . . ." (p. 3). See also Note 73.18.

3.10 ENVIE] In his works Whetstone laments to the point of obsession the power of envy. The English Myrror (1586) is divided into three parts subtitled the Conquests of Envy, Envy Conquered by Virtue, and A Fortress

Against Envy, "this mortall enimie of publike peace and prosperitie." By "envy" the sixteenth century generally understood something akin to malice or hatred.

The Heptameron concludes with a masque (pp. 228-29) in which "the Monster Envy" successfully battles knights and ladies and is overcome only by Aurelia's virtue.

3.20 <u>degenerate from kinde</u>] Degenerate from Nature, from the established order of things. Cf. Guazzo, <u>Civile Conversation</u>, tr. Pettie: "they degenerate not from their kinde" (I, 192).

3.21 <u>maske without visard of excuse</u>] Take part in the masquerade (that is, put on their performance) without even pretending or appearing to have an excuse.

Cf. <u>The English Myrror</u> (1586): "There is no defect of mind nor infirmitie of bodie, but hath his originall of nature, or colour from reason, and by the benefite of the one or the other, receaveth cure: preposterous Envie only except, who degenerateth from kind, and masketh without vizard of excuse." (sig. A1^r)

3.23 <u>barres of their advauncement</u>] "of" is here used in the sense of "to." (<u>OED</u>, of, 58) Cf. 64.3.

3.29-30 <u>a Right noble Italian Gentleman</u>] Segnior Philoxenus. See 4.19.

4.3-5 <u>the full consideration of a dutifull subject, denized by the eternall fame . . . devine Grace</u>] The complete estimation in which the Queen is held by a dutiful subject, who became, as it were, a citizen after hearing of the Queen's fame. That is, Philoxenus, in fact a foreigner to England, is honouring the Queen as though he were an Englishman, so impressed is he by the report of her virtues.

4.16 <u>the civill disputations, and speaches</u>] Social discourses. See Note 1.2.

4.17 <u>well Courted</u>] See Note 1.4.

4.19 <u>Segnior Phyloxenus</u>] From Greek φίλιος = friendly, and ξένος = stranger; hence, philoxenus = friendly to strangers. An appropriate name for a gracious host. But in 171.30 Whetstone translates the name also as "greedy of newes," a definition that suits his then immediate purpose. The practice of creating significant names from Greek roots was widespread among Renaissance writers: we need search for examples no further than Euphues and his friend Philautus. Whetstone's names, however, are rarely drawn from a vacuum: Plutarch in his <u>Moralia</u> refers frequently to a Philoxenus who is a dithyrambic poet and in his <u>Life of Alexander</u> to a general of that name; a Philoxenus appears in Sidney's <u>Arcadia</u> (1590), Book I, Chapter 11.

Segnior Philoxenus, if he were indeed a historical person, has not been identified. The <u>DNB</u> accepts the suggestion by Thomas Corser, in <u>Collectanea Anglo-Poetica</u>, that Whetstone's work is a translation "and that, under the name of Signior Phyloxenus, it is probable that Giraldi Cinthio was intended, from whose tales he had collected his own " (p. 387). Such a statement posits the intriguing situation in which both the original author and his subsequent translator appear as characters in the same work (as Ismarito and Philoxenus); however, Corser's suggestion is easily dismissed in the light of research which has determined that the <u>Heptameron</u>

is obviously indebted to Cintio only for the story of Promos and Cassandra. Any further attempt to identify Segnior Philoxenus with Giovan Battista Giraldi, known as Cintio, Cinzio, or Cinthio, is invalidated by the fact that Cintio died in Ferrara in 1573, whereas Whetstone's Italian journey occurred in 1580.

4.24 <u>a president of behaviours</u>] A model of good conduct, worthy to be imitated. "President" is an obsolete form of "precedent" (<u>OED</u>, precedent, 4); the plural use of "behaviours" in this context is accepted 16th century practice (<u>OED</u>, behaviour, 1b).

4.24-25 <u>indifferent well qualited</u>] Of medium quality, of fine but not outstanding character or social standing. Whetstone's book is designed for the rising upper middle class reader, for the gentleman as opposed to the courtier.

5.2 <u>regarded</u>] The earliest example cited in the <u>OED</u> for the past participle "regarded" is drawn from the dedication to Whetstone's <u>English Myrror</u> (1586): "It then followeth, most regarded Queene . . ." (sig. ¶2^v). "Regard" is one of Whetstone's favorite words (cf. <u>The Rocke of Regard</u>). See Note 9.23.

5.10 <u>Trowchman</u>] Truchman, literally "an interpreter," here used figuratively. A truchman frequently accompanied the presentation of a masque; hence, the term is appropriate in an epistle addressed to a lover of masques. See also 6.5 and Note.

5.19 GEORGE WHETSTONS] "Whetstons" was an alternate spelling of the author's name: it so appears on the title pages of <u>A Remembraunce of George Gaskoigne</u> (1577) and <u>A Remembraunce of Sir James Dier</u> (1582).

Charles Singer, in his otherwise mistaken attempt to prove that George Whetstone was the author of the medical treatise <u>The Cures of the Diseased, in Remote Regions</u> (1598), correctly points out that in Middle English "whetstone" is also spelled "watstone" or "weston" (Singer's edition of <u>The Cures</u>, by George Wateson, n.p.). A character named "Weston" appears to be the author's spokesman in <u>The Censure of a Loyall Subject</u> (1587). Hence, Whetstone's name may very well have been pronounced "Whets-tun" instead of "Whet-stone." See also 8.25 for the spelling "Whetston."

Epistle to the Reader

6.5 <u>Troucheman of a Straungers Tongue</u>] Thomas Corser, in <u>Collectanea Anglo-Poetica</u>, takes the use of "Troucheman" here to imply that Whetstone is making a translation, probably from a work by Cintio. However, Whetstone is using this phrase figuratively to introduce the commonplace protestation that he is more concerned that he write plainly ("declare his meaning") than that he use much rhetorical art or "grace" in rendering into English the discourses he heard (not read) in Italy; and he goes on to state that he is not bound, as is an interpreter, to a specified text (6.12-14). Cf. <u>MMC</u>, sig. ¶2^r: "I dedicate to you (courteous Gentlemen) the Fruits of Noble <u>Alexanders</u> Counselles, as beseeming your worthinesse: I am but his Trouch-man, and your trustie frend." See also 5.10.

6.7 <u>Themistocles</u>] Greek statesman and "a famous capitayne of Athens" (Cooper). He commanded the fleet against Xerxes in 480 B.C. and was responsible for the Athenian victory at the battle of Salamis. This saying is attributed to him by Plutarch (<u>Life of Themistocles</u>, XXIX.3), but Whetstone's immediate source is probably Hoby's Epistle in Castiglione, <u>The Courtier</u> (p. 1).

Explanatory Notes 248

6.20 Questions and Devices] Discussions and dramatic entertainments. The coupling of "Devices" with the verb "sawe presented" makes clear that this is the sense intended by Whetstone, even though the earliest example cited in the OED for this definition is 1588. Debates of "questions," or discorsi, and dialogues were common academic exercises and popular social diversions in the Renaissance; subjects might be frivolous or weighty, ranging from table etiquette to moral philosophy, but the most frequent topic was love. See Introduction, p. lxii.

6.22-23 the Christmas twelvemoneths past] Whetstone claims to have been in Italy in 1580. See Introduction, p. xiii.

7.5 ff. Soranso . . .] The significance of these names is discussed in the notes for p. 23.

7.6-7 President of government] Cf. president of behaviours, 4.24 and Note.

7.9 a discreete methode of talke] Witty and pleasant conversation was essential in social situations. In fact, conversation, the art of talk, was not distinguished from conversation, the art of social intercourse (cf. Guazzo's Civile Conversation). Whetstone's work may be viewed as a manual in the art of conversation in both senses.

7.16 witty] Wise, discreet. In other instances, Whetstone uses the word in the sense of clever or ingenious, and frequently the two senses overlap. For a discussion of "Wit" see W. G. Crane, Wit and Rhetoric in the Renaissance, and Croll in Lyly, p. 2.

7.18-25 the honorable institution of Marriage . . . a Paradice on earth] A paraphrase of the Heptameron's underlying theme, summed up in 36.6-8 in a statement attributed to Plato.

Explanatory Notes   249

7.25 civill and Morall pleasures] The pleasures appropriate to man as both a social and a private being.

8.3-4 injuries received at Roane, Rome, and Naples] A possibly autobiographical incident recounted in The Honorable Reputation of a Souldier (sigs. A2^r-A3^v) may be relevant. Whetstone relates how he and a fellow Englishman were insulted by a "haughtie proude Spainiard" in a garrison town in the Duchy of Milan; a duel was arranged between the Englishman and the Spaniard, but the latter failed to keep the assignation. However, rumors of the encounter preceded the Englishman and he was refused admittance to Rome.

8.4 Roane] Izard (p. 22) points out that Whetstone is most likely referring to Roanne in eastern France rather than to Rouen.

8.6 Suggestioners] Persons who make false statements or representations. Not in OED.

8.21-22 to give a disgrace to ceremonies] To cut short the social formalities. Cf. 202.34.

8.25 Whetston] Another spelling of the author's name. See Note 5.19.

Commendatory Verse

9.1 T.W.] Thomas Watson 1557?-1592. The identification was made by Thomas Park in Heliconia (1815) and is now generally accepted: S. K. Heninger, Jr., in his introduction to Watson's Hekatompathia (Gainesville, Fla.: Scholars' Facsimiles & Reprints, 1964, p. viii) and H. H. Boyle in his unpublished dissertation "Thomas Watson: Neo-Latinist" (UCLA, 1966) agree that this is the first printed English verse by Watson. Educated at Oxford and at the Inns of Court, Watson was a noted classical scholar and a prominent figure in London's literary circle. He was a friend of Lyly, Peele, and Greene; he associated with Walsingham; and he knew Sir Philip Sidney. Watson's works reveal his interest in Italian and Latin authors: his first publication was a Latin translation of Sophocles' Antigone (1581); in 1582 he published Hekatompathia, a sequence of lyrics drawn from the Italian sonneteers; and in 1590 he published a book of Italian madrigals rendered into English.

Watson's path may have crossed Whetstone's on the Continent: in the dedication to Antigone (SR, 31 July 1581), Watson writes that he has recently returned from Italy and France.

9.4-7 Even as the fruictfull Bee . . . culd from the wise] T.W. praises Whetstone for drawing material from numerous sources, from the classics and from continental literature. The metaphor of the bee is a Renaissance commonplace in a variety of literary contexts. (See W. M. Carroll, Animal Conventions in English Renaissance Non-Religious Prose, 1550-1600, New York: Bookman Associates, 1954, pp. 93-94.) It occurs, for instance, in Greene's Alcida (1588) in the commendatory poem signed "E. Percy." Whetstone, however, generally prefers another version of the metaphor, which he first used in his own commendatory poem in Kendall's Flowers of Epigrammes (1577): "In flowers fooles (like Spyders) poyson finde: / The wise (as Bees) win hony from a weede" (sig. a6^v). Cf. Tilley B205 and B208.

9.7 wit] Wisdom, good judgement. Or perhaps, brilliance and quickness of intellect as opposed to wisdom and judgement. See Note 7.16.

9.8 Stage Toy] Watson is not censuring all dramatic presentations, but he is condemning frivolous, trifling plays. In this he agrees with Whetstone who contends, in his Epistle Dedicatory in Promos and Cassandra, that the aim of the stage is to illuminate the mind of man (sigs. $A2^r$-$A3^r$).

9.8 thundring of an Hoast] The opposite of "Stage Toy" may be a weighty drama which preaches and declaims without providing enjoyment to the audience. Or T.W. may be referring to the battles of epic poetry. Whetstone's work is to be neither dramatic nor epic, neither too trivial nor too grave.

9.9 his rare Muse] Source of poetic inspiration. The Muse Urania? See 10.2.

9.9 twixt burnyng fier and frost] Between extremes -- a frequent Renaissance idiom, especially in Whetstone's works (e.g. RR, sig. Cl^r; HRS, sig. Al^v; EM, sig. 2^v). Watson's reference to fire and frost is appropriate in a work that discusses love in marriage, for whereas the courtly lover is tossed between the fire of his love and the frost of his fear or the frost of his lady's disdain, the married lover will find harmony by heeding the voice of common sense. Cf. 73.9 and 149.4.

On the variations of this conceit, see Leonard Forster, The Icy Fire (Cambridge: Univ. Press, 1969).

9.11 the best] Whetstone's models and sources are discussed above throughout the Introduction. They include Castiglione and Guazzo; Boccaccio, Cintio, and Marguerite de Navarre; Guevara and Mexia; Ovid and Plutarch; Lyly and Wotton.

9.15 <u>a naturall common weale</u>] A community that has grown naturally (like a bee-hive). Whetstone absorbs his sources so well that they appear to be his own. Or perhaps T.W. means that Whetstone's writing is life-like, not pretentious.

9.23 <u>regardes</u>] Considerations of questions or problems. The first example cited by the <u>OED</u> to illustrate the plural use of the word in this sense is taken from Whetstone's dedicatory epistle in <u>The English Myrror</u> (1586): "The reach of my duetie . . . simply laboreth to publish these regards, that common faults may be amended" (sig. ¶2^v). Cf. Note 5.2.

9.25 <u>The holy Bush, may wel be sparde, where as the Wine is pure</u>] Tilley W462: Good wine needs no bush (ivy bush, sign). A branch of ivy, the plant sacred to Bacchus as god of wine, served to identify a tavern. Cf. 92.12-13; and <u>EM</u>, sig. ¶4^r.

A favourite Renaissance proverb: writers use it to emphasize their declaration that a good work does not need to be decked out in ostentatious rhetoric. If for "holy Bush" we are to read "holly Bush," I am unable to account for T.W.'s substitution of holly for ivy; however, I believe it more likely that by "holy Bush" T.W. intended "sacred Bush." Cf. <u>OED</u>, holly, 3, 1594 quotation "To take a Taverne and get a Hollibush."

Prefatory Verse

10.1 <u>translated out of Latine</u>] No Latin original of this poem has been discovered. Izard touches upon the possibility that the verse was composed by the Countess of Pembroke, who was sometimes referred to as "Urania" (for example, in Spenser's "Colin Clout's Come Home Again," l. 487), but I find no basis for such a speculation. The theme of Uranie's poem is similar to Wotton's "A Welcome of Peace into Fraunce" (sigs. D1^v-E1^v).

10.2 URANIE] Urania, the Muse of astronomy and, later, of the highest wisdom. Her name became confused with that of Aphrodite Ouranos or Urania, the heavenly Venus, goddess of pure and spiritual love, especially of wedded love, as distinguished from Aphrodite Pandemos, goddess of earthly or sensual love (Plato, Symposium, 180D-181B). Thus Whetstone's Urania is probably the Muse that inspires him to write of married love; she appears as an actual person only as a participant in the masque of the Seventh Day's Exercise (p. 230).

10.2 ISMARITO] The name which Whetstone adopts for himself in this book. See 21.5-6 and Note.

10.3 a Device] A dramatic presentation, in this case a masque. See pp. 227-30

10.5 PANDORA] One of the many mythological names assigned to Queen Elizabeth. Dora and Erwin Panofsky, in Pandora's Box (New York: Pantheon Books, 1962), point out that the sixteenth century recalled the classical Pandora not as the bringer of evils to mankind, but as "all-gifted" or "gift of all," the perfect blend of all things. After 1580, her name was generally used as a term of praise. Thus, Spenser in the "Teares of the Muses" (1591) refers to Queen Elizabeth as "The true Pandora of all heavenly graces" (l. 578). See also 10.30-11.3 and Note.

10.6 JOVE] The Roman ruler of the Gods.

10.7 The mistes of sinne, which from the earth arose] In the Ptolemaic universe, the earth is the seat of sin, of change, corruption, and death.

The regions beyond the sphere of the moon are progressively purer as they approach the perfection of Heaven.

10.8 IRIS] The goddess of the rainbow. She is usually the messenger of Juno, as in Ovid (Met. I.270-1; XI.589), and is so described by Cartari (sig. L2^v). Whetstone may be recalling Homer, who represents Iris as the messenger of Zeus (Iliad II.786 etc.), or he may simply be using the name here in order to create the pun on "Ire" below (10.10). See also 189.11.

10.8.9 to moove . . . the exercise of foes] The words here have military significance. To move = to stir up strife. Exercise = training or drilling troops. Hence, the phrase may be paraphrased as "to incite to military action."

10.10 Ire] Wrath. With an intended pun on Iris. Cf. Wyclif Prov. xxx.33: "He that stirith iris, bringeth forth discordes." (As quoted in OED, ire.)

10.17 Cyllen] Cyllenius is one of the epithets of Hermes or Mercury, the god of learning and the messenger of the gods, who was supposed to have been born on Mount Cyllene (Ovid Met. XIII.146).

10.19 the Region next the grounde] The sphere of the moon, where all corruption and dissension begins. See 10.7 and Note.

10.23 PHAROS light] A lighthouse, named after the famous one built by Ptolemy Philadelphus on the island of Pharos. See 116.4 and Note.

10.23 PHENIX] Phoenix, the fabulous bird of Arabia: "It is unique: it is unparalleled in the whole world. It lives beyond five hundred years." (The Bestiary, p. 125). The reference is to Queen Elizabeth, the light of whose reign attracts Mercury, the bringer of order and the symbol of learning. "Queen Elizabeth placed a phoenix upon her medals and tokens with her favourite motto: 'Semper eadem' ('Always the same'), and sometimes with the motto 'Sola phoenix omnis mundi' ('The sole phoenix of the whole world'); and on the other side, 'Et angliae gloria' ('And the glory of England'), with her portrait full-faced. By the poets of the time, Elizabeth was often compared to the Phoenix." (John Vinycomb, Fictitious and Symbolic Creatures in Art, 1906; rpt. Detroit: Gale Research, 1969, p. 175.) Cf. Cranmer's prophecy in Hen.VIII, V.4. See also 116.5; 33.9; and Notes.

10.25 a fruitfull Ile] England.

10.26 a Queene] Queen Elizabeth.

10.28 Senate] The Queen's Privy Council. According to the OED, the word was so used from 1584.

10.29 For such as fled, for persecutions feare] Elizabeth's reign was noted for its relative religious tolerance. As Lord Chancellor, Hatton also followed a middle course in religious affairs.

10.30-11.3 To whom he gave . . . in everlasting fame] "Pandora, A woman, unto whom sundry goddes gave sundrie giftes. Pallas gave her wisdome, Venus beautie, Apollo musike, Mercurius eloquence. And therefore she was called Pandora, which signifieth, havinge all giftes." (Cooper). See also Note 10.5.

10.31 PALLAS] Surname of Athena, goddess of battle and of wisdom. She

Explanatory Notes 256

was considered to be comparable in beauty to Venus and Juno and contested with them for the prize awarded by Paris (in "The Judgement of Paris"). However, her gift would normally be that of wisdom (see Cooper's statement under 10.30-11.3 above).

10.31 VENUS] Roman goddess of love and beauty.

10.32 PITHOS] A nymph Peitho does sometimes appear in the retinue of Aphrodite, and a Peitho ("Persuasion") is a helpmeet of the Muses in Plutarch Table-Talk IX.14 (Moralia 743 ff.), but Whetstone's Pithos appears to be his own addition to the classical pantheon. Cf. Cooper: "Pitho, or Pithus, The lady and president of eloquence to perswade, called of Ennius Suada, of Horace Suadela."

10.32 DIANS] Diana, Roman name for Artemis, also called Cynthia -- conventional names for Queen Elizabeth -- a virgin goddess.

11.1 nam'd her Grace] Designated her as the one to be favoured. An unusual use of "Grace."

11.6 leake] Like. There is no authority in the OED for this spelling; however, I have not emended it since there is a close analogy, "leeke" and since this word should rhyme with "breake."

11.16 This Silver Pen, meete for a Virgins praise] In heraldry, silver (or "Argent") is a royal metal, and "it signifieth to the bearer thereof Chastitie, virginitie, cleare conscience, and Charitie" (Legh, The Accedens of Armory, sig. B4^r). See also 230.13 and Note.

11.22 Vaticinium URANIES] Urania's prophecy.

12.10-11 over loftye, and too base Love] "loftye" and "base" represent degrees on a social scale.

The first Dayes exercise

13.8 <u>Aestas</u>] Whetstone personifies the Latin noun for "summer."

13.9 <u>Phaebus in his Retrogradation</u>] The falling back of the sun in the sky (away from the zenith). Phoebus, "the shining," is an epithet and later another name of Apollo; Cooper states that this name "is taken for the sonne."

13.11 <u>Hyemps</u>] Latin noun for winter, for stormy weather. "Hiems" occurs in Ovid <u>Met</u>. II.30; XV.212.

13.24-25 <u>a Countrey farre from home</u>] Italy.

13.28 <u>strayed out of knowledge</u>] Wandered into unfamiliar territory; lost. Whetstone is being elaborate.

13.29s.n. <u>Forrest of Ravenna</u>] Ravenna, a city in North-east Italy, was part of the Papal dominions from 1509 to 1859. <u>La Pineta</u> was made famous by Dante (<u>Purgatorio</u> XXVIII.20-21) and Boccaccio (<u>Decameron</u> V.8) and has been eulogized by Byron (<u>Don Juan</u> III.105) as "Ravenna's immemorial wood." "This pine forest, which is believed to be the most ancient and extensive in Italy, is said to have been planted by the Romans as a protection to Ravenna from the ravages of the scirocco. It begins a short distance beyond the church of S. Apollinare in Classe (about 2 1/2 miles from Ravenna), and extends for many miles along the Adriatic coast." (Paget Toynbee, <u>A Dictionary of Proper Names and Notable Matters in</u>

the Works of Dante, rev. Charles S. Singleton, Oxford: Clarendon Press, 1968.)

13.32 Pyne Apple trees] Pine trees. The pine cones were called pine apples, and the fruit discovered later in the New World was called pineapple for its resemblance to the cone.

14.1s.n. River of Poo] Po river, Northern Italy. Cf. RR, sig. B4^r: "In Italie (neare to the river of Poo) there dwelled a noble man."

14.14 well qualyted] The phrase in this context seems to refer to ability rather than rank. Cf. 4.24-25 and 7.14.

14.15 in a servisable order] In a customary manner expressing readiness to serve.

14.24 Bollytyne] Italian "bulletino, bollettino." The word is accepted into English by 1645 as "bolletine," an obsolete form of "bulletin," an official certificate. Montaigne comments that "Over the doors of all the rooms in the hostelry is written: Ricordata della bolleta," "Remember your certificate" (p. 102).

This reference to a warrant of health -- which had to be renewed in each town for fear of the plague -- recalls the frame of the Decameron in which the ten gentlemen and ladies have fled from the plague-stricken city. (Cecioni, "Un adattamento," p. 187).

14.33-34 Pisano é Forresterio. Entrate, e ben venuto.] "Pisan (native of Pisa) and Stranger. Enter and welcome." But why "Pisan"? Or might "Pisano" be Whetstone's or his printer's spelling of "Paesano" ("native")?

15.1ff. Which general invyting . . .] Segnior Philoxenus's palace is Italian in design: Galigani, in "Il Boccaccio nel Cinquecento inglese" (p. 54) suggests that it recalls the palace of Urbino. However, the architectural details mentioned by Ismarito are common to both the princely palaces of Renaissance Italy and the Italian-inspired great houses of sixteenth-century England. The H-plan of the palace emphasizes its symmetry and focuses attention on the main façade. Ismarito approaches the palace by a long drive through a wood or park (p. 13); he is welcomed by a porter at what appears to be the gatehouse (p. 14); the porter conducts him through a court (p. 14) to the main entrance which opens into a great hall, protected from drafts by an ornamental screen (p. 15). The great hall is the center of the general festivities (p. 21); but the "better sort" of guests assemble in the great chamber, and of these, a select few retire after dinner to a "drawing chamber" to participate in their discourses (p. 25). The palace has a chapel for private services (pp. 20, 24), a long gallery in which are displayed maps, portraits and heraldic devices (p. 115), a "chamber of pleasures" (p. 118), a library (p. 169), a private study (p. 170), and a banqueting house for special occasions, as for New Year's Day (p. 200). Ismarito repeatedly admires the plaster ceilings, the elaborate paneling, the tapestries, and the pictorial and emblematic decorations. The extent to which these features are Italianate is indicated by Pearson, <u>Elizabethans at Home</u>, pp. 20-22.

The great country palaces of Theobalds, built by Burghley, and Holdenby, built by Hatton, to entertain the Queen, may have inspired Whetstone's description of Philoxenus's palace. Holdenby, designed by John Thorpe, was begun in 1578. After a visit to the yet unfinished palace in 1579, Burghley wrote to Hatton, "I found a great magnificence in the front or front pieces of the house," praising the "stately ascent from your hall to your great chamber" and the "largeness and lightsomeness" of the chambers (Brook,

Explanatory Notes   260

p. 158). And in 1581, <u>Rich's Farewell to Military Profession</u> pays literary tribute to the magnificence of both Hatton and Holdenby: "Whiche house for the braverie of the buildynges, for the statelinesse of the chambers, for the riche furniture of the Lodginges, for the conveighance of the offices, and for all other necessaries appertenent to a Pallas of pleasure: Is thought by those that have judgement, to be incomparable, and to have no fellowe in Englande, that is out of her Majesties hands . . . . And how many Gentlemen and straungers, that comes but to see the house, are there daiely welcomed, feasted, and well lodged" (sig. B3^v-B4^r).

The entrance to Holdenby was apparently flanked by two giant statues: did these suggest Philoxenus's Welcome and Bountie? At any rate, the parallel between Philoxenus's palace and Holdenby is sufficiently close to flatter Sir Christopher Hatton, Whetstone's hoped-for patron. (Holdenby is discussed in detail in Brook, <u>Sir Christopher Hatton</u>, pp. 158-65; the plans are reproduced in John Thorpe, <u>The Book of Architecture</u>, ed. John Summerson, Glasgow: The Walpole Society, 1966, pp. 93-94 and pl. 85.)

15.30 <u>embost with many curious devises</u>] Andrea Alciati describes in his <u>Emblematum liber</u> (1531) the ways in which emblems may be employed in ornamentation, and Italian artists frequently decorated furnishings, clothes, armor, and apartments with emblems and devices. The gallery of the Palazzo Farnese in Rome, to which Whetstone compares Philoxenus's palace (at 18.5-6), is decorated with devices, as is the ceiling of the atrium of the Villa Farnese near Rome (<u>Encyclopedia of World Art</u>, IV, 731).

15.31 <u>in proper colours</u>] In natural colouring (not in heraldic tinctures).

15.32ff. <u>his devise</u> . . .] The devise (or <u>impresa</u> in Italian) is to be distinguished from the emblem: both are symbols composed of a figure and a motto ("posie"), but whereas the emblem simply gives visual, and often moral, representation to a concept, the device "represents symbolically a proposition, wish, or line of conduct, employing a motto and a figure that reciprocally interpret one another" (Encyclopedia of World Art, IV, 726). Segnior Philoxenus's device is not heraldic: it is a personal symbol that suggests his own attitude or conduct, not a hereditary symbol that identifies his family, rank, or office. As such, it will not appear in heraldic dictionaries.

The emblematic trend was popular in Italy, having been given impetus by Andrea Alciati's Embematum liber (1531) and Paolo Giovio's Dialogo delle imprese militari e amorose (1555), and the device was even more characteristically Italian. Rigorous rules were set forth for the device in Italy, and Philoxenus's device fulfils the five criteria enumerated by Giovio. It combines body (figure) and soul (motto) in proper proportion; it is neither too obvious nor too obscure; it represents something pleasing to the eye (in this case, a bird); it does not contain a human figure; and it has a motto which is brief and which is in a different language (French) from that of the designer of the device (Italian) (Encyclopedia of World Art, IV, 729).

That Whetstone was interested in devices is suggested by the title of a lost work, A Panoplie of Devices, which is included in a list of his books on the verso of the title page of The Enemie to Unthryftinesse (1586).

15.33-34 a fluttering MAVIS fast limed to the bowes] The properties of lime used in snaring birds became a Renaissance symbol for the snares of love.

Tilley B380: The more the bird caught in lime strives the faster she sticks. The example cited from Torriano, 1666, indicates that it was also an Italian proverb. The source is undoubtedly Ovid, Ars Amatoria I.391: "Non avis utiliter viscatis effugit alis."

16.1 Qui me nourit, me destruit] "What feeds me, destroys me." Lime was steam-distilled from the wood of young branches (Albertus Magnus, The Book of Secrets, ed., M. R. Best and F. H. Brightman, Oxford: Clarendon Press, 1973, p. 95 note).

Variations of this motto recur in emblem literature, but usually accompanying a representation of a flame. For instance, Claude Paradin's Heroicall Devices (1591) depicts a burning torch turned upside down and the motto "Qui me alit, me extinguit," the device of the Lord of St. Valier (the father of Diana of Poitiers), who was in exile in Milan: "Which simbole was framed for a certain noblewomans sake, willing to insinuate hereby, that as her beautie and comeliness did please his minde, so might it cast him into danger of his life" (pp. 357-58). The device does not appear in the 1557 edition. In Georgette de Montenay's Emblemes (1571), an inverted candle is pictured with the motto "Quod Nutrit Me Consummat. (The history of the device in emblem literature is traced by Alan R. Young, "Othello's 'Flaming Minister' and Renaissance Emblem Literature," English Studies in Canada, 2 (Spring 1976), 1-7.)

A portrait discovered in 1953 and tentatively identified as that of Christopher Marlowe, by an unknown artist, 1585, pictures a melancholy youth in black accompanied by the motto "Quod me nutruit me destruit." (Roy Strong, The English Icon, London: Paul Mellon Foundation, 1969, p. 353; and A. D. Wraight, In Search of Christopher Marlowe, London: Macdonald, 1965, pp. 63-71.) Did Marlowe appropriate from the Heptameron a motto that Whetstone had encountered in France or Italy?

16.23ff the rule of a Mayden Queene . . .] Panegyrics of Queen Elizabeth by a foreigner (Euphues) occur in Lyly, pp. 237, 432, 440, 447-49.

16.34-17.6 But the vertue of her Shielde . . .] This passage provides a possible interpretation of the action of the masque in the Seventh Day's Exercise, p. 229.

17.4-5 whose vertue shineth . . . as a Diamond in an obscure place] On virtuous deeds shining like a diamond in the dark, see EM, sig. H3^v; Bacon, sig. B2^v; Dier, sig. A4^v. See also 34.30-31.

17.32-33 Cupid and his lover Ciches] The story of Cupid's love for Psyche and the beautiful palace he built for her occurs in Apuleius, The Golden Asse, translated by William Adlington in 1566 (sigs. N3^{r-v}), in which the spelling "Psiches" appears on the title page.

18.2 Tivoly] Tivoli, city near Rome famous for the Villa d'Este, designed by Pirro Ligorio in 1550 for Cardinal Ippolito d'Este. The Villa is even today noted for its magnificent gardens and its beautiful fountains. An etching of the Villa and gardens by E. du Perac appears in The Encyclopedia of World Art, VIII, pl. 432. Montaigne describes the gardens fully but unenthusiastically (pp. 164-66); see also Harl.M., p. 31.

18.4s.n. the Cardinall of Esta] Ippolito II D'Este, Cardinal, 1509-1572. Son of Duke Alfonso I of Ferrara and Lucrezia Borgia. In 1549 he was named governor of Tivoli.

18.5-6 Cardinall Furnesaes Pallace] Alessandro Farnese, 1520-1589, became cardinal at the age of 14. "A highly cultivated man, friend of poets, humanists, and artists, he completed the magnificent Farnese palace in Rome that had been founded early in the reign of Pope Leo X. Sangallo the Younger bagan it, Michelangelo continued it, and Giacoma della Porta completed it." (<u>Italian Renaissance Encyclopedia</u>) Cf. <u>Harl.M.</u>, p. 28.

18.6-7 <u>buylded and beautified, with the ruinous Monuments of Rome</u>] Italian Renaissance architects frequently built on the ruins of classical structures -- for example, the Villa d'Este was transformed from the Roman Valle Gaudiosa -- and their buildings were decorated with classical art. The Farnese family were noted for their collections of classical sculpture.

18.24-25 <u>in the French Courte</u>] If Segnior Philoxenus is 30 to 40 years of age, he was probably at the court of Charles IX, King of France from 1560 to 1574. There he may have known both the Huguenot leader Gaspard de Coligny, killed in 1572 in the St. Bartholomew's Day Massacre ordered by Charles; and Henry Duc d'Anjou, later Henry III of France. The Italian influence at the French court was at its height under Henry III, whose mother was Catharine de'Medici (d. 1589).

18.27-30 <u>he learned to serve God . . . men do</u>] One of several passages in the <u>Heptameron</u> expressing strong Protestant views. Others occur on pp. 26, 30, 44-48, 114-15, 120-24, 170, 199, and 200.

Like Sir Christopher Hatton, Segnior Philoxenus was a convert to Protestantism. Since he had become a Protestant at the French court, he probably had Huguenot connections: this would explain the selection of portraits of Protestant leaders displayed in his gallery (pp. 116-17). Cecioni ("Un adattamento," p. 186) suggests that although Philoxenus and his palace are probably imaginary, Whetstone may have had in mind some Italian connected with the Protestant circle at the court of Ferrara under Renata di Francia. At any rate, Ismarito's gracious host does fuse the virtues of Italy and England: he is both a perfect courtier and a Protestant, and hence morally irreproachable, in addition to being a devoted admirer of Elizabeth (Galigani, "Il Boccaccio nel Cinquecento inglese," p. 56).

18.28-29 painted ceremonies] "That vayne ceremonies do little differ from vayne lyes," a proverb attributed, by Guicciardini, The Garden of Pleasure, to "Master Giovanni della Casa" (sig. E8^r). Cf. Book of Common Prayer, 1559, "Of Ceremonies, why some be abolished, and some retayned" (sigs. a6^v-a7^v); and Ascham, The Scholemaster, pp. 70-71. See also 199.8.

19.11 The Grand Maister of the feast] The person in charge of the ordering of the banquet.

19.15-19 a Cake was cut in peeces . . . Queene of the Christmas pleasures] The idea of choosing a king or queen to preside over the entertainments is of classical origin. In England, the custom persisted in the office of the Master of the Revels. The selection of the ruler by lots placed in a cake was a popular Italian social custom, as Whetstone's note indicates. Variations of this practice are commonplace in continental Renaissance literature, especially in framed tales and discourses and in courtesy books. Two English examples which precede the Heptameron are Edmund Tilney's The Flower of Friendshippe (1577), in which a sovereign is chosen for each day of the discourses (p. 75); and George Gascoigne's The Adventures of Master F.J. (1574), in which a "governor" is chosen by lot (p. 87).

19.20-21 there should be but one to commaund, and all to obay] "God wylleth and ordeinethe that one onlye commaunde all, and that all together obey one" (Guevara, The Diall of Princes, sig. G5^v).

Explanatory Notes   266

This statement has a proverbial ring, but I have been unable to identify it as a proverb. It expresses the Renaissance belief in the importance of hierarchical order and in the doctrine of universal obedience.

19.21 Madona Aurelia] "Aurelia," or "Golden," was a favourite fictional name; it was also the name of an actress performing the part of the innamorata in the commedia dell'arte (Lea, Italian Popular Comedy, p. 500). In 1593 the Heptameron was reissued under the title Aurelia, The Paragon of Pleasure and Princely Delights.

In character and behaviour, Whetstone's Aurelia is very like Boccaccio's Fiammetta (Cecioni, "Un addatamento," p. 187).

19.29 the Sirens sweete songes] Cooper: "three daughters of Achelous and Calliope, which dwelled in an ile betweene Italie and Sicilie, who with their sweete synginge drewe suche unto theim, as passed that sea, and than slewe theim." The story of these mythical creatures, who were later identified with mermaids, first occurs in Homer, Odyssey XII.39-54; 165-200. See also 164.14.

20.22 Heliogabalus] Or Elagabalus. Roman emperor, 218-222, noted for his sensuality, debauchery, extravagance, and cruelty. He constantly sought out delicacies and was supposed to have supped on the tongues of peacocks and nightingales, even offering a reward for a Phoenix for his dinner. Mentioned in Gruget's Mexia, p. 269, but more details are given in MMC, sigs. $D3^v$-$D4^r$.

20.25-29 the eyes of the greater parte . . . faire Gentlewomen] A commonplace in Renaissance prose fiction. Cf. Lyly, p. 34: "And so they sat down; but Euphues fed of one dish which ever stood before him, the

Explanatory Notes   267

beauty of Lucilla." Also Painter, III, 230: "The Gentleman at supper . . . coulde eate little meate, beinge satisfied with the feeding diete of his Amorous eyes."

21.5-6 Cavaliero Ismarito, in Englishe, The Wandring Knight] Italian "smarrito" = lost; stray. Whetstone may also have in mind the traditional wandering affections of the traveller (see 28.7-9).

21.29 the great Hall] The large vestibule which was also used as a reception room or, in this case, as a dining room for the "inferior sort"; not to be confused with the great Chamber (20.8) where the gentlefolk dine.

23.9ff. Queene Aurelia appoynted . . .] That the names of the characters are to be read as epithets is indicated by Whetstone's own comments throughout this passage. Cf. Wotton, who defends his use of "counterfayte names," "lest that I shoulde offend the parties" (Courtlie Controversie, sig. B2^v).

23.10 Fabritio] "The inventor" (in the rhetorical sense). Italian "fabbricare" = to invent, to fabricate. Whetstone may be recalling the Fabricius who is mentioned in Plutarch and in Boethius (II.7) as a Roman consul who could not be bribed and whose name became synonymous with honesty; but he is more likely borrowing the name from the commedia dell'arte in which Fabrizio played the part of a lover (Lea, Italian Popular Comedy, p. 496).

23.11-12 Donna Isabella] A common Italian name in Renaissance fiction: in Tilney's Flower of Friendshippe (1577), Lady Isabella is a lively, emancipated gentlewoman. Isabella and Fabritio are lovers and Franceschina is a serving woman in Li due Trappolini, a scenerio for the commedia dell'arte (Lea, Italian Popular Comedy, pp. 438-40).

23.14 Segnior Soranso] I have discovered no meaning in this name. However, "Soranus," a philosopher, is mentioned in Boethius (I.3).

23.16-17 Don Dondolo] "The double dealer." Spanish "dolo" = fraud, deception, deceit. The Spanish form of address is appropriate since Dondolo is Neapolitan and the Kingdom of Naples was under Spanish rule in the sixteenth century.

23.18 Monsier Bargetto] "A foolish bird." French "bergeretto" = wagtail; or "barge" = godwit.

23.19 Doctor Mossenigo] "The negative one." Latin "mos" = humour, inclination; and "nego" = to say no, to deny. Doctor Mossenigo plays the role of the misogynist and the cynic. He is also the pedant and the old man in love, stock figures in the commedia dell'arte.

23.21 Segnior Faliero] "The deceiver." Latin "fallere" = to deceive; or Italian "fallare" = to err, to be mistaken.

23.28 Maria Belochy] "Of the beautiful eyes." Italian "bello" = beautiful; and "occhio" = eye, look.

23.29-30 whose eye was able to fire a mountaine of Ice] Cf. Tilley F284: To force fire from snow. (Earliest example cited is 1594.) See also 62.5.

23.30 Lucia Bella] "The beautiful one." Italian "lucere" = to shine; and "bello" = beautiful.

23.31 Hellena Dulce] "The charming." Italian "dolce" or Latin "dulcis"= sweet, charming, pleasant.

23.32 Franceschina Sancta] "The virtuous." Latin "sanctus" = pure, virtuous, blameless. "Francesquina" was an actress in the commedia dell'arte (Lea, *Italian Popular Comedy*, p. 504).

23.34 *Katherina Trista*] "The Shrew." Italian "tristo" = perverse, malicious; or Latin "tristis" = harsh, bitter. A sharp-tongued Lady Katherina also appears in *Greenes Farewell to Folly* (sig. F3^v) and, of course, in Shakespeare's *Taming of the Shrew*.

23.34-24.1 *Alvisa Vechio*] "Old woman." Italian "vecchio" = old person. Alvisa is a common Italian name.

24.21-23 *lyke fowles on Saint Valentines day morninge*] Tilley S66: On Saint Valentine's Day all the birds in couples do join. From medieval folklore.

24.28-29 *an advauntage of braverie*] A great deal of finery.

25.4 *a faire Eunucke Boy*] In Italy, boy singers were frequently castrated to preserve the boyish quality of their voices; these *castrati* were much in demand especially in the seventeenth century (*Harvard Dictionary of Music*). Although Renaissance works often mention the practice of solo lute playing after meals -- for example, in Painter's tale of the Duchess of Malfi (III, 39-40) Antonio sings a "sonnet" after dinner to the accompaniment of a lute -- I know of only one other instance in sixteenth-century English fiction in which a eunuch is the performer: in Emanuel Forde's *Parismus* (1598), the hero's mask at the court of Thessaly includes "Eunuches apparelled all in greene" (sig. C3^v).

See also 49.32; 81.15; 119.24; 148.24; 163.16; 175.2; 201.9.

25.25 *sonet*] The fourteen-line sonnet as we know it had not reached its final evolution in Whetstone's time. The "sonnets" collected by Thomas

Watson in his Hekatompathia (1582) are eighteen-line poems. The medieval "sonet" was simply a song, and in the Renaissance the word designated any short lyric but especially a love poem. Gascoigne, in his Certayne Notes of Instruction (1575), recognized the current confusion: "then have you Sonnets, some thinke that all Poemes (being short) may be called Sonets, as in deede it is a diminutive worde derived of Sonare, but yet I can beste allowe to call those Sonets whiche are of fouretene lynes, every line conteyning tenne syllables" (Works, I, 471). In Italy (more so than in England), such poems were generally sung to some instrumental accompaniment: in Painter's story of the Countess of Celant, "the songes of their Love were more common in ech Citizen's mouth, than Stanze or Sonnettes of Petrarch, Played and Fayned upon the Gittrone, Lute, or Lyra" (III, 59).

26.5 sights] Obsolete spelling of "sighs."

26.33-34 they have a custom among them selves, not to live chast] One of Whetstone's attacks on the priesthood; such attacks are characteristic of the novella. See 120.27ff.

27.19-20 as Yron and Flynt, beat together, have the vertue to smite fire] Cf. Tilley F374: Out of two flints smitten together there comes out fire. Lyly, p. 47: "Fire cometh out of the hardest flint with the steel."

That is, only through clashes of opinions would truth be discovered.

27.24 studing] Not an error. The OED cites "studing" as a sixteenth-century form of the present participle for "study."

27.27-30s.n. Wise scilence worketh mor regarde than foolish talke]

Tilley S721: Speak fitly or be silent wisely. (The earliest example cited is 1611.)

For W519, No wisdom to silence, Tilley cites the following example dated 1732: Silence is wisdom, when speaking is folly. Cf. also M1148, More have repented speech than silence (earliest example 1640); and N250, Better say nothing than nothing to the purpose (earliest example 1606).

27.30-21 <u>Floods, when they are most hyest, maketh least noise</u>] Tilley W123: Water runs smoothest where it is deepest. (Still waters run deep.)

28.7-9 <u>Travayler . . . disdayne of Mariage</u>] Renaissance literature abounds in references to the cynicism of travellers (as of Jacques in <u>As You Like It</u>). Cf. Lyly, p. 61: "But alas, Euphues, what truth can there be found in a traveller, what stay in a stranger"; and Pettie, <u>A Petite Pallace</u>, p. 199: "travaylors wordes are not much trusted." However, Whetstone here appears to echo Ascham, <u>The Scholemaster</u>, p. 71: "For commonly they [travellers to Italy] come home common contemners of marriage, and ready persuaders of all others to the same."

28.19-20 <u>Venus, though she love not Diana, yet is she the sworn enemie of Juno</u>] Venus here represents illicit sexual love; Diana, chastity; and Juno, marriage. The rivalry of Venus and Diana is a frequent theme in classical and Renaissance narratives. "Thus, averse to love and under the vow of virginity, Diana is out of all harmony with Venus, the goddess of love, and her son, the sportive Cupid. The contrasting pleasures of the two are thus summed up by Spenser:

> As you [Diana], in woods and wanton wildernesse
> Your glory sett to chace the salvage beasts,
> So my [Venus'] delight is all in joyfulnesse,
> In beds, in bowres, in banckets, and in feasts.
>   <u>F.Q</u>.3.6.22."

(A. E. Randall, The Sources of Spenser's Classical Mythology, p. 49.) See also 33.28, 224.16, and Notes.

28.22 Hymen] Cooper: Himenaeus, "The god of marriage." The word originally referred to the marriage song, but it was personified even in classical times. See also 36.1, 201.9; 201.20.

29.25-27 Marriage is an honourable estate, instituted of God, and embraced of men] A paraphrase from the Book of Common Prayer (1559), "the fourme of solemnization of Matrimonie," sigs. O5^{r-v}.

30.2-3 a vertue uppon necessitie] Tilley V73: Make a virtue of necessity.

In Promos and Cassandra, Whetstone writes "vertue of necessity" (sig. M1^r). See also 31.3.

30.7 Baye] Identified with the laurel in the Renaissance: "The Bay tree is consecrate to Apollo . . . . And it is called Laurell of laude, and so in old tyme it was called" (Guicciardini, The Garden of Pleasure, sigs. C4^{r-v}).

30.8 Daphne . . . Appollo] Ovid relates the story of Apollo's (Phoebus') love for and pursuit of Daphne (Met. I.452-567). She scorned his love; fleeing from him, she prayed for help to her father the river-god Peneus and was turned into a laurel tree. Apollo adopted the laurel as his emblematic plant and made its leaves eternally green.

30.21 in advauntage] To add to the strength of the argument.

30.24-25 Baccus minions] The Bacchae, women who engaged in wild rites at festivals in honor of Bacchus or Dionysius. By calling them "minions"

Whetstone characterizes them as mistresses or paramours of the god.

31.1 <u>as</u> <u>spotted</u> <u>as</u> <u>Labans</u> <u>Sheepe</u>] Surely a proverbial phrase for something that is not genuine or honest, that is based on false grounds, or that is acquired by stratagem. Laban, the father of Leah and Rachel, promises to give Jacob "all the shepe with litle spottes and great spottes" or the spotted goats (the word is imprecise in both the Geneva Bible and the Authorized Version) in his flock. Jacob tricks the stronger sheep into conceiving many speckled and spotted offspring. (Genesis, xxx. 32-43.) The same phrase occurs in <u>EM</u>, sig. C3^r.

31.3 <u>a</u> <u>vertue</u> <u>upon</u> <u>necessytie</u>] See Note 30.2-3.

31.12-13 <u>The</u> <u>Turtle</u> <u>is</u> <u>never</u> <u>merie</u> <u>after</u> <u>the</u> <u>death</u> <u>of</u> <u>her</u> <u>Mate</u>] Tilley T624: As true as turtle to her mate.

The turtle-dove is a symbol of constancy in love and marriage. Whetstone's version of the proverb is closer to Lyly's: "For as the turtle having lost her mate wandereth alone, joying in nothing but in solitariness" (p. 254). See also 73.17 and 226.15.

31.16 <u>unpollitique</u>] The <u>OED</u> definitions of "Impolitic" are not relevant. Whetstone's word appears to refer to creatures that have no political organization, hence, to animals.

31.17-18 <u>by</u> <u>the</u> <u>Impression</u> <u>of</u> <u>Nature</u>] By the influence of Nature, according to natural laws.

31.25-26 <u>the</u> <u>Bay</u> <u>Tree</u> <u>is</u> <u>barren</u> <u>of</u> <u>pleasant</u> <u>fruict</u>] Cf. Tilley C945: Like cypress trees, that have fair leaves but no fruit.

31.29 <u>Sirinx</u> . . . <u>God</u> <u>Pans</u>] Syrinx, an Arcadian wood nymph was loved by Pan; as he pursued her, she prayed for help and was changed by the stream nymphs of Ladon into a bunch of marsh reeds, from which Pan made his pipe (Ovid, Met. I.689-712).

31.31-33 Anaxaretes . . . Iphis . . . Samarin] Anaxarete, a princess of Cyprus, scorns and mocks the love of Iphis because he is of humble birth, and he hangs himself at her door. At the funeral, she looks with indifference upon his corpse until the stony nature of her heart takes possession of her body, and she becomes a stone figure (Ovid Met. XIV. 698-764). But in Ovid, the image stands in the temple of Venus in Salamis ("Salamin" in Golding's translation). See also Pettie, A Petite Pallace, 7.

32.2-6 But in the behalf of Mariage . . . directed and noorished] Stories of faithful lovers are narrated by Ovid in his Metamorphoses. Pyramus and Thisbe are not changed into mulberry trees, but the berries of the tree are colored dark red with Pyramus's blood (IV.115-127). Baucis and Philemon are transformed into an oak and a linden (VIII). Crocus and his beloved Smilax become flowers (IV.283-284). Arcas and his mother (the Great Bear), Hercules, and Julius Caesar are metamorphosed into stars, but these are not lovers. I have not come across stories of lovers being changed into the olive, the pomegranate, or into precious stones.

32.6 directed] Influenced (by the stars).

32.7 In many well governed common wealths] Plato, Laws VI.784. Cf. Guevara, sig. P2^v: "for the man that hath not a wife and children legittymate in his house, cannot have nor hold greate aucthority in the common wealth." See also 206.6-23 and Notes.

32.16-18 you have read a Leafe more then Sainct Katherynes Nun] This statement is proverbial in style, but I am unable to explain the allusion satisfactorily.

Whetstone is possibly referring to St. Catherine of Alexandria who, in 305 A.D., when she was eighteen, is supposed to have disputed with fifty pagan philosophers. She succeeded in converting them through her eloquence, but was put to death on a spiked wheel. Her cult became popular after the tenth century, especially in Italy; she is the patron saint of maidens and of orators and philosophers. In art, one of her attributes is a book representing wisdom.

> Saint Cathern favours learned men, and gives them wisedome hye:
> And teacheth to resolve the doubtes, and alwayes giveth ayde,
> Unto the scolding Sophister, to make his reason stayde.

(Barnaby Googe, The Popish Kingdome . . . by Thomas Naogeorgus [Kirchmeyer], 1570, sig. M2^r.) Hence, the reference to St. Catherine in the context of an argument is appropriate. But why does Whetstone write "Sainct Katherynes Nun"? A nun is a follower, and one of St. Catherine's followers was Joan of Arc, who claimed that the Saint spoke to her directly. "Surely the Lord gave Catherine to Joan of Arc to help her in her debate with the famous theologians . . . Joan of Arc is the Catherine of modern times, indeed of all times" (Encyclopedia of Catholic Saints).

Thus, Ismarito's statement might read, "you are more cunning in argument than Joan of Arc who had Saint Catherine to support her."

32.24-25 The Monsters, Serpents, and loathsome Creatures] The monster is undoubtedly the Minotaur, the offspring of Pasiphae and the bull (Met. VIII); the serpents are Cadmus and his wife (Met. IV); and one loathsome creature is the hermaphrodite resulting from the union of Hermaphroditus and Salmacis (Met. IV).

32.26 Ovide, in his Metamorphosis] Publius Ovidius Naso, 43 B.C.- A.D. 17, was the leading Roman poet of his time. He is best known for the Metamorphoses, a collection of stories from classical and Near Eastern legends, all dealing with changes. It was the great source book for mythology throughout the Middle Ages and the Renaissance. Whetstone probably read Arthur Golding's English translation of the Metamorphoses, the whole of which first appeared in 1567, but there is no reason to doubt that he was also familiar with the Latin text.

32.29 Oedippus] Cooper gives the classical version of the Oedipus myth: "Finally having knowledge at length that by misfortune he had murdered his father at Phocis, and by inceste had knowen his owne mother, so sore it greeved him, that in revengement thereof he pulled out his owne eyes, and lyved ever after in banyshment." Thus, Oedipus blinds himself in horror of his own deeds, not, as Ismarito argues, in horror of his children's vices -- although, according to the myth, he later does curse his sons. Ismarito's mistaken interpretation is repeated by Whetstone in EM: "So outragious was the envy betweene Polineces and Eteocles, as old Oedipus their father scratched forth both his eies because he could not endure to behold the murthers and other deadly mischiefes, inflicted upon the poore Thebanes, in sustaining their unnaturall quarrels" (sig. A4^r). Whetstone may have known Alexander Neville's translation of Seneca's Oedipus (first printed 1563 and revised in 1581); he was undoubtedly familiar with Jocasta (1572), a translation by George Gascoigne and Francis Kinwelmarsh of Euripides' Phoenissae. See also 217.16 and Note.

32.31-32 Marcus Aurelius] Roman Emperor, A.D. 161-180, and philosopher. His son Commodus was exceptional in his bloody cruelty, debauchery, and mad excesses; some accounts suggest that Commodus prevailed upon the physician to poison his father. An unauthentic account of Marcus Aurelius is given by Antonio de Guevara in his Libro Aureo (1527), translated by Lord Berners as The Golden Boke of Marcus Aurelius (1535), and in his Relox de principes (1529), translated by Sir Thomas North as The Diall of Princes (1557). See 171.13-14 and Note.

33.7-8 Dianas band] Diana's followers, that is, maidens. More specifically alluding to the nymphs which accompanied the goddess in her hunts.

33.9 ashes of the Phenix] The Bestiary, on the phoenix: "When it notices that it is growing old, it builds itself a funeral pyre, after collecting some spice branches, and on this, turning its body toward the rays of the sun and flapping its wings, it sets fire to itself of its own accord until it burns itself up. Then verily, on the ninth day afterward, it rises from its own ashes!" (p. 125). In Ovid's version (Met. XV.391-407) no mention is made of flames and ashes, but the legend is a Renaissance commonplace, derived primarily from Pliny X.2.

33.10 some Phenix] Queen Elizabeth. See Notes 10.23 and 116.5.

33.21 Acteon] Actaeon, the hunter who chanced to come across Artemis (Diana) bathing. Angered at being seen naked by a man, she turned him into a stag and he was torn to pieces by his own hounds (Ovid Met. III.138-252).

33.22 Addonis] Adonis, the youth beloved by Aphrodite (Venus). He insisted upon hunting the boar in Arcadia and was fatally wounded; from his blood sprang the anemone (Ovid Met. X.519-559; 708ff.) Ovid makes no reference to any deity seeking revenge on Venus and Adonis, but in other versions Ares (Mars) or Hephaestus (Vulcan) are accused of killing Adonis out of jealousy.

33.28-34.12 _Juno and Diana_ . . .] Goddess of marriage and goddess of virginity. (Cf. 224.16.) Whetstone's descriptions have been traditional since the time of Homer. Diana (Artemis) is also "the goddesse of hunting, and imperiall governesse of pleasant groves, shrub-bearing hils, and christal faced fountaines" (Cartari, sig. H1^v); hence, her proper sphere is the earth. As a huntress, her attributers in art are the bow and quiver of arrows and the greyhound; her favourite game is the hind. Juno (Hera) is often referred to as the Queen of heaven and (in Homer) as "mistress of the thunder and lightning"; as the consort of Jupiter (Zeus) she shares the manna and nectar that are the food and drink of the Olympian gods. Her chariot glistens with gold and silver and carbuncles, "beautiful, adorned, and bespotted round about with starres of gold" (Cartari, sig. L2^r); she is the "goddesse of riches" (sig. L2^v); and in art she is usually crowned and adorned with precious stones.

In his description of the contrast between Diana and Juno, Whetstone is suggesting the contrasts between nature and art, between the simple pastoral life and the elaborate civil life; and in Whetstone's view, the civil and civilized life is more attractive.

See also 28.19-20, 224.16, and Notes.

34.8 _Phaetons wynged Chariot_] Phaeton is usually the son of Helios who borrows the sun's chariot for a day, but there are classical precedents (as in Homer) in which Phaeton, "the shining," is used as an epithet of Helios.

34.14-16 _the Marygoulde_ . . .] Whetstone is here mistaken: the marigold opens its petals to the sun and always faces the sun. Painter's reference is one of many in Renaissance literature: "like the flaring

Marigold flowre, which in the moste fervent heate of the Sommers day, doth appeare most glorious, and upon retire of the nights shadowe, appeareth as though it had never bene the same" (I, p.46). In Claude Paradin's Devises Heroiques (1557), "la fleur du Souci," a flower that turns towards the sun as to God, is the device of Marquerite de Navarre (Menston, Eng.: Scolar Press, 1971, p. 41). See McKerrow's edition of Nashe, II.218,4. The subject has been exhaustively treated in Notes and Queries, Ser. 4, 12 (July-Dec. 1873), 243, 283, 363; Ser. 5, 12 (July-Dec. 1879), 306.

34.15 cloaseth] The OED provides no authority for this spelling of the verb "to close." Lucia Bella is "shut up" and cannot speak.

34.15 Phebus] Phoebus, the sun.

34.23-24 Al is not gold . . . that glistereth] Tilley A146. See also 53.1-2.

34.30-31 a Diamond in the darcke, shineth of her selfe] See 17.4-5 and Note.

35.8-10 who can stop a streame? measure the fire? weygh the winde? or hynder Fancyes passage?] Cf. Lyly, p. 89: "To give reason to fancy were to weigh the fire and measure the wind."

Tilley S927: It is hard (folly, in vain) to strive against the stream.
F288: To weigh the fire and measure the wind.
W417: He that weighs the wind must have a steady hand.
L531: Love will find a way. (Earliest example 1597).

35.21 the Image of himselfe] Children, who become images of God.

36.1 Himen] See Note 28.22; 201.9; 201.20.

36.1-2 as mute as a fishe] Tilley F300. Plutarch, Table-Talk VIII.8 (Moralia 728) points out that fish are silent "because they keep their mouths shut and under restraint."

36.5 the opinion of Plato] I have been unable to find the source of this quotation, if it is a quotation. Cf. 85.13; 146.14; 158.34; and 206.21.

36.21-22 a woman hath no measure in her love, nor mercye in her hate] Tilley W651: A woman either loves or hates to extremes.

36.26 Gundelo] Gondola, a Venetian boat.

36.30 Hyen] Natural historians believed that the hyena could change its sex; hence, it became a symbol of inconstancy. (Pliny VIII.44; Ovid Met. XV.409-10; Topsell, p. 435.) Whetstone gives the legend a new twist: perhaps he is conflating it with the myth of Teresias who, because he had once been a woman, was asked by Juno and Jupiter to judge whether men or women derived more pleasure from love-making (Ovid Met. III.316ff.). See also 228.11.

39.26 Ab re nuntio] "I renounce [it]." For example, in Ecclesiastical Latin, "abrenuntio diabolo et operibus euis" ("I renounce the devil and all his works").

40.4ff DOCTOR MOSSENIGO HIS Satisfaction . . .] The source of this novella is Marguerite de Navarre's Heptaméron 71. Whetstone follows the main features of the original, but he adds the opening anecdote of the painter Parmenio and the final detail of the hanging in the crabtree. Also, Marguerite's version is set in Amboise, the saddler is called Brimbaudier, and the unnamed wife is a good, honest woman.

40.9 _Ophella_] The name is Whetstone's invention. Italian "offella" = tart, cake.

40.10 _Emperour Charles the fift_] Charles I of Spain, 1500-1558, one of the greatest Spanish kings, was the Holy Roman Emperor Charles V from 1519 to 1556. He has a place in art history as the patron of the portrait painter Titian.

40.11 _Parmenio_] I have discovered no such painter. Izard states that "In giving the name of the painter as Parmenio he had apparently confused a general of Alexander the Great with a celebrated painter of the Lombard school . . . commonly called Il Parmigiano" (p. 84). However, it is more likely that Whetstone had no historical person in mind: he was possibly influenced by stories of Titian, and for these stories he appropriated the name of Parmeno, mentioned in Plutarch, _Table-Talk_ V.1 (_Moralia_ 674) as a painter whose realistically mimicked pig became proverbial. Also, "Parmenione" is a character in Boccaccio's _Filocolo_.

40.17ff. _a pleasaunt conceit_ . . .] This anecdote, possibly Whetstone's invention, is an exaggeration of the Renaissance painters' preoccupation with witty devices and emblems. _The Encyclopedia of World Art_ (IV, 730) points out that "Great Italian painters, for example, often painted devices on the covers of portraits. Titian painted a device of love for the portrait of Sperone Speroni. Another was painted by Lorenzo Lotto on the cover of his magnificent portrait of Bernardino de'Rossi."

Cf. Lyly, p. 216: "But as the painter Timanthes could no way express the grief of Agamemnon, who saw his only daughter sacrificed, and therefore drew him with a veil over his face, whereby one might better conceive his anguish than he colour it." From Pliny XXXV.36.

41.4 at a good passe] In a desperate state. This idiom is not in the OED.

41.19 out of fear of her life] No longer fearing that she might survive.

42.4, 16 Thymon of Athens] Cooper: "Timon, A man of Athens, notable for his inhumanitie, and hatynge of the company and society of men." The classical source for the life of this semi-legendary figure is Plutarch, Life of Antony LXX; Whetstone was probably also familiar with Painter, I.28. According to Painter, "He [Timon] had a garden adjoyning to his house in the fields, wherein was a Figge tree, wheruppon many desperate men ordinarily did hange themselves." When he wished to cut down the tree in order to build a house on the site, he charitably announced to the town his intentions so that anyone who planned to hang himself could do so forthwith. Gruget's Mexia (pp. 78-79) mentions a gallows instead of a fig tree.

43.6 report] Common opinion. No authority in OED for precisely this definition.

43.16-17 better to have you a fayned friende . . . then an open enemie] Cf. Tilley F410: It is better to have an open foe than a dissembling friend.

Whetstone has reversed the proverb. See 218.15-16.

43.29 a dio] Italian "addio" = farewell, adieu, goodbye.

Explanatory Notes   283

The seconde Dayes Exercise

44.6-7 Aurora . . . Tithons bed] Aurora, the dawn-goddess, traditionally leaves the bed of her consort, the now immortal Tithonus, to prepare the way for the sun. (For example, Homer, Odyssey V.1-2.) See also 198.11-13.

44.7ff. Phebus . . .] Phoebus, the sun-god, drives his chariot from Oceanus in the east into the heavens, then across the sky, to return via the underworld to Oceanus.

44.8 Caves of Tartessus]. Cf. Cooper: "Tartessus, a citie in the uttermost parte of Spaine"; and Ovid: "Now the setting sun had bathed the Tartessian shores" (Met. XIV.416). Whetstone apparently confuses Tartessus with Tartarus, the classical underworld; hence his reference to the "Caves." See also 180.13.

44.10 Mountaine Oeta] Volcano in central Greece. In Ovid, the road for the sun's chariot is steeply up-hill, but no mention is made of Oeta.

44.11-12 Pyrois and sparklinge Phlegon] Two of the four horses that pull the sun's chariot, named in Ovid Met. II. 153-54.

44.13 Vulcan] Hephaestus, the god of fire, who acts as blacksmith for the gods. His workshop is on Olympus, and the Cyclopes help him to forge lightnings for Zeus.

44.14 Thunderboltes of Jubiter] Zeus, or Jupiter, as god of the sky, has the power to wield thunderbolts. See for example Ovid Met. I.154. The spelling "Jubiter" (also at 100.13; and EM, sig. M8^v) is an infrequent Renaissance variant, and in Aurelia it was emended to "Jupiter."

44.20s.n. The Bed resembleth the Grave] Cf. Tilley S527: Sleep is the image of death.

Whetstone's form of the proverb is not cited by Tilley; it occurs in John Grange, The Golden Aphroditis (1577): "Thy bedde is lyke thy grave" (sig. S1^v).

44.31 Fryer Bugiardo] From the Italian "bugiardo" = liar.

44.32 our Lady was come from Loretto] Loreto, a town near the Adriatic in central Italy, south of Ancona, is the location of the Shrine of the Holy House of the Blessed Virgin (Santa Casa di Loreto), one of the most famous attractions in Italy in the sixteenth century. According to a tradition which was popularized by Teramano's leaflet in 1472, the building was the house of the Virgin Mary in Nazareth: it was made into a church and was transported by angels in 1291 to Tersato in Illyria (Yugoslavia), then in 1294 to Italy, where it moved several times before finding a permanent place in Loreto in 1295. The details of the miracle were inscribed in the sixteenth century on the eastern façade of the basilica (New Catholic Encyclopedia).

Anthony Munday, in The English Romayne Lyfe (1582), comments on the wealth which the pilgrims donate to the shrine: "the Pope finds her a good sweet Lady of Loreto, for the pilgrimage to her, encreaseth his treasure, many thousands in a yere" (sig. H1^{r-v}); he describes the pictures, tapers, and wax cnadles which adorn the shrine, and the gold and silver which ornament the image of our Lady. Munday's comments tally with those of Montaigne, who speaks of crowds of pilgrims and many tradesmen: "There is more show of religion here than in any place I have seen," and "This place is full of miracles without number, for which I refer to the books" (pp. 177-83). Also Harl.M., p. 8.

Whetstone later refers to Loreto with less restraint: in The English Myrror, "Racconati, Maddona de Loreto, Ancona" are mentioned as strongholds of Papacy (sig. H3^v; also C5^v); and in Censure of a Loyall Subject, he attacks "their lewd lie of our ladyes house" (sig. G1^r).

45.2 RACANATI] From 1240 Loreto belonged to the Sees of Recanati and Macerata (New Catholic Encyclopedia, VIII, 993).

45.5 JURY] Jewry; that is, Judea, Palestine.

45.21 blinde Ignoraunce Cave] Cf. Cartari, sig. D1^v: "the darke cave of ignorance."

45.27 as wylye as Serpents] Matthew x.16: "Be ye therefore wise as serpents, and harmless as doves." Cf. Tilley M1162: To have more of the serpent than the dove. Topsell discusses the subtlety of serpents in Serpents, p. 18.

45.31ff. Judas . . .] Matthew xxvii.5.

46.11s.n. Dennis Bull] Meaning uncertain. Aurelia changes the phrase to "Phalaris Bull" here, but not at 77.2, where the poetic metre precludes such a substitution; and The Censure of a Loyall Subject states "so odious as Perillus Bull" (sig. A3^v). Whetstone may indeed have confused the two tyrants of Sicily, Dionysius (Denys or Dennis) and Phalaris. (For the bull of Phalaris, see note 229.29.) The two names are also closely associated in the Gesta Romanorum, XLVIII: "Dionysius records that when Perillus desired to become an artificer of Phalaris, a cruel and tyrannical king . . ."

(trans. C. Swan and W. Hooper, New York: Dover, 1959, p. 84). Gruget's Mexia both recounts the cruelty of Phalaris (p. 140) and states that the first to tame bulls was Denis or Dionysius (p. 253). However, since the name of Phalaris was proverbial in the Renaissance, and since "Dennis Bull" occurs twice in the Heptameron, I am inclined to believe that Whetstone is not mistaken, even though I am unable to explain the allusion.

46.14s.n. Alcaron, a Lawe . . . of Mahomet] "Mahomet being by these means strong and puissant, he made his lawe named the Alcoran: and for that he distrusted the goodnes thereof, he generally forbad all men, upon the paine of death, not so much as to dispute of his lawe" (EM, sig. D5^v). See also EM, sig. M1^r. Gruget's Mexia, p. 51.

46.20-22 the sacred Byble . . . in vulgar Language] The sixteenth-century English translations of the Bible included Coverdale's Bible (1535), the Great Bible (1539), the Bishops' Bible (1568), and the Geneva Bible (1560).

46.25 And synce] The sentence picks up again at 47.8, "By how much more . . . ."

46.26 Alexander Severus] Severus Alexander, Roman Emperor A.D. 222-35. Cooper refers to him as "a man from his childhood of wonderful gravitie and prudence" who made Rome into "a perfecte publike weale." Alexander's reign was one of justice, wisdom, and clemency. Whetstone gives an account of his reforms in A Mirour for Magestrates of Cyties (1584), "Representing the Ordinaunces, Policies, and Diligence, of the Noble Emperour, Alexander (surnamed) Severus, to suppresse and chastise the notorious Vices noorished in Rome." Izard points out that Whetstone is greatly indebted to Sir

Thomas Elyot's _Image of Governaunce_ (1541), but that the three orations attributed to the Emperor in _A Mirour for Magestrates of Cyties_ appear to be original to Whetstone. (For Whetstone's sources, see Izard, pp. 145ff.) See also 206.24.

47.33-34 _his lippes layde on loade_] To lay on load = to deal heavy blows; To lay on by load = to heap or pile on. Hence, his lips moved rapidly (in order to pile on the food).

48.2-3 _Tantalus dinner_] The phrase has proverbial force, meaning "a tantalizing meal." Cooper on Tantalus: "he is in hell tormented in this wyse: He standeth by a fayre ryver, havynge before hym a tree laden with pleasant appuls, and yet he is alwayes thursty and hungry: for as often as he stoupeth to drynke, or holdeth up his handes to gather the appuls, bothe the water and the tree dooe withdrawe them so from hym, that he can not touche theim." See also 86.7-8 and 114.14.

48.4-5 _questions, which he ever aunsweared in a monisillable_] Another Italian social entertainment. A similar example occurs in Bonaventure Des Periers, _Nouvelles Recreations et joyeux devis_, Tale 58, "Of the Monk who Answered Everything in Rhymed Monosyllables." See Izard, pp. 109-10. See also p. 79, p. 164, and Note 164.2.

48.19-20 _Pauca sapienti_] "A few words to the wise." Tilley W781: A word to a wise man is enough.

48.23 _beaten with hys owne sentence_] Tilley W204: To beat one at his own weapon. (Earliest example 1591.)

S802: To be beaten with one's own staff.

Cf. 173.13 s.n.; and 229.30.

48.29 Benedicite] The blessing asked at table.

49.1-3 An olde health rule . . .] Tilley cites this as the first instance of the proverb D340: After dinner sit a while, after supper walk a mile. According to the ODEP, the source is the School of Health at Salerno, "Post prandium stabis, post coenam ambulabis." It also occurs in Bryskett, A Discourse of Civill Life (a translation from Cintio, c. 1582) as "an approved opinion of all antiquitie" (ed. T. E. Wright, p. 74).

49.5 prayse Master] Not in OED.

49.21 to play with fire] Omitted by Tilley, F286. Whetstone's is the first example of this proverb in the ODEP.

49.24 Sampson] The story of Samson and Delilah is told in Judges xvi.4-21. Delilah betrayed Samson by cutting his hair, the source of his strength.

49.30-31 auncient customs . . . lawes incertaine] Cf. Tilley C937: With customs we live well but laws undo us. (Earliest example 1640.)

49.32 Eunuk] See Note 25.4.

50.1-2 this followinge Sonnet, in Italion] No source found.

50.6-7 And yet I lye . . . grypde with payne] Implicit, perhaps, is an image of Tityos who was punished for his passion by being stretched out on the ground while vultures (gripes) tore at his liver.

50.18 Pelops race] Pelops, the son of Tantalus, wooed Hippodamia, the daughter of Oenomaus. Having been warned that his daughter's husband would kill him, Oenomaus had set as a condition of her marriage a race between each suitor and himself; if the suitor was overtaken by Oenomaus, he was speared. Pelops borrowed winged steeds and bribed Oenomaus's charioteer to sabotage his adversary's chariot: Oenomaus was killed in the resulting accident and Pelops wedded Hippodamia.

51.4-5 <u>Impression of nature</u>] the dictate of nature.

51.17 <u>evill served</u>] Poorly provided with game. "Serve" = to drive out game into view of the hawk (Falconry).

51.19-20 <u>flie at checkes</u>] Fly after some lesser game instead of her proper game (Hawking).

51.20-21 <u>rated from riote</u>] Prevented, by scolding, from following the wrong scent (Hunting).

52.33-34 <u>The greatest Clarke . . . proves not alwaies the wisest man</u>] Tilley C409: The greatest clerks are not the wisest men.

53.1-2 <u>He valueth all, that glistereth, Golde</u>] Tilley A146: All is not gold that glisters.
See also 34.23-24.

53.2-3 <u>he esteemeth fayre wordes, as friendly deeds</u>] Cf. Tilley D402: It is better to do well than to say well.

53.3-4 <u>lovely countenaunces, doo spring from a lovyng condition</u>] Tilley F5: A fair face must have good conditions.

53.5s.n. <u>Experience is the best Judge</u>] Possibly proverbial.

53.9-10 <u>the sowre Crab, the savorie Pippin</u>] Cf. Lyly, p. 108: "The sour crab hath the show of an apple as well as the sweet pippin."

53.11s.n. <u>The forme deceiveth</u> . . .] Tilley A285: Appearances are deceitful.

53.17-18 counterfeits will to kinde] Cf. Tilley L286: Like will to like.

53.18-19 Copper holds print, but not touch with Gold] Cf. "but counter-fetes wil unto kinde, Copper may holde print but not bide tutch with golde: even so these hypocrits, as place and opportunitie served, bewraied their beastly natures" (MM, sig. B4^r).

"Touch" = "the touchstone," which tests the fineness of gold. Copper will retain an impression just as well as gold, but it will not abide the touchstone to the same extent (that is, it is not as valuable as gold). Cf. OED, print, sb., A.c., quotation 1400: "The same preent is made, bothe in gold and in copyr."

53.19-20 Fire hid in Ashes, will breake foorth in heat] Cf. Tilley F264: Fire raked up in ashes keeps its heat a long time.

Whetstone's version is closer to that of John Grange in The Golden Aphroditis: "But time trieth troth and bringeth all to light, the smothering heate at length breakes foorth in flame" (sig. R4^v).

53.20-21 water courses stopt, find out new passages] Tilley S929: The stream stopped swells the higher.

54.18-19 a riche young Warde] After the death of the father, an heir or heiress who was a minor was assigned by the Courts, often as a reward, to the guardianship of some gentleman or nobleman, who then controlled the estate. It was a common Elizabethan practice for the guardian to arrange his charge's marriage to his own benefit.

54.29s.n. Love will not be constrained.] Cited by Tilley L499: Love cannot be compelled (forced).

54.34–55.1 no more can forcement enforce the free to fancie] As above.

55.3–7 Petrarke . . .] Petrarch, 1304–1374, Italian poet and humanist. No definite source can be assigned for this quotation, but Izard suggests that a similar passage occurs in Trionfi III (Izard, p. 107). Whetstone does draw on Petrarch for the poems on pages 69, 70, and 72. See also 89.27 and Note.

55.15 which account] In which instance.

55.24 Reason and Love] The opposition of Reason and Love is traditional in the literature of courtly love. A well-known debate between them occurs in the thirteenth-century French poem The Romance of the Rose (ch.21ff.), which was popular in the Renaissance France of Marot and Ronsard.

55.25s.n. Reason and Love, as enemies] Cited in Tilley L517: Love is without reason.

See also 63.10–11.

56.1–4 this Adage . . . .] Cf. John Grange, The Golden Aphroditis (sig. R1^r):

> A Proverbe olde I beare in mynde,
> The whiche I hope will be full true:
> The fallyng out of lovers kynde,
> Is fayned wrath love to renewe.

Tilley F40: The falling out of lovers is the renewing of love.

56.27 taile to taile] I have not found another instance of this phrase. Probably, "in opposite directions."

57.8 in neyther of theyr wretchednesse] In the wretchedness of neither.

57.17ff. The Historie in the reproche of forced Mariage] No known source. But the motif of an arranged marriage joining two families is very common: Whetstone uses it again in The Seventh Day, with a contrasting outcome.

57.19 <u>Cirene</u>] Cyrene (or Cirene in Italian), ancient city in North Africa.

57.20 <u>Tryfo</u>] In Plutarch, <u>Table-Talk</u> IX (<u>Moralia</u> 646ff.), one of the speakers in the dialogues is Trypho, a doctor.

57.24 <u>Sicheus</u>] A Phoenician merchant, the husband of Dido in Virgil, <u>Aeneid</u> IV.20.

58.3-4 <u>though he take impression by sight, rooteth in contemplation</u>] An echo of the Platonic theory of love, as popularized in the Renaissance by Bembo's speech in Book IV of Castiglione's <u>Il cortegiano</u>. "Take impression" = takes hold superficially.

58.19-21 <u>delyght to recount . . . theyr shrewde payments</u>] (The young men) will delight to add up the benefits (pleasures) they receive but will neglect to take into account the damaging payments required for those pleasures.

58.27-29 <u>Salomon deceyved, Sampson subdued, Aristotle derided, and Hercules murthered</u>] Solomon, Samson, and Hercules are traditional Renaissance examples of men deceived by women. (For example, see the poem on this theme by George Gascoigne in <u>The Adventures of Master F.J.</u> [1574], p. 52.) Solomon's thousand "outlandish women" brought him "to idolatrie" (1 Kings xi.1-8); Samson was tricked by Delilah into revealing the secret of his strength (Judges xvi.4-21); and Hercules, the Greek super-hero, was killed by a shirt soaked in poisoned centaur's blood, sent to him by his wife Deianira because she mistakenly thought that it would ensure his love for her (Ovid Met. IX).

But why was Aristotle derided? Cooper may provide a clue when he states that Aristotle "was little of personage, crookebacked, il shapen and strutting." Or is Whetstone thinking of Socrates and his scolding wife?

58.31-59.7 Kinge Demetrius . . . Lamia . . .] The story appears in Plutarch's Life of Demetrius, but Whetstone's immediate source is undoubtedly Painter, II,p.302-4: "One yere and two Moneths before the Death of King Demetrius, his frend Lamia died, who sorowed so mutch hir death, as for the absence and death of hir, he caused the Phylosophers of Athens to entre in this Disputation, Whether the teares and sorow whiche he shed and toke for her sake, were more to be estemed than the riches which he spent in her obsequies and funerall pompes." Painter goes on to relate how Demetrius buried Lamia before his chamber window so that he might lament her.

59.12 reddy in conceyt] Quick in thought.

60.22 Bees ungently used stinge our faces] Cf. Tilley B211: Bees that have honey in their mouths have stings in their tails.

60.28 fowle falle thee] That is, foul befall thee; may something foul happen to you.

60.28s.n. That which is blessing to one, may be a curse to an other] There are a number of proverbs on this subject.

Cf. Tilley M483: One man's meat is another man's poison.

   B51: What baits one banes another.

61.7-8 his finger never akes with my mallice] An idiom that occurs in Painter: "I cannot abide . . . to see your finger ake" (III, pp. 60,154).

Explanatory Notes   294

61.8-9 Forberaunce edgeth the sword of Revenge] Cf. Tilley F584: Forbearance is no quittance.

61.9-10 Choller, though it often strikes, it woundes not muche] Cf. Tilley C359: Choler has more heat than light. (Earliest example 1659.)

61.18-19 the Devill who is the Executioner of Vengeance] The usual proverb is "Vengeance belongs only to God" (Tilley V24), but underlying both statements is the condemnation of revenge -- an attitude shared by the Christian humanists.

61.29-30 Ixions torments, for his ambitious attempting of Junoes love] Angered at Ixion's pursuit of his consort Juno (Hera), Jupiter (Zeus) formed a cloud in her image on which the deceived Ixion begat the centaurs. Because Ixion boasted of his supposed conquest of Juno, Jupiter punished him by attaching him to a fiery wheel perpetually revolving in Hades. See also Note 144.17.

62.5 a Mountaine of Ice] Cf. 23.29-30.

63.10-11 Love quickeneth a mans wit, although it burieth Reason] Cf. Tilley L517: Love is without reason. See also 55.25s.n.

63.14 a light to mischiefe] A way shown to evil-doing.

63.24-26 Mahometians . . .] I have not found the source of this statement, but Whetstone attacks Mahometanism throughout The English Myrror (see for example, sigs. D5^v and M1^r).

64.3 the Barre of his welfare] "of" = to. See 3.23 and Note.

64.14-15 wilfull faultes may be pitied, but deserveth no pardon] Tilley F105: A fault wilfully committed deserves no pardon. (Earliest example is 1596.)

65.10 <u>Metamorphosed into Vipers</u>] No source has been found for this metamorphosis. In <u>The Bestiary</u>, "The Viper (<u>vipera</u>) is called this because it brings forth in violence (<u>vi</u>). The reason is that when its belly is yearning for delivery, the young snakes, not waiting for the timely discharge of birth, gnaw through the mother's sides and burst out to her destruction." The female is supposed to destroy the male at coition, angered at his lust. "Thus both parents perish, the male when he copulates, and the female when she gives birth" (p. 170). The viper traditionally represents disorder in marriage, and in the Renaissance especially it became a symbol of envy. In his examination of Envy in <u>The English Myrror</u> (1586) Whetstone says that "<u>Socrates</u> likeneth envie unto a <u>Viper</u>," for it "will not be bound unto the obedience of nature" (sig. A3^r).

The classical source of these traditions in Pliny X.82; they are retold in Topsell, <u>Serpents</u>, pp. 293ff.

65.33s.n. <u>Sorrowes causeth scilence</u>] Cf. Tilley S664: Small sorrows speak, great ones are silent. (Earliest example is 1587.)

66.10s.n. <u>Good morralitie, is better than evil doctrine</u>] A re-phrasing of Tilley E213: Examples teach more than precepts.

66.14s.n. <u>There is no trustinge of a reconcyled enemye</u>] Cf. Tilley H373 and H378: Take heed of reconciled enemies.

66.15-16 <u>a sneaking dog, that never barkes but bites withall</u>] Tilley D503: A still dog bites sore. (This example cited.)

Cf. also C912: A cur will bite before he bark. (Earliest example 1623.)

67.23 <u>Minervas sheelde</u>] The huge aegis in which is represented the head of Medusa is the standing attribute of Pallas Athene, or Minerva, the goddess of wisdom; it was originally the shield of Zeus, her father (Homer, <u>Iliad</u> V.738ff.; Virgil, <u>Aeneid</u> VIII.433ff.). But what is the source of Aurelia's specific claim that the shield is impervious to poison?

67.30 <u>Euripides</u>] Greek dramatist, 5th century B.C. The source of this poem may be <u>Phoenissae</u>, 524-25, which was translated as <u>Jocasta</u> (1572) by George Gascoigne and Francis Kinwelmarsh. However, Whetstone's version is closer to that of Pettie: "For <u>Ennius</u> saith flatly, there is no friendly or faithfull dealinge to be looked for at any mans handes, in matters pertayninge to a kingdome: and <u>Euripides</u> makes it in a manner lawfull for a kingdomes sake to transgresse the limittes of law, nature, and honesty" (<u>A Petite Pallace</u>, p. 78). See also Lyly, p. 78; and <u>EM</u>, sig. F3^v.

67.33-68.8 <u>In these two thinges</u> . . . <u>a fayre wife</u>] This poem may be paraphrased as follows: In the pursuit of these two things -- the obtaining of a Kingdom and the persuading of a fair women to one's own will -- so sweet is the taste of the final achievement, that men do not fear to destroy their friends with their foes. The reason for this is that exercise of restraint would shrink the scope of the authority which a King might wield as sovereign Judge; and in love, reason does not have the power to restrain the self-conceits of the mind. So that God knows, in danger stands his life, that is a King or hath a fair wife (for others will always strive to steal kingdom or wife).

Cf. Tilley L495: Love and lordship like no fellowship.

68.4 <u>whereas</u>] Read "in which."

68.19 Mask] The masque presented here is not the elaborate dramatic presentation that it became in the England of Ben Jonson and Inigo Jones, but a symbolic parade ending in a dance. The masque in The Seventh Day's Exercise (pp. 227ff.) is an allegorical tableau with action.

Whetstone is once again describing an entertainment that was originally Italian. Edward Hall's Chronicle (1548) describes the first masque at court, held in 1512-13: "On the daie of the Epiphanie at night, the kyng with a xi. other were disguised, after the maner of Italie, called a maske, a thyng not seen afore in Englande" (1809; rpt. New York: AMS, 1965, p. 526). As early as 1573, Italian players performed in masques in England (F. G. Fleay, A Chronicle History of the London Stage, 1559-1642, London: Reeves & Turner, 1890, p. 22, 26).

69.2 Spero, Timeo, Taceo] "I hope, I fear, I am silent."

69.10-12 They agreed to be thus attyred . . . their Mistresses] Through their costumes masquers symbolically revealed their states of mind and their feelings. In Euphues and His England, Philautus says, "It hath been a custom, fair lady, how commendable I will not dispute, how common you know, that Maskers do therefore cover their faces that they may open their affections, and under the colour of a dance discover their whole desires" (Lyly, p. 316).

Whetstone carefully describes the colours of the costumes, for in the Renaissance colours were frequently chosen for their symbolic significance. Russet and murrey suggested low rank or servant status; white symbolized faith, truth, and sincerity; green was a colour for lovers; carnation was worn by gallants; blue (azure blue or watched, a sky blue) represented honor, wisdom, and power; orange tawny (popular at the Tudor courts) suggested pride; popenjay green expressed high hope; yellow revealed arrogance; black symbolized constancy or sadness (Pearson, *Elizabethans at Home*, pp. 593-94). *The Rocke of Regard* discusses the significance of the colors worn by lovers; one youth complains that his "Dye" must change with "wanton moode" (sig. F7^v).

69.20 *Te stante virebo*] "Whilst thou endurest I shall flourish." A common motto (see J. Dielitz, *Die Wahl-und Denkspruche* . . ., 1884; rpt. Vaduz: Kraus, 1963). In Claude Paradin's *Devises Heroiques* (1557) it accompanies a figure of a vine growing around a pyramid (Menston, Eng.: Scolar Press, 1971, p. 72).

69.23 *English Italion*] Probably an English translation out of Italian (see *OED*, English, 3c). Or perhaps English written in the Italian script.

69.24-70.10 *Two Soveraigne Dames . . . of the world*] Derived from the first quatrain of Petrarch's sonnet "Due gran nemiche inseme erano aggiunte" (*Rime* CCXCVII).

69.24 *Beautie and Honestie*] Tilley B163: Beauty and honesty seldom agree.

69.29 *make riot of their Grace*] Put on an extravagant display of their good qualities. *OED* does not cite an example for this use of "riot" before 1649.

70.19 *passion*] A love poem. In Watson's collection of 1582, the *Hecatompathia*, the poems are called "passions" or "Love passions."

70.20-71.7 *Hence burnyng sighes . . . my Mistresse Good*] Derived from the opening of Petrarch's sonnet "Ite, caldi sospiri, al freddo core" (*Rime* CLIII).

70.30 <u>For even as drink, dooth make the Dropsey drye</u>]   Tilley M211: Like a man in a dropsy, the more he drinks the more he may.

See also 94.22-23; 99.11; 189.20-21.

71.18-72.13 <u>Even as the Hart . . . I am your owne</u>]   I have found no specific source for this poem, but the comparison of the lover to a wounded deer is a common Petrarchan conceit.

71.28 <u>Holde this for ease</u>]   Seek ease by doing this.

72.20 <u>in the thought</u>]   In keeping with this idea.

72.21 <u>Basta che spero</u>]   "It is enough that I hope."

72.25-73.12 <u>from shore to sea . . . to live alwaies in hope</u>]   Derived from Petrarch's canzone "Di pensier in pensier, di monte in monte" (<u>Rime</u> CXXIX).

73.9 <u>Twixt Ice and flame</u>]   See Note 9.9, and 149.4.

73.17 <u>Turtle</u>]   The turtle-dove represents constancy in love.   See Note 31.12 and 226.15.

73.18 <u>Parrhasius paynted Table Clothe</u>]   The story originates with Pliny XXX.36; it is recalled by Gruget's Mexia, p. 228. The two most famous classical painters, Parrhasius and Zeuxis, contended with one another. Zeuxis painted a table of fruit to which flew live birds, thinking the grapes to be real. Parrhasius painted only a cloth, which all observers took to be a real sheet: Zeuxis asked Parrhasius to take away the sheet and show his painting. See also Note 3.9.

73.19 <u>rowled</u>]   "Enfolded" or "rolled."

73.20-29 <u>If one firme Faith . . . neede of Grace</u>] Derived from Petrarch's sonnet "S'una fede amorosa, un cor non finto" (<u>Rime</u> CCXXIV).

The thyrd Daies Exercise

75.13 <u>Cesar</u> <u>and</u> <u>Pompey</u> . . .] Pompeius Gnaeus, called Magnus, was defeated by Caesar at Pharsalus in 48 B.C. He then "privily fledde by sea into Aegypte where under the faulse conducte of the Kynge Ptolomeus, he was slayne in a bote, his head beynge stryken of, and his bodie caste on the stronde, where it was poorely buryed" (Cooper). Julius Caesar was killed -- stabbed twenty-three times at the foot of Pompey's statue in the Capitol -- in 44 B.C. at the height of his career.

75.18 <u>Writers</u> <u>adde</u> <u>this</u> <u>Opinion</u>] I am unable to determine whether Whetstone is quoting a specific source.

76.20 <u>upon</u> <u>a</u> <u>quiet</u> <u>thought</u>] In a quiet state of mind.

76.21-22 <u>Boetius</u> <u>of</u> <u>the</u> <u>Consolation</u> <u>of</u> <u>Philosophy</u>] Boethius, Roman aristocrat, humanist, and statesman, 6th century A.D. Put to death for alleged high treason in 525 A.D. His <u>De</u> <u>Consolatione</u> <u>Philosophiae</u> (<u>Consolation</u> <u>of</u> <u>Philosophy</u>) is a Ciceronian dialogue in Latin between Lady Philosophy and the condemned Boethius; many translations were available in the sixteenth century, including those by Chaucer (printed by Caxton in 1478), by John Walton (1525), by George Colvile (1556), and by Queen Elizabeth (1593). Yet Whetstone appropriately chooses to recommend an Italian version.

76.22-23 <u>Cosimo</u> <u>Bartoli</u>] Florentine writer, 1503-1572. Among his varied works is an Italian translation of Boethius, one of three commissioned by Charles V in 1549, published in 1552. (G. Mancini, "Cosimo Bartoli," <u>Archivo</u> <u>Storico</u> <u>Italiano</u>, 76 (1918), 84-135.) Izard mentions that this work is "said to be not without merit" (p. 108).

76.24-77.16 Farewell, bright Golde . . . heavenly knowledge crowne]
No specific source. The theme of the poem -- the rejection of worldly
vanities in favor of philosophy -- echoes the "rejection of love" poems
of the courtly tradition, and it certainly is compatible with a reading
of Boethius.

76.27s.n. SISIPHUS] One of those eternally tormented in Hades. (See
Ovid Met. IV.460;X.44.) Cooper says that "in hell he turneth a stone up
to a great hyll toppe: but whan it is at the toppe, it falleth downe
againe, and reneweth his labour." Hence, Sisiphus is often an emblem of
futility. See also 78.8 and 114.16.

77.2 DENNIS BULL] See 46.11s.n. and Note. Could "Dennis Bull" be
the bull of Dionysius to which Amphion and Zethus bound Dirce to be dragged
to death? Philoxenus refers to Amphion at 78.1-2. This story is represented
in the sculpture group discovered in the early sixteenth century and now
called the Farnese Bull, which Whetstone may have seen at the Farnese
Palace (see 18.5-6s.n. and Note).

77.9 LYNX his eyes] The lynx is a symbol for sharp sight. Lynceus
the Argonaut was supposed to have had extremely keen sight, and this
ability was later attributed to the animal. Topsell refers to "the common
proverb Lynceo perspecacior, for a man of excellent eyesight" (p. 493),
but it is not in Tilley. See also 103.27.

77.11 Cockatrice] A composite creature, generally part bird and part
serpent, said to be hatched from a cock's egg; since the fourteenth century
it has been confused with the Basilisk. One glance from the cockatrice
turns its victim into stone; hence the proverb "The Cockatrice slays by

sight only" (Tilley C495). See Topsell, Serpents, pp. 119ff.

Whetstone may be intending a pun on Cockatrice as a name of reproach for a woman, a whore (OED, earliest example 1599). In this case the grave would be the bed.

77.19-20 bon Giorno] Italian "buon giorno" = good day, good morning.

78.1-2 Amphions Harp gave sence unto stone Walles] The son of Antiope and Zeus, Amphion was given a lyre by Hermes and became an outstanding musician. With his brother Zethus he built the wall around Thebes: the stones moved into position of their own accord to the music of his lyre. He is mentioned in Ovid Met. VI.

78.5 the Paynter Zeuxes] Zeuxis, 4th century B.C., famous painter mentioned by Pliny XXXV.9. Whetstone may be recalling Zeuxis' picture of "Eros in fairest youthful beauty, and as crowned with roses."

78.6-11 Cupid . . . the worke of the Paynter] There is no classical authority for this story. In his study "Blind Cupid," Erwin Panofsky points out that the figure of Cupid was very rarely blind in classical literature and never in classical art. The blindness of Cupid is a medieval addition, growing out of the belief that "love is blind," and appears frequently in Renaissance art and literature: "In fact the discussion of Cupid's blindness or non-blindness kept very much alive in Renaissance literature, with this difference however that it was transferred to a definitely humanistic level and thus tended either to degenerate into a mere jeu d'esprit or to become associated with the Neoplatonic theories of love" (Studies in Iconology, New York: Harper, 1962, p. 123). In philosophical poetry, a bright-eyed "Amore" appears as the opposite of the blind Cupid of the courtly love poetry; these two figures represent spiritual love and sensual passion respectively. By claiming that Cupid is not really blind, that he is only represented in art as being blind, Whetstone has the best of both worlds: he suggests that whereas love is in fact divine, it has nevertheless been debased by man through ignorance.

The question of Cupid's blindness is discussed in <u>Greenes Farewell to Folly</u>, sig. F4^v.

78.8 <u>Sisiphus taske</u>] That is, an impossible or futile task. See Note 76.27 and 114.16.

79.5ff. <u>shee demaunded</u> . . .] Other riddles occur at p. 48 and p. 164.

80.8-9 <u>necessity, is bound unto no law</u>] Tilley N76: Necessity has no law.

80.11-12 <u>a man may offend through rashness, and make amends with repentance</u>] Cf. Tilley H191: He that resolves in haste repents at leisure.

80.27-28 <u>a man can have of a Cat but her skin, and of a begger, but his scrip</u>] Tilley M1167: You can have no more of a cat than his skin. (Whetstone's example cited.)

80.28-30 <u>unles he wil sel</u> . . . <u>the dice maker, the bones of the other</u>] The <u>ODEP</u> cites this as the first example of the proverb "To make dice of one's bones." But Whetstone intends the statement to be understood literally: dice were originally made of bone or ivory.

81.15 <u>Eunuck</u>] See Note 25.4.

81.17-27 <u>To thee I sende</u> . . . <u>with Sacrifice of zeale</u>] I have found no source for this poem.

82.15 hazard upon a charge] Take the risk of making an impetuous attack.

82.24-26 as many deepe woundes with his Pen, as ever he had done with his Launce] Cf. Tilley W839: Words hurt more than swords.

ODEP: The pen is mightier than the sword.

82.24s.n. The dashe of a Pen, is more greevous then the counterbuff of a Launce] Cited by both Tilley (W839) and ODEP. In ODEP, the original reading, "counterbuse," is emended to "counter use."

82.27 an Oke at the Helve of an Axe] Cf. Tilley T496: The oak falls not at the first blow. And A411: He sends the ax after the helve.

"Helve" = handle, so there is no real danger.

83.28-29 where unitie is, small things groweth to great] Tilley U11: In union is strength.

83.32 in the neck] Strongly assailing. (OED, neck, 3c.)

84.32 of two evils the least is to be chosen] Tilley E207: Of two evils choose the least.

85.9-10 to keepe within their teather] To keep within the limits of their ability or position. Cf. "To reach the end of one's tether" (ODEP; not in Tilley).

85.10 to leape within their latchet] To keep within their limits, not to meddle with what does not concern them. "Latchet" = a thong (OED, 1d).

85.13 as Plato sayeth] No source found. Cf. 36.5; 146.14; 158.34; and 206.21.

85.15-16 no man so faultlesse . . . amended] Tilley M116: Every man has his faults. Cited in ODEP.

86.7-8 no man dyneth worse, then hoping Tantalus] See Note 48.2-3. Cf. 114.14.

86.8-10 none are more wetshod . . . the soules (perhaps) wilbe worne] Tilley M619: Who waits for dead men's shoes shall go long barefoot.

86.16s.n. An ungodly childe maketh an unthriftie Father] A denial of the proverb "A sparing father and a spending (prodigal) son." (Tilley F91, earliest example 1586.)

86.27 every offence hath his proper scourge] Tilley S467: Every sin brings its punishment with it.
(Earliest example 1616.)

87.19-20 Plutarke saythe] Plutarch of Chaeronia, philosopher and biographer, 1st century A.D. He was a popular educational writer and had a great influence in the Renaissance, especially through his Lives and Moralia. The major translations include James Sanford's Amorous and Tragicall Tales (1567); Sir Thomas North's The Lives of the Noble Grecians and Romanes (1579), translated from the French of Jaques Amyot; and Philemon Holland's Morals (1603). See also 171.13.

87.29-31 like a Cocke . . . untill he dyeth] Koeppel intensely dislikes this image drawn from cock-fighting (Studien, p. 40).

87.33-34 they go farre that never returne] Cf. Lyly, p. 182: "he runneth far that never returneth." Not in Tilley.

88.7 Ovid sayeth, that Forma numen habet] "Beauty has divinity."

Amores III.3.12.

Quoted also in PC, sig. C2^v.

88.14 Piramus and Thisbie] Frequently cited in the Renaissance as examples of lovers who died for love. Their story is told in Ovid Met. IV.55-166.

88.14-15 Romeus and Juliet] Also a commonplace Renaissance example. The source is Bandello, II.9, which reached England through Boaistuau to be retold by Painter, II.25. Also available was Arthur Broke's poem, The Tragicall Historye of Romeus and Juliet (1562).

88.15 Arnalt and Amicla] I have not been able to identify these lovers. However, if Whetstone intended to suggest "Arnalt and his Friend," he may be referring to the romance Arnalt and Lucenda (1575), translated by Hollyband from the Spanish; or to Arnaut Daniel, praised in Petrarch, Trionfi IV.40-41 as the "Master in love."

88.30 Ovid, Nigidius, Samocratius, Petrarke] See Notes below for p. 89.

89.16-21 Ovid . . . Julia . . .] The poet of love, Ovid died in exile. The popular medieval and Renaissance version of his banishment is referred to by Cooper: "The cause of his exile is uncertaine, savynge some suppose it was for abusynge Julia, daughter of the emperour Augustus." Ovid refers to his own life, including his exile, in the Tristia, which was translated by Thomas Churchyard, Whetstone's acquaintance, in 1572 and reprinted in 1580. The legend is discussed by John C. Thibault in The Mystery of Ovid's Exile (Berkeley: Univ. of Calif. Press, 1964).

89.21 Nigidius] Nigidius Figulus, a friend of Cicero, an active supporter of Pompey, died in 45 A.D. Cooper refers to him as "An auncient Romaine, which was a philosopher, of the secte of Pythagoras, and wrote woonderfully subtilly, about the yere of our lorde .xlviii. he dyed in exyle." Caesar probably exiled him because he took an active part in the civil war on the side of Pompey. Fragments of his work survive in Aulus Gellius, who was probably read by Whetstone, and in other writers.

89.24 <u>Samocratius</u>] I cannot identify this reference. However, its source appears to be Guevara's <u>Epistolas Familiares</u>, correctly translated by Geoffrey Fenton in his <u>Golden Epistles</u> (1582): "<u>Samocratius</u>, <u>Nigidius</u>, and <u>Ovide</u> have written many volumes of the remedie of love, wherein they rather taughte remedie to others, than founde any themselves: for that they all three dyed in persecution, not for the abuses they committed at <u>Rome</u>, but for the loves they practised at <u>Capua</u>" (sig. T5^v). The same trio are mentioned by George Gascoigne in the epistle to his <u>Posies</u> (1575): "I neither take example of wanton Ovid, doting Nigidius, nor foolish Samocratius" (<u>Works</u>, I, 5-6).

89.27-30 <u>Petrarke</u> . . . <u>Madonna Laura</u>] Petrarch fell in love with Laura, he tell us in <u>Rime</u> CCXI, on April 6, 1327, when he first saw her in Avignon. Although she was unattainable, being both married and superlatively virtuous, he remained faithful to his love for her even after she died in the Black Death of 1348. Petrarch's collection of poems, the <u>Rime</u> (or the <u>Canzoniere</u>), addressed to Laura living and dead, popularized the sonnet throughout Europe and established the themes and conventions of love poetry for centuries. Whetstone draws on his works for the poems on pages 55, 69, 70, and 72; and attributes to him the quatrain on page 55.

90.6-8 the Husband wyll leape at a Cruste, and the Wife trot for her Dinner] Tilley C870: To leap at a crust. (Earliest example 1616. The ODEP indicates that Whetstone's is the first recorded use.)

Tilley N79: Need makes the old wife trot.

90.19-20 pleasaunt baytes baineth Fyshe] Cf. Lyly, p. 46: ."Is it not the pleasant bait that causeth the fleetest fish to bite?"

90.21-22 Crocadyles teares, intrappeth Fooles] Tilley C831: Crocodile tears.

The crocodile was popularly supposed to lure its prey by pretending to weep; or, it was supposed to shed tears after devouring its victim. Hence, its tears are a sign of hypocrisy (Topsell, Serpents, pp. 126ff.). See also 164.16 and 177.2-3.

90.31-32 the Mariage must be in poste haste, and the mislikyng at leasure] Tilley H196: Marry in haste and repent at leisure.

Cf. 96.18s.n.

92.12-13 good Wine neede no Ivie Bushe, fyne Marchaundise are solde without a Signe] Tilley W462. See 9.25 and Note.

92.28ff. The Historie in reproofe of rash Mariages . . .] The direct sources for this novella are Marguerite de Navarre's Heptaméron 36 and Painter I, 57. Similar motifs appear in Bandello, Belleforest, and Gruget's Mexia. Painter translates Marguerite de Navaree's tale, and Whetstone appears to be following primarily Painter's version, even echoing his language. Whetstone's additions and alterations make for a more interesting story: he pays more attention to motivations and economic conditions; he attributes Malipiero's forgiveness of Felice to love, not simply to his desire for children; and by including an account of Marino Giorgio's persistent wooing and seduction of Felice, he engages more sympathy for her.

92.30-31 Capo Verdo . . . the capitall Citie, within the kingdome of Naples] "Capua, in ancient times, the chief city of the Campania region of Italy; it was located 16 miles (25 kilometres) north of Neapolis (Naples) on the site of the modern Santa Maria Capua Vetere" (New Encyclopedia Britannica).

93.18-19 striking the yron while it was whote] Tilley I94: It is good to strike while the iron is hot.

93.26ff. And among many an aunciet Gentleman, his Governour . . .] The schoolmaster giving sage advice to Malipiero is reminiscent of the old gentleman lecturing Euphues in Naples (Lyly, pp. 13ff.).

94.22 Periander] Tyrant of Corinth, c. 625-585 B.C., sometimes listed as one of the seven sages of Greece. His home is the scene of Plutarch's "Dinner of the Seven Wise Men" (Moralia 146-164). Whetstone may be recalling the story (recounted by Herodotus and Diogenes Laertius) of Periander's campaign to purge his city of luxury and idleness -- he is supposed to have stripped the Corinthian women of their ornaments -- but I have been unable to locate this exact saying.

94.22-23 a Dropsey: for as drinke encreaseth the drouth of the one] Tilley M211: Like a man in a dropsy, the more he drinks the more he may. See also 70.30; 99.11; 189.20-21.

95.2-3 she will go like a Pecock, and you like a meacock] Proverbial in style, but not listed in Tilley or in ODEP. The peacock is proverbially proud (Tilley P157), and the meacock (according to OED perhaps originally a name of some bird) is meek, sexually weak, effeminate. Cf. example cited by OED for 1719: "For my part I will no more be such a Meacock To deal with the plumes of a Hyde-Park Peacock." Also Shrew, II. i. 305-6.

95.31 looke before you leape] Tilley L429.

96.18s.n. An early marriage, worketh a late repentaunce] Cf. Tilley M694: Marry today repent tomorrow. (Earliest example 1623.) See also 90.31-32.

96.24-25 menaced to punish his oversight (in not regarding him) as Strangers] They were hostile to Malipiero, punishing his oversight (that is, of not considering his parents' wishes) by not giving him any consideration, as if they were strangers to him.

97.9 this braverie was but a blase] Cf. Tilley B167: Beauty is a blaze.

97.28 not in his debt or daunger] Tilley D166: Out of debt out of danger.

M451: He is in every man's debt and danger; that is, "under every man's jurisdiction or power, under an obligation" (Tilley's note).

98.5 A Diamond hath not his grace but in golde] "When the Dyamonde is sette in golde, the mettall honoureth the stone, and the stone the metall" (Legh, The Accedens of Armory, sig. B7^v). For only the most royal metal is suitable for the finest gem. Cf. Wotton, Courtlie Controversie sig. B1^r.

98.9 Piatso Richio] Italian "piazza" = square, market-place; "ricco" = rich.

98.19 their wyves love gadding] Cf. Tilley W695: Women and hens are lost by gadding. (Earliest example 1591.)

99.11-12 as drincke increaseth the dropsies drowth] Tilley M211. See also 70.30; 94.22-23; 189.20-21.

99.12-13 so disdaine, heapeth coales uppon desire] "But so extreme are the passions of love that the more thou seekest to quench them by disdain the greater flame thou increasest by desire" (Lyly, p. 350).

99.13 Teste se ipso] "Himself an (eye) witness."

99.18-20 a pure Sanguine Complection . . . Choller adust] According to medieval physiology, one's temperament was determined by the predominant humour in the body; the four humours were blood, phlegm, choler, and melancholy. Because blood was formerly the chief humour in Marino Giorgio's body, he had been always sanguine or cheerful; now that black bile is uppermost, he is melancholy.

99.23 Galen, Hipocrates] The ancient physicians who were the authorities of medieval and early Renaissance medicine.

Galen of Pergamun, A.D. 129-?199, was court physician in Rome under Marcus Aurelius. His works were revived by the early sixteenth-century humanists -- Thomas Linacre translated them into Latin directly from the Greek (1521-24) -- and some were translated into English by Robert Copland (1541), by John Jones (1574), and by George Baker (1574). Galen was considered to be infallible: "In phisike he was so excellent, as he may justly seeme to be raysed by divine providence, at that time to make perfecte that noble arte" (Cooper).

Hippocrates lived at the time of Socrates (469-399 B.C.); his works are now lost, but <u>Aphorisms</u> attributed to him were translated into English by Humphrey Llwyd (1550?). "If one asks what Hippocrates meant to the Greeks, the Middle Ages, the Renaissance, what he means even today, the answer is that by a complicated historical process he has become the embodiment of the ideal physician" (<u>Oxford Classical Dictionary</u>).

99.24 <u>Paracelsus</u>] Physician and alchemist (1493-1541), whose true name was Philippus Aureolus Theophrastus Bombast von Hohenheim. His works brought new ideas into chemistry and medicine and upset the schoolmen. He criticized the traditional medical authorities, and on June 24, 1527, in front of the University of Basel, he burned the books of Galen and of the Arabian physician Avicenna.

99.26ff. <u>Macrello, the Physition of Love</u> . . .] In late Renaissance prose fiction, love affairs are frequently furthered by an exchange of letters and by the machinations of a go-between.

100.12-14 <u>Acrisius brasen Tower</u> . . . <u>Jubiter</u> . . . <u>Danais love</u>] Learning from an oracle that his daughter's son would slay him, Acrisius, King of Argos, imprisoned his daughter Danae in a brazen subterranean chamber or (according to the Latin poets) in a brazen tower. But Jupiter fell in love with her and descended into her lap in the form of a golden shower: the son was Perseus. "By this fable is signified, that Jupiter sent treasure pryvilye unto Danae, and also to them that had the kepynge of hir, wherewith they being corrupted, suffered Jupiter to enter into the towne, and accomplyshe his pleasure. The fable declareth the force of money and giftes in assauting of chastitie" (Cooper). A classical source is Horace, <u>Odes</u> III.16.1-8.

100.13 Jubiter] An accepted, though infrequent, spelling of Jupiter. See also 44.14.

100.20 the flashe of Rose water] A common Renaissance treatment. Albertus Magnus, The Book of Secrets (c. 1550) credits the rose with the power to restore life (ed. M. R. Best and F. H. Brightman, Oxford: Clarendon Press, 1973, p. 16); and in Gascoigne's The Adventures of Master F.J., "damaske water" is used to revive the hero (p. 86).

100.26s.n. Hope comforteth but Love cureth the Lover] Cf. Tilley H605: If it were not for Hope the heart would break.

102.5 Protheus] Proteus, a sea-god, has the power to take on any shape; he appears as The Old Man of the Sea in Homer, Odyssey IV.384ff., and in Virgil, Georgics IV.387ff. "He also tourned himselfe into sundry fygures, sometyme beynge like a flame of fire, sometyme lyke a bull, an other tyme lyke a terrible serpente . . . . Of him came this proverbe, Proteo mutabilior, more chaungeable then Proteus, applyed to him that in his actes or woordes is unstable" (Cooper).

Tilley S285: As many shapes as Proteus.

103.5 Hercules labours] Hercules "Seemeth to be a generall name geven to men excellynge in strengthe all other of their tyme" (Cooper). He was the son of Jupiter and Alcmena and one of the most famous of Greek heroes. By accomplishing the twelve seemingly impossible tasks imposed upon him by a jealous Juno, he won immortal fame and immortality. The twelve labours feature the Nemean Lion, the Hydra of Lerna, the Boar of Erymanthus, the Hind of Ceryneia, the Birds of Stymphalus, the Augean Stables, the Cretan Bull, the Horses of Diomedes, Geryon, Cerberus, the Apples of the

Hesperides, and the Girdle of the Amazon (for the last, Cooper substitutes the Battle with the Centaurs).

103.25ff. But, O that Furie Jelousie...] The manner in which Malipiero's suspicion is aroused and the way in which he confirms it echoes Painter's story of the Lady of Thurin (I, 43) from Bandello and Boaistuau.

103.27 Lynx his eyes] See Note 77.9.

104.5s.n. Argus] The mythological figure who is said to have a hundred eyes. Juno set him to watch over Io, who had been turned into a white heifer by Jupiter in order to keep her safe from Juno's jealousy. Mercury with his pipes lulled Argus asleep so that Jupiter might possess Io. In anger, Juno placed the eyes of Argus in her peacock's tail. (Ovid Met. I.588-746.) Thus, Argus is a symbol of watchfulness and of jealousy. See also 229.10.

Cf. Tilley E254: As many eyes as Argus.

104.15-16 the Neapolitan to be the severest revenger of dishonor in the world] The contemporary estimate of the Neapolitan character is summed up by Jerome Turler in The Traveiler (1575): "but if you breake promise, they be very sharp revengers of the injurie done unto them, like as they be very mindfull of a good turne receaved" (sig. N5^r). Cf. Nashe, II,298: "The Neapolitane carrieth the bloodiest mind."

104.20s.n. A Judas kisse] Like a Judas Iscariot in its character, traitorous. From Luke xxii.48: "And Jesus said unto him, Judas, betrayest thou the Sonne of man with a kisse?"

Tilley J92: To give one a Judas kiss. (This example cited.)

104.34-105.1 trueth will have passage] Cf. Tilley T591: Truth will come to light (break out). (This example cited in ODEP.)

105.15s.n. Haire, the ornamentes of Chastytie] Painter explains more fully: "for the ornament of the heare doth not appertaine to an adultresse, nor the vayle or other furniture of the head to an unchast woman. Wherefore she goeth so shaven, in token she hath lost her honestie" (II, p. 99).

105.22 Mazar] A mazer is a bowl or drinking-cup; it may also refer to the head. Whetstone is introducing a pun found neither in Marguerite de Navarre nor in Painter.

108.10-14 if every lyke offence . . . baulde men] Not in Painter, but found in Marguerite de Navarre's version of the tale: "If all, ladies, in like case, drank out of like vessels, I am afraid that many a golden cup would be turned into a death's-head" (tr. A. Machen, New York: Knopf, 1927, p. 217).

108.33ff. MOWNTIBANKES] Itinerant entertainers, usually assisted by a professional clown, the Zanni; they originated in Italy. Coryat, who visited Venice in 1608, writes that "the word Mountebank (being in the Italian tongue Monta'in banco) is compounded of two Italian words, Montare, which signifieth to ascend or goe up to a place, and banco, a bench, because these fellowes doe act their part upon a stage, which is compacted of benches or fourmes." These Venetian mountebanks were orators, musicians, actors, and pedlars, whose wares were often "very counterfeit and false"; they frequently played with living vipers. (Quoted in Winifred Smith, The Commedia Dell'Arte, 1912; rpt. New York: Blom, 1964, pp. 30-34.) Topsell repeats an account of mountebanks in Padua who put on a show with vipers, but he points out that the serpents had been rendered harmless (<u>Serpents</u>, p. 4). K. M. Lea, in <u>Italian Popular Comedy</u>, states that Whetstone's descriptions of Mountebanks and improvising comedians (p. 163 below) "show that he was perfectly acquainted with both kinds of professional entertainers" (pp. 345-47).

109.17-18 <u>common Mountebanckers</u>] The mountebanks encountered by Ismarito are unusual in that they were only entertainers and not hawkers of fraudulent goods. K. M. Lea mentions the mountebank called Scotto who was a juggler in England ca. 1579-80 (<u>Italian Popular Comedy</u>, p. 360).

109.32 <u>Virgils Brasen Flayle</u>] The medieval legend of Virgilius tells how the poet-necromancer shut himself in "a goodly castell" with one gate: "And this castell stode without the cytie of Rome and this enteringe of this gate was made with xxiiii yron flayles, and on every syde was there xii men on eche syde, styll a pece smytynge with the flayles never seasynge, the oon after the other; and no man myght cum in without the flayles stode styll but he was slayne" (<u>Early English Prose Romances</u>, 2nd ed., ed. W. J. Thoms, London: Nattali and Bond, 1858, II, 54-55).

110.7 <u>Phrisio</u>] Phriso is a character in <u>The Courtier</u> who is somewhat sceptical of women's virtues.

110.8 <u>winne the Spurres</u>] Tilley S792: He has won the spurs.

110.14 <u>Unsaverie receytes tourne to holsome effectes</u>] This and the following proverbs are variations on a theme, "There is no ill but may turn to one's good" (Tilley I35).

Tilley P327: Bitter pills may have blessed effects.

110.17-18 <u>Nettles . . . maketh Pottage to comforte the heart</u>] The

Roman nettle was widely cultivated in herb gardens for its supposed medicinal properties (Albertus Magnus, The Book of Secrets, ed. M. R. Best and F. H. Brightman, Oxford: Clarendon Press, 1973, pp. 5-6). See also Note 148.28.

110.18-19 the bloude of the Scorpion cureth the biting of the Viper] Cf. Tilley S153: Those that are stung by the scorpion are healed by the scorpion.

Topsell points out that the "oyle of Scorpions" is effective against the poisons of all "other Serpents and venemous beasts" (Serpents, p. 231), and that the Scorpion and the Viper are enemies, for they die by one another's poison (p. 297). See also 112.2-3.

110.26 runne at ryot] Acts without restraint (Hunting).

111.4 used thys circumstaunce] Beat about the bush.

111.9-10 fairest colours soonest staine, as sweetest flowers are blasted with a breath] Tilley F391: The fairest flowers (freshest colors) soonest fade.

111.11-12 the brightest Sunne threateneth suddaine raine] Cf. Tilley S968: Although the sun shines leave not your cloak at home.

111.13 as everye mortall thing hath his imperfection] C. G. Smith, in Shakespeare's Proverb Lore, cites as a proverb not in Tilley, "Nature has given a defect to every thing created" (pp. 90-91).

111.22 Pluto] God of the underworld, of the classical Hades.

112.2-3 the bloud of a Scorpion, cureth the biting of the Viper] See 110.18-19 and Note.

112.23-24 as the rowling Stone gathereth no Mosse] Tilley S885.

Explanatory Notes   318

112.24-25 want of use canckereth Iron] Tilley I91: Iron not used soon rusts.

112.32-113.2 the Gretians . . . poisoned them selves with venemous Cicuta] "Cicuta" is the Latin word for hemlock or for poison extracted from the hemlock. Cf. The Courtier, p. 207:

> In Massilia there was in times past an usage which is thought came out of Greece, and that was, that openly there was poyson laide up meddled with Cicuta, and it was lawfull for him to take it that alledged to the Senate that he ought to bee rid of his life for some discommoditie that hee felt therein, or els for some other just cause: to the entent that who so had suffered too much adversitie, or tasted over great prosperitie, hee might not continue in the one, or change the other.
> . . . I have red an Oration, wherein an unfortunate husband asketh leave of the Senate to dye, and alledgeth that hee hath a just cause, for that he can not abide the continuall wearysomnesse of hys wifes chatting, and had lieffer drinke of that poyson which you say was laid up openly for these respectes, than of his wives scoldinges.

113.5 Diogenes] Philosopher, c. 400-c. 325 B.C. The famous founder of the Cynic sect, so called for its "doggish" nature. Noted for his satirical dialogues, his caustic wit, and his invectives against luxury, Diogenes became a legendary figure. I have not located a source for this anecdote.

The fourth Daies exercise

114.8-19 Orpheus . . . Euridice] "Orpheus, A Thracian borne, sonne of Oegrus, and Polymnia, or (as some write) of Apollo and Calliope, an auncient poete and harper moste excellent. He (as the poetes surmised) dyd with his musicke delyte wylde beastes and infernall spirites, and moved stones with his sweete harmonie: wherby he recovered his wyfe

Eurydice out of hel" (Cooper). Eurydice is killed at her wedding to Orpheus by a serpent's bite. Orpheus seeks her in the underworld, where he addresses the rulers, Pluto and Proserpine, with his lyre. At the sound of his music, the tortures of the tormented -- of Ixion, Tityos, Tantalus, Sisyphus, and the daughters of Belus -- cease, and Pluto is so moved that he grants Orpheus permission to take Eurydice with him, provided he does not look back until he is out of the valley of Avernus. (Ovid Met. X.1-63.) See also 151.7 and 229.13.

114.13-14 the Gripe forbare to teare upon Titius growing hart] "Tityus, the sonne of the Earthe, whom poetes feigned to be slayne by Apollo, because he wolde have ravished Latona his sister: and therefore lieth in hell, havynge an eagle alway eatynge his lyver. And it is also sayd, that his bodie was in length nyne furlongs: witnesse Tibul, which was a poete, and also a great lover, and therefore coulde not lye" (Cooper). In Homer, Odyssey XI.576ff., vultures tear at his liver, which constantly grows back.

114.14 Tantalus] See Note 48.2-3.

114.15 Danaes Daughters] The Danaides, the fifty daughters of Danaus, follow their father's instructions to kill their husbands on their wedding night, and they are punished in Hades by having to pour water forever into a leaky vessel. One source is Ovid, Heroides XIV.

114.16 Sisiphus] See Note 76.27s.n.

114.29-31 where the tongue hath free passage to talke, the heart is occupyed with no great greefe] Cf. Tilley S664: Small griefs speak, great ones are silent.

114.33-34 occasion entertayned him with no other business] At the moment no other business occupied his thoughts.

115.4-5 the Popes Microcosmos at Latteran] The Lateran refers to the group of buildings that stand on the Monte Celio in Rome, now consisting of a Basilica, a Baptistery, and the Lateran Palace. During the Middle Ages, the Lateran was what the Vatican is today -- the center of the government of the Roman Catholic church. Whetstone's reference is to the Palace, which was largely destroyed in 1360 and rebuilt by 1585.

Montaigne reports that on Jan. 26, 1581 he visited "the Vatican to see the statues enclosed in the niches of the Belvedere and the fine gallery that the Pope is erecting for paintings from all parts of Italy, and which is very near its completion" (pp. 130-31); Trechmann's note suggests that Montaigne is referring to "The Galleria Geografica." Galigani also believes that Whetstone is describing "la Galleria (la loggia della Cosmografia?), dove il papa (Pio IV?) aveva raccolta le mappe del mondo" ("Il Boccaccio nel Cinquecento inglese," p. 56, n.120). See also Harl.M., p. 18.

By "Microcosmos" Whetstone intends to emphasize the cosmological significance of the gallery; as the Encyclopedia of World Art points out, during the Renaissance church buildings were frequently intended to be abbreviated images of the universe (III.840-43).

116.2s.n. King Ptolome] Ptolemy II Philadelphus, 308-246 B.C., Macedonian king of Egypt. See also 169.23 and Note.

116.4 a Pharos] "Pharos, A litle yle in Aegipt against the mouthe of Nilus, by the citie Alexandria. In this yle was set a very hyghe towre, wherin were great lightes all the nyghte longe, for the comforte and suretie of them, which were in voiage, either on the sea or the lande. Wherof all other toures made for suche purpose, are called <u>Phari</u>" (Cooper). Pliny states that "The tower is said to have cost 800 talents" (XXXVI.18). Cf. Gruget's Mexia, pp. 447-48. Guevara claims that it was named for the king's lover, "<u>Pharo Dolovina</u>," and became one of the seven great buildings of the world (sig. L4^r). See also 10.23.

116.5 <u>a Phenix</u>] See Notes 10.23 and 33.9. In some versions of the legend, the Phoenix is renewed by the heat of the sun; in any case, the Phoenix with its golden feathers has an affinity for the sun.

Ismarito's witty use of the phoenix device is echoed in an anecdote related by "Weston" in <u>The Censure of a Loyall Subject</u> (1587):

> You put me in remembraunce of a tale that a Gentleman, a traveler once told me, who being at <u>Rome</u>, when Pope <u>Gregorie</u> ther lived, and finding at the English Colledge, over the armes of England, a Phenix dranw, which the Pope did appropriate unto himselfe: the Gentleman dutifully reverensing her majestie as his soveraigne, and Phenix of the worlde, in scorne of the Pope wrote these verses.
> <u>And reason good the Lion should</u>,
>   <u>the Phoenix stand belowe</u>:
> <u>For though the leaves bewray the tree</u>,
>   <u>the fruit the goodnesse showe</u>.
> Applying in secreat zeale, the construction therto, of this sense. The armes of England to leaves as but the generall badge of her kingdome, and the Phenix he did propriat to the vertues of her majestie, as her excellent beautie, and glorie of the world. And of the contrary parte, the matter was wel taken, I know not by what mistaking. (sig. Cl^v)

116.7 <u>Loegria</u>] Logris, an old name for England, after Locrine, a mythical son of Brutus (E. H. Sugden, <u>A Topographical Dictionary to the Works of Shakespeare and His Fellow Dramatists</u>, Manchester, 1925).

116.7 <u>Cambria</u>] A variant of Cumbria (Celtic Cymru) = Wales (Sugden).

116.8 <u>Albania</u>]   Or Albany. The old name for Scotland (Sugden).

116.11 <u>Euxinus Pontus</u>] The ancient name for the Black Sea (Greek "Euxine"). Hence, Elizabeth's influence reaches not only over Great Britain, but also into much of Europe.

116.13 <u>Pharos Europę, non Africę</u>] The guiding light of Europe, not of Africa. Charlemagne also had been called the lighthouse of Europe, in Angilbert's "Carolus Magnus et Leo Papa."

116.22 <u>Phenix</u>] Queen Elizabeth.

116.26-27 <u>a Royall Princesse</u>] Queen Elizabeth.

116.28 <u>a Marchaunt of Venice</u>] The Venetians were famous as traders, and even in Elizabeth's reign there was a Venice Company. Whetstone's claim that Philoxenus thus acquired a portrait of the Queen is credible: Roy Strong, in <u>The English Icon</u> (London: Paul Mellon Foundation, 1969, p. 157), states that such a portrait, dated c. 1580, was "found rolled up in the attic of the Palazzo Reale, Siena, in 1895."

116.29 <u>the Westerne Islands</u>] England and Ireland.

116.33 <u>a goodly Gentleman</u>] Gaspard II de Coligny, seigneur de Chatillon, 1519-1572, Admiral of France. After 1560 he aroused the enmity of the Guise family by demanding religious toleration. His conversion to Protestantism made him the admired leader of the Huguenots. "Although attracted to the Calvinist philosophy, he saw the reformed religion as a system for the maintenance of order, discipline, and justice" (<u>New Encyclopaedia Britannica</u>). In August 1570, he negotiated the Peace of Saint-Germain favourable to the Huguenots. He returned to court in 1571 and grew in favor with Charles IX to the point that his influence over the King threatened Catherine de'Medici: she pressured the King into ordering the massacre of Protestants on St. Bartholomew's Day, 1572, in which Coligny was slaughtered.

Philoxenus was probably at the French court at a time when Coligny's career was at its height (see 18.24-25 and Note). Coligny's portrait is placed next to Queen Elizabeth's as a tribute to the Admiral's championship of the Protestant cause.

When Whetstone discusses the Guise massacre in The English Myrror (sigs. F8^v-G1^r), he refers to both Queen Elizabeth and the Prince of Orange.

116.33 Crowned with a Scepter] Signification not clear. Possibly, "bearing a staff of office." The scepter was not necessarily a symbol of royal authority: the Marshals and the Chancellors of France used batons and maces respectively as heraldic devices. However, there is no example in OED of the use of "Crowned" to mean "bearing." Another possibility is that "Crowned" refers not to Coligny but to his portrait, which might be surmounted with a baton or batons as heraldic supporters within an ornamental frame.

If the phrase were emended to insert a comma after "Crowned" difficulties of literal interpretation disappear. But why would Coligny wear a crown? Perhaps a ducal coronet, which was worn by the Marshals of France? (John Woodward and George Burnett, Woodward's A Treatise on Heraldry, British and Foreign, Rutland, Vt.: Tuttle, 1969, p. 624.)

117.2-3 his Armes, who bare Gu, an Eagle displaied Crowned Ar] On a red ("gules") background, a spread eagle (an eagle with unfolded wings) coloured silver ("argent") and crowned. Whetstone misplaces the "Ar" (argent), which must refer to the eagle, since he provides no other colour for the main heraldic figure, rather than to the crown, which would normally be gold ("Or").

"Gules, an eagle displayed argent, crowned or" are the arms of the French family of Coligny, of the Kingdom of Poland, and of the imperial city of Frankfurt (John Woodward and George Burnett, <u>Woodward's</u> <u>A</u> <u>Treatise</u> <u>on</u> <u>Heraldry,</u> <u>British</u> <u>and</u> <u>Foreign</u>, Rutland, Vt.: Tuttle, 1969, pp. 254-55, 257). A sketch of Coligny's coat of arms may be found in the <u>Grand Larousse Encyclopedique</u>.

Izard (p. 124) mistakenly identifies the coat of arms as belonging to the House of Anjou and hence to Henry III of France. In fact, Henry was entitled to these arms when he was elected King of Poland in 1573 (he abandoned the Polish throne to become King of France in 1574), but we know from a Renaissance account that when he wore the Polish coat of arms, they were incorrectly blazoned:

> Lorsque Henri III fit son entrée à Paris comme roi de Pologne, on connaissait si peu ses armes nouvelles, que Favyn, dans son Théâtre d'honneur, publié en 1620, dit: "Les peintres ignorans, à la vue de hérauts plus ignorans qu'iceulx blasonnèrent les armes de Pologne d'argent et de sable, au lieu qu'elles sont de gueules a l'aigle d'argent. (Lorédan Larchey, <u>Ancien armorial équestre de la Toison d'or et de l'Europe au 15e siècle</u>, Paris: Berger-Levrault, 1890, p. 242.)

117.5 <u>a young Prince</u>] Hercule-François (Francis), 1554-84, Duc d'Alençon, became Duc d'Anjou in 1574 when his brother Henry became King Henry III of France. In August 1578 he was named by the States General "Defender of the Liberties of the Netherlands," and his importance to the Dutch cause increased as he became the suitor of Queen Elizabeth. In September

1580 William of Orange formed an alliance with Anjou, and in the same year the States General were persuaded by William to grant Anjou the title of <u>landheer</u>, "lord of the country," making him the titular hereditary sovereign. Anjou was in the Netherlands in 1578-79 and again in 1582 at William's urging. In November 1581 Anjou arrived in England, hoping to settle the proposed marriage alliance with Elizabeth. When the Queen gave him a ring and a kiss, rumours of their betrothal flew throughout Europe: on November 28, 1581, William of Orange publicly announced the betrothal in Ghent, rejoicing at a match that would join the two allies he most needed, and displayed an allegorical picture on the subject. Anjou left England in February 1582 with no definite commitment from the Queen, took up his new position in the Netherlands as sovereign in place of Philip of Spain, and died in 1584.

For a discussion of these "wooing matters" (Walsingham's phrase), and Hatton's part in them, see Paul Johnson, <u>Elizabeth</u> <u>I</u>; <u>a</u> <u>Study</u> <u>in</u> <u>Power</u> <u>and</u> <u>Intellect</u>, pp. 249ff.

117.10 <u>Hercules Franciscus valesius</u>] Latinized form of "Hercule-François Valois."

117.11 <u>an other counterfeit</u>] That of William I, Prince of Orange, 1533-1584, known as William the Silent, who devoted his life to the liberation of the Netherlands. In 1559, while governor in the Low Countries under Philip II of Spain, he became sympathetic to the Protestants and was converted to Lutheranism. During the popular rising in 1572, he hoped for French support from Coligny, but the St. Bartholomew's Day Massacre destroyed Huguenot influence at the French court, until the Duc d'Anjou emerged as a possible leader in 1578. William's fourth marriage, in 1583, was to Louise de Coligny, daughter of the murdered Huguenot leader. In March 1582 he survived an assassination attempt in Antwerp, but he was fatally shot by a fanatical Catholic on July 10, 1584.

117.12-13 his Posie was, Je le meintiendray] "I will support (uphold) it." The motto of the House of Nassau-Orange is variously cited as "Je maintiendrai," "Je le maintiendrai," or "Je maintiendray Nassau."

In 1580, William of Orange was outlawed by King Philip of Spain. The Apologie of Prince William of Orange against the Proclamation of the King of Spaine (ed. H. Wansink, Leiden: Brill, 1969) was written in December 1580 and first published in Delft in 1581; it ran to sixteen editions in the sixteenth century and was widely translated. By appending the words "je le maintiendrai" to his impassioned plea for freedom and sacrifice, William pledges himself to uphold all that is decided upon for the good of his people.

> The pedestrian English 'I will maintain' does not give the effective meaning of the ancient French, 'Je maintiendray'. It is more than to maintain, it is to uphold, for the word carries in it the sense of mutual obligation, of the oath given by the laying of the overlord's hand on that of the vassal, and of the vassal's within that of his protector. This was the proclamation of William's plighted word to his people: he was sworn, handfasted, to the Netherlands. Indeed -- to the Netherlands; for up to this time the device had been, like all ancient feudal devices, not general but particular to the family of its bearer. The words on his coat of arms were 'Je Maintiendray Nassau'. To omit his family and thereby to endow the narrow phrase with wide significance was a touch of genius. (C. V. Wedgewood, William the Silent, p. 254.)

The motto occurs in the original French text, but not in the English edition of 1581: Whetstone may have read the French version when he was on the continent. He refers to the Apologie in a side note in The English Myrror (sig. D1^r).

Explanatory Notes   327

118.3-4 his mornings sorrowe had beene but a sleepe] Cf. Tilley S662: When sorrow is asleep wake it not. (Earliest example 1595.)

118.9 Phebus] Simply, the sun.

118.28-29 of voluntarie devise] Ingeniously designed to appear as though it were growing naturally, wild. (See OED, voluntary, 11 -- but earliest example cited is 1620.)

119.24 Eunick] See Note 25.4.

119.27-120.12 Care, Care . . . hop for joye] No source found.

119.30 by thee greene yeares with hoarie heares are grownd] Cf. Tilley C82: Care brings grey hair.

120.15 it passed for currant] It was generally accepted. (OED, current, 8. Earliest example cited 1596.)

120.17s.n. One square breaketh no custome] One variation does not upset a custom. OED provides no authority for this usage of "square": the closest approximation is in the sense of "dissension." But compare "To break square": "to interrupt or violate the regular order; commonly in the proverbial phrase, it breaks no square, i.e. does no harm, makes no mischief, does not matter" (OED, break, v.,46).

120.25-26 Fryer Inganno] From Italian "inganno" = deceit, fraud, cheat. "The Deceiver."

120.27ff. The adventure of Fryer Inganno . . .] The motifs of this novella are found in Boccaccio, Decameron IV.2 and VIII.4, two tales which are narrated expressly in order to illustrate the hypocrisy of the religious orders. In the first (IV.2) Brother Alberto pretends to be the Angel

Gabriel in order to seduce Lisetta, and as a punishment he has to endure the torments of flies and hornets until he is rescued by his brother friars. Whetstone's Farina, however, is not as vain and feather-brained as Lisetta, and she is allowed to keep her chastity by means of a bed-trick. Such a substitution occurs in another tale from Boccaccio (VIII.4) in which a rector, who loves a virtuous widow, is tricked by her into going to bed with an ugly scullery maid and is there discovered by the bishop. Whetstone's adaptation of Boccaccio is discussed by Galigani, "Il Boccaccio nel Cinquecento inglese"; and Cecioni, "Un adattamento."

Another version of Decameron IV.2 in English is the tale of "Fryer Onyon" in Tarletons Newes out of Purgatorie (1590).

120.29-30 Appenine Mountaynes] The Apennines (Italian, "Appennino"), mountain range in central Italy.

120.30-31 Sainct Fraunces] Francis of Assisi, c. 1181-1226, founder of the Franciscan order. His body is buried in the church of S. Giorgio in Assisi, where he first preached and where he died. "Many miracles are recorded to have taken place at his tomb" (The Catholic Encyclopedia).

120.32 Farina] "Easily moulded"? From Italian "farina" = flour, meal. The name of a zanni in the commedia dell'arte, an "allusion to the 'lazzo' of flouring the face," occurring in Italy as early as 1585 (Lea, Italian Popular Comedy, pp. 488-89).

121.11s.n. It is said, S. Frances . . .] According to the legend of "The Indulgence of the Portiuncula," St. Francis was assailed by a sudden temptation while he was sitting in his cell in midwinter; he rushed into a garden in an attempt to vanquish his desire and threw himself on brambles which then turned into red and white roses (E. G. Salter, Franciscan Legends in Italian Art, London: Dent, 1905, pp. 112-13).

121.26-28 Blessed art thou . . . countrey-wemen] Galigani ("Il Boccaccio nel Cinquecento inglese," p. 56) points out that this deliberate parody of the Anunciation is not found in Boccaccio.

121.34 his meagre Cripple Image] Whetstone's reference to contemporary images of St. Francis appears to be accurate. George Kaftal states that St. Francis was "Represented in the XIIIth cent. with an emaciated, oblong face, sparce fair hair and a short beard." He was thus depicted in order to suggest his asceticism. (Iconography of the Saints in Central and South Italian Schools of Painting, Florence: Sansoni, 1965, p. 471.)

122.14s.n. Ignoraunce heareth every tale as trueth] Cf. Tilley F456: A fool believes everything.

123.1 Leayda] Italian "laido" = ugly, repellent, filthy, foul.

123.6 without light or leave] Perhaps a deliberate echo of the proverb "Leave is light" (Tilley L170).

123.9 Salve Saincte Francisce] Hail Saint Francis.

123.10-11 Sancte Francisce, ora pro nobis] Saint Francis, pray for us.

123.15 A dolori inferni, libera me Domine] From the pains of hell, deliver me O Lord.

123.23-24 learing lyke the Theefe, that honge on the left side of Christe] Luke xxiii.33: "there thei crucified him, and the evil doers: one at the right hand, and the other at the left." Also xxiii.39-43 and

Mark xv.27,32. Matthew xxvii,38,44 speaks of one of the thieves who cast jeers in Christ's teeth.

124.14-15 the faultes, whiche the Worlde seeeth not, GOD punnisheth not] Cf. Tilley S472: A sin unseen is half pardoned. Guicciardini, The Garden of Pleasure, attributes a version of the proverb to "Boccace" (sig. H3^v).

124.27-28 their evyls are written in their foreheades] Tilley F120: Everyone's faults are (are not) written in their foreheads. (Earliest example in ODEP is 1609.)

125.10ff. The rare Historie of Promos and Cassandra . . .] A prose summary, with minor changes, of Whetstone's play, Promos and Cassandra (1578). For a discussion of the sources of the story and their relation to Shakespeare's Measure for Measure, see especially Geoffrey Bullough, ed., Narrative and Dramatic Sources of Shakespeare (London: Routledge, 1958), II,399-417. Whetstone possibly knew Claude Rouillet's Philanira (1556) and Giraldi Cintio's Ecatommiti VIII.5 (1565), but it appears unlikely that he also knew Cintio's play Epitia (written c. 1573 but not published until 1583). Both Bullough and Izard suggest that it is coincidence that both Whetstone and Cintio (in his Epitia but no in his novella) substitute a felon to be executed in place of Andrugio.

125.14s.n. in a Commedie] Promos and Cassandra (1578), a source for Shakespeare's Measure for Measure (1604). Reprinted in Geoffrey Bullough, ed., Narrative and Dramatic Sources of Shakespeare (London: Routledge, 1958), II,442-513. Prouty, "George Whetstone and the Sources of Measure for Measure" (pp. 131-45), suggests that the play, which is superior to other works of its day, may have been too racy and not sufficiently rhetorical for the taste of the Inns of Court or of the Court itself.

125.12 Corvinus] Matthias I, Corvinus, 1443-1490. Painter, in his tale of A Lady of Bohemia (II.28) describes him thus: "Mathie Corvine, sometime king of Hungarie, aboute the yeare of oure Lorde 1458, was a valiaunt man of Warre, and of goodly personage. Hee was the first that was Famous, or feared of the Turks, of any Prynce that governed that kingdome. And amongs other his vertues, so well in Armes and Letters, as in Lyberallyty and Curtesie he excelled al the Pryncens that raygned in his time" (II, p. 196). Prouty ("George Whetstone and the Sources of Measure for Measure) points out that Corvinus was generally thought of as an administrator of justice.

125.13 Bohemia] Former kingdom in Central Europe, part of Holy Roman Empire. In Promos and Cassandra, Whetstone makes Corvinus king of Bohemia and Hungary. According to Prouty, Corvinus was in fact king of Austria and Bohemia by conquest (pp. 137-38).

125.17 Julio] Prouty identifies this city as Jula, Gyula, or Jula in Eastern Hungary (pp. 138-39).

126.18-19 Soveraigne Justice, is crowned with Laurell, although shee bee gyrt with a Sword] Justice is sometimes represented in art with a sword in one hand and a pair of balances in the other. The laurel, sacred to Apollo, is a symbol of victory and eternity; but the context suggests that the laurel symbolizes mercy.

128.8-9 to leave circumstaunces] To cease beating about the bush.

130.16-17 to judge her yeelding a constrainte] To judge her yielding to be by constraint.

131.6 Hyliogabalus] The Roman emperor Heliogabalus. "He so muche exceeded in detestable leachery and promoting of vyle persones, and rybaldes, that fynally he was hated of all men, and at last slaine and drawen through the city of Rome, and thrown into the ryver of Tyber" (Cooper). Harper's Dictionary of Classical Literature and Antiquities (New York, 1962) refers the reader to Dio Cassius for "the disgusting details." See also Note 20.22.

131.7 Denis of Sicyll] "Denis" is a frequent Renaissance rendering of Dionysius. "It is also the name of twoo kynges of Sicilie, which for their crueltie and avarice were called tyrannes . . . Of both these ye may reade in Plutarke in the life of Dion" (Cooper). Dionysius the Elder, B.C. c. 430-367, tyrant of Syracuse, was especially known for his brutal military despotism.

131.10 Priapus] God of fertility; hence, a figure of lust, whose symbol was the phallus. Mentioned in Ovid Met. IX. Cooper speaks of him with restraint: "Priapus, An ydole, unto whom the paynyms committed theyr gardeynes to keepe. Also a citie of Hellespont."

131.24 Marcus Crassus] Probably Marcus Licinius Crassus (Dives), who shared the consulship with Pompey and Caesar in 55 B.C. Cooper identifies him as "the rychest pryvate person of the Romaines." I have not been able to find Whetstone's source for this statement, but he refers to both Crassus and Marius in EM, sigs. A6^v and N2^v; and CLS, sig. D4^r. Plutarch's

Life of Crassus, III.2 merely states that Crassus cultivated the art of oratory.

131.24 Marius] Marius Gaius, 157-86 B.C., Roman general and seven times consul. Cooper: "Marius, a valiaunt man . . . . He was afterwarde in a civille battayle, overcomme by Sylla in 88 B.C., and in the flyght hyding himselfe among the flagges in a ditch, was drawen out and cast in pryson. At whiche tyme, when a stoute and sterne Frencheman was sent into the pryson to cut of his head, with the majestie of his countenaunce he did so feare hym, that he could not doe it, but rather holpe hym to scape out of pryson." Whetstone repeats the story in EM, sig. N2^V. William Smith (Dictionary of Greek and Roman Biography and Mythology, London: Walton-Murray, 1869) mentions that to the barbarian "the eyes of Marius seemed to dart out fire, and from the darkness a terrible voice shouted out, 'Man, dost thou dare to murder C. Marius?'" See Plutarch's Life of Caius Marius, XXXIX.

132.7 Prometheus] Prometheus had to endure eternal punishment for stealing fire from the gods to give to man. Cooper: "Prometheus, The sonne of Japetus, firste invented makynge of ymages: wherfore the paynyms supposed that he made men, and feigned that he wente up into heaven, and there dyd steale fire to make his ymage have lyfe, wherewith Jupiter beyng wroth, caused him to be bounden on the hill called Caucasus, and an Eagle standing by him eatynge his herte: by the whiche is signified, that he was studious, and a great astronomer." In some versions, Prometheus is first chained to a rock in Tartarus.

132.8-9 such a one as hath had experience . . . of hell] Cf. EM, sig. M1^r: "There is an old saying, Orpheus can describe hell better than Aristotle, . . . and truly in knowledge is assurance, and in report may be error."

133.9-10 chast Lucretias destiny] Two Renaissance versions of this story are Painter I.2, "The Rape of Lucrece," and Shakespeare's poem of the same name. The ultimate source is Livy, but it recurs frequently in classical literature.

The wife of Tarquinius Collatinus, Lucretia was ravished by her husband's kinsman, Sextus Tarquinius; he forced her to submit by threatening to kill her and to lay beside her the body of a murdered slave to show that she had been slain in adultery. After reporting the rape to her father and to her husband, Lucretia stabbed herself to death (for her body had sinned although her mind was pure). Thus, Lucretia is "a singuler paterne of chastitie, both to hir tyme, and to all ages folowinge" (Cooper). See also 138.34.

133.23-24 Byrdes of a feather, would flie together] Tilley B393: Birds of a feather will flock together.

134.7 the River of Stix] The Styx is the principal river, one of nine rivers, of the underworld in Homer and Virgil. It is also a river in Arcadia whose waters were believed to be poisonous. The epithet "loathed" is commonly applied to it. See also 195.31-32.

134.19-20 Hoc facias alteri, quod tibi vis fieri] "Whatsoever ye wolde that men shulde do to you, even so do ye to them" (Matthew vii.12). Tilley D395: Do as you would be done to.

Whetstone cites the Latin version also in RR, sig. K3^r.

134.22-24 if men durst bark as Dogges, manie a Judge in the world would be bewrayed for a thiefe] Cf. Tilley D526: All dogs bark not at him.

A117: All are not thieves that dogs bark at.

135.26s.n. Sive bonum, sive malum, Fama est] "Whether a good thing, or a bad thing, it is fame." The Latin form occurs also at the end of "Cressids complaint," RR, sig. B3^v.

135.27 Pegasus] The winged horse who carries the thunderbolt of Zeus, and is a symbol of immortality. "Fame is almost equivalent to Pegasus and bears some of his attributes. Bocc. says, 'Ego hunc equum famam rerum gestarum arbitror!'" (Lotspeich, Classical Mythology in the Poetry of Edmund Spenser, p. 93.)

138.15ff. The Question that arose . . .] This discussion of the virtues of women is indebted to Castiglione, Book III, pp. 195ff. See Izard pp. 93-97.

In a similar passage in The English Myrror (sig. I4^v), Whetstone cites his source as Guicciardini's Commentaries, Book III.

138.28 Semiramis and her Husbande Ninus] Ninus, a great warrior, is the mythical founder of the Assyrian empire. After his death, his fame was eclipsed by that of his wife Semiramis, who took upon herself the government of the empire, who fought as a man in war, and who built Babylon. The classical source is Diodorus Siculus, II.4-20, but it is retold frequently in the Renaissance (see, for example, Gruget's Mexia, p. 99).

138.29 the Amazon women and Alexender] In mythology, the Amazons are a nation of female warriors in the region of the Black Sea. There is a legend of a meeting of Alexander the Great with an Amazon queen.

138.30-32 Loadice . . . Mithridates her Husband] Mithridates VI, Eupator Dionysus, King of Pontus, 1st century B.C. Cooper: "A puissaunt kyng of Pontus in Asia, of great strengthe both of bodie and mynde, and of singular memory . . . . This man was first overcomme by Sylla, after overthrowen and discomfited by Lucullus, and lastly utterly vanquished by Pompey, and dryven to ende his life with poyson. He is noted of great crueltie: for he killed his wyfe, hir mother, brother, and sister, three yonge sonnes, and as many daughters." Laodice was his sister and also his wife. During his absence, believing a report of his death, she took many lovers; on his return she attempted his life by poison, but he discovered her plans and put her to death.

Cf. Castiglione, p. 206: "Know you not that Mithridates wife and sisters shewed a farre lesse feare of death, than Mithridates himselfe? And Asdruballes wife, than Asdrubal himselfe?"

138.32 Asdruballes Wife, then Asdrubal himselfe] Hasdrubal, Carthaginian general, 3rd century B.C. During the siege of Carthage, he surrendered to Scipio who exhibited him as a suppliant before the deserters holed up in the temple. Rather than yield, they chose to die by setting the temple on fire. "His wife, when the fire was kindling, displayed herself on the walls of the building in the richest attire she could procure, and, having upbraided her husband for his cowardice, slew her two sons, and threw herself, with them, into the burning pile." (Harper's Dictionary of Classical Literature and Antiquities, New York, 1962.)

138.34 Lucretia] See Note 133.9-10.

139.6 <u>Sibels</u>] The Sibyls were originally women prophets or priests of Apollo, of which the most famous is the Cumaean Sibyl (so called after the shrine at Cumae) who delivers the prophecy in Virgil's <u>Eclogue</u> IV and who speaks to Aeneas (<u>Aeneid</u> VI). They were said to have foretold the incarnation of Christ. See Gruget's Mexia, p. 449.

139.21-22 <u>Women receive perfection by men, and men imperfection by Women</u>] Cf. Castiglione, pp. 199-200: "And I remember that I have heard (when it was) that a great Philosopher in certaine Problemes of his, saith: . . . For that in this act, the woman receiveth of the man perfection, and the man of the woman imperfection."

139.23s.n. <u>Aristotles probleames</u>] The <u>Problemata</u>, a compilation, chiefly on natural history, by Aristotle and other writers. The side note in the original text of <u>The Courtier</u> (sig. $2C_4^v$) incorrectly gives the source as Aristotle's <u>Physics</u> I.18. Beauregard suggests the <u>Problemata</u> XXIX, 951a. However, the answer seems to lie in Pettie's <u>Petite Pallace</u>, which attributes a similar saying to Aristotle (pp. 64, 234, 263), a saying which has been traced by Hartman (p. 284, note) to the 1501 edition of the <u>Problemata Aristotelis</u>, IV.10. See also 141.12.

139.33 <u>Sybels</u>] See 139.6 and Note.

140.5-7 <u>As shee that had her Tongue cut . . . the signe of the Gallowse</u>] This is possibly a reference to the Philomela myth. Philomela is "King Pandions daughter of Athens, whom Tereus kyng of Thrace, that had maried hir sister Progne, did ravysh, and that she might not disclose his vilanie, cut out her tongue, and cast hir in pryson. But she beinge very cunnynge in woorkyng and imbrodering, did in such sorte set out the whole matter

in a garment, that any man might understande it, and sent the same by
a servaunt to hir sister Progne, Tereus his wyfe . . . she with speade
escaped from him, and, as poetes feigne, was tourned into a swalowe,
and he into a lapwynge, Philomela into a nightingall" (Cooper). See
Ovid Met. VI.433-674; and Pettie, A Petite Pallace, 2, "Tereus and Progne."
"Theefe" and "Gallows" are to be interpreted metaphorically to refer to
evil-doing in general.

Cf. Castiglione, p. 206: "Then Phrisio, where obstinacie is bent,
no doubt (quoth he) but otherwhile ye shall find some women that will
never chaunge purpose, as she that could no longer call her husband prick-
louse, with her handes made him a signe."

140.8s.n. the trembling passage of death] Castiglione, p. 207: "in
a woman such knowledge and steadinesse in the trembling passage of death"
(but not in reference to Epicaria). The same phrase occurs at EM, sig.
B2^r.

140.8-11 Epicarias . . . Nero . . .] Epicharis was implicated in
a conspiracy against Nero in A.D. 65. Even under torture, she refused
to name any of the conspirators, but strangled herself with her girdle.
This anecdote and that of Leaena occur in Castiglione, p. 206: "Obstinacie
that is bent to a vertuous ende, ought to bee called stedfastnesse, as
in Epicaria a libertine of Rome, which made privie to a great conspiracie
againste Nero, was of such stedfastnesse, that being rent with all the
most cruel torments that could be invented, never uttered any of the
partners."

140.13-16 Leena . . . Hippias . . .] Hippias, tyrant of Athens, 527-510

Explanatory Notes 339

B.C., is constantly confused with his younger brother Hipparchus. "Leaena, A common woman of Athens, who (after Harmodius and Aristogiton hadde slayne Hipparchus the tyranne) beynge tourmented in sundry facions, to the intente she shoulde discover the confederates of that murder, spake not one word, but bytynge in sunder her tounge, she spitte it in the face of Hippias the tyranne, who caused hir to be tourmented" (Cooper). Since Cooper supplies all the details of Aurelia's anecdote, Izard's contention that Whetstone's source must be Castiglione's Courtier is inconclusive.

Cf. Castiglione, p. 206: "What say you of this other, called Leona? In whose honour the Athenians dedicated before the Castle gate, a Lionesse of mettall without a tongue, to betoken in her the steadie vertue of silence. For she being in like sorte made privie to a conspiracie against Tirants, was not agast at the death of two great men her friendes, and for all she was torne with infinite and most cruel torments, never disclosed any of the conspiratours."

The story is found in Pliny and in Plutarch De Garrulitate ("Concerning Talkativeness"), Moralia 505.

140.14s.n. PLIN. lib. 34. Cap. 2.] Pliny, Natural History, Book XXXIV, Chapter 2. But Pliny does not state that Leaena bit out her tongue.

140.19-22 the Athenians . . . her silence] The Athenians honoured Leaena by setting up, in the vestibule of the Acropolis, a bronze statue of a lioness (λέαινα) without a tongue. Pliny does not specify a statue, but Castiglione mentions a "Lionesse of metall."

141.12 the Philosophers Probleames] See Note 139.23s.n.

141.19-20 it is not the quantity, but the quallity that commends]

ODEP: Quality, without quantity, is little thought of. (Earliest example 1604 is similar to Whetstone's version.)

141.20-22 <u>a little Salte, relisheth more then a great deale of Sugar</u>] Cf. Tilley S75: Better eat salt with philosophers of Greece than sugar with courtesans (courtiers) of Italy.

141.22-23 <u>Judeth</u> . . . <u>Cilisions</u>] In the apocryphal Book of Judith, Nebuchadnezzar, ruler of Assyria, subdues Cilicia and other western nations, then assigns his commander-in-chief Holophernes the task of taking vengeance against the rebels. When Holophernes attacks Israelite territory, Judith, an Israelite widow, uses her beauty to gain access to him when he is alone and thus to slay him. Donatello's statue of Judith and Holophernes was displayed in Florence as "A warning to tyrants and a symbol of liberty." "Judeth" and "Nabuchodonosor" are the spellings of the Geneva Bible.

141.25-142.1 <u>Alexandra, the wife of Alexander, King of the Jewes</u> . . .] Alexander Jannaeus, king of the Jews (103-76 B.C.), apparently butchered his own subjects. The source is Castiglione, pp. 205-6:

> Alexandra, which was wife to Alexander king of the Jewes, who after the death of her husband, seeing the people in an uproare, and alreadie runne to weapon to slea the two children which he had left behinde him, for a revenge of the cruel and straight bondage that their father had alwaies kept them in, she so behaved her selfe, that sodainly she aswaged that just furie . . . . she perceiving her children in so great a jeopardie, immediatly caused Alexanders bodie to be cast out into the middest of the market place, afterwarde calling unto her the Citizens, she saide, that she knew their mindes were set on fire with most furie against her husband . . . and therefore shoulde take that bodie of his and give it to be devoured of dogs, and rent it in peeces in the cruellest manner they coulde imagine. But she desired them to take pittie upon the innocent children . . . .
> Of such force were these words, that the raging fury once conceived in all that peoples mindes, was sodenly aswaged, and turned into so tender an affection, that not onely with one

accord, they chose those children for their heades and
rulers, but also to the deade corps they gave a most
honourable buriall.

142.1-4 By what instrument . . . by a Woman] In traditional explications of the Christian story, as man fell through a woman (Eve first tasted the forbidden fruit) so would he be saved through a woman (the Virgin Mary). Mentioned in Castiglione, pp. 202-3.

142.14-15 to nip himself by the nose] Cf. Tilley N237: To pull oneself by the nose.

142.15-17 his Captaine Saint George] Since the thirteenth century, St. George had been patron saint of England, model of knighthood, protector of women. His cult spread during the crusades to make him patron saint of warriors and travellers. The Order of the Garter, an order of knighthood founded by Edward III (c. 1347), adopted him as its patron.

142.19-20 Saint Michael to his Mounte] Michael the Archangel, leader of the heavenly armies in battle, is supposed to have appeared in France in the eighth century -- on the site of Mont Saint-Michel in Brittany. The greatest French order of knighthood, founded by Louis XI in 1469, was the Order of Saint-Michel, limited to thirty-six Chevaliers. Under Charles IX, however, the numbers increased until by 1578 the order was in sufficiently low esteem to be known as "Le Collier a toutes betes."

142.26ff. But where you say Vertue is the Feminine . . .] Cf. 228.12-15.

142.29-34 The old Divines . . .] Cf. Castiglione, p. 199: "And for so muche as one kinde alone betokeneth an imperfection, the Divines of olde time referre both the one and the other to God: Wherefore Orpheus saide that Jupiter was both male and female: And it is read in scripture that God fashioned male and female to his likenesse. And the Poets many times speaking of the Gods, meddle the kindes together."

142.31 <u>Orpheus</u>] The Thracian singer, Orpheus is said to be the founder of Orphism, a religious movement of the 6th and 7th centuries B.C. that reached into the Renaissance through Plato. Poems attributed to Orpheus are the basis for the cult.

The fift Daies Exercise

144.17 <u>Ixion</u>] Cooper: "<u>Ixion</u>, A kyng of Thessalie, who falsely brake promyse with his wives father, and threw him into a pitte of fyre. He also called by Jupiter unto a feaste, styrred Juno to committe adultrie, whiche Jupiter perceivyng, made a cloude like unto Juno, and delivered hir to him, on whom he begatte the people called <u>Centauri</u>. But whan he had avaunted, that he had companied with Juno: he was driven downe into hel, and there bounde to a wheele alwaies tournynge and full of serpentes, as poetes feygne." See also Note 61.29-30. Ixion is mentioned in Ovid <u>Met</u>. X.1 as one of those suffering in Hades, but details of the myth are not given there.

The explication of myths appears to have been a Renaissance social game (cf. 182.9ff.). Soranso's interpretation of the picture of Ixion is the most usual one: Ixion is being punished for his ambition. Ismarito's analysis is more subtle, for he attempts to integrate details from the whole myth, pointing out that Jupiter had invited Ixion to the table of the gods (after purifying him for the murder of his father-in-law). Cf. Wotton, <u>Courtlie Controversie</u> (sig. 2H4^r), where Ixion is an emblem of vanity; and Plutarch's Life of Agis I, where he represents love of glory.

145.19-20 I wyll onely . . . say what I have reade] The following "sermon" (145.22-147.33) by Ismarito is adapted from Antoine du Verdier, Les Diverse Leçons . . . suivans celles de Pierre Messie (1577). For the relevant passages see Izard's Appendix, pp. 263-65.

145.29 dignities] Faculties. No relevant definition in the OED, but Whetstone is appropriating the word from the French "dignitez" in his source, Du Verdier's Mexia (see note above).

146.11-17 And sure the monuments . . . . like Angels] "Monuments" = records (i.e., noble deeds, wise sayings, famous writings, etc.). The monuments by which Alexander, etc. are remembered to this day were the products of the actions of their souls, for it is the nature of the soul to try to make men shine like angels.

146.12 Alexander] Alexander the Great, 356-323 B.C., known as the greatest general of antiquity. See also 168.29 and 218.18.

146.12-13 Julius Cesar] Julius Caesar, 100-44 B.C., the great military leader. See also 75.13 and 218.19.

146.13 Scipio] Probably Scipio Africanus Major, 236-184/3 B.C., Roman general who defeated Hannibal and extended Roman rule in the Mediterranean. Scipio was "The surname of divers noble Romaynes, of the whiche foure were moste excellent, as well in martiall prowesse, as in other moste notable vertues" (Cooper).

146.13 Haniball] Hannibal, 247-183/2 B.C., Carthaginian general, "Adjudged by common consent one of the world's greatest soldiers" (Oxford

Classical Dictionary). See also 218.20.

146.14 Plato] "The prynce of all philosophers (in wysedom, knowledge, vertue, and eloquence, farre exceedyng all other Gentyles)" (Cooper). Whetstone attributes sayings to him at 36.5; 85.13; 158.34; and 206.21.

146.14 Pithagoras] Pythagoras, c. 531 B.C. "A man of excellent witte . . . . He was in sharpenesse of wit passyng al other, and found the subtile conclusions and misteries of arithmetike, musike, and geometrie. Plato wondreth at his wisedome" (Cooper). Pythagoras taught the immortality of the soul and the doctrine of metempsychosis. See Ovid Met. XV.

146.14 Socrates] The Athenian philosopher, 469-399 B.C. See 184.24-25 and Note.

146.14 Solon] Athenian statesman and poet, 6th century B.C.: "he was a man of excellent witte, and called one of the seven wyse men of Greece" (Cooper). Plutarch, in the Life of Solon, states that his chief delight was moral philosophy.

146.31 Microcosmos] A common Renaissance notion: man is a microcosm or "little world" in relation to the universe. Not in Du Verdier's Mexia, Whetstone's source. Cf. MMC, sig. C3^r.

148.24 Eunuck] See Note 25.4.

148.27-149.12 Who prickels feares . . . my Mistresse in my breast] No source found for this poem.

148.28 shall to a Nettle smell] Shall smell a nettle (OED, smell, v., 6) -- and shall thus get stung. Cf. Tilley N134: It is better to be stung by a nettle than pricked by a rose. See also Note 110.17-18.

148.29 through fainte heart, who dooth a Ladie lose] Tilley H302: Faint heart ne'er won fair lady.

148.30 to leade Apes in Hell] Tilley M37: Old maids lead apes in hell.

But the subject of Whetstone's proverb is a man -- an effeminate man.

149.3 Icarus] The son of Daedalus, the craftsman who built the Labyrinth and who was then exiled on Crete. Icarus, "having winges, with his father flew out of the yle of Crete: but whan he flewe hygher than his father commaunded: the waxe, wherewith the feathers of his wynges were glewed, melted with the heate of the sunne. And the feathers fallinge of, Icarus was constraigned to fall into the sea, afterward called Mare Icarium" (Cooper). Daedalus warns his son that he must follow a course midway between earth and heaven lest he soak or scorch the feathers, but Icarus heedlessly attempts to fly to heaven and comes too near the sun. Hence, he is a symbol of foolish aspiration. See Ovid Met. VIII.170ff.

149.4 as fyre and Froste may meete] The poet's wings are so fastened that they might withstand extremes, the extreme passions and torments of love. See Note 9.9, and 73.9.

151.1-6 whightstreaked Carnation Giliflower, was the Metamorphos of a Faire Gentlewoman . . .] No source found for this story.

151.7 Orpheus] As Whetstone's side note indicates, the story of Orpheus and his wife Eurydice is told in Ovid Met. X.1-63. Orpheus loses

Eurydice for the second time because he does not keep the one taboo imposed upon him by Pluto, not to look back at his wife as they leave Hades:

>   when Orphye   did begin
> To dowt him lest shee followed not, and through an eager love
> Desyrous for to see her he his eyes did backward move.
>
> Shee dying now the second tyme complaynd of Orphye naught.
> For why what had shee to complayne, onlesse it were of love
> Which made her husband backe agen his eyes uppon her move?
>   (Ovid Met. X.58-60, 64-66; trans. Arthur Golding, 1567.)

See also 114.8ff. and Note; and 229.13.

151.10 smyling out a scoffe] Smiling in a scoffing manner. No such idiom in OED.

152.11-12 Quo quid difficilius, eo pulchrius] "The more difficult something is, the more admirable it is." A version of Tilley T201. See 191.31-32 and Note.

153.3-4 Ovid saith] In his Ars Amatoria ("The Art of Loving") I.345: "And, grant they or deny, yet are they pleased to have been asked" (Loeb translation). See also I.269-70.

153.4-5 there is no woman, but wil indure the demaund] Cf. Tilley W681: All women may be won.

153.8-9 love spareth no degree] Tilley L505: Love has no respect of persons.

153.11-12 King Cofetua, the Affrican, became enamoured of a Beggar] Cophetua, a king in Africa, is the subject of a ballad in Thomas Percy's Reliques of Ancient English Poetry:

> He cared not for women-kinde,
>   But did them all disdaine.
> But, marke, what hapned on a day,
> As he out of his window lay,

>   He saw a beggar all in gray,
>   The which did cause his paine.
>
> The king marries the beggar maid Penelophon:
>
>   And thus they led a quiet life
>   During their princely raigne;
>   And in a tombe were buried both,
>   As writers sheweth plaine.
>   (ed. H. B. Wheatley, London: Sonnenschein,
>   1889, I, 189-94.)

Cf. Shakespeare, L.L.L. IV.i.65-66; and Romeo II.i.54.

153.12-13 faire Venus, espoused yll favoured Vulcan] Aphrodite (Venus) occasionally appears in Greek myths as the wife of Hephaestus (Vulcan), the god of fire and of the smithy, who is ugly and lame (Homer, Odyssey VIII.266ff.). Whetstone tells the story of Venus, Vulcan, and Mars in The Rocke of Regard (sig. F7^{r-v}).

153.13 Pigmalion doted upon an Image] Pygmalion, a legendary king of Cyprus who fell in love with an ivory statue of a woman. Venus grants his prayer and brings the statue to life. (Ovid Met. X.243ff.; and Pettie, A Petite Pallace, 11.)

153.13-14 Narcissus was drowned in imbrasing his owne shadow] Narcissus was a beautiful youth who scorned all lovers. For rejecting the love of the nymph Echo, Nemesis finally punishes him by making him fall in love with his own reflection in the water: he pines away and is turned into the flower of that name. (Ovid Met. III.346ff.) Much less frequently, he is said to have drowned in the well or pool. (See R. K. Root, Classical Mythology in Shakespeare, p. 88.)

153.15-16 mightie Jove . . . to dallie with simple country trulles] Most of Jupiter's loves were in fact daughters of kings or of minor gods:

a list in Ovid Met. VI.103-14 mentions Asterie, Leda, Antiope, Alcmena, Danae, Aegina, Mnemosyne, and Dio's daughter. But of comparatively lower rank are Callisto, an Arcadian nymph; and Io, the daughter of Inachus the river god.

154.25-30 The Cardinal of Aragon . . . the Duchesse of Malfy . . .] The source is Painter II.23, from Bandello I.26 and Belleforest 19. Because the Duchess of Malfi secretly marries her steward Antonio Bologna, thus dishonouring her house, she and her family are butchered by her two brothers, Ferdinand and the Cardinal of Aragon. Painter points to the moral: "You see the miserable discourse of a Princesse love, that was not very wyse, and of a Gentleman that had forgotten his estate, which ought to serve for a lookinge Glasse to them which bee over hardy in makinge Enterprises, and does not measure their Ability wyth the greatnesse of their Attemptes" (III, p. 3).

155.14-15 crosse her over the thumbes] Tilley T274: To hit over the thumbs. (That is, to reprove sharply, to "rap her knuckles.")

155.30-31 to keepe his Chimney from being fyred] Proverbial in style, but not in Tilley or ODEP. An obvious double entendre.

156.9-10 for the wise to over rule him for a Woodcocke] Tilley W748: To play the woodcock. (Whetstone's is the first example cited in ODEP.) The woodcock, an easily snared bird, is synonymous with a fool, a simpleton.

156.14-15 taking pepper in the nose] Tilley P231. See also 190.3

156.20 the opinion of sundrie Philosophers] No source found for these generalizations.

Explanatory Notes 349

156.22-23 Fortune . . . is blinde] Tilley F604: Fortune is blind.

158.34 as Plato sayeth] No source found. Cf. 36.5; 85.13; 146.14; and 206.21.

159.27s.n. Kytte wyll to kynde] Tilley C135: Cat (Kit) after kind.

160.18 Kyng Astolphus] A possible reference to Ariosto, Orlando Furioso XXVIII.1-75: "Tale of mine Host with Rodomonts invective against women." Astolfo, "whilom king of Lombardy," and a knight share the bed-favors of Fiametta, "the daughter of an Inkeeper in Spaine"; even while lying between the king and the knight, she deceives them by taking a Tapster to bed (Harington's translation, 1591). See Note 161.17.

160.19 three halpenie Juell] Cf. ODEP: Not worth three halfpence.

160.24-25 fell to her kinde] Descended to her true nature.

160.27-161.10 Bianca Maria . . .] This story appears in Painter, II.24, "The Countess of Celant," from Bandello I.4 and Belleforest 20; and in Fenton's Certaine Tragicall Discourses, 7. Whetstone follows Painter's version, even retaining his characters' names, changing only the location (Painter's Pavie becomes Padua).

160.28 Baetta] Whetstone is probably recalling Baia, a town in Southern Italy.

160.29s.n. The Rocke of Regarde] Whetstone's first published work, The Rocke of Regard (1576) is a collection of stories in verse and prose. "The Disordered life of Bianca Maria, countesse of Celaunt" appears in the first part, entitled "The Castle of Delight," in the form of a complaint in rhyme royal (sig. Al^{r}ff.).

161.1 <u>the Counte of Zelande</u>] Painter's Count of Celant.

161.11-14 <u>Andrea Zeno</u> . . . <u>a Cookes Daughter</u> . . .] I have not been able to add to Koeppel's comment that he is in the dark for the source of this reference (<u>Studien</u>, p. 36, note 2).

161.16-17 <u>Ovid Metamorphosis in Latine</u>] Ovid's <u>Metamorphoses</u> was widely read in the Renaissance not only as a storehouse of mythology for poets and painters, but also as a treasury of moral wisdom. The extent of Whetstone's debt to Ovid is indicated throughout the Explanatory Notes. Although the translation by Arthur Golding (published in 1567) was available to Whetstone, I find no specific evidence suggesting that he used the English rather than the Latin version. Thus, the list of books here probably reflects Whetstone's own reading.

161.17 <u>Segnior Lodovicus Regester, in Italian</u>] Possibly a reference to the Italian poet Lodovico Ariosto (1474-1533), called "Divino Lodovico," whose popular and influential romantic epic, <u>Orlando Furioso</u>, published in 1516 and expanded in 1532, reflects the same spirit of play and feeling of nostalgia that permeates the courtesy literature of the time. But why the puzzling "Regester?" Izard accepts as probable Koeppel's conjecture that the "Regester" refers to Cantos XXVIII and XLIII of <u>Orlando Furioso</u> (Koeppel, <u>Studien</u>, p. 37) and mentions a suggestion by R. S. Loomis that "Regester" may be a printer's corruption of "Ariosto" (Izard, p. 106). See Note 160.18.

"Segnior Lodovico" might also refer to Lodovico Guicciardini, whose <u>Commentaries</u>, Book III, is cited by Whetstone as the source for anecdotes of virtuous women in <u>The English Myrror</u> (sigs. I3^r and I4^v); or Lodovico

Dolce, author of <u>Amorosi ragionamenti</u> (1546).

161.18 <u>Amadis de Gaule, in French</u>] An Arthurian romance of Portuguese origin (14th century), the <u>Amadis de Gaula</u> is first known in a Spanish version of 1508. Read as a manual of chivalry and courtesy, it went through thirty editions between 1508 and 1587 and was especially popular in France. Whetstone undoubtedly had in mind the French translation by Nicholas de Herberay, Seigneur des Essarts (1540-48), which was widely read by the Elizabethans. Selections from <u>Amadis</u> were adapted by Thomas Paynell as <u>The Treasurie of Amadis of Fraunce</u> (1567), and Books I and II were translated by Anthony Munday (1589, 1592). The romance had many imitations in England after 1580. It was read "as a courtesy book, a guide to proper behavior and polite manners of knights and ladies in peace and war, and a compendium of speeches, challenges, letters, and rhetorical flourishes for different occasions. Finally it was read as a wonderful treasury of stories, exciting and varied, which ran the gamut from tragedy to farce" (J. J. O'Connor, <u>Amadis de Gaule and Its Influence on Elizabethan Literature</u>, p. 23).

161.18-19 <u>the Pallace of pleasure, in English</u>] William Painter's <u>The Palace of Pleasure</u> (1566-67) is a collection of tales from classical, Italian, and French sources. It introduced the novella into English and became a sourcebook for other writers, especially for dramatists. The <u>Heptameron</u> is indebted to Painter for the story of Felice and Malipiero in The Third Day's Exercise (92.28ff.) and for the story of Bianca Maria (160.27ff.).

161.27-29 <u>chaste Epethia, the welbeloved wife of Hanno Prince of Carthage</u> . . .] Guevara, <u>The Diall of Princes</u>, mentions "Annibal" among the rulers ruined by women (sig. 2C6^v), states that his love for "a yong mayden in the City of Capua" proved a bitter love to him (2D2^r), and links his name with the woman "Tamira" (★★5^r). Cf. Lyly, p. 327; and Munday's Zelauto, III.4. Possibly from Valerius Maximus IX.1.

161.29-31 The vertuous Virginia, espoused to Sextillius . . .] Reference uncertain. Perhaps "Virginea, the daughter of Aureus Virgineus, the Consul Plebeian, the which was forbidden to do sacrifice, for that she was none of the Senatours wives but a Plebeian, as much to saie as a craftes woman, and no gentilmans daughter borne." Her vertue and devotion won her the respect of the Roman patricians, who made her a noblewoman and honoured her after her death with a statue in the Capitol. (Guevara, The Diall of Princes, sig. E2^v, attributed to Livy I.5,10). Whetstone may have confused Guevara's "foundresse" with "laundresse."

162.4 One or two Swallowes, prooves not Summer] Tilley S1025: One swallow makes not summer.

162.14-15 to ron upon the pikes] To rush to destruction. (OED, pike, sb^5, 2b.)

163.16 Eunuke] See Note 25.4.

163.27-32 Comedians of Ravenna . . .] Whetstone appears to be describing a troupe of players of the commedia dell'arte which originated in Italy in the sixteenth century. The production of the commedia dell'arte were based on scenarios that sketched out the action, but the details and the dialogue were improvised and were adapted to each audience. The language was often rhetorical and witty and would appeal to a writer of prose fiction and courtesy books. Companies of commedia dell'arte players were touring

Italy as early as the 1560's. Their plays were introduced at the English court in the 1570's, and one was played at Kenilworth before the Queen in 1575, but in the sixteenth century such performances were not common in England. (New Encyclopedia Britannica; K. M. Lea, Italian Popular Comedy, especially pp. 342-58.) Cf. Montaigne, pp. 103, 118, 240.

164.2ff. certaine Questions . . .] The proposing of philosophical riddles was both a popular Renaissance social pastime and a frequent feature of dialogue literature. Examples are Plutarch Septum Sapientium Convivium "The Dinner of the Seven Wise Men" (Moralia, 153-54); Guevara, The Diall of Princes, sigs. $E5^v-E6^r$, $I3^v$; and Guicciardini, The Garden of Pleasure, sig. $B3^r$. See also pp. 48 and 79.

164.14 the Sirens Songes] That have the power to enchant and charm the hearers. See also 19.29.

164.16 the Crocadiles Teares] See Note 90.21-22.

164.33-34 A Dycer . . . for he teareth God in peeces] Whetstone never passes up an opportunity to attack dicing: such attacks occur frequently in the "Ortchard of repentance" section of The Rocke of Regard, in the epistles in A Mirour for Magestrates of Cyties, and throughout A Touchstone for the Time. See especially the long poem, "Whetstons Invective against Dice":

> The devill is in the rome . . .
> Who chiefely in this hellish house,
> Doth God in peeces teare.   (RR, sig. $N3^r$)

Cf. Chaucer, The Pardoner's Tale, lines 629ff.

165.13-14 to hang the Lyp] To look vexed. (OED, lip, 2.)

166.30-31 everie vertue is commended by his contrarie] Cf. Tilley

C630: Contraries being set the one against the other appear more evident.

Thomas Wilson, The Arte of Rhetorique (1553), points out that this is a saying "in Logique" (sig. S1^r).

166.32 Blacke best setteth foorth White] Tilley B435. (This example cited.)

The syxt Dayes Exercise

168.11 the Mother of confusion] Whetstone is echoing the form of the proverb "Night is the mother of counsel" (Tilley N174). In Wotton's Courtlie Controversie, "the night, mother of confusion" separates two equally matched armies, the two sexes (sig. M1^r). Cf. 198.18.

168.21-22 Peter Mesiere his Cronicle of Memorable things] Pedro Mexia or Mejia (?1499-1551), Spanish humanist and historian who succeeded Antonio de Guevara as chronicler to Charles V. His Silva de varia lección (1541), a compilation of anecdotes and essays on a variety of topics, enjoyed seventeen editions before 1600 and was read throughout Europe. It was translated into English in 1571 by Thomas Fortescue as The Foreste; but Izard shows that Whetstone is indebted to two French versions, Claude Gruget's Les Diverses Leçons de Pierre Messie (1554) and Antoine du Verdier's Les Diverses Leçons (1577). Gruget's book is described on the title page of the 1557 edition as "contenant variables histoires et choses memorables." (Izard, pp. 98-99, 264-77.) Whetstone acknowledges his debt to Mexia in CLS, sig. B3^r, and EM, sig. C2^v; EM also has repeated references to "Ant. Verd."

See also 169.5; and Introduction, p. lxxxvii.

Explanatory Notes   355

168.23-32 Tamberlaine the Great . . .] Timur, Tamberlaine, or Tamerlane, 1336-1405, Turkish conqueror whose life gave rise to many legends; Mexia describes him as a Scythian shepherd who rose to wear the Persian crown and whose empire was divided after his death by the rivalries of his sons (Gruget's Mexia, p. 261). Tamberlaine is described in Chapter 12 of The English Myrror as "a poore labourer, or in the best degree a meane souldiour" (sig. E8^r), and as "a poore shepheard" (sig. Fl^r); the source is given as "Baptista Fulgosius in his collection Campinus florentin, in his history of the Turkes" (sig. E8^r).

168.24 Flagellum Dei] The scourge of God.

168.29 Alexander] Alexander the Great. Mentioned also at 146.12 and 218.18.

168.33-34 Bon giorno] Italian "buon giorno" = good morning, good day.

169.1-2 to geve his solytarinesse, a disgrace] To reproach his solitariness.

169.5 Mesires Cronicles] See 168.21-22.

169.12 Mutius Seavola] Probably Gaius Mucius Scaevola, a legendary Roman. Cooper: "Mutii, were men of a noble familie of the auncient Romains, in the whiche one was called Mutius Scaevola: who at the tyme that Porsena kynge of Tuscanes, layed siege to Rome, came in a beggers apparayle into the campe of Porsena, and intending to have slayne the kyng, slew his secretary. Wherfore he was taken and brought to a great fyre to be burned, into the whyche he wyllyngly thruste his hande that had fayled to slea the kyng, and suffered it to be burned to ashes, affyrmynge that besydes him, there were three hundred that had vowed to make lyke attemptate. Wherewith the kynge beynge abasshed, and fearing their invincible courage, made peace with the Romaynes, takynge pledges of them: and reysyng his siege, departed, without molestyng of them ever after." Whetstone may be referring to Plutarch's statement that Scaevola behaved most nobly and courteously, revealing "out of gratitude what he would not have disclosed under compulsion" (<u>Life of Publicola</u> XVII.4). The story is the basis of Painter I.3. See also <u>HRS</u>, sig. E2^{r-v}; and <u>MMC</u>, sig. D1^r.

169.21-22 <u>the famous Lybrarie of Cosmos de Medicis in Florence</u>] Cosimo, or Cosmo, de Medici, 1389-1464, Florentine merchant prince, banker, and statesman. Interested in the new learning, he patronized many humanists, including Marsilio Ficino, and his palace became the center of literary society in Florence. Three separate libraries were formed by him: the library at the newly rebuilt convent of San Marco, which, endowed with a nucleus of about four hundred books and manuscripts, was the first great public library in Europe; his personal library, which became the foundation of the Laurentian Library; and the library at the Abbey of Fiesole. Although the Marcian Library would have been the most accessible to Whetstone, his note suggests that he is referring to the Medicean Library, the Duke's own collection.

169.23 <u>Ptolomey, surnamed Philodelphus</u>] Cooper: "This Philadelphus was a man of great learnynge, disciple to the philosopher Strato, and built the notable lybrarie of Alexandria, furnished with all maner of woorkes, whiche, to the great losse of learnynge, was burned in the first warre that the Romains had with Alexandria." His library, attached to the Museum, was built in the 3rd century B.C., and aimed at housing copies of the entire body of Greek literature; according to Primaudaye, he "purposely caused seventie and two of the most learned and religious men of Judea to come and translate the holie Bible out of Hebrew into Greek" (The French Academie, sig. G5^r). The tradition apparently originates with Josephus (the Church Father).

See also 116.2s.n. and Note.

171.1 Vegetius] Flavius Vegetius Renatus, Roman author of Epitoma Rei Militaris in four books (c. 400 A.D.), the only surviving ancient account of the Roman military system. His work was available to Whetstone in Caxton's The Book of Fayttes of Armes and Chyvalrye (1489) and in John Sadler's The Foure Bookes of Flavius Vegetius Renatus (1572). "The real importance of Vegetius' work lies perhaps not so much in the mass of information which he gives us about the Roman army . . . as in the very considerable influence which he had upon the military thinking of the Middle Ages and Renaissance" (Oxford Classical Dictionary).

171.4-5 Togatus, as a Romayne Oratour] Latin "togatus" = gowned; wearing the toga as a Roman citizen. Since the toga was obligatory dress on official occasions, it would be worn by orators.

171.5 Paliatus, as a Gretian Phylosopher] Latin "palliatus" = clad in a "pallium," a Greek cloak; that is, clad as a Greek (as opposed to "togatus," clad as a Roman).

171.9 Commentaries] Whetstone undoubtedly had in mind Julius Caesar's memoirs, the Commentaries on the Gallic War and on the Civil War.

171.13 Plutarches Moralles] The Moralia is a collection of short essays on a variety of topics, primarily on moral philosophy. Whetstone's works frequently reveal his indebtedness to the Moralia: for instance, the outline of his story of Phrigius and Pieria (pp. 215ff.) is derived from Plutarch's essay on "The Bravery of Women" (Moralia 253-54). Although Philemon Holland's Morals did not appear until 1603, Amyot's French translation (1572) was read throughout Europe, and selected essays were published in English (for example, James Sanford's Amorous and Tragicall Tales, 1567). But of course, Whetstone (and Philoxenus) would have read Plutarch in Latin. Cf. 87.19-20.

See Introduction, p. lxiii.

171.13-14 Guevaraes Dial of Princes] Antonio De Guevara, c. 1481-1545, Spanish writer, preacher, and official chronicler to Charles V, visited England in 1522. His Libro áureo de Marco Aurelio (1528), claiming to be a collection of the life and letters of Marcus Aurelius, was translated by Lord Berners as The Golden Boke of Marcus Aurelius (1534). A fuller version, the Rélox de principes (1529) was translated by Sir Thomas North as The Diall of Princes (1557). Whetstone's form of the title suggests that he was familiar with North's version. See Introduction, p. lxxxviii.

171.14-15 The Courtier of Count Baldazar, Castillio] Conte Baldassare Castiglione, 1478-1529, diplomat and writer, entered the service of Duke Guidobaldo at Urbino in 1504. In 1506 he visited England to receive the Order of the Garter from Henry VII on Guidobaldo's behalf. In 1528 he published Il libro del cortegiano ("The Book of the Courtier"), usually called Il cortegiano, which is set at the court of Urbino; it quickly became one of the most significant books of the Renaissance. Sir Thomas Hoby's translation (1561) is entitled The Courtyer of Count Baldessar Castilio. See Introduction, p. lii.

171.30 greedy of newes] An interpretation of the meaning of "Philoxenus." See Note 4.19. Cf. Nashe, The Unfortunate Traveller (Works, II, 298).

172.12-13 Count Baldezar] "In his own life Castiglione approached the ideal of the perfect courtier described in his Il libro del cortegiano" (Italian Renaissance Encyclopedia). See Note 171.14-15.

172.28 coram nobis] "In our presence," or "Before the court."

173.3-4 tooke him up so short] Reprimanded him so severely. Cf. OED, short, 5b; and take, 90o.
Tilley M400. (Whetstone's is the first example cited.)

173.5 where you may help, hurt not] See PC, sig. L2^r.

173.13s.n. A scoffer is many times smiten with his owne weapon] Tilley W204: To beat one at his own weapon. (Earliest example in ODEP is 1591.) Guicciardini, The Garden of Pleasure: "That scoffing many tymes lighteth upon the scoffers head (sig. C5^v).
Cf. 48.23, and 229.30.

173.13-15 There would bee . . . robbinge of Headges] If proverbial, I am unable to locate other examples. "Robbinge of Headges" is stealing linen from the hedge where it was left to dry. Cf. I Hen.IV,IV.ii.46.

174.5-6 expounde dreames by contraries] Tilley D588: Dreams go by contraries.

174.17 Palmestrie] Ascham, in The Scholemaster, refers to the interest in palmistry at court, condemning it as an excuse for "fond and filthy talk" (p. 44).

175.2 Eunuke] See Note 25.4.

175.4-19 Regarde my love . . . dies your friende] No source found for this poem.

175.5 the least] The last; that is, "my frostie haires."

177.1-2 The Lyon in his greatest hunger, hurts not the wounded sheepe] Tilley L316: The lion spares the suppliant.
Pliny VIII.19; Topsell, p. 467. Cf. HRS, sig. C4^v.

177.2-4 the Crocadile with teares wassheth the blood from a murthred man] Tilley C831. Whetstone here gives the opposite interpretation to crocodile tears. See 90.21-22 and Note; and 164.16.

177.11 nice, in occasion of suspition] Careful to avoid occasion for suspicion.

177.19 By Sainct Anne] Anna, the Mother of Mary, one of the most popular saints; Anne and Joachim were models of conjugal life.

177.29-33 the House, whose grounde worke is rotten . . .] Tilley F619: Be sure to build on a good foundation.

178.34-179.5 Oulde Wine . . . Fume and Smoake] Cf. Tilley W740: Old wood best to burn, old wine to drink, old friends to trust, and old authors to read.

179.15-16 Gray Haires are nourished, with greene thoughts] Not in Tilley. Cited in ODEP, but no other examples given.

180.2-3 a leg of a Larke, was better then the whole Carkasse of a Kyte] Tilley L186: A leg of a lark is better than the body of a kite. (This example cited.)

180.3-4 woulde none God thank him] Would have none of it, God thank him (for the offer).

180.13 Caves of Tartessus] See 44.8 and Note.

180.31 Acteon] See Note 33.21. Actaeon is depicted in art as sprouting antlers. To be horned is to be cuckolded.

181.5-6 the imbracements of a faire Woman, hastneth an olde man to his Grave] Tilley M348: An old man in love hugs death. (This example cited.) See also 181.25-26.

181.25-27 An olde man amourous . . . health and reputation] See 181.5-6 and Note.

182.1-4 a Beast fourmed like a Unicorne . . .] Since the first description by Ctesias in the 5th century B.C., the unicorn has been confused with the rhinoceros. The Hebrew Re'em was translated in some Biblical texts as "monoceros" or "unicorn," and in others as "rhinoceros." In some early accounts, the unicorn is mild and gentle; in others it is strong and fierce. By the sixteenth century, however, the rhinoceros was generally distinguished from the unicorn, and Edward Topsell is able to provide a realistic picture of the rhinoceros in his Historie of Foure-Footed Beastes (1607), p. 595. Like Topsell, Whetstone is careful to note how the rhinoceros differs from the unicorn (its horn is in its nose), then he goes on to link the unicorn-maiden legend with his "Rhinocerot" (a variant spelling also in Topsell). The third-century Physiologus popularized the belief that the swift and shy unicorn could be trapped only by a fair maid: "A virgin girl is led to where he lurks, and there she is sent of by herself into the wood. He soon leaps into her lap when he sees her, and embraces her, and hence he gets caught" (<u>The Bestiary</u>, p. 21). This story was often illustrated in medieval and Renaissance art; in fact, the Palazzo Farnese (which Ismarito compares to the palace of Segnior Philoxenus, p. 18) has a fresco by Domenichino entitled "Woman with a Unicorn," in which a ferocious unicorn rests its forequarters in the lap of a woman (<u>Encyclopedia of World Art</u>, III, pl. 392). Topsell states that the rhinoceros "is taken by the same meanes that the <u>Unicorne</u> is taken," and falls asleep in the virgin's lap (p. 597).

See Odell Shepard, <u>The Lore of the Unicorn</u> (London: Allen & Unwin, 1930).

182.9ff. <u>The Metamorphose of Rinautus</u> . . .] Narrating stories to explain pictures was an oft-practised Renaissance social and literary pastime; for example, in Greene's <u>Morando</u>, a picture of Europa and the Bull sparks a debate (sig. B2^v). Cf. 144.17ff. As the response of Ismarito's audience suggests (at 183.15-16) -- they are delighted with his witty device -- Whetstone has undoubtedly invented this myth. He combines the unicorn-virgin tale with the legend of Circe; he may also have in mind the tale of Severe who was metamorphosed by Diana into a unicorn as punishment for loving a nymph (Luca Pulci, <u>Driadeo</u> IV.56ff.).

182.11 <u>Rinautus</u>] I have found no source for this story (see note above).

182.13-14 <u>Iland Circeiun</u> . . . <u>the Continent</u>] Circeii, town and isolated promontory on the Italian coast south of Rome, popularly believed to be the abode of Circe. In Homer, Circe dwells on an island, and Cooper calls "Circius" an island.

182.15 Circes] The sources of the Circe legend are Homer, Odyssey X.210ff; Virgil, Aeneid VII.10-20; and Ovid Met. XIV.254ff. In Homer, the goddess Circe lives on an island and exercises her magic to turn Odysseus's men into swine; Odysseus is able to resist her spells with the aid of Hermes and the herb "moly," but he lives with her for a year before resuming his wanderings. The Renaissance, preoccupied with the theme of metamorphosis, was fascinated by Circe. She became the prototype of the witch, the enchantress, and she was generally identified with sexual temptation. The pattern for the moralistic interpretation of the myth, in which man becomes a beast when he allows himself to be governed by passion rather than by reason, was established by Plutarch's dialogue, Bruta Animalia Ratione uti, sive Gryllus ("Beasts are Rational"), Moralia, 985-92. (Whetstone's Rinautus, however, is metamorphosed because he refuses to submit to Circe's passion.) A version of Plutarch's dialogue was published by Giovanni Battista Gelli in 1549 as La Circe; Henry Iden's English translation, Circes, appeared in 1557. Boethius's Consolation of Philosophy (IV.3) devotes a poem to Circe. For a discussion of the Circe myth, see Robert Adams' edition of Gelli, The Circe out of Italian by Mr. Thomas Brown (Ithaca, N. Y.: Cornell Univ. Press, 1963).

Italy was frequently referred to as Circe's court, for it was supposed to transform plain Englishmen into subtle Italians, enchanting them by means of licentious pleasure and the enticements of sin. Cf. Ascham, The Scholemaster, pp. 61-65.

In Greenes Mourning Garment, the "house of great ryot" at which reside the three sisters like Circes, is identified by "the signe of the Unicorne" (sig. D3^v).

Explanatory Notes   364

182.27 Cupid] As the god who forces people to fall in love.

183.1 King Nabucadonizer, in the fourme of an Oxe] Nebuchadnezzar, or Nabuchodonosor, the great king who rebuilt Babylon. "He by the occasion of his great and wonderful dominions, fell into suche pryde, that he woulde have his image honoured for God. Wherfore almighty God, sodeinly transfourmed him into an horrible monster, having the head of an oxe, the feete of a beare, the tayle of a lyon, and did eate hey as a beast" (Cooper). The root text is Daniel iv.30, where Nebuchadnezzar is not actually turned into a beast, but suffers from delusions. In the artistic tradition he is depcited as an animal; in Chaucer he believes himself to be an ox; and in Gower he is metamorphosed into an ox. Whetstone most closely echoes Gower's version in which Nebuchadnezzar suffers because his body is bestial while his mind remains human (Confessio Amantis I.2772-3042). See Penelope Doob, Nebuchadnezzar's Children (New Haven: Yale Univ. Press, 1974), especially Chapter 2.

183.23-24 Robin hoodes penniworthes] Something sold at a robber's price, far below its real value.

Tilley R149. (This example cited in ODEP.)

184.12s.n. No Affliction, but hath his remedie] Tilley G189: God has provided a remedy for every disease.

R70: There is a remedy for everything could men find it.

184.16-17 Ovid and all the amorous Poets] Ovid, as author of the Amores, the Heroides, the Ars Amatoria, and the Remedia Amoris, is pre-eminently the poet of love in the Middle Ages and the Renaissance: Chaucer calls him "Venus clerk" (Hous of Fame, 1. 1487). The other love poets would be Catullus, Gallus, Tibullus, and Propertius.

184.20-21 There is no sore, but hath his salve] Tilley S84: There is a salve for every sore. (This example cited.)

184.24-25 Socrates altred his inclination, by the Studie of Phylosophie] Perhaps a reference to the tradition that in his youth Socrates lived unworthily, even licentiously (Diogenes Laertius, II.20, comp.19). Or is Whetstone referring to the story ascribed to Socrates in Plato's Phaedo (96B), that he first studied natural philosophy before giving himself to the study of moral philosophy and the pursuit of virtue? Cf. TT, sig. I4^r: "Socrates alterd his natural inclination of insolencie by philosophie." See also 146.14.

184.25-26 The Nynivites preserved their Cittie by prayer] Ninevah, a town in ancient Assyria, was to be overthrown in forty days, but its people fasted and prayed until God repented his harsh judgement (Jonah 3).

184.27-28 Virbius dubled his life, by mastering of his disposission] "Virbius, Twyse a man: which name was geven to Hippolytus, the sonne of Theseus, after that Aesculapius hadde brought him agayne to lyfe" (Cooper). Diana arranged to have him resurrected (Ovid Met. XV.545-46). I am not certain why Whetstone says that Virbius mastered his disposition, unless it is a reference to his being a follower of Diana, goddess of chastity.

184.29-185.1 Floradin . . . Persida . . . Pericles . . .] No source found for this allusion.

185.4 Saturne and Venus] Referring both to the planets, which are not in harmony in astrological terms, and to the deities, who represent Old Age and Love.

185.7 <u>Mercurie</u>] Mercury, the Roman equivalent of Hermes, is associated with oratory and with cunning, especially with skill in the use of words. Cooper: "<u>Mercurius</u>, The sonne of Jupiter by Maia, whome poetes faign to have wynges on his head and feete, to signifie, that talke (whiche is represented by the person of Mercurie) dooeth quickely passe through the ayer. He is feigned to be messenger of the Gods, because that by speeche and woordes all thynges are declared. He was coumpted God of eloquence, merchaundyce, feates of activitie, and thefte also."

187.4-5 <u>setteth an edge of her tongue</u>] Makes her speech keener. (<u>OED</u>, edge, sb. 2.)

189.7-8 <u>A prava muliere</u>] "From a perverse (or wicked) woman."

189.11 <u>Iris</u>] Cooper: "The rayne bow." Cf. 10.8 and Note.

189.16-17 <u>soothe his trespasse with an honest shoe</u>] Smooth over the injury with the simulation of honesty (vertue, uprightness). "shoe" = show.

189.20-21 <u>Drinke wil make the Dropsie dry</u>] Tilley M211: Like a man in a dropsy, the more he drinks the more he may.

See also 70.30; 94.22-33; 99.11.

189.25 <u>the shee Devill weareth the hornes</u>] An impossibility. Cf. Tilley D25: The Devil is known by his horns. (Earliest example c. 1592, from Marlowe's <u>Faustus</u>, I.ivA.57: "I'll tell you how you shall know them; all he-devils has horns, and all she-devils has clifts and cloven feet.")

189.30-31 <u>to throwe the house out at the window</u>] To wreak havoc. Tilley H785.

Explanatory Notes   367

190.3 taketh pepper in the nose] Takes offence, becomes angry. Tilley P231.

See also 156.14-15.

190.21-22 pleasure is best seasoned with paine] Cf. Tilley P415: Pleasure is not pleasant unless it cost dear. (Earliest example 1590.)

Tilley P420: There is no pleasure without pain.

190.31 You will kill her with kindnesse] Tilley K51: To kill with kindness.

191.18-22 as Seneca sayeth . . .] Cf. Primaudaye, The French Academie: "Plato also writeth, that it is better for a man not to live at all, then to live wickedly, or in ignorance" (sig. F1^r). And Claude Desainliens (Hollyband), The French School-Master (1573; Menston, Eng.: Scolar Press, 1972): "You know well that it is better to be unborne, then untaught" (p. 90).

I have not been able to determine the classical source.

191.31-32 things that are dearely bought, are of us intirely belooved] Tilley T201: Things hardly attained are highly deemed. (ODEP cites this example for the proverb "Things that are hard to come by are much set by.") Cf. 152.11-12.

192.7-9 how can the Hen succour her Chickens . . .] Francis Meres, Palladis Tamia (1598): "As a Hen doth gather her chickens under her winges, doth defend them against the kite . . ." (sig. D2^r).

192.24 necessitie breake the boundes of nature] Tilley N76: Necessity has no law.

192.26 the custome of Spaine] No source found.

193.2-6 as Ovid devineth . . .] No source found for this quatrain, but the idea is expressed in his Tristia, II.207ff.; and III.73-74.

194.5ff. Laertius lawes . . .] Diogenes Laertius, 3rd Century A.D., author of a book on the lives and doctrines of the ancient philosophers. No source found for this statement.

195.14s.n. It is no striving against the streame] Tilley S927: It is in vain to strive against the stream.

195.32-33 the ryver Stix] The Styx, principal river in Hades. See also 134.7 and Note.

196.2-3 though errour carryed you to Hell gates] Cf. Tilley E179: To err is human, to repent is divine, to persevere is diabolical.

196.5-6 thinges when they are at the worst, begin again to amend] Tilley T216: When things are at the worst they will mend. (Whetstone's is the first recorded example.)

196.8 to deathes doore] Tilley D162: To be at Death's door.

196.19-20 the greefe knowen, the remedye is easie] Tilley D358: A disease known is half cured. (Earliest example 1614.)

The. vii. Dayes Exercise

198.11-13 Aurora . . . Tithon] See Note 44.6-7.

198.18 envying the confusion of night] Disliking the disorderly commotion of the night. Cf. 168.11.

198.32 Janus, God of Time] "The word properly means a gate or barbican
. . . . But to enter house or city one must pass through the gate or the
door; hence Janus tended to become a god of beginnings . . . the first
month of the reformed calendar, Januarius, is his and his festival comes
in it" (Oxford Classical Dictionary). See also 200.21.

198.33-199.4 in the likenes of a Serpent . . .] The ouroboros is
traditionally associated with eternity and time, and with Saturn (Cartari,
sigs. C3^r and D2^r); Janus is god of the year and of Time. Thus, Cartari
links the two: "The Phenicians, as Marcus Tullius and Macrobius report,
understood by Janus, the world: and therefore framed his Image in the
forme of a serpent, holding her taile in her mouth, continually turning
round and circumfered: as that the world doth nourish and feed it selfe,
and the times thereof depending and cohering one of another" (sig. D4^v).

199.8 superstitious Ceremonies] See 18.27-30 and Note.

199.19ff. This order the Italians use . . .] "When the civil year
was initiated in January of the year 135 B.C., the customs associated
with the new year began to be celebrated on this new date. Among these
the most common was the exchanging of gifts given as augurs . . . . These
gifts originally consisted od dried fruit and honey; later silver coins
were given by liegemen to their patrons and by subjects to the emperor.
With the onset of Christianity this custom of giving gifts on New Year's
Day (or on the Epiphany) still persists" (Enciclopedia Italiana, "Capodanno").

Writers in England took advantage of this custom to present new works
to their patrons; for instance, Asham speaks of The Scholemaster as a

"little treatise for a new-year's gift" (p. 15). The Heptameron may have been so intended.

199.30 the Capitole] The Capitoline, one of the Seven Hills of Rome, seat of the Roman government. More specifically, the temple of Jupiter.

199.31 Caesar Augustus] Title given to Roman emperors. Perhaps Whetstone specifically has in mind Augustus Caesar, 63 B.C.-A.D. 14, first Roman emperor.

199.32 so many Countryes, so many customes] Tilley C711: (This example cited.)

200.21 God Janus Feast] Since Janus opened the year and the seasons, his principal festival was New Year's Day. Cf. Guevara, The Diall of Princes, sig. Kl^r: "Of a-solempne feaste the Romaynes celebrated to the God Janus."

See 198.32 and Note.

200.30 Banquetinge House] A separate building for dining, a not uncommon feature of Renaissance palaces.

201.9 Eunuke] See Note 25.4.

201.9 Hymen] God of marriage. See 28.22; 36.1; 201.20.

201.12-29 Even as the Vine . . . the married lyfe] The first two stanzas echo the imagery of Wotton's poem in The Courtlie Controversie, sig. 20$2^r$.

201.12 Even as the Vine, that clasps the tender Elme] Tilley V61: The vine embraces the elm.

201.16 Hymens ryghtes] That is, marriage. "ryghtes" = rites.

201.19 barren thought] Those who think of (and choose to live) barren lives. They breed only the destruction of fame.

201.20 Hymen] God of marriage. See 28.22; 36.1; 201.9.

203.8ff. Upon which incouragement . . .] The following discourse by Segnior Philoxenus is adapted from both Gruget's Mexia, especially Chapter XIV, "De la cordiale amitié de mariage, avec aucuns exemples de l'amour des mariez," and Du Verdier's Mexia, Book IV, Chapter XI. From Mexia's many examples of fidelity in marriage, Whetstone selects Paulina, Darius, Admetus, Artemisia, and Tiberius Gracchus. Izard discusses Whetstone's use of these sources, pp. 99-103, 265.

203.10-21 this holy Institution of Marriage . . . man, and wife] A translation of Du Verdier's Mexia, pp. 272-73. Also a paraphrase of the Book of Common Prayer (1559), sig. O5^r.

203.13-14 Increace, multiply, and replenish the earth] Genesis i.28: "Bring forthe frute and multiplie, and fil the earth."

203.17 Patriarcke Noe] Noah. "Patriarche Noé" in Du Verdier.

203.17-18 to encrease and multiply the earth a new] Genesis ix.1.

203.24-25 You shall be two bodies in one flesh, and no more] Genesis ii.24; and Matthew xix.5-6.

204.6-12 When the stately Dames of Rome . . . Cornelia . . .] Cornelia, the daughter of Scipio Africanus, was the mother of the Gracchi. "This woman was of a mervaylous temperaunce. For on a tyme beynge in company with other ladies of Rome, (beholdynge hir meane apparaile) was demaunded, if she had no better rayment: She, pointynge to hir two sonnes, whiche then wente before hir, answered: Lo here is my fresh apparaile, wherein

I delyte" (Cooper). The source of the anecdote is Valerius Maximus IV.1, who refers not to apparel but to beautiful ornaments or jewels.

204.13-19 When certaine . . . King Darius . . . Olympia . . . Alexander] Olympias was the wife of Philip II of Macedon and the mother of Alexander the Great. The story is not in Plutarch's Life of Alexander.

205.26-32 The Rynge that is geven . . . in conjuge major] A translation of Du Verdier's Mexia, p. 273.

205.31 Propertius] Sextus Propertius, c. 50-c. 16 B.C., Roman poet, one of the literary circle of Maecenas.

205.31-32 Omnis amor magnus, sed aperto in conjuge major] "All love is great, but greater far in open union," Propertius IV.3.49. Quoted in Du Verdier's Mexia.

206.6-23 Licurgus . . . . in the Common wealth] A translation of Du Verdier's Mexia, p. 275. Cf. Guevara, The Diall of Princes, sig. P2^{r-v}; and Thomas Wilson, The Arte of Rhetorique (1553), sigs. F4^r, G1^r.

206.6 Licurgus, the good King of the Lacedemonians] Lycurgus, legendary founder of the Spartan constitution, social institutions, and military system, hence, of the "good order." Plutarch extols his wisdom and justice: "Those which would not marye, he made infamous by lawe. For it was not lawfull for suche to be present, where these open games and pastimes were shewed naked. Furthermore, the officers of the cittie compelled suche as would not marye, even in the hardest time of the winter, to environne the place of these sportes, and to go up and down starcke naked, and to singe a certaine songe made for the purpose against them, which was: that justely were they punished, bicause that lawe they disobeyed. Moreover, when suche were olde, they had not the honour and reverence done them, which old maried men usually received" ("Lycurgus," trans. Sir Thomas North, London, 1579, sig. 3^{r-v}) Cf. Gruget's Mexia, p. 216.

Lacedaemon is the historic name for Sparta, properly for the territory but sometimes also for the city.

206.21 Plato, in his Lawes] Plato Laws IV.721; VI.774. Cf. 36.5; 85.13; 146.14; and 158.34.

206.24-34 The good Emperour, Alexander Severus . . . Mammeas . . . Memmia . . .] Julia Avita Mamaea dominated her son Alexianus, who was subsequently known as Severus Alexander, throughout his reign. Sulpicia Memmia was one of the three wives of Alexander Severus. Izard states that Whetstone is here recalling Sir Thomas Elyot's Image of Governaunce (Izard, p. 101). See Note 46.26.

207.1-5 How wonderfullie, was the Love of Paulina, sage Senecaes Wife . . .] Translated from Gruget's Mexia, p. 221.

Pompeia Paulina was the wife of Seneca the philosopher, Nero's tutor and political advisor. In 65 A.D. Seneca was forced to commit suicide. "She was with her husband at dinner when the centurion came from Nero to tell Seneca that he must die. The philosopher received the intelligence with calmness, embraced his wife, and bade her bear their separation with firmness; but as she begged that she might die with him, he yielded to her entreaties, and they opened their veins together. Nero, however, unwilling to incur a reputation for unnecessary cruelty, commanded her veins to be bound up. Her life was thus spared; and she lived a few years longer" (William Smith, ed. Dictionary of Greek and Roman Biography and Mythology, London: Walton-Murray, 1869).

207.6-12 Quintus Curtius, resiteth, that Kyng Darius . . .] Translated from Gruget's Mexia, p. 221. Plutarch's Life of Alexander XXX also states that Darius lamented the death of his wife.

207.6 Quintus Curtius] Quintus Curtius Rufus, rhetorician and historian, 1st century A.D., published a history of Alexander the Great in Latin in ten books; he is an excellent story-teller. John Brende's version, The Historie of Quintus Curcius, Conteyning the Actes of the Greate Alexander (1553), was highly esteemed throughout the sixteenth century.

207.13-19 King Admetus . . .] Adapted from Gruget's Mexia, p. 221.

Admetus was thus rewarded by Apollo: "he obtained of the destenies, called Parcae, that whan the daye of the death of Admetus shoulde be wounde uppon their spyndels, if he coulde fynde any other, that would willingly die for hym, he hym selfe should escape death at that tyme. Whan the day was come, that Admetus should finishe his life, all men and women, yea father and mother, refused to die: only Alceste his wyfe, preferred the lyfe of hir husbande before her owne" (Cooper). Cf. Pettie, A Petite Pallace, 6, "Alcest and Admetus."

207.20-30 Tiberius Graccus . . . in loosing of him] Adapted from Gruget's Mexia, p. 222. The source is Plutarch's Life of Tiberius Gracchus I.

Tiberius Gracchus was consul in 163 B.C.

207.30 the seven wonders of the worlde] The mausoleum, built of white marble, collapsed before the fifteenth century in an earthquake. The seven wonders are described in Gruget's Mexia, p. 439.

207.31-208.14 the love whiche Queene Artemisia bare to her Husbande

Mausolus . . .] Merely mentioned in Gruget's Mexia, p. 222. The classical sources are Valerius Maximus IV.6; and Aulus Gellius X.18.

Artemisia II succeeded her brother and husband Mausolus as ruler of Caria, 353-352 B.C. Cooper: "The name of a noble princesse, wife to Mausolus, kyng of Caria, of a notable chastitie, and excelled so in love toward hir husband, that whan he was dead, she caused his herte to bee dryed in a vessell of golde into poulder, and by little and little she dranke it up, saiynge: Their two hertes shoulde never departe asonder, and that she thought there mighte bee no woorthy sepulchre made for it, but hir owne bodie. Not withstandyng she made for his bodie such a sepulchre, that for the excellent woorkmanshippe, beautie, and costlinesse, it was taken for one of the mervailes of the worlde: and for the notable fame therof, al sumptuous and great sepulchres, were afterwarde called Mausolaea." Aulus Gellius mentions the literary competition and the names (as in Whetstone) of the famous rhetoricians.

208.10 Theopompus] Theopompus of Chios, born c. 378 B.C., historian, most distinguished pupil of Isocrates.

208.10 Teodectes] Theodectes, c. 375-334 B.C., poet and orator, probably studied under Plato, Isocrates, and Aristotle.

208.10 Naucrites] A disciple of Isocrates.

208.11 Isocrates] Isocrates of Apollonia, disciple of the more famous Isocrates of Athens with whom he is often confused. Cooper: "Isocrates, The name of a famous oratour, of woonderfull eloquence: out of whose schoole proceeded the most excellent oratours of Greece."

208.13s.n. Aul. Gel. in lib. de nocti. atti] Aulus Gellius, c. 130-

Explanatory Notes   376

c. 180 A.D., wrote the Noctes Atticae ("Attic Nights") in twenty books. His work is essentially an expanded commonplace book, a collection of anecdotes, quotations, and stories on a variety of topics, written during the winter evenings to entertain and instruct his children. It appears to have been widely read in the Renaissance.

208.18 Titus and Gisippus] Boccaccio's story of Titus and Gisippus (Decameron X.8) was very popular in the Renaissance as an illustration of perfect friendship. Titus pines away nearly unto death for love of his friend's betrothed, Sophronia, until his friend Gisippus, recognizing that Titus's need is greater than his own, gives the girl to him -- for, says Gisippus, he can always find another wife but not another friend. When Gisippus later finds himself in dire straits, he seeks out his now wealthy friend. Mistakenly believing himself to be slighted by Titus, Gisippus in despair confesses to a murder he did not commit. Titus tries to save him by taking the crime upon himself. Finally the true murderer appears and all is well, Gisippus marrying Titus's sister. The tale entered England through Sir Thomas Elyot's version in The Boke Named the Governour (1531) II.12, the first known English translation of Boccaccio. Whetstone appropriately cites the tale to show that the friendship of man for man is nobler than the love of man for woman.

208.18 Damon and Pithias] Another commonplace example of friendship, this time of classical origin, from Valerius Maximus, IV.7. The story is mentioned in Plutarch, De Amicorum Multitudine ("On Having Many Friends"), Moralia, 93Aff., in which the friends are Damon and Phintias. Cooper: "Damon and Pythias: Twoo philosophers of Pythagoras his secte, in the

league of frendshyppe beyng eche to other moste faythfull. For when
Dionyse the tyranne of Syracuse, had condemned the one of them to death,
and he had required certayne dayes respite to goe home and dispose suche
thynges as he had: the other became suertie for him on this condition,
that if his frende retourned not, he would be content to suffer death
for him. But when he at the daye appointed according to his promyse did
retourne: the tyranne wondryng at their faythfulnesse, pardoned the
offender, and requested that he might be received as thirde into their
knotte and league of amitie."

209.4-5 the Sunne shineth, both upon the good and bad] Tilley S985:
The sun shines upon all alike.

Matthew. v.45: "for he maketh his sunne to arise on the evil and on
the good."

209.5-7 Christe him selfe, was (aswell) Maister to a Theefe, as to
a true Disciple] Perhaps referring to Christ consoling the thieves on
the crosses.

210.15-17 the Rose full blowne . . . the tender Bud] Cf. Tilley
R180: The fairest rose at last is withered.

F391: The fairest flowers soonest fade.

211.14 to get abroade] To acquire means (to make a living) outside
the home.

211.28-31 as Socrates affirmeth . . .] Translated from Du Verdier's
Mexia, p. 275.

211.30 Anaxagoras] Greek philospher, c. 500-c. 428 B.C., the first
to reside in Athens. "A famous philosopher, noble of bloud, but more

noble in vertue and wysdome: whiche abandoning all his possessions, gave him wholy to the studie of naturall phylosophie" (Cooper).

211.31 <u>Archelaus</u>] "One a philosopher, the disciple of Anaxagoras, borne at Miletum, maister to Socrates, brought first naturall philosophy out of Ionia to Athens" (Cooper). 5th century B.C.

213.31 <u>Midas lippes</u>] "<u>Midas</u>, The ryche kynge of Phrygia, who, for his fryndly intertaynement of the God Bacchus, being willed to wyshe what he woulde, with promyse presently to obteyne the same, desyred that what so ever he touched myght foorthwith becomme golde. By whiche wyshe graunted, he tourned castelles and towers into golde. But when he came to eate his meate, and sawe that it also was made golde, being almost famished, he besought Bacchus agayne to take from hym the graunt that he hadde geven hym" (Cooper).

213.32-33 <u>he will be his owne Carver</u>] Tilley C110: To be one's own carver. "To take or choose for oneself, at one's own discretion."

215.5ff. <u>The woorthy Historie of Phrigius and Pieria</u> . . .] Whetstone follows the story outlined by Plutarch in his <u>Mulierum Virtutes</u> ("Bravery of Women") XVI, <u>Moralia</u> 253-54:

> Some of the Ionians who came to Miletus, owing to lively disagreements with the sons of Neileus, went away to Myus and settled there, suffering many ills at the hands of the Milesians; for these made war upon them because of their defection. However, the war was not without truce or intercourse, but at certain festivals the women commonly went to Miletus from Myus. There was among the people of Myus a prominent man named Pythes, who had a wife named Iapygia and a daughter Pieria. As there was a festival in honour of Artemis, and a sacrifice, which they call Neleis, he sent his wife, and daughter, who had asked that they might participate in the festival. The most influential of Neileus's sons, Phrygius by name, fell in love with Pieria,

Explanatory Notes 379

and tried to think what could be done on his part that
would be most pleasing to her. And when she said, "If
only you could make it possible for me to come here often
and many with me," Phrygius was quick to understand that
she wanted friendship and peace for the citizens, and
stopped the war. There was, consequently, in both cities
repute and honour for Pieria, so that the women of Miletus
pray even to this day that their husbands may love them
as Phrygius loved Pieria. (Loeb translation)

Cf. Lyly, p. 108: "yet some have wished to be embraced as Phrigius embraced Pieria"; also p. 381.

215.11 Miletum in Ionia] Ionia was an ancient district on the west coast of Asia Minor. Miletus was the most important of the twelve Ionian cities.

215.21 Myos] Myus was one of the twelve Ionian cities.

217.16 Oedippus] See Note 32.29.

Cooper: "Finally having knowledge at length that by misfortune he had murdered his father at Phocis, and by inceste had knowen his owne mother, so sore it greeved him, that in revengement thereof he pulled out his own eyes, and lyved ever after in banyshment, having his daughter Antigone to leade hym, by whom he was often times preserved, when he would have slaine hymselfe" (Cooper -- italics mine).

218.3-4 though mylde Venus . . . wrathfull Mars . . .] Venus, the goddess of love. Mars (Ares), the god of battle.

218.15-16 her knowen enemy is not so daungerous, as the fayned friend] Tilley F410: It is better to have an open enemy than a dissembling friend. Cf. 43.16-17.

218.18 Alexander] Alexander the Great, who conquered Asia Minor, Persia, and Babylonia into India; Phoenicia and Palestine; and Egypt in Africa. See also 146.12 and 168.29.

218.19 <u>Caesar</u>] Julius Caesar, the great military leader. See also 75.13 and 146.12-13.

218.20 <u>Hanniball</u>] "The sonne of Hamilcar, the moste noble and valiant capitaine of the Carthaginenses, who, makynge warre with the Romaines .XVI. yeres, contended with them in prowesse and policie, wynnynge from them their dominions in Spayne and Italy" (Cooper). See also 146.13.

218.22-23 <u>the life Booke of Fame</u>] Perhaps the living Book of Fame. Or is Whetstone combining the Book of Life (the record of the names of those who shall inherit eternal life) with the Book of Fame?

218.30-31 <u>shame worme the tongue</u>] May shame be a remedy for a blasphemous tongue. (<u>OED</u>, worm, v 3: "to extract the 'worm' from the tongue"-- as a remedy for madness.)

219.1-2 <u>Justice, Pietie, Temperaunce, Concorde and Love</u>] These are the virtues celebrated in the first five books of Spenser's <u>Faerie Queene</u>.

224.16 <u>Juno</u>] In her role as goddess of married love, as opposed to Diana as goddess of chastity. For a discussion of the types of love represented by Diana, Venus, and Juno, see Notes 28.19-20 and 33.28.

224.21 <u>tooke in worth</u>] Took at its proper value. (<u>OED</u>, worth, sb^1.)

225.28 <u>Jupiters wrathe</u>] Simply, the wrath of God.

226.15 <u>white Turtles</u>] Turtle-doves, symbol of constant love and conjugal happiness. See 31.12-13 and 73.17.

227.18-33 <u>a hye Mountain</u> . . . <u>Africa</u>] Cf. Wotton, <u>Courtlie Controversie</u>, sig. 2A3^r: "they entred into a domesticall deserte, so well

and naturally wrought, that Nature confessed hir cunning vanquished by
mans industrye: For the snailes, lizardes, molles, frogs, grashoppers,
shells, flints with all earthly and water beastes, fishes, and foules
were presented so lively amidde the mossy rockes, and all kindes of plantes,
trees, and hearbes, as a man woulde not onely have thought to bee in a
wildernesse of Arabia, and neare some river of Affrica . . . ." But
Wotton's "deserte" is a setting for Bacchus.

227.19 Forestery] Wotton, Courtlie Controversie, sig. 2A3^r: "forrestrie."
For the English signification, "a vast extent of trees," the OED cites
no example before 1823; but Wotton is translating directly from the French.

227.25 Camelions] Cameleopards or giraffes. Topsell, sig. K2^v.

227.26 beasts of honor] Animals used in heraldry to represent certain
virtues. In his discussion of heraldic animals, including the lion,
leopard, hart, unicorn, bull, boar, ram, and horse, Gerard Legh in The
Accedens of Armory refers to "any beast of more honor" (sig. G3^r).

227.34 by a still motion] By a silent or secret process of movement.

228.6 Diana attired all in whyte] White as the colour of chastity,
of purity. See also 28.19.

228.7 the nyne Muses] Cooper: "The Muses: whiche were maydens, whome
poetes feygned to bee the daughters of Jupiter and Memorie, and that
they weare ladyes and governours of poetrie and Musyke. They were in
numbre nyne, or after some but three. Some call them gevers of eloquence,
and dooe name them goddesses." The usual list includes Calliope (heroic
epic), Clio (history), Euterpe (flute music), Terpsichore (lyric poetry
or dance), Erato (lyric poetry or hymns), Melpomene (tragedy), Thalia

(comedy), Polyhymnia (mimic art), and Urania (astronomy).

228.11 the Hyen] See 36.30 and Note.

228.12-15 the ful power of vertue . . . both kindes] Cf. 142.26ff.

228.16 Monster Envy] See Note 3.10.

228.20 the golden age] In classical mythology and literature, the Golden Age was the period when Saturn or Cronus ruled the world, the earliest age of man. It was a time of innocent happiness, of peace, love, and harmony. Men lived close to nature without agriculture or industry, without strife, and without civilization. Many of the deities then lived on earth. The Golden Age was followed by a Silver Age, a Bronze Age, and the present Iron Age. See Hesiod, Works and Days, 109ff.; Ovid Met. XV.99ff.; and Guevara, The Diall of Princes, I.31.

Harry Levin points out in The Myth of the Golden Age in the Renaissance (Bloomington: Indiana Univ. Press, 1969) that this motif was common in Renaissance pageantry, especially in Florence (pp. 38-40).

228.23 Parnassus] Mount Parnassus in Greece, sacred haunt of the Muses.

229.10 more warie then Argus] See Note 104.5s.n.

229.11 the Tormenters of Hell] Pluto and Proserpine, rulers of the underworld.

229.12 Inachus Oten Pipe] Inachus was a river-god, the father of Io. (In Cooper, he is the first king of the Argives.) But when Argus was set by Juno to guard Io, he was overcome with the pipes of Mercury (Hermes), not of Inachus. In Golding's translation of Ovid's Metamorphoses,

Mercury uses an "oten Reede" to pipe Argus to sleep.

229.13 Orpheus passionate Musick] See 114.8, 151.7, and Notes.

229.19 Non vi, sed virtute] "Not by might, but by virtue." Whetstone adopted this as his motto on the title page of A Mirour for Magestrates of Cyties (1584) in the form, "Virtute, Non Vi."

The title of a poem in Kendall's Flowers of Epigrammes, to which Whetstone contributed a commendatory verse, is "By Vertue Not Vigour" (sig. M4^r). Cf. EM, sig. ¶3^r: "the saying of morall Diogenes, Vertue onely conquereth Envy"; and M4^v.

229.20 with a Myrrour] Parallels include EM, sigs. ¶2^v; M6^v; and Dier, sig. B4^v.

In EM, Queen Elizabeth is the conqueror of envy. See also 16.34.

229.29 As Phallaris, dyd to Perillus] Phalaris, tyrant of Acragos, 6th century B.C., noted for his cruelty. Cooper: "Phalaris, A cruell tyranne of Agrigentine, who mervaylously delighted in the devise of new and straunge punishementes. Wherefore one Perillus a cunnynge woorkeman, thynkynge to have great thankes and a large rewarde, invented a bull of brasse, into the which if one weare put, and a fyre made underneath, the voyce of his crying should be like the belowyng of a bull. The tyranne in steede of rewarde, to trie this newe devise, first burned in it Perillus himselfe, and after hym many other." The story is told in Gruget's Mexia, p. 140; Guevara's The Diall of Princes, I.46; and Painter, II.10. Among the classical sources are Ovid, Ars Amatoria I.653-54; Tristia III.39-54; and Pliny XXXIV.19.

229.30 die with the weapon, thou preparst for other] Cf. Tilley

W204: To beat one at his own weapon. (Earliest example cited 1591.)
See also 48.23, and 173.13s.n.

229.32 the Nymphe Chlora] Cooper: Chloris, "Also the goddesse of flowers, otherwyse called Flora." Whetstone conflates the two names.

229.33ff. a Shield . . .] Whetstone has taken the description of this shield from Gerard Legh's The Accedens of Armory:

> The first whereof is a looking glasse of Cristall,
> in a fielde of greene, which signifieth prudence . . .
> The second is a paire of ballaunce of Silver,
> in a fielde blewe, which signifieth, Justice . . .
> The third, is a piller of Porphiere, in a
> golden field, which signifieth Fortitude . . .
> The fowerth is a Jugge and cuppe of Ruby rock,
> in a field silver . which signifieth temperance . . . .
> (sigs. A6^r-A7^r)

Thus, the shield given to Aurelia symbolizes the four cardinal virtues and differs from Legh's shield only in a detail of the fourth quarter. Legh's shield is pictured on the title page of The Accedens of Armory, a book which discusses heraldry in dialogue form, which is dedicated "To the honorable assembly of gentlemen in the Innes of Court and Chauncery," and which ends with a description of the speaker's reception at the Inns of Court, where he enjoys the generous hospitality of "Palaphilos." Whetstone's use of this device at such a prominent point in the book suggests a significance which I have not yet defined, but it surely argues a close connection between Whetstone and the Inns of Court.

In Primaudaye, The French Academie, the cardinal or civil virtues make possible "the excellent order of all humane things" and protect society from disorder and confusion (sig. C5^v).

230.6-7 a Garland of Roses, parted, perpale, ARGENT, and GULES] The garland is described in heraldic terms. "Parted" = party, parti-coloured. "Party per pale" = having two different qualities, hence, half-and-half. "Argent" = silver or white. "Gules" = red. Thus, the garland is composed of mixed red and white roses.

230.13 The Silver Pen, and Verses] In Grange, The Golden Aphroditis, Sir N.O seeks out the Muses in the Arbor of Amitie to solicit a gift for the nymph A.O.; Melpomene dips a silver pencil in a well and writes verses on the cover of a goblet which she presents to him (sig. L4^r).

See also 11.16 and Note.

230.14 URANIE] See 10.2 and Note.

230.14-15 in the forefrunt of this Booke] See pp. 10-11.

230.17-18 the Cock was ready to sing his midnight song] The tradition that the cock crows at midnight at Christmas does not seem relevant here, for it is said to crow on Christmas Eve, not on New Year's night. The clue to interpretation of this line is provided by Thomas Tusser's Five Hundred Pointes of Good Husbandrie (1580):

> Experience teacheth, as true as a clock:
>   how winter might passeth, by marking the cock.
>
> Cock croweth at midnight, times few above six,
>   with pause to his neighbour, to answere betwix.
> At three a clock thicker, and then as ye knowe:
>   like all in to Mattens, neere daie they doo crowe.
>   (sig. S2^r)

GLOSSARY

The following list includes (1) words which predate the earliest example in the OED for the sense in which they are used in the Heptameron, and (2) obsolete words which may be obscure or confusing to a reader who is not an Elizabethan specialist. No attempt has been made to gloss all obsolete words, only those whose meanings are not immediately apparent from their context. OED predatings are marked by an asterisk, the date of the OED example being cited at the end of each entry.

The words are spelled as they appear in the Heptameron; variants such as those caused by interchangeable "i" and "y" or "c" and "s" have been grouped under the spelling which occurs first in the text. If a word is used in a particular sense more than three times in the Heptameron, only the first example is cited, followed by "etc." When a word is used in both current and obsolete senses, only examples of the latter are cited. The comment "(see note)" indicates that the word is discussed in the explanatory notes. Nouns are normally listed in the singular, and verbs in the infinitive form.

The authority for all definitions is the Oxford English Dictionary.

```
*abased 74.15, 106.28 lowered (1652)
*abilyties 58.1 faculties, talents (1587)
 able 158.32 wealthy
*a bylling 188.9 caressing
 abylytie 85.19 etc. wealth, means
*accomodated 17.31, 96.33 equipped, furnished (1597)
 acquire 152.34 to require
*acquired 55.15 gained, obtained by one's own efforts (1606)
*Acteon 144.31 to cuckold (1615)
*addopted 21.3 christened, named anew (1601)
 adventure 15.17 etc. chance occurrence, fortune
```

advertisement 58.13 warning
*affect 29.5 etc. to prefer, to be fond of, to love (1593)
affected 153.17, 184.7, 219.22 those in love
*affectedlye 32.28 with fondness; 92.11 sincerely (1596)
affectionated 154.14, 205.8s.n. affectionate
affie 22.12, 62.11, 75.24 to trust, confide
agreable 204.30 agreeing together
Alcaron 46.14 the Koran
Almain 19.10 a German
Almayne 70.18, 227,18, 230.10 a kind of dance
amiable 54.10 worthy to be loved
amisse 149.26 misdeed
*Anotomy, Annotomie 105.10, 106.22 skeleton, mummy (1589)
annoy 119.31, 120.5 annoyance, discomfort
appalled 91.26 made pale
*apparaunce 133.6 display, show (1591)
arrivyng 15.22 bringing
*Arte, names of 174.19 words of art, technical terms (1628)
*aslant 227.24 across in a slanting direction (1602)
aspeckt 185.4 relative positions of heavenly bodies
*assemblies 117.9 social gatherings (1590)
astonied 133.7 amazed, astonished
attache 72.4 to seize, lay hold of
Audit Bagges 97.19 money bags
avouch 66.32 to cite as authority
awaie with 87.3 tolerate, put up with
*awkeward 83.4 unfavourable (1587)
*Bacheler 185.14 a novice (1604)
Balme 221.28 to anoint
*bane 165.34 to harm, hurt (1601)
bare 139.18, 227.4, 227.5 worthless
base, bace 158.20s.n. etc. low in social scale
bended 69.1 striped or banded
best 90.8, etc. most superior in rank or station
bestow 86.34 to place; 190.27 to settle in marriage
better sort 1.6 etc. superior in rank or station (see note)
bewray 53.15 etc. to reveal, expose; to betray
blinde 217.27 misleading
*bloome 197.5 to bring into bloom (1592)
*Bollytyne 14.24 bolletine, bulletin (1645)
*brave mynded 1.11, 171.22 of excellent mind (1617)
*broade waking 198.19 fully awake (1583)
Bullice 53.8 bullace, a wild plum
Burgoys 151.31 Burgeyse, a female citizen

*call 90.20 a decoy-bird (1595)
*callumner 217.17 calumniator (1614)
camelion 227.25 camelopard or giraffe
canker 53.7 an inferiour kind of rose
canvass 42.34 to beat
capitall 136.4 deadly, mortal

Glossary 388

carraine 87.6 carrion
cates 15.11 bought delicacies
Cattel 227.29 worthless creatures
*Champion 38.4 champaign, a plain (1589)
*charged 147.19, 220.33 burdened, laden (1583); sore charged 53.24 hard pressed
check, v. 140.29 to rebuke
check, n. 51.20 false swoop (in hawking) (see note)
chirurgion 80.24 a surgeon
choller 48.25 bile, one of the four humours, supposed to cause anger
choller adust 99.20 black bile, supposed to cause melancholy
chopped 195.31 snapped up
Christall 146.27 of the cyrstalline heaven (in the Ptolemaic system)
cicuta 113.2 poison extracted from the hemlock
citterne 76.18 cithern
*circumstaunce 111.4, 128.9 circumlocution (1597) (see note)
civill 1.2 etc. refined, well-bred; social (see note); 19.3 seemly, decent; *31.19 non-ecclesiastical (1592)
*clapping 225.2 striking hands in token of a bargain (1599)
*clarkely 177.22 clerkly, skilfully (1594)
clawing 47.22 flattering, fawning
cloying 48.21 impeding, obstructing; overloading with food
cognizance 116.19 knowledge, understanding
*Comedians 163.23 etc. comic actors (1601)
comfortable 130.20 reassuring; 133.16 comforting
*commaund 28.5 to hold in check (1586)
common 93.29 to converse, talk
*compasse 154.5 to embrace (1590)
Complection 99.19, etc. collection of humours, temperament, constitution
conceite 185.32 judgement; reddy in conceyt 59.12 quick in thought (see note)
*conseight 111.28 self-conceit (1605); 111.16 idea, thought
*conclude 27.18 to result in (1639); 157.6 to close with
conditions 22.2 etc. personal qualities, manners
confounde 201.18 to destroy
*conjure downe 121.17 to subdue (by magic), with a baudy innuendo
Conscience 17.11 inmost thought; 93.24 a matter of conscience
*Consort 68.30 company of musicians (1587)
*construction 126.14 interpretation (1586)
*contentment 223.27 delight (1586)
contrary 184.20 to do what is contrary to
controulment 68.3 restraint
*conveiances 18.3 ingenious devices (1596)
convenient 16.16 appropriate, suitable
*coosen 97.30 to cozen, deceive (1583)
corsive 41.17 a caustic remedy; 178.23 something that consumes
*counsellinge, counsaylyng 36.3, 207.18 that counsels (1628)
counterbuff 82.26s.n. blow in contrary direction
course 60.28 to worry, persecute
Courted 1.4, 4.17 courtier-like (see note)
Coyfe 98.27 coif, head-covering
Crannelle 14.2 cranny

*crased 107.21, 133.14 damaged, ruined (1590)
*cross, v. 75.10 to contradict (1589)
*crosse, n. 142.21 a crossing (1599)
*crosse, a. 174.12 contrarious (1588)
*cunning 45.1 etc. skilful, in bad sense (1590); 228.34 full of knowledge
cunningest 52.31 most learned
curbed 146.5 bent, bowed
curiousnesse 18.8 beauty, elaborateness
custom 56.32 to accustom

Dame 30.28, 124.19, 204.6 superior of a nunnery
dammage 42.4 misfortune
daunger, v. 216.33 to expose to danger
daunger, n. 97.28 power; 137.23, 209.15 harm
daungerous 27.11 etc. harmful
dead 179.1 flavourless
defende 86.17 to ward off
defray 98.4 to cover the expenses of
*delicate 200.30 graceful, elegant (1583)
denized 4.4 made a citizen
deserve 148.10 requite
determination 133.9, 138.30 intention decided on
device 10.3, 163.29 dramatic representation; 23.16 witty expression; 68.19 design
devine 193.2 to explain
devise 68.20 etc. to converse, talk
devotion 84.19 disposal; alms
*devotionate 224.15 full of devotion (1864)
dignities 145.30s.n. faculties (see note)
discomforted 230.9 discomfitted
*disgrace 8.22 etc. disparagement, reproach (1586) (see note)
dishearited 87.22 disinherited
dishonest, v. 130.4 to defile
dishonest, a. 52.20, 52.23, 121.12 dishonourable, unchaste
dishonesty 86.32, 88.18 unchastity
dispatch 15.19 dismissal
dispence 94.31 expenditure
dispoil 17.29 to undress
distemperature, distemprature 114.20 etc. disordered condition of the humours, ailment
*Divines 142.29 non-Christian writers on theology (1587)
documente 7.15 instruction, warning
domesticall 227.29 cultivated
*Domesticke 109.23 tame (1620)
droyle 148.30, 159.11 drudge
drye 71.27 barren; 229.4 not drawing blood, severe

Eav't 109.11 eft
engrave 59.6, 207.33 to entomb
easye conceited 150.30 of small intelligence
*egall, v. 146.32 to equal (1591)
egall, a. 149.8, 187.32 equal, equally reciprocated

Element 40.19, 40.22 the sky
emprise 30.19 renown, glory; 139.23, 225.18 value
encounter 224.21 to address each other;*221.15 to go to meet (1603)
entertaine 7.26 etc. to receive; to take into one's service; to greet,
 to deal with; to treat; *to keep occupied; *to while away (time)
entrayles 192.21 bowels; children
envie 215.25 etc. hostile feeling, ill-will, malice
envying 198.18 disliking (see note)
*Equipage 44.30 apparel (1645); 225.15 state of being equipped (1600)
erect 203.10 to found
*errant 58.29 deviating from the correct standard (1609)
exercise 4.22 etc. customary occupation; 10.9 action of drilling troops;
 23.2 an academic disputation
exhibition 85.3 maintenance, support
exordium 145.18s.n. the beginning of a discourse
*expect 21.16, 43.23 to anticipate (1601)
*expose 96.31 to offer publicly, put up for sale (1610)
*Extasie 103.10 ecstasy, trance (1598)
*eye 191.29 to keep in view (1590)

factions 133.28 actions, doings
faine, fayne 43.16 etc. to feign, to represent in fiction
familiar 16.14 affable, courteous
fantasie 52.30, 61.2 to take a fancy
Father in law 191.8, 191.26, 192.16 stepfather
*favor 198.28 token of affection (1588)
fearefull 34.7 timid
Fee 177.20 a prize
fianced 93.19 affianced
*Fillet 132.19 thread (1590)
Firmament 146.28 the eighth heaven, or the sphere of the fixed stars,
 in the Ptolemaic system
*flashe 100.20 a sprinkling (1615)
flat 56.25 absolute
*flatterie 185.6 deception (1600)
fleete 73.4 to float, sail
*florish 52.30 rhetorical ornament (1603); 158.15 ostentatious embellish-
 ment (1588)
*folowyng 210.2 succeeding, resulting
foode 55.25 feud
*Forestery 227.19 trees (1712) (see note)
forme 61.1 beauty
forstoode 184.22 opposed, withstood
fowlded 6.11 folded, rolled up
frantick 89.27 extremely foolish
friende 104.32, 105.21 lover
furnish 163.20 to fill, occupy

gage 212.21 to engage, to put up as security
Geate 15.5 jet, black marble
*generall 109.21 all collectively (1591)
gettinges 94.34 gains, earnings

Ghostly Father 136.11 father confessor
give 55.5 to gyve, to fetter
*governe 186.24 predominate (1596)
government 1.8 etc. behaviour, conduct (see note); *104.22 management
Grace 10.27 good fortune; 11.1 the one to be favoured (see note);
    68.1 pleasantness of flavour; 68.5 efficacy
Granado 71.11 from Granada
Grand Maister 19.11 the chief officer of the household
gree 81.22 in gree: with goodwill
greefe 192.20 disease
grin 123.12 snare
Gripe 114.13 vulture
*grose witted 22.33 dull, stupid (1587)
*grounded 170.8 "floored," "gravelled" (1597)

grudge 47.22s.n., 224.27 ill-will
grype 50.7 to afflict
Gyves 50.18 shackles, fetters

*handmayde 29.22 female personal attendant (1592)
*Headsman 127.8 executioner (1601)
heardle 144.17 to hurdle, hurtle: to whirl; or hartheled: to raddle,
    to fasten to the spokes of a wheel
homely 162.17 domestic
honest 58.29 etc. virtuous, chaste; respectable
horne wood 180.5 horn mad: enraged
hye 11.7 to hie, to hasten

illustre 202.18 to light up
Imagynation 75.10 a scheming; 110.23, 185.1 thought, feeling; 117.1
    by imagination: through images; *153.22 impression as to what is
    likely
impertinent 148.21, 200.22, 230.16 irrelevant, unrelated
*imployment 223.21 employment, service (1593)
Importunities 102.31 troubles
imprice 48.12 value
*inabled 178.13 unabled, lacking strength (1597)
inconveniences 12.6 etc. mischiefs, misfortunes; 4.26 etc. improprieties
indifferencie 156.26 fairness
indifferent 29.6 impartial; 4.24, 90.9 not extreme, of medium quality;
    143.8 of either gender; 192.4 impartially pertinent; 217.1 of neutral
    disposition
indifferently 119.5 fairly
*indiscression 157.15, 212.6 indiscreet act (1601)
indure 153.4 endure: to submit to
infirme 205.14 shaky, fickle
Ingenious 208.25 talented
inhabylytie 153.30 lack of means
*inroll 17.25 enroll: to place upon a list (1613)
Intendment 145.30, 145.33, 146.20 faculty of understanding
intercoursed 1.16, 12.18 alternated; 228.3 run through
intreat 19.11, 153.21 to treat

*jadish 51.16 vicious, ill-tempered (1589)
jangling 56.3 angry, squabbling
Jorneyes 98.23 business, affairs
Judgement 174.20 astrological conclusion

kallender 169.30 calendar: chronological list of documents
*Kitchynstuffe 159.22, 159.32 kitchen maid (1637)

langour 73.21 mental suffering
latchet 85.10 loop, thong (see note)
*lated 38.8 belated (1592)
Lawnes 98.27 articles of dress made from fine linen
least 175.5 last
leave 58.23 to neglect; 94.18, 113.22 to stop; 128.8 to cease speaking
   (of)
lewde 134.26 etc. wicked, base
life 218.23, 227.6 living (see note)
light, v. 186.2 to meet, come across
light, a. 189.9 burning brightly
lightly 94.21, 181.9s.n. probably, most likely
livings 57.24 etc. property, wealth, possessions
longes 72.8 belongs
loppe of 90.16 cut at, loppings of

*malice 56.16, 205.16 to entertain, or to regard with, malice (1587)
manners 52.6, 210.20 customs, moral behaviour
Mansion 10.28, 45.13 abiding place

matching 54.2, 159.17, 186.21 marrying
Mavis 15.34 song-thrush
Mazar 105.22, 108.12 drinking-cup; the head
meacock 95.3 weakling, coward, spiritless man, some kind of bird (see note)
*meale 81.25 to spot, stain (1603)
*meanest 129.28 least, smallest (1585)
meates 147.22, 176.25 kinds of food, "dishes"
*mende 152.13 to improve (1603)
merrit 101.17 due reward or punishment
Millaine 69.6 cloth from Milan
Minion 144.30, 188.13 lover
*Mispriser 206.14 a despiser (1586)
*Moderne 117.19 modern (1585)
*monument 148.8s.n. portent (1590); 31.34 mark, indication
moove 10.8, 218.30 to stir up strife, to excite
motion 26.11 etc. emotion, agitation, inclination; 134.14 motions
   of excuse: excusable grounds
*Mumpes 188.9 woman (1598)
Murrey 69.1 mulberry colour

necessarie 17.31 etc. useful
*negligent 150.8 due to negligence (1606)
nice *177.11, 212.8 particular, careful (1584); 183.24 intricate

Glossary   393

niceness 115.27 reserve, shyness
nonce 109.10 for the nonce: expressly
note 66.27, 122.26s.n., 198.6 stigma, reproach
Novell 18.12 a novelty
*Nimphes 224.18 young women, maidens (1584)

office 172.33 room connected with kitchen
officious 14.30 eager to serve
once 52.19 once for all, to sum up
open 58.34, 125.3 to reveal, declare
order 95.13 etc. suitable action; 24.14 etc. customs; 41.22, 86.11 to take order: to take steps (to)
*ordinary 62.17 etc. of the usual kind (1590); 108.12 of everyday occurrence, abundant (1597)
Orphant 98.33 orphan
*overcharge 60.13 excessive load (1611)
*overcharged 114.18, 133.4 overloaded (1593)
overpayse 61.5 to outweigh
*over rule 193.32 to make judgement on
*over ruled 139.21 authoritatively decided (1593)
over watching 143.23 want of sleep

parle 223.29 to discuss terms; 224.31 to talk in conference
Parsonage 186.6 personage: personal appearance, figure
partes 33.24 etc. acts; 93.16 talents
parted 230.6 parti-coloured: *Party per pale, half-and-half (1616) (Heraldry)
participate 127.26, 137.32 to share
Partlet 212.26 neckerchief, collar, or ruff
passe, at a good 41.4 in a desperate state (see note)
passage 207.17 departure, death
passenger 53.27 wayfarer
passion 70.19 etc. poem marked by deep emotion; *76.14 fit of strong feeling (1590); 109.26 amorous feelings (1588)
*pausyng 200.23 lingering, dwelling upon (1719)
pearch 159.26 to set oneself up
physicke 36.31s.n., 41.2 remedy
pikes 162.15 to run upon the pikes: to rush to destruction (see note)
pine Apple trees 13.32 pine trees (see note)
pitifull 45.1 etc. pious; compassionate
plausible 58.10. 226.27 deserving of applause, commendable; 124.6 pleasing, acceptable
playes 206.10 amusements
Plot 154.2 ground-plan of building
popenjay 73.14 color of green parrot
Porphier 230.3 porphyry
powled 108.13 polled: shorn, shaven
*prayse Master 49.5 (see note)
president 4.24 etc. precedent (see note); 215.10 model, exemplar
present 6.14 existing at that time
*presume 62.12 rely upon (1586)
prevent 59.15 etc. to forestall

Glossary   394

*previleadg 79.31 to privilege: to authorize (1592)
pride 24.2 the prime, sexual desire; 180.8 splendour, display
privitie 84.16, 96.7 private knowledge; 205.8 legal relationship
proloyning 56.30 purloin: to steal
*promise 97.11 to afford ground of expectation (1594)
prove 9.18 prosper; 25.24 to have experience of, to suffer
purchase 54.18 acquisitions; prize
push 58.9 an attack

quallytie 15.14 rank or position; *174.17s.n. an accomplishment (1584),
    228.8 functions
*qualited 4.25 etc. qualitied (1600) (see note), 14.14 capable
questions 6.20 etc. discourses, disputes, debates (see note)
quicke 220.23 strongly felt
quicknesse 58.2 life, vitality
*quid pro quo 164.17 something for something (1591)
quited 61.8s.n. removed

*raise 176.3 to produce (a sound) (1590)
rancke 115.10, 117.15 in a rank: in a line
Rapines 216.15 acts of violent robbery or pillage
rascall 169.13 forming the rabble; *173.9 wretched, mean (1585);227.28 inferio
reaking 73.25 reeking
*realish 50.3 to give a relish to (1586); 153.30 to be pleased or satisfied
    with (1594)
reasoned of their affayres 224.30 discussed their business
reave 1.16 etc. to rob, remove; 203.34 to plunder
recognisance 17.23 recognition or acknowledgement
recomfort 76.17 to soothe, console
recorded 76.6 recalled, recollected
recount 58.19 to reckon, count up
recounting 99.29 considering, weighing
refell 111.5 etc. refute, disprove
refer 19.23 to defer, postpone
*regard v. 157.31 to consider, take into account (1586); 54.27 to take
    care, to see to it
regard n. *4.2 etc. esteem, affection (1591); 6.29 etc. estimation,
    importance, value
*regestre 155.2 to set down (1597)
*report v. 139.11 to give an account of (1602)
Reporte n. 75.22 fame; *43.6 common opinion; 194.19 rumour, common talk
repose 84.10 to confide, place trust in
reputation 152.21 in reputation: in the general estimate
resembled 118.30 imitated, depicted
reservyng of 87.4 with proper respect for
*resited 167.16 recited (1630)
*resolved 104.1 satisfied or convinced (1585)
restraint 46.11 a prohibition
*retrograding 192.28 fall back or revert to inferior position (1613)
Rhinocerot 182.2s.n. Rhinoceros
Rialtie 17.22, 20.21 royalty, royal pomp
*riot 69.29 extravagant display (1649) (see note); 110.26 runne at ryot
    to act without restraint (see note)

Glossary   395

riote 51.21 following wrong scent (see note)
Russet 160.20 coarse reddish-brown cloth worn by peasants

*salute 224.9 to pay a complimentary visit to (1585)
 salve 130.11 to preserve; 174.8 to anoint with salve
 Sarcenet 69.5 very fine soft silk
*scandall v. 42.10 to revile (1601)
*scandall n. 57.7 defamatory talk (1596)
 Scarpines 69.8 light shoes (It. scarpino)
*scourge 86.27 punishment
 scrip 80.28 small bag, satchel
 Scullerie 172.29 area of kitchen
 seem 175.18 to befit, beseem
*selfe conceyghtes 68.6 self-conceit: wilful thought (1602)
*Senate 10.28, 17.1 Privy Council (1584)
 serve 51.17 to drive out game into view (see note); served with 161.12
    treated by
*servisable 14.15 expressing readiness to serve (1586)
 set 20.23 to sit at table
 shaddowe 117.22 portrait; 150.6 unreal appearance
 shadow 228.4 to shade
*shell 174.26 in the shell: unhatched (1601)
 shift 97.26 to make a living by one's own devices; *104.33 to slip
    off unobserved (1590)
 shiftlesse 28.14, 192.12 helpless, void of cunning
 shoe 189.17 show (see note)
 shrewd 42.11s.n. having dangerous consequences; 58.21 hurtful, injurious;
    *103.33s.n. coming close to the truth (1588)
 shrinck 74.28 to withdraw from
 Siene 156.27, 156.32 Scion
 sight v. 32.33, 72.27 to sigh
 sight n. 26.5, 73.25, 120.4 sigh
*Simbole 116.17 symbol (1590)
*simplicity 193.27 instance of lack of ordinary knowledge (1592)
*simplye 34.33, 111.14s.n. absolutely (1590)
 Skreene 15.3 partition dividing a room
 skyl 99.24 to have knowledge of
 sleightly 27.9 craftily, subtly
 slender 94.28 deficient in energy, lax
 slope 72.17 sloping, slanting
 slowe 148.31 sloe
 slut 189.31 kitchen-maid
 slutishly 161.12, 212.27 despicably, immorally
 smally 54.28, 58.5 to a small extent, very little
 smoulder 174.26 to smother
 smugge 121.9 trim, neat
 sollace 25.24 pleasure, delight
 some 50.14 etc. a certain
*soothe 189.16 to smooth or gloss over (1587)
*soothing 180.29 flattering (1599)
 spedie 13.30 advantageous, helpful
 speede 88.2 to fare well
 spent 186.2 farre spent: in an advanced state of tiredness or age
    (1591), deprived of force

spright 120.3 spirit
square 212.33 dispute, quarrel
stand with 145.21 to agree with
standing Cup 230.4 cup having a foot or base
starke naught 85.25 utterly worthless
starklyng 77.25 showing signs of fear, quaking
stately 204.6 haughty;*227.11, 228.5 splendid (1593); *230.10 dignified (1593)
stockes 69.8 stockings
straingenesse 160.9 coldness, aloofness
strange 38.14 unfriendly, reserved
*streaked 118.5 marked with lines (1595) (see note)
*stripe 40.15 stroke or lash of whip (1830)
studie 50.19 to set deliberately to do something
subject 147.17 substance
subtill *81.32 working imperceptibly (1601)
succour 13.15 shelter, refuge
succourer 158.33 one who aids
*suddayne 42.18 impromptu (1591); 44.26 of the suddaine: suddenly
suffering 125.21 permission, tolerance
sufficiencie 27.34, 179.15 ability, competency
Suffrage 189.7 prayer
*Suggestioner 8.6 person who makes false statements or representations (not in OED)
suggestion 28.34 etc. false representation or charge
*Superficies 229.24 surface layer (1603)
superstitious 18.29 etc. irrational, idolatrous, excessive; 148.8 extremely particular
surmise 28.1, 37.6 allegation, charge
*survaye 17.24 to examine (1592)
sute 151.8 suit: pursuit
suter 114.11 suitor: petitioner, suppliant
Sympathie *204.30s.n. harmony of disposition (1596)

table 40.19, 40.21 picture; *79.9 the company at dinner (1602); 115.23 writing-tablet
*table Booke 184.31 pocket note-book (1596)
Tables of Memorie 225.20 memorial tablet
tablet 199.15 ornament, jewellery
Taffata 68.32, 69.17, 73.14 glossy silk; 69.4 of the nature of taffeta
tardie 37.33 to take tardy: to surprise
Tawny 71.8 brown-yellow colour; cloth of a tawny colour
teather 85.10 beyond one's tether: beyond the limits of one's ability
tedious 189.23 painful
teene 129.7 anger, malice
temperature 138.26 combination of humours in the body; temperament
tender over 130.18 careful of the welfare of
tendrynge 137.7 being concerned for or solicitous about
*testimonie 37.22 proof or evidence (1597)
thrift 56.26 prosperity
*thriving 196.13s.n. prospering, fortunate (1607)
towardlinesse 117.6, 215.16 willingness, tractableness

trafique, Trafick 98.31, 223.32 intercourse, communication
travell 8.16 etc. outcome, product; literary work; 44.11 etc. labour, hardship
travel, travail 145.6s.n. etc. to labour, to journey
*Trowchman 5.10, 615 truchman: interpreter (1585)
Trull 21.30, 153.16 girl, wench
Trumpe 75.23 one who proclaims loudly
*tyrannise 64.6 to rule tyrannically (1588)

*unappalled, unapauled 207.7, 216.11 not dismayed, not enfeebled (1606)
uncivill 119.10s.n., 141.26 not civilized, barbarous
*undertaken 51.22 taken in hand (1592)
*unnecessarily 65.18 needlessly (1594)
unpartiall 141.13 impartial, fair
*unpollitique 31.16 not having social organization or government
unquiet 194.14 to disturb the quiet of
*unseemyng 33.24 unbecoming, unseemly (with direct object, 1592)
unsufficient 22.19 insufficient, incompetent, unfit
unthrift 196.13s.n. spendthrift, prodigal
unwittie 175.21 deficient in intelligence, ignorant

Venetians 68.32 Hose or breeches originally introduced from Venice
venter, v. 28.12 to venture, to take the risk of
venter, n. 162.12, 191.34 hazard or peril
*Ventoy 69.18, 98.25 From Italian ventaglio, a fan; or French ventail (1602)
*vestall 226.23 chaste, virgin (1595)
*vexation 75.26 a grief or affliction (1594)
*via 161.12 by way of (1779); or Via, a woman's name? (see note)
*violents 67.10, 83.9 violent passions (1619)
*voluntarie 118.29 growing naturally, spontaneously (see note) (1620)
*voutchsafe 126.6 to make a grant of (1587)

*warde 154.12 to avert, keep off (1586)
warnyng 81.13 summons, command for attendance
*warrant 82.17, 90.11 justifying reason
waspissest 175.25 most waspish, irascible
watchod 71.9 watchet, light blue colour
waterishly 179.6 dimmed by watery vapours
waye 54.28 to weigh, to value; 149.22 to care
weeke 41.13 wick
whot 59.13 hot
will, v. 187.1 to entreat; n. 186.32 acquiescence
Will, n. 145.30 etc. power or capacity of willing; 204.33, 221.9 inclination (1594); wish in wyll 149.8 object of desire. Cf. wish in desire 153.26
winne 56.30 to steal, to make profit
wist 36.9 etc. knew
wit 9.7 etc. wisdom, good judgement; 19.27 etc. mental capacity, intellect
*witsafe 27.27 vouchsafe: to deign to give (1597); 101.27, 107.3 to grant, to agree graciously

wittie, witty 7.16 wise, discreet (see note); *113.17, 163.22 cunning, ingenious (1602)
worme 218.30 to extract the worm, as a remedy against madness (see note)
worth 81.23 take in worth: to take at its proper value
wotte 177.32 God wotte: used to emphasize the truth of a statement
wracke 56.6 devastation, destruction
wreake 200.16 to gratify
wrothe 120.10 angry, wrathful

Index of Proper Names

Acrisius 100.12
Acteon 33.21, 180.31
Addonis 33.22
Admetus 207.13
Aestas 13.8
Africa 227.33
Albania 116.8
Alexander 138.29, 146.12, 168.29, 204.15, 218.18
Alexander, King of the Jewes 141.25
Alexander Severus 46.26, 206.24
Alexandra 141.25
Alvisa Vechio 23.23 etc.
Amadis de Gaule 161.18
Amazon 138.29
Amicla 88.14
Amphion 78.1
Anaxagoras 211.30
Anaxaretes 31.31
Andrugio 125.31 etc.
Anne, Sainct 177.19
Appenine 120.29
Appollo 30.8
Arabia 227.33
Aragon, Cardinal of 154.25
Archelaus 211.31
Argus 104.5s.n., 229.10
Aristotle 58.28, 139.23s.n.
Arnalt 88.14
Artemisia 207.32
Asdrubal 138.32
Astolphus, Kyng 160.18
Athenians 140.19
Augustus 89.6
Aulus Gellius 208.13s.n.
Aurelia 7.11 etc.
Aurora 44.6, 198.11
Baccus 30.24
Baetta 160.28
Bartoli, Cosimo 76.22-23
Bergetto 7.5 etc.

Bianca Maria 160.27
Boetius 76.21
Bohemia 125.13
Borrihauder 40.7
Botrevicus, Joannes 2.18
Bugiardo, Fryer 44.31
Caesar Augustus 199.31
Cesar, Caesar 75.13, 218.19, 146.13
Cambria 116.7
Camenae 2.4
Capitole 199.30
Capo Verdo 92.30
Cassandra 125.10 etc.
Castillio, Count Baldazar 171.15
Charles the fift 40.10
Chion 61.21
Chlora 229.32
Ciches 17.33
Cilisions 141.23
Circeiun 182.14
Circes 182.15
Cirene 57.19
Claros 2.4
Clearches 57.21
Cofetua, King 153.12
Cornaro 106.2
Cornelia 204.7
Corvinus 125.12
Crassus, Marcus 131.24
Cupid 17.32, 182.27
Cyllen 10.17
Damon 208.18
Danaus 100.14, 114.15
Daphne 30.8
Darius 204.14, 207.6
Demetrius, Kinge 58.31
Denis of Sicyll 131.7
Dennis 46.11s.n., 77.2
Diana 10.32, 28.19, 33.7, 33.28, 215.30, 228.6
Diogenes 112.5, 113.5
Dondolo 7.5 etc.

Index of Proper Names 400

Elisa 57.25
Epethia 161.27
Epicaria 140.8
Esta, Cardinall of 18.4s.n.
Euridice, Eurydice 114.12,
    151.8s.n.
Euripides 67.30
Euxinus Pontus 116.11
Fabritio 23.10 etc.
Faliero 23.21 etc.
Farina 120.32
Felice 93.3
Floradin 184.29
Franceschina Santa 7.13 etc.
Fraunces, Saint 120.31
Furnesae, Cardinall 18.5
Galen 99.23
George, Saint 142.15
Giorgio, Marino 98.33
Gisippus 208.18
Gretians 112.32
Guevara 171.13
Haniball 146.13, 218.20
Hanno 161.28
Hatton, Sir Christopher 3.1
Heliogabalus, Hyliogabalus
    20.22, 131.6
Hellena Dulce 23.31
Hercules 58.28, 103.5
Hermes, Vicount 160.33
Hipocrates 99.23
Hippias 140.14
Homer 182.13
Hyemps 13.11
Hymen, Himen 28.22, 36.1, 201.9,
    201.16, 201.20
Icarus 149.3
Inachus 229.10
Inganno, Fryer 120.26
Ionia 215.11
Iphis 31.32
Iris 10.8, 189.11
Isabella 23.12 etc.
Ismarito 21.5 etc.
Isocrates 208.11
Ivry 45.5
Ixion 61.29, 144.17
Janus 198.32, 200.21
Jones, Richard 1.22
Jove 10.6, 153.15
Jubiter 44.14, 100.13

Judeth 141.22
Julia 89.6
Juliet 88.14
Julio 125.17
Juno 28.20, 33.28, 224.16
Katherina Trista 23.34 etc.
Katheryne, Sainct 32.17
Laban 31.1
Lacedemonians 206.6
Laertius 194.5
Lamia 58.33
Latteran 115.5
Laura 89.27
Leayda 123.1
Leena 140.13
Licurgus 206.6
Loadice 138.30
Lodovicus 161.17
Loegria 116.7
Loretto, Laureta 44.32
Lucia Bella 7.12 etc.
Lucretia 133.9, 138.34
Macrello 99.26
Mahometians 63.24
Malfy, Duchesse of 154.26
Malipiero, Antonio 92.34
Malipiero, Marco 92.33
Mammeas 206.26
Marcus Aurelius 32.31
Maria Belochi 7.12 etc.
Marius 131.24
Mars 218.4
Mausolus 207.32
Medicis, Cosimos de 169.22
Memmia 206.27
Mercurie 185.7
Mesiere, Peter 168.21, 169.5
Michael, Saint 142.20
Midas 213.31
Miletum 215.11
Minerva 67.23
Mithridates 138.31
Mossenigo, Doctor 23.19 etc.
Muses 228.7
Myos 215.21
Nabucadonizer 183.1
Naples 8.4, 92.31
Narcissus 153.13
Naucrites 208.10
Neapolitan 104.15
Nebeus 215.13

Index of Proper Names 401

Nero 140.11
Nigidius 88.30, 89.21
Ninus 138.28
Nynivites 184.26
Oedippus 32.29, 217.16
Oeta, Mountaine 44.10
Olympia 204.15
Ophella 40.9
Orpheus 114.8, 142.31, 151.7,
    229.13
Ovide 32.26, 88.7, 88.30, 151.5s.n.
    153.3, 161.16, 184.16, 193.2
Padua 161.7
Pallas 10.31
Pan 31.29
Pandora 10.5
Paracelsus 99.24
Parmenio 40.11
Parnassus 228.23
Parrhasius 3.9, 73.18
Paulina 207.1
Pegasus 135.27
Pelops 50.17
Periander 94.22
Pericles 184.30
Perillus 229.29
Persida 184.30
Petrarke 55.3, 88.30, 89.27
Phaebus, Phebus 13.9, 44.7, 118.9
Phaeton 34.7
Phallaris 229.29
Pharos 10.23, 115.33s.n., 116.4,
    117.30
Phlegon 44.12
Phrigius 198.5 etc.
Phrisio 110.7, 113.12
Phyloxenus, Segnior 4.19 etc.
Piatso Richio 98.9
Pieria 198.5 etc.
Pieriae 2.5
Pigmalion 153.13
Piramus 88.14
Pithagoras 146.14
Pithias 208.18
Pithos 10.32
Plato 36.5, 85.13, 146.14, 158.34,
    206.21
Pliny 140.14s.n.
Plutarke 87.19, 171.13
Pluto 111.22, 114.8
Polina 125.33

Pompey 75.13
Poo, River of 14.1s.n.
Priapus 131.10
Prometheus 132.7
Promos 125.10 etc.
Propertius 205.31
Protheus 102.5
Provolo, Philippo 93.4
Ptolomey, King 116.2s.n., 169.23
Pyrois 44.11
Pythes 215.22
Quintus Curtius 207.6
Racanati 45.2
Ravenna 151.31, 163.27
Ravenna, Forrest of 13.29s.n.
Rinautus 182.11
Roane 8.4
Rome 8.4, 204.6
Romeus 88.14
Salomon 58.27
Samarin 31.33
Samocratius 88.30, 89.24
Sampson 49.24, 58.28
Saturne 185.4
Scapardon, Giaccomo 160.28
Scipio 146.13
Seavola, Mutius 169.12
Semiramis 138.28
Seneca 191.14s.n., 191.18, 207.2
Sextillius 161.30
Sibels, Sybels 139.6, 139.33
Sicheus 57.24 etc.
Sirens 19.29, 164.14
Sirinx 31.29
Sisiphus 76.27s.n., 78.8, 114.16
Socrates 146.14, 184.24, 211.28
Solon 146.14
Soranso 7.5 etc.
Spaine 192.26
Stix 134.7, 195.33
Tamberlaine the Great 168.23
Tantalus 48.2, 86.8, 114.14
Tartessus, Caves of 44.8, 180.13
Teodectes 208.10
Themistocles 6.7
Theopompus 208.10
Thisbie 88.14
Thymon of Athens 42.4, 42.16
Tiberius Graccus 207.20
Tithon 44.7, 198.13
Titius 114.14

Titus 208.18
Tivoly 18.2
Tryfo 57.20
Uranie 10.2, 230.14
Vegetius 171.1
Venus 10.31, 28.19, 153.12, 185.4, 218.3
Virbius 184.27

Virgil 109.32
Virginia 161.29
Vulcan 45.13, 153.13
W., T. (Thomas Watson) 9.1
Zelande, Counte of 161.1
Zeno, Andrea 161.11
Zeuxes 78.5

Index of Stories

	page
Borrihauder and Ophella. (Doctor Mossenigo his Satisfaction) Source: Heptaméron 71.	40
Felice and Malipiero. (The Historie in reproofe of rash Mariages) Sources: Heptaméron 32, Painter I.57.	92
Fryer Inganno and Farina. (The Adventure of Fryer Inganno) Sources: Boccaccio IV.2, IV.8.	120
Phrigius and Pieria. (The woorthy Historie of . . .) Source: Plutarch Moralia 253F.	215
Promos and Cassandra. (The rare Historie of . . .) Source: Cintio VIII.5.	125
Rinautus. (The Metamorphose of Rinautus) No known source.	182
Sicheus and Elisa. (The Historie in reproche of forced Mariage) No known source.	57

Index of First Lines of Poems

	page
Care, Care, goe pack, thou art no mate for me	119
Even as the Hart, a deadly wounde, that hath	71
Even as the Vine, that clasps the tender Elme	201
Farewell, bright Golde, thou glory of the worlde	76
From shore to sea, from dales to mountaines hie	72
Hence burnyng sighes, which sparckle from desyre	70
I that some times of Nuptiall rites	193
If one firme Faith, one Hart uncharg'd with frawd	73
In these two thinges, a Kingdome to obtaine	67
Regarde my love, but not my frostie haires	175
The Prince, the Peere, the Subject and the slave	55
To thee I sende, thou fayrest of the fayre	81
To realish Love, I taste a sowrie sweete	50
Two Soveraigne Dames, Beautie and Honestie	69
Who prickels feares, to pluck the lovely Rose	148

LIST OF WORKS CONSULTED

The following list does not include works of general reference or works used only in compiling the Explanatory Notes. Reel numbers are given for texts consulted in the University Microfilms series of STC books (Ann Arbor, Mich.).

The list is divided into two sections: Primary Texts, including Whetstone's works, and Secondary Sources.

Primary Texts

Whetstone's Works

The Censure of a Loyall Subject. Richard Jones, 1587. STC 25334. (Reel 371)

The English Myrror. J. Windet for G. Seton, 1586. STC 25336. (Reel 553)

The Honorable Reputation of a Souldier. Richard Jones, 1585. STC 25339. (Reel 401) -- Another edition, Leyden, 1586. STC 25340. (Reel 371)

A Mirour for Magestrates of Cyties. Richard Jones, 1584. Contains An Addition: Or Touchstone for the Time. STC 25341. (Reel 1047) -- Re-issued in 1586 as The Enemie to Unthryftinesse. STC 25341.5 (Reel 1262)

A Mirror of Treue Honnour and Christian Nobilitie, Exposing the Life, Death, and Vertues of Frauncis Earle of Bedford. Richard Jones, 1585. STC 25342. (Reel 401)

A Remembraunce of the Life, Death, and Vertues, of Thomas Late Erle of Sussex. John Wolfe and Richard Jones, 1583. STC 25344. (Reel 401)

A Remembraunce of the Precious Vertues of the Right Honourable and Reverend Judge, Sir James Dier. John Charlewood, 1582. STC 25345. (Reel 371)

A Remembraunce of the Wel Imployed Life, of George Gaskoigne, Esquire.
For Edward Aggas, 1577. STC 25346. In Certayne Notes of Instruction
in English Verse, by George Gascoigne. Ed. Edward Arber. Westminster:
Constable, 1901. pp. 15-29.

A Remembraunce, of the Woorthie Life of Sir Nicholas Bacon. (J. Kingston)
for Myles Jennyngs, 1579. STC 25343. (Reel 553)

The Right Excellent and Famous Historye, of Promos and Cassandra. (John
Charlewood for) Richard Jones, 1578. STC 25347. (Reel 553)

The Rocke of Regard. (H. Middleton) for Robert Waley, 1576. STC 25348.
(Reel 553)

Sir Phillip Sidney, His Honorable Life, His Valiant Death, and True Vertues.
(T. Orwin) for Thomas Cadman, 1587. STC 25349. (Reel 371)

Other Works

Alberti, Leon Battista. The Family in Renaissance Florence. A translation
by Renee Neu Watkins of I Libri Della Famiglia (1434). Columbia: Univ.
of South Carolina Press, 1969.

Ariosto, Ludovico. Orlando Furioso. Trans. Sir John Harington (1591). Ed.
Robert McNulty. Oxford: Clarendon Press, 1972.

Ascham, Roger. The Scholemaster (1570). Ed. R. J. Schoeck. Don Mills,
Ont.: Dent, 1966.

Bandello. Tragical Tales. Trans. Geoffrey Fenton (1567). Ed. Hugh Harris.
London: Routledge, 1923.

Boccaccio, Giovanni. Amorous Fiammetta (1587). Trans. Bartholomew Young.
Ed. Edward Hutton. London: Navarre Society, 1952.

----------. Boccaccio on Poetry; Being the Preface and the Fourteenth and
Fifteenth Books of Boccaccio's Genealogia Deorum Gentilium. Ed. Charles
G. Osgood. 1930; rpt. New York: Liberal Arts Press, 1956.

----------. The Decameron. Trans. Frances Winwar. New York: Modern
Library, 1955.

----------. A Pleasaunt Disport of Divers Noble Personages. Trans. H. G.
London, 1567. STC 3180. (Reel 197)

Boethius. The Consolation of Philosophy. Trans. "I. T." (1609). London:
Heinemann, 1946. (Loeb Classical Library).

Bryskett, Lodowick. A Discourse of Civill Life (1606). Literary Works. Ed. J. H. P. Pafford. n.p. Gregg Internat'l Publishers, 1972.

----------. A Discourse of Civill Life (1606). Ed. Thomas E. Wright. Northridge, Calif.: San Fernando Valley State College, 1970.

Castiglione, Baldassare. The Book of the Courtier. Trans. Sir Thomas Hoby (1561). London: Dent, 1928. (Everyman's Library)

----------. The Courtyer. Trans. Sir Thomas Hoby. London, 1561. STC 4778. (Reel 311)

Cyvile and Uncyvile Life. London, 1579. STC 15589. (Reel 474) -- Also in Inedited Tracts. Ed. W. C. Hazlitt. New York: Burt Franklin, 1868.

Della Casa, Giovanni. A Renaissance Courtesy-Book: Galateo, of Manners and Behaviours. Trans. Robert Peterson (1576). Ed. J. E. Spingarn. Boston: Merrymount Press, 1914.

Elyot, Sir Thomas. The Book Named The Governor (1531). Ed. S. E. Lehmberg. London: Dent, 1962. (Everyman's Library)

Fortescue, Thomas. The Foreste, or Collection of Histories. London, 1571. STC 17849. (Reel 436)

Gascoigne, George. Complete Works. Ed. John W. Cunliffe. Cambridge: Univ. Press, 1907.

----------. A Hundreth Sundrie Flowres. Ed. Charles T. Prouty. Univ. of Missouri Studies, 17. Columbia: Univ. of Missouri, 1942.

Grange, John. The Golden Aphroditis. London, 1577. STC 12174.

Greene, Robert. Alcida: Greenes Metamorphosis [1588]. London, 1617. STC 12216. (Reel 1173)

----------. Greenes Farewell to Folly. London, 1591. STC 12241. (Reel 344)

----------. Greenes Groats-worth of Witte. London, 1592. STC 12245. (Reel 838)

----------. Greenes Mourning Garment. London, 1590. STC 12251. (Reel 1101)

----------. Mamillia; a Looking Glass for the Ladies of England. London, 1583. STC 12269. (Reel 568)

----------. Mamillia, The Second Part of the Triumph of Pallas. London, 1593. STC 12270. (Reel 344)

----------. Morando, The Tritameron of Love. London, 1584. STC 12276. (Reel 385)

----------. *Perimedes the Blacke-smith*. London, 1588. STC 12295. (Reel 344)

----------. *The Repentance of Robert Greene*. London, 1592. STC 12306. (Reel 568)

Guazzo, Stefano. *The Civile Conversation*. Books I-III trans. George Pettie, 1581. Book V trans. Bartholomew Young, 1586. Ed. Sir Edward Sullivan. 2v. London: Constable, 1925.

Guevara, Antonio de. *The Diall of Princes*. Trans. Thomas North. London, 1557. STC 12427. (Reel 299)

----------. *The Diall of Princes*. Trans. Sir Thomas North. Ed. K. N. Colvile. London: Philip Allan, 1919.

Guicciardini, Ludovico. *The Garden of Pleasure*. Trans. James Sanford. London, 1573. STC 12464. (Reel 1069)

Harvey, Gabriel. *Pierces Supererogation, or a New Prayse of the Old Asse*. London, 1593. STC 12903. (Reel 345)

Heywood, John. *A Dialogue of Proverbs* (1546). Ed. Rudolph E. Habenicht. Univ. of California Publ., English Studies, 25. Berkeley: Univ. of California Press, 1963.

Kendall, Timothy. *Flowers of Epigrammes*. London, 1577. STC 14927. (Reel 251)

Legh, Gerard. *The Accedens of Armory*. London, 1568. STC 15389. (Reel 261)

Lyly, John. *Euphues: the Anatomy of Wit; Euphues & His England*. Ed. Morris William Croll and Harry Clemons. 1916; rpt. New York: Russell, 1964.

Marguerite de Navarre. *L'Heptaméron*. Ed. Michel Francois. Paris: Garnier, 1964.

----------. *The Heptameron*. Trans. Arthur Machen. New York: Knopf, 1924.

Meres, Francis. *Palladis Tamia; Wits Treasury*. Ed. Arthur Freeman. 1598; facsimile rpt. New York: Garland, 1973. STC 17834.

Mexia, Pedro. *Les Diverses Leçons de Pierre Messie*. Trans. Claude Gruget. Lyon: Thomas Soubron, 1592. (1st ed. 1554)

Montaigne, Michel de. *The Diary of Montaigne's Journey to Italy in 1580 and 1581*. Trans. E. J. Trechmann. New York: Harcourt, 1927.

Munday, Anthony. *The English Romayne Lyfe*. London, 1582. STC 18272. (Reel 426)

Nashe, Thomas. Works. 5v. Ed. Ronald B. McKerrow. Oxford: Basil Blackwell, 1958.

Painter, William. The Palace of Pleasure (1566-67). Ed. Joseph Jacobs. 3v. 1890; rpt. New York: Dover, 1966.

Pettie, George. A Petite Pallace of Pettie His Pleasure (1576). Ed. Herbert Hartman. London: Oxford Univ. Press, 1938.

Plutarch. Moralia. 15 vols. London: Heinemann, 1957-69. (The Loeb Classical Library)

Primaudaye, Pierre de la. The French Académie. Trans. T. Bowes. London, 1586. STC 15233. (Reel 257)

Rich, Barnabe. Rich's Farewell to Military Profession, 1581. Ed. Thomas Mabry Cranfill. Austin: Univ. of Texas Press, 1959. STC 20996.

Robson, Simon. A New Yeeres Gift. The Courte of Civill Courtesie. London, 1582. STC 21135. (Reel 351) (1st ed. 1577)

Rollins, Hyder Edward, ed. The Paradise of Dainty Devices (1576-1606). Cambridge, Mass.: Harvard Univ. Press, 1927.

Spenser, Edmund. The Faerie Queene. Ed. J. C. Smith. 2v. Oxford: Clarendon Press, 1909.

Starkey, Thomas. England in the Reign of King Henry the Eighth. A Dialogue Between Cardinal Pole and Thomas Lupset (c. 1538). Ed. J. M. Cowper. London: EETS, 1871. (EETS extra ser. 12)

Thomas, William. The History of Italy (1549). Ed. George B. Parks. Ithaca, N. Y.: Publ. for the Folger Shakespeare Library by Cornell Univ. Press, 1963.

Tilney, Edmund. The Flower of Friendshippe. London, 1577. Ed. Ralph Glassgow Johnson. Diss. Univ. of Pittsburgh, 1961. (1st ed. 1568, entitled A Brief and Pleasaunt Discourse of Duties in Mariage.)

A True Description and Direction of What is Most Worthy to be Seen in All Italy (c. 1600). Harleian Miscellany. 1810; rpt. New York: AMS, 1965. V, 1-41.

Turler, Jerome. The Traveiler (1575). Ed. Denver Ewing Baughan. Facsimile rpt., Gainesville, Fla.: Scholars' Facsimiles & Reprints, 1951. STC 24336.

Wateson, George. The Cures of the Diseased in Forraine Attempts of the English Nation. Ed. Charles Singer. 1598; facsimile rpt. Oxford: Clarendon Press, 1915. STC 25106.

Webbe, William. A Discourse of English Poetrie. London, 1586. STC 25172. (Reel 401)

Wotton, Henry. A Courtlie Controversie of Cupids Cautels. London, 1578. STC 5647. (Reel 879)

Secondary Sources

Allen, Don Cameron, ed. Francis Meres's Treatise "Poetrie." Univ. of Ill. Studies in Language and Literature, 16 (Sept.-Dec. 1933), 345-500.

Anders, H. R. D. Shakespeare's Books. Berlin: G. Reimer, 1904.

Barber, Richard. The Knight and Chivalry. London: Longman, 1970.

Barbu, Zevedei. Problems of Historical Psychology. London: Routledge, 1960.

Beach, Donald Marcus. "Studies in the Art of Elizabethan Prose Narrative." Diss. Cornell Univ., 1959.

Beauregard, David Napoleon. "A Critical Edition of George Whetstone's Heptameron of Civill Discourses, 1582." Diss. Ohio State Univ., 1967.

Bond, R. Warwick. "Euphues and Euphuism: Introductory Essay." The Complete Works of John Lyly. Oxford: Clarendon Press, 1902. I, 119-75.

Borinski, Ludwig. "The Origin of the Euphuistic Novel and Its Significance for Shakespeare." Studies in Honor of T. W. Baldin. Ed. Don Cameron Allen. Urbana: Univ. of Illinois Press, 1958.

Bornstein, Diane. Mirrors of Courtesy. Hamden, Conn.: Archon, 1975.

Branca, Vittore. Boccaccio: the Man and His Works. Trans. Richard Monges. New York: New York Univ. Press, 1976.

Brook, Eric St. John. Sir Christopher Hatton. London: Cape, 1946.

Burckhardt, Jacob. The Civilization of the Renaissance in Italy. Trans. S. G. C. Middlemore. 1878; rpt. New York: Modern Library, 1954.

Bush, Douglas. Mythology and the Renaissance Tradition in English Poetry. New rev. ed. New York: Norton, 1963.

Cecioni, Cesare G. "Un adattamento di due novelle del Boccaccio nello 'Heptameron of Civil Discourses' di George Whetstone (1582)." Il Boccaccio nella Cultura Inglese e Anglo-Americana. Ed. Giuseppe Galigani. Firenze: Olschki, 1974. pp. 185-91.

Clements, Robert J. "Anatomy of the Novella." *Comparative Literature Studies*, 9 (March 1972), 3-16.

Corser, Thomas. *Collectanea Anglo-Poetica*. Part XI: *Remains, Historical and Literary*, CXI. London: The Chetham Society, 1883.

Crane, Thomas Frederick. *Italian Social Customs of the Sixteenth Century and Their Influence on the Literature of Europe*. Cornell Studies in English, 5. New Haven: Yale Univ. Press, 1920.

Crane, William G. *Wit and Rhetoric in the Renaissance*. Columbia Univ. Studies in English and Comparative Literature, 129. 1937; rpt. Gloucester, Mass.: Peter Smith, 1964.

Croll, Morris W. "Introduction: The Sources of the Euphuistic Rhetoric." *Euphues: the Anatomy of Wit; Euphues & His England*, by *John Lyly*. 1916; rpt. in *Style, Rhetoric, and Rhythm*, Princeton: Princeton Univ. Press, 1966.

Davis, Walter R. *Idea and Act in Elizabethan Fiction*. Princeton: Princeton Univ. Press, 1969.

De Bruyn, Jan. "A Study of Seventeenth-Century Courtesy and Conduct Literature as a Revelation of the Concept of the English Gentleman." Diss. Univ. of London, 1951.

Deligiorgis, Stavros. *Narrative Intellection in the Decameron*. Iowa City: Univ. of Iowa Press, 1975.

Dorsten, J. A. Van. *Poets, Patrons, and Professors: Sir Philip Sidney, Daniel Rogers, and the Leiden Humanists*. Leiden: Univ. Press, Publ. for the Sir Thomas Browne Inst., 1962.

Eccles, Mark. *Christopher Marlowe in London*. Cambridge, Mass.: Harvard Univ. Press, 1934.

Einstein, Lewis. *The Italian Renaissance in England*. 1902; rpt. New York: Burt Franklin, n.d.

Ernle, Rowland Edmund. *The Light Reading of our Ancestors*. London: Hutchinson, 1927.

Fellheimer, Jeannette. "The Englishman's Conception of the Italian in the Age of Shakespeare." Diss. Univ. of London, 1935.

Frye, Northrop. "Varieties of Literary Utopias." *The Stubborn Structure*. Ithaca, N. Y.: Cornell Univ. Press, 1970. pp. 109-34.

Galigani, Giuseppe. "Il Boccaccio nel Cinquecento inglese." *Il Boccaccio nella Cultura Inglese e Anglo-Americana*. Firenze: Olschki, 1974. pp. 27-57.

Gelernt, Jules. _World of Many Loves: The Heptameron of Marguerite De Navarre_. Univ. of North Carolina Studies in Comparative Literature, 38. Chapel Hill: Univ. of North Carolina Press, 1966.

Greene, Thomas. "The Flexibility of the Self in Renaissance Literature." _The Disciplines of Criticism_. Ed. Peter Demetz, Thomas Greene, and Lowry Nelson, Jr. New Haven: Yale Univ. Press, 1968. pp. 241-64.

Griffith, T. Gwynfor. _Bandello's Fiction; an Examination of the Novelle_. Oxford: Basil Blackwell, 1955.

Habenicht, Rudolph E. "Introduction." _A Dialogue of Proverbs_ by John Heywood. Univ. of California Publications, English Studies, 25. Berkeley: Univ. of California Press, 1963. pp. 1-94.

Hale, J. R. _England and the Italian Renaissance_. London: Faber, 1954. (Especially Chapter I, pp. 11-36.)

Hart, Walter Morris. "The Narrative Art of the Old French Fabliaux." _Anniversary Papers by Colleagues and Pupils of George Lyman Kittredge_. Boston: Ginn, 1913. pp. 209-16.

Highet, Gilbert. _The Classical Tradition: Greek and Roman Influence on Western Literature_. 1949; rpt. New York: Oxford Univ. Press, 1957.

Howard, Clare. _English Travellers of the Renaissance_. London: Lane, 1914.

Howard, Donald R. "Renaissance World-Alienation." _The Darker Vision of the Renaissance_. Ed. Robert S. Kinsman. Berkeley: Univ. of California Press, 1974. pp. 47-76.

Howell, Roger. _Sir Philip Sidney: The Shepherd Knight_. Boston: Little, 1968.

Hunter, G. K. _John Lyly; The Humanist as Courtier_. London: Routledge, 1962.

Huizinga, Johan. _Homo Ludens; A Study of the Play Element in Culture_. 1949; rpt. London: Temple Smith, 1970.

Izard, Thomas C. _George Whetstone: Mid-Elizabethan Gentleman of Letters_. 1942; rpt. New York: AMS, 1966.

Javitch, Daniel. "Poetry and Court Conduct: Puttenham's _Arte of English Poesie_ in the Light of Castiglione's _Cortegiano_." _MLN_, 87 (May 1972), 865-82.

----------. "Rival Arts of Conduct in Elizabethan England: Guazzo's _Civile Conversation_ and Castiglione's _Courtier_." _Yearbook of Italian Studies_ (1971), 178-98.

Jeffery, Violet M. John Lyly and the Italian Renaissance. Bibliothèque de la Revue de Littérature Comparée, 53. Paris: Honore Champion, 1928.

Johnson Paul. Elizabeth I; a Study in Power and Intellect. London: Weidenfeld & Nicolson, 1974.

Johnson, Ralph Glassgow. "A Critical 3rd Edition of Edmund Tilney's The Flower of Friendshippe, published in 1577, Edited, with Introduction, Notes, and Glossary." Diss. Univ. of Pittsburgh, 1961.

Jones, Joseph R. Antonio de Guevara. Boston: Twayne, 1975.

Jusserand, J. J. The English Novel in the Time of Shakespeare. Trans. Elizabeth Lee. New ed. 1890; rpt. London: Benn, 1966.

Kelso, Ruth. The Doctrine of the English Gentleman in the Sixteenth Century. Univ. of Illinois Studies in Language and Literature, 14. Urbana: Univ. of Illinois, 1929.

Koeppel, Emil. Studien zur Geschichte der Italienischen Novelle in der Englischen Litteratur des Sechzehnten Jahrhunderts. Strassburg: Trubner, 1892.

Krailsheimer, A. J. "The Heptameron Reconsidered." The French Renaissance and Its Heritage; Essays Presented to Alan M. Boase. Ed. D. R. Haggis et al. London: Methuen, 1968. pp. 75-92.

----------, ed. The Continental Renaissance 1500-1600. Harmondsworth, Middlesex: Penguin, 1971. pp. 299-487.

----------, ed. Three Sixteenth-Century Conteurs. London: Oxford Univ. Press, 1966.

Lathrop, Henry Burrowes. Translations from the Classics into English from Caxton to Chapman 1477-1620. 1932?; rpt. New York: Octagon, 1967.

Lea, Kathleen M. Italian Popular Comedy. Oxford: Clarendon Press, 1934.

Lewis, C. S. English Literature in the Sixteenth Century Excluding Drama. Oxford: Clarendon Press, 1954.

Lievsay, John L. The Elizabethan Image of Italy. Ithaca, N. Y.: Publ. by Cornell Univ. Press for the Folger Shakespeare Library, 1964.

----------. The Englishman's Italian Books, 1550-1700. Philadelphia: Univ. of Pennsylvania Press, 1969.

----------. Stefano Guazzo and the English Renaissance 1575-1675. Chapel Hill: Univ. of North Carolina Press, 1961.

Long, Percy Waldron. "From Troilus to Euphues." *Anniversary Papers by Colleagues and Pupils of George Lyman Kittredge*. Boston: Ginn, 1913. pp. 367-76.

Lotspeich, Henry Gibbons. *Classical Mythology in the Poetry of Edmund Spenser*. 1932; rpt. New York: Octagon, 1965.

McFarlane, I. D. *Renaissance France 1470-1589*. London: Benn, 1974.

McLean, Andrew Miller. "Early Tudor Prose Dialogues: A Study in Literary Form." Diss. Univ. of North Carolina at Chapel Hill, 1971.

Martines, Lauro. "The Gentleman in Renaissance Italy: Strains of Isolation in the Body Politic." *The Darker Vision of the Renaissance*. Ed. Robert S. Kinsman. Berkeley: Univ. of California Press, 1974. pp. 77-93.

Mason, John E. *Gentlefolk in the Making*. Philadelphia, Pa.: Univ. of Pennsylvania Press, 1935.

Mazzeo, Joseph Anthony. *Renaissance & Revolution: Backgrounds to Seventeenth-Century English Literature*. New York: Random, 1967. Especially Ch. 3: "Castiglione's *Courtier*: The Self as a Work of Art," pp. 131-60.

Miller, Edwin Haviland. *The Professional Writer in Elizabethan England*. Cambridge, Mass.: Harvard Univ. Press, 1959.

Mohrmann, Gerald P. "*The Civile Conversation*: Communication in the Renaissance." *Speech Monographs*, 39 (March 1972), 193-204.

Nelson, William. *Fact or Fiction; The Dilemma of the Renaissance Storyteller*. Cambridge, Mass.: Harvard Univ. Press, 1973.

O'Connor, John J. *Amadis de Gaule and Its Influence on Elizabethan Literature*. New Brunswick, N. J.: Rutgers Univ. Press, 1970.

Pallikunnen, Augustine G. "The Treatment of Virtues and Vices in the Courtesy Literature of the Sixteenth Century." Diss. Duquesne Univ., 1970.

Parks, George B. "The Decline and Fall of the English Renaissance Admiration of Italy." *Huntington Library Quarterly*, 21 (1967-68), 341-57.

----------. *The English Traveler To Italy*. Vol. I. Stanford, Calif.: Stanford Univ. Press, 1954.

----------. "The First Italianate Englishmen." *Studies in the Renaissance*, 8 (1961), 197-216.

----------. "Introduction." *The History of Italy (1549)* by William Thomas. Ithaca, N. Y.: Publ. for the Folger Shakespeare Library by Cornell Univ. Press, 1963.

Pearson, Lu Emily. *Elizabethans at Home*. Stanford, Calif.: Stanford Univ. Press, 1957.

Pierce, Frank. *Amadis de Gaula*. Boston: Twayne, 1976.

Powell, Chilton Latham. *English Domestic Relations 1487-1653*. Columbia Univ. Studies in English and Comparative Literature. New York: Columbia Univ. Press, 1917.

Prouty, Charles T. *George Gascoigne: Elizabethan Courtier, Soldier, and Poet*. New York: Columbia Univ. Press, 1942.

----------. "George Whetstone and the Sources of *Measure for Measure*." *Shakespeare Quarterly*, 15 (1964), 131-45.

Pruvost, René. *Matteo Bandello and Elizabethan Fiction*. Bibliothèque de la Revue de Littérature Comparée, 113. Paris: Champion, 1937.

Raleigh, Walter. "Introduction." *The Book of the Courtier*. London: David Nutt, 1900. pp. vii-lxxxviii.

Randall, Alice Elizabeth (Sawtelle). *The Sources of Spenser's Classical Mythology*. 1896; rpt. New York: AMS, 1970.

Rhodes, Clifford. *The Necessity for Love: the History of Interpersonal Relations*. London: Constable, 1972.

Roche, Thomas P. "The Nature of Faeryland." *The Kindly Flame*. Princeton: Princeton Univ. Press, 1964. pp. 31-50.

Rodax, Yvonne. *The Real and the Ideal in the Novella of Italy, France and England; Four Centuries of Change in the Boccaccian Tale*. Chapel Hill: Univ. of North Carolina Press, 1968.

Root, Robert Kilburn. *Classical Mythology in Shakespeare*. Yale Studies in English, 19. 1903; rpt. New York: Gordian Press, 1965.

Rossetti, William Michael. "Italian Courtesy-Books." *Queene Elizabethes Achademy*. London: EETS, 1869. (EETS extra ser. 8, pt. 2.)

Rouse, W. H. D. "Introduction." *Shakespeare's Ovid*. 1904; rpt. Carbondale: Southern Illinois Univ. Press, 1961.

Rowen, Herbert H., ed. *The Low Countries in Early Modern Times*. New York: Walker, 1972.

Ryan, Lawrence V. "Book Four of Castiglione's *Courtier*: Climax or Afterthought?" *Studies in the Renaissance*, 19 (1972), 156-79.

Schlauch, Margaret. *Antecedents of the English Novel 1400-1600*. London: Oxford Univ. Press, 1963.

Scott, Mary Augusta. *Elizabethan Translations from the Italian*. 1916; New York: Burt Franklin, 1969.

Sheavyn, Phoebe. *The Literary Profession in the Elizabethan Age*. 2nd ed. Rev. J. W. Saunders. Manchester: Manchester Univ. Press, 1967.

Smith, Charles G. *Shakespeare's Proverb Lore: His Use of the Sententiae of Leonard Culman and Publilius Syrus*. Cambridge, Mass.: Harvard Univ. Press, 1963.

----------. *Spenser's Proverb Lore; With Special Reference to His Use of the Sententiae of Leonard Culman and Publilius Syrus*. Cambridge, Mass.: Harvard Univ. Press, 1970.

Starnes, DeWitt T. *Renaissance Dictionaries: English-Latin and Latin-English*. Austin: Univ. of Texas Press, 1954.

Starnes, DeWitt T. and Ernest William Talbert. *Classical Myth and Legend in Renaissance Dictionaries*. Chapel Hill: Univ. of North Carolina Press, 1955.

Steadman, John M. "Renaissance Dictionaries and Manuals as Instruments of Literary Scholarship." *New Aspects of Lexicography*. Ed. Howard D. Weinbrot. Carbondale: Southern Illinois Univ. Press, 1972. pp. 17-35.

Stone, Donald. *From Tales to Truths: Essays on French Fiction in the Sixteenth Century*. Analecta Romanica, 34. Frankfurt am Main: Vittorio Klostermann, 1973.

Strong, R. C. and J. A. Van Dorsten. *Leicester's Triumph*. Leiden: Univ. Press, Publ. for the Sir Thomas Browne Institute, 1964.

Tetel, Marcel. *Marguerite De Navarre's Heptameron: Themes, Language, and Structure*. Durham, N. C.: Duke Univ. Press, 1973.

Thompson, Elbert N. S. "Books of Courtesy." *Literary Bypaths of the Renaissance*. Freeport, N. Y.: Books for Libraries Press. 1924? pp. 127-71.

Tilley, Arthur. *The Literature of the French Renaissance*, Vol. I. 1904; rpt. New York: Hafner, 1972.

Tilley, Morris Palmer. *Elizabethan Proverb Lore in Lyly's Euphues and in Pettie's Petite Pallace*. Univ. of Michigan Publications, Language and Literature, 2. New York: Macmillan, 1926.

Tonkin, Humphrey. *Spenser's Courteous Pastoral: Book Six of the Faerie Queene*. Oxford: Clarendon Press, 1972.

Trilling, Lionel. *Sincerity and Authenticity*. Cambridge, Mass.: Harvard Univ. Press, 1972.

Turner, Celeste. *Anthony Mundy, an Elizabethan Man of Letters*. Univ. of California Publ. in English, 2. Berkeley: Univ. of California, 1928. pp. 1-234.

Valency, Maurice and Harry Levtow, eds. "Introduction." *The Palace of Pleasure; an Anthology of the Novella*. New York: Capricorn, 1960. pp. 1-28.

Wedgwood, C. V. *William the Silent: William of Nassau, Prince of Orange, 1533-1584*. New Haven: Yale Univ. Press, 1944.

Weiss, Roberto. *Humanism in England During the Fifteenth Century*. Medium aevum monographs, 4. Oxford: Basil Blackwell, 1941.

Wheeler, Charles Francis. *Classical Mythology in the Plays, Masques, and Poems of Ben Jonson*. Princeton: Princeton Univ. Press for the Univ. of Cincinnati, 1938.

Whigham, Frank Frederick. "'Fayned Showes and Forgerie': Courtesy and Political Suasion in English Renaissance Literature." *Dissertation Abstracts International*, 37 (1977), 4380A (Univ. of California, San Diego).

Wilson, Charles. *Queen Elizabeth and the Revolt of the Netherlands*. London: Macmillan, 1970.

Wilson, F. P. "The Proverbial Wisdom of Shakespeare." *Shakespearian and Other Studies*. Ed. Helen Gardner. Oxford: Clarendon Press, 1969. pp. 143-75.

Wright, Herbert G. *Boccaccio in England from Chaucer to Tennyson*. London: Athlone Press, 1957.

Wright, Louis B. *Middle-Class Culture in Elizabethan England*. 1935; rpt. Ithaca, N. Y.: Publ. for the Folger Shakespeare Library by Cornell Univ. Press, 1958.

For Product Safety Concerns and Information please contact our EU
representative GPSR@taylorandfrancis.com
Taylor & Francis Verlag GmbH, Kaufingerstraße 24, 80331 München, Germany

www.ingramcontent.com/pod-product-compliance
Lightning Source LLC
Chambersburg PA
CBHW071231300426
44116CB00008B/987